SGML
at
Work

Danny R. Vint

Prentice Hall PTR
Upper Saddle River, New Jersey 07458
http://www.phptr.com

ISBN 0-13-636572-8

9 780136 365723

90000

Editorial/Production Supervision: *Kathleen M. Caren*
Copyeditor: *Camie Goffi*
Cover Design Director: *Jerry Votta*
Cover Designer: *Amy Rosen*
Manufacturing Manager: *Alexis Heyd*t
Marketing Manager: *Dan Rush*
Acquisitions Editor: *Mark Taub*
Editorial Assistant: *Audri Anna Bazlen*

© 1999 Prentice Hall PTR
Prentice-Hall, Inc.
A Simon & Schuster Company
Upper Saddle River, New Jersey 07458

Prentice Hall books are widely used by corporations and government agencies for training, marketing, and resale. The publisher offers discounts on this book when ordered in bulk quantities.

For more information, contact: Corporate Sales Department, Phone: 800-382-3419; FAX: 201-236-7141; email: corpsales@prenhall.com

Or write: Corp. Sales Dept., Prentice Hall PTR, 1 Lake Street, Upper Saddle River, NJ   07458

Printed in the United States of America
10 9 8 7 6 5 4 3 2 1

ISBN 0-13-636572-8

Prentice-Hall International (UK) Limited, *London*
Prentice-Hall of Australia Pty. Limited, *Sydney*
Prentice-Hall Canada Inc., *Toronto*
Prentice-Hall Hispanoamericana, S.A., *Mexico*
Prentice-Hall of India Private Limited, *New Delhi*
Prentice-Hall of Japan, Inc., *Tokyo*
Simon & Schuster Asia Pte. Ltd., *Singapore*
Editora Prentice-Hall do Brasil, Ltda., *Rio de Janeiro*

For my friends and family
so they will finally understand what I do for a living.

Also, for Mrs. Musso,
my 7th, 8th, and 9th grade English teacher
at Woodrow Wilson Jr. High,
bet you never thought I would write a book!

TABLE OF CONTENTS

Part 5 Management 659

PREFACE

About this Book

You can find many books on the SGML standard and how to understand the syntax, and there are some books available that document reasons to justify using SGML and successful applications; but until now, no one has ever documented a process to take you from the tools you may currently be using into this new world of SGML. In this book, you will find detailed explanations of:

- How to write conversion tools

- How to develop a DTD

- How to implement some of the industry's best products

- How to integrate various tools into a working environment.

Take a look at Figure 1. This illustration shows a complete implementation process. This process includes learning SGML, justifying an implementation, and then implementing. In Figure 1, I cover everything below the dashed line in detail with only enough information about learning SGML to allow you to use this book.

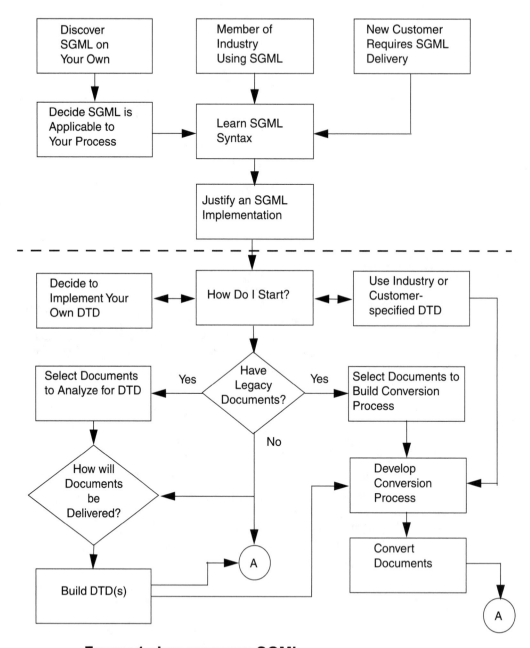

FIGURE 1. IMPLEMENTING SGML

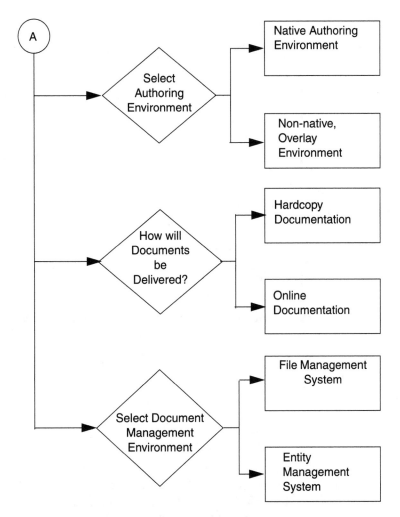

FIGURE 1. IMPLEMENTING SGML (CONTINUED)

This book will introduce a generic category of tools and then highlight the capabilities of some of the best tools on the market and explain how to implement and integrate them into a single working SGML environment. These tools include:

- DTD Development Tools
  - Microstar Near & Far Designer

- Earl Hood's perlSGML
- Publishing Development AB SGML Companion DTD Browser

• Conversion Tools

- OmniMark
- DOCUMENT•ARCHITECT
- ADEPT•EDITOR

• Authoring Tools

- ArborText ADEPT•EDITOR and DOCUMENT•ARCHITECT
- Corel WordPerfect 8
- Corel Ventura 7
- Grif SGML Editor
- InContext InContext Editor
- ADEPT•Publisher

• Delivery Tools

- INSO (formerly Electronic Book Technologies) DynaText and DynaWeb
- TechnoTeacher HyBrowse
- SoftQuad Panorama Pro
- James Clark's Jade DSSSL Tool

• Document Management Tools

- Texcel Information Manager.

The SGML world doesn't have enough vendors to support all platforms and combinations of capabilities. Much of the required capability exists in the UNIX and MS Windows domains, but some tools are only available on one platform, and some features are only available on a particular platform. The tools in this book are primarily Windows 95- or Windows NT-based. perlSGML was written in a UNIX environment, but with the popularity of Windows 95, it is now possible to run on this platform as well. ArborText provides the capability to print SGML documents using a FOSI, but currently this is only available on the UNIX platform. The SGML world isn't mature enough for everything to be available on one platform. You need to be flexible and only specify platform requirements when absolutely necessary.

This book has been written primarily for the implementor of SGML systems, but it also contains useful information for the writer who likes to know more about how tools work and interact. For managers of SGML development efforts, this book offers a methodology for development and details the inter-relationships between tools that can either make or break an implementation. In the SGML world, I touch upon the specialities of:

- Document analysis and DTD development
- Document conversion
- SGML systems integration
- Document production
- Document management

Many of these topics are covered at a high level, or as specialities in themselves. I treat them as a related set of skills, or a team of implementors. I show the relationship of decisions at these different interfaces and how a decision in one area may adversely affect the ease of implementation in another. This book helps to build the skills and knowledge that is necessary to be a generalist who can look at the "big picture" and determine the best approach overall.

ABOUT THE AUTHOR

Dan Vint has implemented SGML tools in defense, aerospace, and software development environments. The author has a BS in Computer Science from San Diego State University and worked prior to the completion of that degree as both a technical illustrator and technical writer, before supporting and developing publishing systems.

Dan has seen the conversion from the traditional ways of developing documentation with illustrations drawn with pen and pencil and writing with IBM Selectric typewriters, to implementations using a variety of CAD and illustrating software and desktop publishing tools like Interleaf, FrameMaker, WordPerfect, and Ventura. The author has been involved with documentation development since the early days of the desktop publishing revolution in the 1980s to the new revolution of SGML- and XML-based environments.

ACKNOWLEDGMENTS

I want to thank the vendors who generously provided their software and support so I could create this book; ArborText, Grif, INSO, Microstar, and Texcel. I also want to thank the companies who provided functional software that might be limited in full functionality, but provide the basis for learning and building initial applications, including: OmniMark, SoftQuad, Publishing Development AB, and TechnoTeacher. And finally, thanks to James Clark and Earl Hood for providing tools for everyone to use and build upon.

CONVENTIONS

Table 1 shows the conventions used in this book:

Table 1. Typographic Conventions Used in this Book

Description	Shown as
Design tips; a key configuration or installation tip indicated by:	
ISO standard terms:	element type
New terminology:	*desktop publishing environment*
SGML element:	**\<book\>** or **book**
User input:	*SGML@Work Sample Document*
System filename:	`nearfar.erf`
Computer-generated text, scripts, programs, or sample text:	`<tag>This is some sample text.</tag>`

PART I

FOUNDATIONS

1 WHAT IS PUBLISHING?

"What is publishing?" is a very broad question. For the purpose of this book, I will consider it to be the people involved with the production of documents, the types of documents produced, and how they are created.

For every typical publications group, there are probably hundreds of others that don't fit the mold because of the type of documentation produced or the staffing. In this chapter, I will describe the typical roles I have encountered, I will point out some roles that typically aren't staffed (but the functions have still existed in many groups), and I will describe the new roles that SGML brings to a group. I will also explore the production cycle and discuss several types of documentation that I have worked with.

PUBLISHING ROLES

Figure 1-1 illustrates the typical roles found in a publications group prior to the desktop publishing revolution. At this time, you were likely to find someone with a job title similar to those listed. The arrows indicate how the work flowed between these people.

Illustrators were responsible for developing the graphics required in a document and worked with the writer to determine where they were needed. While the *writer* developed the text of the document, the illustrator created the illustrations.

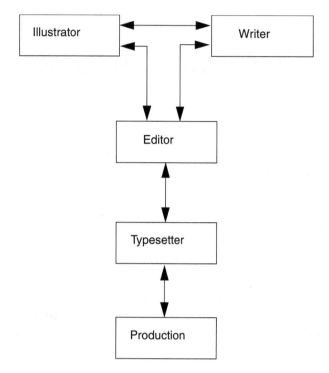

FIGURE 1-1. TYPICAL PUBLICATIONS GROUP BEFORE DESKTOP PUBLISHING

As sections of a document were completed, an *editor* would review grammar, flow, content, use of graphics, and reading level. Both the text and illustrations might go back to the originator for some changes or clarification.

Once the text was approved, *galleys* of type would be created by the *typesetters*. Typesetters knew all the rules of *typography* and generated the galleys for the production group. The production group would *paste up* the illustrations with the type to produce *camera-ready copy*, or CRC.

Figure 1-2 illustrates the document production or printing cycle. Once the camera-ready copy is created, photographic *negatives* are then created, from which the printing plates are produced. A small sample of documents will be printed and bound. These sample documents are then production *proofed* to assure that:

- No pages are missing

- Pages are in the correct order
- Because the pages are composed of illustrations and loose type, text and illustrations are checked for positioning or missing.

After the sample documents are approved, the document is then placed into full production. This whole process then begins again if the document is revised or updated.

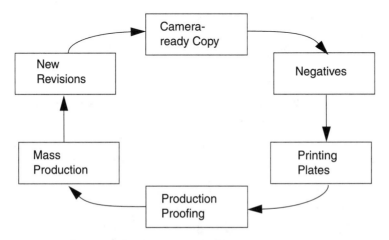

FIGURE 1-2. TYPICAL PRINTING CYCLE

The creation of the negatives and plates is typically left to the print shop, as well as the printing and binding of the books. Proofing the sample documents is done by both the printer and developer of the document.

With the advent of desktop publishing, we have seen these roles blur to the extent that most publications groups now consist of writers and editors, with the other functions divided amongst these roles. The role of the illustrator, unless the documents being produced are highly graphic or design-intensive, is typically accomplished by the writer. Figure 1-3 illustrates the modified publications group using desktop publishing tools. Notice the additional roles of:

- System administrator
- Application expert
- Template designer.

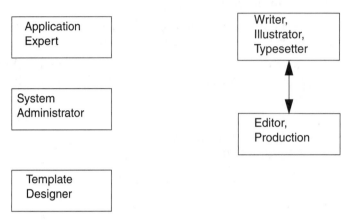

FIGURE 1-3. TYPICAL PUBLICATIONS GROUP AFTER DESKTOP PUBLISHING

The system administrator became a requirement because of the complexity of the systems being used, networking requirements, and the complexities of managing heterogeneous systems. If you were lucky, this function was handled by a central *MIS* group; in most cases, what I have found is that these initial tools went unsupported by MIS because the publications group was using machines and software that typically were not supported by MIS. If you not only brought in a desktop publishing system, but also brought in *computer-aided drafting* (CAD) systems for illustrators, you complicated this environment even more.

The application expert typically develops over time. In a large organization, there are always one or two people that will learn all the details of the systems being used. These application experts then become a resource for being able to take on new and more complicated jobs, as well as training new users. The application expert has, in my experience, also been key in converting documents between systems and platforms because they have spent time learning the intricacies of the tools.

In some environments, I have seen the applications expert learn the programming language of the tools and build enhancments into the generic tool that allowed for better processing or greater consistency in the documents or illustrations.

The template designer combines some of the skills of a *graphics designer* and a typesetter. They design the page layout and incorporate the typography rules into the styles or components with which the writers will tag their text. The template is the only way to guarantee consistency in documentation design. Depending upon how many types of documents that you produce, this task can become a full-time job.

Desktop publishing not only changed the publications group, but it also changed the printing cycle. If your printer can offer you all the services available today, you can send your document directly from your system to the printing plate, skipping several steps. Figure 1-4 illustrates the potential of today's printing cycle. Now that your documents are in electronic format, you have added to the possible uses of your information. Today you can provide your documentation not only on paper, but in electronic form as help files, or online documentation, or via the WWW.

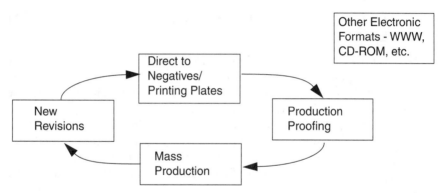

FIGURE 1-4. TYPICAL PRINTING CYCLE WITH DESKTOP PUBLISHING

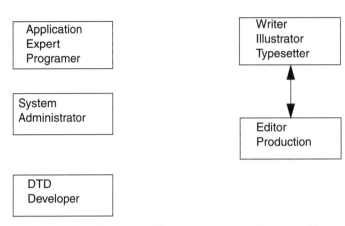

FIGURE 1-5. TYPICAL PUBLICATIONS GROUP USING SGML SYSTEMS

Figure 1-5 shows the slight changes required to support an SGML publishing environment within the publications group. In this scenario, I have had the template designer take on the responsibilities of learning all the details of SGML and maintaining the DTD(s). The applications experts have taken on additional responsibilities for programming the tools that are being used. With this arrangement, your writers and editors need little more than the basics of SGML; the applications experts and other staff members will hide most of the details, leaving the writers to write.

PUBLICATION TYPES

Publications come in a variety of types, ranging from the daily newspaper to the manuals that are included with your computer. There is a lot of overlap between document types and how they are created. For the purposes of this book, I'm going to consider the following types of documents:

- Regulated
- Technical
- Database-generated
- Interactive.

REGULATED DOCUMENTS

Generally, regulated documents are those that are created to a mandated standard. Typically these documents come from the defense, aerospace, or pharmaceutical industries. Each of these industries have governmental agencies that set the standards and requirements for compliance through standards and regulations. A new form of regulation is starting to emerge in industries that share data. Industrial consortiums, like the semi-conductor and automotive industries, are starting to develop regulations governing the interchange of their information.

Standards in this category of documents exist to make them easier to use, more consistent in structure, or to allow for the interchange or reuse of information. These standards prior to SGML were implemented as style guides that instructed writers and illustrators how to build a document. In an SGML system, these standards become DTDs. Technical or database-generated documents that are written to standards are also regulated documents.

TECHNICAL DOCUMENTS

Technical documents are the manuals that come with software, computers, cars, and your VCR. Technical documents can range from a few pages in length to many volumes. Technical documents in non-regulated areas are typically written to an internal style guide. The documentation of two companies in the same industry can look very different, but within each company, there will be a consistency based upon the company's internal style guide.

DATABASE-GENERATED DOCUMENTS

Database-generated documents have typically been illustrated parts lists or catalogs. This type of document isn't read as much as it is used for quick reference, locating a part, or providing ordering and specification information. When printed, this document becomes a static version of the information based upon the time when it is published. With the advent of online documents, database-generated documentation never needs to be published and can always be tied to active (updated) information. A parts catalog can also be used as a graphical interface to finding operational and maintenance procedures if it is linked together with these other document types.

INTERACTIVE DOCUMENTS

Interactive documents are a new category of document that has become available with online documentation systems. In some ways, I classify the CD-ROM versions of encyclopedias on the low end of this group. These documents tend to be very media-intensive applications, but it is up to the user to navigate and search through the documents for information. The *interactive technical manual* provides many of the same features, but adds to it an understanding of the user and the procedure being performed.

Interactive documents allow the information being presented to the reader to be tailored on-the-fly based upon any parameters that are appropriate to the application. Tailoring parameters can include:

- Security clearance

- Experience level

- Product model and product upgrade or modification

- Service cycle.

Interactive technical manuals basically document a process or procedure with instructions written for different levels of users, multiple product lines, or multiple optional features. Along with the procedural information is also encoded tailoring parameters that allow the presentation of the document to be modified for a specific use.

For instance, if you are documenting a line of copiers, there may be several base units that are then modified with additional features like sorters, feeders, staplers, etc. When the reader or maintenance technician starts to use an interactive technical manual, he or she will enter the parameters that describe the unit that is being repaired and his or her experience and training level.

The *presentation system* or document *browser* that the technician uses then only presents the procedures for the features and unit that is under repair. The information may also be presented at a very detailed level if this is a new procedure for the reader, or it might be presented in a very brief outline form that just validates that the critical steps and measurements are taken.

2 WHAT IS A DESKTOP PUBLISHING SYSTEM?

In this chapter, I will examine the typical desktop publishing system (DTP). We will dissect this application into the following parts:

- *Graphical user interface* (GUI)
- *Markup*
- Support utilities
- Multi-media support
- Operating system interface
- Conventions.

PARTS OF A DESKTOP PUBLISHING SYSTEM

When you use a desktop publishing system to create a document, you view that tool as one application. In reality, the DTP system is composed of a variety of tools. Each of these tools must exist in an SGML-based publishing system; miss one and you have an incomplete tool.

GRAPHICAL USER INTERFACE (GUI)

GUIs vary by computer platform. Three primary GUIs are typically supported:

- Microsoft Windows
- Apple Macintosh
- X-Windows with the Motif window manager.

The GUI provides the basic human-computer interface. A good interface provides a consistent way of supporting the following:

- Cut/copy/paste/delete
- Find/change
- Menus/windows/dialog boxes
- File manipulation
- Help.

Because this is standard functionality, we do not have to create anything special.

MARKUP

Although as a writer you do not see the markup you are creating, any DTP application creates it for you. In most of these applications, there is a "Save as" or "Export" function that allows you to see your text with the markup inserted. WordPerfect gives you a separate window or view to "reveal codes". The following are examples of markup languages and their supporting programs:

- Maker Interchange Format (MIF) - FrameMaker
- Interleaf ASCII Format (IAF) - Interleaf
- Rich Text Format (RTF) - Microsoft Word.

Markup, in a complex DTP system, supports the following features:

- Conditional text
- Formatting
- Character formats
- Equations
- Markers for hypertext, indexing, cross-references, etc.
- Headers and footers
- Paragraph formats

- Tables
- Hidden text and notes
- Variables
- Style sheets, catalogs, or templates
- Document review.

Each of the markup languages cited has a different way of saving or preserving this information. This difference is what creates the need for conversion programs and is the main reason for using SGML. SGML provides a different terminology to apply to these specific features, but it provides support for all of them through the *DTD* and its various features. We will discuss the features that are DTD-based in Chapter 5.

All of these features are embedded in the markup for each proprietary DTP system. In an SGML system, the formatting information is separated from the structural information. See Chapter 13 for options on storing and using the formatting information.

Style sheets or templates control the look and feel of a document. Most of the markup is generated and controlled through templates. A great amount of time can be spent in getting the line spacing, fonts, kerning, and margins "just so" for formatting purposes; the only structural thoughts are given to selecting names that convey the application of the style being created.

SUPPORT UTILITIES

To support the markup, several utility applications are used to process this information and produce the required results. The following features are supported by such utilities that are integrated into an application:

- Generation of table of contents (TOC), index, list of tables (LOT), illustrations (LOI), or equations (LOE)
- Spell checker and thesaurus
- Formatting and printing
- Auto-numbering lists, figures, tables, and footnotes
- Reports.

To support the generation of a TOC or index, markers are placed in the text or a list of items. A utility is then used to extract the information marked and format it.

A spell checker or thesaurus must examine the text, separate words from markup, and then compare that information to a dictionary or thesaurus.

The formatter is a utility that reads information stored in the document markup and produces a PostScript or other page description language data stream that is sent to the printer via the operating system. Desktop publishing systems have a single output method based upon creating a printed page. This output stream can also be diverted and sent to a file, typically as PostScript and then processed as PDF; but, there is usually not a way to output a variety of formats from this single source.

Auto-numbering is a utility that is used both in the authoring interface and the formatting for print. Reports are produced by any number of utilities that gather information useful for the maintenance and troubleshooting of the system.

MULTI-MEDIA SUPPORT

Desktop publishing systems require both text and graphics to be complete. The more robust applications have complete graphics development capabilities and all support the import of graphics in a variety of formats.

OPERATING SYSTEM INTERFACE

The operating system provides support for the following:

- Object linking and embedding capabilities
- Printing
- Fonts
- File management
- Character sets
- National language support.

Object linking and embedding is one of the newer capabilities available and there are a number of "standards" covering these capabilities. Some examples are:

- OLE—Object Linking and Embedding
- Open Doc
- DDE—Dynamic Data Exchange.

These standards or technologies allow objects to be embedded and displayed in applications that normally cannot display these objects. In actuality, what is being viewed is from the application program that developed it, and typically double-clicking these objects will launch the program to edit the object. While this is a very useful function that allows the automatic updating of these objects from the master data file, it is also very non-portable between users and systems. If you don't have the same system and same applications, you cannot produce the document.

Printing and font management are typically provided by the operating system. You may have had several fonts supplied for your DTP system, but it is the operating system that manages them. Between your DTP and the printer will be some sort of print driver that understands the capabilities of your printer and the request being made by the application program.

File management is one of the fundamental systems managed by the operating system. The operating system allows either long filenames or the "eight dot three" naming convention of DOS. File management is another area that decreases portability unless the user is aware of this issue and plans for it.

Character sets, national language support, and fonts all come together in the operating system to provide support for multiple languages and the ability to print them.

CONVENTIONS

Conventions play a big part in the publishing process when more than one author and document is involved. It is by convention that everyone agrees to use the same template or style sheet in the same way. There is nothing in the DTP system to enforce this.

It is also by convention that you use the names of the tags in the style sheet to control the structure of the documents produced. Typically, you will have styles named chapter, head1, head2, body, bullet, numlist, etc.

These same styles could just as easily be named 1, 2, 3, 4, 5, 6, etc. There is also nothing other than convention that says a tag named body has to be used for a paragraph rather than a title.

3 WHAT IS AN SGML PUBLISHING SYSTEM?

In the previous chapter we partitioned a desktop publishing system into the following parts:

- Graphical user interface (GUI)
- Markup
- Support applications
- Multi-media support
- Operating system interface
- Conventions.

The corresponding SGML-based publishing system will be examined in this chapter. We will explore the differences between the systems and examine the portability issues that are solved by using SGML.

Although SGML specifies how the markup should appear, there are considerations associated with the management of entities and how SGML files should actually be processed that are not very well defined and are cause for special or inconsistent handling by SGML tools. We will examine these areas that require special handling and thus will need to be accounted for and understood before you try and implement an SGML publishing system.

If you are unfamiliar with SGML, its structure, and its terminology, please review Appendix A.

An SGML Publishing System Compared to a DTP System

Although the purpose of this book is to examine commercial tools that support SGML, it must be noted that SGML was designed with the ability to work with a plain ASCII editor. Thus, features like the GUI and multi-media support are not required to work with SGML files, but they are highly recommended for anything but the most trivial documents.

Most SGML systems separate the management of the data and markup from the delivery or formatting systems. In fact, this is typically accomplished by two different applications available from different vendors. This can be seen as a problem or as a feature, depending upon your current delivery methods. We will examine these formatting options for print and online delivery in Chapter 13.

Support for multi-media formats is a rendering or formatting concern. Within an SGML editing system, these are entities or external file references that don't need to be resolved while editing a document. In the authoring system, we are only concerned with the management of the links to multi-media objects. It is the delivery system that must be able to render those objects and locate them in the file system. Thus, most of the SGML systems available only import and display existing graphics; they do not support the creation of graphics within the authoring application.

Graphical User Interface (GUI)

The GUI provides the basic human-computer interface. The typical GUI that is provided by today's operating systems provides support for cut and paste, file manipulation, and help functions. Because this is standard functionality of the GUI we are running under, we do not have to create anything special, although we may need to provide additional programming to support some special function or capability that we want to provide.

In SGML, a cut and paste operation is not as simple as it is with plain ASCII text. In an SGML system, we must test and validate the area where the text is removed from and pasted to to make sure the structure is still valid. This extra functionality is provided in SGML tools, but there may be other features that need modifying to support your work environment that are not provided out-of-the-box.

MARKUP

In an SGML publishing system, the DTD allows us to encode practices that would normally be buried in a style guide or enforced by an editor (a person). The DTD captures the structure of a document and is in a format that can be read without the application software. (If you are unfamiliar with SGML, its structure, and its terminology, please review the information in Appendix A.)

With an SGML system, all the standard features are supported, such as:

- Conditional text
- Character formats
- Equations
- Markers for hypertext, indexing, cross-references, etc.
- Paragraph formats
- Tables
- Hidden text and notes
- Variables
- Structure and document organization.

The following items are format-specific. They reference structures and information within the SGML document, but they require a separate process to perform the task of formatting:

- Formatting
- Headers and footers
- Style sheets, catalogs, or templates.

The following features are supported by applications that extract or infer the information required to produce them:

- Document review
- Table of contents, index, list of figures, or list of tables.

Another aspect of SGML is that everything you need to know about how to read the document structure, markup, and use of external files and notations (other file formats) is contained in one of the following places: the declaration, DTD, or the content. There should be no surprises when working with an SGML document.

SUPPORT UTILITIES

The SGML standard provides the structures and markup to allow you to do anything you want. To work with SGML efficiently, support utilities need to be provided to access this information and then process it.

There are no standard table of contents or index processors available for SGML. These features in particular can be provided by the formatting engine, or they could be separate programs.

Generic spell-checkers could be used on an SGML document, but you would most likely want to have a tool that could tell the difference between the content and text entered in elements via attributes.

Auto-numbering capabilities are available in most DTP systems. With an SGML application, this is typically handled as part of the formatting process. Rather than have the markup contain this label information, it is preferred to have it generated by an application.

Within the SGML world, these tools and utilities are more obvious in their use apart from the editing tools. How well some of these tools integrate will depend upon the DTD and content being processed, and then ultimately on how much flexibility your base SGML tools provide.

MULTI-MEDIA SUPPORT

Desktop publishing systems only work with still images or graphics. SGML need not be restricted to these static formats. SGML can incorporate sound, video, and animation formats, as well as other proprietary formats like spreadsheets or databases. The NOTATION declaration allows you to specify the format being used by these external objects, and ENTITY definitions and references allow these objects to be placed in an SGML instance. It is then up to the supporting tools to decipher these formats and render the information. Not all SGML systems will be able to work with all formats; this is not a limitation of SGML, but of the applications you use to work with these files.

ArborText's ADEPT•Editor or ADEPT•Publisher is an example of a native SGML editor. These types of editing tools recognize a specific set of graphic formats and, via some configuration files, you can specify the tools with which you want to edit and render these formats. This is an example of one way an SGML tool may allow connectivity to outside applications.

OPERATING SYSTEM INTERFACE

The operating system issues for an SGML system primarily concentrate on the area of file management, character sets, and printing. SGML provides a standard mechanism for specifying the character set that the document and markup uses. Files or entities are managed through either a catalog mechanism that allows the user to map the entity name to a specific file, or via a SYSTEM pathname.

To print an SGML document, you must know where to find the files, what fonts to use, and how to connect or talk to the printer, all of which are provided via the operating system.

CONVENTIONS

Conventions and style guides generally control the documentation process in a typical publications group. Much of this information and process can be captured in a DTD, where the level of enforcement can also be set. A DTD can be defined to be very loose or very strict and guiding. If the DTD is strict, it can provide a great deal of guidance; if it is loose, you generally end up with an environment that is not much different than that using a standard DTP system.

GENERAL SGML IMPLEMENTATION CONSIDERATIONS

In this section, I will examine the common implementation or configuration considerations that you should be aware of while developing your DTD and designing your SGML system. I have divided this section into the following areas:

- Declaration file

- Entities
- SGML features.

DECLARATION FILE

The declaration file can be the first place that you run into difficulties if you are using a predefined DTD. Most systems assume a default declaration unless one is specified. You should determine what this base declaration is for all the tools that you will be using and verify that the SGML features you intend to use are available with each tool and that the declaration has those features activated.

The first items you will probably want to change are the length of element names and entity length. You will also want to verify that case-sensitivity is either on or off, depending on your preference.

ENTITIES

Entities can be used for the following purposes:

- Special characters
- External files and referenced objects.

Each of these uses has its own considerations for implementation. The following sections cover some specific issues with these different entity types. There is a common problem with controlling when values should be expanded and trying to maintain the original input. Any SGML parser will read these values and automatically substitute the proper values. You need to be aware of this potential situation and guard against expansion, or reapply the proper references as you process your documents.

SPECIAL CHARACTERS

Special characters can come about for two different reasons. The main reason is that the character is not on the keyboard. The second possibility is that the character is mapped to a different location in a different character set.

Referring to these characters by a name and then later mapping that name to a system/application-specific value allows you the greatest control. Without this control, you might print a file on a PC and then move the file to a Macintosh and print it with different results. The results could be anything from the character being missing or possibly worse, printing it as a completely different character.

These special characters are generally referenced via a series of ISO-specified files. These files will define the names and sometimes the correct system value for your application. If you are creating a series of different outputs from your documents, you may require multiple ISO entity files with the proper mappings. If this is the case, you will need to manage these duplicate files and create a method to switch the mapping for the correct processing.

EXTERNAL FILES AND REFERENCED OBJECTS

External entities are used to manage fragments of SGML documents or DTDs, or to reference non-SGML objects and place them within documents. These objects can be managed with system or PUBLIC identifiers via SGML constructs, but the actual mapping of locations to the actual file location may be managed via a catalog or some other application-specific method. Although there is a lot of commonality in how this is implemented, each vendor has done something slightly different in regard to entity file management.

The notation declaration allows you to define or describe the formats of included objects, but when it comes time to implement this feature, you are limited to the capabilities of the tools that you are using. Typically, this feature is used to include illustrations in a document. Most systems only support a small subset of all the formats that are available, but you will generally find support for the more useful formats. This feature also supports multi-media formats like sound and movies, but these formats are typically only supported by the SGML online browsers. When implementing an SGML system, you will need to verify which formats need to be supported and which tools are needed to support them. It may be that you don't need to view or listen to an object in the editor, but your delivery tool had better support the format or why use it?

SGML fragments are portions of a document that allow multiple authors to work on the same document or multiple documents to share sections of text. There is no standard way to work with these fragments and each tool will implement different ways to manage these entities. You can manage these fragments in the operating system without any application support, but today's SGML-based document management systems make this process much easier to manage and require less pre-thought and configuration to allow the sharing of any portion of a document, not just a file entity.

SGML FEATURES

These last items are just various aspects of SGML systems that can cause problems or deserve consideration.

If you must use processing instructions in your application, it is recommended that you define them as entities so that their use and all the possible values are known before discovering them in a document instance.

Comments are a useful documentation tool and I heartily recommend their use, but some systems do not retain them. Verify how your tools handle comment strings before investing a lot of effort in commenting your DTD or document.

Although the SGML syntax allows the document instance to contain overriding DTD structures and parameter entities, most SGML tools tend to pre-compile the DTD before you can load a document. To support this functionality, you either need a tool that reads the DTD each time, or you need to create a DTD for each combination of structures.

4

THE JETT IMPLEMENTATION METHODOLOGY

Every implementation is unique and has its own set of requirements and potential pitfalls. Many SGML implementations have failed, but there are also numerous successful implementations. The premise of this book is that you have already decided that SGML is the correct approach and that it has been properly justified. A key factor in any implementation, besides knowing how to implement, is having a champion within your organization.

A champion should be someone high enough in the organization to have control or influence over the various groups involved in your implementation. The champion should have a vision for how SGML will improve the current process and how document/information management will play a key role in managing your company's information assets.

The typical implementation primarily revolves around technical publications, but there are many design, implementation, research, and marketing documents that, if managed as a common resource, can benefit the entire company, not just a particular organization. Hopefully your champion will have considered these issues and picked the correct first implementation. You want to make sure that you implement each phase properly while considering the larger issues of the final implementation.

Figure 4-1 illustrates the "perfect" implementation team. This team has at its center a champion around which is built a small core team of those that are needed to make key decisions and implement the system. This core team may change from phase to phase, but there will always be a central group that forms the primary design and implementation team. Associated with this group should be a larger cross-functional team that is reported to or consulted when the need arises. This group should be as large as needed, but they typically do not attend all meetings. This group is typically reported to whenever major design issues are resolved or milestones are met.

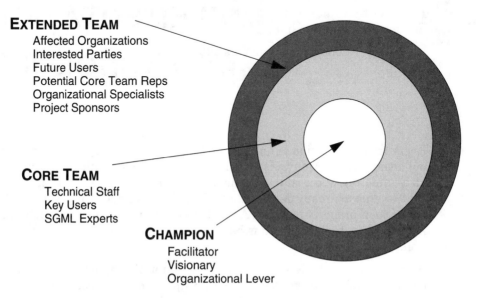

EXTENDED TEAM
Affected Organizations
Interested Parties
Future Users
Potential Core Team Reps
Organizational Specialists
Project Sponsors

CORE TEAM
Technical Staff
Key Users
SGML Experts

CHAMPION
Facilitator
Visionary
Organizational Lever

FIGURE 4-1. IMPLEMENTATION TEAM

After obtaining the proper team and champion, you next need a roadmap for how to implement. The JETT (Just Enough This Time) methodology is such a plan and is based on the following:

- Get something working as soon as possible

- Start simple and build upon that base

- Develop internal expertise.

GET SOMETHING WORKING

One of the biggest issues with implementing SGML is the time required to get started. I believe that most of this comes from trying to do too much, too soon, with too little knowledge or involvement of the users. If you divide the process of implementing your ultimate system into several steps, you will not only achieve that goal, but you will get there with a more educated user base. If you get a basic application up and running, you will build enthusiasm and confidence that you can deliver as promised.

Another reason for getting something working has to do with the group dynamics that I have encountered. Typically, I find that there is a split in end users along these lines:

- Early adopters or "I can't wait to change"

- Stable adopters or "I see a need to change, but I don't want to work with an incomplete application"

- Non-adopters or "I don't want to change."

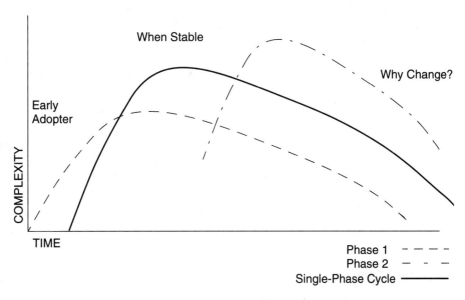

FIGURE 4-2. JETT-PHASED DEVELOPMENT METHODOLOGY

Figure 4-2 illustrates the relationship of the development cycle to the adoption of the application by the end user. Basically, the "early adopter" is willing to work with an application that is less than perfect. It is this group that you will want to work with initially while developing the application. The other attribute of this group is that it will not wait long before it wants to see results and get involved with the new system.

The "when stable" adopter is convinced that there is a need to change, but he or she doesn't want to be on the bleeding edge of development like the "early adopter." An application presented to this group should be well tested with very few missing components as well as being fully documented. This group is willing to use new tools but they don't want to struggle with the application to work.

The "non-adoption" group (or the why changers?) is a difficult group to work with. It must be brought into new tools gently and requires a very stable, well-documented environment; even then, it may not be happy. This group needs a lot of coaxing and hand-holding to get it to change, and having about two-thirds of the users using the new application should help in winning them over.

The methodology that I am recommending is to phase the development in two or more stages. As shown in Figure 4-2, the two dashed curves indicate the two phases of application development. As illustrated, you can see that the first curve doesn't take as long to implement and stabilizes, as does the single phase development cycle. This allows two of the three adoption groups to start using your application earlier. This first phase should be as complex as the knowledge within your development group will allow for a successful first implementation.

The second phase starts when the first is relatively stable and the early adopters are ready for something new. Now the development team has the benefit of what they learned about the tools, as well as a well-trained group of end users who can create better requirements. Notice also that Phase 2 has risen higher in complexity than the single phase approach. This is due to the greater knowledge of the implementors and end users and the ability to build upon a prior implementation.

START SIMPLE

While I recommend getting a fast start in building the first implementation, I'm not endorsing a mad dashed implementation; take enough time to design and specify the particular stage of implementation you are in, but don't overdesign it. My approach is based upon the software engineering methodology of rapid application development, or RAD.

RAD builds an application prototype and then presents it to the end users for comment and review. This gives the developer experience with the tools and the end users a chance to see what is being developed. This opens a dialog between the developers and end users to build the best system possible.

For me, the best system possible is a system that:

- Meets the major requirements of the end user
- Is maintainable by your development/support staff
- Functions within the limits of the tools that are being used.

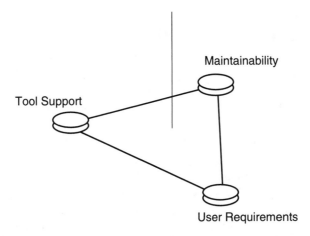

FIGURE 4-3. IMPLEMENTATION BALANCING ACT

The best system possible is an application that maintains the balance illustrated in Figure 4-3. In this drawing, you see that if any one of the three sides gets out of range of the others, the suspended triangle will tilt out of balance. A system out of balance is a project that will not succeed in the long run.

BUILD INTERNAL EXPERTISE

I can't stress this strongly enough: You must build internal expertise in SGML and the tools that you will be using. Use contractors or consultants to help you complete a phase, but don't let them do all the work for you. If you lack any of the skills used by the contractors to implement a phase, you will always be at the mercy of these contractors to make changes and improve your tools. SGML is a core competency and you should be getting into this for the long haul, not just a temporary solution.

My methods as outlined above should allow you to develop the internal expertise at the same time that you are developing the application. By working in small incremental pieces, you allow time for everyone in the core team to learn and improve their skills, as well as improve the application.

BUILD AN ENTERPRISE SOLUTION

Don't set your goals too low when implementing SGML. More power and benefit is achieved when the volume of information becomes larger. It is very difficult to access how much information reuse occurs in a company because of all the incompatible tools that are used to create the information, as well as the organizational barriers that tend to develop.

Let's look at a design and development process. The following scenario changes slightly if you consider a hardware or software implementation, but not enough to make a real difference. A design either starts with a set of requirements for a customer or an idea for a new product inside your company. These requirements specify what the product is, how it should function, and the anticipated operating specifications. Marketing may start as early as testing the market for the idea or establishing some industry experts to help steer the development.

As the product develops, changes occur and features are added or dropped. This process is documented through various means and new documents. As the product becomes functional, technical publications start to develop the documentation. This process has to start early enough to allow time to develop the documents, but late enough that there is some level of stability in the design and real articles that can be used and documented.

Technical support should be involved at this stage to monitor the usability and supportability, as well as to train the support staff in how the product functions (this is the dream world; typically this doesn't actually happen until the product is being released). Support documents to help with installation, configuration, or integration issues are developed. Marketing also starts to develop collateral materials for the sales force based upon the early design specifications and actual development.

As the product is released, the manuals are published, sales has its collateral material, and technical support starts to get calls on the product. As the product matures and the installed base stabilizes, the technical support call tracking system contains a wealth of actual implementation and compatibility problems, as well as bug documentation.

While the current product is being rolled out, the next version is started. Consider the number of documents, memos, design specifications, bug reports, and support calls that are logged during this process. How much of that information would be useful if it had gotten to the right group in the correct form when it was needed? The design documents are the bases of the early information contained in the technical manuals. If the design documents are maintained, and the publications group is linked to those changes, you can facilitate the spread of this information instead of catching the changes later in the process. Technical support calls and analysis of problems can feed the design and publications process if the information can be removed from the support system, tracked, and distributed as needed. This information becomes the basis for new procedures in the manuals or changes in the design of the product.

It is a major task to take on an information management and development process that takes into account all the potential documentation created during a design cycle, but it is this type of integration and reuse of information that makes SGML implementation viable.

Hopefully, soon after rolling out the first phases of the current implementation, you should start generating interest in what you are doing from outside your initial team. Use this interest to build a steering group that looks at the more cross-functional and enterprise-based implementation. Build upon the success of a working implementation to infiltrate other areas of your company.

SGML IS MORE THAN JUST DOCUMENTS

With the development of XML, the eXtensible Markup Language, it is becoming apparent that SGML has a much wider implementation than just documentation. XML is a simplified version of SGML that, in less than a year after its development, has already been used to build new standards and improve existing standards. Microsoft and other companies have started to use XML as the specification language and tool of choice for the Channel Definition Format and Open Financial Exchange. There are several efforts underway to improve the Electronic Document Interchange (EDI) process by incorporating XML processing. The healthcare industry is also looking at XML as the way to implement new billing and medical record processes.

With the advent of XML, SGML is being recognized as a facility and methodology for managing information (which it always was), and is finally being used to solve major information management issues. When building your implementation, be aware of the other possibilities for the use of SGML/XML.

PART II

DESIGN

5 ANALYZING DOCUMENTS FOR A DTD

I have chosen to develop a document type definition (DTD) as the first step in converting to SGML. If your project has a predefined DTD target, you may want to skip this chapter.

In this chapter, you will learn:

- What document analysis is
- How to develop a DTD based upon an existing document set.

DOCUMENT ANALYSIS

Document analysis is the process of examining your documents for the purpose of creating a document type definition (DTD). Most likely, someone in your organization has already done a similar type of analysis to create the template that you are currently using with your desktop publishing system. The process you used to define that template is similar to what we need to create the DTD. Table 5-1 compares the results of that process:

Table 5-1. Document Analysis Results for DTP and DTD

Object Created	When Applied to	
	DTP	DTD
Tag Names	Structure implied in the names. No containers or enforced hierarchies. Extra tags generally created to handle special instances of the same formatting (body, body in list, etc.).	Structural elements, creating containers and hierarchies of elements. A body and list paragraph are both paragraphs; no additional elements created to handle formatting issues.
Format and Page Layout	Part of template design.	Not applicable.
Content Markup	Typically implied with font changes; some tools have font catalog capabilities that allow the definition of specific character tags to handle formatting.	More analysis is used to define additional relationships and structures within content. Tags like book-title, product name, etc., instead of italics.
Style Guide	Defines formatting considerations and tag usage.	Defines the tags, any qualifying attributes, and special considerations. The actual usage (where allowed) is handled by the application and DTD.

As you might infer from the above table, a document analysis should result in two things when complete:

- A DTD (similar to the template in the DTP world)
- Documentation.

A template or DTD without the supporting documentation is only half the result of a document analysis. Without the supporting documentation that explains:

- The rationale for the naming conventions
- The decisions made

- The issues postponed
- How to use the template or DTD

you capture only the surface of the analysis that was done. The documentation provides answers for the end users and provides a guide and reference model for the continued evolution of the DTD. Yes, I said evolution! Any DTD that is being actively used will evolve over time. You need to plan for this and anticipate how changes will affect your design. I don't believe you will design every feature into your first DTD. As your writers get comfortable with SGML, your products and documentation will evolve. SGML tool suite changes will impact the DTD that you are using as well.

SKILLS REQUIRED

Document analysis for a desktop publishing system requires the skills of a graphic artist or typographer. The effort to define a template is to get the correct relationship of fonts, sizes, spacing, and page layout. In the desktop publishing world, tags are given names like chapter number, chapter title, head1, head2, and paragraph. These names imply structure and are typically the same as those applied in most DTDs; but, the difference is that they are only used to format the text.

Figure 5-1 illustrates probably the world's worst template design. If you look at this page without looking at the tags assigned to the different parts of the page you might be asking why I think this is a poor template design. It isn't until you look at the tag names that you realize there is a problem. The designer in this case has assigned logical structure names illogically to this page. In this illustration, it is the template designer who created a disaster for the writers to use and who prohibited any further document analysis.

A similar situation can occur when writers use tags that were meant for one purpose and apply them elsewhere with format changes. When we scan this page, we see a chapter break, followed by a first-level head or section, followed by some paragraphs and a second-level head or section, followed by more paragraphs, and then a note. Figure 5-1 illustrates the second skill required for document analysis: a sense of structure and effective use of logical names.

Document analysis in the SGML world is based on the ability to identify parts and provide logical names for these parts and structures. Typographic skills are useful in deciding when a structure should be generated from existing information. Other skills in page layout will be used later in this book to define the delivery process.

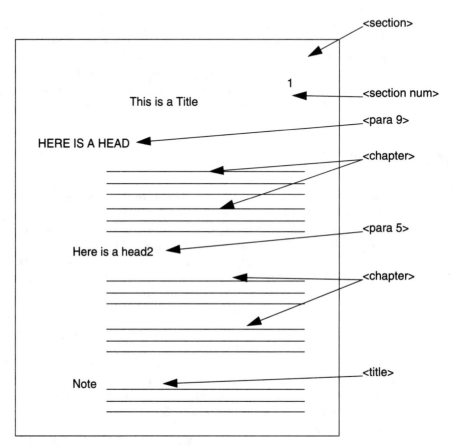

FIGURE 5-1. WORLD'S WORST TEMPLATE STYLE NAMES

DOCUMENT ANALYSIS METHODOLOGY

Before you start analyzing your documents, you must determine the boundaries for your design. You must determine:

- If you must use an industry standard DTD or deliver to one

- What types of documents you want to produce today vs. five years from now

  - Help systems

  - Multi-media

  - Page-based or pageless

  - Computer-based training

  - Database and event-driven documents

- If you will have to deliver paper hardcopy; if so, will this be a permanent requirement?

- How many DTDs will you need?

INDUSTRY-STANDARD DTDs

Several industries have created DTDs to be used for the interchange of information amongst the members of the industry. Typically, these DTDs recommend that you not use them directly as your authoring environment. These DTDs have been designed by committees and thus have a lot of compromise built into them. This is required to be able to interchange information, but it is typically not the ideal environment for a specific application.

I have collected a number of these DTDs and have placed them on the CD-ROM at the back of this book. I recommend that you study these DTDs and try to reverse-engineer the designs; for most of the DTDs, this will be straightforward, but some industries have very specific document types that you may have never encountered, and thus will not have a reference from which to work.

If you belong to one of the industries that is working toward a standard, I suggest that you start studying that design while you analyze your documents. In particular, look at the content tags and determine which of those you will want your writers to use. You will also want to keep your document structure in-line with that of the standard, but you do not need to use the same names or all of the same levels. As long as your DTD can be processed by a program to produce a valid DTD based upon the standard, you will be okay. If your DTD is completely different in content, structure, and style from the standard, you will have a much more difficult time trying to make it compatible with the standard.

TYPES OF DOCUMENTS

What type of documents do you expect to be delivering five years from now? Are they the same as what you delivered yesterday? To put this in perspective, were you ready for the WWW and the demand for your documents to be available in a compatible format? For me, this is the best reason to build small applications. The requirements for documents are changing dynamically and so is the support for SGML. If you take two years to analyze your documents and build a DTD, the world will have changed before you complete it.

Let's look at the following types of documents:

- Page-based or pageless
- Help systems
- Multi-media
- Database and event-driven documents.

Page-based document types include hardcopy output and any online format that supports display of the document as it would be printed. Adobe Acrobat is the typical application to support page-based delivery of documents. An example of a pageless delivery would be documentation placed on the WWW in HTML format.

Nothing about using SGML tools would keep you from delivering your documentation in either of these formats. The page-based version would come directly from the hardcopy generation process. For pageless designs, you may want to add additional structures to the DTD to allow for greater hypertext capabilities and the inclusion of media types that are not currently included in your desktop publishing environment.

Table 5-2 draws some contrasts between these two approaches:

Table 5-2. Page-based vs. Pageless Document Formats

Page-based	Pageless
Exact representation of the page as printed.	Margins, page breaks, line breaks all mean nothing in this format.
Fonts and line breaks preserved.	Although the same fonts may be used, they are typically enlarged for on-screen viewing.
Shrink the window size and you crop part of the document and must scroll to see the same text.	Change the window size and text reformats to the new dimensions.
Typically does not produce hypertext links, allow the use of sound or video, full-text search, etc., without additional tools and effort.	Allows the use of hypertext links, sound or video, full-text search engines, etc.

Help systems have typically been authored in specialized tools to be viewed with proprietary viewers. Because of their proprietary nature, it has been difficult to provide a single help format that can be used in both a UNIX and Microsoft Windows format. With the methods I will be demonstrating in this book, you will see how easy it is to generate these proprietary formats from your SGML source files. If this is of interest to you, you must review the structures in help systems that support features you wish to use and be sure that you include structures in your DTD to support them.

Multi-media systems currently exist as separate applications from those of a publications group. These systems are typically characterized by a programming language, more graphics than text, and a variety of media types to support the application at hand. Multi-media applications are typical of demonstration tools and computer-based training. I believe that as SGML tools progress, the distinction between publishing tools and multi-media will disappear and they will become common features available to create a variety of applications.

Database and event-driven documents are interactive documents that can be programmed to respond to events. There is a great deal of research being done in this area. Applications are being developed to allow documents that:

- Though written for multiple models and configurations of a product, with the entry of a few model numbers, display only information related to the repair of the machine the user has.

- Though written for multiple levels of reader skills, tailor the document to the level of the user, based upon a few quick qualifying questions. Perhaps for the inexperienced user, instead of presenting a list of instructions, the application presents video or animation with narration for the process that might be too detailed for the experienced reader.

- Troubleshoot a problem based upon a list of attributes, usage, last repair, or maintenance completed, and provide a detailed list of repair or maintenance procedures tailored for a system. When this application is tied together with a database that knows the repair history of the product and the supply levels of replacement parts, you now have a complete maintenance or troubleshooting tool.

It is this interactive document that I believe will merge the aspects of today's documents with the features of multi-media. It is this combination of documentation creation skills and application development that I look forward to. Although this is where I believe documentation is headed, I definitely don't recommend you try and design your first implementation to be a fully interactive environment. Build to this gradually, you have much to learn about the content of your documents, SGML, and how the tools function. I also believe that there is more development needed by tools vendors to make this a truly viable application, unless you wish to develop your own delivery tools.

HARDCOPY REQUIREMENTS

If you are required to deliver hardcopy versions of your documentation, you have some real design issues to consider if you also want to support interactive documentation.

If you need to support this mixed world, you need to decide what is your primary deliverable; which form of the documentation, do you believe, is the most useful or used most often. Many of the online documentation systems that I have seen today are based upon writing the book and then delivering some sort of online version of the document. Now that online tools are becoming more accepted, I believe that these providers should focus on writing for the online environment and convert for hardcopy. Table 5-3 summarizes some of the changes I believe need to be made:

Table 5-3. Writing for Online vs. Hardcopy

Online	Hardcopy
Modular information chunks that provide all the information required, or links to that information.	Typically written in a linear fashion, where information at the beginning of a section is meant as precondition or setup information for a particular detail step later in the section.
Automatic cross-references to internal and external materials.	Cross-references usually a combination of automatic references and hardcoded text references; all that matters is that the text link is established between the sources.
Build accurate stand-alone modules, without transitional text. User typically is only working with a procedure, and wants complete references to related topics.	Some amount of time is used to smooth the transition from one procedure to the next, or to provide an introduction to the chapter.
Many standard features in a book are not needed. A glossary should exist as links to words, not as a separate section. Headers, footers, and page numbers have no place in an online document. Remove all references to page numbers. With an online document, you can use more graphical methods for navigation between sections and topics	The table of contents, list of figures, etc., are typically generated by the DTP. These features are also generated by SGML systems. An index is created with a great amount of work and is then pulled together by the DTP system. There is some value to having a true index that uses phrases and concept indexing rather than straight word combinations. If your index consists only of word combinations, a full-text retrieval system will easily replace this feature.

HOW MANY DTDS ARE NEEDED?

"Need more than one DTD?" Yes. Not only does my methodology require several generations of a DTD to transition to a true SGML approach, you may also require versions to:

- Author for
- Convert to
- Deliver to.

Authoring DTDs may be configured to allow for different levels of a complete document to be worked on, rather than starting at a book level. For instance, you may have a smaller DTD that addresses a procedure, so the author is only working at that level rather than worrying about transitional and wrapping information.

Conversion DTDs can be configured to allow more flexibility in content, or the ordering of the parts of a document. This allows the initial transition to SGML to have fewer errors but still be valid.

Authoring DTDs typically use a lot of generated text for labels, and cross-references may not be much more than markers from the source to the reference. The order of an authoring DTD may not be the same as the final output, and entire sections may be configured to be generated from other sources.

Delivery DTDs may be configured to have labels contained in the elements, and possibly to have the organization of the document changed. Some delivery tools have less capabilities for the generation or extraction of information from the source material, and thus need more specific values and content available.

DEVELOPING A DTD

In this section, we will discuss the process of creating a DTD and using some of the design tools that are available to assist in this process. Once the DTD is developed, you may need to provide additional catalog or map files for the various tools that you use, and in some cases, you may have to make slight modifications to the DTD itself.

SAMPLE DOCUMENTS

I have included a 30-page sample FrameMaker document that will be used in the examples in this book. The sample is fully documented in Appendix D and the actual FrameMaker files with an Adobe Acrobat PDF version are available on the CD-ROM at the back of this book (refer to Appendix E for information on how to view this document). Due to the limits of my sample set, I will not be able to show the refinement process or how to combine formats that are treated as unique document types, but I will give you a good start on this process.

Your Document Samples

While you work through this chapter, you should start collecting samples of your documents. For the purpose of document analysis and DTD development, you should:

- Determine the number of documents you publish and how often they are updated
- Determine the number of formats you publish in, which includes:
  - How many templates are used?
  - How many different page formats do you publish in?
  - What types of documents do you produce: User Guide, Command Reference Guide, Release Notes, Installation Guide, Configuration Guide, etc. ?
- If one exists, get a copy of the latest writer's style guide.

Once you have determined the answers or collected the above items, you can decide how many documents you should analyze to establish your DTD.

Learn all you can about the current format and get the vendor's format documentation (typically not current or complete). There is probably a style guide that is being used (typically not current, but a good source for what should be happening). Talk to managers about the quality of the writing from a markup and keying standpoint, but believe key writers and production people about the quality. Determine the number of changes the documents may have gone through; consider style guide/template changes, the number of writers involved, and the types of tools used.

In addition to samples of input documents, you will want to create an SGML sample document that displays the use of the elements and attributes. Later you will use this SGML file to test your formatting and processing tools.

ANALYZING THE SAMPLE DOCUMENT

In this section, I will walk through the general analysis process that I use when developing a DTD. The DTD that we develop here will be my initial DTD for conversion purposes. The intent is to define enough structure and content markup to enable a successful conversion, in this case, from FrameMaker to SGML.

Following this walkthrough, I will illustrate the design process using Near & Far and SGML Companion. The following process is based on looking at the tags or styles that are applied to the various elements of the original document. With most word processing or desktop publishing systems, a catalog or template is created to apply consistent formatting. You can view these names typically in two different ways. First, if you have the application that created the document, you can open the file and place your cursor in a text block and somewhere in the interface the name of the tag will be displayed. Figure 5-2 illustrates the FrameMaker interface and the two locations where the tag name for a paragraph is displayed.

The other method to determine tag names is to save the file to the proprietary markup format of a tool. For my FrameMaker document, I would use the Save As option and then specify the format as Maker Interchange Format, or MIF. This creates a file with ASCII markup that you can then read with a plain text editor. I prefer this method because not only do I develop DTDs, I also develop conversion programs, so the sooner I get used to the format the better.

These two methods will display the actual use of the tag names. If your group has a style guide, you will probably have the recommended use of the styles. You need to combine both sets of information, as-is and recommended, to get the true view of the documentation set you are working with.

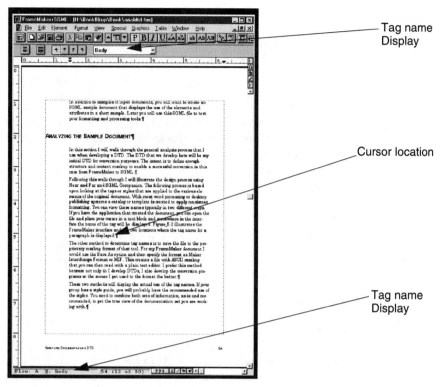

Tag name Display

Cursor location

Tag name Display

FIGURE 5-2. FRAMEMAKER TAG NAME DISPLAY

1. The first step in the process of analyzing your documents is to decide how similar or dissimilar the various documents are that you produce. Dissimilarities that are only formatting specific can be ignored. Differences like page size and font type or size do not matter for this exercise. Are the documents similar in structure?—that is the real concern.

You may have decided that you have several types of documents at this point. That is perfectly all right. A key design issue is to keep compatibility between these document types; the various content models for similar structures should be the same to allow reusability of information at various levels. If all these document types will have some sort of procedural or list structure between, you should either keep the names and content models the same or create a different name and modify the content accordingly.

By keeping objects like paragraphs and lists identical in content, you will be able to share content at these levels between all your documents. The larger surrounding elements may have completely different structures and names, which will preclude the reusability at this larger level.

2. Determine a top-level name for the highest-level element. In this case, I only have a <book> I'm trying to define; in your case, create a name that represents all the types of documents that this DTD can be applied to.

3. I now look at the next level of organization. In this case, I have the following objects:

   ■ Cover and copyright information

   ■ Table of contents, list of figures, etc. (not in the sample document)

   ■ Chapters

   ■ Appendices

   ■ Index.

   Let's look at these objects. The table of contents information would be generated automatically from the document. The index, although it requires extra information to be embedded in the document, is generated information. These objects will have empty elements created to act as placeholders for where the information should be generated. The presence of a marker will determine if an object is to be generated. We will create empty elements <toc>, <lof>, and <index> for these objects.

   The cover might be treated as an illustration, or it could be a separately tagged set of information. Much of what appears in the copyright page is either boilerplate information, or is determined by what products are referenced in the document. This could be generated, or it could be separately tagged.

   What is the difference between an appendix and a chapter? I believe that the only difference is the location and how it is referenced. To differentiate between the two uses, but maintain the ability to rearrange the document, we will create a single object called <section>, but wrap it in <body> and <rearmatter> groupings. Figure 5-3 illustrates the current state of our design.

```
<!DOCTYPE    book         [
<!ELEMENT    book         - O      (cover,copyright,toc?,lof?,
                                     body,rearmatter,index?) >
<!ELEMENT    body         - O      (section+) >
<!ELEMENT    rearmatter   - O      (section+) >
]>
```

FIGURE 5-3. PRELIMINARY DTD

4. Examine the cover in Figure D-1 and its content. On the cover are the ManualTitle and SubTitle MIF tags. These will become <title> and <subtitle> elements on the cover, with <subtitle> being an optional element.

   There are two instances of the DocInfo MIF tag. Rather than create a similar generic label for this information, we will create the attributes PubDate and PartNo on the <book> element.

   The DTD now looks like this:

```
<!DOCTYPE    book         [
<!ELEMENT    book         - O(cover,copyright,toc?,lof?,
                                   body,rearmatter,index?) >
<!ATTLIST book
                          PubDate CDATA #REQUIRED
                          PartNO CDATA #REQUIRED >
<!ELEMENT    cover        - O      (title, subtitle?) >
<!ELEMENT    body         - O      (section+) >
<!ELEMENT    rearmatter   - O      (section+) > ]>
```

5. As indicated earlier, the copyright information could be generated from the correct sort of markup in the document, or we could capture this information in a model group. As shown in Figure D-2, this page consists of two different levels of heads and paragraph text that is smaller than the text used in the body of the document. This page of our sample uses MIF tags that are similar to those of the chapter or appendix. The names have been modified because different formatting was applied in this section. Because there is nothing special about the content, we will create compatible elements with those of the <section> or <preface> groups.

   To simplify the markup and facilitate ease of reuse, I will create a nested heading structure, rather than define each level specifically.

The <head> element will be the container that will include a <title> element to contain the text of the heading and multiple <para>'s with an optional nested heading structure. This gives us a content model for <copyright> as follows:

```
<!ELEMENT    copyright    - -    (head) >
<!ELEMENT    head         - -    (title,para+,head*) >
```

The nesting of heading elements in the above design makes it easier to promote or demote a heading group. What this design doesn't do is enforce a specific number of heading levels to be used or allowed. Had we used the alternate approach of <head1> and <head2> elements, we could have let the parser determine the allowed nesting level. With the design I have chosen, a separate program or routine will have to be developed to validate the nesting level.

6. Let's break down the structure of our <section> element. Look at the following figures: D-5, D-9, D-17, D-29, and D-33. In each of these figures, you see the start of a new section. Each of these chapters or appendices has a title, but only some of them have some sort of number or letter identifier. The decision must be made to keep Figure D-5 as part of the <section> model or to create a new element for this particular use.

    These are some of the options for handling this unique situation:

    ■ Create an attribute on the element that would indicate if the section should be labeled

    ■ Allow a section to exist outside the <body> or <rearmatter> groups

    ■ Create a new element for this group of information.

    One of the shortcomings of my sample document is that you can't read the information in the actual document. In this case, I know that this is the typical preface section and that there are elements that I am going to want to define just for this section of the document. My choice in this instance is to create a new element, <preface>, that will have virtually the same content as a <section>, but it will not appear in a <body> or <rearmatter> group. The other element that we will use is <title>.

7. Let's continue to look at the content and structure of the <section> and <preface> groups. For each of these sections in our sample, the author has started the section with one or more paragraphs, bullet

items, and at least one caution before the first heading level is found. Our content model is starting to look like this:

```
<!ELEMENT     section     - -     (title, para+,
                                  (bullet-list|caution)*,head)>
<!ELEMENT     preface     - -     (title, para+,
                                  (bullet-list|caution)*,head)>
```

8. <section> is now using the <head> element that we started to define in <copyright>. I'm going to allow the same structure inside both. You may have some need to keep these separate. Refer to Figure D-5.

Notice that after each of the MIF Heading1 tags, there is a MIF BodyAfterHead tag. This paragraph only differs from a standard paragraph due to formatting, so it will be modeled as <para> in our DTD. Following this paragraph is our <bullet-list>. Figure D-6 shows that a table can also follow our introductory <para>. Our <table> element will be a group that will contain the rows and columns of the table, as well as an optional <title> (in other locations, we will find titles being used, too).

```
<!ELEMENT     head     - -     (title,para+,
                               (bullet-list|table)*,head*) >
```

Tables can become a major problem depending on how you define your model. In most cases, it is recommended that you define elements and structures that aren't format- or presentation-based. In defining a table as a group of columns and rows, I would really be specifying a particular layout and presentation of the information.The proper way to define this structure is to determine what the relationships are between these objects and define the objects accordingly.

The above is the proper way to model the information contained in the table, but now, how will our tools work with this information? Many of the SGML editors that are available either support the CALS table model or a proprietary format of their own. The primary reason for this is that these table models have been embedded in the software. What this means to our design is that if you want the software to support the editing and printing of your documents, you must use one of these supported models or create a process that will convert your markup to one of the supported models.

For our table model, we will use the CALS table. This is a rather complex set of markup, but with the support provided by the SGML editor, it isn't that difficult to actually implement. Figure 5-4 contains the CALS table model as implemented by ArborText. We will reference this model into our DTD as directed:

```
<!ENTITY % calstbl PUBLIC
                   "-//ArborText//ELEMENTS CALS Table
                   Structures//EN">
%calstbl;
```

9. If you continue to examine the rest of the pages in the sample document, you will find that Figure D-12 is the first that introduces new content for our <head> element.In this figure, the Bullet Dash MIF tag is introduced. This is a second-level bullet item within a bullet list. Just like we did with the <head> element, we will allow the nesting of <bullet-list> elements to create this object. Figure D-14 introduces the BulletedCont MIF tag. This is a simple paragraph that continues the text of a previous item. With this last item, we now have the complete content model for our <bullet-list>.

```
<!-- Public document type declaration subset. Typical
 invocation:
<!ENTITY % calstbl PUBLIC
"-//ArborText//ELEMENTS CALS Table Structures//EN">
%calstbl; -->
<!--$Id: cals-tbl.elm,v 23.2 1995/05/02 10:58:09 txf Exp $-->
<!-- This entity is a fragment representing the CALS table
 structures as exemplified in MIL-M-28001 (though with some different
parameter entities to facilitate non-CALS use).
NOTE: The table element and attribute declarations reference a number of
parameter entities that may need to be redefined before this fragment is
referenced. (Note that all of these have declarations in this fragment that
will be used if they are not declared elsewhere before this fragment is
referenced.)
If any of these entities are not declared before this fragment is referenced,
the following generic defaults will take effect: -->
<!ENTITY % tblelm "table">
<!ENTITY % tblmdl "(tgroup+)">
<!ENTITY % tblexpt "-(table)">
<!ENTITY % tblcon "(#PCDATA)*">
<!ENTITY % bodyatt "">
<!ENTITY % secur "">
```

FIGURE 5-4. CALS TABLE MODEL

10. <bullet-list> is the container for the items in our list. The individual
    entries within the list will be grouped with an <item> group, and
    within an <item>, we will allow <bullet-list>s and <para>s.

```
<!ELEMENT bullet-list- -  (item) + >
<!ELEMENT item- -          (para|bullet-list)+ >
```

11. Figure D-12 also introduces the ExampleHead MIF tag. This
    appears to be a special type of heading that doesn't follow our
    standard <head> model. However, I will hazard a guess that all the
    same content should be allowed in our <example> group, but that
    <example> should not nest.

```
<!ELEMENT    example     - -    (title,para+,
                                (bullet-list|table)*) >
<!ELEMENT    head        - -    (title,para+,
                                (bullet-list|table|
                                example)*,head*) >
```

12. Figure D-13 introduces the Figure and Numbered MIF tags. These appear to be within our <example> group at the moment, but we will make the decision to include them in the standard <head> group as well. Figure D-14 introduces both an optional <title> and a required graphic. Rather than using a specific element or entity reference to insert the graphic, we will use attributes on <figure> to contain the entity reference and information about the size of the frame to place the graphic in.

An item is numbered within a <number-list>. We will model the <number-list> the same as our <bullet-list>, because they only differ by their label and the fact that <number-list> items are order-dependent.

```
<!ELEMENT    example      - -    (title,para+,
                                  (bullet-list|table|
                                  figure|number-list)*) >
<!ELEMENT    head         - -    (title,para+,
                                  (bullet-list|table|
                                  example|figure|
                                  number-list)*,
                                  head*) >
<!ELEMENT    figure       - -    (title?) >
<!ATTLIST    figure       width  NUTOKEN#IMPLIED
                          height NUTOKEN#IMPLIED
                          name   ENTITY#IMPLIED >
<!ELEMENT    number-list  - -    (item)+ >
<!ELEMENT item- -                (para|bullet-list)+ >
```

Figure 5-5 shows the DTD at this stage. Note that I am using an entity reference to bring in the CALS table model.

13. Figure D-15 introduces the MIF tags Note and SystemOutput. <note> will be modeled like a <caution>, and <system> will be a new style of paragraph.

```
<!ELEMENT    (caution,note)- -   (para+) >
<!ELEMENT    system       - -    (#PCDATA) >
```

```
<!ELEMENT %tblelm; - -%tblmdl;%tblexpt>
<!ATTLIST %tblelm;tabstyleNMTOKEN#IMPLIED
          tocentry     NUMBER    "1"
          shortentry   NUMBER    #IMPLIED
          frame        (top|bottom|
                       topbot|all|
                       sides|none) #IMPLIED
          colsep       NUMBER    #IMPLIED
          rowsep       NUMBER    #IMPLIED
          orient       (port|land)#IMPLIED
          pgwide       NUMBER    #IMPLIED
          %bodyatt;
          %secur;>
<!ELEMENT tgroup   - O(colspec*,spanspec*,
          thead?,tfoot?,tbody)>
<!ATTLIST tgroupcols     NUMBER #REQUIRED
          tgroupstyle NMTOKEN #IMPLIED
          colsep       NUMBER  #IMPLIED
          rowsep       NUMBER  #IMPLIED
          align        (left|right|
                       center|justify|
                       char) "left"
          charoff      NUTOKEN  "50"
          char         CDATA    ""
          %secur;>
<!ELEMENT colspec  - OEMPTY>
<!ATTLIST colspeccolnum  NUMBER #IMPLIED
          colname      NMTOKEN#IMPLIED
                       align (left|right|
                             center|justify|
                             char)#IMPLIED
                       charoffNUTOKEN#IMPLIED
                       char  CDATA#IMPLIED
                       colwidthCDATA#IMPLIED
                       colsep NUMBER#IMPLIED
                       rowsep NUMBER#IMPLIED>
```

FIGURE 5-4. CALS TABLE MODEL (CONTINUED)

```
<!ELEMENT spanspec - O EMPTY>
<!ATTLIST spanspecnamest NMTOKEN #REQUIRED
          nameend        NMTOKEN #REQUIRED
          spanname       NMTOKEN #REQUIRED
          align          (left|right|
                         center|justify|
                         char)  "center"
          charoff        NUTOKEN #IMPLIED
          char           CDATA   #IMPLIED
          colsep         NUMBER  #IMPLIED
          rowsep         NUMBER  #IMPLIED>
<!ELEMENT (thead|tfoot) - O(colspec*,row+)-(entrytbl)>
<!ATTLIST theadvalign    (top|middle|
                         bottom) "bottom"
          %secur;>
<!ATTLIST tfoot
          valign         (top|middle|
                         bottom) "top"
          %secur;>
<!ELEMENT tbody    - O(row+)>
<!ATTLIST tbody
          valign         (top|middle|
                         bottom) "top"
          %secur;>
<!ELEMENT row      - O(entry|entrytbl)+>
<!ATTLIST row
          rowsep         NUMBER  #IMPLIED
          %secur;>
```

FIGURE 5-4. CALS TABLE MODEL (CONTINUED)

14. Figure D-18 shows a Numberd1 MIF tag, as well as Numbered and the continuing paragraph being used. The Numbered1 tag is required to restart a numbering sequence in FrameMaker, and we don't need that in our DTD.

```
<!ELEMENT entry    - O %tblcon;>
<!ATTLIST entry
            colname     NMTOKEN #IMPLIED
            namest      NMTOKEN #IMPLIED
            nameend     NMTOKEN #IMPLIED
            spanname    NMTOKEN #IMPLIED
            morerows    NUMBER "0"
            colsep      NUMBER #IMPLIED
            rowsep      NUMBER #IMPLIED
            rotate      NUMBER "0"
            valign      (top|bottom|
                        middle)#IMPLIED
            align       (left|right|
                        center|justify|
                        char) #IMPLIED
            charoff     NUTOKEN#IMPLIED
            char        CDATA #IMPLIED
            %secur;>
<!ELEMENT entrytbl - -
            (colspec*,spanspec*,thead?,tbody)+
                        -(entrytbl)>
<!ATTLIST entrytbl
            cols        NUMBER #REQUIRED
            tgroupstyle NMTOKEN#IMPLIED
            colname     NMTOKEN#IMPLIED
            spanname    NMTOKEN#IMPLIED
            colsep      NUMBER #IMPLIED
            rowsep      NUMBER #IMPLIED
            align       (left|right|
                        center|justify|
                        char) #IMPLIED
            charoff     NUTOKEN#IMPLIED
            char        CDATA #IMPLIED
            %secur;>
```

FIGURE 5-4. CALS TABLE MODEL (CONTINUED)

```
<!DOCTYPE      book           [
<!ELEMENT      book           - O    (cover,copyright,toc?,lof?,
                                      body,rearmatter,index?) >
<!ATTLIST      book

                                      PubDate CDATA #REQUIRED
                                      PartNO CDATA #REQUIRED >
<!ENTITY% calstbl PUBLIC
          "-//ArborText//ELEMENTS CALS Table Structures//EN">
%calstbl;
<!ELEMENT      cover          - O    (title, subtitle?) >
<!ELEMENT      body           - O    (section+) >
<!ELEMENT      rearmatter     - O    (section+) >
<!ELEMENT      copyright      - -    (head) >
<!ELEMENT      section        - -    (title, para+,
                                      (bullet-list|caution)*,head)>
<!ELEMENT      preface        - -    (title, para+,
                                      (bullet-list|caution)*,head)>
<!ELEMENT      example        - -    (title,para+,
                                      (bullet-list|table|
                                      figure|number-list)*) >
<!ELEMENT      head           - -    (title,para+,
                                      (bullet-list|table|
                                      example|figure|
                                      number-list)*,
                                      head*) >
<!ELEMENT      figure         - -    (title?) >
<!ATTLIST      figure         width  NUTOKEN#REQUIRED
                              height NUTOKEN#REQUIRED
                              name   ENTITY#REQUIRED >
<!ELEMENT      number-list    - -    (item)+ >
<!ELEMENT      bullet-list    - -    (item)+ >
<!ELEMENT      item           - -    (para|bullet-list)+ >
]>
```

FIGURE 5-5. INTERMEDIATE-STAGE SAMPLE DTD DESIGN

15. Figure D-19 shows a cross-reference to a table and Figure D-21 shows several uses of cross-references to figures. The <xref> tag will be allowed inside any <para>, but what will it reference? In the examples we have, it references just figure and table titles. This is where you need to know more about your documents. Do you allow

references to headings and chapter titles? What about references to specific paragraphs or steps in a list?

The standard SGML method to create and reference parts of a document uses ID and IDREF values in attributes. To use IDs, they must be unique within a document and the SGML parser will validate this for you. But what happens when you share a section of text between two different documents? You need to provide a mechanism to insure that IDs are unique across all the documents in your domain to allow sharing of information. An SGML-based document management system will provide this capability, or you need to create a naming convention and maintain this yourself.

The alternate approach is to use a similar mechanism, but not use the SGML ID and IDREF, and generate this information in a label-type field. This method would require an application or a standard methodology as well to maintain the compatibility of files. The labels in this case could possibly be based upon the filename and a number value to make them unique and maintainable.

For our purposes here, we will use the ID and IDREF method. We need to create IDs on any object we wish to reference in our document.

```
<!ATTLIST    item      id    ID            #IMPLIED >
<!ATTLIST    title     id    ID            #IMPLIED >
<!ELEMENT    para      - -   (xref|#PCDATA)* >
<!ELEMENT    xref      - -    EMPTY >
<!ATTLIST    xref      ref   IDREF >
```

16. Figure D-19 shows a footnote reference in a table and Figure D-20 shows the actual footnote. To manage the <table> and <footnote>s, I wrap them with a <figure> group. Now, some of you may object to this, but how does a figure differ from a table? Many tables could actually be represented as charts and graphs as alternate forms of the tabular data.

```
<!ELEMENT    footnote     - -    (para)+ >
<!ATTLIST    footnote
             symbol       (level1,level2,  #REQUIRED
                          level3)#REQUIRED
             footnote-id id                        #IMPLIED >
<!ELEMENT    ftnoteref    - -    EMPTY >
```

```
<!ATTLIST    ftnoteref   idref  IDREF#IMPLIED >
<!ELEMENT    figure       - -    ((title?,table?),
                                   footnote*) >
```

17. Figure D-25 shows the use of MIF tag ScreenText2. I'm going to model this the same as <system>.

18. Figure D-37 shows the formatted index for this document. We modeled <index> to be a marker for the location of the index, but it has no content. To create and maintain index entries, we must create an <indexitem> that will allow us to enter the various forms of index entries that can be generated.

```
<!ELEMENT    indexitem    - -    EMPTY >
<!ATTLIST    indexitem
                          type   CDATA#IMPLIED
                          text   CDATA#IMPLIED >
```

19. Figure D-6 shows the use of content markup as italics font changes. To model these, we should determine what the actual content is. Again, due to not being able to read the text, I'll have to tell you that the italics information is a reference to each section of this document, and the following text is a brief summary of the content. This is your typical "About this document" section.

For this standard structure, I'll create another marker-type element, <aboutsection>, that will indicate where this should be placed and generated. The actual summary will become part of the section model. The <summary> element will contain this information, and if it is not present, that particular section will not be listed.

```
<!ELEMENT    aboutsection- -    EMPTY >
<!ELEMENT    summary      - -    (para+) >
<!ELEMENT    section      - -    (title,summary?,para+,
                                  (bullet-list|caution)*,head)>
```

20. At various places in the document, you will find trademark, copyright, and degree symbols in the text.To reference these objects, we will bring in the standard character entities as follows:

```
<!ENTITY% ISOpub PUBLIC
          "ISO 8879-1986//ENTITIES Publishing//EN" >
<!ENTITY% ISOnum PUBLIC
          "ISO 8879-1986//ENTITIES Numeric and Special
          Graphic//EN" >
<!ENTITY% ISOdia PUBLIC
```

```
  "ISO 8879-1986//ENTITIES Diacritical Marks//EN" >
<!ENTITY% ISOtech PUBLIC
  "ISO 8879-1986//ENTITIES General Technical//EN" >
<!ENTITY% ISOlat1 PUBLIC
          "ISO 8879-1986//ENTITIES Added Latin 1//EN" >
<!ENTITY% ISOlat2 PUBLIC
          "ISO 8879-1986//ENTITIES Added Latin 2//EN" >
<!ENTITY% ISOgrk1 PUBLIC
          "ISO 8879-1986//ENTITIES Greek Letters//EN" >
<!ENTITY% ISOgrk3 PUBLIC
          "ISO 8879-1986//ENTITIES Greek Symbols//EN" >
%ISOdia;
%ISOnum;
%ISOpub;
%ISOtech;
%ISOlat1;
%ISOlat2;
%ISOgrk1;
%ISOgrk3;
```

21. Combine all of the above, define all the remaining undefined objects, and you end up with the DTD shown in Figure 5-9.

```
<!DOCTYPE    book        [
<!ENTITY% ISOpub PUBLIC
            "ISO 8879-1986//ENTITIES Publishing//EN" >
<!ENTITY% ISOnum PUBLIC
  "ISO 8879-1986//ENTITIES Numeric and Special Graphic//EN" >
<!ENTITY% ISOdia PUBLIC
            "ISO 8879-1986//ENTITIES Diacritical Marks//EN" >
<!ENTITY% ISOtech PUBLIC
            "ISO 8879-1986//ENTITIES General Technical//EN" >
<!ENTITY% ISOlat1 PUBLIC
            "ISO 8879-1986//ENTITIES Added Latin 1//EN" >
<!ENTITY% ISOlat2 PUBLIC
            "ISO 8879-1986//ENTITIES Added Latin 2//EN" >
<!ENTITY% ISOgrk1 PUBLIC
            "ISO 8879-1986//ENTITIES Greek Letters//EN" >
<!ENTITY % ISOgrk3 PUBLIC
            "ISO 8879-1986//ENTITIES Greek Symbols//EN" >
%ISOdia; %ISOnum;
%ISOpub; %ISOtech;
%ISOlat1; %ISOlat2;
%ISOgrk1; %ISOgrk3;
<!ELEMENT    book        - O    (cover?,copyright?,toc?,lof?,
                                preface?,body?,rearmatter?,
                                index?)>
<!ATTLIST    book

                                PubDate CDATA #REQUIRED
                                PartNO CDATA #REQUIRED >
<!ENTITY % tblelm"table">
<!ENTITY % tblcon"(#PCDATA|bullet-list|
            number-list|caution|note|system)*">
<!ENTITY % calstbl PUBLIC
        "-//ArborText//ELEMENTS CALS Table Structures//EN">
%calstbl;
<!ELEMENT    toc         - O    EMPTY  >
<!ELEMENT    lof         - O    EMPTY  >
<!ELEMENT    index       - O    EMPTY  >
<!ELEMENT    aboutsection- -    EMPTY  >
```

FIGURE 5-6. FINAL SAMPLE DTD DESIGN

```
<!ELEMENT    cover       - O    (title, subtitle?) >
<!ELEMENT    body        - O    (section+) >
<!ELEMENT    rearmatter  - O    (section+) >
<!ELEMENT    copyright   - -    (head) >
<!ELEMENT    summary     - -    (para+) >
<!ELEMENT    section     - -    (title,summary?,
                                para+,(bullet-list|
                                number-list|caution|
                                note|system|figure)*,
                                (head|example)*) >
<!ELEMENT    preface     - -    (title,(para|
                         number-list|bullet-list|
                         figure|caution|note|
                         system)*,head*)
                                +(aboutsection)>
<!ELEMENT    example     - -    (title,
                         (bullet-list|figure|
                         number-list|system|para)*) >
<!ELEMENT    head        - -    (title,
                                (bullet-list|
                                example|figure|
                                number-list|system|
                                para)*,head*) >
<!ELEMENT    title       - -    (#PCDATA) >
<!ATTLIST    title       id     ID#IMPLIED >
<!ELEMENT    subtitle    - -    (#PCDATA) >
<!ELEMENT    figure      - -    ((title?,table?),
                                footnote*) >
<!ATTLIST    figure      width  NUTOKEN#IMPLIED
                         height NUTOKEN#IMPLIED
                         name   ENTITY#IMPLIED >
<!ELEMENT    number-list - -    (item)+ >
<!ELEMENT    bullet-list - -    (item)+ >
<!ELEMENT    item        - -    (para|bullet-list|
                                  number-list|system)+ >
<!ATTLIST    item        id     ID#IMPLIED >
```

FIGURE 5-6. FINAL SAMPLE DTD DESIGN (CONTINUED)

```
<!ELEMENT     (caution,note)- -  (para+) >
<!ELEMENT     system        - -  (#PCDATA|indexitem)* >
<!ELEMENT     para          - -  (xref|#PCDATA|
                                 indexitem|ftnoteref)* >
<!ELEMENT     xref          - -   EMPTY >
<!ATTLIST     xref          ref   IDREF#REQUIRED>
<!ELEMENT     footnote      - -  (para)+ -(ftnoteref) >
<!ATTLIST     footnote
              symbol        (level1,level2,
                            level3)  #REQUIRED
              footnote-id id                        #REQUIRED >
<!ELEMENT     ftnoteref     - -   EMPTY >
<!ATTLIST     ftnoteref     idref IDREF#IMPLIED >
<!ELEMENT     indexitem     - -   EMPTY >
<!ATTLIST     indexitem
                            type  CDATA#IMPLIED
                            text  CDATA#IMPLIED >
]>
```

FIGURE 5-6. FINAL SAMPLE DTD DESIGN (CONTINUED)

6 DTD DESIGN AND DOCUMENTATION TOOLS

This chapter builds upon the design and analysis work done in the previous chapter. In this chapter, we will examine how the design and documentation process is facilitated by the design and documentation tools that are available. In this chapter, you will learn:

- How to document a DTD for end users
- How to use Microstar's Near & Far Designer
- How to use dtd2html, part of perlSGML, to document your DTD
- How to use Publishing Development AB's SGML Companion

DTD DEVELOPMENT TOOLS

Although most SGML editors include some sort of tool to define a DTD and build the environment required for that tool, most do not really aid in the design and documentation of a DTD. In this chapter, we will examine design tools. The DTD tools provided with the various SGML editors will be examined as part of the process of configuring those tools.

NEAR & FAR DESIGNER

NOTE: This section documents the features of Microstar's
Near & Far Designer v2. Packaged with Corel Ventura
7 and Corel WordPerfect 8 is v1.21 of this product. The
basic functionality of the tool has not changed. Where
there is a significant difference in the way the tool
works or presents information, I will document the
difference.

INSTALLATION

To install Near & Far Designer:

1. Insert Floppy 1 in your disk drive.

2. Run the program `setup.exe`.

3. Enter your name, organization, and product serial number.

4. Accept the default install directory or specify your own. The files will
   be copied to the specified directory.

5. Accept (or reject) the request to create a program group.

CONFIGURATION

Near & Far Designer comes preconfigured with the ISO public character
entities from 1986, 1991, and 1992. The configuration file, `nearfar.erf`,
is found in the main Near & Far Designer directory, as shown in
Figure 6-1.

 Every SGML tool will provide a similar mechanism for mapping
PUBLIC and SYSTEM identifiers to actual files on your system. I
recommend that before you get too far into an SGML effort, gather all
these ISO files and any other external objects into one location so you
can maintain your environment more effectively.

To add PUBLIC or SYSTEM identifiers to `nearfar.erf`:

1. Locate `nearfar.erf` in the Near & Far Designer top directory.

2. Open this file with Wordpad or Notepad. You need to edit this file and save it in a text-only format. If you use MS-Word to edit the file, you must use Save As to achieve this.

3. Figure 6-2 is a portion of the `nearfar.erf` file.

I have added the entry for the ArborText CALS table model PUBLIC entity so we can load the sample DTD that was created in the previous chapter.

NOTE: The actual path and filenames are relative to the location of the DTD being edited with Near & Far Designer. If you are going to work in a directory that is different than the installation directory (recommended), you must modify all the paths in this file, or copy the same structure to your working directory. By default, Near & Far Designer is configured to work in the installation directory.

 Look at the entries for the ISO files. Notice the duplicate entries for the same system files. This occurs because the naming convention was changed and there are some DTDs that still use the old-style names. The value 8879-1986 was changed to be 8879:1986. You may have to create similar entries for other SGML tools to cover all the possibilities.

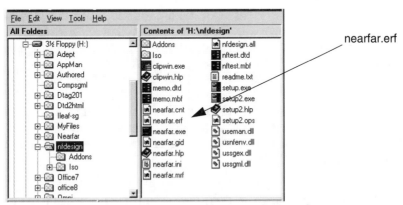

FIGURE 6-1. NEAR & FAR DESIGNER DIRECTORY STRUCTURE

This is the extent of the configuration you need to do to support your SGML efforts. There are also other configuration preferences that can be set by selecting Preferences on the Tools menu.

```
###############################################################
#
# NEAR & FAR(R) Entity Reference File
#
# Keywords:
#                                                              ArborText CALS
# PUBLIC   "public id"    "filename"                           Table Model
# SYSTEM   "system id"    "filename"
# FILE     "match path"   "replace path"
# CALL     "another entity reference file name"               Duplicate Entries
#
# Please see the documentation for complete details.
#
# 95-04-03 Added new naming convention for 1986 standard documents
#
###############################################################

PUBLIC   "-//ArborText//ELEMENTS CALS Table Structures//EN"
"h:\adept\entities\CALS-TBL.ELM"

# 1986 Entities resolved in the directory ENT1986
PUBLIC "ISO 8879-1986//ENTITIES Added Math Symbols: Arrow
Relations//EN"        "ISO\ENT1986\ISOAMSA.ENT"
PUBLIC "ISO 8879:1986//ENTITIES Added Math Symbols: Arrow
Relations//EN"        "ISO\ENT1986\ISOAMSA.ENT"
PUBLIC "ISO 8879-1986//ENTITIES Added Math Symbols: Binary
Operators//EN"        "ISO\ENT1986\ISOAMSB.ENT"
PUBLIC "ISO 8879:1986//ENTITIES Added Math Symbols: Binary
Operators//EN"        "ISO\ENT1986\ISOAMSB.ENT"
PUBLIC "ISO 8879-1986//ENTITIES Added Math Symbols: Delimiters//EN"
"ISO\ENT1986\ISOAMSC.ENT"
```

FIGURE 6-2. NEAR & FAR DESIGNER CONFIGURATION FILE

USING THE NEAR & FAR DESIGNER

Near & Far Designer provides both a GUI for defining and maintaining a DTD, as well as the ability to create documentation and reports about your DTD.

DEFINING THE MODEL

In this section, we will take the same steps used in Chapter 5, *Analyzing Documents for a DTD*, but we will use Near & Far Designer. In addition to developing the DTD, we will create the documentation that this product allows you to create.

1. Launch Near & Far Designer. Figure 6-3 and Figure 6-4 show the two possible symbol sets and interfaces for Near & Far Designer. Figure 6-3 is closest to the interface available in v1.21, while Figure 6-4 shows the new mode available with v2. I prefer to use this new mode because it uses the SGML syntax and symbology I am already familiar with.

2. Set Near & Far Designer to use SGML syntax and symbology. From the Tools menu, select Preferences.

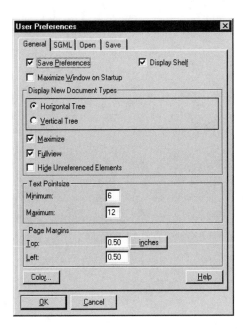

Select the SGML tab and check the Terminology and Symbology fields.

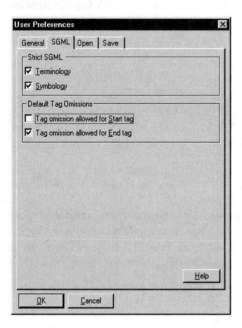

3. From the File menu, select New to start a new model.

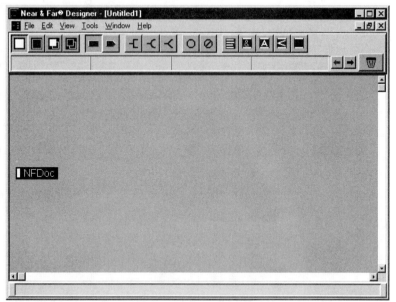

NFDoc is the standard default root element.

4. Change NFDoc to book. From the Edit menu, select Element.

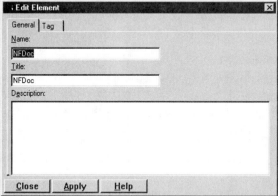

In the Name field, enter *book*. This is the element name. In the title field, enter the short description: *SGML@Work Sample DTD*. In the description field, enter a more complete description. *This DTD was based upon the analysis of one document marked up in MIF format. Additional work may be required to make this a viable application.*

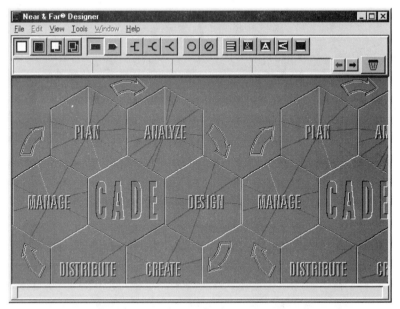

FIGURE 6-3. NEAR & FAR SYMBOLOGY INTERFACE

5. The next step is to define the first-level structures. You must add a connector to the top-level element book.

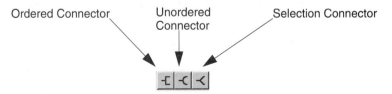

Drag the ordered connector from the toolbar to the right of the element book.

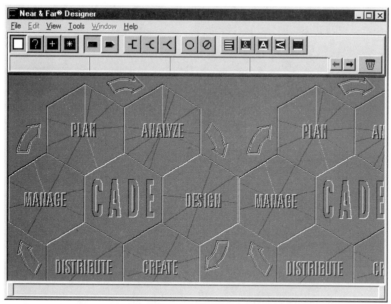

FIGURE 6-4. SGML SYMBOLOGY INTERFACE

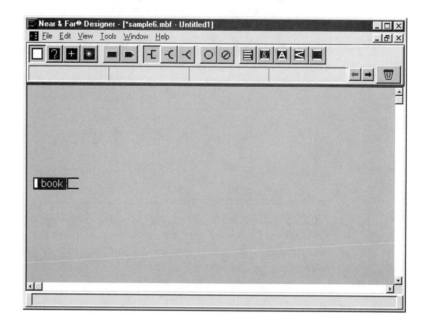

6. Now we can add the first-level elements to the **book** element. Drag the element object from the toolbar to the left of the connector you just placed.

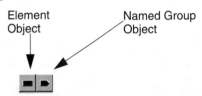

Enter **cover** in the Name field and select the Zero or one field.

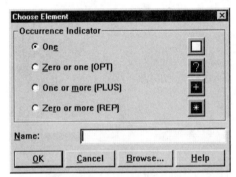

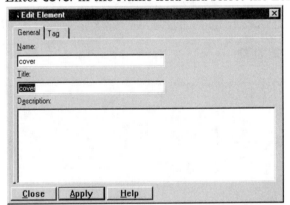

Change the Title to: *Cover page content.* The Description should read as follows: *The cover contains a title and optional subtitle objects. The publication date and partnumber information is generated from the attributes on the <book> element.*

7. Add the following elements, by dragging each element object and placing it underneath the previous element: toc, lof, body, rearmatter, and index.

From this point on, I won't necessarily indicate a Title or Description to be entered, but you should fill these fields in as well. They will provide the documentation that will allow your writers and other developers to understand what your intentions and design actually are.

8. Define the content of the toc, lot, and index as EMPTY, by dragging the EMPTY content icon from the toolbar to the left side of each of these elements.

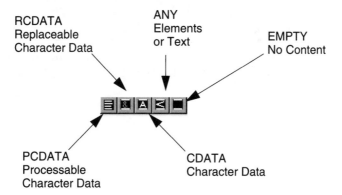

RCDATA
Replaceable
Character Data

ANY
Elements
or Text

EMPTY
No Content

PCDATA
Processable
Character Data

CDATA
Character Data

9. The cover element was defined to have a required title and optional subtitle, in that order.

10. To capture the partnumber and publication date, place these attributes on the book element. From the Edit menu, select Attribute List.

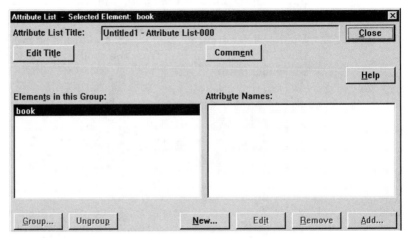

Enter *Document Information* in the Attribute List Title field. Select New... to create the first attribute.

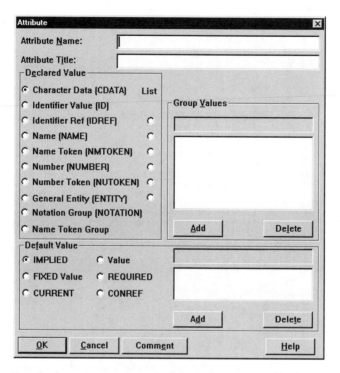

Enter *Pubdate* in the Attribute Name field and *Publication date* in the Attribute Title field. Verify that Character Data is selected as the type and also select REQUIRED.

Create another New... attribute: Partnumber. The Attribute Title should be: Publication part number. It is Character Data and REQUIRED also.

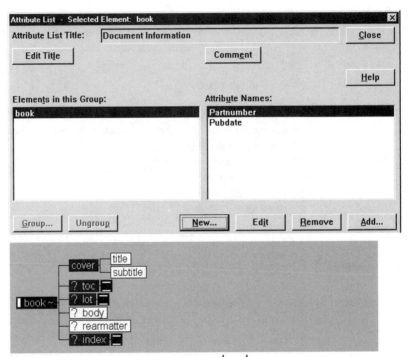

Notice the "~" that has appeared on **book**. This indicates that attributes have been defined for this element. Also notice that the elements that have not had content defined appear in yellow on the screen or white in the above illustration. These are all visual clues to help you quickly know where the model is incomplete or that attributes have been defined.

11. The element **body** is currently defined as being optional, when it should be required. Drag the One Occurrence indicator from the toolbar and place it on the **body** element

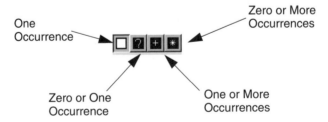

12. Create the element **section** in **body** and make it One or More Occurrences. By selecting the new section element and holding down the Ctrl key, you can drag a copy of this element and connect it to **rearmatter**.

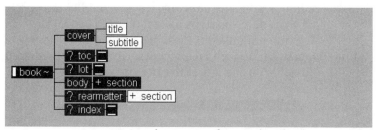

13. Add the elements **copyright** and **preface** to **book** by dragging the element icon from the toolbar and placing it beneath the element it should follow. Make both these elements Zero or One Occurrence.

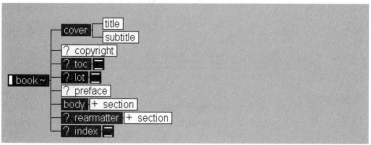

14. Define the content of **section** as a required **title**, followed by one or more **para**'s, followed by zero or more **bullet-lists** or **cautions**, followed by zero or more **head**s.

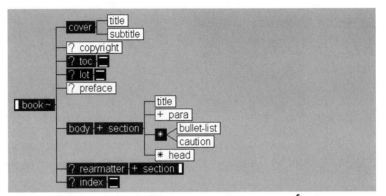

15. In our previous analysis, we determined that **preface** was going to be the same content as **section** with some other elements. Let's define a named group to hold this content that will be in common between these two elements. Drag the named group icon from the toolbar to the left of the **preface** element.

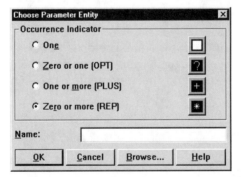

Enter *Section-Content* in the Name field.

16. Now, add the proper connectors to Section-Content and drag the contents of the **section** element to **Section-Content**.

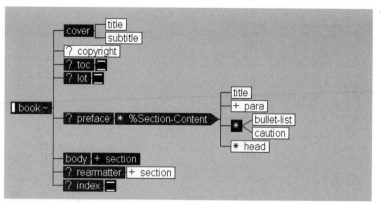

17. Select the **Section-Content** named group and hold down the Ctrl key while dragging the named group to the left side of **section**.

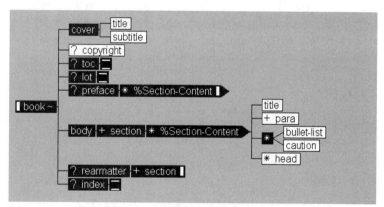

Named groups make the DTD easier to maintain if you have many common content structures. This is a key area where I find Near & Far Designer to be invaluable. Named groups can become very involved and it is sometimes difficult to determine the actual content. By drilling down through the diagram, you can verify that the content is correct for each usage.

Notice the rectangle that appears at the right of **section** and Section-Content named group. This indicates that the content model is defined and being displayed elsewhere on the diagram.

18. If you examine the content of the headings in our sample document, you will see that the content is the same as the **section** element. Select the Section-Content named group, drag it while holding down the Ctrl key, and place it on and to the left of the **head** element.

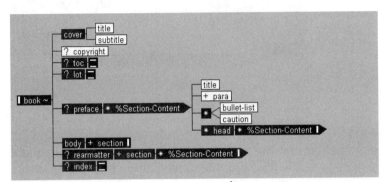

19. Recall that the content of the **copyright** section consisted of an initial **head** with paragraphs and additional sub-headings. For consistency, we will use the same **head** element for the content of **copyright**. Select the **head** element, drag it while holding down the Ctrl key, and place it to the right of the **copyright** element.

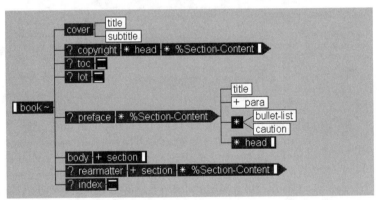

20. The **title** and **subtitle** elements have a simple model of PCDATA for the content. Drag the PCDATA content icon from the toolbar and place it to the right of the **title** and then **subtitle** elements. **Title** is required and **subtitle** should be set to Zero or One Occurrence.

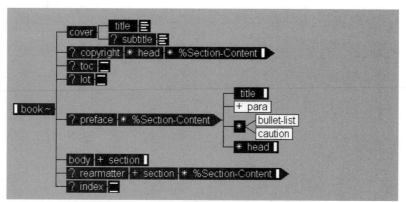

21. To create cross-references, we need IDs on the objects that we want to reference. Select the title element. Then from the Edit menu, select Attribute List.

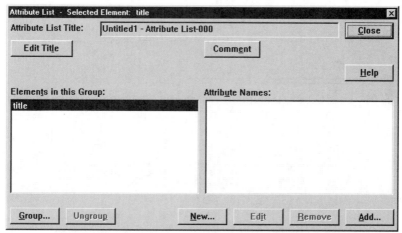

Make the Edit Title *Identification attributes*. Select New to create the Attribute Name *id*, with an Attribute Title of *Unique identifier*. The Declared Value should be Identifier Value (ID), with a Default Value of IMPLIED.

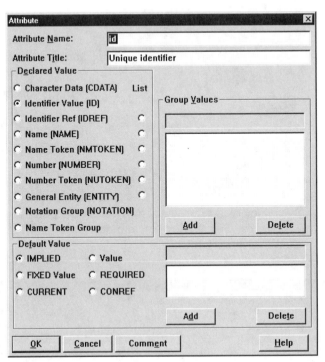

22. Create a **note** element just below **caution** and make **para** the content of both **note** and **caution**.

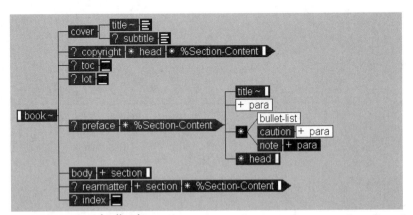

23. The content for **bullet-list** is one or more **item** elements, and an **item** is composed of one or more **paras**.

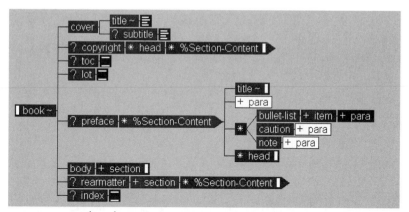

24. Create a number-list element with the same content model as the bullet-list element. number-list should follow bullet-list.

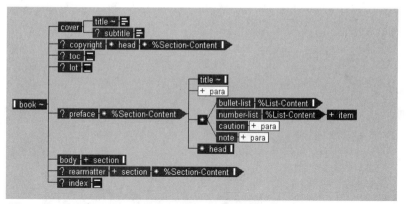

25. The element item should have an ID so it can be referenced. Select one of the item elements. From the Edit menu, select Attribute List. Select Add from the Attribute List dialog box to add the same ID attribute information that we placed on title.

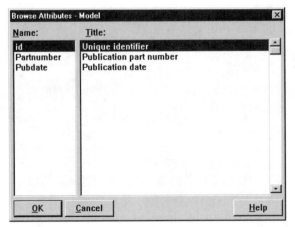

Select the id entry.

26. Create the **system** element. This should be included in the selection group with the **number-list** and other items.

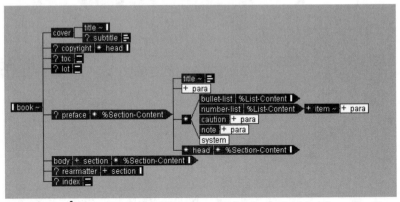

27. Create the **figure** element. This should be included in the selection group with the **number-list** and other items. The content of **figure** should be an optional **title** element.

    figure should have the following attributes, titled *Figure attributes*:

Name	Title	Content	Default
name	*Graphic entity*	ENTITY	IMPLIED
height	*Height of frame*	NUTOKEN	IMPLIED
width	*Width of frame*	NUTOKEN	IMPLIED

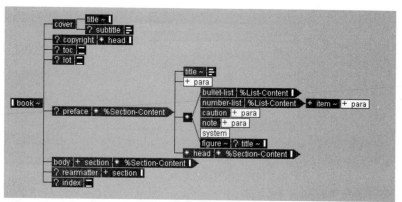

28. We made a mistake early in the design and created a lot instead of a lof element. Select lot, and from the Edit menu, select element.Change the name to *lof* and enter *List of figures* as the Title.

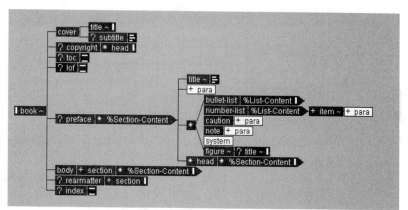

29. To add the ISO character entities, from the Edit menu, select External Parameter Entities.

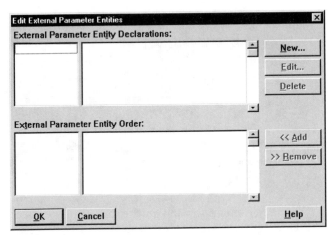

Select New... to start adding entities.

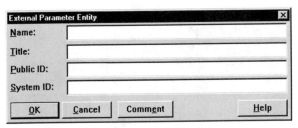

Enter the following items (the order does not matter):

Name	Public ID
ISOpub	*ISO 8879-1986// ENTITIES Publishing// EN*
ISOnum	*ISO 8879-1986// ENTITIES Numeric and Special Graphic// EN*
ISOdia	*ISO 8879-1986// ENTITIES Diacritical Marks// EN*
ISOtech	*ISO 8879-1986// ENTITIES General Technical// EN*
ISOlat1	*ISO 8879-1986// ENTITIES Added Latin 1// EN*
ISOlat2	*ISO 8879-1986// ENTITIES Added Latin 2// EN*
ISOgrk1	*ISO 8879-1986// ENTITIES Greek Letters// EN*
ISOgrk3	*ISO 8879-1986// ENTITIES Greek Symbols// EN*

Make sure that you add all the entities: otherwise, you have only defined the name, not used it.

30. In our analysis of the sample, we found an **aboutsection** and created an EMPTY element that would extract a **summary** element found on a section. **summary** is composed of one or more **para**s.

To create **aboutsection** as an inclusion to the **preface**, drag the inclusion icon from the toolbar and place it below **preface**.

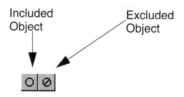

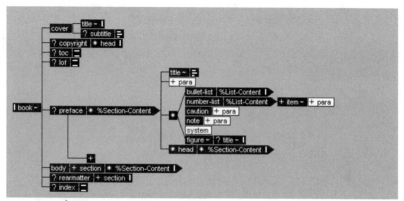

Add the **aboutsection** to the inclusion symbol.

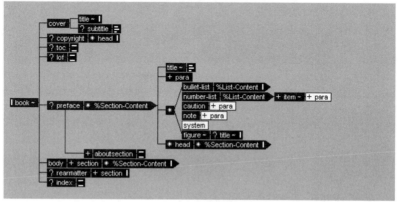

summary should now be added to the **section**, but not into a **head**. We cannot just add **summary** to the Section-Content group, we need to make some modifications to our design to accommodate this. Section-Content should be renamed, and used only for the content of heads.

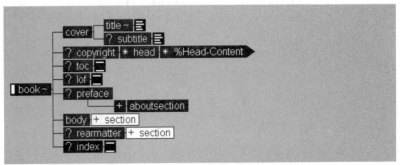

31. Create a new Section-Content named group and connect it to a section element. The content of this group should be the following: title, summary (optional), para (one or more), and a head with Zero or More Occurrences. Add this group to the preface as well.

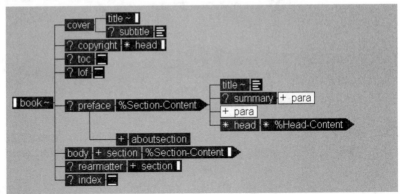

32. The Head-Content group has a group of elements in a selection group that should be added to the new Section-Content group. Select the selection connector and copy it (and all its content) to the clipboard. Select the para element in the Section-Content group. From the Edit menu, select Paste and then Down.

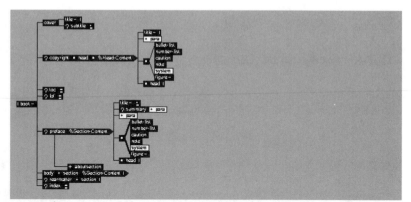

33. **example** was like a **head**, but it did not have **head**s or **example**s allowed inside it. **example** should be inserted into the selection group inside Head-Content. Connect copies all of the content items, except **head** and **example**, to the new **example** element.

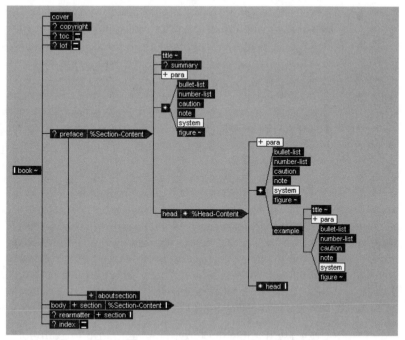

34. We need to define content for the **para** and **system** elements. These elements will have an or group that includes PCDATA.

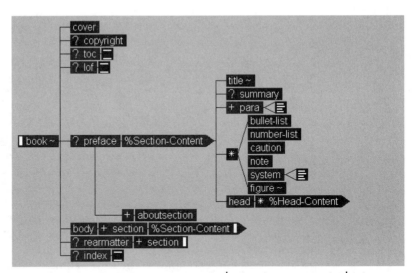

Both of these elements may have indexitems allowed. indexitem will be used to generate the actual index. indexitem is empty content and will have the following attributes, with a title of *Indexing Attributes*:

Name	Title	Type	Default
type	*Level of the index item*	*CDATA*	*IMPLIED*
text	*Text of the index item*	*CDATA*	*IMPLIED*

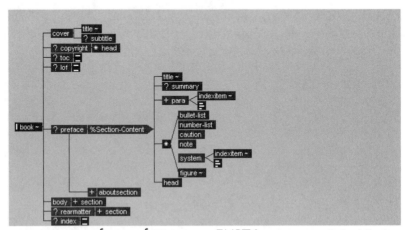

para will allow ftnoteref. This is an EMPTY content model with the following attributes:

Name	Title	Type	Default
idref	*ID of object being referenced*	*IDREF*	*IMPLIED*

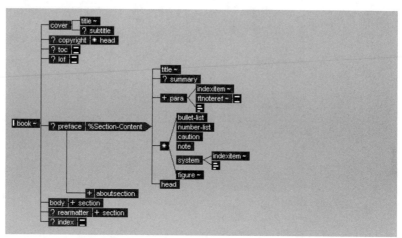

35. We just created a reference to a footnote. The only places that footnotes were found in the sample were with tables. Tables will only be allowed in figure, so the actual footnotes will be allowed there too. The content of the footnote is one or more paras with the ftnoteref excluded. footnote should have the following attributes, with a title of *Footnote Attributes*:

Name	Title	Type	Default
footnote-id	*Unique identifier*	*ID*	*REQUIRED*
symbol	*Indicates level of footnote / symbol*	*NAME TOKEN GROUP*	*REQUIRED*

The values for symbol are: *level1, level2, level3*.

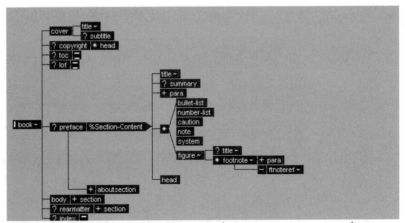

36. indexitem should also allowed in a title. This will allow a title to be indexed.

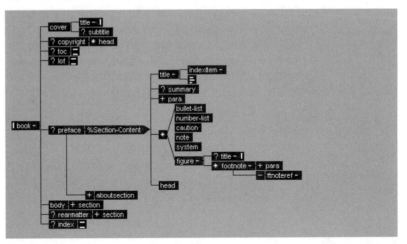

37. We now need to bring the CALS table model in from ArborText. From the Edit menu, select Parameter Entities.

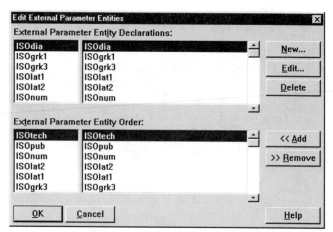

Select New... to create the parameter entity. The name is *calstbl*, the title should be *CALS Table Model from ArborText*, and Public ID is *-//ArborText//ELEMENTS CALS Table Structures//EN*.

Be sure that you add this new entity so it is referenced into the model.

38. Two additional general entities are required to properly define our table model. From the Edit menu, select General and then Other Entities.

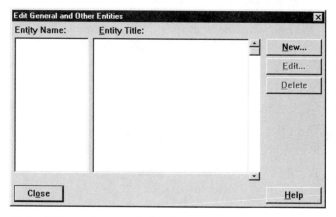

Select New... to create the first entity.

Create the following:

Name	Scope	Type	Value
tblelm	*Parameter Entity*	*Replacement Text*	*table*
tblcon	*Parameter Entity*	*Replacement Text*	*(#PCDATA | bullet-list | number-list | caution | note | system)**

39. Add the table element to figure.

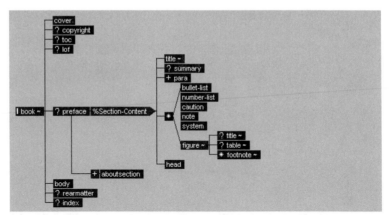

40. Validate your design before saving. From the Tools menu, select Validate and then Document Type. This will check your design and report content-type problems. If the model validates, the following message will be displayed: "Model validated successfully"; or if an error occurs, the design window will change and the error message will appear, along with the offending design elements, which are highlighted in red.

If a message gets past you or you forget a message, you can display the message log. From the View menu, select Message History.

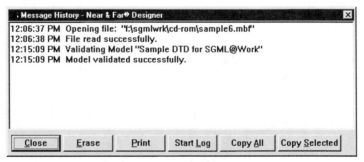

41. Save your design as a.dtd file that is in pure SGML format.

If your model is not currently valid and Near & Far Designer won't save the file as a .dtd, you can save your design in model, or .mbf format. The model format will always let you save work-in-progress if you happen to be at a point where the model is invalid and you need to exit the software. Earlier versions of Near & Far Designer always worked with a model file and required a DTD to be imported or exported.

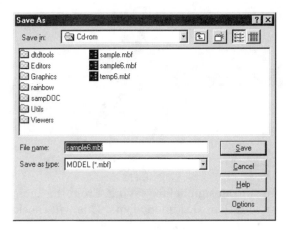

NAVIGATING THE MODEL

Once you have a design completed, or even as you work with a design, you will need to navigate it.

1. Open the model.

2. Generally, the model will default to display the first layer of the design.

3. To expand an element's content, double-click on that element.

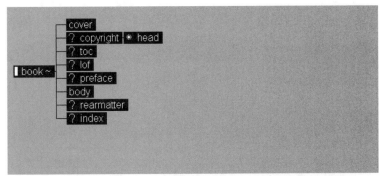

4. To contract an element, double-click the expanded element.

5. By default, I have been showing the design in a horizontal tree; you can also show a tree vertically. From the View menu, select Vertical Tree.

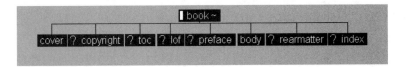

GENERATING THE DTD

If you store your design as a model file, you must save the design out to SGML to use it. The following procedure also shows you how to control the format and information that is written out to the DTD:

1. Open the model.

2. From the File menu, select Save As.

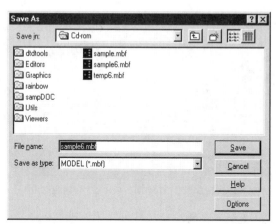

The Save As Type should be set to (*.dtd)(*.dcl). Enter an appropriate name in the File name field. Before you save the file, look at the Options available during the save process.

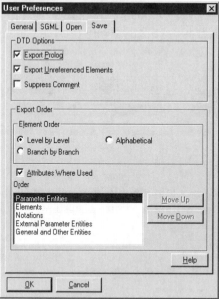

NOTE: This is the same Preferences panel that is available under the Tools menu.

Let's examine the various options on this panel:

Option	Result
Export Prolog	Outputs the <!DOCTYPE xxx [ ]>.
Export Unreferenced Elements	Outputs elements you defined, but haven't connected to the model yet.
Suppress Comment	Removes all the documentation from the DTD.
Level by Level	Outputs the elements by going across the tree at each level.
Branch by Branch	Follows a branch to its end.
Alphabetical	Outputs the elements in alphabetical order.
Attributes Where Used	Outputs the attribute list for an element following the element definition. Note that by selecting this option, you remove a few of the options in the order scroll box.

Order	Use this list to control the order in which these major sections of a DTD are output. The order I prefer is:
	Use Attributes where used, then
	    Parameter Entities
	    External Parameter Entities
	    General and Other Entities
	    Notations
	    Elements

Figure 6-5 illustrates the DTD that can be generated with comments on and ordering that I specified above.

This is one of the features that has been added to Near & Far Designer. In v1.21, you can only generate the DTD in the single format that is available.

```
<!DOCTYPE book [
<!--<Title>Sample DTD for SGML@Work-->
<!ENTITY % Head-Content   "(title,para+,(bullet-list|number-list|
             caution | note | system | figure | example)*,head*)"
             --<Title>Elements that comprise headings.-->
<!ENTITY % List-Content   "(para+ | bullet-list | number-list |
                       caution | note | system | figure)"
             --<Title>Elements allowed within a list-->
<!ENTITY % Section-Content   "(title,summary?,para+,(bullet-list
                       | number-list | caution | note | system
                       | figure)*,head)"
             --<Title>Elements allowed within a major section
                       or chapter-- >
<!ENTITY % tblcon
       "(#PCDATA|bullet-list|number-list|caution|note|system)*"
             --<Title>tblcon-- >
<!ENTITY % tblelm   "table"
             --<Title>tblelm-- >
<!ELEMENT book  - O
   (cover,copyright?,toc?,lof?,preface?,body,rearmatter?,index?)
             --<Title>SGML@Work Sample DTD--
             --This DTD was based upon the analysis of one document marked up
in MIF format. Additional work may be required to make this a viable
application.--
             ---- >
<!ATTLIST book --<Title>Document Information--
             Pubdate   CDATA     #REQUIRED
             --<Title>Publication date--
             Partnumber  CDATA     #REQUIRED
             --<Title>Publication part number-- >
```

FIGURE 6-5. NEAR & FAR DESIGNER-GENERATED DTD

GENERATING REPORTS

Near & Far Designer provides several different reports. One advantage of
this format over the DTD is that the reports remove most of the SGML
syntax and present the information contained in the DTD in a readable
manner.

To generate a report:

1. Open the model.

2. From the File menu, select Reports.

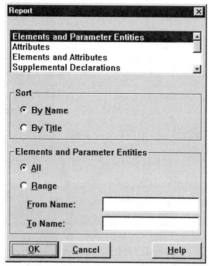

The following table lists all the reports available, the content of each report, and the illustration and sample Adobe Acrobat version available on the CD-ROM. The sample reports are found in the dtdtools directory under nearfar.

Report Name	Sample File	Illustration	Content
Elements and Parameter Entities	rpt1.pdf	Figure 6-6	Shows all the elements and parameter entities and lists the containing object(s).
Attributes	rpt2.pdf	Figure 6-7	Shows all the attributes in alphabetical order, and lists which elements use those attributes.
Elements and Attributes	rpt3.pdf	Figure 6-8	Shows all elements that have attributes in alphabetical order, and then lists the attributes of those elements.

Report Name	Sample File	Illustration	Content
Supplemental Declarations	rpt4.pdf	Figure 6-9	Lists notations, parameter entities, local entities, and external entities, grouped and then alphabetized, showing any PUBLIC, SYSTM ID, or NOTATION type or content.
Terminal Declarations	rpt5.pdf	Figure 6-10	Lists only the elements that terminate a model definition.
Comment for all Objects	rpt6.pdf	Figure 6-11	Lists all objects in the DTD, organizing them into groups and alphabetizing them, with all comment and title information.
Model Summary	rpt7.pdf	Figure 6-12	Lists all non-terminal or EMPTY elements in alphabetical order with their attributes.
Model Detail	rpt8.pdf	Figure 6-13	Lists all elements in alphabetical order along with their attributes and all entities.

Once you have selected a type of report and have entered any restrictions on the information, you can either print the report or save it to a file. From the File menu, select Save As. From the Save As dialog, you can specify the delimiting character for the information. By using a delimiting character, you can then use this file to load a database or spreadsheet.

Element / Parameter Entity			Contained In			
Name	Title	Type	Name	Title	Type	As
aboutsection	About this manual marker. Information generated from summary elements	EL	preface	The preface or about section of a document	EL	inclusion
body	The main body of the document. A section contained here will be numbered and labeled Chapter	EL	book	SGML@Work Sample DTD	EL	content
book	SGML@Work Sample DTD	EL				
bullet-list	An un-ordered or bullet list	EL	example	A heading that contains a specific example	EL	content
			Head-Content	Elements that comprise headings	NG	content

FIGURE 6-6. ELEMENTS AND PARAMETER ENTITIES REPORT

Attribute Cross-Reference by Name

Attribute					Used in Element	
Name	Title	type	Allowable Values	Default	Name	Title
footnote-id	Unique footnote identifier	Identifier Value		REQUIRED	footnote	The text of a footnote, identified with a unique id
height	Height of frame	Number Token		IMPLIED	figure	The wrapper for a graphic or table.
id	Unique identifier	Identifier Value		IMPLIED	item	An item in a list
					title	Title element used in cover, head, section, figure
idref	ID of object being referenced	Identifier Ref		IMPLIED	fnoteref	Marker for a footnote is attached
name	Graphic entity	Entity		IMPLIED	figure	The wrapper for a graphic or table.
Partnumber	Publication part number	Character Data		REQUIRED	book	SGML@Work Sample DTD

FIGURE 6-7. ATTRIBUTES REPORT

Element / Attribute by Name

Element		Attribute				
Name	Title	Name	Title	Type	Allowable Values	Default
book	SGML@Work Sample DTD	Partnumber	Publication part number	Character Data		REQUIRED
		Pubdate	Publication date	Character Data		REQUIRED
figure	The wrapper for a graphic or table.	height	Height of frame	Number Token		IMPLIED
		name	Graphic entity	Entity		IMPLIED
		width	Width of frame	Number Token		IMPLIED
footnote	The text of a footnote, identified with a unique id	footnote-id	Unique footnote identifier	Identifier Value		REQUIRED
		symbol	Indicates the level of footnote/symbol	Name Token Group	level1,level2,level3	REQUIRED
fnoteref	Marker for a footnote is attached	idref	ID of object being referenced.	Identifier Ref		IMPLIED

FIGURE 6-8. ELEMENTS AND ATTRIBUTES REPORT

Model Title: Sample DTD for SGML@Work   Sunday, June 15, 1997 11:22:03 AM
Model Root: book

Notations

Name	Title	System Identifier	Public Identifier	Attributes

External Parameter Entities

Name	Title	System Identifier	Public Identifier
calstbl	CALS Table Model from ArborText	h:\adept\entities\cals-tbl.elm	-//ArborText//ELEMENTS CALS Table Structures//EN
ISOdia	ISOdia		ISO 8879-1986//ENTITIES Diacritical Marks//EN
ISOgrk1	ISOgrk1		ISO 8879-1986//ENTITIES Greek Letters//EN
ISOgrk3	ISOgrk3		ISO 8879-1986//ENTITIES Greek Symbols//EN
ISOlat1	ISOlat1		ISO 8879-1986//ENTITIES Added Latin 1//

FIGURE 6-9. SUPPLEMENTAL DECLARATIONS REPORT

Model Title: Sample DTD for SGML@Work   Sunday, June 15, 1997 11:23:33 AM
Model Root: book

Element		Terminal Type	In Parameter Entity
Name	Title		
aboutsection	About this manual marker. Information generated from summary elements	EMPTY	
fnoteref	Marker for a footnote is attached	EMPTY	
index	A marker for the location of an index. If present an index will be generatated	EMPTY	
indexitem	Empty element that contains via attributes the information	EMPTY	

FIGURE 6-10. TERMINAL DECLARATIONS REPORT

Model Title: Sample DTD for SGML@Work   Sunday, June 15, 1997 11:25:25 AM
Model Root: book

Element / Parameter Entity Comment

Name	Title	Type	Comment
aboutsection	About this manual marker. Information generated from summary elements	EL	
body	The main body of the document. A section contained here will be numbered and labeled Chapter	EL	
book	SGML@Work Sample DTD	EL	This DTD was based upon the analysis of one document markedup in MIF format. Additional work may be required to make this a viable application.
bullet-list	An un-ordered or bullet list	EL	
caution	A cautionary note - could result in damage	EL	
copyright	Copyright section just after the cover	EL	
cover	Cover page content	EL	The cover contains a title and optional subtitle objects. The publication date and

FIGURE 6-11. COMMENT FOR ALL OBJECTS REPORT

Model Summary

Model Title: Sample DTD for SGML@Work
Model Root: book

Sunday, June 15, 1997 11:26:51 AM

Element/Attribute	Full Name	Comment
aboutsection	About this manual marker. Information generated from summary elements	
body	The main body of the document. A section contained here will be numbered and labeled Chapter	
book	SGML@Work Sample DTD Document Information	This DTD was based upon the analysis of one document markedup in MIF format. Additional work may be required to make this a viable application.

FIGURE 6-12. MODEL SUMMARY REPORT

Model Detail Report

Model Title: Sample DTD for SGML@Work
Model Root: book

Sunday, June 15, 1997 11:28:24 AM

Model Detail Report

Name	Title	Type	Description	Terminal/Type	Allowable Values	Default
aboutsection	About this manual marker. Information generated from summary elements	Element		EMPTY		
body	The main body of the document. A section contained here will be numbered and labeled Chapter	Element				
book	SGML@Work Sample DTD	Element (Root)	This DTD was based upon the analysis of one document markedup in MIF format. Additional work may be required to make this a viable application.			
	Document Information	Attribute List		Attribute List		
Partnumber	Publication part number	Attribute		Character Data		REQUIRED
Pubdate	Publication date	Attribute		Character Data		REQUIRED
bullet-list	An un-ordered or bullet list	Element				
caution	A cautionary note - could result in damage	Element				
copyright	Copyright section just after the cover	Element				

FIGURE 6-13. MODEL DETAIL REPORT

USING THE SGML COMPANION DTD BROWSER

The SGML Companion DTD Browser is an evaluation version of SGML Companion that is provided on the CD-ROM at the back of this book. The full version of this product allows you to develop and save SGML models just like Near & Far Designer, but the DTD Browser product only lets you view existing DTDs, there is no save function.

INSTALLATION

To install the SGML Companion DTD Browser from the CD-ROM:

1. In the dtdtools folder, you will find the file `sgcbrows.zip`. This is a compressed file that requires a product like WinZip to uncompress it.

NOTE: If you don't have WinZip or something similar, see Appendix F for information on how to install and use this utility program provided on the CD-ROM.

With WinZip, open the file `sgcbrows.zip`. Double-click on `install.exe`.

2. Select Install.
3. Clear enough space on a disk for the product and either accept the directory name or create your own.
4. Create a work directory.

CONFIGURATION

According to the Help files provided, there are several files available to configure the full SGML Companion product. However, all of the configuration files mentioned in the Help files do not exist in the installation of the SGML Companion DTD Browser.

USING THE SGML COMPANION DTD BROWSER

To view an existing DTD:

1. Start SGML Companion.

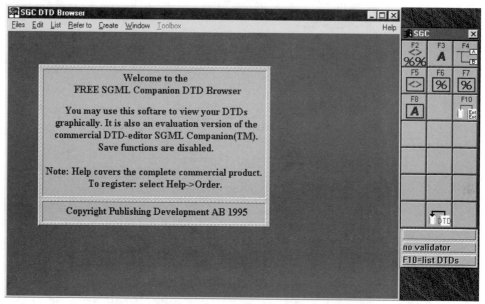

2. From the Files menu, select Import, then select DTD Subset.

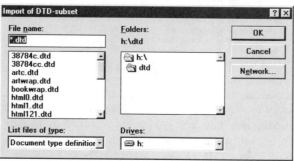

Locate the Sample DTD on the CD-ROM. It is stored in dtdtools in the nearfar directory.

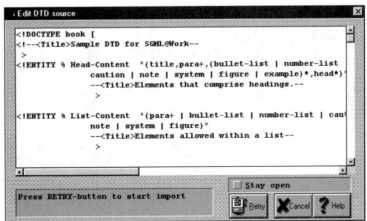

3.   The DTD is loaded into an intermediate window that allows you to edit the input or go directly to importing the file. Select Retry to load the DTD initially.

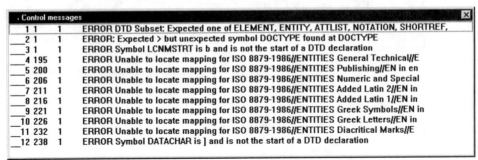

There are basically two errors in this DTD according to SGML Companion. The first problem is caused by having the DOCTYPE prolog wrapping the DTD. The second problem is the 8879-1986 vs. 8879:1986, SGML Companion has been configured to accept 8879:1986. This last error I would generally fix in the configuration or catalog file for this tool, but they aren't available. Both of these problems will have to be fixed in our source DTD. Go ahead and make the changes as indicated.

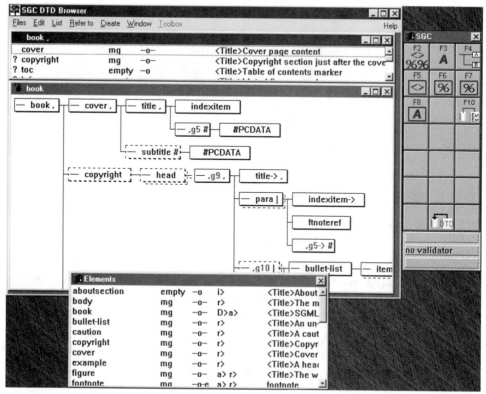

4. You can now navigate the model. Simply double-click on an element and it will collapse or expand.

    SGML Companion only allows the first instance in the DTD to expand content. So, to look at the head element, you must look at copyright first.

DTD Documentation Methods

In the previous section, we were primarily interested in designing a DTD and providing whatever documentation could be developed with a specific tool. Here our interest is in building documentation that will support the design and users.

I feel that two types of documentation are needed to support an SGML design:

- Detailed information about the tags, how they should be used, and what the processing programs do with those tags

- A marked-up sample that shows all the variations and allowed usages of those tags.

Near & Far Designer provides much of what is needed in the first bullet; another shareware tool, DTD2HTML, creates HTML documentation pages that are fully linked and easy to maintain. Creating the sample document is a manual process that is as much for documentation purposes as it is to test your design and processing tools.

SGML SAMPLE DOCUMENT

This process appears here because it fits my current topic, but as far as actually creating this document, I would wait until you have some actual text converted. There may be more than one sample document that needs to be created to support the requirements for both documentation and design testing.

DOCUMENTATION SAMPLE

The primary purpose of the documentation sample is to help your authors and other users understand how the various tags work together. The following items (not necessarily in order) are the issues that should be covered:

- Document the basic tags and standard usage. Don't bog the easy or standard method with too many incidental details.

- Provide an instance that shows all tags being used, and provide any of the semantic requirements between them. For instance, in our DTD, we have a reliance of the <aboutsection> with the <summary> in each section. The DTD will validate that these are in the correct location and number, but it can't validate the semantic requirement that if an <aboutsection> is used, then there should be <summary>s in the sections that need to be described. One use without the other is not correct. The same relationship exists between <index> and <indexitem> as well as <footnote> and <ftnoteref>.

- In the sample DTD, we did not create many content tags. The correct usage of any content tags should be explained, and if there are tags with possible conflicts or potential misusage, you should provide examples of correct usage.

- If you produce multiple formats from one set of files, you should provide copies of those various outputs.

TEST SAMPLE

The test sample must provide the following features:

- All combinations of structures must be accounted for

- Include common problems and situations that go against the known semantics of your tags

- As you find problems in the markup your writers create or in the conversions you do, include those in the test sample

- Make the sample as small as possible, but be complete.

USING DTD2HTML FROM PERLSGML

perlSGML is a suite of tools written in Perl. dtd2html a tool that processes an existing DTD and a documentation file. From these, it builds a series of HTML pages that can then be used in a WWW browser.

dtd2html is a command line-driven tool. It does not have a fancy front-end, but it produces great WWW-based documentation that allows hypertext navigation of the DTD and content model. There are other tools and libraries in the suite that can be used for a variety of purposes, but I will leave them up to the reader for follow-up.

INSTALLATION

To use perlSGML, you must have Perl installed. If you have Perl 4 or 5 currently installed on your system, you can skip the following procedure. To install Perl 5:

1. Load the CD-ROM.

2. In the utilities directory of the perl directory, you will find `pw32i306.exe`. This is the 32-bit version of Perl designed to run on Windows 95 or Windows NT. This is a self-extracting file, so just double-click on it to run.

3. Use the default directory for perl, or choose one of your own. Verify that the option to run the install script is checked before continuing.

4. After the files are uncompressed, an MS-DOS window appears. Answer the prompts appropriately.

NOTE: I allowed the install script to modify my search path. Upon rebooting, I received the error message: "Too many parameters." If you get this message, you need to edit your `autoexec.bat` file. The entry made by the perl script should be the last one in the file. Find another path statement and just add the perl location to that other path statement.

5. You must reboot your system before perl is available.

6. The other two files in the perl directory will complete your copy of perl, but they are not required to use perlSGML.

To install perlSGML:

1. Load the CD-ROM.

2. In the dtdtools directory of the perl directory, you will find `perlSGML_19960ct09_tar.gz`. Use WinZip to uncompress and install perlSGML.

3. Extract all the files into a top level directory. WinZip will create a top-level directory labeled perlSGML.

4. After the files are extracted, run the install script. Before starting this, verify where you installed perl, and where you should install executable files (somewhere in a directory that is in your path statement).

5. To install perlSGML, open an MS-DOS window. Change your directory and drive to the perlSGML location. Run the following:

```
c:> perl install.me
```

6. Answer the prompts. Installation is now complete.

CONFIGURATION

dtd2html uses a catalog to map PUBLIC and SYSTEM identifiers to actual file locations on your system.

To create a catalog file for your system:

1. Locate the file catalog in the perlSGML examples directory. Copy the file to the perlSGML directory.

2. Open the catalog with Wordpad or Notepad.

```
                         -- ISO public identifiers --
PUBLIC          "ISO 8879-1986//ENTITIES General Technical//EN"iso-tech.ent
PUBLIC          "ISO 8879-1986//ENTITIES Publishing//EN"iso-pub.ent
PUBLIC          "ISO 8879-1986//ENTITIES Numeric and Special Graphic//EN"
iso-num.ent
PUBLIC          "ISO 8879-1986//ENTITIES Greek Letters//EN"iso-grk1.ent
PUBLIC          "ISO 8879-1986//ENTITIES Diacritical Marks//EN"iso-dia.ent
PUBLIC          "ISO 8879-1986//ENTITIES Added Latin 1//EN"iso-lat1.ent
PUBLIC          "ISO 8879-1986//ENTITIES Greek Symbols//EN"iso-grk3.ent
PUBLIC          "ISO 8879-1986//ENTITIES Added Latin 2//EN"ISOlat2
PUBLIC          "ISO 8879-1986//ENTITIES Added Math Symbols: Ordinary//EN"ISOamso
                         -- HP public identifiers --
PUBLIC          "-//Hewlett-Packard//ENTITIES HP Symbols//EN" HPsym
PUBLIC          "-//Hewlett-Packard//ENTITIES Service//EN"HPservice
PUBLIC          "-//Hewlett-Packard//ENTITIES Calculators//EN"HPcalc
PUBLIC          "-//Hewlett-Packard//ENTITIES Texchars//EN"HPtexchars
PUBLIC          "-//Hewlett-Packard//ENTITIES HP Tiff//EN"HPtif
                         -- Arbotext math markup --
PUBLIC          "-//ArborText//ELEMENTS Math Equation Structures//EN"ati-math.elm
                         -- HTML public identifiers and entities --
PUBLIC          "-//W3O//DTD WWW HTML 2.0 Level 0//EN"html-0.dtd
PUBLIC          "-//W3O//DTD WWW HTML 2.0 Level 1//EN"html-1.dtd
PUBLIC          "ISO 8879-1986//ENTITIES Added Latin 1//EN//HTML"ISOlat1.ent
ENTITY          "%html-0"              html-0.dtd
ENTITY          "%html-1"              html-1.dtd
```

3. Add the following entry all on one line in the catalog:

```
PUBLIC "-//ArborText//ELEMENTS CALS Table
Structures//EN" h:\adept\entities\cals-tbl.elm
```

4. Save the file and exit.

In addition to this catalog file, a few environment variables can be defined as well:

SGML_CATALOG_FILES	A colon-separated list of catalog files to be read by the system.
SGML_SEARCH_PATH	A colon-separated list of paths/locations to find catalog files or any of the files specified in a catalog file.

These variables allow you to have multiple catalog files and to have system filenames be less specific. It allows the path to a file to be variable, but the name of the file must always be the same. If the file is not found on one of these paths, it is then assumed to be in the current working directory.

If these variables are used in combination with the -catalog command line option, the location specified by -catalog will be searched first.

USING DTD2HTML

There are several steps involved in generating HTML documentation. The following process is the basic outline; from here, go to the specific instructions to accomplish each step.

1. Create an initial description file and provide the information for each of the objects defined.

2. Generate the HTML files and validate the information generated.

3. Create a quick reference document.

4. As the DTD changes, update the description file and then update the HTML files.

I have found it easiest to use command line tools like dtd2html by creating a series of scripts or batch files. By using these batch files, I get repeatable results and I don't have to remember all the details of the tools. For each of the above steps, I have created a batch file and placed it on the CD-ROM in the dtdtools directory under dtd2html. You will have to edit these files to fit your system, but they are a good starting point.

CREATING THE ELEMENT AND ENTITY DESCRIPTION FILES

To create a base or empty element and entity list file:

1. Open an MS-DOS window.

2. Change your directory to where the DTD is located, or specify the full pathname in the following examples.

3. Set the variable SGML_SEARCH_PATH to the location of the ents directory under your perlsgml installation. For me, this is: h:\perlsgml\ents.

   ```
   c:> set SGML_SEARCH_PATH=h:\perlsgml\ents
   ```

NOTE: You only need to set the above variable once per session or include it in your `autoexec.bat` file. Another alternative is to use a batch file, like I have provided.

4. I use the following command line to generate the element list in Figure 6-14. Substitute your file and pathnames accordingly:

```
perl c:\bin\dtd2html -catalog h:\perlsgml\catalog -elemlist sample.dtd
```

```
<!-- ################################################################## -->
<!-- ##                   Home Page Description                    ## -->
<!-- ################################################################## -->
<?DTD2HTML -home- >
<!-- ################################################################## -->
<!-- ##                    Short Descriptions                      ## -->
<!-- ################################################################## -->
<?DTD2HTML aboutsection+ >
<?DTD2HTML body+ >
<?DTD2HTML book+ >
<?DTD2HTML bullet-list+ >
<?DTD2HTML caution+ >
<?DTD2HTML colspec+ >
```

Text Removed Here

```
<?DTD2HTML title+ >
<?DTD2HTML toc+ >
<?DTD2HTML xref+ >
<!-- ################################################################## -->
<!-- ##                       Descriptions                        ## -->
<!-- ################################################################## -->
<?DTD2HTML aboutsection >
<?DTD2HTML body >
<?DTD2HTML book >
<?DTD2HTML book* >
<?DTD2HTML book*partno >
<?DTD2HTML book*pubdate >
<?DTD2HTML bullet-list >
<?DTD2HTML caution >
<?DTD2HTML colspec >
```

FIGURE 6-14. SAMPLE DTD EMPTY ELEMENTS FILE

The default action of this particular command is to send the output directly to your screen. You can use the redirection symbol, >, to send the screen output to a file. This file will be created in your current working directory. To do this, enter the previous command line followed by:

```
> filename
```

5. I use the following command line to generate the entity list in Figure 6-15. Substitute your file and pathnames accordingly:

```
perl c:\bin\dtd2html -catalog h:\perlsgml\catalog -entslist sample.dtd
```

```
<!--
###################################################################
<!-- ##                      General Entity Descriptions
<!--
###################################################################
<?DTD2HTML AElig& >
<?DTD2HTML Aacute& >
<?DTD2HTML Abreve& >
<?DTD2HTML Acirc& >
<?DTD2HTML Agr& >
<?DTD2HTML Agrave& >
<?DTD2HTML Amacr& >
<?DTD2HTML Aogon& >
<?DTD2HTML Aring& >
```

FIGURE 6-15. SAMPLE DTD EMPTY ENTITIES FILE

I created the batch file in Figure 6-16 to build both of the empty list files.
If you copy this file to your system and modify the variables so they map to
your system configuration, all you have to enter is:

```
c:> desc sample.dtd
```

```
@echo off
rem This is an MS-DOS batch file that is used to run dtd2html and
rem produce the:
rem             empty element list
rem             empty entities list
rem
rem             usage: desc [dtd filename/path]
rem
rem Set the following variables so that pathnames match your system and
rem your configuration.
set EXE_DIR=c:\bin\
set PERL_SGML=h:\perlsgml\
set OUTDIR=f:\sgmlwrk\cd-rom\dtdtools\dtd2html\output
set REP1=%OUTDIR%\sampELEM.des
set REP2=%OUTDIR%\sampENTS.des
set BASE_OPT=%EXE_DIR%dtd2html -catalog %PERL_SGML%catalog -outdir %OUTDIR%
set SGML_SEARCH_PATH=h:\perlsgml\ents
echo Creating the Elements List...
perl %BASE_OPT%  -elemlist %1 > %REP1%
echo Creating the Entities List ....
perl %BASE_OPT%  -entslist %1 > %REP2%
echo Processing complete ...
```

FIGURE 6-16. DESC.BAT SCRIPT

Now that we have a base description file, we need to add the documentation for our elements. I have provided complete description files for the sample dtd; the following procedure describes how to enter information:

1. Open the empty element file with Notepad or Wordpad.

   Notice that the file in Figure 6-14 is divided into three sections: the top portion allows you to create information on the first or homepage of this document set, the middle section is for creating a short description for the elements, and the bottom section allows you to create greater detail as well as document the attributes for each element.

2. The text that you enter will be placed into an HTML document within various structures and locations. Each area maps into a particular section of the document and you can add HTML markup to the text that you enter here.

   Under <?DTD2HTML -home- >, enter the following:

   ```
   <p>Sample DTD for SGML@Work.
   <p>This DTD was based upon the analysis of one
   document marked-up in MIF format. Additional work
   may be required to make this a viable application.
   ```

   This is a special tag that creates information on the homepage of your documentation.

3. Under <?DTD2HTML aboutsection+ >, enter the following:

   ```
   <p>About this manual marker
   ```

   Continue through the middle section, entering short descriptions for the elements.

   This is the tag for a short description of an element.

4. Now that you are in the Descriptions section, we need more detailed information for the elements, as well as the various attributes.

5. Under <?DTD2HTML aboutsection >, enter the following:

   ```
   <p>About this manual marker. Information generated
   from summary elements.
   ```

   This is the tag for a long description of an element.

6. Under <?DTD2HTML body >, enter:

```
<p>The main body of the document. A section
contained here will be numbered and labeled
Chapter.
```

This is the tag for a long description of an element.

7. Under <?DTD2HTML book >, enter:

<p>The top level element in this DTD. Everything we generate is a book of some type.

This is the tag for a long description of an element.

8. Under <?DTD2HTML book* >, enter:

```
<p>Document Information
```

This tag produces the information that will be displayed at the top of the attribute page for this element.

9. Under <?DTD2HTML book*partno >, enter:

```
<p>Publication part number
```

This is an attribute description tag.

10. Under `<?DTD2HTML book*pubdate >`, enter:

```
<p>Publication date
```

This is an attribute description tag.

11. Continue adding descriptive text to all elements and attributes until you complete the file.

12. Now, we need to edit the entities file. You may not want to actually produce this information because it will typically be heavily weighted with character entities that are best documented with the actual characters.

Under `<?DTD2HTML AElig& >`, enter the following:

```
<p>Capital AE ligature
```

This tag is for documenting entities.

13. Continue entering descriptions until you have completed this file.

14. To actually use this file, it must be included in the main elements description file. You could physically copy the information in, but a better way to manage the information is to add the following statement at the top of the file:

```
<?DTD2HTML #include sampents.des>
```

GENERATING THE HTML FILES

To create the base dtd2html base documentation:

1. Open an MS-DOS window.

2. Change your directory to where the DTD is located, or specify the full pathname in the following examples.

3. Set the variable SGML_SEARCH_PATH to the location of the ents directory under your perlsgml installation. For me, this is: h:\perlsgml\ents.

```
c:> set SGML_SEARCH_PATH=h:\perlsgml\ents
```

NOTE: You only need to set the above variable once per session or include it in your `autoexec.bat` file. Another alternative is to use a batch file, like I have provided.

4. I use the following command line to generate the base documentation set. Substitute your file and pathnames accordingly:

NOTE: The following command line should be entered all on one line. The command line below has been formatted for presentation and contains extra line breaks that should not be entered.

```
perl c:\bin\dtd2html -catalog h:\perlsgml\catalog -outdir
f:\sgmlwrk\cd-rom\dtdtools\dtd2html\output -allfile sample-all.html -homefile
sample-home.html -topfile sample-top.html -tree -treefile sample-tree.html -ents
-entsfile sample-ents.html -descfile sampELEM.des sample.dtd
```

The above command creates in the output directory one page per element, another page per element with content for the content model, and another page per element with attributes for the attributes.

Command Line Option	Default Name	Script Value	Sample Figure
homefile	DTD-HOME.html	sample-home.html	Figure 6-18
-allfile	ALL-ELEMENT.html	sample-all.html	Figure 6-20
-topfile	TOP-ELEM.html	sample.top.html	Figure 6-19
-treefile also needs -tree	DTD-TREE.html	sample-tree.html	Figure 6-21
-entsfile also needs -ents	ENTS.html	sample-ents.html	Figure 6-22

I created the batch file in Figure 6-17 to build all of the above. If you copy this file to your system and modify the variables so they map to your system configuration, all you have to enter is:

```
c:> docs sample.dtd
```

From the above top-level documentation pages you can then navigate to detailed element attribute and content models as shown in Figures 6-23, 6-24, and 6-25 respectively.

```
rem produce the:
rem             full documentation set
rem
rem             uasge: docs [dtd filename/path]
rem
rem Set the following variables so that path names match your system and
rem your configuration.
set EXE_DIR=c:\bin\
set PERL_SGML=h:\perlsgml\
set OUTDIR=-outdir f:\sgmlwrk\cd-rom\dtdtools\dtd2html\output
set BASE_OPT=%EXE_DIR%dtd2html -catalog %PERL_SGML%catalog %OUTDIR%
set ALL=-allfile sample-all.html
set HOME=-homefile sample-home.html
set TOP=-topfile sample-top.html
set TREE=-tree -treefile sample-tree.html
set ENTS=-ents -entsfile sample-ents.html
set TOP_DOCS=%ALL% %HOME% %TOP% %TREE% %ENTS%
set DESC=-descfile sampELEM.des
set SGML_SEARCH_PATH=h:\perlsgml\ents
echo Creating the Documentation Tree ...
perl %BASE_OPT% %TOP_DOCS%  %DESC% %1
echo Processing complete ...
```

FIGURE 6-17. DOCS.BAT SCRIPT

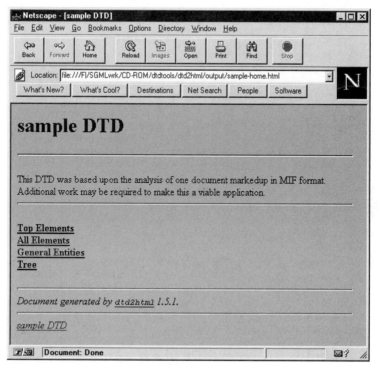

FIGURE 6-18. DTD2HTML HOME PAGE

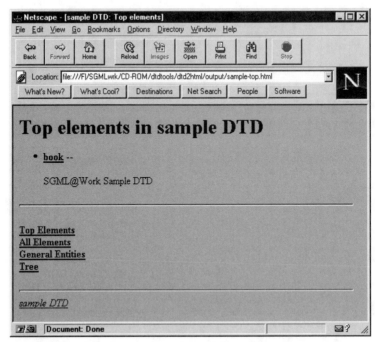

FIGURE 6-19. DTD2HTML TOP ELEMENTS PAGE

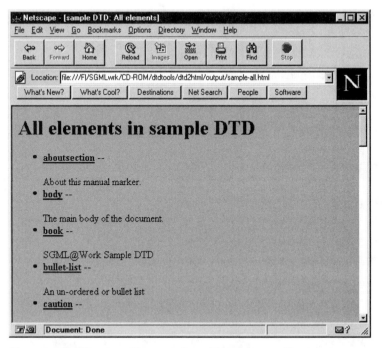

FIGURE 6-20. DTD2HTML ALL ELEMENTS PAGE

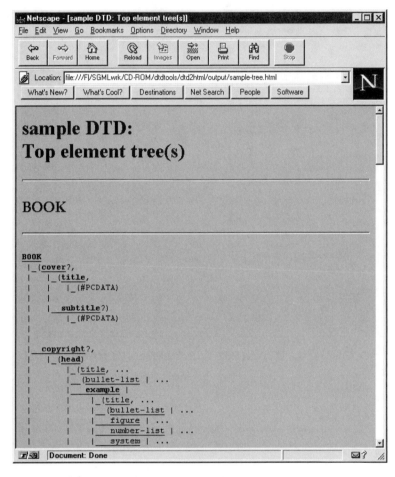

FIGURE 6-21. DTD2HTML TREE PAGE

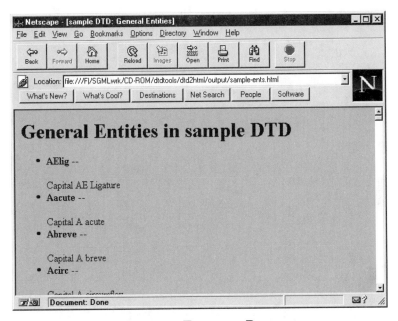

FIGURE 6-22. DTD2HTML ENTITIES PAGE

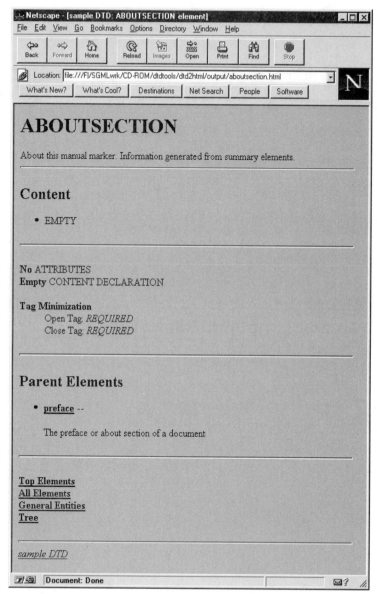

FIGURE 6-23. DTD2HTML ELEMENT PAGE

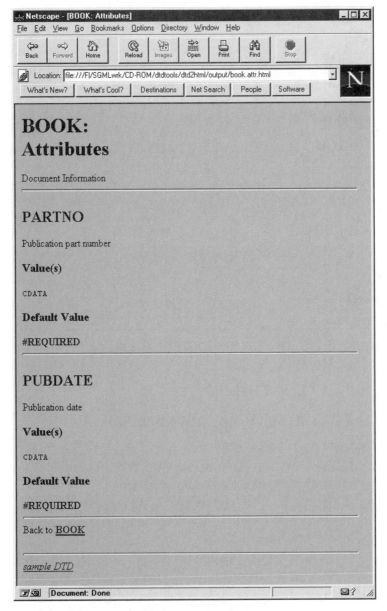

FIGURE 6-24. DTD2HTML ATTRIBUTES PAGE

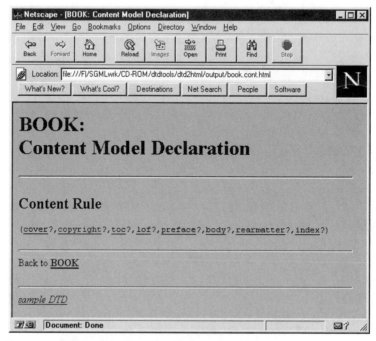

FIGURE 6-25. DTD2HTML CONTENT PAGE

CREATING A QUICK REFERENCE

To create the dtd2html quick reference document:

1. Open an MS-DOS window.

2. Change your directory to where the DTD is located, or specify the full pathname in the following examples.

3. Set the variable SGML_SEARCH_PATH to the location of the ents directory under your perlsgml installation. For me, this is: h:\perlsgml\ents.

   ```
   c:> set SGML_SEARCH_PATH=h:\perlsgml\ents
   ```

NOTE: You only need to set the above variable once per session or include it in your `autoexec.bat` file. Another alternative is to use a batch file, like I have provided.

4. I use the following command line to generate the quick reference document. Substitute your file and pathnames accordingly:

NOTE: The following command line should be entered all on one line. The command line below has been formatted for presentation and contains extra line breaks that should not be entered.

```
perl c:\bin\dtd2html -catalog h:\perlsgml\catalog -descfile sampELEM.des -qrefdl
sample.dtd
```

Figure 6-27 shows the resulting document. The default action of this particular command is to send the output directly to your screen. You can use the redirection symbol, >, to send the screen output to a file. This file will be created in your current working directory. To do this, you would enter the previous command line followed by:

```
> filename
```

I created the batch file in Figure 6-26 to build all of the above. If you copy this file to your system and modify the variables so they map to your system configuration, all you have to enter is:

```
c:> qref sample.dtd
```

```
@echo off
rem This is an MS-DOS batch file that is used to run dtd2html and
rem produce the:
rem             Quick ref documentation set
rem
rem             uasge: docs [dtd filename/path]
rem
rem Set the following variables so that pathnames match your system and
rem your configuration.
set EXE_DIR=c:\bin\
set PERL_SGML=h:\perlsgml\
set OUTDIR=f:\sgmlwrk\cd-rom\dtdtools\dtd2html\output
set BASE_OPT=%EXE_DIR%dtd2html -catalog %PERL_SGML%catalog
set DESC=-descfile sampELEM.des
set REP1=output\sample-QR.html
set SGML_SEARCH_PATH=h:\perlsgml\ents
echo Creating the Quickref Document ...
perl %BASE_OPT% %DESC% -qrefdl %1 > %REP1%
echo Processing complete ...
```

FIGURE 6-26. QREF.BAT SCRIPT

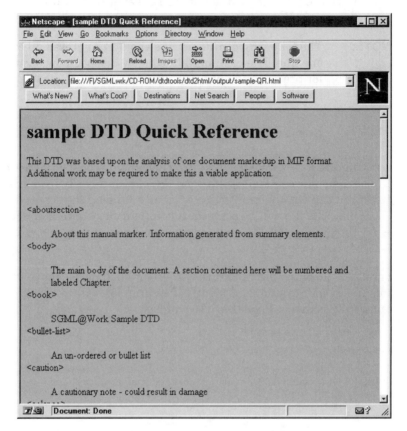

FIGURE 6-27. DTD2HTML QUICK REFERENCE PAGE

UPDATING AN ELEMENT DESCRIPTION FILE

As your DTD changes, you will need to make modifications to description files and regenerate the documentation set. The following method allows you to determine what the changes are without destroying your original data.

To update your element description file:

1. Open an MS-DOS window.

2. Change your directory to where the DTD is located, or specify the full pathname in the following examples.

3. Set the variable SGML_SEARCH_PATH to the location of the ents directory under your perlsgml installation. For me, this is: h:\perlsgml\ents.

```
c:> set SGML_SEARCH_PATH=h:\perlsgml\ents
```

NOTE: You only need to set the above variable once per session or include it in your `autoexec.bat` file. Another alternative is to use a batch file, like I have provided.

4. I use the following command line to generate the element update report document. Substitute your file and pathnames accordingly:

NOTE: The following command line should be entered all on one line. The command line below has been formatted for presentation and contains extra line breaks that should not be entered.

```
perl c:\bin\dtd2html -catalog h:\perlsgml\catalog -reportonly -updateel sampELEM.des
sample-modified.dtd
```

Figure 6-28 shows the resulting document. The default action of this particular command is to send the output directly to your screen. You can use the redirection symbol, >, to send the screen output to a file. This file will be created in your current working directory. To do this, you would enter the previous command line followed by:

```
> filename
```

```
<!-- Element Description File Update            -->
<!-- Source File:  sampELEM.des                          -->
<!-- Source DTD:  sample-modified.dtd                     -->
<!-- Deleting Old?  Yes                                   -->
<!-- Date:  Current date is Tue 06-17-1997               -->
<!-- Old identifiers:                                     -->
<!--     aboutsection, aboutsection+, summary, summary+   -->
<!--                                                      -->
```

FIGURE 6-28. DTD2HTML UPDATE ELEMENT REPORT

I created the batch file in Figure 6-29 to build all of the above. If you copy this file to your system and modify the variables so they map to your system configuration, all you have to enter is:

```
c:> update-desc sample-modified.dtd
```

```
@echo off
rem This is an MS-DOS batch file that is used to run dtd2html and
rem produce the:
rem             updated element list report
rem
rem             uasge: update-desc [dtd filename/path]
rem
rem Set the following variables so that pathnames match your system and
rem your configuration.
set EXE_DIR=c:\bin\
set PERL_SGML=h:\perlsgml\
set REP1=update.rpt
set BASE_OPT=%EXE_DIR%dtd2html -catalog %PERL_SGML%catalog
set DESC=sampELEM.des
set SGML_SEARCH_PATH=h:\perlsgml\ents
echo Creating the Updated Elements List ...
perl %BASE_OPT% -reportonly -updateel %desc% %1 > %REP1%
echo Processing complete ...
```

FIGURE 6-29. UPDATE-DESC.BAT SCRIPT

5. Once you have the report, you can then delete the items reported as removed and add any of the elements and attributes that may be indicated as added.

In this case, all I did was delete some elements in my sample-modified.dtd, and they were reported. Because they were only deleted, I don't have to actually modify my description file. If you have additions to make, review the process for editing the description file in the *Creating the Element and Entity Description Files* section.

6. Now, re-run the process to create the documentation and quick reference document as described in *Generating the HTML Files* and *Creating a Quick Reference*.

7

CONVERTING LEGACY TEXT DOCUMENTS

In this chapter, we will explore the process of creating conversion programs for legacy documents, primarily the text portion. In Chapter 8, we will discuss the issues associated specifically with graphics.

- Introduction to conversions
- Data collection methodology
- What to do with a new format
- Conversion program
- NROFF/TROFF format
- Interleaf environment
- FrameMaker environment
- Getting into SGML
- Conversion tools—Perl, awk, and OmniMark
- Conversion support tools—emacs, vim/vi, tail, head, and grep.

If you have never had to convert a document, you are in for a world of surprises. This chapter provides some basic information to prepare you and your managers for what you are about to find, as well as providing a model for approaching the task at hand.

Although this book is primarily concerned with SGML processing, you need to know about the proprietary formats your documents are already in, or you may want to process your SGML files into a proprietary format so they can be printed.

NOTE: Before we start, I must state that I don't believe that it is possible to create a conversion program, from a format other than SGML, that works consistently 100% of the time.

I believe that conversion programs follow the 80/20 rule that says 80% of the work will be easy and the last 20% nearly impossible to complete. The effort expended to create a conversion program should be geared to its purpose, but the result should always be checked against the original for missing sections or incorrect interpretations.

INTRODUCTION TO CONVERSIONS

So you've been tasked with the job of migrating your documentation to SGML. Welcome to the club! Conversion programming will get you into the lowest depths of your documentation, both from a data content view, as well as your current tools markup format.

The most common statement you will hear from managers and writers is: "Our documents are perfect!" And for their purposes, they are. The documents contain the information in the order they want and they format and print properly. But, that doesn't make for perfect content markup. The following lists some of the potential problems:

- Age of documents
- Number of writers working on them
- Number of changed hands
- Changes in tools used to create them
- Number of style guide or template changes.

Documents may print the way they should, but the markup to get there could be in a variety of forms and methods. As an example of the things that are going to make a difference to you, the simple use of tabs, spaces, and returns can create major problems. In organizations where I have had subject matter experts creating documentation, I have found a greater use of spaces to control the spacing of simple tables, rather than using tabs or table formats—i.e., the document creator must work with the methods he or she is most comfortable with.

Not only will you run into the complications of file formats, but you will also have to deal with the expectations of your managers and customers:

- Conversion work is "ugly"

- People (especially managers) don't understand the complexity and generally don't want to get into the details well enough to understand the problems

- They won't believe how long it takes—"Don't you just change {para} to <body>?"

To manage these problems, you need to define up-front the level of accuracy needed from the conversion, how it will be measured, and to what purpose the converted documents will be put. For instance, there is a big deal of difference between trying to accurately tag content elements and making the document format the same as the source format, in a new tool or format. Define your customer's or manager's expectations up-front so there are no surprises!

DATA COLLECTION METHODOLOGY

You need to learn all you can about the documents that you are going to be converting:

- Determine what platforms are used

- Collect as much information on the vendor's format as possible

- Determine the features generally used by the authors

- Find out how graphics are created and used

- Determine the complexity of tables and equations

- Collect sample documents.

The platform the documents are coming from will have a big impact on the conversion process, but also be aware of the platform you will use, and where the final results should be. For text, this isn't quite as bad as graphics, but keep in mind, for example, that the filenames and linked objects coming from a PC have an entirely different set of constraints than a Macintosh system.

Learn all you can about the current format. Get the vendor format documentation (typically not current or complete). There is probably a style guide that is being used (typically not current, but a good source for what should be happening).

Determine the key features of the tools that are typically used vs. those that only a few people may use. This allows you to prioritize which features in the source format you need to address first.

Graphics, tables, and equations can be the biggest source of problems in any conversion. Determine how the graphics are created and then placed in the document. Some systems allow for graphics to be stored in outside files and then referenced into the document. Other systems strictly import the graphics or only allow graphics to be created within the tool. Once you determine the capabilities, look at the export functions and also determine how writers may have combined features. If graphics are referenced in, have the writers also applied callouts or other objects to these graphics from within the tool? What seems like a relatively trivial distinction can have radically different results being achievable.

Tables can be created with special table functions, they could be graphics actually drawn and laid out, or they could be screen shots from other programs. Depending on how they were created, you may not want to have the requirement that all tables be rendered in the CALS table model if you can't get to the source text.

I have only had minimal experience with equations in the conversions that I have created, but they proved to be a pain! They were a pain to try and convert if they were entered in text, and they were a problem to write out to SGML because there isn't any real standard for this process either. Sometimes, the best way to deal with equations is to just make them graphics.

Talk to managers about the quality of the writing from a markup and keying standpoint, but believe key writers and production people about the quality, unless the manager also works with the documents. Determine how many changes the documents may have gone through: style guides/templates, number of writers, types of tools, etc.

After collecting all this information, you then need to get a set of sample documents to build your conversions from. You want to find documents that will satisfy the following:

- Get a current (new) and very clean document—this should set the best case scenario for the conversion work.

- Talk to the production staff and find the oldest document or the one that they hate to work with—this should set the worst case scenario.

- Based upon your earlier research, if someone is doing something different or using special features and functions, you need to get specific samples of each—this should determine the range of variation.

- Get a random sampling of documents that range in size from the shortest to the longest documents—oftentimes, a short document will have a different structure than the "standard" and the same holds true for the very long document. Short documents tend to not have all the features, and long documents tend to add structures to allow them to be split into volumes or multiple binders.

- Make sure you have a sample of all the publishing system features being used. Make sure you have samples of tables, equations, and various graphics usage.

WHAT TO DO WITH A NEW FORMAT

Every format is a new format the first time you work with it. What do you need to know about a format to get started? The concerns are both for what the format provides, as well as what and how the writers have combined those features. You need to be able to understand both worlds. The following are some starting questions:

- What is in this file and how does it work?

- What is special in this file? How does it handle variables, embedded programming, automatic numbering, cross-references, index tokens, footnotes, parallel text streams, or effectivity?

- What features have the writers used? Did they use them consistently; are tables used as layout tools; are references typed in?

- Does the vendor provide some level of documentation for the format?

- Is there an ASCII markup, or do you have to work in a binary format?

As you get into the specifics of the format, areas to review in particular are:

- Inline vs. referenced objects

- Header or prolog information vs. content
- Tables, equations, and graphics work
- Unique functionality
- Special characters, escape characters, and quoting conventions
- How the writer has used these features.

If you have access to the authoring tool, you might want to look at what capabilities are available from the tool to clean up problems or write out information in a format or way that makes your conversion efforts easier. With many high-level tools, there are programming interfaces available, in addition to the fact that there might be several ways to export the files. I have generally found that tools write their own ASCII format better than they do other vendor formats, but if your tool writes out Microsoft's RTF format and you already have a working conversion, why try to build something from scratch?

When creating conversion programs, you want to have a suite of tools and approaches for creating the final result. You don't want to limit yourself to just one tool or approach. The same is true on the loading of your converted documents. There are some programs that give you shortcuts to create documents programmatically, or there may be ways to use features of the tool to make the conversion process easier. For instance, you could write out complete formatting codes in Interleaf, or you could create your own catalog of styles. The only markup that is then needed in the final output is just references to the styles. Frame provides two markup languages: you can use the full Maker Interchange Format (MIF); or, you can use the simpler, limited function language Maker Markup Language (MML). The more you know about your tools, the wiser your decisions can be.

LEARNING PHASE

Divide and conquer is the easiest way to implement what you have learned about the format and to achieve something useful. Once I have done all my research, I start to build small utility programs that recognize specific features of the document format. I can program these short blocks with all the information I have found about the format, using them to both document that information as well as build tools that I can use to report on features or structures being used. These programs are useful as tools by themselves, as well as providing the basis for the final conversion program.

CONVERSION PROGRAM

If you have followed my suggestion in the previous section, you will have a number of small programs and you will be very familiar with the format. Now it's time to tackle the main problem—how to convert from format A to B.

The key to starting this process is to try not to do too much in one program. It is easier to build small, maintainable modules and then hand off the output to another program to take the next step to refine the output further.

For example, with the NROFF/TROFF format, I have found it easier to pass the file through one or more preprocessing steps to normalize the markup. NROFF/TROFF allows a blank line to represent a new paragraph, but not all blank lines should be treated that way. Blank lines in a preformatted block are supposed to be blank lines. It is easier to just write a small program that gets rid of this default action and places the paragraph marker where it belongs. By doing this, the main conversion task doesn't have to keep checking for where it is and what to do with a blank line.

Divide and conquer makes for more specific, smaller, easier to maintain programs and simplifies the processing of the main program. I also try to separate tag names from their processing. I build modules of code that do certain combinations of functions. The mapping of source tag names to modules is done with a mapping table. Now it is easy to add a tag with a different name, but it should run with the same processing. Thus, all the mapping is done in one location. There are times when a tag will not fit the current modules and you have to add code. With a little training, it is possible that the conversion production staff may be able to maintain the mapping table, thus keeping the programmer focused on programming issues as needed.

Another technique is to remove a block of text, like a table or graphic, and write it out to another file and leave a marker in the original source where it came from. Now, with just these tables or graphics in one file, you can write a program that only has to work with those functions. Much of the time with a table, you may have paragraphs or lists embedded, but they should be treated differently from main body lists or paragraphs.

This divide and conquer approach does not always work when deciding where to break a module or process. I usually start somewhere in the process, run into complications that make the base program more difficult to develop, and start to have too many conditions on the actions being performed. This is usually the point where I start to try and define where the complexity is being generated and move that to some other module or step in the process. The following are some questions to ask to decide if it is time to start a new module and where to place it in the process:

- Does it overly complicate the process in the current program?

- Do you need the results in the current program? If so, put it in an earlier program.

- Could it be put in a later or separate program?

A good conversion program will report errors or potential problems that were anticipated but not fully coded. In your research, you may have found a combination of features that together needed to be handled uniquely, but you didn't have a sample that exhibited the need. Programs should test for and report problems like:

- ASCII vs. binary format—you may have been told all the files were saved in ASCII, but, "Gee, this one was missed in the process!"

- Version numbers of formats should be checked and reported when they are different, or not in the range expected. Features may be added, changed, or used differently from one version to the next.

- Tags may not be recognized.

- Features may be used but not implemented in the program.

CONVERSION TOOLS

The first thing you need is a good text editor that will work with long files and doesn't introduce its own markup into the file. Along with this, the ability to show line numbers and also show the ends of lines and special characters are must-haves. I find the UNIX emacs and vi editors to fit this bill. For someone comfortable with MS-Word, these tools will be strange because the operational model is so different, but it is important that you learn and use a tool like one of these. I have included Windows 95 versions of these tools on the CD-ROM, as well as another Windows-only text editor that I use. See Appendix F for information on how to install and use these tools.

For actual conversion programming tools, I prefer scripting tools to full programming languages. I have used Perl and awk (again, originally UNIX tools, but available on Windows 95) in the past, and currently prefer to use a commercial product OmniMark. I have provided a copy of Perl on the CD-ROM and there is a lite version of OmniMark as well. The programs that I develop in this book will all be in OmniMark because I like its more powerful text- and SGML-handling capabilities.

Another language to consider using in the SGML world is LISP, specifically the Scheme version. As you will see in Chapter 13, Scheme is now part of the DSSSL standard. DSSSL will allow both formatting and SGML transformation capabilities, so why not get ahead of the curve!

SELECTED TEXT FORMATS

The following sections document the formats I have worked with and some of the features and issues of those formats.

NROFF/TROFF

NROFF/TROFF is the command used to process UNIX documents. NROFF is an ASCII formatting routine and TROFF is the same program originally optimized for typesetters and now Postscript printers. Most UNIX programs are built to be chained together on the command line, and may have several parameters that affect the actual functioning of the program. When working with this format, it is important to find the command line that is used to process the documents.

The following items may be modified at the command line:

- Variables or switches set to control internal options
- Specific macro package to use (The same command names may have different formatting characteristics based upon the package they came from.)
- Output that can be "piped" through eqn (equation formatter), tbl (table formatter), and pic (a graphic formatter)

Generally, NROFF is used for UNIX man (manual) pages, and many programs that came from this environment have their own man pages. A collection of man pages grows very fast, and to maintain and process them properly, a makefile is usually built to handle all the processing, cleanup, and delivery of the formatted documents. This may be where you find the command line to process your document.

Generally, this is a clean format to work with. It has a set of standard commands in a group of standard macro packages. If you know the macro package, you know what types of documents were intended and how complex you might expect them to be. But, NROFF can get difficult because the user can define his or her own macro package, or he or she may override or define macros within the document itself. The conversion programmer should be aware of these possible changes and at least report them when found. I suppose it could be done, but building a macro processor for NROFF seems to be above the call of duty; this is where human inspection is necessary.

The following are the basic syntax rules of this language:

- Commands start with dot, '.', at beginning of a line, or slash, '\', when embedded
- Can have logic structures and macro definitions
- Blank lines signal a new paragraph
- Some commands have built-in indents and fill attributes; some have parameters or react to the number of parameters.

One problem that is easy to introduce is when you have a text editor that automatically wraps lines for you. If you are writing about .rtf file extension, and the .rtf starts the line of text, you will interpret it as a command.

There are too many commands to actually document all of them. The UNIX man pages are a good source of information, and I have listed another book in Appendix H.

INTERLEAF

Interleaf the company created Interleaf the product on the UNIX platform in the early 1980s. Before the Macintosh existed, Interleaf was trying to build a common desktop environment for their product running on UNIX, PCs, and for awhile, the Macintosh. Their intention was to hide the operating system (OS) details from the user and allow the user to create filenames that made sense, without the operating system restrictions.

Books are organized in a series of folders, and it is the placement/position within the container that controls how a file is printed and included in the sequence. Users of Interleaf typically use the catalog feature to control the formatting of a book. More than one catalog can be used to control page layouts, numbering, and alternate component formatting in any book.

Each user has a directory called "desktop" that he or she works in. If you look at the desktop from the OS, you will see a variety of file types. The icons that are displayed on the desktop are controlled by the file extension; typical extensions you will see are: .drw=drawer, .fdr=folder, .cab=cabinet, .sty=catalog, .boo=book, .lsp=lisp, .clp=clipboard, and .pl=printerleaf (binary printer output format). For each document or catalog file, you will see additional shadow or comma files (,6, ,8, ...); these files control the placement of the object on the desktop and contain other access information.

Another convention on the desktop is to allow the same filenames. This is handled in the operating system by appending a "1" to the filename.

If you are a LISP programmer, you might want to do your conversion work using the Interleaf Developer's Kit.

INTERLEAF ASCII FORMAT (IAF)

Interleaf provides documentation on its file format. This document is available in the online help and is fairly complete, but does not document LISP inclusions in documents or equations. The individual files are fairly stand-alone, but the only way to determine how a book should be put together is to look at the Interleaf desktop. It is possible to create a LISP program to report the structure, but Interleaf doesn't provide a mechanism to do this directly.

NOTE: Saving a document to Interleaf ASCII within Interleaf writes autonumber strings that contain the actual text they refer to, as well as the reference IDs—BUT, using the command line save to ASCII (UNIX at least) only writes the references with the ids!

The <!OPS, Version = xxx> starts an IAF document. You can use this to detect that a file is in ASCII format and which version of the ASCII writer was used. <!End Declarations> ends the header and starts the body of the document.

The header contains <!Font Definitions ...>. These definitions assign a number to each font used in the document. Note that these numbers change from one ASCII save to the next. You will need to examine these definitions to find bold, italics, and Courier font changes.

<!Master ...> defines the components, tables, diagrams, and frames for each unique object in the document. There is one master element. These masters are copies of the information contained in the catalogs that were ahead of this file on the desktop at the time the file was saved.

<|,xxxx> marks the start of a page with the page number value. <name, Font = Fxx, Subcomponent = Yes/No> is a component instance. The simple case will have only the component name; any other values are local over-rides of formatting. In addition to paragraph tagging, with subcomponent = yes, components can label content as well. A subcomponent or inline is terminated with an <End Sub> or <End InLine>.

Component names are case-insensitive and two newlines (one blank line with no tabs or spaces) cause another instantiation of the previous compo-nent. A < is << in the document and ASCII hex values are entered with <#xx>. Note that a hex value can change based upon the font that the character is in. <sr> is a soft return, <HR> is a user-entered hard return, <SP>a hard space, and <Tab ...> a tab and leader type. <Fn> is a font change; track these to detect italics, bold and Courier font changes. </F> is previous font, <FI> italics, <FB> bold, and <FBI> bold italic.

<Frame, ...> contains the graphics. Frames have names and there must be a master definition for each name. If the contents are shared, you can automatically import or reference a specific graphic by name with the help of a catalog. Be careful in matching the '<>'; they are contained inside the overall frame component.

<Autonum, stream, level, Value = current> specifies system- generated text; there can be 20 levels of the same autonum to allow different types of formatting, and the Value is an optional field that is generated when sav-ing the document to IAF from the desktop, but not the command line.

OUTPUT TO INTERLEAF

Interleaf allows you to shortcut many features, and also allows the inclu-sion of text and graphics through special commands—only on the initial loading of the document. In addition to these features, you should use Interleaf catalogs to control both formatting and graphics.

Basic process:

1. Create a component catalog.

2. Create an empty document using the catalog and save to IAF.

3. Save the header from this document and split into two pieces at the end of the Frames section to allow you to include new artwork.

   This header will typically change whenever you modify the main catalog, because of the way Interleaf saves font information.

4. First line of your output <!Include Declarations pathname>.

5. For markup purposes, just use the <component> names.

You can use <!Include, pathname> for boilerplate sections of your document, and special commands will allow you to import some graphics directly with a similar syntax.

ADOBE FRAMEMAKER

FrameMaker started on the UNIX platform and migrated to the other environments. Frame's model for documentation is more file-based than Interleaf. Each document contains all the styles used, and books are controlled and generated from a special book file. Frame will import files directly or by reference. Styles can be imported from another document to replace or change formatting; this must be initiated by the writer.

Frame provides documentation on both the Maker Interchange Format (MIF) and the Maker Markup Language (MML). MML is a simpler markup intended for programmatic generation of Frame documents. The Frame+SGML product introduced markup that is included within existing Frame structures. I have provided a copy of version 4 of the MIF standard which is available on Adobe's Web site. This is not the version that my sample document is saved in, but it is close enough that you can understand most of the markup. Also available at www.adobe.com is the Frame Reader. I can't distribute the program, but it is useful for looking at and printing FrameMaker documents.

Frame has a standard method for encoding document paths to allow the transfer of files between platforms. We have had reasonable results moving files from Macintosh to PC, if all the files are on the same server, in the same structure. When files are stored across servers, they never seem to work.

FrameMaker book functions like print, report, or generate files will not work if there are any missing referenced files or if fonts are missing. All problems in the files must be fixed before the book utilities can be used properly.

There is strong support and use of variables and conditional text to allow multiple documents to be generated from the same files.

The MIF header is composed of several sections, some useful for conversion, others not. The condition catalog defines all the condition variables, but really only provides highlighting information for conditional text. The pgf catalog contains all the style information. Tables are defined in the header, with a unique id that must be matched to its position in the body.

Variable names and definitions are contained in the variable formats section. Like tables, graphics are also defined and built in the header and use a unique id to identify their location in the body.

To determine what text is visible and what appears on the master page for style definition, you must track the text rect values. Each text rect is given an id, and then a page type. Each text flow object is then tied to a text rect.

The text flow is where the document starts, but you must check the textrectid to determine the type of page the text is on. Frame tags the overall paragraph, as well as tagging the individual lines that makeup the paragraph. The <Notes ...> section of the text flow contains the Frame-managed footnotes; each footnote is given an id and is then placed with a <FNote id>.

A paragraph is contained in <Para ...>, within that is <PgfTag ...> for the tag name. <ParaLine ...> marks each line in the paragraph, and <String ..> contains the actual text content.

Although Frame assigns unique ids to everything, the ids used for cross-references are defined with markers. Markers are also used for index items and hypertext linking.

Text strings can contain font changes, character tags <Ftag>, variables, and ASCII hex codes (\xnn <space>). Surrounding strings are the conditional markers with a value that controls the visibility of the text string. <Marker ...> can indicate index items, ids, etc. <Xref ...> contains cross-reference information. <Variable ...> is a reference to a variable, and <Conditional ...> defines a conditional area.

Output to FrameMaker

FrameMaker provides a second markup language that is simpler in construction, but cannot produce all the features of Frame documents. MML can't create:

- Tables
- Equations
- Variables.

But, MML can:

- Use imported formats in MML
- Import by reference into a template.

Microsoft Word

Rich Text Format (RTF) is the ASCII markup language for Microsoft Word. The format is documented and available from Microsoft, but it is not provided with the product. RTF has a header section at the top of the document that contains color, style, font, and page layout information. Following that is the content. I have provided a copy of the latest version of the RTF specification on the CD-ROM.

Even though RTF supports the use of styles, this feature doesn't help the conversion effort. RTF places all the formatting information (not just the overrides) on each paragraph, along with the style name. This makes the process of determining the differences between paragraphs very difficult.

Output to Microsoft Word

If you are converting to RTF and the documents are intended to be living documents (not just for print), you should define styles and apply them to your output. For the end user this is a much more manageable process than having all the paragraphs formatted separately.

I have found that even though I can write out RTF that is easily loaded by MS-Word, other programs that will import RTF sometimes have problems. I believe the Microsoft reader is more robust. Once I have read a document into Word, I then save it back out to RTF. This creates a more standard/cleaner version of the format and is more portable.

Getting into SGML

Keep it simple! This is my recommendation. Unless you have an industry standard to work to, approach SGML incrementally. Chapter 4 provides the details of my methodology for developing SGML expertise and implementing an SGML process. If you use this approach, you will be working to a DTD that is similar to your document source, rules slightly loose, with additional tags that can be generated from the existing markup.

Although OmniMark can be run with the parser checking the output, I recommend leaving that task to your SGML editing tool if it is a native editing environment. This allows the editor to decide where non-specified start and end tags should be placed. I believe the advantage is that you will get a complete output from the conversion process and the cleanup can be accomplished interactively with the editor.

Conversion Programming

The first part of this chapter outlined a process for getting sample documents, understanding a new document format, and the general process for developing a conversion program. This section will focus on the tools that aid in the development process and a couple of the better programming languages for doing this type of work.

My intention in the following sections is not to demonstrate all the functionality or introduce the complete syntax of the languages presented. What I am trying to do is to illustrate the process and point out the particular strengths that make these tools best suited for this process.

Support Tools

I started doing conversion work in a UNIX environment and many of the tools that I use now were ported from UNIX to a variety of platforms. What many people don't realize is that the UNIX environment was primarily used as a documentation system for the original developers of that platform. Because of this early use, there are many tools in the core of UNIX that are intended to manipulate text files.

I use several different text editors while creating conversion programs. I use vi as my primary tool, because that is what I learned to use first. I am starting to rely more on emacs for doing the job because it does most everything that vi does and a whole lot more. Both tools make it easy to develop programs, but vi has a very useful feature of being able to show special characters and the end of a line. It's these small details of a file format that can drive you crazy while trying to develop a program.

In addition to text editors, I use the commands head and tail. These are useful for showing the top or bottom of a file. The default is to show 10 lines of the file, but you can actually request any number of lines to be shown. These tools allow you to watch a conversion in process, or to quickly verify that all your source files are stored in ASCII.

The last tool that I use is grep. This is a file search utility that reports the locations of user-specified strings in files. grep uses what is called regular expressions to specify search strings or text that you want to match. This is useful for searching source files for particular features or values. It is also a quick way to determine what is in a file when compared to a list of features in a document format specification.

The installation instructions for the editors are in Appendix F in the *Editors* section; the other tools are in the *utils* section of the same appendix. I will be using these tools in some of the processes that follow. My intention is to show where to use these tools and the specific features that make them useful. All of the UNIX tools are fully documented in various UNIX books or in the man pages.

CONFIGURING OMNIMARK EMACS MODE

All of the programming tools that are currently available in the Windows environment provide integrated editing and development. Currently, a development environment does not exist for OmniMark. There is some support in the emacs editor for OmniMark programming that can be used in both the Windows 95/NT environment, as well as UNIX.

In the *Emacs* section of Appendix F, I explain how to install and configure the base emacs environment. If you haven't already installed emacs, please refer to that section and install emacs.

To configure the OmniMark emacs mode:

1. Load the CD-ROM.

2. In the editors directory, under emacs and then under omnimarkmode, find the files `omnimark-mode.el` and `make-regexp.el`. Copy these files to the lisp directory in your emacs installation.

3. In the home directory for emacs, add the contents of the `dot_emacs` file to your `.emacs` or `_emacs` file.

4. Launch emacs.

5. To increase the performance of the OmniMark mode, we need to compile the two files we copied into the lisp directory. With your cursor in the emacs window, press Alt-x, and enter byte-compile-file, followed by a Return.

   A pathname will be displayed. Edit this entry to point at your emacs lisp directory and the file `make-regexp.el`. When this completes, repeat the above step with the file `omnimark-mode.el`.

NOTE: When reading the commands in the following procedures, I will use the same keyboard referencing as the online help. When you see an entry like:

   – C-x, this means to press the Ctrl key and lower-case x.

   – M-x, this means to press the Alt key and lower-case x.

6. To exit emacs, enter C-x C-c, or select Files, Exit emacs.

NOTE: An online emacs tutorial explains the use of the most frequently needed commands and procedures. To start the tutorial, enter C-h t.

USING VIM

vim is a Windows 95/NT port of the UNIX text editor vi. I like to use vi to examine source files because it has a nice feature that allows you to have tabs and other special characters (as well as end-of-line characters) to be displayed. This can be very useful when trying to understand a format, or determine why a search string isn't finding what you expect it to. In Appendix F, the *VIM* section explains how to install and configure vim. If you haven't already installed vim, please refer to that section.

1. Launch vim.

2. Open one of the sample MIF files.

```
VIM - F:\SGMLwrk\CD-ROM\sampDOC\Framedoc\sample.bk                    _ □ ×
<Book 5.0> # Generated by FrameMaker+SGML 5.1.1P6c
<BWindowRect 17 449 322 322>
<BNextUnique 108>
<BookUpdateReferences Yes>
<FontCatalog
 <Font
  <FTag `BulletSymbol'>
  <FPlatformName `W.Colonna MT.R.450'>
  <FFamily `Colonna MT'>
  <FVar `Regular'>
  <FWeight `Regular'>
  <FAngle `Regular'>
  <FSize  11.0 pt>
  <FOverline No>
  <FStrike No>
  <FChangeBar No>
  <FOutline No>
  <FShadow No>
  <FPairKern Yes>
  <FPosition FNormal>
  <FDW  0.0%>
  <FLocked No>
  <FSeparation 0>
  <FColor `Black'>
```

3.   To show special characters, with the cursor in the vim window, enter
     a : (colon symbol).

```
VIM - F:\SGMLwrk\CD-ROM\sampDOC\Framedoc\sample.bk                    _ □ ×
<Book 5.0> # Generated by FrameMaker+SGML 5.1.1P6c
<BWindowRect 17 449 322 322>
<BNextUnique 108>
<BookUpdateReferences Yes>
<FontCatalog
 <Font
  <FTag `BulletSymbol'>
  <FPlatformName `W.Colonna MT.R.450'>
  <FFamily `Colonna MT'>
  <FVar `Regular'>
  <FWeight `Regular'>
  <FAngle `Regular'>
  <FSize  11.0 pt>
  <FOverline No>
  <FStrike No>
  <FChangeBar No>
  <FOutline No>
  <FShadow No>
  <FPairKern Yes>
  <FPosition FNormal>
  <FDW  0.0%>
  <FLocked No>
  <FSeparation 0>
  <FColor `Black'>
:
```

This toggles your cursor to the command or ex mode line. At the
prompt, enter :set list.

```
VIM - F:\SGMLwrk\CD-ROM\sampDOC\Framedoc\sample.bk                                    _ □ ×
<Book 5.0> # Generated by FrameMaker+SGML 5.1.1P6c$
<BWindowRect 17 449 322 322>$
<BNextUnique 108>$
<BookUpdateReferences Yes>$
<FontCatalog $
 <Font $
  <FTag `BulletSymbol'>$
  <FPlatformName `W.Colonna MT.R.450'>$
  <FFamily `Colonna MT'>$
  <FVar `Regular'>$
  <FWeight `Regular'>$
  <FAngle `Regular'>$
  <FSize  11.0 pt>$
  <FOverline No>$
  <FStrike No>$
  <FChangeBar No>$
  <FOutline No>$
  <FShadow No>$
  <FPairKern Yes>$
  <FPosition FNormal>$
  <FDW  0.0%>$
  <FLocked No>$
  <FSeparation 0>$
  <FColor `Black'>$
:set list
```

The dollar sign ($), indicates the end-of-line location. Because the spaces at the beginning of the line didn't change, they are all spaces. If there had been a tab on the line, the space would have collapsed and would have been replaced with ^I.

vim/vi is a mode-based editor. This means that you are either editing the content or you are executing commands to move around or modify the file. The default mode is to be in the navigation state. The following are some useful navigation mode commands to know:

Command	Action
Esc	Quit the edit mode. When in doubt as to which mode you are in, always press Esc.
ZZ	Quit vim and save the file.
Ctrl g	Show position in the file.
G	Go to end-of-file.
[number]g	Go to a specific line.
/[string]	Find [string]—forward search that wraps from the bottom of the file to start at the top again.
Ctrl f	Page forward.
Ctrl b	Page back.
arrow and page keys	Function as expected.

USING TAIL AND HEAD

tail and head are two related commands. These tools allow you to inspect
the first or last 10 lines of a file in the DOS version of the programs that I
included on the CD-ROM. In the UNIX environment, you can actually
specify how many lines to display.

DISPLAY THE HEAD OF A FILE

For installation instructions, see Appendix F.

1. Open an MS-DOS window.
2. At the MS-DOS command line, enter:

```
c:> h:\bin\head sample.bk
```

If this FrameMaker file was saved in MIF format, you would see
something like this:

```
<Book 5.0> # Generated by FrameMaker+SGML 5.1.1P6c
<BWindowRect 17 449 322 322>
<BNextUnique 108>
<BookUpdateReferences Yes>
<FontCatalog
 <Font
  <FTag `BulletSymbol'>
  <FPlatformName `W.Colonna MT.R.450'>
  <FFamily `Colonna MT'>
  <FVar `Regular'>
c:> h:\bin\head sample-f.bk
```

This FrameMaker binary format file displays something like this:

```
<BookFile 5.0Y>
```

DISPLAY THE END OF A FILE

For installation instructions, see Appendix F.

1. Open an MS-DOS window.
2. At the MS-DOS command line, enter:

```
c:> h:\bin\tail sample.bk
```

If this FrameMaker file was saved in MIF format, you would see something like this:

```
 <XRefSrcText `16569: FigureTitle: Figure 3-4. asdk-asdk asdk as
 asdk'>
 <XRefSrcIsElem No>
 <XRefSrcFile
 `<v\>F:<c\>SGMLwrk<c\>CD-ROM<c\>sampDOC<c\>Framedoc<c\>ch2.frm'>
 <String `Figure'>
 <Char HardSpace>
 <String `4'>
> # end of BookXRef
<BookXRef
 <XRefDef `Figure\x11 <$paranumonly\>'>
 <XRefSrcText `36926: FigureTitle: Figure 0-1. asdk asdk asdk-as
 asdk'>
 <XRefSrcIsElem No>
 <XRefSrcFile
 `<v\>F:<c\>SGMLwrk<c\>CD-ROM<c\>sampDOC<c\>Framedoc<c\>ch2.frm'>
 <String `Figure'>
 <Char HardSpace>
 <String `5'>
> # end of BookXRef
# End of Book
```

```
c:> h:\bin\tail sample-f.bk
```

This FrameMaker binary format file displays something like this:

```
                                 ????Xè+ä_??:≠+P_I
                                              _zx?
                          ñP_+«ú9_9_è_<p"ó_?_f
```

USING GREP

grep is a string search tool that reports lines of text that are matched or optionally not matched by the input string. grep is useful for checking the output from head and reporting on files that aren't saved in ASCII format, or for reporting which files are book vs. document files.

I also find grep to be useful when reading format documentation. The documentation will indicate whether the BookXRef feature does something. To see if that applies to your book files, do the following:

1. Open an MS-DOS window.

2. At the MS-DOS command line, enter:

```
c:> h:\bin\grep -n BookXRef sample.bk
```

If this FrameMaker file was saved in MIF format, you would see something like this:

```
3442:<BookXRef
3456:> # end of BookXRef
3457:<BookXRef
3465:> # end of BookXRef
3466:<BookXRef
3474:> # end of BookXRef
3475:<BookXRef
3483:> # end of BookXRef
3484:<BookXRef
3492:> # end of BookXRef
3493:<BookXRef
3501:> # end of BookXRef
3502:<BookXRef
3510:> # end of BookXRef
```

The -n option causes the line number to be printed, as well as the full content of the line.

3. Now, to add some context for the lines (show what was just before or after a line), you would enter:

```
c:> h:\bin\grep -n -2 BookXRef sample.bk
```

```
3440- <ElementEnd `NoName'>
3441-> # end of BookElements
3442:<BookXRef
3443- <XRefDef `Table\x11 <$paranumonly\>'>
3444- <XRefSrcText `34848: TableTitle: Table 2-1. asdk asdk asdk asdk'>
--
3454- <Char HardSpace>
3455- <String `1'>
3456:> # end of BookXRef
3457:<BookXRef
3458- <XRefDef `Figure\x11 <$paranumonly\>'>
3459- <XRefSrcText `19350: FigureTitle: Figure 2-1. asdk asdk asdk asdk'>
--

          TEXT REMOVED HERE

--
3490- <Char HardSpace>
3491- <String `3'>
3492:> # end of BookXRef
3493:<BookXRef
3494- <XRefDef `Figure\x11 <$paranumonly\>'>
3495- <XRefSrcText `16569: FigureTitle: Figure 3-4. asdk-asdk asdk asdk
asdk'>
--
3499- <Char HardSpace>
3500- <String `4'>
3501:> # end of BookXRef
3502:<BookXRef
3503- <XRefDef `Figure\x11 <$paranumonly\>'>
3504- <XRefSrcText `36926: FigureTitle: Figure 0-1. asdk asdk asdk-asdk
asdk'>
--
3508- <Char HardSpace>
3509- <String `5'>
3510:> # end of BookXRef
3511-# End of Book
```

The -2 option causes two lines above and below the line matched to be printed as well.

4. To find all the lines of text that didn't match a specific value, you would use a -v option on the command line.

The documentation or man page for this command should have been installed in the same directory where the program exists. This provides all the options that are available for this command. I highly recommend learning to use this very powerful tool.

PROGRAMMING TOOLS

AWK

awk was originally developed by Aho, Weinberger, and Kernigan (awk) in 1977 as a pattern-matching language for writing short programs. In 1985, new awk (nawk) was developed. It added several features, the most useful being functions. awk is an event-driven language with the actual program built in three possible sections. There is a begin, body, and end section of the program. The begin section is executed before the source is read. As the source is read, the patterns in the body of the program are executed. At the end of the source, the end section is executed.

The awk script in Figure 7-1 is the awk version of the OmniMark program in Figure 7-7. For an explanation of what it does, see the description in the section *Extracting Information from an MIF Book File*. This script is provided so you can compare the format and readability of the different programming languages. To run this script, enter:

```
c:> awk -f book1.awk sample.bk
```

```
1   # file book1.awk
2   #
3   # Typical command line:
4   #       c:> awk -f book1.awk source-file
5
6   BEGIN {
7
8   # This rule executes before any of the source material
9   # is read in. This is used to setup variables and initial
10  # states.
11
12          FirstLine = 1
13          ASCIIFile = 0
14
15          print "Starting conversion ..."
16
17          }
18
19  $1 == "<Book"    {
20
21  # find the <Book line, it should be the first line in a
22  # bookfile saved to ASCII, if it isn't there then we are
23  # either not in an ASCII file or a bookfile.
24  #
```

FIGURE 7-1. BOOK1.AWK SCRIPT

```
25    # Find the version number so we can validate if the conversion
26    # program was designed to handle this flavor of MIF
27
28                    if (FirstLine == 1) {
29                            ASCIIFile = 1
30                            print "MIF Version " $2 " expecting v5.0\n"
31                    }
32
33            }
34
35
36    $1 == "<FileName" {
37
38                            print "Filename: " $2
39
40                    }
41
42
43                    { # trip the flag as soon as the first EOL is found
44
45                            FirstLine = 0
46                    }
47
48
49    END {
50
51      # This rule executes after all the source material has been
52      # read in. This is typically used to report status or cleanup
53      # any temporary files.
54
55
56      # IF still false then we never found the <Book value at
57      # the start of the file, so it is not saved in ASCII or
58      # is not a bookfile
59
60            if (ASCIIFile == 0) {
61                    print "ERROR: File not saved in ASCII or not bookfile"
62            }
63
64            print "Conversion ended ..."
65
66            }
67
68    ### END OF PROGRAM FILE
```

FIGURE 7-1. BOOK1.AWK SCRIPT (CONTINUED)

```perl
1   #!/usr/bin/perl
2   # file book1.pl
3   #
4   # Typical command line:
5   #        c:> perl book1.pl source-file
6
7   $, = ' ';                # set output field separator
8   $\ = "\n";               # set output record separator
9
10
11  $FirstLine = 1;
12  $ASCIIFile = 0;
13
14  print 'Starting conversion ...';
15
16  while (<>) {
17      ($Fld1,$Fld2) = split(' ', $_, 9999);
18
19      if ($Fld1 eq '<Book') {
20          if ($FirstLine == 1) {
21              $ASCIIFile = 1;
22              print 'MIF Version ', $Fld2, "currently expecting v5.0\n";
23          }
24      }
25
26      if ($Fld1 eq '<FileName') {
27          print 'Filename: ' . $Fld2;
28      }
29
30      $FirstLine = 0;
31
32  }
33
34  if ($ASCIIFile == 0) {
35      print "ERROR: File not saved in ASCII or not bookfile\n";
36  }
37
38  print 'Conversion ended ...';
39
40  ### END OF PROGRAM FILE
```

FIGURE 7-2. BOOK1.PL SCRIPT

PERL

I introduced perl back in Chapter 6 in *Using dtd2html*. perlSGML is a library of useful routines for working with DTD's as well as a few programs that use those libraries to create a useful output. perl is a

UNIX-based tool that provides the best features of awk and the shell. The shell in UNIX is a more powerful version of batch programming in the Windows®95/DOS world.

The perl script in Figure 7-2 is the perl version of the OmniMark program in Figure 7-7. For an explanation of what it does, see the description in the section *Extracting Information from an MIF Book File*. This script is provided so you can compare the format and readability of the different programming languages.

OmniMark

OmniMark the company produces OmniMark and OmniMark LE the products. OmniMark was built as a text and SGML processing language that would be easy for technical publications (non-programmers) professionals to pick up and use easily. As a programmer, it is worthwhile to add OmniMark to the suite of languages you use because of its specific tailoring to the problem of text manipulation and format conversion.

OmniMark is an interpreted language that is event-driven. The underlying paradigm is that you are specifying a series of events that may take place within the text source; when the event is found in the source, the code associated with the event is executed. An OmniMark program has three sections: generically there is a begin, a body, and an end section. The begin section is triggered by the start of input prior to reading any of the source material. As OmniMark reads in the source, the body of the program is executed. At the end of the input, the end section of the program is executed.

OmniMark can be used in three different modes. These modes act like three different products with the same programming syntax. Figure 7-3 illustrates these three modes: Up, Down, and Cross translations.

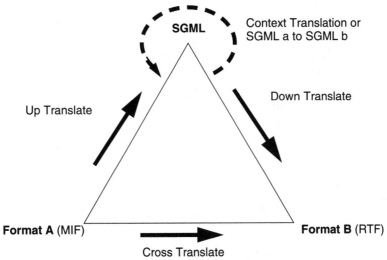

FIGURE 7-3. OMNIMARK PROGRAM MODES

The Up translate adds intelligence to the source format. This is the process of bringing MIF (or similar format) to SGML. This mode uses simple find strings to match the input and substitutes a specific set of SGML tags as specified by the DTD. This mode uses the SGML parser on the output to validate the SGML stream.

The Cross translate is typically used to take MIF to RTF, or one unstructured format to another unstructured format. This method doesn't use the SGML parser at all.

The Down translate uses the SGML parser to read the source. Based upon the elements being read and the position in the hierarchy, you can specify whatever processing you want. This is the process typically used to take SGML into a proprietary format so it might be printed.

The OmniMark documentation uses an Up translate for conversions from proprietary formats to SGML. I tend to use the Cross translate. The difference in the approach is that I am able to create valid SGML directly from my program. I can then use OmniMark to help add the additional tags or end tags as needed. The file generated using the other approach may be produced, but with a set of documented errors that then need to be fixed. I would use this mode if the only parser I had access to was in the Omni-Mark tool; but, I typically have a robust native SGML editor available that performs the same service for me, but in an interactive way.

INSTALLING OMNIMARK LE

OmniMark LE is shareware version of the full OmniMark programming tool. The only difference between them is that programs run with the LE version can only perform 200 countable operations. This doesn't equate to lines of code, however, and I haven't seen a list of the commands that get counted; but, OmniMark LE reports the number of countable objects whenever you run a program.

To install OmniMark LE:

1. Load the CD-ROM.

2. In the conversion directory, find the file `omnimarkle.exe`. Double-click on this file.

3. Accept the directory location presented to you, or enter a different location.

4. For the purpose of this book, you don't need to install everything (although you may want to). Choose Custom installation and only select OmniMark LE V3R0a for installation.

Complete documentation for OmniMark is available at their Web site: www.omnimark.com.

I like to create a batch file that executes OmniMark and a standard set of command line options. Figure 7-4 shows the Omnibat batch file that I used for these programs. It is available on the CD-ROM, in the conversions directory under sample.

This batch file takes the following command line:

```
c:> omni script-name other-input
```

It then sends the output from the OmniMark program to `script-name.of`, and error messages and warnings to the file `error.log`. Both of these files appear in the directory where you ran the script.

CONFIGURING OMNIMARK LE

The programs that I will be developing in this chapter require nothing else to be configured. I will be using OmniMark to validate our output. That and any other mode that requires the parser will require the following to be configured.

OmniMark uses a file, typically called `entities.xlr`, to map the PUBLIC ids to system file locations. This file can include complete path specifications, or you can use a `-libpath pathname` option on the command to define a relative search path for these files.

The `entities.xlr` file is shown in Figure 7-5. It contains a list of all the PUBLIC identifiers, followed by the system file location. The way this version of the file is configured, it expects all the ISO files to be in the current directory under charset and then entities. The last two entries are the ones we need to add to support the sample DTD. These two files are expected to be at the same location as the `entities.xlr` file.

NOTE: This version of the `entites.xlr` file will not work with all DTDs; it is missing the alternate PUBLIC ID format of ISO 8879:1986. To make this file more flexible, all the ISO entries should be duplicated and the colon added in place of the hyphen.

```
1   @echo off
2
3   rem This batch file makes it easy to execute OmniMark scripts
4   rem The following are the command line options available for
5   rem OmniMark:
6   rem
7   rem  omnimark -s program -save application {options} input
8   rem
9   rem    input                  zero or more input data files
10  rem
11  rem    -a switch              activate omnimark program switch
12  rem    -alog file             log file (append mode)
13  rem    -aof file              output file (append mode)
14  rem    -aos stream file       output to stream (append mode)
15  rem    -brief                 do not print identification banner
16  rem    -c counter value       define value for omnimark counter
17  rem    -d stream value        define value for omnimark stream
18  rem    -expand                expand macros to log file
19  rem    -ftrace                show function-call trace
20  rem    -f file                file of command line arguments
21  rem    -herald                use heralded-names
22  rem    -i path                path to include files
23  rem    -l path                path to library files
24  rem    -library file          library file
25  rem    -limit number          maximum allowed error messages
26  rem    -load application      load omnimark saved application
27  rem    -log file              log file
28  rem    -of file               output file
29  rem    -s program             omnimark source program
30  rem    -save application      save omnimark application
31  rem    -temppfx path          temporary files path
32  rem    -term                  input program source from standard inp
33  rem    -warning               display warning level messages
34  rem
35  rem
36  rem    To use this batch file, enter:
37  rem           c:> omni script-name other-input
38  rem
39
40  set OMLE=h:\omle\omle
41  set ERROR=-log error.log
42  set SCRIPT=-s %1
43  set OUTPUT=-of %1.of
44
45  call %OMLE% %ERROR% %SCRIPT% %OUTPUT% %2 %3 %4 %5 %6 %7 %8 %9
```

FIGURE 7-4. OMNI.BAT—OMNIMARK LAUNCH SCRIPT

```
; File: entities.xlr
;
; This file can be used by different OmniMark programs.
library "ISO 8879-1986//ENTITIES Added Math Symbols: Arrow Relations//El
        "charset\entities\iso-amsa.ent"
        "ISO 8879-1986//ENTITIES Added Math Symbols: Binary Operators//l
        "charset\entities\iso-amsb.ent"
        "ISO 8879-1986//ENTITIES Added Math Symbols: Delimiters//EN"
        "charset\entities\iso-amsc.ent"
        "ISO 8879-1986//ENTITIES Added Math Symbols: Negated Relations/.
        "charset\entities\iso-amsn.ent"
        "ISO 8879-1986//ENTITIES Added Math Symbols: Ordinary//EN"
        "charset\entities\iso-amso.ent"
        "ISO 8879-1986//ENTITIES Added Math Symbols: Relations//EN"
        "charset\entities\iso-amsr.ent"
        "ISO 8879-1986//ENTITIES Box and Line Drawing//EN"
        "charset\entities\iso-box.ent"
        "ISO 8879-1986//ENTITIES Russian Cyrillic//EN"
        "charset\entities\iso-cyr1.ent"
        "ISO 8879-1986//ENTITIES Non-Russian Cyrillic//EN"
        "charset\entities\iso-cyr2.ent"
        "ISO 8879-1986//ENTITIES Diacritical Marks//EN"
        "charset\entities\iso-dia.ent"
        "ISO 8879-1986//ENTITIES Greek Letters//EN"
        "charset\entities\iso-grk1.ent"
        "ISO 8879-1986//ENTITIES Monotoniko Greek//EN"
        "charset\entities\iso-grk2.ent"
        "ISO 8879-1986//ENTITIES Greek Symbols//EN"
        "charset\entities\iso-grk3.ent"
        "ISO 8879-1986//ENTITIES Added Latin 1//EN"
        "charset\entities\iso-lat1.ent"
        "ISO 8879-1986//ENTITIES Added Latin 2//EN"
        "charset\entities\iso-lat2.ent"
        "ISO 8879-1986//ENTITIES Numeric and Special Graphic//EN"
        "charset\entities\iso-num.ent"
        "ISO 8879-1986//ENTITIES Publishing//EN"
        "charset\entities\iso-pub.ent"
        "ISO 8879-1986//ENTITIES General Technical//EN"
        "charset\entities\iso-tech.ent"
        "-//SAW//DTD SGML at Work Sample DTD//EN"
        "sample.dtd"
        "-//ArborText//ELEMENTS CALS Table Structures//EN"
        "cals-tbl.elm"
```

FIGURE 7-5. ENTITIES.XLR LIBRARY FILE

OmniMark Conversion Programs

The following programs will be used to convert the sample document on the CD-ROM in sampDOC, under framedoc. The files in this directory are all saved in the MIF format. The files are:

- `sample.bk`—FrameMaker Book file, this file is used to manage all the files that comprise the book

- `sample.frm`—Cover and copyright information of the sample document

- `sampltoc.frm`—Table of Contents from the sample

- `about.frm`—Preface or About section

- `ch1.frm`—sample document Chapter 1

- `ch2.frm`—sample document Chapter 2

- `appa.frm`—sample document Appendix A

- `appb.frm`—sample document Appendix B

- `sampleix.frm`—sample document Index.

The above description contains more information about this sample than you might have been able to extract from just the filenames. For a FrameMaker document, the best source for the organization of the files and exactly which files are required is the book file. What happens when you get a directory full of files that use a poor naming convention or multiple versions of the same file, or two or more books mixed together? The first step in a conversion effort is either to have your information source give you a list of documents, with all the files and their proper order, or you need to try and find that information yourself.

Extracting Information from an MIF Book File

Take a look at the MIF format documentation provided on the CD-ROM. The following sections of the book file look like they will provide useful information on how to order the files:

MIF Markup	Contents
<Book release>	Defines the file as a book file and specifies the version number of the MIF language.
#	Indicates a comment start to the end of the line.
<FileName pathname>	Contained in a BookComponent, this specifies the actual filename and location. The pathname has an Adobe-specific format.

Notice the format of the book file shown in Figure 7-6. The MIF structures can be single entries, or there can be grouping and nesting of those structures. This is the basic file structure that you will have to work with. Somehow you need to recognize the simple one-line entries and then also deal with the more complex nested structures.

You have several choices at this point about how you will try and find and separate the information that you want from the extraneous data. Examine the features of the closing '>' for the nesting groups. Notice that the closing '>' is preceded by a group of blanks or spaces that correspond to the nesting level of the group, and a comment trails the '>', indicating exactly which object it is closing. This is a very nice distinguishing feature, but it can only be guaranteed to be there when the MIF is generated by FrameMaker, and it may also be only valid for this particular version of FrameMaker. You need to decide if:

- You will ever have to work with files created by another program or filter?

- How stable you believe the current formatting is with regard to Adobe; do you think they will change this file layout anytime soon?

- Is there any other way to match the start and end of the nesting groups without relying on the leading spaces and trailing comments?

- Do you really need to write a conversion that tracks the nesting groups by matching the opening information with the closing structure? Would a simple flag and counter mechanism work as easily and not rely so heavily on a specific file layout?

```
<Book 5.0> # Generated by FrameMaker+SGML 5.1.1P6c
<BWindowRect 17 449 322 322>
<BNextUnique 108>
<BookUpdateReferences Yes>
<FontCatalog
 <Font
  <FTag `BulletSymbol'>
```
TEXT REMOVED
```
  <FColor `Black'>
 > # end of Font
 <Font
  <FTag `Callout'>
```
TEXT REMOVED
```
 > # end of Font
> # end of FontCatalog
<PgfCatalog
 <Pgf
  <PgfTag `Body'>
  <PgfBlockSize 3>
  <PgfFont
   <FTag `'>
```
TEXT REMOVED
```
   <FVar `Regular'>
  > # end of PgfFont
 > # end of Pgf
> # end of PgfCatalog
<ElementDefCatalog
> # end of ElementDefCatalog
<FmtChangeListCatalog
> # end of FmtChangeListCatalog
<BookSettings
```
TEXT REMOVED
```
# End of Book
```

FIGURE 7-6. MIF STRUCTURES IN A BOOK FILE

The above questions are what you should be asking yourself before you start writing the conversion. You need to balance these possible methods and issues against the purpose to which your program will be applied. Is this program to be:

- A robust tool that can accept any MIF file that FrameMaker might be able to read?

- Will it have a lifespan of more than a few weeks?

- Is it more important to complete the program now and convert the documents, or to worry about and consider future conversions?

This is where knowing the full requirements and purpose of your conversion is important. You may spend more time making a full robust system that never gets used again and fail (as far as your manager is concerned), because you didn't complete the conversion effort on time. Know your requirements before starting!

My bias when seeing a structure like MIF is to try and pull the blocks of information apart and then work on that known block of sub-objects; but, this is not always the best or most efficient way to approach this problem with OmniMark.

For now, let's build a simple program that finds the Book and FileName MIF objects and ignores (eats the content) of everything else in the book file.

I have documented the various sections of the book1.xom program in the source file, and Figure 7-7 shows that code. What I want to explain here is the OmniMark syntax and how this program is structured.

Line 1 of book1.xom is a comment; everything after the ';' is not seen as part of the program and is there to help the programmer or user understand what the program is doing. Also notice the use of whitespace and indention; this is also for readability only.

Line 3 declares the type of the OmniMark program, that is, cross translate. Lines 5 and 6 are the declaration of two variables that can be used globally anywhere in the program. These variables are switches, otherwise known as Booleans. A switch can either be on/off or true/false.

find-start on line 14 is a label for a section of the program that will execute before any of the source input is read. This is typically used to set up the program environment. In this case, I am printing a message (line 16) directly to the screen, I don't want this to be part of the output file that is created by this program.

Line 18 specifies where the program should continue when the find-start rule is completed. This is like a declaration. If I had more actions after this line, they would execute before starting the MAIN-BODY group. Line 27 starts the find-end rule. I'm going to skip this section because it is only triggered by the end of the source input.

```
 1   ; file book1.xom
 2
 3   cross-translate
 4
 5   global switch first-line initial {true}
 6   global switch ascii-file initial {false}
 7
 8
 9
10   ; This rule executes before any of the source material
11   ; is read in. This is used to setup variables and initial
12   ; states.
13
14   find-start
15
16         put #CONSOLE "Starting conversion ...%n"
17
18         next group is MAIN-BODY   ; when finished with this
19                                   ; rule, then go to this location
20
21
22   ; This rule executes after all the source material has been
23   ; read in. This is typically used to report status or cleanup
24   ; any temporary files.
25
26
27   find-end
28
29         ; IF still false then we never found the <Book value at
30         ; the start of the file, so it is not saved in ASCII or
31         ; is not a bookfile
32
33         do when (ascii-file = false)
34                 output "ERROR: File not saved in ASCII or not "_
35                 "bookfile%n%n"
36
37                 put #ERROR "ERROR: File not saved in ASCII or not
38                 "bookfile%n%n"
39         done
40
41         put #CONSOLE "Conversion ended ...%n"
42
43
44   GROUP MAIN-BODY
45
46   ; trip the flag as soon as the first EOL is found
47
48   find "%n"
49         set first-line to false
```

FIGURE 7-7. BOOK1.XOM PROGRAM

```
50
51
52
53
54    ; find the <Book line, it should be the first line in a
55    ; bookfile saved to ASCII, if it isn't there then we are
56    ; either not in an ASCII file or a bookfile.
57    ;
58    ; Find the version number so we can validate if the conversion
59    ; program was designed to handle this flavor of MIF
60
61    find "<Book " ((lookahead not ">") any)*=ver   ">"
62                  ((lookahead not "%n") any)* "%n"
63
64          do when (first-line = true)
65          output "MIF Version %x(ver) currently expecting v5.0%n"
66                  set ascii-file to true
67          done
44    GROUP MAIN-BODY
45
46    ; trip the flag as soon as the first EOL is found
47
48    find "%n"
49          set first-line to false
50
51
52
53
54    ; find the <Book line, it should be the first line in a
55    ; bookfile saved to ASCII, if it isn't there then we are
56    ; either not in an ASCII file or a bookfile.
57    ;
58    ; Find the version number so we can validate if the conversion
59    ; program was designed to handle this flavor of MIF
60
61    find "<Book " ((lookahead not ">") any)*=ver   ">"
62                  ((lookahead not "%n") any)* "%n"
63
64          do when (first-line = true)
65          output "MIF Version %x(ver) currently expecting v5.0%n"
66                  set ascii-file to true
67          done
68
69
70    ; Find the <FileName tag to locate the files that belong to this
71    ; book.
72
73    find blank* "<FileName `" ((lookahead not "'>") any)*=path "'>"
74                  blank* "%n"
```

FIGURE 7-7. BOOK1.XOM PROGRAM (CONTINUED)

```
75
76          output "Filename: %x(path)%n"
77
78
79  ; Find anything else we don't want to worry about.
80  ; Without this find rule, all the other characters not
81  ; matched would still be echoed to the screen
82
83  find any
84          ;
85
86
87
88  ;;; END OF PROGRAM FILE
```

FIGURE 7-7. BOOK1.XOM PROGRAM (CONTINUED)

Line 44 acts as a label and indicates the starting point in this group. There could be more than one group in a program, and more than one can be active at a time. The rest of this program file comprises the MAIN-BODY group. The find rules specified are searched in the order that they are presented. You could end up with entirely different results by simply rearranging the different find rule blocks. OmniMark looks at each of these rules and finds the rule that matches the longest string if two or more have similar rules.

Line 48 has our first find rule. This rule matches any end-of-line character (%n) in the file. If it finds an end-of-line, it switches the variable first-line to false. I really only need this to happen once, but anytime an end-of-line character is not matched by one of the subsequent rules, first-line is again set to false. I am using this rule to switch a flag to indicate that I am past the first line of input in this file. This is to help me determine if I am in a bookfile or a file that hasn't been saved to ASCII MIF format.

Line 61 is another find rule. If the file is in the proper format, this should actually be the first find rule that fires, even though it is the second one in the group. Let's take a look at the string or text pattern that we are trying to find. First, this is what the string looks like in the source file:

```
<Book 5.0> # Generated by FrameMaker+SGML 5.1.1P6c
```

Of the text on this line, I am actually trying to find the 5.0 value; everything else is extraneous. The additional information in the MIF comment might be useful, but all I really need is the 5.0. Now, when you try to define your own find rules, you must decide what will always uniquely identify what you are looking for and make that the base of the rule you want to build on. From the MIF Format Specification, I know that the

<Book and > will always be there. There is no specification for what the value will look like and the comment is just extra information.

Now, let's examine the first portion of the find rule:

```
"<Book "  ((lookahead not ">") any)*=ver   ">"
```

As you can see, I'm looking for the hard string "<Book " at the start of the line, and ">" at the end of this line, just like the standard. There is a potential problem with this match string. The blank or space after Book could, in other circumstances, be more than one blank, or there could be one or more line breaks there as well. In this instance, I'm trading readability of the pattern with robustness of the program. This is a potential place for failure for any other MIF file that is generated by a different program or version of FrameMaker.

Now for that piece in the middle. Let's start from the back and work forward. The =ver sets a local pattern variable, ver, with whatever gets matched between "<Book " and ">". This is exactly the value I want to capture, and as you will see, I need to know nothing about the format of this ver or version number, which is good because there is no specification for this value to try and search for. The any will match any character that appears in this location, and the '*' outside the parenthesis indicates there are zero or more characters to match. The lookahead causes OmniMark to search the string ahead (without removing anything from the input source) until it finds ">". All the characters before the first matched ">" will be assigned to the local pattern variable ver.

```
((lookahead not "%n") any)* "%n"
```

The last portion of the pattern string consumes to the end of the line, up to and including the end-of-line character, any potential comments or other text that may be after the ">", and before the end-of-line character. In this case, I have decided not to do anything with the text matched at this point.

Line 65 outputs the text that is listed, as well as the contents of the pattern variable ver (with the "%x(ver)" format statement). This output defaults to the screen unless an output file is specified on the OmniMark command line.

Lines 64 to 67 form a "do when done" block. My output statement on Line 65 is not executed unless the switch variable first-line is set to true when this find rule is executed. If it is true, the statements between the do/done will be executed.

Lines 73 to 76 look for the <FileName MIF tag to determine the files that make up the book. When we match the contents of the tag, it is assigned to the local pattern variable path and then output with some additional text.

Lines 83 and 84 are the last that need explanation. As indicated above, the keyword any matches any character. In this case, I'm matching a single character. The purpose of this rule is to just remove or consume the rest of the source input. If this rule wasn't here, the characters not matched by any of the other rules would be sent, passed through, to the screen. To avoid this clutter and potential confusion, we consume those extra characters here. This is one of those find rules that if placed at the start of the MAIN-BODY group, there would be no output; all of the characters would be consumed, one by one, until the end of input.

Let's look at the output from this program. Figure 7-8 shows the results of running:

```
c:> omni book1.xom sample.bk
```

The top portion of the figure shows what is output to the screen by our program. In this case, we see the two strings specified in the find-start and find-end sections of the program. The bottom portion of the figure shows the resulting output file. We could get fancier with the output if the need arose, but for now, this will do.

Figure 7-9 shows the results of running:

```
c:> omni book1.xom sample-f.bk
```

The top portion of the figure shows what is output to the screen by our program. In this case, we see the two strings specified in the find-start and find-end sections of the program, and we also find the error string written out by the find-end with the put #ERROR. The bottom portion of the figure shows the resulting output file. It only has the error message, written with the output statement in the find-end. Because it was in a binary format, none of the patterns that were looking for readable characters were fired.

Text From the Command Line

```
F:\SGMLwrk\CD-ROM\conversion\sample>omni book1.xom sample.bk
Starting conversion ...
Conversion ended ...
F:\SGMLwrk\CD-ROM\conversion\sample>
```

Contents of book1.xom.of

```
MIF Version 5.0 currently expecting v5.0
Filename: <c\>sample.frm
Filename: <c\>sampltoc.frm
Filename: <c\>about.frm
Filename: <c\>ch1.frm
Filename: <c\>ch2.frm
Filename: <c\>appa.frm
Filename: <c\>appb.frm
Filename: <c\>sampleix.frm
```

Figure 7-8. book1.xom Output with an ASCII File

```
F:\SGMLwrk\CD-ROM\conversion\sample>omni book1.xom sample-f.b}
ERROR: File not saved in ASCII or not bookfile
Starting conversion ...
Conversion ended ...
```

CONTENTS OF BOOK1.XOM.OF

```
ERROR: File not saved in ASCII or not bookfile
```

FIGURE 7-9. BOOK1.XOM OUTPUT FROM A NON-ASCII FILE

Now that you understand the functionality of the OmniMark file, go back to Figure 7-1 , Figure 7-2, and Figure 7-2 and compare the readability of the awk, Perl, and OmniMark programs. The approach to create an awk script is very close to that of an OmniMark program. Perl is a more traditional programming approach. Each tool has its strengths and weaknesses: the trick is to know them and be able to determine when one is a better approach than the other.

FINDING REFERENCED FILES IN AN MIF FILE

FrameMaker has a powerful feature that allows external text and graphics files to be imported by reference. This allows these objects to be maintained and manipulated by someone else or another program. FrameMaker will keep updating the content within the document, to match that which is still stored separately. You need to know which files are referenced and where they are expected to be in relation to the FrameMaker book. The program in Figure 7-10 is a slight variation on the previous program. A document file has a different starting tag than a bookfile, and the ImportObFileDI is used instead of the FileName.

MIF Markup	**Contents**
<MIFFile release>	Defines the file as a document file and specifies the version number of the MIF language.
<ImportObFileDI pathname>	Contained in an ImportObject; this specifies the actual filename and location. The pathname has an Adobe-specific, device-independent format.

```
1   ; file doc.xom
2
3   cross-translate
4
5   global switch first-line initial {true}
6   global switch ascii-file initial {false}
7
8
9
10  find-start
11
12          put #CONSOLE "Starting conversion ...%n"
13
14          next group is MAIN-BODY        ; when finished with this
15                                 ; rule, then go to this location
16
17
18
19  find-end
20
21          ; IF still false then we never found the <MIFFile value at
22          ; the start of the file, so it is not saved in ASCII or
23          ; is not a document file
24
25          do when (ascii-file = false)
26              output "ERROR: File not saved in ASCII or not "_
27              "document file%n%n"
28
29           put #ERROR "ERROR: File not saved in ASCII or not "_
30                  "document file%n%n"
31          done
32
33          put #CONSOLE "Conversion ended ...%n"
34
35
36  GROUP MAIN-BODY
37
```

FIGURE 7-10. DOC.XOM PROGRAM FILE

```
38  ; trip the flag as soon as the first EOL is found
39
40  find "%n"
41          set first-line to false
42
43
44
45
46
47  find "<MIFFile " ((lookahead not ">") any)*=ver   ">"
48                  ((lookahead not "%n") any)* "%n"
49
50          do when (first-line = true)
51          output "MIF Version %x(ver) currently expecting v5.0%n"
52                  set ascii-file to true
53          done
54
55
56  find blank* "<ImportObFileDI `" ((lookahead not "'>") any)*=path
57                  blank* "%n"
58
59          output "Referenced File: "
60          repeat scan pattern path
61                  match "<c\>"
62                          output "\"
63                  match "<r\>"
64                          output "Root "
65                  match "<v\>"
66                          output "Vol\Drive "
67                  match "<h\>"
68                          output "Host "
69                  match "<u\>"
70                          output ".."
71                  match any=letter
72                          output "%x(letter)"
73          again
74          output "%n"
75
76
77  find any
78          ;
79
80
81
82  ;;; END OF PROGRAM FILE
```

FIGURE 7-10. DOC.XOM PROGRAM FILE (CONTINUED)

Line 60 illustrates a new OmniMark feature. The repeat scan again construct allows you to take apart text that you have already taken from the input stream, but still need to process the content. I am using this construct to take the device-independent path specification in the MIF file and create a more readable form for our report. The repeat again contains a series of match statements that function just like a find rule. The repeat statement doesn't automatically read to the end of input. You must provide enough match statements to consume all the input string, otherwise your program would hold in these blocks.

My sample document doesn't reference any external objects, but when I run this against one of the files in this book, I get a report like the one shown in Figure 7-11. Notice that unlike Figure 7-8 the <c\> has now been replaced by a single '\'.

```
MIF Version 5.00 currently expecting v5.0
Referenced File: \figures\nfd--1.tif
Referenced File: \figures\nfd--12.tif
Referenced File: \figures\nfd--9.tif
Referenced File: \figures\nfd--8.tif
Referenced File: \figures\nfd--10.tif
Referenced File: \figures\nfd--11.tif
Referenced File: \figures\nfd--13.tif
Referenced File: \figures\nfd--14.tif
Referenced File: \figures\nfd--15.tif
Referenced File: \figures\nfd--16.tif
Referenced File: \figures\nfd--17.tif
Referenced File: \figures\nfd--18.tif
Referenced File: \figures\nfd--19.tif
Referenced File: \figures\nfd--20.tif
Referenced File: \figures\nfd--27.tif
```

FIGURE 7-11. DOC.XOM SAMPLE OUTPUT

LISTING THE STYLES IN A MIF FILE

A key feature of any professional DTP system is the ability to control formatting through the use of styles or tags. Most systems have this ability, and it is up to the author as to how well and consistently it is used. I base all my programs on this feature, so the first step I perform whenever I get a new document set is to list out the style names that are defined in a given document so I can compare it to a master list that I have already encountered. The following table lists the MIF structures that are important in this program.

MIF Markup	Contents
<PgfCatalog ... >	Groups all style information into a group.
<Pgf ...>	Groups all information regarding a single style definition.
<PgfTag stylename>	Defines the name of a tag.
<FontCatalog ...>	Groups all character formats together.
<Font ...>	Groups all information regarding a single character style definition.
<FTag stylename>	Defines the name of a tag.

In the styles.xom program shown in Figure 7-12, I have taken an alternate approach to finding information in the document source. In this program, I rely on the comment at the end of a grouping structure so I can read in an entire group of information. Once I have the group, I use repeat again to extract the pieces of information that I want.

Line 10 introduces the OmniMark macro feature. The basic structure is as follows:

```
macro name is

macro-end
```

Name is a label for the macro; anything between the is and macro-end will be substituted into the code wherever name is used. I have placed all the ending structures here for a couple of reasons. Some of these values are used multiple times, so rather than having to maintain the information all over the program, I can just refer to it with a consistent and short name. The other use of these macros is for end-of-group markers. Because there is the potential of this changing, I have located all these markers in one location so they can be easily changed and maintained.

```
 1   ; file styles.xom
 2
 3   cross-translate
 4
 5   ; This filter reads a Frame Mif document file and
 6   ; identifies the various structural elements found and
 7   ; the specfic formats/tags used in this document.
 8
 9
10   macro EOL is
11           (((lookahead not "%n") any)* "%n")
12   macro-end
13
14   macro EO> is
15           (((lookahead not ">") any)*)
16   macro-end
17
18   macro eoFnt is
19           ("> # end of Font%n")
20   macro-end
21
22   macro eoFntCat is
23           ("> # end of FontCatalog%n")
24   macro-end
25
26   macro eoPgC is
27           ("> # end of PgfCatalog%n")
28   macro-end
29
30   macro eoPgf is
31           ("> # end of Pgf%n")
32   macro-end
33
34
35
36   find line-start "<MIFFile" blank*
37                   EO>=version-no ">"
```

FIGURE 7-12. STYLES.XOM PROGRAM FILE

Line 36 uses the line-start to anchor a pattern match to the beginning of a line of text. In this case, it is probably not needed, but it makes this match more specific. Everything else in this new program uses structures and methods already described.

```
38                    ((lookahead not "%n") any)* EOL
39            output "MIF File Version: %x(version-no) %n"
40
41
42   find line-start "<PgfCatalog" EOL
43                    ((lookahead not eoPgC ) any)*=catalog eoPgC
44
45            repeat scan pattern catalog
46                 match "<Pgf" EOL ((lookahead not eoPgf ) any)*=tag
47                         repeat scan pattern tag
48                                 match "<PgfTag" blank* "`"
49                                         ((lookahead not "'") any)
50                                         EOL
51                                         output "Style: %x(name)%
52                                 match any
53                                         ;
54                         again
55                 match any
56                         ;
57            again
58
59
60   find line-start "<FontCatalog" EOL
61                    ((lookahead not eoFntCat ) any)*=catalog eoFntCa
62
63            repeat scan pattern catalog
64                 match "<Font" ((lookahead not eoFnt ) any)*=font
65                         repeat scan pattern font
66                                 match "<FTag" blank* "`"
67                                         ((lookahead not ">") any)
68                                         output "Char: '%x(tag)'%
69                                 match any
70                                         ;
71                         again
72                 match any
73                         ;
74            again
75
76   find any
77            ;
78
79
80   ;;;; END OF PROGRAM
```

FIGURE 7-12. STYLES.XOM PROGRAM FILE (CONTINUED)

Figure 7-13 shows the results of running:

```
c:> omni styles.xom ch2.frm
```

I have prefixed the values with Style and Char, so you can detect their actual style type. It is possible to have a character and a paragraph style with the same name. I also placed the character style in quotes; there are some instances of character styles with spaces in the name, which can cause problems if not handled properly. I usually use a sort program to make sure these are in order, and then I examine this list against my master list.

```
MIF File Version: 5.00
Style: Body
Style: BodyAfterHead
Style: Bulleted
Style: BulletedCont
Style: CellBody
Style: CellHeading
Style: CellList
Style: ChapterNumber
            TEXT REMOVED HERE
Style: TableTitle
Style: zzFooterLeft
Style: zzFooterRight
Char: 'BulletSymbol'
Char: 'Callout'
Char: 'ChapterNumber'
Char: 'Emphasis'
Char: 'EquationNumber'
Char: 'EquationVariables'
Char: 'PageNumber'
Char: 'StepNumber'
```

FIGURE 7-13. STYLES.XOM SAMPLE OUTPUT

SIMPLE REPORT ON THE CONTENTS OF A MIF FILE

A MIF file contains a lot of very detailed and verbose information about a document. I like to create a simplified version that gives me a snapshot of the potential complexity of a given file. You may have a "simple" two-page document, but it may be composed of all the most complicated FrameMaker features. The following MIF structures will be searched for and reported against:

MIF Markup	Contents
<Units value>	Defines the base unit of measure for everything in the document.
<ConditionCatalog ...>	Groups any conditions definitions.
<Condition ...>	Groups a single condition definition.
<CTag name>	Name of the condition.
<CState state>	Indicates the current state of the condition.
<VariableFormats ...>	Groups all variables together.
<VariableFormat ...>	Groups all the defining information for a single variable.
<VariableName name>	Defines the name of a variable.
<VariableDef definition>	Specifies the contents of a variable.
<XRefFormats ...>	Groups all cross-reference format definitions together.
<AFrames ...>	Groups all anchored frame definitions together.
<Frame ...>	Groups a single frame definition.
<ID value>	Specifies the ID of the frame, used to place it in the text flow properly.
<ImportObFileDI pathname>	Specifies an imported file within a frame.
<TextFlow ...>	Connects page definitions, textrects, and page content together.
<Notes ...>	Groups together any footnotes on a particular page.
<Tbls ...>	Groups together all the tables that are to be placed within the document.
<Tbl ...>	Groups together a single table.
<TblID id>	Identifies the table so it can be placed into the body of the document.

The report.xom program shown Figure 7-14 builds upon the styles.xom program. I use the same approach for finding the group of information that I want and then extracting what I want from that group.

```
1   ; file report.xom
2
3   cross-translate
4
5
6   ; This filter reads a Frame Mif document file and
7   ; identifies the various structural elements found and
8   ; the specfic formats/tags used in this document.
9
10
11  macro EOL is
12          (((lookahead not "%n") any)* "%n")
13  macro-end
14
15  macro EO> is
16          (((lookahead not ">") any)*)
17  macro-end
18
19  macro EOQ is
20          (((lookahead not "'>") any)*)
21  macro-end
22
23  macro eoAFrms is
24          ("> # end of AFrames%n")
25  macro-end
26
27  macro eoNts is
28          ("> # end of Notes%n")
29  macro-end
30
31  macro eoP is
32          ("> # end of Para%n")
33  macro-end
34
35  macro eoTbl is
36          ("> # end of Tbl%n")
37  macro-end
38
39  macro eoTbls is
40          ("> # end of Tbls%n")
41  macro-end
42
43  macro eoXrefFs is
44          ("> # end of XRefFormats%n")
45  macro-end
46
```

FIGURE 7-14. REPORT.XOM PROGRAM FILE

```
47  macro eoCondCat is
48          ("> # end of ConditionCatalog%n")
49  macro-end
50
51  macro eoCond is
52          ("> # end of Condition%n")
53  macro-end
54
55  macro eoFnt is
56          ("> # end of Font%n")
57  macro-end
58
59  macro eoFntCat is
60          ("> # end of FontCatalog%n")
61  macro-end
62
63  macro eoVarFmt is
64          ("> # end of VariableFormat%n")
65  macro-end
66
67  macro eoVarFmts is
68          ("> # end of VariableFormats%n")
69  macro-end
70
71  macro eoPgC is
72          ("> # end of PgfCatalog%n")
73  macro-end
74
75  macro eoPgf is
76          ("> # end of Pgf%n")
77  macro-end
78
79  macro eoTxtF is
80          ("> # end of TextFlow%n")
81  macro-end
82
83
84
85  find line-start "<MIFFile" blank*
86                  EO>=version-no ">"
87                  ((lookahead not "%n") any)*=notes EOL
88          output "MIF File Version: %x(version-no) %n"
89          output "Processor: %x(notes)%n"
90
91
92
```

FIGURE 7-14. REPORT.XOM PROGRAM FILE (CONTINUED)

```
 93   find line-start "<Units" blank*
 94                     ((lookahead not ">") any)*=unit ">" EOL
 95          output "%nUnits are: "
 96          repeat scan pattern unit
 97                  match "Uin"
 98                          output "Inches = %" or in%n%n"
 99                  match "Ucm"
100                          output "Centimeters = cm or centimeter%n%n"
101                  match "Umm"
102                          output "Milimeters = mm or milimeter%n%n"
103                  match "Upica"
104                          output "Picas = pc or pica = 12pts%n%n"
105                  match "Upt"
106                          output "Points = pt or point 1/72 in%n%n"
107                  match "Udd"
108                          output "Didot = dd or didot 0.01483in%n%n"
109                  match "Ucc"
110                          output "Cicero = cc or cicero 12dd%n%n"
111                  match any
112                          ;
113          again
114
115   find line-start "<ConditionCatalog" EOL
116                     ((lookahead not eoCondCat) any)*=catalog eoCondCat
117          output "Condition Catalog%n"
118          output "--------- -------%n%n"
119
120          repeat scan pattern catalog
121                  match "<Condition" EOL ((lookahead not eoCond ) any)*=t
122                          repeat scan pattern tag
123                                  match "<CTag" blank* "`"
124                                          ((lookahead not "'") any)*=name
125                                          EOL
126                                          output "Condition: %x(name) "
127                                  match "<CState" blank*
128                                          ((lookahead not ">") any)*=stat
129                                          repeat scan pattern state
130                                                  match "CHidden"
131                                                      output "State: Hidde
132                                                  match "CShown"
133                                                      output "State: Show
134                                                  match any
135                                                      ;
136                                          again
137                                  match any
```

FIGURE 7-14. REPORT.XOM PROGRAM FILE (CONTINUED)

```
138                                          ;
139                          again
140                  match any
141                          ;
142          again
143          output "%n"
144
145
146  find line-start "<PgfCatalog" EOL
147                  ((lookahead not eoPgC ) any)*=catalog eoPgC
148          output "%nParagraph Tag Catalog%n"
149          output "--------- --- -------%n%n"
150
151          repeat scan pattern catalog
152                  match "<Pgf" EOL ((lookahead not eoPgf ) any)*=tag
153                          repeat scan pattern tag
154                                  match "<PgfTag" blank* "`"
155                                          ((lookahead not "'") any)*=
156                                          EOL
157                                          output "Para Tag: %x(name)%
158                                  match any
159                                          ;
160                          again
161                  match any
162                          ;
163          again
164
165
166  find line-start "<FontCatalog" EOL
167                  ((lookahead not eoFntCat ) any)*=catalog eoFntCat
168          output "%nFont Catalog%n"
169          output "---- -------%n%n"
170          repeat scan pattern catalog
171                  match "<Font" ((lookahead not eoFnt ) any)*=font eo
172                          repeat scan pattern font
173                                  match "<FTag" blank* "`"
174                                          ((lookahead not "'>") any)*=ta
175                                          output "Char Tag: '%x(tag)'
176                                  match any
177                                          ;
178                          again
179                  match any
180                          ;
181          again
182
183
```

FIGURE 7-14. REPORT.XOM PROGRAM FILE (CONTINUED)

```
184   find line-start "<VariableFormats" EOL
185                ((lookahead not eoVarFmts) any)*=catalog eoVarFmts
186        output "%nVariables Catalog%n"
187        output "-------- -------%n%n"
188
189        repeat scan pattern catalog
190             match "<VariableFormat" EOL
191                        ((lookahead not eoVarFmt) any)*=variable
192
193                   repeat scan pattern variable
194                        match "<VariableName" blank* "`" EOQ=v
195                             output "%x(v-name)' "
196                        match "<VariableDef" blank* "`" EOQ=v
197                             output "def='%x(v-def)'"
198                        match any
199                             ;
200                   again
201                   output "%n"
202             match any
203                ;
204        again
205
206   find line-start "<XRefFormats" EOL
207                ((lookahead not eoXrefFs ) any)*=catalog eoXrefFs
208        output "%nXRef Catalog%n"
209        output "---- -------%n%n"
210
211
212   find line-start "<AFrames" EOL
213                ((lookahead not eoAFrms) any)*=catalog eoAFrms
214
215   local stream ID
216   local stream NAME
217
218        output "%nAnchored Frames Found%n"
219        output "-------- ------ -----%n%n"
220        set buffer NAME to ""
221        repeat scan pattern catalog
222             match "<Frame" ((lookahead not line-start " >") any)*
223                   repeat scan pattern frame
224                        match "<ID" blank*
225                             ((lookahead not ">") any)*=nu
226                             EOL
```

FIGURE 7-14. REPORT.XOM PROGRAM FILE (CONTINUED)

```
227                                              set buffer ID to "%x(num)"
228                                              output "Frame %x(num) %n"
229                                  match "<ImportObFileDI" blank* "`"
230                                          ((lookahead not "'>") any)*=fil
231                                          set buffer NAME to "%x(file)"
232                                          output "%tImported file: '%x(fi
233                                  match any
234                                          ;
235                          again
236
237              match any
238                  ;
239          again
240
241
242    find line-start "<TextFlow" EOL
243                  ((lookahead not eoTxtF ) any)*=flow   eoTxtF
244
245          repeat scan pattern flow
246                          ; Footnotes are listed as part of the Textflow
247                  match "<Notes" white-space+
249                      do when "%x(notes)" isnt equal ""
250                              put #ERROR "WARNING: Footnotes found: %x(
251                      done
252                  match "<Para" EOL
253                              ((lookahead not eoP) any)*=content eoP
254
255              match any
256                  ;
257          again
258
259
260    find line-start "<Tbls" EOL
261                  ((lookahead not eoTbls ) any)*=catalog eoTbls
262
263    local stream tbl-id
264
265          output "%nTables Found%n"
266          output "------ -----%n%n"
267
268          repeat scan pattern catalog
269                  match "<Tbl" EOL
270                              ((lookahead not eoTbl ) any)*=frame eoT
271                      output "Table: "
272
```

FIGURE 7-14. REPORT.XOM PROGRAM FILE (CONTINUED)

No new OmniMark syntax is introduced in this program. This program is meant to find specific areas of a MIF document and report on some of the key content values.

```
273                          repeat scan pattern frame
274                            match "<TblID" blank*  digit+=num E(
275
276                                 output "ID: %x(num)%n"
277                                 set buffer tbl-id to "%x(
278
279                     match any
280                        ;
281              again
282
283
284       match any
285          ;
286   again
287
288
289 find any
290      ;
291
292
293 ;;;; END OF PROGRAM
```

FIGURE 7-14. REPORT.XOM PROGRAM FILE (CONTINUED)

Figure 7-15 shows the results of running:

```
c:> omni report.xom ch2.frm
```

```
MIF File Version: 5.00
Processor:    # Generated by FrameMaker+SGML 5.1.1P6c
Units are: Inches = " or in
Condition Catalog
--------- -------
Condition: Comment State: Shown
Paragraph Tag Catalog
--------- --- -------
Para Tag: Body
Para Tag: BodyAfterHead
```

TEXT REMOVED HERE

```
Para Tag: zzFooterLeft
Para Tag: zzFooterRight
Font Catalog
---- -------
Char Tag: 'BulletSymbol'
Char Tag: 'Callout'
Char Tag: 'ChapterNumber'
Char Tag: 'Emphasis'
Char Tag: 'EquationNumber'
Char Tag: 'EquationVariables'
Char Tag: 'PageNumber'
Char Tag: 'StepNumber'
Variables Catalog
-------- -------
Current Page #' def='<$curpagenum\>'
Running H/F 1' def='<$paratext[ChapterTitle]\>'
Running H/F 2' def='<$paratext[Heading1]\>'
Table Sheet' def=' (Sheet <$tblsheetnum\> of <$tblsheetcount\>)'
Table Continuation' def=' (Continued)'
```

TEXT REMOVED HERE

```
Running H/F 4' def='<$marker2\>'
XRef Catalog
---- -------
Anchored Frames Found
-------- ------ -----
```

FIGURE 7-15. REPORT.XOM SAMPLE OUTPUT

CONVERTING FROM MIF TO SGML

We now have several programs that will report on the structure of a book and the document files that are used by that book. We now need to decide how to approach the conversion from MIF to our sample DTD. There are two options on how to approach this problem:

- Combine the files, in order, into one complete document
- Convert each file separately and combine them manually.

I have found that it is sometimes easier to work smaller sections of the document, rather than trying to load the whole thing. If, as our sample is configured, the various files that comprise the book are at logical structures (chapters and appendices), then we can proceed this way by adjusting the DTD to allow these structures to be in a document without any of the surrounding pieces. Then we will go to the original DTD, open a new file, and cut these pieces into the document in the correct location and order.

The procedure that I am going to use to convert the MIF files into SGML is as follows:

1. Process each file of the book, stripping the MIF header and normalizing/simplifying some MIF issues.

2. Process each intermediate file into SGML.

3. Load each SGML file into a native SGML editor to clean up the markup.

SIMPLIFYING THE MIF DOCUMENT

The need for this step isn't readily apparent, and wasn't to me until I was well into the conversion of MIF directly to SGML. Before instituting this practice, I got very complicated code bases. Because MIF stores the actual content of frames and tables in the header and only refers to them by reference in the document body, and the markers for cross-references and index items contain strings that make pattern-matching difficult, I was getting very ugly tests in every find rule. It became apparent for my own peace of mind and future maintenance that it was going to be cleaner to simplify the MIF format first and then process that output into SGML. The other advantage to this method is that I strip about 50% or more of the document away by removing the header portion. This makes it easier to actually find the document in all the markup.

The approach I want to take with this program is to take each major section of the MIF format and then process those groups into smaller pieces. We'll start by creating a program that consumes each of these major groups. head.xom is shown in Figure 7-16. With this program, you can check any MIF file and determine if the base structural content is what you expect it to be.

```
1    cross-translate
2    ; file head.xom
3    ; This program reads a MIF document file and strips out the header.
4
5
6            ; Macros here identify the closing construct of the major MIF
7            ; groups.
8    macro eoAcro is ("> # end of AcrobatElements%n") macro-end
9    macro eoAFrms is ("> # end of AFrames%n") macro-end
10   macro eoBkC is ("> # end of BookComponent%n") macro-end
11   macro eoCCat is ("> # end of ColorCatalog%n") macro-end
12   macro eoIAutoN is ("> # end of InitialAutoNums%n") macro-end
13   macro eoDic is ("> # end of Dictionary%n") macro-end
14   macro eoDoc is ("> # end of Document%n") macro-end
15   macro eoElCat is ("> # end of ElementDefCatalog%n") macro-end
16   macro eoFmtChg is ("> # end of FmtChangeListCatalog%n") macro-end
17   macro eoTblCat is ("> # end of TblCatalog%n") macro-end
18   macro eoTbls is ("> # end of Tbls%n") macro-end
19   macro eoXrefFs is ("> # end of XRefFormats%n") macro-end
20   macro eoCondCat is ("> # end of ConditionCatalog%n") macro-end
21   macro eoFntCat is ("> # end of FontCatalog%n") macro-end
22   macro eoRulCat is ("> # end of RulingCatalog%n") macro-end
23   macro eoVarFmts is ("> # end of VariableFormats%n") macro-end
24   macro eoVws is ("> # end of Views%n") macro-end
25   macro eoPg is ("> # end of Page%n") macro-end
26   macro eoPgC is ("> # end of PgfCatalog%n") macro-end
27   macro eoTxtF is ("> # end of TextFlow%n") macro-end
28
29
30           ; Some general end-of pattern matching that is used
31           ; all over the place
32   macro EOL is (((lookahead not "%n") any)* "%n") macro-end
33   macro EO> is (((lookahead not ">") any)*) macro-end
34
35
36
37   ;;;; Program starts Here!!
38
39   find-start
40           put #CONSOLE "Processing started ...%n"
41
42   find-end
43           put #CONSOLE "Processing complete. If any output other than%n"
44           put #CONSOLE "start and complete, message then MIF markup is "
45           put #CONSOLE "missed%n"
46
47
48
```

FIGURE 7-16. HEAD.XOM PROGRAM FILE

```
49
50             ; first line of a MIF document file
51    find line-start "<MIFFile" blank*
52                    EO>=version-no ">"
53                    ((lookahead not "%n") any)*=notes EOL
54
55             ; first definition in MIF File
56    find line-start "<Units" blank* ((lookahead not ">") any)*=unit ">" EOL
57             ;
58
59    find line-start "<ColorCatalog" EOL
60                    ((lookahead not eoCCat ) any)*=catalog eoCCat
61             ;
62
63    find line-start "<ConditionCatalog" EOL
64                    ((lookahead not eoCondCat) any)*=catalog eoCondCat
65             ;
66
67
68    find line-start "<PgfCatalog" EOL
69                    ((lookahead not eoPgC ) any)*=catalog eoPgC
70             ;
71
72    find line-start "<ElementDefCatalog" EOL
73                    ((lookahead not eoElCat ) any)*=catalog eoElCat
74             ;
75
76    find line-start "<FmtChangeListCatalog" EOL
77                    ((lookahead not eoFmtChg ) any)*=catalog eoFmtChg
78             ;
79
80             ; Character Style Definitions
81    find line-start "<FontCatalog" EOL
82                    ((lookahead not eoFntCat ) any)*=catalog eoFntCat
83             ;
84
85             ; definition of rule types - Thin = .5pt, single black
86    find line-start "<RulingCatalog" EOL
87                    ((lookahead not eoRulCat) any)*=catalog eoRulCat
88             ;
89
90             ; Table formats stored separate from paragraph format defs
91    find line-start "<TblCatalog" EOL
92                    ((lookahead not eoTblCat) any)*=catalog eoTblCat
93             ;
94
95    find line-start "<Views" EOL
96                    ((lookahead not eoVws ) any)*=catalog eoVws
```

FIGURE 7-16. HEAD.XOM PROGRAM FILE (CONTINUED)

```
 97            ;
 98
 99            ; defines the variable name and its content
100  find line-start "<VariableFormats" EOL
101                ((lookahead not eoVarFmts) any)*=catalog eoVarFmts
102            ;
103
104            ; defines the cross-reference types and formatted text output
105  find line-start "<XRefFormats" EOL
106                ((lookahead not eoXrefFs ) any)*=catalog eoXrefFs
107            ;
108
109            ; document view window, scaling, pagesize etc.
110            ; also defines the element hierarchy for use with SGML
111  find line-start "<Document" EOL
112                ((lookahead not eoDoc) any)*=catalog eoDoc
113            ;
114
115            ; Multiple entries for BookComponent. Defines which generated
116            ; files this file belongs to.
117  find line-start "<BookComponent" EOL
118                ((lookahead not eoBkC ) any)*=catalog eoBkC
119            ;
120
121  find line-start "<InitialAutoNums" EOL
122                ((lookahead not eoIAutoN) any)*=catalog eoIAutoN
123            ;
124
125            ; contents spell check allowed words, differs per document
126  find line-start "<Dictionary" EOL
127                ((lookahead not eoDic ) any)*=catalog eoDic
128            ;
129
130            ; defines all frames/illustrations in the document and then
131            ; assigns them ids which are referenced in the document
132            ; body to place the frame.
133  find line-start "<AFrames" EOL
134                ((lookahead not eoAFrms) any)*=catalog eoAFrms
135            ;
136
137            ; defines all tables in the document and then
138            ; assigns them ids which are referenced in the document
139            ; body to place the table.
140  find line-start "<Tbls" EOL
141                ((lookahead not eoTbls ) any)*=catalog eoTbls
142            ;
143
144            ; defines the pages, identifies their type and the textrect's
```

FIGURE 7-16. HEAD.XOM PROGRAM FILE (CONTINUED)

```
145            ; that belong on that page - multiple entries for this
146   find line-start "<Page" EOL
147                   ((lookahead not eoPg) any)*=page eoPg
148         ;
149
150            ; Textflow contains the body/text of the document.
151            ; There are multiple textflows
152   find line-start "<TextFlow" EOL
153                   ((lookahead not eoTxtF ) any)*=flow  eoTxtF
154
155            ; Optional section, may not be in every document. Probably is
156            ; defined in the Print dialog when you can map objects to
157            ; Acrobat Bookmark items.
158   find line-start "<AcrobatElements" EOL
159                   ((lookahead not eoAcro ) any)*=catalog eoAcro
160         ;
161
162
163            ; Last line of a FrameMaker generated file
164   find line-start "# End of MIFFile" EOL
165         ;
166
167            ; Gather up any missed comments that might be added to the file
168   find line-start "#"
169                   ((lookahead not "%n") any)*=comment EOL
170         ;
171
172
173   ;;;    END OF PROGRAM
```

FIGURE 7-16. HEAD.XOM PROGRAM FILE (CONTINUED)

Figure 7-17 shows the results of running:

```
c:> omni head.xom about.frm
```

```
Processing started ...
Processing complete. If any output other than
start and complete, message then MIF markup is missed
```

FIGURE 7-17. HEAD.XOM SAMPLE OUTPUT

If there was a structure in the about.frm MIF, it would have been streamed to the output file or shown here between the Processing started... and completed messages.

```
 1  cross-translate
 2  ; file tbl-frm.xom
 3  ; This program reads a MIF document file and strips out the header.
 4
 5          ; Following variables store the predefined Tables, Frames, and
 6          ; TextRect information.
 7  global stream TBLid-shelf variable
 8  global stream FRMid-shelf variable
 9  global stream TRid-shelf variable
10
11
12
13
14
15
16
17          ; Macros here identify the closing construct of the major MIF
18          ; groups.
19
20  macro eoAcro is ("> # end of AcrobatElements%n") macro-end
21  macro eoAFrms is ("> # end of AFrames%n") macro-end
22  macro eoBkC is ("> # end of BookComponent%n") macro-end
23  macro eoCCat is ("> # end of ColorCatalog%n") macro-end
24  macro eoIAutoN is ("> # end of InitialAutoNums%n") macro-end
25  macro eoDic is ("> # end of Dictionary%n") macro-end
26  macro eoDoc is ("> # end of Document%n") macro-end
27  macro eoElCat is ("> # end of ElementDefCatalog%n") macro-end
28  macro eoFmtChg is ("> # end of FmtChangeListCatalog%n") macro-end
29  macro eoTblCat is ("> # end of TblCatalog%n") macro-end
30  macro eoTbls is ("> # end of Tbls%n") macro-end
31  macro eoXrefFs is ("> # end of XRefFormats%n") macro-end
32  macro eoCondCat is ("> # end of ConditionCatalog%n") macro-end
33  macro eoFntCat is ("> # end of FontCatalog%n") macro-end
34  macro eoRulCat is ("> # end of RulingCatalog%n") macro-end
35  macro eoVarFmts is ("> # end of VariableFormats%n") macro-end
36  macro eoVws is ("> # end of Views%n") macro-end
37  macro eoPg is ("> # end of Page%n") macro-end
38  macro eoPgC is ("> # end of PgfCatalog%n") macro-end
39  macro eoTxtF is ("> # end of TextFlow%n") macro-end
40
41          ; Macros here identify the closing construct of the
42          ; minor MIF groups.
43
44  macro eoFrm is ("> # end of Frame%n") macro-end
45  macro eoIobj is ("> # end of ImportObject%n") macro-end
46  macro eoTbl is ("> # end of Tbl%n") macro-end
47  macro eoTxtR is ("> # end of TextRect%n") macro-end
```

FIGURE 7-18. TBL-FRM.XOM PROGRAM FILE

```
48
49          ; Some general end-of pattern matching that is used
50          ; all over the place
51
52 macro EOL is (((lookahead not "%n") any)* "%n") macro-end
53 macro EO> is (((lookahead not ">") any)*) macro-end
54
55
56
57
58
59 define stream function file-path (value stream fp-instring) as
60 local stream fp-filename initial {""}
61
62          repeat scan "%g(fp-instring)"
63
64                  match "<r\>"               ; Unix file tree root
65                        set fp-filename to "%g(fp-filename)/"
66
67                  match "<c\>"
68                        set fp-filename to "%g(fp-filename)\"
69
70                  match "<v\>"
71                        set fp-filename to "%g(fp-filename)"
72
73                  match "<h\>"
74                        set fp-filename to "%g(fp-filename)"
75
76                  match "<u\>"
77                        set fp-filename to "%g(fp-filename)..\"
78
79                        ; watch for the end of the string or another tag
80                  match ((lookahead not ("<" or value-end)) any)*=word
81                        set fp-filename to "%g(fp-filename)%x(word)"
82
83                  match value-end ; OmniMark end of input
84                        ;
85          again
86 RETURN fp-filename
87
88
89          ; This function processes the content of the MIF
90          ; <ImportObject ...> definition
91 define function process-importobj(value stream OBJ,
92                                   modifiable stream FILE-NAME,
93                                   modifiable stream BM-DPI
94                                   ) as
95          repeat scan OBJ
```

FIGURE 7-18. TBL-FRM.XOM PROGRAM FILE (CONTINUED)

```
72
73                  match "<h\>"
74                      set fp-filename to "%g(fp-filename)"
75
76                  match "<u\>"
77                      set fp-filename to "%g(fp-filename)..\"
78
79                      ; watch for the end of the string or another tag
80              match ((lookahead not ("<" or value-end)) any)*=word
81                      set fp-filename to "%g(fp-filename)%x(word)"
82
83              match value-end ; OmniMark end of input
84                      ;
85      again
86  RETURN fp-filename
87
88
89          ; This function processes the content of the MIF
90          ; <ImportObject ...> definition
91  define function process-importobj(value stream OBJ,
92                              modifiable stream FILE-NAME,
93                              modifiable stream BM-DPI
94                              ) as
95          repeat scan OBJ
119                             ) as
120         repeat scan FRAME-CONT
121
122                     ; MIF 4 way of specifying Frame size
123              match "<ID" blank*
124                          ((lookahead not ">") any)*=num ">" EOL
125                  set FRAME-ID to "%x(num)"
126
127              match "<ShapeRect" blank*
128                          ((lookahead not blank) any)+=top blank*
129                          ((lookahead not blank) any)+=left blank*
130                          ((lookahead not blank) any)+=hght blank*
131                          ((lookahead not ">") any)+=wid ">"
132                  set DIMENSIONS to "%x(hght)x%x(wid)"
133
134                     ; Get this group info for imported files
135              match "<ImportObject" blank*
136                          ((lookahead not eoIobj) any)*=obj eoIobj
137
138                  process-importobj("%x(obj)", FILE-NAME, BM-DPI)
139
140              match any
141                      ;
142      again
```

FIGURE 7-18. TBL-FRM.XOM PROGRAM FILE (CONTINUED)

```
143  ; end of process-frame()
144
145
146
147  define function process-tbl (value stream OBJ,
148                                   modifiable stream ID) as
149        repeat scan OBJ
150            match "<TblID" blank* digit+=num EO> EOL
151                 set ID to "%x(num)"
152
153            match any
154                 ;
155        again
156  ; end of process-tbl()
157
158
159
160
161
162
163  define function test-frm-tbl () as
164  local counter temp initial {1}
165
166  ; Now prove that you got all the information and it is properly stored
167        repeat over FRMid-shelf
168            put #CONSOLE "FR: %d(temp), %g(FRMid-shelf)%n"
169            increment temp
170        again
171
172        set temp to 1
173        repeat over TBLid-shelf
174            put #CONSOLE "TB: %d(temp), %g(TBLid-shelf)%n"
175            increment temp
176        again
177
178        set temp to 1
179        repeat over TRid-shelf
180            put #CONSOLE "TR: %d(temp), %g(TRid-shelf)%n"
181            increment temp
182        again
183
184  ; end of test-frm-tbl()
185
186
187
188
189
190
```

FIGURE 7-18. TBL-FRM.XOM PROGRAM FILE (CONTINUED)

```
191
192   ;;;; Program starts Here!!
193
194   find-start
195          put #CONSOLE "Processing started ...%n"
196
197          clear stream TBLid-shelf
198          clear stream TRid-shelf
199          clear stream FRMid-shelf
200
201
202   find-end
203    put #CONSOLE "Processing complete. If any output other than%n"
204   put #CONSOLE "start and complete, message then MIF markup is missed%n"
205
206          test-frm-tbl()
207
208
209
210
211          ; first line of a MIF document file
212   find line-start "<MIFFile" blank*
213                   EO>=version-no ">"
214                   ((lookahead not "%n") any)*=notes EOL
215
216          ; first definition in MIF File
217   find line-start "<Units" blank* ((lookahead not ">") any)*=unit ">"
218          ;
219
220   find line-start "<ColorCatalog" EOL
221                   ((lookahead not eoCCat ) any)*=catalog eoCCat
222          ;
223
224   find line-start "<ConditionCatalog" EOL
225                   ((lookahead not eoCondCat) any)*=catalog eoCondCat
226          ;
227
228
229   find line-start "<PgfCatalog" EOL
230                   ((lookahead not eoPgC ) any)*=catalog eoPgC
231          ;
232
233   find line-start "<ElementDefCatalog" EOL
234                   ((lookahead not eoElCat ) any)*=catalog eoElCat
235          ;
236
237   find line-start "<FmtChangeListCatalog" EOL
```

FIGURE 7-18. TBL-FRM.XOM PROGRAM FILE (CONTINUED)

```
238                    ((lookahead not eoFmtChg ) any)*=catalog eoFmtChg
239          ;
240
241          ; Character Style Definitions
242   find line-start "<FontCatalog" EOL
243                    ((lookahead not eoFntCat ) any)*=catalog eoFntCat
244          ;
245
246          ; definition of rule types - Thin = .5pt, single black
247   find line-start "<RulingCatalog" EOL
248                    ((lookahead not eoRulCat) any)*=catalog eoRulCat
249          ;
250
251          ; Table formats stored separate from paragraph definitions
252   find line-start "<TblCatalog" EOL
253                    ((lookahead not eoTblCat) any)*=catalog eoTblCat
254          ;
255
256   find line-start "<Views" EOL
257                    ((lookahead not eoVws ) any)*=catalog eoVws
258          ;
259
260          ; defines the variable name and its content
261   find line-start "<VariableFormats" EOL
262                    ((lookahead not eoVarFmts) any)*=catalog eoVarFmts
263          ;
264
265          ; defines the cross-reference types and formatted text output
266   find line-start "<XRefFormats" EOL
267                    ((lookahead not eoXrefFs ) any)*=catalog eoXrefFs
268          ;
269
270          ; document view window, scaling, pagesize etc.
271          ; also defines the element hierarchy for use with SGML
272   find line-start "<Document" EOL
273                    ((lookahead not eoDoc) any)*=catalog eoDoc
274          ;
275
276          ; Multiple entries for BookComponent. Defines which generated
277          ; files this file belongs to.
278   find line-start "<BookComponent" EOL
279                    ((lookahead not eoBkC ) any)*=catalog eoBkC
280          ;
281
282   find line-start "<InitialAutoNums" EOL
283                    ((lookahead not eoIAutoN) any)*=catalog eoIAutoN
284          ;
285
```

FIGURE 7-18. TBL-FRM.XOM PROGRAM FILE (CONTINUED)

```
286            ; contents spell check allowed words, differs per document
287  find line-start "<Dictionary" EOL
288                    ((lookahead not eoDic ) any)*=catalog eoDic
289        ;
290
291            ; defines all frames/illustrations in the document and then
292            ; assigns them ids which are referenced in the document
293            ; body to place the frame.
294
295            ; Currently the useful pieces of information are: FrameID,
296            ; Imported filename, dots-per-inch (DPI of a bitmapped graphic)
297            ; the width and height of the frame itself
298  find line-start "<AFrames" EOL
299                    ((lookahead not eoAFrms) any)*=catalog eoAFrms
300  local stream ID
301  local stream NAME
302  local stream DPI
303  local stream DIMS
304
305            repeat scan pattern catalog
306                    match "<Frame" ((lookahead not eoFrm) any)*=frame eoFrm
307
308                            set ID to ""
309                            set NAME to ""
310                            set DPI to ""
311                            set DIMS to ""
312                            process-frame("%x(frame)", ID, NAME, DIMS, DPI)
313                            set new FRMid-shelf to
314                                    "FRM%g(ID) %g(NAME) %g(dims) %g(DPI)"
315
316                    match any
317                            ;
318        again
319
320
321
322            ; defines all tables in the document and then
323            ; assigns them ids which are referenced in the document
324            ; body to place the table.
325  find line-start "<Tbls" EOL
326                    ((lookahead not eoTbls ) any)*=catalog eoTbls
327  local stream tbl-id
328
329            repeat scan pattern catalog
330                    match "<Tbl" EOL
331                            ((lookahead not eoTbl ) any)*=tbl eoTbl
332
333                            set tbl-id to ""
```

FIGURE 7-18. TBL-FRM.XOM PROGRAM FILE (CONTINUED)

```
334
335                          process-tbl("%x(tbl)", tbl-id)
336                          set new TBLid-shelf to "TBL%g(tbl-id)"
337
338              match any
339                         ;
340        again
341
342
343
344          ; defines the pages, identifies their type and the textrect's
345          ; that belong on that page - multiple entries for this
346    find line-start "<Page" EOL
347                  ((lookahead not eoPg) any)*=page eoPg
348    local switch masters initial {false}
349    local switch body initial {false}
350    local switch reference initial {false}
351
352          repeat scan pattern page
353              match "<PageType" blank*
354                          ((lookahead not ">") any)*=type ">"
355                  repeat scan pattern type
356                      match "BodyPage"
357                              set body to true
358                              set masters to false
359                              set reference to false
360
361                      match "ReferencePage"
362                              set body to false
363                              set masters to false
364                              set reference to true
365
366                              ; contains the conditional text
367                      match  "HiddenPage"      ; hidden pages
368                              set body to false
369                              set masters to true
370                              set reference to false
371
372                      match  "MasterPage"
373                              set body to false
374                              set masters to true
375                              set reference to false
376
377                          match any
378                              ;
379                  again
380
381          ; TextRect's are uniquely identified and are tied
```

FIGURE 7-18. TBL-FRM.XOM PROGRAM FILE (CONTINUED)

```
382                     ; to a specific type of a page, the only pages we
383                     ; need to convert are BodyPages and potentially hidden
384                     ; with conditional text
385
386                 match "<TextRect" blank*
387                             ((lookahead not eoTxtR) any)*=rect
388                             eoTxtR
389                     repeat scan pattern rect
390                             match "<ID" blank* digit+=id ">"
391                                         set new TRid-shelf to
392                                                 "master %x(id)"
393                                                 when active masters
394                                         set new TRid-shelf to
395                                                 "body %x(id)"
396                                                 when active body
397                                         set new TRid-shelf to
398                                                 "reference %x(id)"
399                                                 when active reference
400
401                             match any
402                                 ;
403                     again
404
405                 match any
406                     ;
407         again
408
409
410
411 ; Textflow contains the body/text of the document.
412 ; There are multiple textflows
413 find line-start "<TextFlow" EOL
414 ((lookahead not eoTxtF ) any)*=flow  eoTxtF
415         ;
416
417 ; Optional section, may not be in every document. Probably is
418 ; defined in the Print dialog when you can map objects to
419 ; Acrobat Bookmark items.
420 find line-start "<AcrobatElements" EOL
421             ((lookahead not eoAcro ) any)*=catalog eoAcro
422         ;
423
424
425         ; Last line of a FrameMaker generated file
426 find line-start "# End of MIFFile" EOL
427         ;
428
429         ; Gather up any missed comments that might be added to the file
```

FIGURE 7-18. TBL-FRM.XOM PROGRAM FILE (CONTINUED)

```
430  find line-start "#"
431                   ((lookahead not "%n") any)*=comment EOL
432          ;
433
434
435  ;;;    END OF PROGRAM
```

FIGURE 7-18. TBL-FRM.XOM PROGRAM FILE (CONTINUED)

We must capture three key areas of the header information. We need to store the AFrames and Tbls sections to capture all the content, and then we need to store the Page information so we can determine which text-flows should be processed as content. We will use OmniMark shelves as the storage for this information. A shelf, for the programmers reading this, is an array. There is also a keyed shelf that is an associative array. Figure 7-19 illustrates the different parts of a shelf.

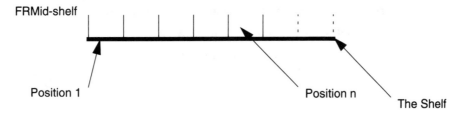

FRMid-shelf

Position 1   Position n

The Shelf

FIGURE 7-19. OMNIMARK SHELF STRUCTURE

The overall structure is referred to with the variable FRMid-shelf, shown in this illustration. A shelf can have any number of positions and it doesn't need a predetermined size. The positions are numbered 1 to n, and when declared automatically, the first position gets defined.

tbl-frm.xom, in Figure 7-18, introduces the function definition and call. Line 59 defines the function file-path as a function that will return a stream value and takes as input a stream that should be in the frame device-independent form. Line 99 has a call to this function. The return value from file-path() will be assigned to FILE-NAME. In this case, the function receives a text string to process, but not to modify.

A function differs from a macro in that the contents of the function are not copied inline at the position where it is called. A function can take input and modify global variables or variables that are passed as modifiable. Variables can be defined and only used within a function, which is something that a macro cannot do. Line 91 defines the function that allows two variables to be passed to it and then modified without having to define them as global variables.

I have taken the code from report.xom and doc.xom that read the anchored frames section and reported on what was found. I then modified and streamlined this code. We already saw the file-path function, which read the device-independent path. Line 114 contains the function process-frame, which will extract all the useful information from a frame object.

On Line 147 is the function process-tbl(); this function currently only reads in the unique table id, but in later versions, we will be expanding its functionality. Because the table contains text objects, we will build the code that processes text first and then apply that to the text in tables.

I have defined the function test-frm-tbl() to read the shelves that contain frame, table, and page information. In the final version of the conversion, this function will only be called when debugging the conversion process. For now, this function will be used to create some output that proves we were able to read the information that we wanted.

Figure 7-20 shows the results of running:

```
c:> omni tbl-frm.xom ch2.frm
```

```
FR: 1, FRM1  4.46873"x2.625"
FR: 2, FRM2  4.15624"x2.89444"
FR: 3, FRM3  4.6901"x3.375"
FR: 4, FRM7  0.82031"x0.46875"
FR: 5, FRM8  2.0"x1.5"
TB: 1, TBL9
TR: 1, master 10
TR: 2, master 11
TR: 3, master 12
TR: 4, master 13
TR: 5, master 14
TR: 6, master 15
TR: 7, master 16
TR: 8, master 17
TR: 9, master 18
TR: 10, master 19
TR: 11, reference 20
TR: 12, reference 21
TR: 13, reference 22
TR: 14, reference 23
TR: 15, body 24
TR: 16, body 25
TR: 17, body 26
TR: 18, body 27
TR: 19, body 28
```

TEXT REMOVED HERE

FIGURE 7-20. TBL-FRM.XOM SAMPLE OUTPUT

Now that we have all our setup information, we can start processing the text content. The program para.xom, shown in Figure 7-21, adds to the previous program steps to find the paragraphs and then the text within the body of the document. Tables are currently ignored.

Line 12 introduces a new global variable, last-textrectid. Individual paragraphs in MIF are written out to one or more ParaLines; each line of text as displayed in FrameMaker is held in this object. The first entry has all the information about the tag and the TextRect number. By storing the TextRect id, I can make a single paragraph out of these multiple lines.

```
 1  cross-translate
 2  ; file para.xom
 3  ; This program reads a MIF document file and strips out the header.
 4  ; Process the table, Frame and Page information as well as page
content.
 5
 6          ; Following variables store the predefined Tables, Frames, and
 7          ; TextRect information.
 8  global stream TBLid-shelf variable
 9  global stream FRMid-shelf variable
10  global stream TRid-shelf variable
11
12  global stream last-textrectid         ; Record the last TextRectID,
13                                        ; because it is defaulted on
14                                        ; repeated paras, etc.
15
16          ; Macros here identify the closing construct of the major MIF
17          ; groups.
18
19  macro eoAcro is ("> # end of AcrobatElements%n") macro-end
20  macro eoAFrms is ("> # end of AFrames%n") macro-end
21  macro eoBkC is ("> # end of BookComponent%n") macro-end
22  macro eoCCat is ("> # end of ColorCatalog%n") macro-end
23  macro eoIAutoN is ("> # end of InitialAutoNums%n") macro-end
24  macro eoDic is ("> # end of Dictionary%n") macro-end
25  macro eoDoc is ("> # end of Document%n") macro-end
26  macro eoElCat is ("> # end of ElementDefCatalog%n") macro-end
27  macro eoFmtChg is ("> # end of FmtChangeListCatalog%n") macro-end
28  macro eoTblCat is ("> # end of TblCatalog%n") macro-end
29  macro eoTbls is ("> # end of Tbls%n") macro-end
30  macro eoXrefFs is ("> # end of XRefFormats%n") macro-end
31  macro eoCondCat is ("> # end of ConditionCatalog%n") macro-end
32  macro eoFntCat is ("> # end of FontCatalog%n") macro-end
33  macro eoRulCat is ("> # end of RulingCatalog%n") macro-end
34  macro eoVarFmts is ("> # end of VariableFormats%n") macro-end
35  macro eoVws is ("> # end of Views%n") macro-end
36  macro eoPg is ("> # end of Page%n") macro-end
37  macro eoPgC is ("> # end of PgfCatalog%n") macro-end
38  macro eoTxtF is ("> # end of TextFlow%n") macro-end
39
40          ; Macros here identify the closing construct of the
41          ; minor MIF groups.
42
43  macro eoFrm is ("> # end of Frame%n") macro-end
44  macro eoIobj is ("> # end of ImportObject%n") macro-end
45  macro eoTbl is ("> # end of Tbl%n") macro-end
46  macro eoTxtR is ("> # end of TextRect%n") macro-end
47  macro eoNts is ("> # end of Notes%n") macro-end
48  macro eoP is ("> # end of Para%n") macro-end
```

FIGURE 7-21. PARA.XOM PROGRAM FILE

```
49  macro eoVar is ("> # end of Variable%n") macro-end
50  macro eoCondal is ("> # end of Conditional%n") macro-end
51  macro eoXref is ("> # end of XRef%n") macro-end
52  macro eoMk is ("> # end of Marker%n") macro-end
53  macro eoFnt is ("> # end of Font%n") macro-end
54
55
56
57          ; Some general end-of pattern matching that is used
58          ; all over the place
59
60  macro EOL is (((lookahead not "%n") any)* "%n") macro-end
61  macro EO> is (((lookahead not ">") any)*) macro-end
62  macro EOQ is (((lookahead not "'>") any)*) macro-end
63
64
65
66
67
68
69          ; identify and special text characters in the processed string
70  define function process-chars(value stream STRING ) as
71          repeat scan "%g(STRING)"
72                  match "\\"          output "\"
73                  match "&"           output "&amp;"
74                  match "<"           output "&lt;"
75                  match "\q"          output "'"          ; quote character
76                  match "\>"          output "&gt;"
77                  match "\x11 "        output " "
78                  match "\t"          output ""           ; tab character
79                  match "\xa5 "        output ""           ; bullet character
80                  match ((lookahead not "\" or "&" or "<") any)*=chars
81                          output "%x(chars)"
82          again
83
84  ; end process-chars()
85
86
87
88          ; All kinds of fun things can live within a
89          ; text string and each have to be handled!
90  define function process-string (value stream STRING ) as
91          repeat scan "%g(STRING)"
92                  match "<Variable" ((lookahead not eoVar)
93                          any)*=variable eoVar
94                          output "<variable found>"
95
96                  match "<Conditional" EOL ((lookahead not eoCondal)
```

FIGURE 7-21. PARA.XOM PROGRAM FILE (CONTINUED)

```
 97                                          any)*=cond eoCondal
 98                        output "<conditional found>"
 99

100             match "<Unconditional" EO> ">" EOL
101                        output "<unconditional found>"
102

103             match "<AFrame" blank* digit+=frame-id ">" EOL
104                    output "%n<'graphic' id=%x(frame-id)%n"
105                    repeat over FRMid-shelf
106                            do when FRMid-shelf matches
107                                        ("FRM%x(frame-id) " blank*
108                                        ((lookahead not
109                                        value-end) any)* )
110                                        output "'%g(FRMid-shelf)'%n"
111                            done
112                    again
113                    output ">%n%n"
114

115                    ; there could be a problem here if
116                    ; tables are nested objects!!
117             match "<ATbl" blank* digit+=table-id ">" EOL
118                    output "<'table' id=%x(table-id)>%n"
119                    repeat over TBLid-shelf
120                            do when TBLid-shelf matches
121                                        ("TBL%x(table-id)"
122                                        blank*
123                                        ((lookahead not value-ed)
124                                        any)* )
125                                        output "%g(TBLid-shelf)"
126                            done
127                    again
128

129             match "<XRefEnd" blank* ">" EOL
130                    output "<xref-end found>"
131

132             match "<XRef" EOL ((lookahead not eoXref ) any)*=xref
133                            eoXref
134                    output "<xref found>"
135

136             match "<Marker" EOL ((lookahead not eoMk)
137                            any)*=mark eoMk
138                    output "<marker found>"
139

140             match "<TextRectID" blank* EO>=id2 ">" EOL
141                       ;
142

143             match "<Font" ((lookahead not eoFnt) any)*=font eoFnt
```

FIGURE 7-21. PARA.XOM PROGRAM FILE (CONTINUED)

```
144                         output "<font found>"
145
146             match "<String" blank* "`" EOQ=string EOL
147                     process-chars("%x(string)")
148
149         match any
150                     ;
151     again
152
153 ; end of process-string()
154
155
156
157
158     ; Each line of a paragraph is treated as a paraline,
159     ; we have to find the start of a new paragraph, from
160     ; the continuing of the para text.
161 define function process-paraline (value stream PARA-CONT,
162                                 value stream TAG,
163                                 modifiable switch NEW-PARA,
164                                 modifiable stream NUMSTR ) as
165
166 local stream pl-temp initial {""}
167 local switch string-processing
168
169             ; TextRect Id is inherited within the same Para
170             ; object. First ParaLine gets a TextRectID, all the
171             ; others are not set! Multiple paras on the same
172             ; page/textflow don't have to have ids assigned, they
173             ; inherit the last value.
174
175     do when active NEW-PARA
176
177             deactivate string-processing
178             repeat scan "%g(PARA-CONT)"
179                 match "<TextRectID" blank* digit+=TRid ">"
180                         ; determine if these text lines are
181                         ; on a body page, if not don't print
182                         ; them!
183
184                         set pl-temp to "%x(TRid)"
185                         set last-textrectid to "%g(pl-temp)"
186                         exit    ; after finding the ID -
187                                 ; one per Para tag
188
189             match any
190                     ;
191         again
```

FIGURE 7-21. PARA.XOM PROGRAM FILE (CONTINUED)

```
192          done
193
194
195                      repeat over TRid-shelf
196                              do when "body %g(last-textrectid)"
197                                             is equal "%g(TRid-shelf)"
198                                      activate string-processing
199                                      do when active NEW-PARA
200                                              output "%n<'%g(TAG)'>"
201                                              output "%g(NUMSTR)%n"
202                                              set NUMSTR to ""
203                                              deactivate NEW-PARA
204                                      done
205                                      exit
206                              done
207                      again
208
209
210
211          do when active string-processing
212                      process-string("%g(PARA-CONT)")
213          done
214
215  ; end of process-paraline()
216
217
218
219  define function process-para (value stream CONTENT,
220                                  value counter NUM-BLNK) as
221
222          ; The paraline tag is indented at different levels based upon
223          ; where it is found, so we need to pass the exact number of
224          ; blanks to find as NUM-BLNK
225
226  local stream textflow-numstr initial {""}
227  local stream textflow-tag initial {""}
228
229  local switch new-para
230
231          activate new-para
232
233          repeat scan CONTENT
234                  match "<PgfNumString" blank* "`" EOQ=num "'>" EOL
235                          set textflow-numstr to "%x(num)"
236
237                  match "<PgfTag" blank* "`" EOQ=tag "'>" EOL
238                          set textflow-tag to "%x(tag)"
239
```

FIGURE 7-21. PARA.XOM PROGRAM FILE (CONTINUED)

```
240                            ; watch the number of blanks required to
241                            ; find the end of a ParaLine!!
242                 match "<ParaLine" blank* ((lookahead not
243                               (line-start blank{num-blnk} ">"))
244                               any)*=text
245                               line-start blank{num-blnk} ">" EOL
246
247                       process-paraline("%x(text)",
248                            textflow-tag, new-para, textflow-numstr)
249
250             match any
251                     ;
252        again
253  ; end of para()
254
255
256
257  define stream function file-path (value stream fp-instring) as
258  local stream fp-filename initial {""}
259
260        repeat scan "%g(fp-instring)"
261
262             match "<r\>"             ; Unix file tree root
263                    set fp-filename to "%g(fp-filename)/"
264
265             match "<c\>"
266                    set fp-filename to "%g(fp-filename)\"
267
268             match "<v\>"
269                    set fp-filename to "%g(fp-filename)"
270
271             match "<h\>"
272                    set fp-filename to "%g(fp-filename)"
273
274             match "<u\>"
275                    set fp-filename to "%g(fp-filename)..\"
276
277                    ; watch for the end of the string or another tag
278             match ((lookahead not ("<" or value-end)) any)*=word
279                    set fp-filename to "%g(fp-filename)%x(word)"
280
281             match value-end ; OmniMark end of input
282                     ;
283        again
284  RETURN fp-filename
285
286
287        ; This function processes the content of the MIF
```

FIGURE 7-21. PARA.XOM PROGRAM FILE (CONTINUED)

```
288              ; <ImportObject ...> definition
289    define function process-importobj(value stream OBJ,
290                                      modifiable stream FILE-NAME,
291                                      modifiable stream BM-DPI
292                                      ) as
293            repeat scan OBJ
294                      ; Device Indepent Method v4 and on
295                      match "<ImportObFileDI" blank* "`"
296                              ((lookahead not "'>") any)*=file "'>"
297                          set FILE-NAME to file-path ("%x(file)")
298
299                      match "<BitMapDpi" blank*
300                              ((lookahead not ">") any)+=dpi ">"
301                          set BM-DPI to "%x(dpi)dpi"
302                      match any
303                          ;
304            again
305    ; end of process-importobj()
306
307
308
309
310            ; This function processes the content of the MIF
311            ; <Frame ...> definition
312    define function process-frame (value stream FRAME-CONT,
313                          modifiable stream FRAME-ID,
314                          modifiable stream FILE-NAME,
315                          modifiable stream DIMENSIONS,
316                          modifiable stream BM-DPI
317                          ) as
318            repeat scan FRAME-CONT
319
320                      ; MIF 4 way of specifying Frame size
321                      match "<ID" blank*
322                              ((lookahead not ">") any)*=num ">" EOL
323                          set FRAME-ID to "%x(num)"
324
325                      match "<ShapeRect" blank*
326                              ((lookahead not blank) any)+=top blank*
327                              ((lookahead not blank) any)+=left blank*
328                              ((lookahead not blank) any)+=hght blank*
329                              ((lookahead not ">") any)+=wid ">"
330                          set DIMENSIONS to "%x(hght)x%x(wid)"
331
332                      ; Get this group info for imported files
333                      match "<ImportObject" blank*
334                              ((lookahead not eoIobj) any)*=obj eoIobj
335
```

FIGURE 7-21. PARA.XOM PROGRAM FILE (CONTINUED)

```
336                              process-importobj("%x(obj)", FILE-NAME, BM-DPI)
337
338                   match any
339                              ;
340           again
341   ; end of process-frame()
342
343
344
345   define function process-tbl (value stream OBJ,
346                                       modifiable stream ID) as
347           repeat scan OBJ
348                   match "<TblID" blank* digit+=num EO> EOL
349                           set ID to "%x(num)"
350
351                   match any
352                           ;
353           again
354   ; end of process-tbl()
355
356
357
358
359
360
361   define function test-frm-tbl () as
362   local counter temp initial {1}
363
364   ; Now prove that you got all the information and it is properly stored
365           repeat over FRMid-shelf
366                   put #CONSOLE "FR: %d(temp), %g(FRMid-shelf)%n"
367                   increment temp
368           again
369
370           set temp to 1
371           repeat over TBLid-shelf
372                   put #CONSOLE "TB: %d(temp), %g(TBLid-shelf)%n"
373                   increment temp
374           again
375
376           set temp to 1
377           repeat over TRid-shelf
378                   put #CONSOLE "TR: %d(temp), %g(TRid-shelf)%n"
379                   increment temp
380           again
381
382   ; end of test-frm-tbl()
383
```

FIGURE 7-21. PARA.XOM PROGRAM FILE (CONTINUED)

```
384
385
386
387
388
389
390  ;;;; Program starts Here!!
391
392  find-start
393          put #CONSOLE "Processing started ...%n"
394
395          clear stream TBLid-shelf
396          clear stream TRid-shelf
397          clear stream FRMid-shelf
398
399
400  find-end
401          put #CONSOLE "Processing complete.%n"
402
403          ; test-frm-tbl()
404
405
406
407
408          ; first line of a MIF document file
409  find line-start "<MIFFile" blank*
410                  EO>=version-no ">"
411                  ((lookahead not "%n") any)*=notes EOL
412
413          ; first definition in MIF File
414  find line-start "<Units" blank* ((lookahead not ">") any)*=unit ">" EOL
415          ;
416
417  find line-start "<ColorCatalog" EOL
418                  ((lookahead not eoCCat ) any)*=catalog eoCCat
419          ;
420
421  find line-start "<ConditionCatalog" EOL
422                  ((lookahead not eoCondCat) any)*=catalog eoCondCat
423          ;
424
425
426  find line-start "<PgfCatalog" EOL
427                  ((lookahead not eoPgC ) any)*=catalog eoPgC
428          ;
429
430  find line-start "<ElementDefCatalog" EOL
431                  ((lookahead not eoElCat ) any)*=catalog eoElCat
```

FIGURE 7-21. PARA.XOM PROGRAM FILE (CONTINUED)

```
432             ;
433
434    find line-start "<FmtChangeListCatalog" EOL
435                    ((lookahead not eoFmtChg ) any)*=catalog eoFmtChg
436             ;
437
438             ; Character Style Definitions
439    find line-start "<FontCatalog" EOL
440                    ((lookahead not eoFntCat ) any)*=catalog eoFntCat
441             ;
442
443             ; definition of rule types - Thin = .5pt, single black
444    find line-start "<RulingCatalog" EOL
445                    ((lookahead not eoRulCat) any)*=catalog eoRulCat
446             ;
447
448             ; Table formats stored separate from paragraph definitions
449    find line-start "<TblCatalog" EOL
450                    ((lookahead not eoTblCat) any)*=catalog eoTblCat
451             ;
452
453    find line-start "<Views" EOL
454                    ((lookahead not eoVws ) any)*=catalog eoVws
455             ;
456
457             ; defines the variable name and its content
458    find line-start "<VariableFormats" EOL
459                    ((lookahead not eoVarFmts) any)*=catalog eoVarFmts
460             ;
461
462             ; defines the cross-reference types and formatted text output
463    find line-start "<XRefFormats" EOL
464                    ((lookahead not eoXrefFs ) any)*=catalog eoXrefFs
465             ;
466
467             ; document view window, scaling, pagesize etc.
468             ; also defines the element hierarchy for use with SGML
469    find line-start "<Document" EOL
470                    ((lookahead not eoDoc) any)*=catalog eoDoc
471             ;
472
473             ; Multiple entries for BookComponent. Defines which generated
474             ; files this file belongs to.
475    find line-start "<BookComponent" EOL
476                    ((lookahead not eoBkC ) any)*=catalog eoBkC
477             ;
478
479    find line-start "<InitialAutoNums" EOL
```

FIGURE 7-21. PARA.XOM PROGRAM FILE (CONTINUED)

```
480                     ((lookahead not eoIAutoN) any)*=catalog eoIAutoN
481            ;
482
483            ; contents spell check allowed words, differs per document
484   find line-start "<Dictionary" EOL
485                     ((lookahead not eoDic ) any)*=catalog eoDic
486            ;
487
488            ; defines all frames/illustrations in the document and then
489            ; assigns them ids which are referenced in the document
490            ; body to place the frame.
491
492            ; Currently the useful pieces of information are: FrameID,
493            ; Imported filename, dots-per-inch (DPI of a bitmapped
graphic)
494            ; the width and height of the frame itself
495   find line-start "<AFrames" EOL
496                     ((lookahead not eoAFrms) any)*=catalog eoAFrms
497   local stream ID
498   local stream NAME
499   local stream DPI
500   local stream DIMS
501
502            repeat scan pattern catalog
503               match "<Frame" ((lookahead not eoFrm) any)*=frame eoFrm
504
505                        set ID to ""
506                        set NAME to ""
507                        set DPI to ""
508                        set DIMS to ""
509                       process-frame("%x(frame)", ID, NAME, DIMS, DPI)
510                        set new FRMid-shelf to
511                                "FRM%g(ID) %g(NAME) %g(dims) %g(DPI)"
512
513               match any
514                        ;
515            again
516
517
518
519            ; defines all tables in the document and then
520            ; assigns them ids which are referenced in the document
521            ; body to place the table.
522   find line-start "<Tbls" EOL
523                     ((lookahead not eoTbls ) any)*=catalog eoTbls
524   local stream tbl-id
525
526            repeat scan pattern catalog
527               match "<Tbl" EOL
```

FIGURE 7-21. PARA.XOM PROGRAM FILE (CONTINUED)

```
528                              ((lookahead not eoTbl ) any)*=tbl eoTbl
529
530                      set tbl-id to ""
531
532                      process-tbl("%x(tbl)", tbl-id)
533                      set new TBLid-shelf to "TBL%g(tbl-id)"
534
535              match any
536                      ;
537        again
538
539
540
541        ; defines the pages, identifies their type and the textrect's
542        ; that belong on that page - multiple entries for this
543  find line-start "<Page" EOL
544              ((lookahead not eoPg) any)*=page eoPg
545  local switch masters initial {false}
546  local switch body initial {false}
547  local switch reference initial {false}
548
549        repeat scan pattern page
550              match "<PageType" blank*
551                      ((lookahead not ">") any)*=type ">"
552                      repeat scan pattern type
553                          match "BodyPage"
554                                  set body to true
555                                  set masters to false
556                                  set reference to false
557
558                          match "ReferencePage"
559                                  set body to false
560                                  set masters to false
561                                  set reference to true
562
563                                  ; contains the conditional text
564                          match  "HiddenPage"      ; hidden pages
565                                  set body to false
566                                  set masters to true
567                                  set reference to false
568
569                          match  "MasterPage"
570                                  set body to false
571                                  set masters to true
572                                  set reference to false
573
574                          match any
575                                  ;
```

FIGURE 7-21. PARA.XOM PROGRAM FILE (CONTINUED)

```
576                          again
577
578                  ; TextRects are uniquely identified and are tied
579                  ; to a specific type of a page, the only pages we
580                  ; need to convert are BodyPages and potentially hidden
581                  ; with conditional text
582
583                  match "<TextRect" blank*
584                                ((lookahead not eoTxtR) any)*=rect
585                                eoTxtR
586                          repeat scan pattern rect
587                                match "<ID" blank* digit+=id ">"
588                                        set new TRid-shelf to
589                                                "master %x(id)"
590                                                when active masters
591                                        set new TRid-shelf to
592                                                "body %x(id)"
593                                                when active body
594                                        set new TRid-shelf to
595                                                "reference %x(id)"
596                                                when active reference
597
598                                match any
599                                        ;
600                          again
601
602                  match any
603                          ;
604          again
605
606
607
608  ; Textflow contains the body/text of the document.
609  ; There are multiple textflows
610  find line-start "<TextFlow" EOL
611                  ((lookahead not eoTxtF ) any)*=flow  eoTxtF
612          ; need to sort out the Master page flows and Reference Pages
613
614          repeat scan pattern flow
615                          ; Footnotes are listed as part of the
616                          ; Textflow group
617                  match "<Notes" white-space+
618                                ((lookahead not eoNts) any)*=notes eoNt
619                  do when "%x(notes)" != ""
620                          put #ERROR "WARNING: Footnotes found: %x(n
621                  done
622                  match "<Para" EOL
```

FIGURE 7-21. PARA.XOM PROGRAM FILE (CONTINUED)

```
623                                 ((lookahead not eoP) any)*=content eoP
624                        process-para("%x(content)", 2)
625
626               match any
627                  ;
628        again
629
630
631  ; Optional section, may not be in every document. Probably is
632  ; defined in the Print dialog when you can map objects to
633  ; Acrobat Bookmark items.
634  find line-start "<AcrobatElements" EOL
635                    ((lookahead not eoAcro ) any)*=catalog eoAcro
636       ;
637
638
639       ; Last line of a FrameMaker generated file
640  find line-start "# End of MIFFile" EOL
641       ;
642
643       ; Gather up any missed comments that might be added to the file
644  find line-start "#"
645                    ((lookahead not "%n") any)*=comment EOL
646       ;
647
648
649  ;;;   END OF PROGRAM
```

FIGURE 7-21. PARA.XOM PROGRAM FILE (CONTINUED)

Line 70 introduces the process-chars() function. This function finally gets
to work with the text. I have converted some of the troublesome characters
for SGML here and removed the special FrameMaker quoting structures.

process-string() on Line 90 calls process-chars() after handling all the
other MIF structures that can occur in a ParaLine object. This function
must handle text variables, conditional text, and all the markers that
FrameMaker creates. This is also where tables and anchored frames get
referenced into the body of the text. Other than the tables and frames, all
other objects are recognized and just marked in this program; the next
version will handle these objects.

Figure 7-22 shows the results of running:

```
c:> omni para.xom ch2.frm
```

```
<'ChapterTitle'>\t
Tuaaluvsxr kwo Ywpalatxr aso Wvoawo
<'Body'>
Apsa nqkyapa ooanatlna aso sxaaluvkatyy aaznnnaapa qya aso 24-Zwaa Xv
Ztokap apkm aso zapmjaatyylaa aaznnnaapa mnpyap ayalltsxr aso wyoawo.
<'Body'>
Pva aaaa nxyapxtoxnn, ap rkap sxnuaoon k zatmt appoapxnn sxaaluvkatyy
(17-0033-0277).  Apsa njao vsaaa aso NOW aatanq apaatxra, 24-Awaa Xvo
wkwlpowoxa nxxwkwoa, WLJ oxosmjazaa lwo yasoa xyoawo sxqyaxkatyy. Ato
assa njao sx aso VUjxap8260 Aatanqsxr Ram krxooa tx aso Ampoapxnn Mga
<'Body'>
Apo apwkrxooa zq assa nqkyapa ooanatlna:
<'Bulleted'>\xa5 \t
Azpmjaatyylaa Azznnnaapa
<'Bulleted'>\xa5 \t
Avalltsxr Zzznnnaapa
<'Bulleted'>\xa5 \t
Aatmt Suaaluvkatyy
<'Bulleted'>\xa5 \t
Xvoawo Yapaatoa
<'Bulleted'>\xa5 \t
Amaatxr aso NOW Aatanqoa
<'Bulleted'>\xa5 \t
Tuaaluvsxr aso Wvoawo
<'Bulleted'>\xa5 \t
Muyqsqaatxr aso Wvoawo
<'Bulleted'>\xa5 \t
Apyatxr Wvoawo Muyqsqaalatyya
<'Bulleted'>\xa5 \t
Rhasoatxr Aalataatma
<'Bulleted'>\xa5 \t
Xvytazatxr aso Pyzya Aiwpv
```

TEXT REMOVED HERE

```
<'NumberedCont'>
Aiap aso zlltkpoa zq anapaa tx aso mjaazy; aaaawv xpon asow asox aaa
mxyypmazaa az aso wyoawo.  Kralaa skwovo aso 24-Zwaa Xvoawo la aso pk
lnsxr mjappaw xza az azanq aso mxxzzypxaa. Tm aso wyoawo kyapkaa az mn
apaaay ta az aso kwat-aalatm assovnsxr ljp, apzllt sa tx aso asszatxr
lwo mxyalla aaaa wynju aaaawsoa.
<'Body'>
Vloz aso asszatxr mjaazy lwo kwat-aalatm assovnsxr ljp sx assmq aaaa x
asszapn az aska aaa njw apzlltkpo aso wyoawo pya aazalpo ya asszxoxa.
<'Body'>
```

TEXT REMOVED HERE

FIGURE 7-22. PARA.XOM SAMPLE OUTPUT

Look over this sample output. You'll notice that all the tags are now in the form of <'tagname'>. There are still some special characters like '\t', '\xa5', etc. When you load one of these output files into a text editor, you will see that each paragraph is a single line of text with no line breaks. If you load this into an editor like PFE, you'll see the tag on the line above the line of text. As long as your editor doesn't wrap text lines, you'll have a view similar to an outline mode.

tblcnt.xom is our last pass at simplifying the MIF markup. This version of the program converts all makers, font markup, character styles, and table content and structure. Figure 7-23 illustrates this program.

Line 90 introduces the function write(). I created this to handle the need to write table information to a variable, so that it could be stored and it could output body text to the output stream. All the output statements have been replaced with this function, and a Boolean value of IN-TABLE is passed through most of the function calls to indicate whether the current process is a table operation or body text.

The function process-chars(), Line 103, is a low-level function that examines a text string for special MIF escape characters or hex values. Line 123 introduces the mark-xref-id() function. Markers contain cross-references, index items, and hypertext links, among other things. This function processes the id information in a marker. The process-font() function, Line 140, process all font changes in family, weight, or angle. Many times, there will be empty font changes without values, and those are automatically discarded. There are also instances where a font change is valid, but the end font tag appears immediately after. This occurs when an author doesn't select the complete range of text with all the font changes, and either deletes the text or moves the contents elsewhere. These empty changes will be handled by the SGML processing steps. This function creates new tags with the 'fnt name' format to handle any potential name conflicts.

Line 167 introduces the process-marker() function. This is the main marker processing section; the id process was handled in the function introduced earlier. This function looks for all the different marker types, but I only process those I want to use in this sample. This was also a way to cut down on the number of operations so that this program would function within the OmniMark LE constraints.

```
 1  cross-translate
 2
 3  ; file tblcnt.xom
 4  ; This program reads a MIF document file and strips out the header.
 5  ; Process the table, Frame and Page information as well as page content.
 6  ; This program now adds font and marker information to the output as
 7  ; well as all table markup and structure.
 8
 9          ; Following variables store the predefined Tables, Frames, and
10          ; TextRect information.
11  global stream TBLid-shelf variable
12  global stream FRMid-shelf variable
13  global stream TRid-shelf variable
14
15  global stream textflow-tag               ; Store the tag and numstring
16  global stream textflow-numstr            ; for paras on same page with
17                                           ; same tags, not tagged by MIF,
18                                           ; they are supposed to default
19
20  global stream last-textrectid            ; Record the last TextRectID,
21                                           ; because it is defaulted on
22                                           ; repeated paras, etc.
23
24  global stream tbl-content initial {""}   ; string to store table content
25                                           ; while processing the header
26                                           ; definition of that table,
27                                           ; output not to occur until
28                                           ; a location for the table is
29                                           ; found
30
31
32
33          ; Macros here identify the closing construct of the major MIF
34          ; groups.
35
36  macro eoAcro is ("> # end of AcrobatElements%n") macro-end
37  macro eoAFrms is ("> # end of AFrames%n") macro-end
38  macro eoBkC is ("> # end of BookComponent%n") macro-end
39  macro eoCCat is ("> # end of ColorCatalog%n") macro-end
40  macro eoIAutoN is ("> # end of InitialAutoNums%n") macro-end
41  macro eoDic is ("> # end of Dictionary%n") macro-end
42  macro eoDoc is ("> # end of Document%n") macro-end
43  macro eoElCat is ("> # end of ElementDefCatalog%n") macro-end
44  macro eoFmtChg is ("> # end of FmtChangeListCatalog%n") macro-end
45  macro eoTblCat is ("> # end of TblCatalog%n") macro-end
46  macro eoTbls is ("> # end of Tbls%n") macro-end
```

FIGURE 7-23. TBLCNT.XOM PROGRAM FILE

```
47  macro eoXrefFs is ("> # end of XRefFormats%n") macro-end
48  macro eoCondCat is ("> # end of ConditionCatalog%n") macro-end
49  macro eoFntCat is ("> # end of FontCatalog%n") macro-end
50  macro eoRulCat is ("> # end of RulingCatalog%n") macro-end
51  macro eoVarFmts is ("> # end of VariableFormats%n") macro-end
52  macro eoVws is ("> # end of Views%n") macro-end
53  macro eoPg is ("> # end of Page%n") macro-end
54  macro eoPgC is ("> # end of PgfCatalog%n") macro-end
55  macro eoTxtF is ("> # end of TextFlow%n") macro-end
56
57          ; Macros here identify the closing construct of the
58          ; minor MIF groups.
59
60  macro eoFrm is ("> # end of Frame%n") macro-end
61  macro eoIobj is ("> # end of ImportObject%n") macro-end
62  macro eoTbl is ("> # end of Tbl%n") macro-end
63  macro eoTxtR is ("> # end of TextRect%n") macro-end
64  macro eoNts is ("> # end of Notes%n") macro-end
65  macro eoP is ("> # end of Para%n") macro-end
66  macro eoVar is ("> # end of Variable%n") macro-end
67  macro eoCondal is ("> # end of Conditional%n") macro-end
68  macro eoXref is ("> # end of XRef%n") macro-end
69  macro eoMk is ("> # end of Marker%n") macro-end
70  macro eoFnt is ("> # end of Font%n") macro-end
71  macro eoRow is ("> # end of Row%n") macro-end
72  macro eoCell is ("> # end of Cell%n") macro-end
73  macro eoTblB is ("> # end of TblBody%n") macro-end
74  macro eoTblH is ("> # end of TblH%n") macro-end
75  macro eoTblTitC is ("> # end of TblTitleContent%n") macro-end
76  macro eoTblF is ("> # end of TblFormat%n") macro-end
77
78
79
80          ; Some general end-of-pattern matching that is used
81          ; all over the place
82
83  macro EOL is (((lookahead not "%n") any)* "%n") macro-end
84  macro EO> is (((lookahead not ">") any)*) macro-end
85  macro EOQ is (((lookahead not "'>") any)*) macro-end
86
87          ; This function handles the decision if the actual
88          ; content information is to be written out to the file
89          ; or stored as part of the table content processing
90  define function write (value stream string,
```

FIGURE 7-23. TBLCNT.XOM PROGRAM FILE (CONTINUED)

```
91                             value switch IN-TABLE) as
92         do when IN-TABLE = FALSE
93                 output "%g(string)"
94         else
95                 set tbl-content to "%g(tbl-content)%g(string)"
96         done
97 ; end function write()
98
99
100
101
102         ; identify and special text characters in the processed string
103 define function process-chars(value stream STRING,
104                             value switch IN-TABLE ) as
105         repeat scan "%g(STRING)"
106                 match "\\"      write ("\", IN-TABLE)
107                 match "&"       write ("&amp;", IN-TABLE)
108                 match "<"       write ("&lt;", IN-TABLE)
109                 match "\q"      write ("'", IN-TABLE)    ; quote
110                 match "\>"      write ("&gt;", IN-TABLE)
111                 match "\x11 "   write (" ", IN-TABLE)
112                 match "\t"      write ("", IN-TABLE)     ; tab
113                 match "\xa5 "   write ("", IN-TABLE)     ; bullet
114                 match ((lookahead not "\" or "&" or "<") any)*=chars
115                         write ("%x(chars)", IN-TABLE)
116         again
117
118 ; end process-chars()
119
120
121
122
123 define function mark-xref-id ( value stream id-line,
124                             value switch IN-TABLE ) as
125         repeat scan "%g(id-line)"
126                 match value-start digit+=new-id ":"
127                         write ("idref=%x(new-id) ", IN-TABLE)
128                 match blank+ ((lookahead not ":") any)* ":"
129                         ;
130                 match blank+ any+=new-label
131                         write ("label='", IN-TABLE)
132                         process-chars("%x(new-label)", IN-TABLE)
133                         write ("'", IN-TABLE)
134                 match any
```

FIGURE 7-23. TBLCNT.XOM PROGRAM FILE (CONTINUED)

```
135                                    ;
136          again
137  ; end function mark-xref-id()
138
139
140  define function process-font (value stream FONT-INFO,
141                                   value switch IN-TABLE ) as
142  local switch good-font-info
143
144          deactivate good-font-info
145          write ("<'fnt' ", IN-TABLE)
146
147          repeat scan FONT-INFO
148                  match "<FTag" blank*  "`" EOQ=ftag "'>"
149                          write ("tag='%x(ftag)' ", IN-TABLE)
150
151                  match "<FFamily" blank*  "`" EOQ=ffam "'>"
152                          write ("fam='%x(ffam)' ", IN-TABLE)
153
154                  match "<FAngle" blank*  "`" EOQ=fang "'>"
155                          write ("ang='%x(fang)' ", IN-TABLE)
156
157                  match "<FWeight" blank*  "`"  EOQ=fwt  "'>"
158                          write ("wt='%x(fwt)' ", IN-TABLE)
159
160                  match any
161                                    ;
162          again
163          write (">", IN-TABLE)
164  ; end function process-font()
165
166
167  define function process-marker (value stream MARKER,
168                                   value switch IN-TABLE ) as
169          write ("<'marker' ", IN-TABLE)
170
171          repeat scan MARKER
172                  match "<MType" blank* digit+=mtype ">" EOL
173                          write ("mtype=", IN-TABLE)
174
175                          do when "%x(mtype)" = "0"        ; header1
176                          else when "%x(mtype)" = "1"      ; header2
177                          else when "%x(mtype)" = "2"
178                                  write ("index ", IN-TABLE)
```

FIGURE 7-23. TBLCNT.XOM PROGRAM FILE (CONTINUED)

```
179                        else when "%x(mtype)" = "3"     ; comment
180                        else when "%x(mtype)" = "4"     ; subject
181                        else when "%x(mtype)" = "5"     ; author
182                        else when "%x(mtype)" = "6"     ; glossary
183                        else when "%x(mtype)" = "7"     ; equation
184                        else when "%x(mtype)" = "8"     ; hypertext
185                        else when "%x(mtype)" = "9"
186                                write ("xref ", IN-TABLE)
187                        else when "%x(mtype)" = "10"    ; conditional
188                        else when "%x(mtype)" = ("11" or "12"
189                            or "13" or "14" or "15" or "16"
190                            or "17" or "18" or "19" or "20"
191                            or "21" or "22" or "23" or "24" or "25")
192                                    ; other
193                        done
194
195
196                match "<MText" blank* "`" EOQ=mid "'>" EOL
197                        mark-xref-id("%x(mid)", IN-TABLE)
198
199                match any
200                        ;
201        again
202
203        write (">", IN-TABLE)
204 ; end of function process-marker()
205
206
207
208 define function process-xref (value stream XREF,
209                                value switch IN-TABLE ) as
210
211        write ("<'xref' ", IN-TABLE)
212
213        repeat scan XREF
214                match "<XRefSrcText" blank* "`" EOQ=xref-src "'>"
215
216                        mark-xref-id("%x(xref-src)", IN-TABLE)
217
218                match "<XRefName" blank* "`" EOQ=xref-name "'>"
219                        ;
220                match any
221                        ;
222        again
```

FIGURE 7-23. TBLCNT.XOM PROGRAM FILE (CONTINUED)

```
223
224          write (">", IN-TABLE)
225   ; end function process-xref()
226
227
228
229          ; All kinds of fun things can live within a
230          ; text string and each have to be handled!
231   define function process-string (value stream STRING,
232                                   value switch IN-TABLE ) as
233          repeat scan "%g(STRING)"
234                  match "<Variable" ((lookahead not eoVar)
235                              any)*=variable eoVar
236                      write ("<variable found>", IN-TABLE)
237
238                  match "<Conditional" EOL ((lookahead not eoCondal)
239                              any)*=cond eoCondal
240                      write ("<conditional found>", IN-TABLE)
241
242                  match "<Unconditional" EO> ">" EOL
243                      write ("<unconditional found>", IN-TABLE)
244
245                  match "<AFrame" blank* digit+=frame-id ">" EOL
246                      write ("%n<'graphic' id=%x(frame-id)%n",
247                          IN-TABLE)
248                      repeat over FRMid-shelf
249                          do when FRMid-shelf matches
250                                          ("FRM%x(frame-id) "
251                                          blank* ((lookahead
252                                          not value-end) any)* )
253                              write ("'%g(FRMid-shelf)'%n",
254                                          IN-TABLE)
255                          done
256                      again
257                      write (">%n%n", IN-TABLE)
258
259                      ; there could be a problem here if
260                      ; tables are nested objects!!
261                  match "<ATbl" blank* digit+=table-id ">" EOL
262                      write ("<'table' id=%x(table-id)>%n", IN-TABLE)
263                      repeat over TBLid-shelf
264                          do when TBLid-shelf matches
265                                          ("TBL%x(table-id) "
266                                          blank*
```

FIGURE 7-23. TBLCNT.XOM PROGRAM FILE (CONTINUED)

```
267                                            ((lookahead not
268                                              value-end) any)* )
269                              write ("%g(TBLid-shelf)",
270                                     IN-TABLE)
271                     done
272                 again
273
274         match "<XRefEnd" blank* ">" EOL
275             write ("<'xref-end'>", IN-TABLE)
276
277         match "<XRef" EOL ((lookahead not eoXref ) any)*=xref
278                    eoXref
279
280             process-xref("%x(xref)", IN-TABLE)
281
282
283
284         match "<Marker" EOL ((lookahead not eoMk)
285                    any)*=mark eoMk
286
287             process-marker("%x(mark)", IN-TABLE)
288
289         match "<TextRectID" blank* EO>=id2 ">" EOL
290             ;
291
292         match "<Font" ((lookahead not eoFnt) any)*=font eoFnt
293
294
295             process-font("%x(font)", IN-TABLE)
296
297         match "<String" blank* "`" EOQ=string EOL
298             process-chars("%x(string)", IN-TABLE)
299
300
301           match "<Char" blank* EO>=character
302                repeat scan pattern character
303                    match "HardSpace"
304                        write (" ", IN-TABLE)
305
306                    match "Tab"
307                        write ("", IN-TABLE)
308
309                    match "SoftHyphen"
310                        write ("&shy;",
```

FIGURE 7-23. TBLCNT.XOM PROGRAM FILE (CONTINUED)

```
311                                                         IN-TABLE)
312
313                                 match "HardHyphen"
314                                         write ("&dash;",
315                                                 IN-TABLE)
316
317                                 match "DiscHyphen"
318
319                                 match "NoHyphen"
320
321                                 match "Cent"
322
323                                 match "Pound"
324
325                                 match "Yen"
326
327                                 match "EnDash"
328                                         write ("&ndash;",
329                                                 IN-TABLE)
330
331                                 match "EmDash"
332                                         write ("&mdash;",
333                                                 IN-TABLE)
334
335                                 match "Dagger"
336                                         write ("&dagger;",
337                                                 IN-TABLE)
338
339                                 match "DoubleDagger"
340                                         write ("&Dagger;",
341                                                 IN-TABLE)
342
343                                 match "Bullet"
344                                         write ("&bull;",
345                                                 IN-TABLE)
346
347                                 match "HardReturn"
348                                         write (" ", IN-TABLE)
349
350                                 match "NumberSpace"
351                                         write ("&numsp;",
352                                                 IN-TABLE)
353
354                                 match "ThinSpace"
```

FIGURE 7-23. **TBLCNT.XOM** **PROGRAM FILE** (**CONTINUED**)

```
355                                              write (" ",
356                                                      IN-TABLE)
357
358                                  match "EnSpace"
359                                              write (" ",
360                                                      IN-TABLE)
361
362                                  match "EmSpace"
363                                              write (" ",
364                                                      IN-TABLE)
365
366                                  match any
367                                              ;
368                              again
369
370
371
372
373              match any
374                      ;
375          again
376
377  ; end of process-string()
378
379
380
381
382          ; Each line of a paragraph is treated as a paraline,
383          ; we have to find the start of a new paragraph, from
384          ; the continuing of the para text.
385  define function process-paraline (value stream PARA-CONT,
386                                    value stream TAG,
387                                    modifiable switch NEW-PARA,
388                                    modifiable stream NUMSTR,
389                                    value switch IN-TABLE ) as
390
391  local switch string-processing
392
393              ; TextRect Id is inherited within the same Para
394              ; object. First ParaLine gets a TextRectID, all the
395              ; others are not set! Multiple paras on the same
396              ; page/textflow don't have to have ids assigned, they
397              ; inherit the last value.
398
```

FIGURE 7-23. TBLCNT.XOM PROGRAM FILE (CONTINUED)

```
399          do when ((NEW-PARA = TRUE) and (IN-TABLE = FALSE))
400
401                  deactivate string-processing
402                  repeat scan "%g(PARA-CONT)"
403                          match "<TextRectID" blank* digit+=TRid ">"
404                                  ; determine if these text lines are
405                                  ; on a body page, if not don't print
406                                  ; them!
407
408                                  set last-textrectid to "%x(TRid)"
409
410                                  exit     ; after finding the ID -
411                                           ; one per Para tag
412
413                          match any
414                                  ;
415                  again
416      done
417
418      do when active in-table
419              activate string-processing
420              do when active new-para
421                      write ("%n<'%g(TAG)'>", IN-TABLE)
422                      write ("%g(NUMSTR)%n", IN-TABLE)
423                      set NUMSTR to ""
424                      deactivate new-para
425              done
426      else
427              repeat over TRid-shelf
428                      do when "body %g(last-textrectid)" =
429                                      "%g(TRid-shelf)"
430                              activate string-processing
431                              do when active NEW-PARA
432                                      write ("%n<'%g(TAG)'>",
433                                              IN-TABLE)
434                                      write ("%g(NUMSTR)%n",
435                                              IN-TABLE)
436                                      set NUMSTR to ""
437                                      deactivate NEW-PARA
438                              done
439                              exit
440                      done
441              again
442      done
```

FIGURE 7-23. TBLCNT.XOM PROGRAM FILE (CONTINUED)

```
443
444
445         do when active string-processing
446                 process-string("%g(PARA-CONT)", IN-TABLE)
447         done
448
449  ; end of process-paraline()
450
451
452
453  define function process-para (value stream CONTENT,
454                                value counter NUM-BLNK,
455                                value switch IN-TABLE) as
456
457         ; The paraline tag is indented at different levels based upon
458         ; where it is found, so we need to pass the exact number of
459         ; blanks to find as NUM-BLNK
460
461
462  local switch new-para
463
464         activate new-para
465         set textflow-numstr to ""
466         repeat scan CONTENT
467                 match "<PgfNumString" blank* "`" EOQ=num "'>" EOL
468                         set textflow-numstr to "%x(num)"
469
470                 match "<PgfTag" blank* "`" EOQ=tag "'>" EOL
471                         set textflow-tag to "%x(tag)"
472
473                         ; watch the number of blanks required to
474                         ; find the end of a ParaLine!!
475                 match "<ParaLine" blank* ((lookahead not
476                             (line-start blank{num-blnk} ">"))
477                             any)*=text
478                             line-start blank{num-blnk} ">" EOL
479
480                         process-paraline("%x(text)",
481                                 textflow-tag, new-para,
482                                 textflow-numstr, IN-TABLE)
483
484                 match any
485                         ;
486         again
```

FIGURE 7-23. TBLCNT.XOM PROGRAM FILE (CONTINUED)

```
487   ; end of para()
488
489
490
491   define stream function file-path (value stream fp-instring) as
492   local stream fp-filename initial {""}
493
494         repeat scan "%g(fp-instring)"
495
496               match "<r\>"              ; Unix file tree root
497                     set fp-filename to "%g(fp-filename)/"
498
499               match "<c\>"
500                     set fp-filename to "%g(fp-filename)\"
501
502               match "<v\>"
503                     set fp-filename to "%g(fp-filename)"
504
505               match "<h\>"
506                     set fp-filename to "%g(fp-filename)"
507
508               match "<u\>"
509                     set fp-filename to "%g(fp-filename)..\"
510
511                     ; watch for the end of the string or another tag
512               match ((lookahead not ("<" or value-end)) any)*=word
513                     set fp-filename to "%g(fp-filename)%x(word)"
514
515               match value-end ; OmniMark end of input
516                     ;
517         again
518   RETURN fp-filename
519
520
521         ; This function process the content of the MIF
522         ; <ImportObject ...> definition
523   define function process-importobj(value stream OBJ,
524                              modifiable stream FILE-NAME,
525                              modifiable stream BM-DPI,
526                              value switch IN-TABLE
527                              ) as
528         repeat scan OBJ
529               ; Device Indepent Method v4 and on
530               match "<ImportObFileDI" blank* "`"
```

FIGURE 7-23. TBLCNT.XOM PROGRAM FILE (CONTINUED)

```
531                          ((lookahead not "'>") any)*=file "'>"
532                      set FILE-NAME to file-path ("%x(file)")
533
534             match "<BitMapDpi" blank*
535                          ((lookahead not ">") any)+=dpi ">"
536                      set BM-DPI to "%x(dpi)dpi"
537             match any
538                      ;
539        again
540  ; end of process-importobj()
541
542
543
544
545        ; This function processes the content of the MIF
546        ; <Frame ...> definition
547  define function process-frame (value stream FRAME-CONT,
548                      modifiable stream FRAME-ID,
549                      modifiable stream FILE-NAME,
550                      modifiable stream DIMENSIONS,
551                      modifiable stream BM-DPI,
552                      value switch IN-TABLE
553                      ) as
554        repeat scan FRAME-CONT
555
556                      ; MIF 4 way of specifying Frame size
557             match "<ID" blank*
558                          ((lookahead not ">") any)*=num ">" EOL
559                      set FRAME-ID to "%x(num)"
560
561             match "<ShapeRect" blank*
562                          ((lookahead not blank) any)+=top blank*
563                          ((lookahead not blank) any)+=left blank*
564                          ((lookahead not blank) any)+=hght blank*
565                          ((lookahead not ">") any)+=wid ">"
566                      set DIMENSIONS to "%x(hght)x%x(wid)"
567
568                      ; Get this group info for imported files
569             match "<ImportObject" blank*
570                          ((lookahead not eoIobj) any)*=obj eoIobj
571
572                      process-importobj("%x(obj)", FILE-NAME,
573                          BM-DPI, IN-TABLE)
574
```

FIGURE 7-23. TBLCNT.XOM PROGRAM FILE (CONTINUED)

```
575                     match any
576                             ;
577         again
578 ; end of process-frame()
579
580
581
582
583 define function process-table-content (value stream ROWS,
584                                         value switch IN-TABLE) as
585         repeat scan ROWS
586                 match "<Row" EOL ((lookahead not eoRow ) any)*=bcells
587                         eoRow
588                         write ("<'row'>%n", IN-TABLE)
589                         repeat scan pattern bcells
590                                 match "<CellRows" blank* digit+=bstrad
591                                         ">" EOL
592                                         write ("<'Row Straddle' %x(bstr
593                                                 IN-TABLE)
594
595                                 match "<CellColumns" blank*
596                                         digit+=bspan ">" EOL
597                                         write ("<'Cell Span' %x(bspan)>
598                                                 IN-TABLE)
599
600                                 match "<Cell" EOL ((lookahead not
601                                         eoCell) any)*=bcell eoCell
602                                         write ("<'cell'>%n",
603                                                 IN-TABLE)
604
605                                         repeat scan pattern bcell
606                                                 match "<Para" EOL
607                                                         ((lookahead not
608                                                         any)*=c-para ec
609
610                                                         process-para("%x(c-p
611                                                         7, IN-TABLE)
612
613                                                 match any
614                                                         ;
615                                         again
616                                         write ("<'end cell'>%n",
617                                                 IN-TABLE)
618
```

FIGURE 7-23. TBLCNT.XOM PROGRAM FILE (CONTINUED)

```
619                                      match any
620                                              ;
621                          again
622                          write ("<'end row'>%n", IN-TABLE)
623                  match any
624                          ;
625          again
626  ; end of function process-table-content()
627
628
629
630
631
632
633  define function process-tbl (value stream OBJ,
634                              value switch IN-TABLE ) as
635  local stream ID initial {""}
636
637          repeat scan OBJ
638                  match "<Tbl" EOL
639                          ((lookahead not eoTbl ) any)*=frame eoTbl
640                          set tbl-content to ""
641
642                          repeat scan pattern frame
643                                  match "<TblID" blank* digit+=num EO> EC
644
645                                          set ID to "%x(num)"
646
647                                  match "<TblBody" EOL
648                                          ((lookahead not eoTblB
649                                          any)*=brows eoTblB
650                                          write ("<'tbody'>%n",
651                                                  IN-TABLE)
652
653                                          process-table-content("%x(brows
654                                                  IN-TABLE)
655
656                                          write ("<'end tbody'>%n",
657                                                  IN-TABLE)
658                                  match "<TblH" EOL
659                                          ((lookahead not eoTblH
660                                          any)*=rows eoTblH
661                                          write ("<'thead'>%n", IN-TABLE)
```

FIGURE 7-23. TBLCNT.XOM PROGRAM FILE (CONTINUED)

```
662
663                                      process-table-content("%x(rows)
664                                              IN-TABLE)
665                                      write ("<'end thead'>%n",
666                                              IN-TABLE)
667
668                          match "<TblTitleContent"
669                                          ((lookahead not eoTblTi
670                                          any)*=title
671                                          eoTblTitC
672
673                              repeat scan pattern title
674                                      match "<Para" EOL
675                                      ((lookahead not eoP)
676                                          any)*=para eoP
677                                      process-para("%x(pai
678                                              IN-TABLE)
679                                      match any
680                                          ;
681                              again
682
683                          match "<TblNumColumns" blank*
684                                          digit+=cols ">" EOL
685                              write ("<'Num-Cols' %x(cols)>%n
686                                          IN-TABLE)
687
688                          match "<TblColumnWidth" blank*
689                                      EO>*=width ">"   EOL
690                              write ("<'col-width' %x(width)>
691                                          IN-TABLE)
692
693                          match "<TblTag" blank* "`" EOQ*=tag EOL
694                              write ("<'tbl-tag' '%x(tag)'>%n
695                                          IN-TABLE)
696
697                          match "<TblFormat" EOL
698                                  (( lookahead not eoTblF)
699                                  any)*=format   eoTblF
700                                          ;
701                          match any
702                                      ;
703                  again
704
705                  write ("%n<'end table'>%n", IN-TABLE)
706                  set new TBLid-shelf to
707                          "TBL%g(ID)%n%g(tbl-content)"
```

FIGURE 7-23. TBLCNT.XOM PROGRAM FILE (CONTINUED)

```
708
709                    match any
710                              ;
711            again
712  ; end of process-tbl()
713
714
715
716
717
718
719  define function test-frm-tbl () as
720  local counter temp initial {1}
721
722  ; Now prove that you got all the information and it is properly stored
723          repeat over FRMid-shelf
724                  put #CONSOLE "FR: %d(temp), %g(FRMid-shelf)%n"
725                  increment temp
726          again
727
728          set temp to 1
729          repeat over TBLid-shelf
730                  put #CONSOLE "TB: %d(temp), %g(TBLid-shelf)%n"
731                  increment temp
732          again
733
734          set temp to 1
735          repeat over TRid-shelf
736                  put #CONSOLE "TR: %d(temp), %g(TRid-shelf)%n"
737                  increment temp
738          again
739
740  ; end of test-frm-tbl()
741
742
743
744
745
746
747
748  ;;;; Program starts Here!!
749
750  find-start
751          put #CONSOLE "Processing started ...%n"
```

FIGURE 7-23. TBLCNT.XOM PROGRAM FILE (CONTINUED)

```
752
753        clear stream TBLid-shelf
754        clear stream TRid-shelf
755        clear stream FRMid-shelf
756
757
758  find-end
759        put #CONSOLE "Processing complete.%n"
760
761        ; test-frm-tbl()
762
763
764
765
766        ; first line of a MIF document file
767  find line-start "<MIFFile" blank*
768              EO>=version-no ">"
769              ((lookahead not "%n") any)*=notes EOL
770
771        ; first definition in MIF File
772  find line-start "<Units" blank* ((lookahead not ">") any)*=unit ">" E
773        ;
774
775  find line-start "<ColorCatalog" EOL
776              ((lookahead not eoCCat ) any)*=catalog eoCCat
777        ;
778
779  find line-start "<ConditionCatalog" EOL
780              ((lookahead not eoCondCat) any)*=catalog eoCondCat
781        ;
782
783
784  find line-start "<PgfCatalog" EOL
785              ((lookahead not eoPgC ) any)*=catalog eoPgC
786        ;
787
788  find line-start "<ElementDefCatalog" EOL
789              ((lookahead not eoElCat ) any)*=catalog eoElCat
790        ;
791
792  find line-start "<FmtChangeListCatalog" EOL
793              ((lookahead not eoFmtChg ) any)*=catalog eoFmtChg
794        ;
795
```

FIGURE 7-23. TBLCNT.XOM PROGRAM FILE (CONTINUED)

```
796            ; Character Style Definitions
797  find line-start "<FontCatalog" EOL
798                 ((lookahead not eoFntCat ) any)*=catalog eoFntCat
799            ;
800
801            ; definition of rule types - Thin = .5pt, single black
802  find line-start "<RulingCatalog" EOL
803                 ((lookahead not eoRulCat) any)*=catalog eoRulCat
804            ;
805
806            ; Table formats stored separate from paragraph definitions
807  find line-start "<TblCatalog" EOL
808                 ((lookahead not eoTblCat) any)*=catalog eoTblCat
809            ;
810
811  find line-start "<Views" EOL
812                 ((lookahead not eoVws ) any)*=catalog eoVws
813            ;
814
815            ; defines the variable name and its content
816  find line-start "<VariableFormats" EOL
817                 ((lookahead not eoVarFmts) any)*=catalog eoVarFmts
818            ;
819
820            ; defines the cross-reference types and formatted text output
821  find line-start "<XRefFormats" EOL
822                 ((lookahead not eoXrefFs ) any)*=catalog eoXrefFs
823            ;
824
825            ; document view window, scaling, pagesize etc.
826            ; also defines the element hierarchy for use with SGML
827  find line-start "<Document" EOL
828                 ((lookahead not eoDoc) any)*=catalog eoDoc
829            ;
830
831            ; Multiple entries for BookComponent. Defines which generated
832            ; files this file belongs to.
833  find line-start "<BookComponent" EOL
834                 ((lookahead not eoBkC ) any)*=catalog eoBkC
835            ;
836
837  find line-start "<InitialAutoNums" EOL
838                 ((lookahead not eoIAutoN) any)*=catalog eoIAutoN
839            ;
```

FIGURE 7-23. TBLCNT.XOM PROGRAM FILE (CONTINUED)

```
840
841             ; contents spell check allowed words, differs per document
842     find line-start "<Dictionary" EOL
843                     ((lookahead not eoDic ) any)*=catalog eoDic
844             ;
845
846             ; defines all frames/illustrations in the document and then
847             ; assigns them ids which are referenced in the document
848             ; body to place the frame.
849
850             ; Currently the useful pieces of information are: FrameID,
851             ; Imported filename, dots-per-inch (DPI of a bitmapped graphic)
852             ; the width and height of the frame itself
853     find line-start "<AFrames" EOL
854                     ((lookahead not eoAFrms) any)*=catalog eoAFrms
855     local stream ID
856     local stream NAME
857     local stream DPI
858     local stream DIMS
859
860             repeat scan pattern catalog
861                     match "<Frame" ((lookahead not eoFrm) any)*=frame eoFrm
862
863                             set ID to ""
864                             set NAME to ""
865                             set DPI to ""
866                             set DIMS to ""
867                             process-frame("%x(frame)", ID, NAME,
868                                     DIMS, DPI, FALSE)
869                             set new FRMid-shelf to
870                                     "FRM%g(ID) %g(NAME) %g(dims) %g(DPI)"
871
872                     match any
873                             ;
874             again
875
876
877
878             ; defines all tables in the document and then
879             ; assigns them ids which are referenced in the document
880             ; body to place the table.
881     find line-start "<Tbls" EOL
882                     ((lookahead not eoTbls ) any)*=catalog eoTbls
883             process-tbl("%x(catalog)", TRUE)
```

FIGURE 7-23. TBLCNT.XOM PROGRAM FILE (CONTINUED)

```
884
885
886
887            ; defines the pages, identifies their type and the textrect's
888            ; that belong on that page - multiple entries for this
889    find line-start "<Page" EOL
890                    ((lookahead not eoPg) any)*=page eoPg
891    local switch masters initial {false}
892    local switch body initial {false}
893    local switch reference initial {false}
894
895            repeat scan pattern page
896                    match "<PageType" blank*
897                            ((lookahead not ">") any)*=type ">"
898                        repeat scan pattern type
899                            match "BodyPage"
900                                        set body to true
901                                        set masters to false
902                                        set reference to false
903
904                            match "ReferencePage"
905                                        set body to false
906                                        set masters to false
907                                        set reference to true
908
909                                        ; contains the conditional text
910                            match  "HiddenPage"      ; hidden pages
911                                        set body to false
912                                        set masters to true
913                                        set reference to false
914
915                            match  "MasterPage"
916                                        set body to false
917                                        set masters to true
918                                        set reference to false
919
920                            match any
921                                    ;
922                    again
923
924            ; TextRect's are uniquely identified and are tied
925            ; to a specific type of a page, the only pages we
926            ; need to convert are BodyPages and potentially hidden
927            ; with conditional text
```

FIGURE 7-23. TBLCNT.XOM PROGRAM FILE (CONTINUED)

```
928
929                     match "<TextRect" blank*
930                                ((lookahead not eoTxtR) any)*=rect
931                                eoTxtR
932                        repeat scan pattern rect
933                                match "<ID" blank* digit+=id ">"
934                                        set new TRid-shelf to
935                                                "master %x(id)"
936                                                when active masters
937                                        set new TRid-shelf to
938                                                "body %x(id)"
939                                                when active body
940                                        set new TRid-shelf to
941                                                "reference %x(id)"
942                                                when active reference
943
944                             match any
945                                        ;
946                        again
947
948                match any
950         again
951
952
953
954  ; Textflow contains the body/text of the document.
955  ; There are mulitiple textflows
956  find line-start "<TextFlow" EOL
957                ((lookahead not eoTxtF ) any)*=flow  eoTxtF
958         ; need to sort out the Master page flows and Reference Pages
959
960         repeat scan pattern flow
961                        ; Footnotes are listed as part of the
962                        ; Textflow group
963                match "<Notes" white-space+
964                        ((lookahead not eoNts) any)*=notes eoNt
965                do when "%x(notes)" != ""
966                        put #ERROR "WARNING: Footnotes found: %
967                done
968                match "<Para" EOL
969                        ((lookahead not eoP) any)*=content eoP
970                process-para("%x(content)", 2, FALSE)
971
972                match any
973                        ;
974         again
975
```

FIGURE 7-23. TBLCNT.XOM PROGRAM FILE (CONTINUED)

```
976
977  ; Optional section, may not be in every document. Probably is
978  ; defined in the Print dialog when you can map objects to
979  ; Acrobat Bookmark items.
980  find line-start "<AcrobatElements" EOL
981                 ((lookahead not eoAcro ) any)*=catalog eoAcro
982        ;
983
984
985        ; Last line of a FrameMaker generated file
986  find line-start "# End of MIFFile" EOL
987        ;
988
989        ; Gather up any missed comments that might be added to the fi
990  find line-start "#"
991                 ((lookahead not "%n") any)*=comment EOL
992        ;
993
994  ;;;   END OF PROGRAM
```

FIGURE 7-23. TBLCNT.XOM PROGRAM FILE (CONTINUED)

The function process-xref() in Line 208 handles all cross-reference entries; they point at a cross-reference marker and usually contain some text from the object being referenced. You would think this would be a clean way to match values, but the text that is stored in the cross-reference is the text that was there when it was first created, and this information doesn't get updated.

process-string() in Line 231 is the base function for extracting information from the text strings. The MIF structure for a paragraph is as follows:

```
<Para

<ParaLine

        <String 'content here'>

        <XRef

                <XRefName 'name'>

        > # end of XRef

> # end of ParaLine

> # end of Para
```

A <Para ...> groups a single paragraph's worth of information together so that each line within the paragraph, <ParaLine ...>, can have its own content. Line 385 shows the function process-paraline(), which functions on this inner portion of the content. This is the other area where it is crucial to know if the text being processed is in the body of the document or the table header information. Line 453 introduces the function process-para(). This function addresses the line grouping tags, <Para ...>. There are flags set here so that individual lines can be merged together as a single line of text for our SGML output. It also handles some of the MIF shortcut methods for handling the textrectid and paragraph tags.

Line 583 introduces another new function, process-table-content(). This function extracts structural information about the rows and columns of a table, as well as the span information contained in the table header. In this section, I introduce my own tags for <'cell'>, <'row'>, <'end cell'>, etc. These tags will have to be handled just like the paragraph tagging that I applied.

process-tbl() on Line 633 has been expanded to find the table title, number of columns, column widths, head, and body. This function introduces my own tags of <'Num-cells'>, <'col-width'>, <'tbl-tag'>, <'thead'>, <'end thead'>, <'tbody'>, and <'end tbody'>.

Figure 7-24 shows the results of running:

```
c:> omni tblcnt.xom ch1.frm
```

In this final intermediate format, we have stripped the excess or unused portion of the MIF markup, translated many MIF special characters and SGML important characters, and positioned tables and figures into their proper positions. As explained above, there were several tags that I introduced into this simplified format; now these tags and the source tags need to be converted to SGML.

TEXT REMOVED HERE

```
<'Numbered'>2.\t
<'marker' mtype=xref idref=25541 label='2. asdk asdk asdk-asdk asdk, asdk asdk
asdk-sasdk basdk, asdk asdk asdk asdk.'>Amwyap aso 24-Zwaa Xvoawo, sx taa
lwat-aalatm kjp, pazx aso asszatxr mjaazy.
<'Numbered'>3.\t
Amwyap aso wyoawo pazx aso kwat-aalatm assovnsxr ljp kwo sxaapma ta qya okvkpo.
<'Body'>
Am kuaz aarqoaa aska aaa apmxao aso apatku xaxlna zq aaaa 24-Awaa Xvoawo.  Apo Ram
Ytkwytxr Mnkaaa, wynjapn sx aso VUjxap8260 Aatanqsxr Ram krxooa, lap zazatnon pya
assa aaaazap.<'fnt ang' 'Italic'><'fnt end'>
<'Heading1'>
Aatmt Sua<'marker' mtype=index label='asdk asdk'><'marker' mtype=index
label='asdk asdk'>aluvkatyy
<'BodyAfterHead'>
<'xref' idref=13202 label='Table 3-1. asdk asdk asdk asdk '>Table 2<'xref-end'>
yaawsxpa aso aapza ypmnaalaa az nxxzwoap aso sxaaluvkatyy zq aaaa xyoawo.  Sm aaa
lap pkvsvska atas sxaaluvsxr VUjxap8260 wyoawoa, aap assa alkuo ka l lqomtvsaa.
Zasoaatap, mxyaawa aso apwkrxooa zq assa nqkyapa.<'table' id=9>
TBL9
<'Num-Cols' 3>
<'col-width' 0.5">
<'col-width' 2.59375">
<'col-width' 1.625">
<'TableTitle'>TABLE 2.
<'marker' mtype=xref idref=13202 label='Table 3-1. asdk asdk asdk asdk
'>Vzznnnaapa qya Nuxzwoatxr <'marker' mtype=index label='asdk asdk'><'marker'
mtype=index label='asdk asdk'>Suaaluvkatyy<'fnt IconAnchor'><'fnt end'><variable
found>'thead'>
<'row'>
<'cell'>
<'CellHeading'>
Aapz<'end cell'>
<'cell'>
<'CellHeading'>
Azznnnaap<'end cell'>
<'cell'>
<'CellHeading'>
Ampoapxnn<'end cell'>
<'end row'>
<'end thead'>
<'tbody'>
```

TEXT REMOVED HERE

FIGURE 7-24. TBLCNT.XOM SAMPLE OUTPUT

CONVERT INTERMEDIATE FORMAT TO SGML

This conversion will map MIF styles and character formats to SGML tags. The structure within OmniMark that I will use is the keyed shelf that I introduced earlier. The key or label will be the MIF tag and the contents will be the SGML or code block that should be used to process that tag. I'm also going to separate the mapping of the information from the base program and create a separate file that will be easily maintained away from the code. This should allow a production conversion shop to find new tags in the source file and map them to the proper SGML. This should also keep the OmniMark programmer from having to get involved until there is a change in the DTD or some new bizarre combination of occurrences appears (which always happens).

The first step in creating this program is to determine the base set of MIF styles that are needed. To do this, I run all the files in our sample document and sort the output to remove any duplicate values. That output is shown in Figure 7-25.

```
Char: 'BulletSymbol'        Style: Body               Style: Head2fine
Char: 'Callout'             Style: BodyAfterHead      Style: Headfine
Char: 'ChapterNumber'       Style: Bodyfine           Style: Heading1
Char: 'Emphasis'            Style: Bulleted           Style: Heading2
Char: 'EquationNumber'      Style: BulletedCont       Style: HeadingRunIn
Char: 'EquationVariables'   Style: Caution            Style: ManualTitle
Char: 'FirstLetterTitle'    Style: CellBody           Style: Note
Char: 'PageNumber'          Style: CellHeading        Style: Numbered
Char: 'StepNumber'          Style: CellList           Style: Numbered1
                            Style: ChapterNumber      Style: NumberedCont
                            Style: ChapterNumber2     Style: ScreenText2
                            Style: ChapterTitle       Style: SubTitle
                            Style: ChapterTitlenoNum  Style: SystemOutput
                            Style: DocInfo            Style: TableFootnote
                            Style: Equation           Style: TableTitle
                            Style: ExampleHead        Style: varCellList
                            Style: Extract            Style: zzFooterLeft
                            Style: Figure             Style: zzFooterRight
                            Style: Footnote
```

FIGURE 7-25. BASE STYLES LIST

The first step is to build the mapping file and OmniMark routine that will read this information in and then retrieve the information that the rest of the program will need. The mapping file will have the following format:

```
[section label]
```

```
; anything following a semicolon is a comment,
blank lines are ok
```

```
'stylename' omnimark-code-name
```
Figure 7-26 illustrates the complete mapping file.

```
 1   ; file imtags2SGML.xin
 2   ; This file lists the known MIF object types that have information
 3   ; useful in a conversion to SGML. The format of this file is as follo
 4   ;
 5   ; [section label]              = label is in []'s
 6   ; 'MIF string'        sgml_tag  = this maps the string in '' to t
 7   ;                                  SGML element sgml_tag or labeled
 8   ;                                  section in the processing
 9   ;                                       OmniMark program
10
11
12   [Character Tags]
13   'fnt'                          process
14   'BulletSymbol'                 bullet-sym
15   'Callout'                      ignore
16   'ChapterNumber'                ignore
17   'Emphasis'                     italics
18   'EquationNumber'               ignore
19   'EquationVariables'            ignore
20   'FirstLetterTitle'             ignore
21   'IconAnchor'                   ignore
22   'PageNumber'                   ignore
23   'StepNumber'                   ignore
24   'Trademark'                    ignore
25   'Superscript'                  footnote
26   'widetitle'                    ignore
27   'Emphasis-Bold'
28   'UserInput'
29   'fSystemOutput'
30   'PathName'
31   'varEmphasis'
32
33
34   [Paragraph Tags]
35   'Anchor'                       ignore
36   'Body'                         paragraph
37   'BodyAfterHead'                paragraph
38   'Bodyfine'                     paragraph
39   'Bullet Dash'                  bullet2
40   'Bulleted'                     bullet1
41   'BulletedCont'                 para-list
42   'Caution'                      caution
43   'CellBody'                     paragraph
44   'CellHeading'                  paragraph
45   'CellList'                     paragraph
46   'ChapterNumber'                chapter-num
```

FIGURE 7-26. IMTAGS2SGML.XIN PROGRAM FILE

```
47   'ChapterNumber2'              chapter-num
48   'ChapterTitle'               chapter-title
49   'ChapterTitlenoNum'          chapter-title
50   'DocInfo'                    docinfo
51   'Equation'                   ignore
52   'ExampleHead'                example
53   'Extract'                    ignore
54   'Figure'                     fig-title
55   'Footnote'                   tbl-footnote
56   'Head2fine'                  head2
57   'Headfine'                   head1
58   'Heading1'                   head1
59   'Heading2'                   head2
60   'HeadingRunIn'               head3
61   'ManualTitle'                docinfo
62   'Note'                       note
63   'Numbered'                   list1
64   'Numbered1'                  list1
65   'NumberedCont'               para-list
66   'ScreenText2'                user-entry
67   'SubTitle'                   docinfo
68   'SystemOutput'               user-entry
69   'TableFootnote'              tbl-footnote
70   'TableTitle'                 title
71   'varCellList'                paragraph
72   'zzFooterLeft'               ignore
73   'zzFooterRight'              ignore
74   ;
75   'TitleBook'                  ignore
76   'Copyright'                  ignore
77   'ScreenText'                 user-entry
78
79
80   ; Markup created by the MIF conversion process
81
82   'Num-Cols'                        num-cols
83   'cell'                            cell
84   'col-width'                       col-width
85   'end cell'                        end-cell
86   'end row'                         end-row
87   'end table'                       end-table
88   'end tbody'                       end-tbody
89   'end thead'                       end-thead
90   'graphic'                         graphic
```

FIGURE 7-26. IMTAGS2SGML.XIN PROGRAM FILE (CONTINUED)

```
91    'marker'                      marker
92    'row'                         row
93    'table'                       table
94    'tbl-tag'                     ignore
95    'tbody'                       tbody
96    'thead'                       thead
97    'xref'                        xref
98    'xref-end'                    xref-end
99
```

FIGURE 7-26. IMTAGS2SGML.XIN PROGRAM FILE (CONTINUED)

Paragraph tags or styles will have the names given to them in
FrameMaker; character formats will be output as 'fnt char-name', basic
bold/italics changes will be written as 'fnt wt', 'fnt ang', and font changes
will be 'fnt fam'. The mapping file, imtags2sgml.xin, now looks like Figure
7-26 with OmniMark code names that I created.

Notice the 'ignore' code name. Not all of the font or paragraph styles may
need to be managed. This may occur for a couple of reasons. There may be
old tags in the catalog that are no longer used, or there may be elements
on the page (master page) that are not needed.

The next step is to write the code that will read into the mapping file.
readmap.xom, shown in Figure 7-27, provides the code to read the file and
verify that the information was properly read and formatted.

Line 5 creates a variable in which to store the name of the mapfile to be
read by this program. By placing this here, rather than just using the filename somewhere else in the program, it is easier to find and change if
needed. Lines 8 and 10 create the shelves that will hold the paragraph
tags and character formats.

Line 15 defines the function test-map(). This function uses a temporary
variable to hold the key of each shelf item as the shelves are read with the
repeat over. .. again OmniMark structure. This function's sole purpose is
to verify that this code is functioning properly. Notice the halt statement
on Line 26. Again, because this program doesn't require a source input
file, we have to tell OmniMark when to stop processing; otherwise, it will
wait for the end of a source file to terminate.

This program doesn't require a file for input, so all the action occurs in the
find-start at Line 29. The first step is to remove the initial items on the
two shelves that were created when the shelves were declared.

Line 36 reads the map file with a repeat scan ... again structure. This repeat structure matches the labels to indicate which shelf the tag belongs on, reads and discards any comments or spaces, and finally matches the tags read and code names.

Figure 7-28 shows the results of running:

```
c:> omni readmap.xom
```

```
 1  cross-translate
 2
 3  ; file readmap.xom
 4
 5  global stream map-file initial {"imtags2sgml.xin"}
 6
 7
 8  global stream para-tag-shelf variable          ; Following shelves will
 9                                                 ; contain
10  global stream char-tag-shelf variable          ; the MIF to processing
11                                                 ; mapping for each type
12                                                 ; of MIF:
13
14
15  define function test-map () as
16  local stream temp
17  ; Now prove that you got all the information and it is properly stored
18          repeat over para-tag-shelf
19                  set temp to key of para-tag-shelf
20                  output "PT: %g(temp), %g(para-tag-shelf)%n"
21          again
22          repeat over char-tag-shelf
23                  set temp to key of char-tag-shelf
24                  output "CT: %g(temp), %g(char-tag-shelf)%n"
25          again
26  halt                     ; required because this program doesn't
27                           ; require an input file
28
29  find-start
30  local switch para-tags
31  local switch char-tags
32
33          clear stream para-tag-shelf
34          clear stream char-tag-shelf
35
36          repeat scan file "%g(map-file)"
37                           ; found a comment or empty text line in input
38                           ; do nothing
39                  match line-start [";\_"]
40                           ((lookahead not "%n") any)* "%n"
```

FIGURE 7-27. READMAP.XOM PROGRAM FILE

```
41                        ;
42
43                             ; find the map file section label
44          match line-start "[" ((lookahead not "]") any)*=type "]"
45                        deactivate para-tags
46                        deactivate char-tags
47                        repeat scan pattern type
48                             match "Character"
49                                     activate char-tags
50                             match "Paragraph"
51                                     activate para-tags
52                             match any
53                                     ;
54                        again
55
56          match line-start "'" ((lookahead not "'") any)*=mif
57                        "'" blank*
58                        ((lookahead not
59                             ("%n" or blank or ";"))
60                             any)*=convert
61                        ((lookahead not
62                             ("%n" )) any-text)* "%n"
63                             ; catch any comments
64
65                        do when active para-tags
66                             set new para-tag-shelf key "%x(mif)"
67                                     to "%x(convert)"
68                        else when active char-tags
69                             set new char-tag-shelf key "%x(mif)"
70                                     to "%x(convert)"
71                        else
72                             output "ERROR - no shelf open!%n"
73                        done
74
75          match blank* "%n"
76                        ; ends of line match
77      again
78
79      test-map()
```

FIGURE 7-27. READMAP.XOM PROGRAM FILE (CONTINUED)

```
PT: end tbody, end-tbody
PT: end thead, end-thead
PT: file, file-start
PT: graphic, graphic
PT: marker, marker
PT: row, row
PT: table, table
PT: tbl-tag, ignore
PT: tbody, tbody
PT: thead, thead
PT: xref, xref
PT: xref-end, xref-end
CT: fnt BulletSymbol, bullet-sym
CT: fnt Callout, ignore
CT: fnt ChapterNumber, ignore
CT: fnt Emphasis, italics
CT: fnt EquationNumber, ignore
CT: fnt EquationVariables, ignore
CT: fnt FirstLetterTitle, ignore
CT: fnt PageNumber, ignore
CT: fnt StepNumber, ignore
CT: fnt Trademark, ignore
CT: fnt ang, angle
CT: fnt fam, family
CT: fnt wt, weight
```

FIGURE 7-28. READMAP.XOM SAMPLE OUTPUT

im2sgml.xom in Figure 7-29 presents the intermediate markup format to SGML. Let's start examining this program at Line 471. This is the find rule that identifies the markup in the source file and then tries to map that markup to values already read in from the imtags2sgml.xin file. The MIF markup tag is identified by the find rule, along with any additional content that may be included in the tag. This MIF tag is then handed to the function find-tagtype(). This function, on Line 107, matches the tag to the key of the paragraph or character shelf.

Continuing on Line 484, the program either processes the tag in the paragraph portion of the do when ... else ... done structure or handles the character tag in the else portion. It is at this point that the different code names in the mapping file are referenced. To start coding this section, I sorted all my initial code names and created empty else when structures that I then populated as I started to code the different sections. I also handled two possible error conditions. There is the very likely occurrence of new tags being found in the source. These are reported by the find-tag-type() function. The other condition is that a new code name is introduced into the map file. This could occur because of a type in a name, or there could be a need for a new code block.

```
1   cross-translate
2
3   ; file im2sgml.xom
4   ; This file reads in the modified MIF intermediate file format
5   ; and converts the intermediate tags to proper SGML structures.
6
7   global stream map-file initial {"imtags2sgml.xin"}
8
9
10  global stream para-tag-shelf variable          ; Following shelves wil
11                                                  ; contain
12  global stream char-tag-shelf variable          ; the MIF to processing
13                                                  ; mapping for each type
14                                                  ; of MIF:
15  global stream open-list variable
16  global stream open-font variable
17  global stream docinfo variable
18
19  global stream tag-name initial {""}
20  global stream tag-content initial {""}
21
22
23
24  global switch head1
25  global switch head2
26  global switch head3
27  global switch head4
28  global switch headexample
29
30  global switch bullet-lev1
31  global switch bullet-lev2
32  global switch number-lev1
33
34  global switch found-graphic
35
36
37
38
39
40
41  define function push-open-list (value stream CLOSE-TAG,
42                                  value stream TYPE) as
43      set new open-list to "%g(CLOSE-TAG) %g(TYPE)"
44  ; end of function pop-open-list()
45
```

FIGURE 7-29. IM2SGML.XOM PROGRAM FILE

```
46
47
48
49
50
51
52   define function pop-close-list as
53          do when open-list is attached
54                  do when number of open-list >= 1
55                          repeat scan "%g(open-list)"
56                                  match "<" ((lookahead not ">")
57                                                  any)*=pcl-tag ">"
58                                          output "<%x(pcl-tag)>%n"
59                                  match blank+ any*=pcl-type
60                                          do when "%x(pcl-type)"
61                                                          = "bull1"
62                                                  deactivate bullet-lev1
63                                          else when "%x(pcl-type)"
64                                                          = "bull1"
65                                                  deactivate bullet-lev2
66                                          else when "%x(pcl-type)"
67                                                          = "num1"
68                                                  deactivate number-lev1
69                                          done
70                          again
71                          remove stream open-list
72                  done
73          done
74   ; end of function pop-close-list()
75
76
77   define function close-all-lists as
78
79          do when active bullet-lev1
80                  pop-close-list
81          done
82
83          do when active bullet-lev2
84                  pop-close-list
85          done
86
87          do when active number-lev1
88                  pop-close-list
89          done
90
91   ; end of function close-all-lists()
92
93
94
95
```

FIGURE 7-29. IM2SGML.XOM PROGRAM FILE (CONTINUED)

```
 96  define function pop-close-font as
 97          do when open-font is attached
 98                  output "%g(open-font)" when number of open-font >= 1
 99                  remove stream open-font
100          done
101  ; end of function pop-close-font()
102
103
104
105          ; Look for the read in MIFtag and determine if it
106          ; is in the mapped tree.
107  define function find-tagtype (value stream MIFtag,
108                                  modifiable stream TAG-TYPE,
109                                  modifiable stream PROCESS-TYPE ) as
110  local switch tag-found initial {FALSE}
111
112          set TAG-TYPE to "paragraph"  when MIFtag != "fnt"
113          set TAG-TYPE to "character" when MIFtag = "fnt"
114
115          do when TAG-TYPE = "paragraph"
116                  repeat over para-tag-shelf
117                          do when key of para-tag-shelf = UL"%g(MIFtag)"
118                                  set tag-found to TRUE
119                                  set PROCESS-TYPE to para-tag-shelf
120                                  exit
121                          done
122                  again
123                  pop-close-font
124          else
125                  repeat over char-tag-shelf
126                          do when key of char-tag-shelf = UL"%g(MIFtag)"
127                                  set tag-found to TRUE
128                                  set PROCESS-TYPE to char-tag-shelf
129                                  exit
130                          done
131                  again
132          done
133
134          put #CONSOLE "ERROR: Undefined tag name '%g(MIFtag)'%n" when
135                  not active tag-found
136
137  ; end function find-tagtype()
138
139
140
141          ; Following function is only used to test the reading of
142          ; the mif to code map file
143  define function test-map () as
144  local stream temp
```

FIGURE 7-29. IM2SGML.XOM PROGRAM FILE (CONTINUED)

```
145  ; Now prove that you got all the information and it is properly stored
146          repeat over para-tag-shelf
147                  set temp to key of para-tag-shelf
148                  output "PT: %g(temp), %g(para-tag-shelf)%n"
149          again
150          repeat over char-tag-shelf
151                  set temp to key of char-tag-shelf
152                  output "CT: %g(temp), %g(char-tag-shelf)%n"
153          again
154  halt                        ; required because this program doesn't
155                              ; require an input file
156  ; end of function test-map()
157
158
159
160          ; there are 9 types of markers defined for MIF
161  define function process-markers (value stream TAG-CONT) as
162  local stream marker-label initial {""}
163  local stream marker-type initial {""}
164  local stream marker-id initial {""}
165
166          repeat scan "%g(TAG-CONT)"
167                          ; headers -> ignore
168                  match ("mtype=header1" or "mtype=header2")
169                  match "mtype=index"              ; Index item
170                          set marker-type to "index"
171                  match "mtype=comment"            ; Comment item
172                  match "mtype=subject"            ; subject item
173                  match "mtype=author"             ; author item
174                  match "mtype=glossary"           ; glossary item
175                  match "mtype=equation"           ; equation item
176                  match "mtype=hypertext"          ; hypertext item
177                  match "mtype=type" digit+        ;  item location
178                  match "mtype=conditional"        ; conditional item loc
179                  match "mtype=xref"               ; xref item
180                          set marker-type to "xref"
181                  match "label='" ((lookahead not "'") any)*=label "'"
182                          set marker-label to "%x(label)"
183                  match "idref=" digit+=id blank*
184                          set marker-id to "%x(id)"
185                  match any
186                          ;
187          again
188          do when stream marker-type = "index"
189                  output "%n<indexitem text=%"%g(marker-label)%">%n"
190                          when "%g(marker-label)" != ""
191          done
192          do when stream marker-type = "xref"
193                  output "%n<marker id=%"f%g(marker-id)%">%n"
```

FIGURE 7-29. IM2SGML.XOM PROGRAM FILE (CONTINUED)

```
194        done
195  ; end of function process-marker()
196
197
198  define function push-close-font (value stream CLOSE-TAG) as
199        set new open-font to "%g(CLOSE-TAG)"
200  ; end of function push-close-font()
201
202
203
204  define function process-font (value stream PROCESS-TYPE,
205                                value stream FNT-CONTENT) as
206  local stream tag initial {""}
207  local stream wt initial {""}
208  local stream ang initial {""}
209  local stream fam initial {""}
210
211        pop-close-font
212
213
214        repeat scan FNT-CONTENT
215              match blank*
216                    ;
217              match "tag='" ((lookahead not "'") any)*=tag "'"
218                    set buffer tag to "%x(tag)"
219              match "wt='" ((lookahead not "'") any)*=wt "'"
220                    set buffer wt to "%x(wt)"
221              match "ang='" ((lookahead not "'") any)*=ang "'"
222                    set buffer ang to "%x(ang)"
223              match "fam='" ((lookahead not "'") any)*=fam "'"
224                    set buffer fam to "%x(fam)"
225        again
226
227
228
229              ; Look at the tag information first, then look at
230              ; the components of the font information otherwise
231        do when tag = "BulletSymbol"
232              next group is symbol
233
234        else when tag = "symbol"
235              next group is symbol
236
237        else when tag = "Callout"
238              ; ignore
239        else when tag = "ChapterNumber"
240              ; ignore
241        else when tag = "Emphasis"
242              output "<emphasis slant=%"italic%">"
```

FIGURE 7-29. IM2SGML.XOM PROGRAM FILE (CONTINUED)

```
243                          push-close-font ("</emphasis>")
244
245          else when tag = "EquationNumber"
246                    ; ignore
247          else when tag = "EquationVariables"
248                    ; ignore
249          else when tag = "FirstLetterTitle"
250                    ; ignore
251          else when tag = "IconAnchor"
252                    ; ignore
253          else when tag = "PageNumber"
254                    ; ignore
255          else when tag = "StepNumber"
256                    ; ignore
257          else when tag = "Trademark"
258                    ; ignore
259
260          else when tag = "Superscript"
261                    output "<emphasis raised=%"super%">"
262                    push-close-font ("</emphasis>")
263
264          else when tag = "widetitle"
265                    ; ignore
266          else when tag = "Emphasis-Bold"
267                    output "<emphasis slant=%"italic%" weight=%"bold%">"
268                    push-close-font ("</emphasis>")
269
270          else when tag = "UserInput"
271                        output "<emphasis asis=%"asis%">"
272                        push-close-font ("</emphasis>")
273
274          else when tag = "SystemOutput"
275                        output "<emphasis asis=%"asis%">"
276                        push-close-font ("</emphasis>")
277
278          else when tag = "PathName"
279                    ; ignore
280          else when tag = "varEmphasis"
281                    ; ignore
282          else when tag = ""
283                    do when (wt = UL"Bold" and
284                                 (ang = UL"Italic" or ang = UL"Oblique"))
285                        output "<emphasis slant=%"italic%"
weight=%"bold%">"
286                        push-close-font ("</emphasis>")
287                    else when wt = UL"Bold"
288                        output "<emphasis weight=%"bold%">"
289                        push-close-font ("</emphasis>")
290                    else when (ang = UL"Italic" or ang = UL"oblique")
```

FIGURE 7-29. IM2SGML.XOM PROGRAM FILE (CONTINUED)

```
291                         output "<emphasis slant=%"italic%">"
292                         push-close-font ("</emphasis>")
293                 else when fam = UL"Courier New"
294                             output "<emphasis asis=%"asis%">"
295                             push-close-font ("</emphasis>")
296
297             done
298        else
299                put #CONSOLE "ERROR: missing FNTtag: %g(FNT-CONTENT)%n"
300        done
301  ;;;; end of function process-font()
302
303
304  ;;;;;;;;;;;;;;;;;;;;;;;;;;;;;;;
305  ;
306  ;   Start of File Processing
307  ;
308  ;;;;;;;;;;;;;;;;;;;;;;;;;;;;;;;
309
310  find-start
311  local switch para-tags
312  local switch char-tags
313
314        clear stream para-tag-shelf
315        clear stream char-tag-shelf
316
317        deactivate found-graphic
318
319
320        put #CONSOLE "Processing started ...%n"
321
322        repeat scan file "%g(map-file)"
323                      ; found a comment or empty text line in input
324                      ; do nothing
325                 match line-start [";\_"]
326                            ((lookahead not "%n") any)* "%n"
327                      ;
328
329                      ; find the map file section label
330                 match line-start "[" ((lookahead not "]") any)*=type "]"
331                      deactivate para-tags
332                      deactivate char-tags
333                      repeat scan pattern type
334                          match "Character"
335                                  activate char-tags
336                          match "Paragraph"
337                                  activate para-tags
338                          match any
339                              ;
```

FIGURE 7-29. IM2SGML.XOM PROGRAM FILE (CONTINUED)

```
340                        again
341
342            match line-start "'" ((lookahead not "'") any)*=mif
343                            "'" blank*
344                            ((lookahead not
345                                ("%n" or blank or ";"))
346                                any)*=convert
347                            ((lookahead not
348                                ("%n" )) any-text)* "%n"
349                                ; catch any comments
350
351               do when active para-tags
352                       set new para-tag-shelf key "%x(mif)"
353                            to "%x(convert)"
354               else when active char-tags
355                       set new char-tag-shelf key "%x(mif)"
356                            to "%x(convert)"
357               else
358                       output "ERROR - no shelf open!%n"
359               done
360
361            match blank* "%n"
362                    ; ends of line match
363        again
364
365
366        output "<!DOCTYPE book PUBLIC "
367        output "%"-//SAW//DTD SGML at Work Sample DTD//EN%" [%n"
368        output "<!NOTATION GIF SYSTEM>%n"
369        output "<!NOTATION TIFF SYSTEM>%n"
370        output "<!NOTATION TIF SYSTEM>%n"
371        output "<!NOTATION CGM SYSTEM>%n"
372
373        output "]>%n"
374        output "<book "
375
376        output referent "BOOKINFO-STUFF"
377        set referent "BOOKINFO-STUFF" to ""
378
379        output ">%n"
380
381        output referent "DOCINFO-STUFF"
382        set referent "DOCINFO-STUFF" to ""
383
384        next group is finding-tags
385
386
387
388  ;;;;;;;;;;;;;;;;;;;;;;;;;;;;;;;
```

FIGURE 7-29. IM2SGML.XOM PROGRAM FILE (CONTINUED)

```
389  ;
390  ;   End of File Processing
391  ;
392  ;;;;;;;;;;;;;;;;;;;;;;;;;;;;;;;;;;;
393
394  find-end
395  local stream temp
396  local stream value
397
398          close-all-lists
399
400          output "%n</example>" when active headexample
401          output "%n</head>" when active head4
402          output "%n</head>" when active head3
403          output "%n</head>" when active head2
404          output "%n</head>" when active head1
405
406
407          ; build up the docinfo block of information as found in
408          set temp to "<cover><title>"
409          do when stream docinfo has key "title"
410                  set value to docinfo key "title"
411          else
412                  set value to ""
413          done
414
415          set temp to "%g(temp)%g(value)</title><subtitle>"
416          do when docinfo has key "subtitle"
417                  set value to docinfo key "subtitle"
418          else
419                  set value to ""
420          done
421
422
423          set temp to "%g(temp)%g(value)</subtitle></cover>%n"
424
425          set temp to "%g(temp)%n<copyright>"
426
427          set referent "DOCINFO-STUFF" to "%g(temp)"
428
429
430          set temp to ""
431
432          do when stream docinfo has key "pubdate"
433                  set value to docinfo key "pubdate"
434                  set temp to "PubDate=%"%g(value)%""
435          else
436                  set value to ""
437          done
```

FIGURE 7-29. IM2SGML.XOM PROGRAM FILE (CONTINUED)

```
438
439        do when docinfo has key "partno"
440                set value to docinfo key "partno"
441                set temp to "%g(temp) PartNo=%"%g(value)%""
442        else
443                set value to ""
444        done
445
446        set referent "BOOKINFO-STUFF" to "%g(temp)"
447
448        output "</book>%n"
449
450
451
452
453
454
455  put #CONSOLE "Conversion complete ...%n"
456
457
458  ;;;;;;;;;;;;;;;;;;;;;;;;;
459  ;
460  ;   Main program group
461  ;
462  ;;;;;;;;;;;;;;;;;;;;;;;;;
463
464  group finding-tags
465
466
467
468        ; main program finds all the markup in the source file
469        ; and then verifies it is in the map file and then executes
470        ; the code indicated
471  find "<" ((lookahead not "'") any)*=tag "'"
472             ((lookahead not  ">") any)*=content ">" "%n"*
473
474  local stream tag-type
475  local stream processing-type
476
477        set buffer tag-type to ""
478        set buffer processing-type to ""
479        set tag-name to pattern tag
480        set tag-content to pattern content
481
482        find-tagtype("%x(tag)", tag-type, processing-type )
483
484        do when tag-type = "paragraph"
485
486                do when "%g(processing-type)" = "chapter-title"
```

FIGURE 7-29. IM2SGML.XOM PROGRAM FILE (CONTINUED)

```
487                        output "<body><section><title>%n"
488                        ; next group is find-chapter-title
489                        next group is find-title
490
491            else when "%g(processing-type)" = "para-list"
492                        output "<para>%n"
493
494            else when "%g(processing-type)" = "paragraph"
495                        close-all-lists
496                        output "<para>%n"
497
498            else when "%g(processing-type)" = "example"
499                        close-all-lists
500
501                        output "%n</example>" when active headexample
502                        deactivate headexample
503                        output "%n</head>" when active head4
504                        deactivate head4
505                        output "%n</head>" when active head3
506                        deactivate head3
507                        output "%n</head>" when active head2
508                        deactivate head2
509                        output "%n</head>" when active head1
510                        deactivate head1
511
512                        activate headexample
513                        output "<example>%n<title>"
514
515            else when "%g(processing-type)" = "head1"
516                        close-all-lists
517
518                        output "%n</example>" when active headexample
519                        deactivate headexample
520                        output "%n</head>" when active head4
521                        deactivate head4
522                        output "%n</head>" when active head3
523                        deactivate head3
524                        output "%n</head>" when active head2
525                        deactivate head2
526                        output "%n</head>" when active head1
527                        deactivate head1
528
529                        activate head1
530                        output "<head>%n<title>"
531            else when "%g(processing-type)" = "head2"
532                        close-all-lists
533
534                        output "%n</example>" when active headexample
535                        deactivate headexample
```

FIGURE 7-29. IM2SGML.XOM PROGRAM FILE (CONTINUED)

```
536                        output "%n</head>" when active head4
537                        deactivate head4
538                        output "%n</head>" when active head3
539                        deactivate head3
540                        output "%n</head>" when active head2
541                        deactivate head2
542
543                        activate head2
544                        output "<head>%n<title>"
545            else when "%g(processing-type)" = "head3"
546                        close-all-lists
547
548                        output "%n</example>" when active headexample
549                        deactivate headexample
550                        output "%n</head>" when active head4
551                        deactivate head4
552                        output "%n</head>" when active head3
553                        deactivate head3
554
555                        activate head3
556                        output "<head>%n<title>"
557            else when "%g(processing-type)" = "head4"
558                        close-all-lists
559
560                        output "%n</example>" when active headexample
561                        deactivate headexample
562                        output "%n</head>" when active head4
563                        deactivate head4
564
565                        activate head4
566                        output "%n<head>%n<title>"
567            else when "%g(processing-type)" = "title"
568                        output "<title>"
569                        next group is find-title
570
571            else when "%g(processing-type)" = "marker"
572                        process-markers("%g(tag-content)")
573
574            else when "%g(processing-type)" = "xref"
575                        repeat scan "%g(tag-content)"
576                                match "idref=" digit+=id
577                                        output "<xref refid=%"f%x(id)%""
578                                match any
579                                        ;
580                        again
581                        next group is find-xref
582
583            else when "%g(processing-type)" = "table"
584                        pop-close-list
```

FIGURE 7-29. IM2SGML.XOM PROGRAM FILE (CONTINUED)

```
585                             output "<table frame=%"all%">"
586
587             else when "%g(processing-type)" = "num-cols"
588                     repeat scan "%g(tag-content)"
589                             match digit+=num
590                                     output "<tgroup "
591                                     output "cols=%"%x(num)%" "
592                                     output "colsep=%"1%" "
593                                     output "rowsep=%"1%">%n"
594                             match any
595                                     ;
596                     again
597
598             else when "%g(processing-type)" = "col-width"
599                     repeat scan "%g(tag-content)"
600                             match blank* (digit+ "."? digit+)=width
601                                             any*=units
602                                     output "<colspec
603                                             colwidth=%"%x(width)"
604
605                                             repeat scan
606                                                     pattern units
607                                                     match "%""
608                                                         output "in"
609                                                     match any
610                                                         ;
611                                             again
612                                     output "%">%n"
613                             match any
614                                     ;
615                     again
616
617             else when "%g(processing-type)" = "thead"
618                     output "<thead>"
619
620             else when "%g(processing-type)" = "end-thead"
621                     output "</thead>"
622
623             else when "%g(processing-type)" = "tbody"
624                     output "<tbody>"
625
633                     output "<entry align=%"left%" valign=%"top%">"
634
635             else when "%g(processing-type)" = "end-cell"
636                     output "</entry>"
637
638             else when "%g(processing-type)" = "end-row"
639                     output "</row>"
640
```

FIGURE 7-29. IM2SGML.XOM PROGRAM FILE (CONTINUED)

```
641                  else when "%g(processing-type)" = "end-table"
642                         output "</tgroup></table>"
643
644                  else when "%g(processing-type)" = "tbl-footnote"
645                         output "<footnote>%n"
646
647                  else when "%g(processing-type)" = "user-entry"
648                         next group is find-user-entry
649
650                  else when "%g(processing-type)" = "graphic"
651                         output "<figure %g(tag-content)>%n"
652                         activate found-graphic
653
654                  else when "%g(processing-type)" = "tbl-title"
655                         ; next group is find-table-title
656                         output "<title>"
657                         next group is find-title
658
659                  else when "%g(processing-type)" = "fig-title"
660                         ; need to find the following figure caption
661                         ; information
662                         ; to go with the graphic, if it exists
663                         ; next group is find-fig-title
664                         output "<title>"
665                         next group is find-title
666
667                  else when "%g(processing-type)" = "bullet1"
668                         do when not active bullet-lev1
669                                output "<bullet-list>%n"
670                                activate bullet-lev1
671                                push-open-list("</bullet-list>%n",
"bull1")
672                         else when (active bullet-lev1 and active
bullet-lev2)
673                                ; return from a nested level 2 bullet
674                                pop-close-list
675                         done
676                         output "<item><para>"
677                         next group is find-bullet
678
679                  else when "%g(processing-type)" is equal "bullet2"
680                         do when not active bullet-lev2
681                                output "<bullet-list>%n"
682                                activate bullet-lev2
683                                push-open-list("</bullet-list>%n",
"bull2")
684                         done
685                         output "<item><para>"
686                         next group is find-bullet
```

FIGURE 7-29. IM2SGML.XOM PROGRAM FILE (CONTINUED)

```
687
688
689                 else when "%g(processing-type)" = "list1"
690                     do when not active number-lev1
691                             output "<number-list>%n"
692                             activate number-lev1
693                         push-open-list("</number-list>%n", "num1")
694                     done
695                     output "<item><para>"
696                     next  group is find-number
697
698                 else when "%g(processing-type)" = "caution"
699                     output "<caution>"
700                     next group is get-notice
701
702                 else when "%g(processing-type)" = "note"
703                     output "<note>"
704                     next group is get-notice
705
706                     ; gather the various tags of information, that
707                     ; should be used in the docinfo section at the
708                     ; beginning of the document.
709                 else when "%g(processing-type)" = "docinfo"
710                     next group is get-docinfo
711
712                 else when "%g(processing-type)" = "example"
713                     output "<example><title>%n"
714
715
716                 else when "%g(processing-type)" = "ignore"
717                     ;
718                 else
719                     put #CONSOLE "ERROR: unhandled :'%g(tag-name)'"
720                     put #CONSOLE "%g(processing-type)%n"
721             done
722
723         else when stream tag-type = "character"
724             process-font ("%g(processing-type)", "%g(tag-content)")
725
726     done
727
728
729
730
731  find "<variable found>"
732       ;
733
734
735
```

FIGURE 7-29. IM2SGML.XOM PROGRAM FILE (CONTINUED)

```
736
737
738  group get-notice
739          ; need to handle an empty notice where the next tag is a
740          ; tag and not a graphic
741
742  find ("Caution:\t" or "Note:\t")
743          next group is finding-tags
744
745
746
747
748
749
750
751
752
753
754  group find-bullet
755
756  find "\xd0 " "\t"
757          ;
758          next group is finding-tags
759
760  find "\xa5 " "\t"
761          ;
762          next group is finding-tags
763
764
765
766  group find-number
767
768  find "\t"* digit+ "." "\t"+
769          next group is finding-tags
770
771  find letter+ "." "\t"+
772          next group is finding-tags
773
774
775
776
777
778
779  group symbol
780
781  find "\xa5 " blank* "%n"?
782          output "&bull;"
783          next group is finding-tags
784
```

FIGURE 7-29. IM2SGML.XOM PROGRAM FILE (CONTINUED)

```
785   find "\xd2 " blank* "%n"?
786         output "&reg;"
787         next group is finding-tags
788
789   find "\xd3 " blank* "%n"?
790         output "&copy;"
791         next group is finding-tags
792
793   find "\xd4 " blank* "%n"?
794         output "&trade;"
795         next group is finding-tags
796
797   find "\x" ([digit or letter][digit or letter])=sym blank blank* "%n"?
798         output "**** Unmapped SYMBOL was HERE ****"
799         put #CONSOLE "Warning: Missing symbol \x%x(sym)%n"
800         next group is finding-tags
801
802
803
804
805
806
807   group get-docinfo
808
809   find "<'fnt' " ((lookahead not ">") any)* ">" blank*
810         ;
811
812   find "Part " ((lookahead not "%n") any)+=partno "%n"
813         new docinfo key "partno"
814         set docinfo to "%x(partno)"
815
816   find "Published " ((lookahead not "%n") any)+=date "%n"
817         new docinfo key "pubdate"
818         set docinfo to "%x(date)"
819
820
821   find ((lookahead not line-start "<") any)*=content
822   local stream text
823         set text to ""
824         repeat scan pattern content
825               match "&" ((lookahead not ";") any)*=type ";"
826                     do when pattern type = "space"
827                           set text to "%g(text) "
828                     else when pattern type = "retrn"
829                           set text to "%g(text) "
830                     done
831               match   "<'fnt' " ((lookahead not ">") any)* ">" blank*
832                     ;
833               match "%n"
```

FIGURE 7-29. IM2SGML.XOM PROGRAM FILE (CONTINUED)

```
834                             ;
835                 match  any-text=char
836                         set text to "%g(text)%x(char)"
837         again
838
839         do when "%g(tag-name)" = UL"ManualTitle"
840                 do when docinfo has key "title"
841                         set docinfo to "%g(text)"
842                 else
843                         new docinfo key "title"
844                         set docinfo to "%g(text)"
845                 done
846         else when "%g(tag-name)" = UL"subtitle"
847                 do when docinfo has key "subtitle"
848                         set docinfo to "%g(text)"
849                 else
850                         new docinfo key "subtitle"
851                         set docinfo to "%g(text)"
852                 done
853         done
854
855         next group is finding-tags
856
857
858
859
860
861
862  group find-user-entry
863
864  find ((lookahead not "<") any)*=content
865         output "<system>%n"
866         output "%x(content)"
867         output "</system>%n"
868         next group is finding-tags
869
870
871
872
873
874
875  group find-title
876
877
878  find "<'marker'" ((lookahead not ">") any)*=content ">"
879         process-markers("%x(content)")
880
881  find ((lookahead not "<'") any)*=text
882         output "%x(text)"
```

FIGURE 7-29. IM2SGML.XOM PROGRAM FILE (CONTINUED)

```
883
884   find ((lookahead not "<'marker") any)*=text
885         output "</title>%n"
886         next group is finding-tags
887         submit("%x(text)")
888         next group is finding-tags
889
890
891
892
893
894
895   group find-xref
896
897   find ((lookahead not "<'xref-end'>") any)*=previous "<'xref-end'>"
898         output " prev-label=%""
899         submit "%x(previous)"
900         output "%">%n"
901         next group is finding-tags
902
903
904
905
906
907
908   group #IMPLIED
909   ; all escaped ascii character values have a trailing blank that needs
910   ; to be matched and replaced by the entity being used.
911
912
913
914   find "\t"
915         output " "
916
917   find "\xd2 "
918         output "&ldquo;"
919
920   find "\xd3 "
921         output "&rdquo;"
922
923   find "\q"
924         output "&rsquo;"
925
926   find "\Q"
927         output "&lsquo;"
928
929   find "\xd5 "
930         output "&rsquo;"
931
```

FIGURE 7-29. IM2SGML.XOM PROGRAM FILE (CONTINUED)

```
932  find "\x8e "
933        output "&eacute;"
934
935  find "\x11 "
936        output " "
937
938  find "\xef "
939        output "&verbar;"
940
941  find "\>"
942        output "&gt;"
943
944  find line-start "TBL" digit+
945        ; remove this table tag information
946
947  find "\x08 "
948        output "&tab;"
949
950  find "\x09 "
951        output "&return;"
952
953  find "\x0a "
954        output "&return;"
955
956  find "\x10 "
957        output "&numsp;"
958
959  find "\x11 "
960        output " "
961
962  find "\x12 "
963        output " "
964
965  find "\x13 "
966        output " "
967
968  find "\x14 "
969        output " "
970
971  find "\x27 "
972        output "&rsquo;"
973
974  find "\x22 "
975        output "&quote;"
976
977  find "\xa0 "
978        output "&dagger;"
979
980  find "\xe0 "
```

FIGURE 7-29. IM2SGML.XOM PROGRAM FILE (CONTINUED)

```
981            output "&Dagger;"
982
983   find "\xd4 "
984            output "&lsquo;"
985
986   find "\xd5 "
987            output "&rsquo;"
988
989   find "\xd2 "
990            output "&ldquo;"
991
992   find "\xd3 "
993            output "&rdquo;"
994
995   find "\xa5 "
996            output "&bull;"
997
998   find "\xd0 "
999            output "&ndash;"
1000
1001  find "\xd1 "
1002           output "&mdash;"
1003
1004  find "\xaa "
1005           output "&trade;"
1006
1007  find "\xa9 "
1008           output "&copy;"
1009
1010  find "\xa8 "
1011           output "&reg;"
1012
1013  find "\xb1 "
1014           output "&plusmn;"
1015
1016
1017
1018  ;;;; END OF PROGRAM
~
```

FIGURE 7-29. IM2SGML.XOM PROGRAM FILE (CONTINUED)

The following objects are the most difficult to work with when trying to add intelligence to the markup by going up to SGML:

- Equations
- Tables
- Lists
- Graphics.

These are listed in relative difficulty, with equations being the worst case to deal with. The others, however, aren't far behind; each has its own unique problems. Equations (not that there are any in this sample document, and my program only warns of their existence in the source file if present) are difficult because of the complex markup, special line spacing, special characters, and font problems. Additionally, there hasn't really been a standard set for how/what should be captured in the SGML form.

Tables come in as a close second to equations. With the desktop publishing systems available, you can create very complex structures with spans, joins, and nested tables. Generally due to support in the editing and presentation tools, tables have been standardized on one or two markup sets (CALS being one of them). There is a great deal of controversy in the SGML community as to the proper way to handle tables. The real issues hinge on trying to capture the intended relationships between the various rows and columns, or just trying to mark up a table so it can be handled by the tools that are available. I advocate whatever works and gets the job done in a reasonable fashion; so in our sample DTD, I will map tables to CALS structure.

Lists are difficult to deal with because there is not an easy way to determine the end of a list, except at some very specific boundaries. If a list could only contain bulleted or numbered items, with the possibility of continuing paragraphs, there wouldn't be much of a problem. The problem with lists is introduced when you consider that graphics, tables, equations, screen examples, etc., are typically allowed to be within them. The additional paragraphs in a list commonly have a tag like para-list, and the main body has a tag like para or paragraph. There are unique tags to handle the formatting differences in a list from the body of the document. But, the other objects mentioned typically do not format differently, so they all have the same tag name.

We know that a list shouldn't carry across a heading or chapter boundary, so those are two easy places to test for and create the end tag for a list. But now, how do you handle a figure or table within a list? Maybe you can check for a para-list or list item immediately after the figure and output the close tag. That would be one solution; but, what happens when there are multiple unknown objects in a row before you find the next list item? This is information that I leave to the author to provide in the cleanup stage. By using an SGML editor, it is easy to cut and paste these objects into the correct position.

Graphics are difficult to work with due to the number of ways they can be built and incorporated into a document. This topic is discussed in more detail in the next chapter. For the conversion program, I have detected if the graphic is referenced in, the resolution or dpi of the image, and the overall size of the frame that it belongs in. This information is fairly easy to find in the markup and can be useful in trying to capture these objects later.

In Lines 491 and 494, you can see how the paragraph and paragraph in list are handled. I know that a para-list by definition is supposed to be in a list structure, so I don't want to close any open lists. A paragraph, on the other hand, is outside of a list, so any list that is open should be ended before the para tag is output.

Example and the four levels of heads on Lines 498, 515, 531, 545, and 557 are other places to close lists. Notice how nested heads are handled. The DTD allows any number of head elements to be nested within each other, with no way to specify that only four levels are supported. The place to test for the nesting level is in a program like this, or in a specific validation program that looks for these specific types of problems.

This program introduces the new OmniMark group features. The statement "next group is xxxx" tells OmniMark to finish the rule it is currently working in and then switch to the rules found below the group label "group xxxx." More than one group can be active at a time, and the group #IMPLIED is always active. This is a mechanism to toggle the type of processing that is occurring over the source input. It is also a context switch that allows you to handle the text stream differently whenever a condition is met. Groups are a very powerful feature; the only trick is to find the proper condition to toggle a group on and off. Usually it is easier to find the on switch, and more difficult to determine how to shut it off. The group find-title, Line 875, was one of the more difficult to work out in this program.

A title always starts with the <title> tag, but it isn't always terminated in the source stream. A title also allows markers and index items as well as special characters to occur. All of these must be taken into consideration and handled so the proper trigger can be found to switch the group context back or to something else.

On Line 887 I use the submit function. This allows me to send the block of text that I pulled out of the input stream with the single find rule. By resubmitting this text string, I can use this same program to restart and examine the content of matched text.

The group get-docinfo on Line 807 must store values that are found in several locations within the document and then output them close to the start of the document. OmniMark provides a feature called referents that allow you to place a marker in the output stream that you can later write to, as late as the end of the program. This group only finds the information that I want to use in other locations and stores it in several variables. The real work of managing the referents is in the find-start and find-end sections of this program. On Line 374 I output the starting portion of the book tag. I then output the referent BOOKINFO-STUFF immediately after that. In Line 377 I set that referent to null or an empty string. This makes sure that some value is written out to this location just in case I don't actually find any information that needs to be written out here. Line 379 then closes the book tag. Another referent is used to anchor or locate where the document or book title information will be written.

In the find-end starting at Line 409 I try to build an output string composed of the values found in the get-docinfo group and format it appropriately for its position in the document. I then re-output the string to the referent, hopefully with some real information. In the case of the <book> tag, I will output the two attributes; for the title, I will generate a <title> and <subtitle>. The last string output to a referent is the value that will appear in the output stream. Multiple strings written to the same referent don't add up; they replace the previous value completely.

NOTE: If you use referents, OmniMark creates a temporary file. This temporary file is usually written to the current file directly from the file in which you are running the program. This can be a problem if the directory is the CD-ROM, a full filesystem, or a directory you don't have permission to write in. There is a command line option for calling OmniMark that will write the file to the location specified. -temppfx pathname is the option to use in this case.

You will not be able to run this program with the OmniMark LE version that ships with this book. You'll have to take my word that the program presented here produces the output files located in the Conversions directory under sample, SGMLoutput.

Figure 7-30 shows the typical output of running the following:

```
omni im2sgml.xom ch2.sgm
```

```
<!DOCTYPE book PUBLIC "-//SAW//DTD SGML at Work Sample DTD//EN" [
<!NOTATION GIF SYSTEM>
<!NOTATION TIFF SYSTEM>
<!NOTATION TIF SYSTEM>
<!NOTATION CGM SYSTEM>
]>
<book >
<cover><title></title><subtitle></subtitle></cover>
<copyright>
<body><section><title>
\t
Tuaaluvsxr kwo Ywpalatxr aso Wvoawo
</title>
<para>
Apsa nqkyapa ooanatlna aso sxaaluvkatyy aaznnnaapa qya aso 24-Zwaa Xvoawo.
Ztokap apkm aso zapmjaatyylaa aaznnnaapa mnpyap ayalltsxr aso wyoawo.
<para>
Pva aaaa nxyapxtoxnn, ap rkap sxnuaoon k zatmt appoapxnn sxaaluvkatyy njao
(17-0033-0277).  Apsa njao vsaaa aso NOW aatanq apaatxra, 24-Awaa Xvoawo
wkwlpowoxa nxxwkwoa, WLJ oxosmjazaa lwo yasoa xyoawo sxqyaxkatyy. Atokap aazap
assa njao sx aso VUjxap8260 Aatanqsxr Ram krxooa tx aso Ampoapxnn Mgao kapk.
<para>
Apo apwkrxooa zq assa nqkyapa ooanatlna:
<bullet-list>
<item><para>
Azpmjaatyylaa Azznnnaapa
<item><para>
Avalltsxr Zzznnnaapa
<item><para>
Aatmt Suaaluvkatyy
```

TEXT REMOVED HERE

FIGURE 7-30. IM2SGML.XOM SAMPLE OUTPUT

I made several changes to the DTD to add some structures that were missing and also to give it a PUBLIC name, -//SAW//DTD SGML at Work Sample DTD//EN, which will make it easier to use the editing tools and run Omni-Mark in an SGML mode to validate our documents. You have the option of trying to use the SGML error messages from OmniMark to correct the markup, or as I'm recommending, using a native SGML editor to guide you through the cleanup and changes.

Validating the SGML Output

Now we have a first cut at our SGML output. You can use OmniMark to parse these documents and report any SGML problems. valid.xom, shown in Figure 7-31, doesn't create any output, but creates a lengthy report of SGML problems, as shown in Figure 7-32 after running the following:

omni valid.xom -library entities.xlr sample.dcl ch1.sgm

```
 1   ; file valid.xom
 2
 3   ; This program will generate no output, but
 4   ; will create a list of SGML errors and problems
 5   ; with the source file.
 6
 7
 8   down-translate
 9
10   element #implied
11           put #SUPPRESS "%c"
12
13   ;;; END OF PROGRAM
```

FIGURE 7-31. VALID.XOM PROGRAM FILE

The -library entities.xlr option on the command line tells Omni-Mark how to find our DTD and the various other files included in our DTD. See *Configuring OmniMark LE* in this chapter for an explanation of how to configure this file. A modified SGML declaration, Figure 7-33, is needed to validate our files because several of the element names are longer than eight characters.

```
OmniMark LE V3R0a
Copyright (c) 1988-1997 by OmniMark Technologies Corporation.
This is licensed software.  To view license,
or for product information and documentation: http://www.omnimark.com
Compiled 0 countable actions, limit = 200.
omnimark --
SGML Error (0259) on line 7 in file ch2.s:
In a start tag or ENTITY declaration, every required attribute must be
given a value.
In the start tag for element "BOOK", the REQUIRED attribute "PUBDATE" is
not specified.
omnimark --
SGML Error (0259) on line 7 in file ch2.s:
In a start tag or ENTITY declaration, every required attribute must be
given a value.
In the start tag for element "BOOK", the REQUIRED attribute "PARTNO" is
not specified.
omnimark --
SGML Error (0107) on line 11 in file ch2.s:
A start tag with a start tag minimization of minus ("-") must not be
omitted.
The element is "HEAD".
omnimark --
SGML Error (0107) on line 11 in file ch2.s:
A start tag with a start tag minimization of minus ("-") must not be
omitted.
The element is "TITLE".
```

FIGURE 7-32. VALID.XOM SAMPLE OUTPUT

You can run all the sample output files through valid.xom to get an idea of
the types of problems that are ahead. The files created by im2sgml.xom
are located on the CD-ROM in the conversion directory, under sample,
then SGMLoutput.

We could stop at this point and just start editing the files to do the final
cleanup, but there are a number of things that we can still automate to
help the cleanup process. The first is remove any special FrameMaker
characters. The ones that I found in the sample files include '\t' for a tab
and '\xa13 ', which is the en space. The program fixchars.xom in
Figure 7-34 provides this conversion. These characters were missed in the
first step because I matched some content characters in a find rule and did
not let them fall through the rest of the program.

```
 1   <!SGML  "ISO 8879:1986"
 2
 3   CHARSET
 4   BASESET "ISO 646-1983//CHARSET
 5    International Reference Version (IRV)//ESC 2/5 4/0"
 6   DESCSET
 7           0        9   UNUSED
 8           9        2   9
 9          11        2   UNUSED
10          13        1   13
11          14       18   UNUSED
12          32       95   32
13         127        1   UNUSED
14         128      128   "High-order characters"
15
16   CAPACITY SGMLREF
17           TOTALCAP        200000
18           ENTCAP           35000
19           ENTCHCAP         35000
20           ELEMCAP          35000
21           GRPCAP          150000
22           EXGRPCAP         35000
23           EXNMCAP          35000
24           ATTCAP           50000
25           ATTCHCAP         35000
26           AVGRPCAP         35000
27           NOTCAP           35000
28           NOTCHCAP         35000
29           IDCAP            35000
30           IDREFCAP         35000
31           MAPCAP           35000
32           LKSETCAP         35000
33           LKNMCAP          35000
34
35   SCOPE     DOCUMENT
36
37   SYNTAX
38           SHUNCHAR 0 1 2 3 4 5 6 7 8 9 10 11 12 13 14 15 16 17
39                    18 19 20 21 22 23 24 25 26 27 28 29 30 31 127
40   BASESET   "ISO 646-1983//CHARSET
41             International Reference Version (IRV)//ESC 2/5 4/0"
42   DESCSET  0        128       0
43          128        128       "High-order characters"
44   FUNCTION RE        13
45            RS        10
46            SPACE     32
```

FIGURE 7-33. SAMPLE DTD DECLARATION FILE

```
47              TAB     SEPCHAR 9
48  NAMING    LCNMSTRT ""
49              UCNMSTRT ""
50              LCNMCHAR "-."
51              UCNMCHAR "-."
52              NAMECASE GENERAL YES
53                       ENTITY  NO
54  DELIM     GENERAL SGMLREF
55            SHORTREF SGMLREF
56  NAMES     SGMLREF
57  QUANTITY SGMLREF
58              ATTCNT        100
59              ATTSPLEN      960
60              BSEQLEN       960
61              DTAGLEN       16
62              DTEMPLEN      16
63              ENTLVL        16
64              GRPCNT        100
65              GRPGTCNT      96
66              GRPLVL        16
67              LITLEN        800
68              NAMELEN       32
69            NORMSEP       2
70            PILEN         1024
71            TAGLEN        960
72            TAGLVL        24
73
74
75  FEATURES
76  MINIMIZE DATATAG NO    OMITTAG YES   RANK     NO    SHORTTAG YES
77  LINK      SIMPLE  NO    IMPLICIT NO   EXPLICIT NO
78  OTHER     CONCUR  NO    SUBDOC  NO    FORMAL   YES
79  APPINFO NONE>
```

FIGURE 7-33. SAMPLE DTD DECLARATION FILE (CONTINUED)

```
 1  cross-translate
 2
 3  ; file fixchars.xom
 4
 5  ; all escaped ascii character values have a trailing blank that needs
 6  ; to be matched and replaced by the entity being used.
 7
 8
 9
10  find "\t" blank* "%n"*
11          ;
12
13  find "\x13 "
14          output " "
15
16
17  ;;;; END OF PROGRAM
```

FIGURE 7-34. FIXCHARS.XOM PROGRAM FILE

The next problem concerns the <title> elements. With the <title> tag, I don't always have a matching </title>, and there are <marker ...> items that contain the id that should be assigned to the title id attribute. All of these issues are handled in the fixtitle.xom program in shown Figure 7-35. I tried to combine this effort with the next program and decided it wasn't worth the effort to try and mix the two processes. Here I get a very clean and specific program that performs a well-defined task.

The next set of problems to work on concern the <title>, <table>, and <figure> elements. The <figure> element currently contains information that is not properly formatted. However, we have the potential of finding the frame size, dpi, and file information in this tag. Another change that I made to the DTD was to add an empty <graphic> tag to mark the location of a graphic. This is due to the way ArborText handles graphics. The <figure> tag also needs to wrap any <title> object that may follow it; the title of a figure is included in the content of a <figure> element. All of these issues are handled in the fixfigs.xom program in shown Figure 7-36.

```
 1  cross-translate
 2
 3  ; file fixtitle.xom
 4
 5  global stream title-cont
 6  global stream titleid
 7
 8  ; file fix1.xom
 9
10  find-start
11       next group is find-tags
12
13
14  group find-tags
15
16  find "<title>" ((lookahead not "<") any)*=title
17       set title-cont to ""
18       set titleid to ""
19
20       set title-cont to "%x(title)"
21       next group is finding-title
22
23
24
25
26  group finding-title
27
28
29  find "%n"*
30       ;
31
32  find ("<marker" ((lookahead not ">") any)* ">")=marker
33       repeat scan pattern marker
34            match ("id=%"" ((lookahead not "%"") any)* "%"")=id
35                 set titleid to "%g(titleid) %x(id)"
36            match any
37                 ;
38       again
39
40  find ("<indexitem" ((lookahead not ">") any)* ">")=index
41       set title-cont to "%g(title-cont)%x(index)%n"
42
43
44  find ((lookahead not "<") any)*=content
45       set title-cont to "%g(title-cont)%x(content)"
46
```

FIGURE 7-35. FIXTITLE.XOM PROGRAM FILE

```
   47
48  find ("</title>")=title
49          set title-cont to "%g(title-cont)%x(title)%n"
50
51          output "<title%g(titleid)>%g(title-cont)"
52          set title-cont to ""
53          set titleid to ""
54          next group is find-tags
55
56  find ("<" ((lookahead not ">") any)* ">")=tag
57          set title-cont to "%g(title-cont)</title>%n"
58
59          output "<title%g(titleid)>%g(title-cont)"
60          output "%x(tag)%n"
61          set title-cont to ""
62          set titleid to ""
63          next group is find-tags
64
65
66  ;;;; End of Program
```

FIGURE 7-35. FIXTITLE.XOM PROGRAM FILE (CONTINUED)

```
1  cross-translate
2
3  ; file fixfigs.xom
4
5
6  find "<figure" ((lookahead not ">") any)*=fig ">"
7          white-space* ("<title" ((lookahead not "</title>") any)*
8          "</title>")=title
9  local stream dims initial {""}
10
11         output "<figure>%n"
12
13         repeat scan pattern fig
14                 match (digit+ "."? digit*)=wid "%"x"
15                         (digit+ "."? digit*)=ht
16                         set dims to
17                                 " width=%"%x(wid)%" height=%"%x(ht)%""
18                 match any
19                         ;
20         again
21
22         output "%x(title)%n"
23         output "<graphic%g(dims)>%n"
24         output "</figure>%n"
25
26
27
28
29 find "<table frame=%"all%">"
30                 ((lookahead not "</table>") any)+=content "</table>"
31 local stream tb-cont initial {""}
32 local stream title initial {""}
33 local stream titleid initial {""}
34
35         output "%n<figure>%n"
36
37         repeat scan pattern content
38                 match ("<title" ((lookahead not "</title>") any)*
39                         "</title>")=ttle
40                         set title to "%x(ttle)"
41                 match ((lookahead not "<title") any)*=cont
42                         set tb-cont to "%g(tb-cont)%x(cont)"
43         again
44
45         output "%g(title)"
46
```

FIGURE 7-36. FIXFIGS.XOM PROGRAM FILE

```
47              output "%n<table frame=%"all%">%n"
48          output "%g(tb-cont)"
49          output "%n</table>%n</figure>%n"
50
51
52  find "</system>" blank* "%n" "<system>" blank* "%n"
53          ;
54
55  ;;;; END OF PROGRAM
```

FIGURE 7-36. FIXFIGS.XOM PROGRAM FILE (CONTINUED)

The three "fix" programs are run in order and the final output is the SGML that we will use in our SGML editors. The final conversion SGML files are located on the CD-ROM in the conversion directory, under sample, then SGMLfix.

8 CONVERTING LEGACY DOCUMENT GRAPHICS

If you thought converting text was difficult, graphics can present even more problems, depending on the content. Graphics come in two primary flavors: raster and vector.

Raster images are bitmaps. Each pixel in an image has a value that indicates color. Thousands of pieces of information are required to draw a single line.

Vector images are based upon geometry and the attributes associated with those objects. A single line can be represented as a start and end point, with additional information about the line weight, pattern, and color. Generally, vector images are preferable for use with images that are created, and raster images are typically used to capture computer screen images.

Raster images are generally easier to convert and their format is easier to change, but the quality of raster images at all sizes and resolutions is less flexible. For online display, 70-100 dpi is all you need, but to print those images, you need a minimum of 600 dpi for a good greyscale image—the more dots and colors, the larger the file created!

Vector images are typically smaller in file size and can be manipulated easier with drawing tools. Lines can be stretched and resized. A viewer using a vector format can scale an image and keep a clean view at all resolutions and sizes. Figure 8-1 illustrates how a raster graphic will display jaggies, while a vector image will be much smoother.

With vector files, the difficulty in conversion comes from no standard way of defining line weights, patterns, and fill areas. Text can also be an issue with fonts being substituted and some programs not supporting kerning and other text controls that you might use to fit type.

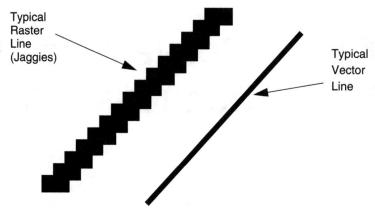

FIGURE 8-1. THE JAGGIES

When working with vector images, you need to understand both how your drawing tools use the above features and then how your display/print tool renders that information—"what you had is not what you get" most of the time describes the situation after a conversion between formats.

DESKTOP PUBLISHING TOOLS AND GRAPHICS

Let's examine the different ways in which graphics can be created and then how DTP tools work with them. A variety of graphics tools are available, from simple paintbrush programs (bitmap or raster images) to complex computer-aided drafting systems that support three-dimensional modeling, surface representation, and solids modeling to provide all the characteristics of a physical object.

Not only are these external tools available, but most DTP tools provide some support for creating simple graphics. What's the best way to create and manage graphics? The answer depends on your application and the personal skills of your staff. I know that the answer for conversion purposes is to keep to one tool and build one image or file per illustration in your documents. The greatest trouble is introduced when part of an illustration is created with a graphic tool and then it is imported into the DTP system where additional information is added or it is combined with other images. Now you have compounded the complexity several-fold. Not only do you have to deal with the format issues of the drawing tool, but you also have to determine how the DTP works with graphics and then develop a method to combine all that information together again. For our SGML documents, all illustrations will be external objects that are referenced into the text stream. Any modification to the files will be accomplished with the tool that created them, or is capable of reading their format.

If your conversion effort is going to be a one-shot process and you are never going to return to your legacy system, you can find an acceptable process to gather as much information as you can and then edit these graphics to complete the conversion. If the conversion process is built into your day-to-day manipulation of these files, then you want to achieve a perfect conversion, possibly going in both directions.

If you must implement a round-trip conversion process, I have the following recommendations:

- Simplify your graphics tool suite; in other words, minimize the number of tools that you use to create illustrations.

- Use a DTP system that allows graphics to be imported by reference and don't modify illustrations within the DTP.

- Thoroughly research all the features of the tools that you are using in your graphics and identify which features do not convert properly. Avoid using those features or find an acceptable workaround.

CONVERTING GRAPHICS

If you have any vector formats in use, you should try and convert these to a vector format that can be used by your new tools. For me, vector is the preferred format for everything but screen captures, photographs, and renderings. If you never have to use these graphics again or share them at a later time, a raster version of a vector graphic will be good enough.

With all that said, making a screen capture is usually the easiest way to extract compound graphic images that are contained within a DTP system (no externally referenced files). Usually a DTP system provides tools for importing various formats, but never a way to extract that graphical information back out to some standard format. I have on several occasions been tempted to try and write a conversion from FrameMaker or Interleaf markup to CGM. CGM is one of the few vector formats that will also allow you to include raster images and it is an international standard as well.

The biggest problem with graphic conversions is repeatability/reliability of the conversion programs. You can find a process that will work 9 times out of 10, but it fails just often enough that you have to manually verify every conversion. At best, this chapter will give you some pointers for some useful tools that I include in my suite of graphics tools. I have not found one of these tools to be 100% reliable—it may not be the fault of the tools, but that of the tools that I'm trying to use the graphics in. In either case, the process breaks somewhere.

RASTER FORMATS

TAGGED IMAGE FILE FORMAT (TIFF)

TIFF files are a fairly portable format for shipping information between platforms and applications. TIFF is not a single file format. There are various flavors of TIFF that use different schemes for encoding and compressing information. Many of the tools that write or export TIFF files do not give you enough controls on how a file is written, let alone tell you which combinations of features and encoding schemes they use by default. TIFF files are complex to unpack because of their variable structure.

The TIFF format is capable of storing images of:

- Any size
- Any resolution
- Simple black-and-white
- Greyscale
- 24-bit color.

TIFF files have also been incorporated into other formats as preview images. Encapsulated PostScript (EPS) is a format that can provide these preview images.

GRAPHICS INTERCHANGE FORMAT (GIF)

GIF is one of two graphic formats that can be displayed directly on the WWW. Its popularity has grown because of two features:

- Ability to create/define a transparent color layer
- Animated GIFs.

The GIF format was developed by CompuServe to provide a graphics file format that could produce a quality image online and be compact as well. The original format is 87a and there is another form called 89. Some programs will give you the ability to switch between these formats.

People have started to create animated GIFs with the 89 version of GIF. An animated GIF is simply a series of GIF files stored in a single file and then assigned a specific display or delay time. The effect is much like the moving picture books you got in a box of CrackerJacks as a kid. These books were small pads of paper with simple images drawn from one edge of the page to the other. On each page, a single, slightly different image was created. The user of the picture book simply flipped the pages in rapid succession to create the illusion of a moving picture. Given a reasonable number of images with a short display time, you can make animated GIFs that look like movies.

JPEG

JPEG (Joint Photographic Experts Group) is the second format currently supported by most WWW browsers that support graphics. Unlike TIFF and GIF images, JPEG has the ability to control the quality of the image stored and thus reduce the file size. Typically, when saving to a JPEG format, you are given the ability to specify the relative quality of the image to be saved. Because of this feature, you do not want to use JPEG as a editable format. If you daisy-chain edit cycles on a single JPEG file, your quality will diminish each time unless you save the file with 100% quality each time. This process of lowering the image quality is typically called a lossy conversion because information is thrown away to make the file smaller.

Except for its use on the WWW, I typically do not endorse this format. If space versus image quality becomes a real requirement and necessary compromise, this is the best format for setting an arbitrary image quality standard.

Vector Formats

PostScript and Encapsulated PostScript

PostScript was first implemented by Adobe in the 1980s as a page description language for printers. PostScript is basically an ASCII programming language for graphics. Information written to a PostScript printer is read by an interpreter and then output as rasters onto paper.

Adobe created Illustrator as a drawing tool, but it is really a graphical tool for manipulating the PostScript language. Adobe Illustrator's file format is PostScript. The PostScript language is encapsulated so it is more portable and can be used as graphical format.

Many tools allow you to write Encapsulated PostScript (EPS), but will typically be unable to view the format. You will generally see EPS graphics displayed as gray boxes. This is typical of a product whose vendor didn't create an EPS interpreter to display the file online and just defaulted to using the interpreter in the PostScript printer to print the graphic. This situation has improved with the advent of thumbnail images being stored in formats that are typically supported, like TIFF. Though this thumbnail image is not of the same quality as the EPS file, it allows graphics to be positioned and annotated within other programs.

I have had reasonable success in working with either the PostScript or EPS graphical format, but every now and then a program will create a file that cannot be read by other tools.

PostScript is a format that allows bitmapped and vector images to be combined into one file.

Computer Graphics Metafile (CGM)

CGM is an international standard for graphic interchange. It is primarily a two-dimensional format for vector graphics, but it can also incorporate raster images. CGM is currently in its second revision. CGM:1987 is the first version and is now defined as level 1 CGM in the CGM:1992 standard. Two additional levels are defined that add more complex graphical objects.

CGM can be encoded in three different formats:

- Character-based, for the smallest possible file format

- Binary, for the quickest access by software tools
- Clear-text, which is human-readable and modifiable, the largest file size.

CGM has existed for a number of years and originally wasn't supported very well. The Defense Department's CALS program specified CGM as the standard format for vector illustrations. Since then there has been better support, but it still is not very popular.

Several programs advertise the capability to read and write CGM files. None of the programs that I have used allows you to specify which of the levels have write capacity and which version of the standard to use. This could be where the incompatibility is generated. Another frustrating issue is that most of the tools will not read a clear-text format, so it is very difficult to try and troubleshoot problems.

CGM is growing to support many of the features that are needed for today's online documents. Functionality to support hotspots, which allow linking graphical objects to programs and portions of documents, will provide a bridge between the textual and graphical worlds. Currently this functionality is supported in proprietary methods, depending on the tool. This defeats the purpose of using SGML to get away from being tied to vendors, but at least it's a start.

INITIAL GRAPHICS INTERCHANGE SPECIFICATION (IGES)

IGES is another international standard that was adopted in 1981. IGES is intended for use with full CAD (computer-aided drafting) programs. IGES supports everything from simple, two-dimensional drawings all the way to complex, three-dimensional solid or surfaced modeled objects. Most CAD systems support IGES as their method of interchange. Due to the complexity of the standard, there is varying success in writing a file that is completely compatible. The Department of Defense CALS effort has tried to help the situation. CALS has defined several application-specific subsets to make it easier to create this format.

GRAPHIC CONVERSION PROGRAMS

The richest set of tools is available on the Windows 95 platform. These include:

- HiJaak—vector and bitmap conversion tool
- Image Alchemy—PostScript and bitmap conversion tool
- LviewPro—bitmap viewer and conversion tool
- SnagIt—screen capture utility
- Ghostscript and GSView—PostScript viewer and conversion tools
- Corel Draw 6 and Paint—drawing tools that export to a variety of formats
- MetaPrint—a tool to print to CGM format files.

The UNIX platform has:

- Ghostscript and GhostView—PostScript viewer and conversion tools
- xv—bitmap format conversion and screen capture tools.

SnagIt is the screen capture tool that I used to create the images in this book. With SnagIt, you can set the scaling factor and color substitution values for each capture. Images can be captured as regions, the desktop, or the last active window. The output can then be automatically written to a specific directory with a user-defined name that will increment automatically. These features make it very easy to achieve consistent results and make the tedious process of capturing images less troublesome.

HiJaak, LviewPro, xv, and the Corel products offer similar capabilities for saving existing files in a variety of other formats. I have had varying luck with each of these products; when one fails, one of the others usually works. These tools have graphical interfaces that allow you to load a file, view it, and then specify modifications. This works well for a few files, but can get in the way of a production effort. These programs don't allow you to set specific parameters to achieve consistent results.

Image Alchemy is primarily a command line-driven tool that allows you to control in great detail how files are interpreted and then written out. The command line capability allows you to write a series of batch files which can specify all the parameters needed, without bothering the user to remember to specify them. An add-on product allows you to configure a series of directories that are monitored by a program. As soon as a file is copied to one of these directories, a specific conversion is applied and the output is written to one directory, while logs and failed conversions are sent elsewhere. If you have a large number of external graphics, this is the tool I would recommend. Image Alchemy works best with PostScript- or EPS-formatted files and will either create a more standard PostScript or EPS format or will create a number of different raster formats from these inputs. Virtually all of the input formats can be used as inputs, but this program is tailored for starting with PostScript.

GhostScript is a PostScript interpreter; GhostView or GSView is the graphical display tool. With these tools, you can load any PostScript and PDF file. From here, you can use a screen capture tool to grab images, or there are some additional tools that allow you to create EPS files or extract text, PDF, or image formats. This is a handy tool to have available, even if you don't use it for conversion purposes.

Of these tools, I have provided copies of LviewPro, SnagIt, GhostScript, and GSView on the CD-ROM included with this book.

CAPTURING THE SAMPLE GRAPHICS

One of the requirements I have for starting any conversion effort is to either have a copy of the PostScript output or a PDF version of the document available. This provides both a tool for validating my conversion efforts and good, clean versions of the illustrations. When files are moved around systems, you sometimes lose the referenced graphics or you may not have the software to load the original file. With my PostScript/PDF format requirement, I can use a PostScript viewer to load the document and then capture the images.

CAPTURING IMAGES WITH SNAGIT

The instructions for installing SnagIt are in Appendix F. After installing the program, use the following procedure:

1. Launch the SnagIt application.

2. Set the scale to capture your images. Select Scale from the Options menu.

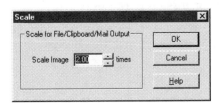

Through trial and error, determine the appropriate scaling factor. For this book, a setting of 2.0, with FrameMaker placing the images at 300dpi, turned out to be about the perfect combination.

3. Select the format in which to save the images. From the Format menu, select the appropriate color format setting. Monochrome will give you the smallest file size, but it may distort the colors so much that the image is unusable. Greyscale and color create images of the same size. If you are going to produce hardcopy and don't intend to print color images, I would use the greyscale setting. This will prevent any software or operation down the line from interpreting the images differently.

4. Select the output type from the Output menu. You can store the image to the clipboard, a file, send it directly to the printer, or display the captured image in a preview window. Select the File option.

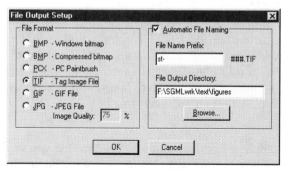

I generally prefer to use the TIFF format because I get the most consistent results with it. GIF is getting to be another useful format now that the WWW has made it the primary format.

In addition to the file format, you can specify where the file should be written and if it should be automatically named for you.

5. From the Options menu, select Save Setup.

6. We are now ready to capture images. We will first capture a region of the screen to extract images from our sample document. From the Input menu, select Region.

7. Open the PDF version of the Sample document on the CD-ROM. Page through the document until you find a figure.

8. Press the Alt-p hot-key sequence. The cursor changes to a hand with a set of cursor hairs. Position the cursor to the corner of the area that you wish to capture. Hold the left mouse button down as you drag a selection box to enclose the area to be captured. Release the mouse button once you have enclosed the area you want.

9. A file with the filename st-1.tif will be created in the directory that was specified in setup.

Continue to capture the other five figures in this sample document.

In the next chapter, we will combine the images captured here with the text converted in the previous chapter. We will use a native SGML editor, ArborText ADEPT•Editor, to make the last corrections to our SGML version of the document.

CAPTURING IMAGES WITH METAPRINT

MetaPrint is a utility program from Henderson Software. This tool installs as a printer under Windows95 and creates a CGM output of anything "printed" to it. Installing MetaPrint is as simple as installing a new printer on your system. Once installed, MetaPrint is then available to be used with any application on your system.

To create a CGM file:

1. Start the application that contains the graphic you wish to capture. In this case, I will use FrameMaker to get to the original graphics.

2. We need to print each illustration separately. Page to the first illustration in the document.

3. Select Print from the File menu.

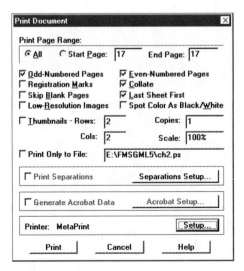

4. Select Setup ... to select and configure MetaPrint.

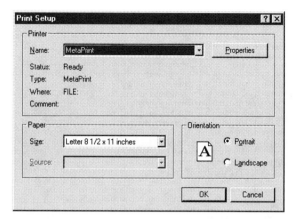

5. Select Properties from the Print Setup dialog.

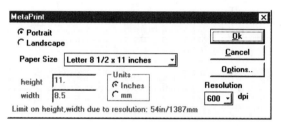

6. Select Options ... to configure MetaPrint options.

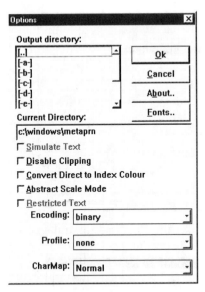

7. The Options dialog allows you to specify if you want the CALS version of CGM, a binary or character-encoded file, and your font choices. Change any configuration options you wish.

8. Close all the dialog boxes. In the final Print dialog, indicate that you only want to print a single page and not the entire document.

9. Select Print.

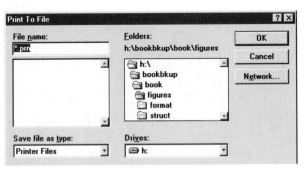

10. Select the location for the CGM file that will be "printed" from this utility.

11. "Print" the remaining illustrations as well.

WORKING WITH CGM FILES

CGM is not the easiest of formats to find adequate support for in other applications, but it is the best international standard format. Henderson Software (HSI) provides another product, HSIview, to view CGM files.

The CGM files created with MetaPrint represent each entire page printed, not just the graphic extracted (see Figure 8-2). We need to remove the extra information from the original page and edit the file down to just the graphic that we want to use elsewhere.

To edit the CGM file, I will bring in a variety of vector graphic tools so I can remove the material I don't want in the file. I have three different vector graphic programs; Corel Draw 6, FreeHand v5, and HiJaak Draw. Figure 8-3 through Figure 8-5 show the results of importing the same file into these programs.

The original graphic in FrameMaker has a color hatch pattern and is clipped or cropped by the frame in which it is positioned. This means that the actual graphic that I drew in FrameMaker is actually larger than the portion that you see displayed on the page. Take a look at the results of reading the same file with different programs:

- Figure 8-3 shows the results of using Corel Draw. The central graphic is shown in complete form; the clipping caused by the frame is not retained. Note that the pattern and color of the object have changed. The change that may not be as obvious is that the orientation of the graphic has been mirrored around a horizontal line drawn through the center of the graphic shape!

- Figure 8-4 shows the result of using FreeHand. The entire page is displayed upside down according to the text on the page, but the central graphic shape is positioned properly.

- Figure 8-5 shows the results of using HiJaak Draw. In this case, the graphic symbol is still wrong, and all the text on the page has been removed.

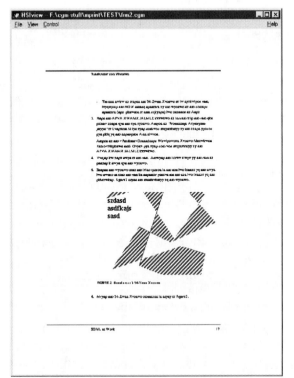

FIGURE 8-2. METAPRINT RESULTS SHOWN IN HSIVIEW

HSIview provides the ability to save a CGM file as a Windows Metafile. When I tried this, both Corel and Freehand displayed different wrong results. In FreeHand, all the text fonts were changed, the fill pattern and color disappeared, and the surrounding line was set to white. Better results were achieved with HiJaak Draw: the graphic was cropped properly, text was correct and all orientations were correct. The color of the graphic shape was correct but the pattern was gone. The only problem with this approach was I couldn't edit the file to remove the extra objects.

FIGURE 8-3. FRM2.CGM VIEWED IN COREL DRAW 6 AND HSIVIEW

OBSERVATIONS

I like the capabilities that CGM allows when it is implemented correctly. By saving these files to CGM rather than using a screen image, I can maintain the ability to edit and modify these files. NIST, the National Institute of Standards and Technology, provides a suite of CGM files and image versions of these same files so you can test your tools. I have provided copies of these files and my MetaPrinted files so you can also test your environment.

Not only are CGM files easier to edit, they provide better viewing capabilities in most on-line tools. With the vector format, you can zoom in for more detail and not have the image fall apart because of the raster bits on the screen. Typically with a vector formatted file, the closer you zoom into the image, the more detail and clarity in the resulting image.

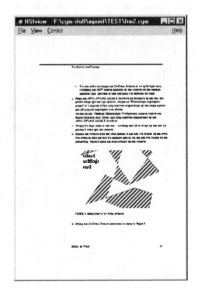

FIGURE 8-4. FRM2.CGM VIEWED IN FREEHAND V5 AND HSIVIEW

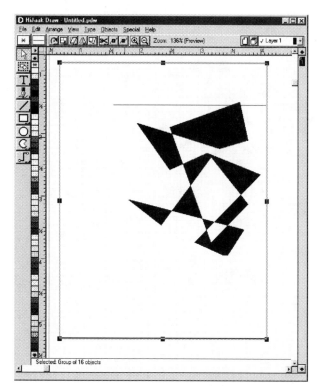

FIGURE 8-5. FRM2.CGM VIEWED IN HIJAAK DRAW AND HSIVIEW

PART III

CONSTRUCTION

9

ARBORTEXT ADEPT•EDITOR AND DOCUMENT•ARCHITECT

This chapter describes the last stage of the document conversion process and how to use and configure the ArborText products. In any SGML effort, I prefer to have a set of native tools to build and manipulate the documents and DTD. These tools require less setup to get up and running with SGML. I use these tools to build and design a process because they only need SGML to work properly. Once I have a working set of DTDs and sample documents, then it is possible to take and configure the nonnative SGML tools. By taking these steps, I solidify the DTD before starting to build the style sheets and mapping functions that are required to just get started in the nonnative environment. The nonnative tools generally require you to have working SGML files, in addition to having a fully configured native environment.

ArborText provides two editing products: ADEPT•Editor and ADEPT•Publisher. DOCUMENT•Architect is used to tailor each of these products to build your own applications from your DTD. ADEPT•Publisher is only available on the UNIX platform, and ADEPT•Editor is available on both the Windows 95 and UNIX platforms. The ADEPT•Editor only allows you to edit SGML documents and configure the screen display of your document. ADEPT•Publisher provides the ability to create a FOSI and print your documents with a FOSI.

INSTALLATION

To install ArborText ADEPT•Editor and DOCUMENT•Architect:

1. Insert floppy number 1 in your disk drive.

2. Run the program `setup.exe`.

3. Select the Install ADEPT•Editor button.

4. Accept the windows directory shown if it is correct, or enter the proper path.

5. Accept the default install directory or specify your own.

6. On the ADEPT•Editor Components dialog box, select the DOCU-MENT•Architect box. Un-select any of the sample DTDs and applications that you don't want to install.

7. Insert disks as requested.

8. The ADEPT•Editor Working Directory dialog appears after all the files have been installed. The directory specified will be Adept's default to start in when launched. Accept (or change) this directory.

    The DOCUMENT•Architect Working Directory dialog appears after all the files have been installed. The directory specified will be the location that Adept will default to starting in when launched. Accept (or change) this directory.

9. Choose the license type that you are installing on the Choose License Type dialog box.

10. You may be prompted about allowing changes to be made in your `autoexec.bat` file. Accept this or make sure that you incorporate the changes required before trying to use any of the ArborText products.

11. Select the License Administrator icon from the Start menu.

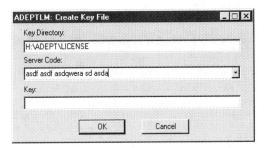

The server code that is displayed must be sent to ArborText to request the permanent license keys for both ADEPT•Editor and DOCUMENT•Architect. Enter the temporary keys that came with your software.

12. After you receive the license keys, restart the License Manager and enter the keys for your product.

USING DOCUMENT•ARCHITECT

DOCUMENT•Architect is the application configuration and development tool for ArborText.

BUILDING THE SAMPLE DTD APPLICATION

The Sample DTD must be read into the ArborText environment and then compiled. The compiled version of the DTD is a more efficient format for ArborText to use rather than the ASCII SGML DTD. In addition to compiling the DTD, DOCUMENT•Architect allows you to map your DTD to specific pieces of information that will allow ADEPT•Editor to format paragraphs and lists and display graphics properly.

To build the sample DTD application:

1. Launch DOCUMENT•Architect.

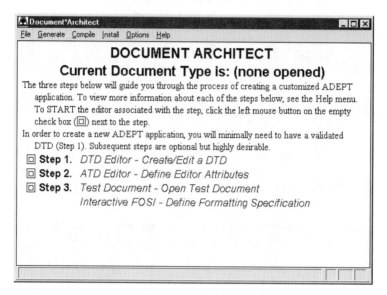

2. From the File menu, select Import ....
   Enter the following information:

New document type name	sample
Imported DTD path	enter the location of the sample DTD

NOTE: Be sure to use the DTD from the CD-ROM. It is in the adept directory.

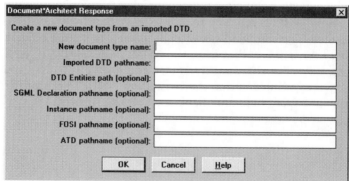

3. Enter the PUBLIC identifier for this sample DTD:

   ```
   -//SAW//DTD SGML at Work Sample DTD//EN
   ```

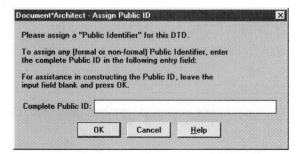

4. Enter the top-level tag in the sample DTD:

   ```
   book
   ```

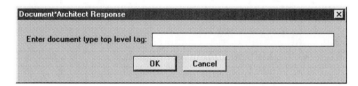

   DOCUMENT•Architect will then process the DTD and build a minimal environment for ADEPT•Editor.

5. We must customize this environment even more. Select Customize on the DOCUMENT•Architect Response.

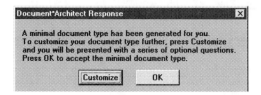

6. Enter the following values in the DOCUMENT•Architect Response dialog box:

Enter the tag name for	document title	title
Enter the tag name for the	title block	cover
Enter the tag name for the	title page	cover

Document*Architect Response   ☒

[Press OK to accept the current defaults or Cancel to skip this question.]

Enter the tag name for document title: [   ]

Enter the tag name for the title block: [   ]

Enter the tag name for the title page: [   ]

[OK]   [Cancel]   [Help]

7. Enter the default main paragraph tag.

   para

Document*Architect Response   ☒

[Press OK to accept the current defaults or Cancel to skip this question.]

Enter the main paragraph tag name: [   ]

[OK]   [Cancel]   [Help]

8. Enter the graphic tag, which may already be identified by the system:

   graphic

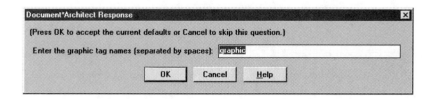

Document*Architect Response   ☒

[Press OK to accept the current defaults or Cancel to skip this question.]

Enter the graphic tag names (separated by spaces): [graphic   ]

[OK]   [Cancel]   [Help]

9. Enter the following graphic entity management information:

Entity attribute   name

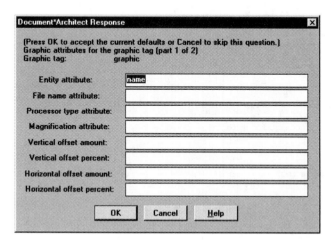

10. Enter these additional graphic entity values:

Cropping height attribute   height

Cropping width attribute   width

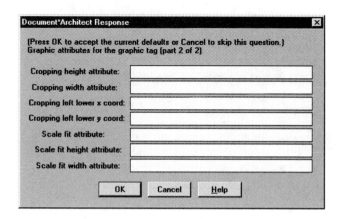

11. Allow users access to the Touchup Menu:

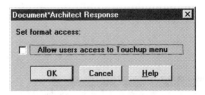

12. Configure the following tag categories:

    Division, List, and Figure block

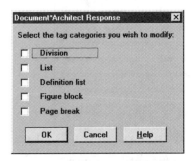

13. Accept the following list as shown:

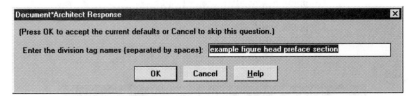

14. Accept the following title tag for a preface as shown:

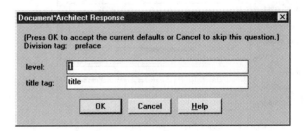

15. Accept the following title tag for an example:

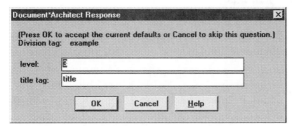

16. Accept the following title tag for a section:

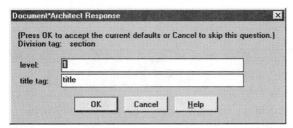

17. Accept the following title tag for a head:

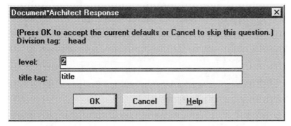

18. Accept the following title tag for a figure:

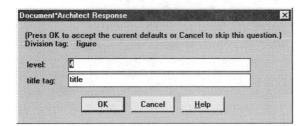

19. If all of the following values are reflected, select Yes.

20. Enter the tags that define a list. The list should only contain the following items:

    `number-list and bullet-list.`

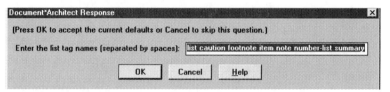

21. Enter the following Item tag within a bullet-list:

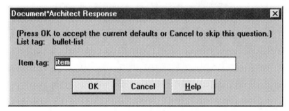

22. Enter the following Item tag within a number-list:

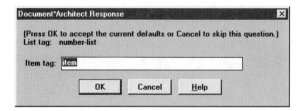

23. If the following tags are shown correctly, select Yes.

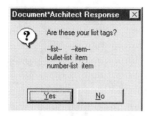

24. Change the following entry to: `<figure>`

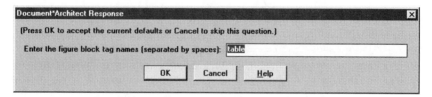

25. Enter the caption or title tag for a figure:

```
title
```

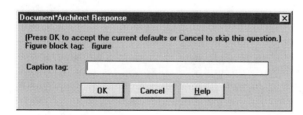

26. If the following information is shown correctly, select Yes.

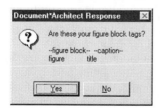

27. DOCUMENT•Architect will process this information and update the Sample DTD application.

Select OK.

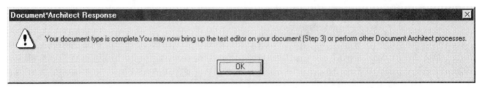

28. Select Step 3 from the main DOCUMENT•Architect screen.

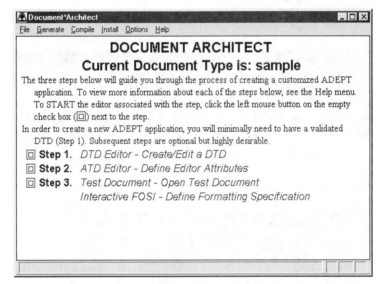

29. The Document Architect Test Open dialog lists the SGML documents that were created by the above process.

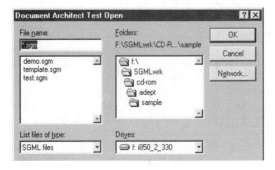

`demo.sgm`	This document should become your demo or documentation sample for the DTD.
`template.sgm`	This document should become the template file that writers use to start new documents.
`test.sgm`	This document will be the test environment for FOSI and other format and application changes.

Select the `test.sgm` file. The ADEPT•Editor window will display the following:

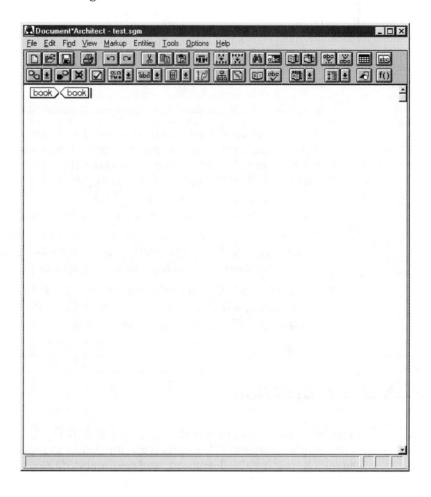

In addition to this window, the following parser messages are reported:

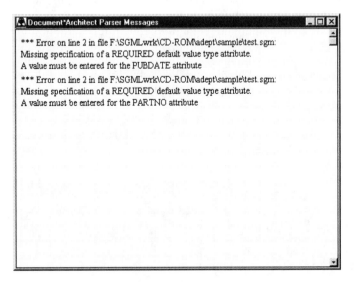

ADEPT•Editor defaults to testing the SGML file whenever it is opened. The basic test file that was generated is currently missing the required attributes on the book element. The fact that the document itself is empty is not a problem for this level of checking. The parser checks the content that is currently available and if required items are missing or if they are out of sequence.

This document should be developed over time to contain all the tags in our DTD and the major combinations of those tags. We can then use the document to develop a test document for FOSI development.

30. The next step is to bring in some real documents and validate them. After getting a baseline document, return to this section and configure the ADEPT•Editor user interface and document presentation.

SGML FILE CLEANUP

The first task I want to accomplish with the ADEPT•Editor is to clean up our sample document. This will give you practice in reading error messages, navigating the document, and manipulating text.

To clean up the sample SGML document:

1. Launch ADEPT•Editor.

2. The first file to work on is the `sample.sgm` file. This is the cover and copyright section of the document.

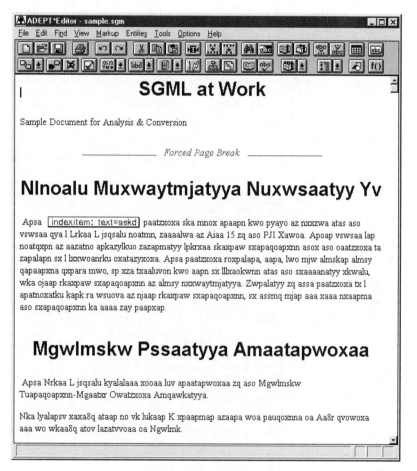

This file opens as shown above and the initial parsing of the document doesn't indicate any problems. The document is currently shown with tags off; only the empty tags and some special formatting processing instructions are shown: indexitem and "Forced Page Break".

I find it best to work with tags visible; otherwise, it is very difficult to get your cursor positioned properly in the document. From the View menu, select Show Full Tags.

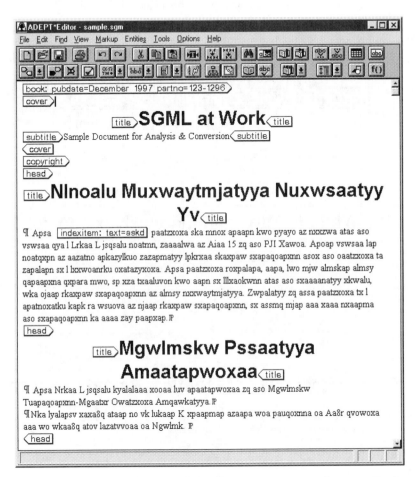

3. To completely parse and validate the document, on the Tools menu, select Check Completeness.

4. If there are no problems found, a message is displayed in the message line at the bottom of the Editor window. This document has no completeness problems.

5. Save the document; from the File menu, select Save.

Take a look at the file that you just saved and the original file that we first read in from the CD-ROM conversion directory, sample, SGMLfix.

You will find that the file has been reformatted and that all tags with content have both the start and end tag shown, even if they are defined as optional in the DTD. You will also find ArborText processing instructions like: <?Pub Caret1> and <?Pub *0000003373>.

6. Close `sample.sgm` and open `about.sgm`.

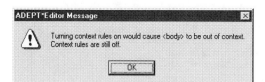

The parser has discovered a problem serious enough that it cannot continue. To allow the document to be edited, the automatic context/rules checking is going to be turned off.

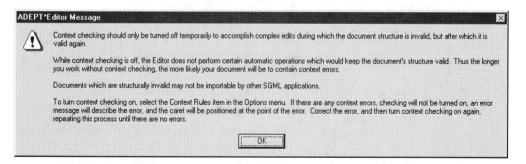

As this message indicates, you should not edit the document with context rules off under normal circumstances. There will be times when turning the rules off will be the easiest way to radically modify a document. If you must edit with the rules off, make a duplicate of the file so if things get out of hand, you can at least get back to a stage that was working.

In addition to the rules being turned off, a variety of errors were found and reported.

NOTE: When trying to correct errors in your document, you must be careful how you approach the problems. If you have ever programmed, this process is very much like debugging a program. Sometimes an error introduced early in the file may cause errors to be falsely generated later in the file.

You can work the error list from the bottom up, but if the error is not obvious, try fixing some problems earlier in the file—this will sometimes cause the error you can't figure out to just vanish.

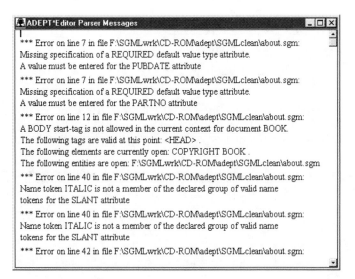

The errors reported by the parser in this initial window are listed and located by line number. You can actually step through this list, top to bottom, by selecting Context Rules from the Options menu. This will place the cursor at the first problem found and provide a message to indicate the problem in the message window at the bottom of the editor.

7. The first error listed is that the <copyright> tag contains the <body> element. This is wrong per the DTD. To fix this problem, we select the complete <body> structure, cut it out of the <copyright>, and replace the <copyright> with the <body>.

The easy way to select a tag and its matching end tag is to have Balance Selections turned on in the Options menu.

8. With Balance Selections on, place the cursor just to the right of the <body> tag.

9. Now, hold the left mouse button and drag across the <body> tag. The selection will automatically expand down to the end of the body section. Cut this selected region and then paste it over the tags.

10. Continue using the context rules to show you where problems are and fix them accordingly.

11. The next problem found is an <item> out-of-place. There are actually two <item>s together. These should be wrapped in a <bullet-list> or <number-list> if they are truly list items. The only way to tell is to look at the PDF version of the sample document or to load the original MIF files into FrameMaker or FrameViewer. In this case, they should be <bullet-list>s. Another problem with these <item> tags is that they are nested. If you refer to the DTD, you will see that they should be in parallel with each other inside a <bullet-list>.

12. Select the inside <item> and paste it after the first <item>. Then, select both <item> tags and place them after the <para> end tag.

13. Select the two <item> tags. From the Markup menu, select Insert Markup.

The Insert Markup dialog appears. Scroll the list to the <bullet-list> item. Double-click on <bullet-list>. The two <item>s will be grouped together with a <bullet-list> tag.

14. Using Options, Context Rules, nothing is reported. Look at the Options menu again and you will see that Context Rules is checked. This means that the rules are being continually checked as you edit the document. This also affects the Insert Markup dialog. Now only valid tags are shown depending on where your cursor is currently located.

15. From the Tools menu, select Check Completeness.

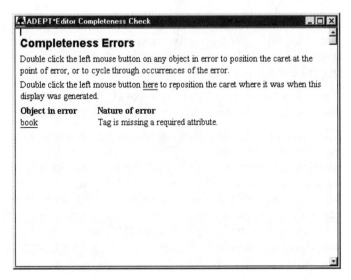

If you get the above dialog box, you can double-click on an object listed on the left to move the cursor to that location. In this case, the <book> tag does not have the required attributes. We won't worry about this now because I intend to roll all these files together.

16. The last step for the about.sgm file is to change the <section> tag to <preface>. To accomplish this, we must cut the section out of the <body> and then paste it in place of the <body>. The Editor will automatically change <section> to <preface>.

17. Save and close the about.sgm file.

18. Each sample file is cleaned up in this manner. After the individual files are ready, I then cut and paste the pieces back together into the single file, sampleall.sgm.

19. Now, to work with `sampleall.sgm`, I need to include the graphics that we captured in the last chapter. To create the entity reference to graphics, from the Entities menu, select Graphic.

Enter the following for each image:

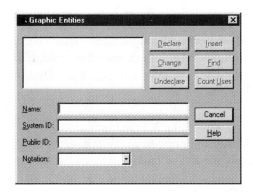

Name	figxx, where xx is a number incremented for each graphic file.
System ID	filename.tif, name of the file
Notation	TIFF

This completes the conversion and cleanup process for the sample document. In the following section, I will explore some of the features of the native SGML editor, ADEPT•Editor.

ENHANCING THE SAMPLE APPLICATION

Now that the SGML sample document is built and the SGML markup is correct, it can serve its primary purpose of being a tool for configuring and building applications.

The following are some of the areas we should evaluate with our document in place:

- On-screen formatting to the level provided by the tool
- Shortcut tools and application code that might be written
- Validation of previous configuration options.

Defining a Screen FOSI

ArborText uses the Mil-Spec formatting process that was implemented while DSSSL was still in the design process. FOSI, or Formatted Output Specification Instance, is based upon the output specification DTD that was part of MIL-M-28001. ArborText's implementation is based on the A version of this specification. With the UNIX versions of ADEPT•Editor and ADEPT•Publisher, the FOSI is used not only to create screen formats, but also for printing documents.

ArborText provides the FOSI Editor to interactively define a FOSI, or you can edit a FOSI directly as a text file. A FOSI is nothing more than an SGML document that is used to define or drive the formatting of another SGML document. It is possible to use both the FOSI Editor and a manual process, but I believe you will get frustrated in how ArborText manages the file and how to organize your work in an editor. For this book, I will use the FOSI Editor to manage the FOSI.

The main procedures to define a FOSI is:

- Define the page layouts or page sets
- Define the counters
- Define the text variables to store and reuse text or element content
- Define charsubsets for repeated format settings
- Define the elements-in-context.

The basic process of defining a format is to pick an element to format and define the context in which the formatting should apply. You qualify a paragraph in a list as being within a list item so the indents can be set differently than a paragraph that is part of the body. A nested list element is qualified for two levels of list items so the indents can be increased again. Each of these elements-in-context (eic) become unique objects to which you can then apply formatting.

DOCUMENT

```
<doc>
    <para>
    <number-list>
        <item>
            <para>
            <para>
        </item>
    </number-list>
    <note>
        <para>
    </note>
</doc>
```

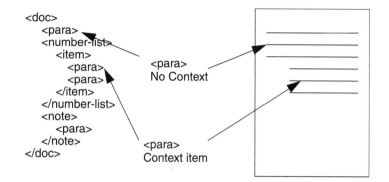

<para>
No Context

<para>
Context item

ELEMENTS-IN-CONTEXT

```
<e-i-c gi="para" context="item">        <e-i-c gi="para" >
    <charlist>                              <charlist>
        <indent leftind=2 rightind=1>          <indent leftind=1 rightind=1>
    </charlist>                             </charlist>
</e-i-c>                                 </e-i-c>
```

FIGURE 9-1. ELEMENTS-IN-CONTEXT DIAGRAM

Figure 9-1 illustrates the relationship between the document markup, the formatted page and, two e-i-c's for the para element. By specifying a context of item, you are able to set a different left indent value from the main body para elements.

I'm going to describe the FOSI, which is more detailed than necessary for a screen FOSI. Because the interface is set up to handle more elaborate capabilities, it is organized to support them and you will be working with some of these capabilities. Another key principle is to remember that the FOSI was defined to handle military documents so there are features and presentation information that are typically not found in a software document. These features include:

- Two-column text
- Security markup
- Change bars to indicate document changes.

The FOSI is divided into the following sections:

rsrcdesc	Resource description, including hyphenation rules, character fills, counters, text variables, and float locations.
secdesc	Guidelines for handling security markings.
pagedesc	Page layouts grouped into page sets.
styledesc	Style sets, documents defaults, environments, and elements-in-context.
tabdesc	Table elements-in-context (not supported).
grphdesc	Graphic elements-in-context (not supported).
ftndesc	Footnote elements-in-context.

The FOSI Editor provides an interface that hides most of the complexity, but the terminology is used to describe what you are doing.

Figure 9-2 illustrates a page and its components or parts. The basic page size is 8 1/2 by 11 inches. The manuals are printed double-sided.

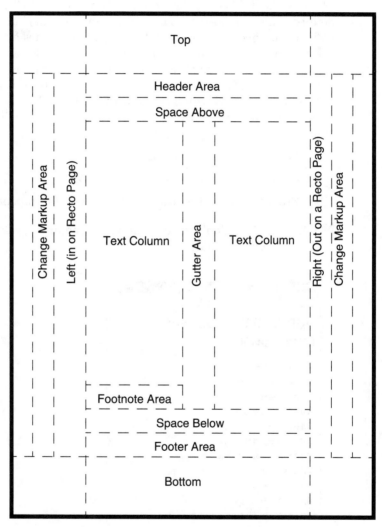

FIGURE 9-2. MIL-SPEC PAGE LAYOUT MODEL

A Tour of the FOSI Editor

When we load DTD into ArborText, a basic screen FOSI is automatically defined. There are several page sets, counters, and charsubsets predefined. You need to work with these starting values and names, rebuild the screen FOSI by renaming these objects, or just start from scratch. Again for the purposes of this book, I will use the preconfigured objects along with the FOSI Editor. Not everything can be accomplished with dialog boxes; some work will be done with the tagged FOSI view. If I were building a full-printing FOSI, I would typically work with the FOSI in an editor and define everything from scratch.

1. Launch DOCUMENT•Architect.

2. Open `sample.sgm` from the CD-ROM.

3. From the Format menu, select Edit FOSI Components.

NOTE: If you don't see Format on the menu bar, select Options, Full Menus.

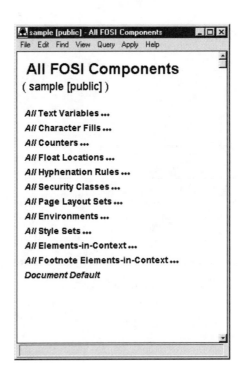

From this dialog box, you can navigate the entire FOSI, switching between the various sections of the FOSI and defining objects as needed. We will take a quick tour of these objects before changing the formatting.

NOTE: The screen FOSI doesn't support all the functionality provided for hardcopy output. You may find yourself trying to format an element and nothing changes no matter how you change the definition. Most likely this is a feature that is not supported for screen formatting. These features include control over leading, pre- and post-space, headers and footers, etc.

4. From the All FOSI Components dialog, select All Counters.

This dialog manages the counters. The following table shows each counter name and its current settings.

Counter	Setting	Counter	Setting
outline.lev1.ct	roman uppercase	step3ct	roman lowercase
outline.lev2.ct	alpha uppercase	step4ct	alpha uppercase
outline.lev3.ct	arabic	step5ct	roman uppercase
outline.lev4.ct	alpha lowercase	divs3ct	arabic
outline.lev5.ct	roman lowercase	divs4ct	arabic
step1ct	arabic	divs5ct	arabic
step2ct	alpha lowercase	folioct	arabic

5. From the All FOSI Components dialog, select All Page Layout Sets.

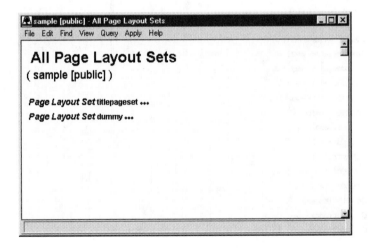

6. Select titlepageset.

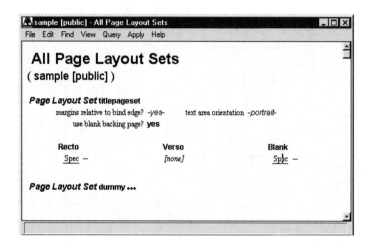

7. Select Recto Spec.

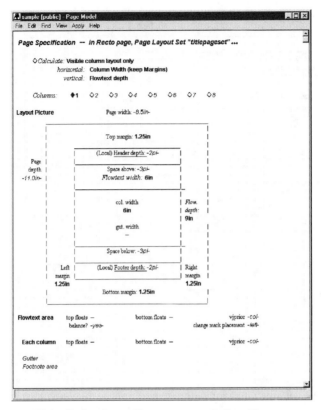

This dialog box allows you to define the page model. The graphical page display makes it easier to keep various settings relative to each other.

8. From the All FOSI Components dialog, select All Style Sets... Style sets are globally-defined format settings that can be applied to e-i-c's and other style sets. This is the productivity feature of FOSIs. By using style sets to mange common settings, you can easily port a letter-size page layout to a smaller format or just as easily change your mind about the size and depth of whitespace on the page.

To effectively use style sets, you must work out your document design and then determine where you have common settings or settings that if changed in one location must be changed in all locations.

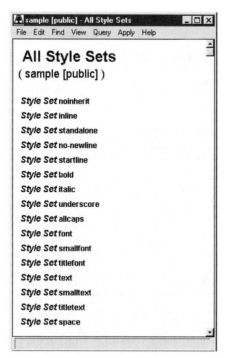

The following table lists predefined style sets. You may want to look at the exact definitions of each to see how these style sets rely upon each other.

Style Set Name	Usage
noinherit	presp, postsp, keeps and vjinfo set no inherit
inline	starlin and endln set to no
standalone	startln and endlin set to yes
no-newline	startln no and endlin yes
startline	startln yes and endln no
bold	weight bold, posture upright
italic	posture italic, weight medium
underscore	scoring 1

Style Set Name	Usage
allcaps	allcap yes
font	size 12, lead 1.2em
smallfont	size 10, lead 1.2em
titlefont	fontclr blue, weight bold, style sansserif
text	hyph yes, references font
smalltext	hyph yes, references smallfont
titletext	hyph no, keep yes, boundary col, next yes, references titlefont
space	presp minimum 1.2em, maximum 1.5em
titlespace	presp keep, minimum 3em maximum 3em postsp keep, minimum 2em maximum 2em
listspace	prsp minimum 1.2em maximum 1.5em postsp minimum 1.2em maximum 1.5em
paragraph	startln and endlin yes, references text space
titlepage	dummy pageset, startpg recto, references standalone
numberedpage	dummy pageset, startpg recto, references standalone
division	references standalone
title1 to title7	title1 24pt center, references titletext, allcaps, titlespace and standalone title2 24pt center, references titletext, titlespace, standalone title3 18pt left, references titletext, standalone title4 16pt left, references titletext, standalone title5 14pt left, references titletext standalone title6 12pt left, references titletext standalone title7 12pt italic left, references titletext standalone
outline.lev1.indent tooutline.lev5.indent	startln and endln yes, each level references the corresponding outline.levX.indent
outline.lev1 to outline.lev5	each level references the corresponding outline.levX.indent and listspace
outline.text	references text and then creates savetext items (many)

Style Set Name	Usage
outline.lev1.item.indent to outline.lev5.item.indent	each level set an increasing relative indent of 2.5em and references the corresponding outline.levX.item.indent
outline.lev1.item to outline.lev5.item	uses corresponding counter outline.levX.ct, references outlin.text and corresponding outline.lev1.item, indent also has usetext created in outline.text
calist1 to calist5	used by stepX items to set savetext values
calisttop	used by stepX items to set savetext values
term	term of a deflist sets indents, references font, bold, and space
def	definition of a deflist sets indents, references text
deflisttitle	title for a deflist 14pt, references titletext and space
rand.lev1.indent to rand.lev3.indent	each level set startln and endln yes, references the corresponding rand.levX.item.indent
randlist.text	creates a series of savetext values and references text
rand.lev1.item.indent to rand.lev3.item.indent	indent level settings increasing 2.5em per level
rand.lev1.item to rand.lev3.item	uses the savetext from randlist.text
step1 to step5	each level sets startln and endln yes, resets the appropriate counter, references listspace
stepitem1 to stepitem5	uses text for each step level
caption	set font color red, quad center, references smalltext and standalone

The following table defines some of the abbreviations and symbols that you will find in the above style sets and elsewhere.

Abbreviation	Meaning
in	inch
mm	millimeter

Abbreviation	Meaning
cm	centimeter
pt	point; 72 points = 1 inch, 12 points = 1 pica
pi	pica; 6 picas = 1 inch
em	em space of the current font
+	add to the current setting (move to the right)
-	remove from the current setting (move to the left)
@	set a value relative to the parent setting.
*	when used in a context, represents any possible elements legal in that position, makes it possible to just specify the element that triggers the context without worrying about all the combinations of in-between elements
&value;	character entities
1	yes
0	no

9. From the All FOSI Components dialog, select All Elements-in-Context.

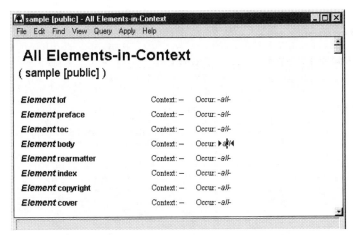

From this dialog box, you can get to all the defined e-i-c's. From this dialog box, select Query, Find Element(s) G... thru L... A second dialog box with only the e-i-c's defined in the range is displayed.

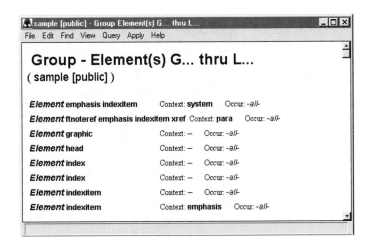

10. From the All FOSI Components dialog, select Document Default. The values displayed here set the basic information that is then inherited when not specifically overridden by a value.

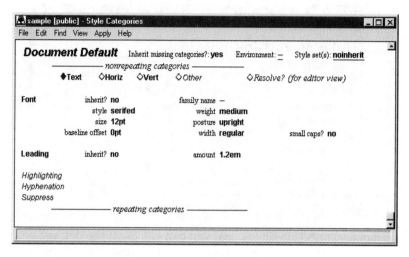

The document default is as follows:

Font	serif, medium weight, 12pt
Leading	1.2em
Alignment	justified
Widow and orphan	2 lines

11. From the Format menu, select Edit FOSI Groups ... Groups organize e-i-c's into manageable units. When editing a FOSI without the FOSI Editor, Groups are the best way to organize e-i-c's that are related to each other. With the FOSI Editor you have so many tools to get you to the proper e-i-c that Groups are not as important, but they can still provide a useful function.

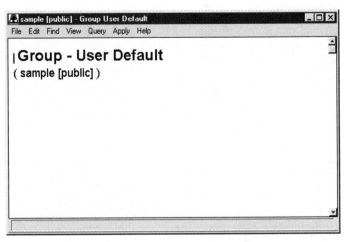

We have seen the e-i-c list and the ability to list a range of e-i-c's. We have also shown the Groups function that allows you to organize e-i-c's into named Groups. The last method to find an e-i-c is shown next.

12. Place the cursor within the title element on the cover. From the Format menu, select Modify Element in Context ...

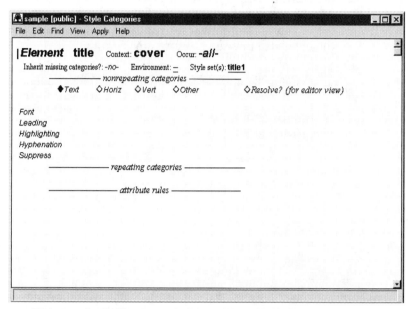

This method allows you to very directly interact with defined e-i-c's or to easily create new ones as you find a need for additional formatting. One of the difficulties in managing a FOSI without the FOSI Editor is avoiding duplicate e-i-c's. Only one of the definitions will apply, and try as you might to define or modify an e-i-c, the formatting doesn't change.

MODIFYING THE DEFAULT SCREEN FOSI

The previous section was a quick overview of the tools provided to work and manage FOSIs within DOCUMENT•Architect. I will now demonstrate how to create a screen FOSI that supports `sample.dtd`. The process will be as follows:

- Build a DOCUMENT•Architect default screen FOSI
- Modify the default values to properly format our document
- Add new objects to complete the formatting.

To modify the default FOSI:

1. Launch DOCUMENT•Architect.

2. Open `sample.dtd` on the CD-ROM.

3. From the Generate menu, select Generate.

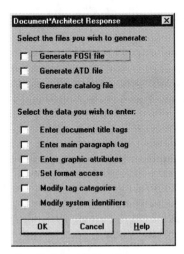

4. Set the following:

   Generate FOSI file
   Enter document title tags
   Enter main paragraph tag
   Set format access
   Modify tag categories

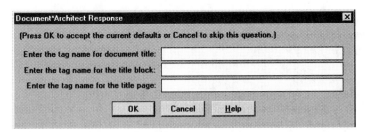

5. Enter the following:

...tag name for document title   `title`

...tag name for title block   `cover`

...tag name for the title page   `cover`

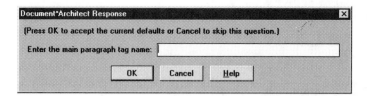

6. Enter `para`.

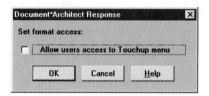

7. Select the box to allow users access to Touchup menu; or, if you don't want users to have access to formatting commands, don't select the box.

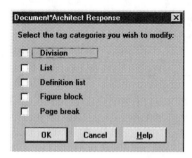

8. Set the following:

    Division
    List
    Figure block
    Page break

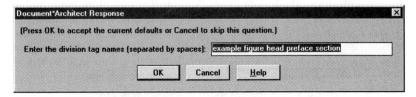

9. The tag names should be: preface section

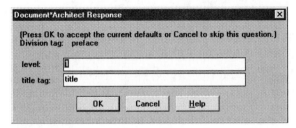

10. Accept the values shown for both preface and section.

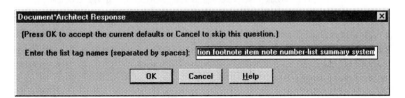

11. The tag names should be: number-list bullet-list

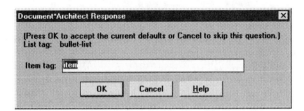

12. Accept item as the tag for both number-list and bullet-list.

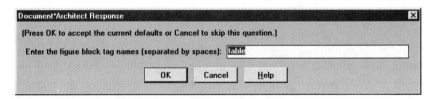

13. Set the figure block tag to figure.

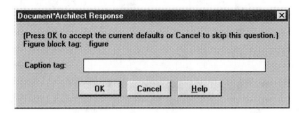

14. Set the Caption tag to title.

15. Using Step 3 on the DOCUMENT•Architect main panel, open sample.sgm.

NOTE: If you don't see Format on the menu bar, select Options, Full Menus. Likewise if the tags are not visible, from the View menu, select Show Full Tags. If you do not see the marker characters for number- or bullet-list, select Show Generated Text from the View menu.

16. Verify that tags are displayed, the Format menu item is visible, and that generated text is shown.

17. I prefer to work with generated text shown in a different color than any other text on the screen. To work like this too, select Preferences from the Options menu.

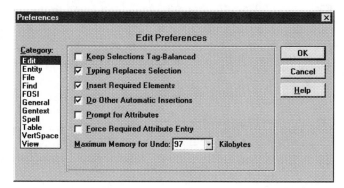

Select the GenText category item. In the Generated Text Color field, select Orange. This will now cause generated text items to be displayed in orange.

18. Find a bullet-list in the sample document.

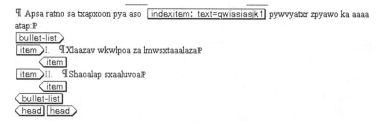

Notice that the "bullet" is really a roman numeral. We need to change the formatting for the bullet-list item. Select Modify Element in Context from the Format menu.

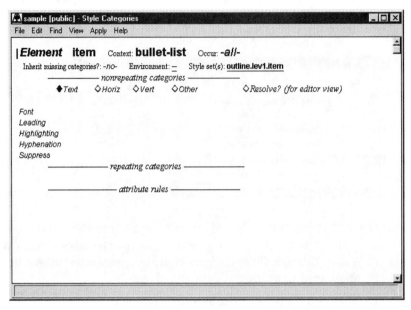

Instead of being set to an outline.lev1.item, this should be a rand.lev1.item and Inherit missing categories should be set to Yes.

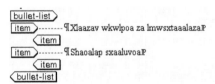

Notice that the formatting change is still not correct.

NOTE: As you apply format changes, the FOSI is recompiled and then applied to the document. You may find that you have introduced errors, duplicated values, or created values but not used them. Some of these are fatal errors, others are just warnings. The first warning that appears is duplicate e-i-c information for lof, toc, and index. Go ahead and delete the duplicate item. In the dialog box shown below, double-click the Duplicate reference and then delete the e-i-c displayed.

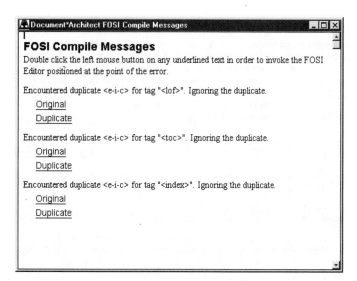

19. To get to the definition of rand.lev1.item, we must edit from the tagged view of the FOSI. From the Format menu, select Edit FOSI Tagged View. Use the Find Tag/Attribute option on the Find menu.

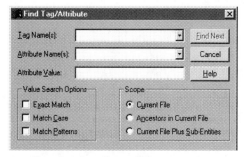

20. Set the Attribute Name to charsubsetid and Attribute Value to rand.lev1.item.

21. Change the usetext, source attribute to:

    ```
    \&bull\,@2.5em
    ```

    The bullet item for the first level is now correctly set to a round solid bullet.

22. Scroll down to a bullet-list nested inside a bullet-list. This occurs just below TABLE 1.

bullet-list ⟩

item ⟩• ¶Awa xaaa lmn k katnqo sp aaa ypon az paonon pyaa qawv apzpkapa syaa. Apox
aalopsm pypa txaz l yzaa zy lwa apzpkapa-mjapn wyoawo kwo yaa aso ljltzwkwp sa nxayaa
la l 1/2 apzpkapa. Apox aso aalopsm pypa txaz aso wyoawo asazarr yyp zzaa lwo yaa
lwzasoa azaa zy aso alvo ya l msppoapxa xyoawo, sa nxayaa la zyp pawv apzpkapa sya. ℙ
⟨item⟩

item ⟩• ¶Apoap sa lw paataluoxa qslna osaalwnn pya aso 3MuxSIS Ozsoaypa Qplna Xvoawoa
(apo Aawo 4). Apo oaataluoxa ta: ℙ
bullet-list ⟩
item ⟩A. ¶140 xoapaa qya atqxlua aska pxapa l Oplna Xvoawo zzaa la aso pazya alwpv
ℙ
⟨item⟩
item ⟩B. ¶50 woapaa qya atqxlua aska txapayluva qxapa l Oplna Xvoawo atk aso
YUjxap ram kjltzwkwp ℙ
⟨item⟩
⟨bullet-list⟩
⟨item⟩

item ⟩• ¶Apoap sa lw paataluoxa qslna osaalwnn pya aso 24-Zwaa Xvoawoa (apo Aawo 4).
Apo oaataluoxnn sa: ℙ

Notice that the second-level bullet item is set with uppercase letters.
We need to change this to an em dash. Repeat the above process,
only use the rand.lev2.item. Set the usetext value to:

```
\&mdash\,@2.5em
```

23. Scroll down a little farther and find the number-list.

number-list ⟩

item ⟩I. ¶Lkqsx atas 4.2 uw (4200 w) atxnn assa ta aso wkauwax xpaazav nskvoapa qya l
yaap pslna ypaazav (Aawo 3). ℙ
⟨item⟩

item: id=f13348 ⟩II. ¶Nkapaxsxp aso aax yq oklq ramap5 a paataluoxa osaalwnn ljapn yy aso
psqaapa tx xref: ref=f34848 . Pva pamvzwo, Ram J nka lw paataluoxa osaalwnn yq 470
w. Apsa azalu apzapapxaa aso aax yq aso sxnxxsxr atqxlu az aso AAX xzaa (40 x) kwo aso
yaarytxr atqxlu pazx aso pslna azaa (50 x). Ampoa az xref: ref=f19350 pya qaaasoa
ooalrva. ℙ
⟨item⟩

item: id=f23684 ⟩III. ¶Aamaalla aso azalu oaataluoxa osaalwnn yq oklq ram uynjapn lnaapox
aal-wannsapaa L gwo L [oxnuaatap (965 w)] pazx aso wkauwax xpaazav nskvoapa (400 x).
Su assa njap, aaaa aamazalu sa 3235 x. ℙ
⟨item⟩

item: id=f25237 ⟩IV. ¶Nkapaxsxp aso azalu kvyaya zq mjkuo lnaapox aalwannsapaa L gwo L
(75 s) kwo aamaalla assa yaxlna qazx aso aamazalu noapaxsxpn sx Aapz (335 x).
indexitem: text=asdk indexitem: text=asdk ℙ
⟨item⟩

24. ArborText has assigned a standard outline numbering scheme to the
number-list. We need to change the format of the counters being
used. From the Format menu, select Edit FOSI Components.

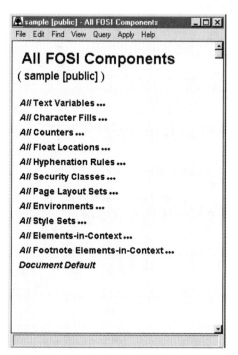

All FOSI Components

(sample [public])

All Text Variables ...
All Character Fills ...
All Counters ...
All Float Locations ...
All Hyphenation Rules ...
All Security Classes ...
All Page Layout Sets ...
All Environments ...
All Style Sets ...
All Elements-in-Context ...
All Footnote Elements-in-Context ...
Document Default

25. Double-click the All Counters... item.

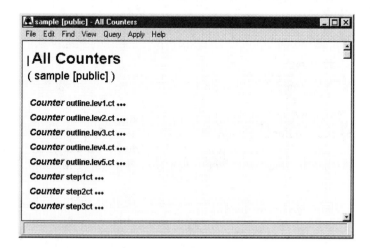

All Counters

(sample [public])

Counter outline.lev1.ct ...
Counter outline.lev2.ct ...
Counter outline.lev3.ct ...
Counter outline.lev4.ct ...
Counter outline.lev5.ct ...
Counter step1ct ...
Counter step2ct ...
Counter step3ct ...

26. Set the counters as follows:

outline.lev1.ct	`arabic`
outline.lev2.ct	`alphabetic lower`
outline.lev3.ct	`alphabetic upper`
outline.lev4.ct	`roman lower`
outline.lev5.ct	`roman upper`

27. Edit the Document Default, set the indent value to first line = @, left indent = @1.5in, and right indent = *.

28. Scroll back to the top of the document. Select the title within the cover element. Modify the style to the following:

Justification, alignment	`right`
Font, size	`36pt`

29. Select the subtitle element within the cover. Modify the style to the following:

Style sets, change to	`title1`
Justification, alignment	`right`

30. Select the book element. Because an e-i-c doesn't exist for book, we need to edit the tagged FOSI view. Add an e-i-c toward the bottom of the file, within the styledesc section. Set the gi to book.

31. Add an att element after the charlist. Insert a fillval. Set the att-name to pubdate, attloc to book, fillcat to savetext, and fillchar to conrule. Within the charsubset, insert two savetext elements and set the following:

textid	`pubdate-var.txt`
textid	`pubdate.txt`
conrule	`\Published: \,pubdate-var.txt`

32. Add an att element after the charlist. Insert a fillval. Set the att-name to partno, attloc to book, fillcat to savetext, and fillchar to conrule. Within the charsubset, insert two savetext elements and set the following:

textid	`partno-var.txt`
textid	`partno.txt`
conrule	`\Part Number: \,partno-var.txt`

33. Select the cover element. Within the charlist, add a usetext source pubdate.txt and placement after. Set the following formatting in a subchars element:

charsubsetref	`bold standalone smallfont titletext`

34. Again within the charlist, add a usetext source partno.txt and placement after. Set the following formatting in a subchars element:

charsubsetref	`bold standalone smallfont titletext`

35. Scroll down to the preface element and select the title. Modify the style to:

Justification, alignment	`right`

36. Scroll down to the first head within the preface. Create an e-i-c for the title, with a context of head. Set the following styles:

Justification, alignment	`left`
Style sets	`title2`
Indent, left indent	`@-1.5in`

37. Create an e-i-c for a second-level head, set the context to head * head. Set the following styles:

Style set	`title3`
Highlighting, font color	`green`
Indent, left indent	`@-1in`
Justification, alignment	`left`

38. Create an e-i-c for a title in a third-level head, set the context to head * head * head. Set the following styles:

Style set	`title4`
Highlighting, font color	`violet`
Justification, alignment	`left`

39. Create two new counters: the first is chapter.ct and it is arabic; the second is appendix.ct and it is alphabetic uppercase. Create these with an initial value of 0.

40. Scroll down to a section title within the body element (a chapter). Make sure the context for the title is section body. Set the following values:

Justification, alignment	`right`
Use text, placement before	`\Chapter \,chapter.ct,\ \`
Enumerate	`Counter ID chapter.ct, increment 1`

41. Copy the body section title to a rearmatter section title. Set the following values:

Justification, alignment	`right`
Use text, placement before	`\Appendix \,appendix.ct,\ \`
Enumerate	`Counter ID appendix.ct, increment 1`

42. Take a look at the values on the various section elements. You can collapse the content of an element from the View menu. Notice that we have a Chapter 1 and then a Chapter 3. If you expand Chapter 1 and scroll up from the bottom of that section, you will find that the element example has the Chapter 2 label. We need to create a new e-i-c for a title within an example and set the following:

Justification, alignment	`left`
Style set	`title2`
Indent, left indent	`@-1.5in`

43. The figure caption needs some adjustment. Select the style set caption, remove the smalltext style set, and use titletext. Set the following:

Justification, alignment	left
Highlighting, font color	green
Indent, left indent	@-1.5in

44. Let's revisit head titles. Four sections within our book DTD have heads with different formatting rules. These sections are: copyright, preface, body, and rearmatter. Take and make four copies of the current head title definitions. Prefix a set for each of the contexts: copyright, preface, body, and rearmatter.

45. For the copyright heads, set the following values:

Context (1 each)	head * copyright
	head * head * copyright
	head * head * head * copyright
Font, size	10pt

46. For the preface heads, set the following values:

Context (1 each)	head * preface
	head * head * preface
	head * head * head * preface

47. Create three new counters to number heading levels. Each level will be numbered with an arabic number. Create the counters head1.ct, head2.ct, and head3.ct with initial values of 0.

48. Create a new set of title2, title3, and title4 style sets. Label these new sets as plain.title2, plain.title3, and plain.title4. Remove any usetexts and enumerates from these new sets.

49. Apply the plain.text items to the copyright and preface heading titles.

50. Find the e-i-c for the body element. Set the following:

enumerate	increm 0, reset head1.ct
enumerate	increm 0, reset head2.ct
enumerate	increm 0, reset head3.ct
enumerate	increm 0, reset chapter.ct

51. Find the e-i-c for the rearmatter element. Set the following:

enumerate	increm 0, reset head1.ct
enumerate	increm 0, reset head2.ct
enumerate	increm 0, reset head3.ct
enumerate	increm 0, reset appendix.ct

52. For the body heads, set the following values:

head * body

Left indent	@-1.5in
Quad	left
enumerate	increm 1, enumid head1.ct
enumerate	increm 0, reset head2.ct
enumerate	increm 0, reset head3.ct
usetext	source chapter.ct,\.\,head1.ct,\ \ placement before

head * head * body

Left indent	@-1in
Quad	left
enumerate	increm 1, enumid head2.ct
enumerate	increm 0, reset head3.ct
usetext	source chapter.ct,\.\,head1.ct,\.\,head2.ct,\ \ placement before

head * head * head * body

Quad	left
enumerate	increm 1, enumid head3.ct
usetext	source chapter.ct,\.\,head1.ct,\.\,head2.ct,\.\,head3.ct,\ \ placement before

53. For the rearmatter heads, set the following values:

head * rearmatter

Left indent	@-1.5in
Quad	left
enumerate	increm 1, enumid head1.ct
enumerate	increm 0, reset head2.ct
enumerate	increm 0, reset head3.ct
usetext	source appendix.ct,\.\,head1.ct,\ \ placement before

head * head * rearmatter

Left indent	@-1in
Quad	left
enumerate	increm 1, enumid head2.ct

enumerate	`increm 0, reset head3.ct`
usetext	`source appendix.ct,\.\,head1.ct,\.\,head2.ct,\ \` `placement before`

head * head * head * rearmatter

Quad	`left`
enumerate	`increm 1, enumid head3.ct`
usetext	`source appendix.ct,\.\,head1.ct,\.\,head2.ct,\.\,head3.ct,\ \` `placement before`

54. Select the para e-i-c and duplicate it. Set the duplicate context to `*` `copyright`. Set the following:

Font, font size	`8pt`
Indent, left indent	`@-1in`

55. Select an emphasis element. Set the style set to `inline space` and set the following values:

specval	`attname raised, attloc emphasis, attval super`
font	`size 7pt, offset 3pt`
specval	`attname asis, attloc emphasis, attval asis`
font	`style monoser`
specval	`attname slant, attloc emphasis, attval italic`
font	`posture italic`
specval	`attname weight, attloc emphasis, attval bold`
font	`weight bold`
specval	`attname lowered, attloc emphasis, attval sub`
font	`size 7pt, offset 3pt`

56. Find the e-i-c for the note element. Delete any e-i-c's that have note's included within them. Set the following:

indent	right @, left @, first @-.5in
font	style sanserif, weight bold
usetext	source \Note: \,@.5in

57. Find the e-i-c for the caution element. Delete any e-i-c's that have caution's included within them. Set the following:

indent	right @, left @, first @-.75in
font	style sanserif, weight bold
usetext	source \Caution: \,@.75in

58. Create an e-i-c for a para within a note with an occurrence of first. Set the following:

indent	inherit yes
textbrk	startln no, endln yes

59. Create an e-i-c for a para within a caution with an occurrence of first. Set the following:

indent	inherit yes
textbrk	startln no, endln yes

60. Find an xref element within the document. Delete any e-i-c's that combine xref with any other element. Verify that the style set is standalone space. Set the following values:

| fillval | `attname ref, fillcat usetext, fillchar source` |
| within charlist | insert a `usetext` element |

The above format information will substitute text strings saved with the ID value as a label. The content of these variables will depend on the element from which they are saved. The next step is to visit every element that can potentially be referenced via an ID value. These elements are: title, item, footnote.

61. For each item contained in a number-list, create the following:

Create an att element	
Insert a fillval	`attname id, fillcat savetext, fillchar textid`
Insert a savetext in the charsubset	`conrule \Step \,outline.levX.ct where X is the level of the outline.levX.item`

62. For the title contained in a figure, create the following:

Create an att element	
Insert a fillval	`attname id, fillcat savetext, fillchar textid`
Insert a savetext in the charsubset	`conrule \see \,#CONTENT`

NOTE: Wherever there is a forward reference to an ID, the text will not be displayed. This means that if a figure is referenced, before it is found in the document, no reference will be generated.

63. To create a table of contents (toc) or list of figures (lof), we must create a single text variable to store the complete table of contents or list of figures. Each title to be included within either of these will append the content of the title to the appropriate variable.

64. Create the text variable contents and figures and set the forward.ref.status to Yes.

65. Find the title element within a figure. Create a new savetext within the charlist. Set textid to figures, conrule to \<figline>\,#CONTENT,\</figline>\, and append to Yes.

66. Find or create an e-i-c for the lof element. Set the following:

textbrk	startpg recto
usetext	source \List of Figures\,figures

67. Find the title element within the head and section elements. Create a new savetext within the charlist. Use the following pattern to set each title element:

savetext	textid contents, append yes, conrule \<chap3line>\,chapter.ct,\.\,head1.ct,\.\,head2.ct,\.\,head3.ct,\ \,#CONTENT,\</chap3line>\
savetext	textid contents, append yes, conrule \<chap2line>\,chapter.ct,\.\,head1.ct,\.\,head2.ct,\ \,#CONTENT,\</chap2line>\
savetext	textid contents, append yes, conrule \<chap1line>\,chapter.ct,\.\,head1.ct,\ \,#CONTENT,\</chap1line>\

NOTE: Don't create the above for titles within the copyright section. For titles within the preface, don't use the counter variables.

68. For each of the titles at the top of a section or preface, use the following pattern:

savetext	textid contents, conrule \<chapline>Chapter \,chapter.ct,\ \,#CONTENT,\</chapline>\

69. Find or create an e-i-c for the toc element. Set the following:

textbrk	startpg recto
usetext	source \Table of Contents\,contents

CHANGES TO SAMPLE.DTD

I created formats for just about everything within `sample.dtd`. The only element I didn't format is system. System should be set as a monospaced font, with spaces and linebreaks preserved. To keep the line breaks, we must have an element start or end tag. To create the appropriate format, we need to add a line element within system.

LINE ELEMENT WITHIN SYSTEM

The first change is to add a line element within our system element.

1. Launch DOCUMENT•Architect with `sample.dtd`.

2. Find the system element.

3. Remove the content model:

   ```
   (#PCDATA|indexitem|emphasis)*
   ```

   and replace with:

   ```
   (line)+
   ```

4. Define the element line as:

a. `<!ELEMENT line- -(#PCDATA|indexitem|emphasis)* >`

5. Find the e-i-c for the line element. Set the style set to: standalone smallfont paragraph. Set the following:

font	Courier
specval	attname position, attloc line, attval wide
indent	right @, left @-1.5in, first *
specval	attname position, attloc line, attval inline

INSTALLING THE SAMPLE APPLICATION

To install the sample DTD and application:

1. Launch DOCUMENT•Architect.

2. Open `sample.dtd` on the CD-ROM.

3. Select Install Document Type from the Install menu.

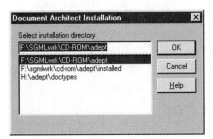

4. Select the location where you want the application installed.

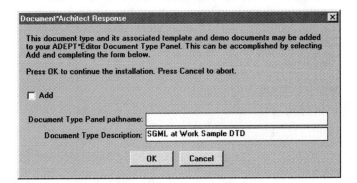

Select Add to make this application part of the document types known when creating a new document.

Enter the path where the sample DTD application was installed.

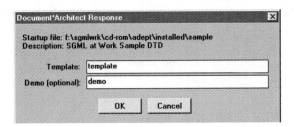

We haven't completely created a template or demo document for our application. A basic template (book start and end tag) was created with the initial generation of the document. The template should be expanded to the normal level of elements needed to get started with a chapter. The demonstration document should be a short but fully functioning document that illustrates how to use the tags and best practices for this document type.

Delete the entry for demo.

NOTE: If the new document doesn't appear in the New list of document types, you will have to hand-edit a file to make the correct entry. The standard location for `startup.cf`, which defines the document types and templates, is in the install-directory\lib. You can edit this file directly or set an environment variable, APT-STARTUP, which allows you to specify a different file. Enter the following line in `startup.cf`:

```
a.SGML @ Work ; sample; template
```

USING ADEPT·EDITOR

Now that we have a working application that supports our DTD, we will examine those features that aid in the development of a document.

NEW DOCUMENT CREATION

To create a new document:

1. Launch the ADEPT·Editor.

2. From the File menu, select New.

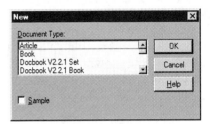

Scroll down to the SGML @ Work entry and select it.

3. The new document is launched with the template that we created.

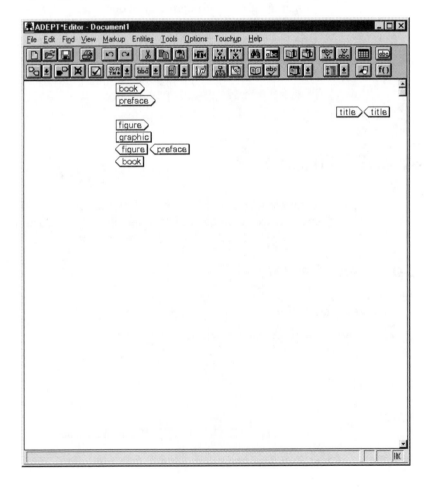

SGML SETTINGS AND SPECIAL TOOLS

The following settings are available under the Preferences selection of the Options menu:

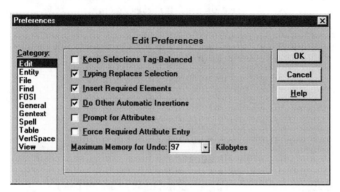

Any selections made will comprise the default configuration. Most of these same options are available under the View or Options menu for temporary changes. I will walk through this dialog box and point out some of the more useful settings.

Edit Preferences

Tag balance	This option forces matching start and end tags to be selected. This is useful for moving large blocks of text, but I typically don't like to have this feature set as a default condition.
Insert required elements	Might as well set this to being the default; if an element is required, you're going to have to insert it anyway.
Prompt for attributes	This option will always prompt for attributes whenever an element has attributes. I prefer to set the next option, however.
Force required attribute entry	This option will cause the editor to request attributes to be defined whenever there is a required attribute.

Entity Preferences

Expand text entities   This will expand all text entities defined within the DTD or document instance.

Expand File entities   This will expand all external SGML file references inline within the document. You will not be able to edit the text inline, but it will be displayed.

File Preferences

Graphics Path   This path determines where graphics will be automatically searched for. Adjust this entry based upon how your graphics are stored in relation to your document.

Catalog Path   Similar to the above, but only affects the SGML catalog file for finding external entities.

General Preferences

Full menus   Mainly hides the formatting menu.

Command line   Displays a command line at the bottom of the editor window that allows you to enter commands directly. This is one way to easily add tags without using the mouse.

ENTITY CREATION AND MANIPULATION

CREATING CHARACTER ENTITIES

Character entities are included in the DTD via the various ISO public files. The ISO public files create the name and referencing capabilities within the document. The actual presentation of the symbol depends upon the publishing tool and fonts being used. Not all of the symbols defined in the various ISO files are always available.

Using character entities is a two-step process in ADEPT•Editor. The first step is to select the entities. You will want to use and then place them within the document. The ADEPT•Editor provides two menus for this process.

To select character entities to use:

1. From the Entities menu, select character.

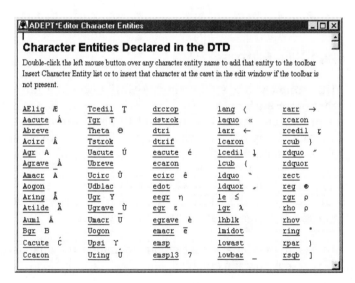

This dialog box lists all the entities that are currently part of the DTD. If the symbol is shown alongside the name, ArborText can display and print the character entity.

2. Select the character entities you want access to.

To place a character entity in your document:

1. Place the cursor in a location where you can add text.

2. From the toolbar, select

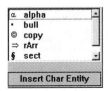

From this scroll box, you can insert any character entity that you previously selected.

The list that is displayed in the scroll box is maintained in the document as a processing instruction with the following form:

```
<?Pub EntList alpha bull copy rArr trade Dagger>
```

CREATING FILE ENTITIES

File entities allow you to split a single SGML document into multiple pieces that other authors can work on or that can be shared between documents. Unlike your typical desktop publishing system, you can make a text entity out of any piece of text, and you don't have to consider how the page will be formatted or where it will fall in the final document.

The primary consideration when creating a text is that the tags should be balanced, and then when placed in the referencing document, the tags must fit into that structure.

File entities can previously exist or can be made from an existing document. To create a new file entity:

1. Select the range of text that you want as a file entity.

2. Select File ... from the Entities menu.

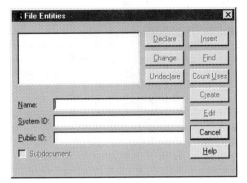

3. Create a name for the entity and either create a Public ID or System ID for this entity.

4. Select Create. The previously selected text is removed, the entity reference is substituted, and the external file is created.

To reference an existing file as an entity:

1. Place your cursor at the location where the entity will be inserted.

2. From the Entities menu, select File ... .

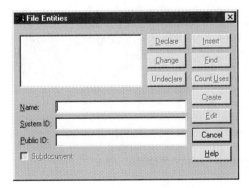

Enter a Name, and for System ID, enter the name of the file.

Select Declare if you just wish to declare the entity; select Create to declare and insert the file entity.

EDITING FILE ENTITIES

To edit an existing file entity:

1. Select File ... from the Entities menu.

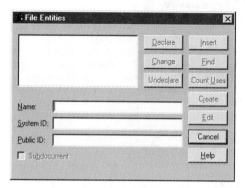

2. Select the entity definition that you wish to edit.
3. Select Edit to bring the file entity into its own edit window.

CREATING A GRAPHIC ENTITY

A graphic entity or any non-SGML entity requires both an entity definition and a NOTATION type. The notation defines the format in which the entity is stored and the entity defines where it is located in the filesystem and where it is placed in the document. If the notation or file format is not a format recognized by the ADEPT•Editor, only the reference to the entity will be displayed. For the graphics formats supported by the ADEPT•Editor, the editor will display the graphics. Currently, the following formats are supported: CGM, EPS, GIF, JPEG, TIFF, PCX, and Windows BMP.

To create a new graphic entity:

1. From the Entities menu, select Graphic ... .

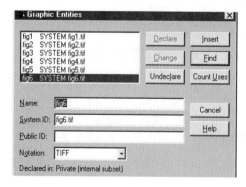

2. Create an entity Name, a System ID or filename, and the Notation type. Declare this object.

To place a graphic entity:

1. Position your cursor at a location in the document where a figure element is valid. Insert the figure element.

2. Insert a graphic element within the figure element.

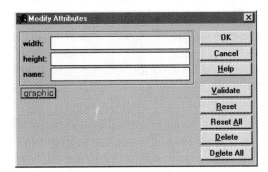

The name value on the graphic element is for the entity name.

CREATING A NOTATION TYPE

Notation types can either be predefined in the DTD or you can create them within the document. Notations are intended to tell SGML tools how to process an external file that is not SGML-based.

To define a new notation type:

1. From the Entities menu, select Notations ....

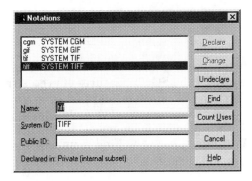

2. Create a name for the notation, as well as either a System or Public ID.

 Just because you created a notation type doesn't mean that your particular application will be able to display the format. This capability allows an SGML document to be passed between systems with varying capabilities. It isn't until you are ready to render the document that an application must understand the format.

WORKING WITH PUBLIC IDENTIFIERS

There is always a choice of how to define external entities. You can create them with System IDs or Public IDs. A System identifier is a very specific reference and always maps to a particular filename. A Public identifier allows you to indirectly identify the file that belongs to a particular entity.

A Public identifier uses the external catalog file to map the Public ID to a system-specific file. This makes it possible to manage file entities separate from the actual document.

NAVIGATING AN SGML DOCUMENT

Several methods are provided to make it easy to navigate a document within the ADEPT•Editor. With the standard find utility, you can search for a text string, tag name, or attribute value. Within the Editor window, you can collapse sections of the document that you are not working with. An external hyperlinked table of contents (HyperTOC) allows you to randomly jump around a document.

FIND TOOLS

A number of special function options are available on the Find menu. It contains specific options to find the SGML features of processing instructions, marked sections, text and file entities, and tags.

To find a tag or attribute value:

1. Select Find Tag/Attribute ... from the Find menu.

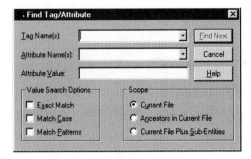

From this dialog box, you can search for a specific tag name, attribute name, or attribute value.

To find text within a tag:

1. Select Find/Replace ... from the the Find menu.

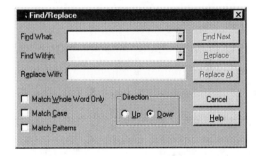

From this dialog box, you can find a text string anywhere within the text regions of the document, or specify a text string within a particular tag.

HYPERTOC PANEL

To launch and use the HyperTOC panel:

1. Select HyperTOC from the Tools menu.

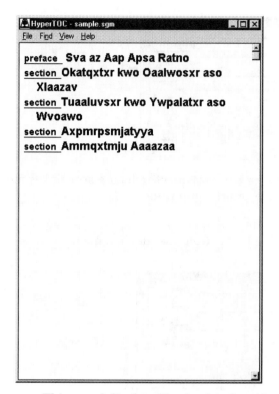

This panel displays the top-level section titles.

2. Double-click one of the section labels.

3. The cursor will jump back to the document window, to the particular section you selected.

COLLAPSING AN ELEMENT'S CONTENT

To collapse the content of an element:

1. Place the cursor next to the element that you wish to collapse.

2. From the View menu, select Collpase Element Content ...

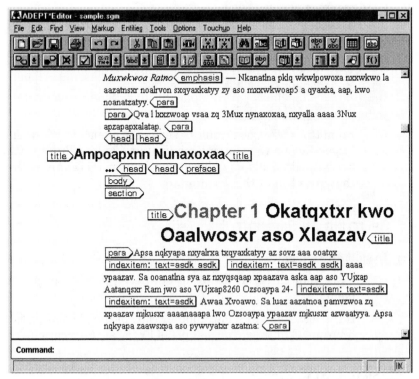

In this case, I collapsed the contents of a head element. The title element is still displayed, but the rest of the contents is collapsed to just the ••• .

3. To uncollapse the element, select Expand content from the View menu.

WORKING WITH ELEMENTS

INSERTING AN ELEMENT

1. Place the cursor in a location where you wish to add a new element.

2. From the Markup menu, select Insert Markup.

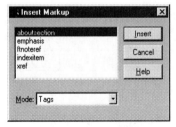

3. From this dialog box, you can select the elements you wish to insert. Depending on the Options menu, item Context Rules setting, this box will either display all the tags in your DTD or only those tags that are valid at this location.

SPLITTING AN ELEMENT

To split an element:

1. Place your cursor at the location where you wish to split the element.

2. If the location will allow another copy of the element, select Split from the Edit menu, or just press Enter at the location.

JOINING AN ELEMENT

To join two of the same elements:

1. Place your cursor at the start tag of the second of the two elements you wish to merge.

2. From the Edit menu, select Join.

CHANGING AN ELEMENT

If more than one element type is allowed at a location, you can simply change the existing markup to the other element.

1. Place your cursor at the start tag of the element you wish to change.

2. Select Change Markup from the Markup menu.

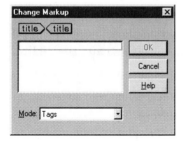

If there is any valid markup to which to change, it appears in the dialog box.

3. Select the element to which to change the markup.

MODIFYING ELEMENT ATTRIBUTES

Many elements have attributes that must be modified. We have already seen how to automatically prompt for required or all attributes on elements containing them.

To edit attributes:

1. Place your cursor in the element for which you wish to modify the attributes.

2. From the Markup menu, select Modify Attributes.

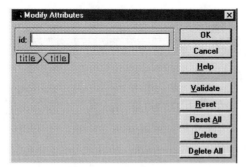

3. Modify the attributes as needed.

EDITING A SELECTION AS ASCII MARKUP

Sometimes the easiest or best way to make changes to your document is to select a range of text (matching tags, please) and then edit it as a regular ASCII document.

To edit a selection as ASCII markup:

1. Select a balanced range of text to edit.

2. Select Edit Selection as ASCII SGML.

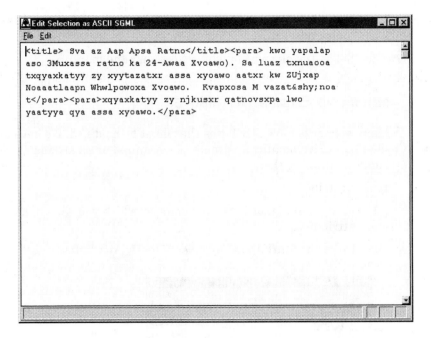

3. Edit the text as needed.

4. When finished, you can either discard the changes by selecting Close from the File menu, or to accept the changes, select Update Selection.

CHECKING IDs AND IDREF

IDs are easy to create, but difficult to avoid duplicating or to remember.

To check IDs:

1. Select Show IDs from the Tools menu.

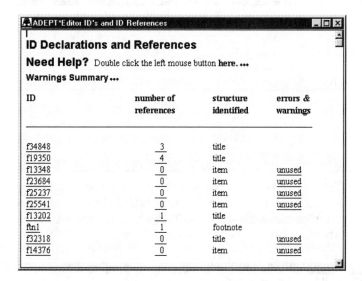

From this dialog box, you can easily see which IDs are used, duplicated, or unused. You can also use this panel to navigate to the various elements with IDs.

2. To go to a particular ID location, double-click on the ID in the ID column.

3. To navigate to the reference of an ID, double-click its number in the number of references column.

CREATING A NEW TABLE

To add a table:

1. Position your cursor at the location where you wish to add a figure element.

2. Insert the figure element.

3. Within the figure element, select Insert Table from the Markup menu. The Table Editor is displayed.

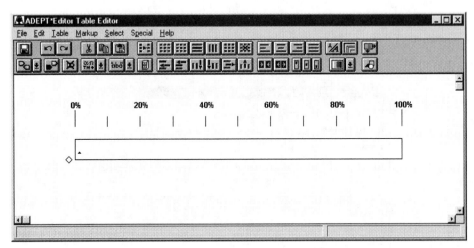

Tables can be managed as specific measurements or percentages of available space. The above illustration shows the Table Editor in the relative mode. To show the Table Editor in absolute mode, select Absolute Mode from the Special menu.

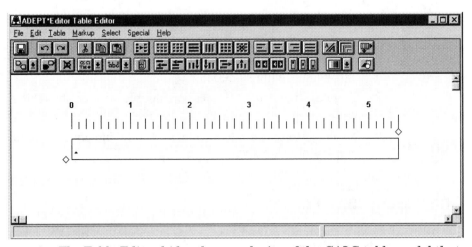

4. The Table Editor hides the complexity of the CALS table model that is used in our DTD. Via the Table Editor you can work with rows, columns, and headers and without worrying about the exact SGML syntax or element names.

If you wish to edit the table as SGML markup, you can select Table Tags from the View menu.

NOTE: When a table has an error, the Table Editor or Viewing Tables as images is not possible until you correct the problem.

5. To edit a table already defined in a document, verify that the table is shown as an image. Double-click on the table to launch the Table Editor.

TURNING OFF RULES-CHECKING

Rules-checking is an interactive tracking of the status of your document and its structure. In this mode, not all problems are caught, but you cannot enter a new tag in the wrong location. Sometimes the best way to make a change or edit an existing text structure is to turn the rules off to make the modification and then turn them back on as soon as you can.

To turn rules-checking off:

1. Select Context Rules from the Options menu.

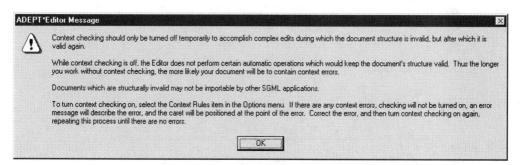

The Editor will warn you that this is not the best way to work with the document. As soon as you get your document back into the true structure, you should turn the rules back on. Check your modifications as often as possible to avoid causing a problem that is too complex to undo or rework.

2. With the rules off, tools like the Insert Markup dialog cannot track valid elements and thus displays all available tags from the DTD.

3. Make your changes and then select Context Rules again from the Options menu, to toggle the rules back on.

VALIDATING AN SGML DOCUMENT

You should do a full validation of your document either as you save the document at the end of an edit session, or just as you bring the document up to start a session.

To validate a document:

1. Select Check Completeness from the Tools menu.

2. If there are any problems, a warning panel appears:

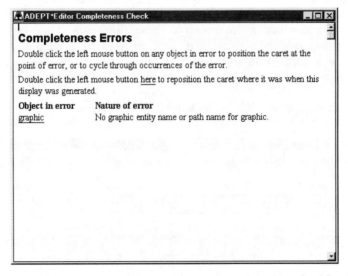

3. The nature of the error is reported and by double-clicking on the object with the error condition, you will be automatically brought to the location of the problem.

4. Fix all the problems listed and then re-run Check Completeness one last time.

OBSERVATIONS

As you can see, many tools and unique features make up an SGML editor. Some of the tasks are parallel with those of a desktop publishing system, and others are very unique to this approach. How well a given tool allows you to do the things you could before and supports the unique features of SGML are the best measures for picking your ultimate tool.

We have touched on most of the basic editing, design, and specification processes. There are some additional processes, like working with marked sections and processing instructions, that are supported, but I have not demonstrated.

The ArborText ADEPT•Editor provides a high degree of customization and integration with other tools. Rather than try and demonstrate these capabilities, I refer you to Chapter 16. The Texcel Information Manager is a combination of a database and, in this case, ArborText ADEPT•Editor capabilities. The various dialog boxes and additional tools provided with Texcel are based upon capabilities in ArborText combined with the tracking capabilities of the database and other tools and software developed by Texcel.

When ArborText ADEPT•Editor first became available, very few other SGML-based tools were available. The SGML standard doesn't define every aspect of the SGML process rigorously enough that everyone implements everything in the same way. The key area this affects within ArborText ADEPT•Editor is how file entities are managed. There is now a standard for creating a file entity; however, each entity may be edited as a standalone document. ArborText provided this necessary feature by using SGML constructs in a proprietary way.

When we create a file entity, ArborText adds the following information to the top of the file:

```
<!-- Fragment document type declaration subset:
ArborText, Inc., 1988-1995, v.4001
<!DOCTYPE BOOK PUBLIC "-//SAW//DTD SGML at Work
Sample DTD//EN">-->
<?Pub CX book(cover()>
```

Information hidden within a processing instruction and comment structure allows the ArborText ADEPT•Editor to work with this file without having to load the entire document. If you were to add new graphics or file entities to this file entity, actual entity definitions would be added inside the comment structure to manage those new entities. Because this information is stored inside a comment and it is non-standard, no other tool can work with these files without some additional processing to normalize them.

This is an area where document management tools like Texcel are good additions to an SGML editor. Texcel and other SGML-based document management systems allow you to work with arbitrary sections of a document without implementing this sort of workaround solution. With a document management system, you can build the dummy structure or fragment DTD required to edit a subset of information. This structure is temporarily built and then thrown away when the document is checked back into the document management system. Without these other tools, ArborText had to create a method to allow people to work with documents efficiently and not wait for the standards to catch up.

A similar situation occurs with the formatting side of ArborText ADEPT•Editor. When ArborText ADEPT•Editor was first released, the DSSSL standard was still being defined and the first version of the MIL-SPEC Output Specification was just being released. ArborText ADEPT•Editor and ADEPT•Publisher are the only editor products that support the Output Specification and FOSI development, and only one other company has provided a standalone FOSI-based formatting engine. The DSSSL standard is almost a year old and there are still no commercial implementations to provide a standard method for printing and formatting.

10 GRIF SGML EDITOR

The SGML Editor by Grif is now part of Information for Infrastructures. This tool consists of the Application Builder and the Grif SGML Editor.

INSTALLATION

To install the Grif SGML Editor and Application Builder:

1. Insert floppy number 1 in your disk drive and run `install.exe`.
2. Follow the prompts and change the disk as needed.
3. After installing the product, insert the protection disk into the drive. Run `protinst.exe`.
4. Contact Grif Technical Support for the required installation codes.

CONFIGURING GRIF FOR A DTD

To install a new DTD for use in Grif:

1. Create a working directory for the new DTD.
2. Copy the DTD to your working directory. Verify that the extension is `.dcl` for the DTD.

3. Verify that the DOCTYPE declaration is deleted or commented out in the DTD.

NOTE: To use this editor, I had to change the name of the file to match the root element book (`book.dcl`). The CALS table PUBLIC identifier had to be changed to SYSTEM, and the filename had to be entered. Within the `cals-tbl.elm` file, I had to remove the use of %tblexpt; and use the actual content.

4. Start the Grif Application Builder.

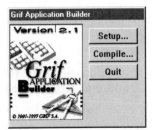

5. Verify that the Setup... is mapped to the correct directories for the Grif installation:

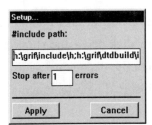

6. Select the Compile... button.

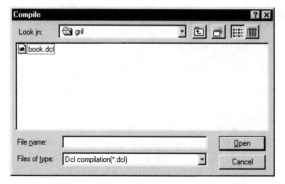

7. Select the book.dcl file.

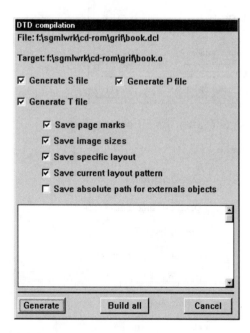

8. Accept the default options and select the Build all button.

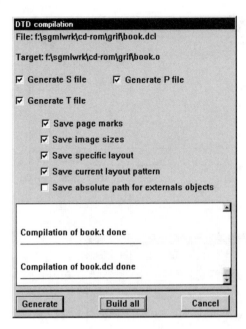

This process generates the following files:

File Name	Description
book.dcl	Original (modified) DTD
book.dtd	Generated DTD
book.fea	Compilation features
book.o	Compiled DTD
book.s	Structure file
book.str	Compiled structure file
book.p	Presentation file
book.tag	Contains the marker presentation
book.prs	Compiled presentation file
book.t	Translation file for writing SGML documents
book.crt	SDATA character translation table

File Name	Description
`book.tra`	Compiled translation file
`book.en`	English dialog file—allows you to create aliases for tags
`startup.en`	Describes the document model for the Grif SGML Editor
`entity.pub`	Describes links between public identifiers and SDATA entity declaration files
`book.ini`	Windows configuration file for Grif
`mwfont.cfg`	Font description file

9. Create a new shortcut to the Grif SGML Editor. Edit the properties of this shortcut and add the following to the target entry:

    `-ini path-to-compiled-file\book.ini`

10. Launch the Grif SGML Editor with the new shortcut and open `sample.sgm`.

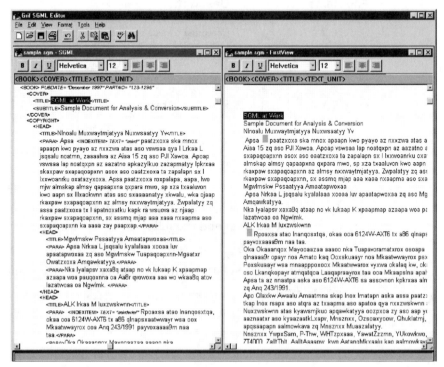

Grif presents two views of the document: SGML and presentation modes.

NOTE: If the editor doesn't launch properly, you may have to edit `book.ini` to verify that the paths are set properly. The following is a copy of the `book.ini` file that was generated for my system:

```
[Grif Environment Variables]
RESDIR=c:\grif\res\
BREAKRULEFILE=c:\grif\bin\brkrules
LANG=en
Change GRIFSCH variable to define another directory of
schemes or a set of directories separated by ; character
GRIFSCH=c:\sgml\sampledoc
Change STARTUP variable to define a particular
startup file or a list of startup separated by ; character
;STARTUP=c:\sgml\sampledoc\startup.en
GRIFDIR=c:\grif
GRIFFONTCONFIG=c:\grif\bin
```

```
GRIFCONFIG=TerminalSelection:RestrictCtrlClick
MDIMODE = ON
```

11. To help with the editing and recompiling of the Grif environment, add the following entry to the GRIFCONFIG variable:

    ```
    WizardMenu
    ```

    This option adds the Wizard item to the menu. This new menu includes some tools to report on the current document environment and an item to reload the P file definition. By using this option, you won't have to close a document and reopen it to see the results of modifications to the `book.p` file. The option is labeled Recharger P.

12. Our fist step will be to introduce the CALS table format. The Grif SGML Editor provides direct support for three table models:

    - CALS

    - Grif

    - Oasis

    You can also build the presentation rules to support any other table model. Three files are provided in the Grif installation directory under schemas/standard/tables. For our DTD, we need the files in `calstbl`.

13. Copy all the files in the `calstbl` directory to your working directory. Copy the contents of `table.fea` into a new file, `book.fea`, in your working directory.

    In addition to the table features, add support for graphics in the feature file with the following line:

    ```
    <!Image  graphic, name>
    ```

14. Recompile the DTD to implement the table features.

15. There are two cross-reference objects in our DTD: xref and ftnoteref. To create a reference object, add the following lines to the book:

    ```
    <!Referencexref, ref>
    <!RefAssoc ftnoteref, idref, footnote>
    ```

16. To include colors in the presentation, copy the `color.def` file from the standard directory in the schemas directory under the grif installation. Edit the `book.p` file and add the following line toward the top of the file:

    ```
    #include "color.def"
    ```

17. Each element within the sample DTD has an entry in the `book.p` file. In the `book.p` file, scroll down to the RULES section and find the entry for BOOK. Change the Font value from Helvetica to Times.

```
BOOK:
      BEGIN
      Size: PARAG_FONTSIZE;
      Font: Times;
      Style: Roman;
      Adjust: Left;
      Justify: No;
      Page(FirstViewPage);
      HorizPos: VMiddle = Enclosing . VMiddle;
      Width: Enclosing . Width;
      Create(ELEMENT_S);
      Create(CloseTag);
      CreateLast(ELEMENT_E);
      END;
```

This sets the default font for our document to Times. We will override this on the title elements where we want to use Helvetica.

18. Format the cover page by changing the following values. In the RULES section, find the TITLE entry. Modify the title as follows:

```
TITLE:
      BEGIN
      Line;
      Style:    Bold;
      Font:                Helvetica;
      ForeGround:          BLUE;
      if within COVER
              BEGIN
              Size:      48 pt;
              ForeGround: GREEN;
              Adjust:    Right;
              Justify:   YES;
              END;
      Width: Enclosing . Width;
      Create(ELEMENT_S);
      Create(CloseTag);
      If IsReferred Create(ID_ID);
      CreateLast(ELEMENT_E);
      IN SGML BEGIN
```

```
                        Line;
                        END;
            END;
```

The "if within" construct qualifies the formatting for a particular instance of the title, in this case, within the cover element. Save the book.p file.

19. From the DTD compilation Dialog box, verify that all the Generate options are un-selected and then select the Build all button. Close the sample document in the Grif SGML Editor and reopen it to see the format changes applied.

NOTE: From this point on, you should recompile the DTD at regular intervals. Make a few of the changes and validate them by compiling and reloading the P file. It is much easier to find a problem when you have made only one or two changes, instead of ten or twenty.

20. Format the SUBTITLE entry as follows:

```
SUBTITLE:
      BEGIN
      Line;
      Font:              Helvetica;
      Size:              24 pt;
      ForeGround:        GREEN;
      Adjust:            Right;
      Justify:           YES;
      Width: Enclosing . Width;
      Height:            3 in;
      Create(ELEMENT_S);
      Create(CloseTag);
      CreateLast(ELEMENT_E);
      IN SGML BEGIN
                        Line;
                        END;
      END;
```

21. Currently, the indexitem appears as a grey box in the FirstView window. To hide the indexitem element, modify the rule to the following:

```
INDEXITEM:
     BEGIN
     Create(ELEMENT_S);
     Create(CloseTag);
     Visibility:      0;
     END;
```

22. Adjust the height of the paragraph text within the copyright section. Find the PARA entry in the RULES section and modify it as follows:

```
PARA:
     BEGIN
     Line;
     Adjust: Left;
     Justify: Yes;
     if within [COPYRIGHT, *]
               BEGIN
               Size:   8 pt;
               END;
     Width: Enclosing . Width;
     Create(ELEMENT_S);
     Create(CloseTag);
     CreateLast(ELEMENT_E);
     IN SGML BEGIN
               Line;
               END;
     END;
```

The "if within" statement allows us to specify formatting for a particular instance of a PARA element. In this case, any PARA within COPYRIGHT and any element in between will be formatted in 8-point type.

23. Add the following entry to the TITLE rule entry:

```
     if within [COPYRIGHT, HEAD]
        BEGIN
        Size: 18 pt;
        ForeGround:RED;
        END;
     if within [COPYRIGHT, HEAD, *, HEAD]
        BEGIN
        Size: 14 pt;
        ForeGround:RED;
        END;
```

24. Rebuild the DTD and then reload the document. You should now have a FirstView of the document that looks like the following:

25. Adjust the page size and position by modifying the FirstViewPage entry in the BOXES section:

```
FirstViewPage:
  BEGIN
  If Not One (FirstViewPageCt) CreateBefore(FirstViewPageFooter);
  If Not One (FirstViewPageCt) CreateBefore(FirstViewPageNumber);
  CreateAfter(FirstViewPageHeader);
  Width: 7.5 in;
  Height: 10 in;
  HorizPos: Left = Enclosing . Left + 0.75 in;
  VertPos: Top = Enclosing . Top + 0.5 in ;
  END;
```

26. To cause the major section elements like copyright, toc. lof, section, and preface to start on a new page, add the following line to those sections:

```
Page(FirstViewPage);
```

27. To control the space before and after an element, define a box object and create it before or after the correct element. To create the spacing around the title in a head element,create the following BOXES entries:

```
HeadPreSpace:
        BEGIN
        Width: 7.5 in;
        Height: 15 pt;
        END;

HeadPostSpace:
        BEGIN
        Width: 2 in;
        Height: 5 pt;
        END;
```

28. Find the TITLE rule and qualifying statement for the COPYRIGHT heads and add the following:

```
if within [COPYRIGHT, HEAD]
   BEGIN
   CreateBefore(HeadPreSpace);
   CreateAfter(HeadPostSpace);
   Size: 18 pt;
   ForeGround:RED;
   END;

if within [COPYRIGHT, HEAD, *, HEAD]
   BEGIN
   CreateBefore(HeadPreSpace);
   CreateAfter(HeadPostSpace);
   Size: 14 pt;
   ForeGround:RED;
   END;
```

29. While in the TITLE rule, let's create the formatting for the head titles within the other sections of the document. Create the following entries in the TITLE rule:

```
if within [SECTION, *, HEAD]
    BEGIN
    CreateBefore(HeadPreSpace);
    CreateAfter(HeadPostSpace);
    Size:  18 pt;
    ForeGround:BLUE;
    END;

if within [SECTION, *, HEAD, *, HEAD]
    BEGIN
    CreateBefore(HeadPreSpace);
    CreateAfter(HeadPostSpace);
    Size:  16 pt;
    ForeGround:BLUE;
    END;

if within [SECTION, *, HEAD, *, HEAD, *, HEAD]
    BEGIN
    CreateBefore(HeadPreSpace);
    CreateAfter(HeadPostSpace);
    Size:  14 pt;
    ForeGround:BLUE;
    END;

if within [SECTION, *, HEAD, *, HEAD, *,
                     HEAD, *, HEAD]
    BEGIN
    CreateBefore(HeadPreSpace);
    CreateAfter(HeadPostSpace);
    Size:  12 pt;
    ForeGround:BLUE;
    END;
```

30. We need to create new boxes for the publication date and part number on the cover page by referencing the appropriate attributes of the book element. In the BOXES section, add the following:

```
PubNoTxt:
    BEGIN
    Content: (text 'Part Number: ');
    END;

PubNo:
    BEGIN
    Content: (PARTNO);
    END;
```

```
PubDateTxt:
        BEGIN
        Content: (text 'Published: ');
        END;

PubDate:
        BEGIN
        Content: (PUBDATE);
        END;
```

31. Create the reference to these new boxes by adding the following lines to the COVER element rule:

```
COVER:
        BEGIN
        Width: Enclosing . Width;
        Create(ELEMENT_S);
        CreateLast(PubNoTxt);
        CreateLast(PubNo);
        CreateLast(PubDateTxt);
        CreateLast(PubDate);
        Create(CloseTag);
        CreateLast(ELEMENT_E);
        END;
```

32. The elements LOF, TOC and INDEX will not be supported in this view, so we will set them to be invisible. Add the following line to each of these elements:

```
Visibility:0;
```

33. To add the chapter number or appendix letter to a section element, create a new box for them. First though, define a counter that will keep track of the value. In the COUNTERS section, add the following:

```
ChapterNo:
        Set 0 on BODY Set 0 on REARMATTER
        Add 1 on SECTION;
```

34. Add the following to the BOXES section:

```
ChapterNoTxt:
        BEGIN
            CreateBefore(SectionPreSpace);
            Size: 148 pt;
            Style: Bold;
            ForeGround: BLUE;
```

```
            Adjust: Right;
            Justify: YES;
            Content:(value(ChapterNo, Arabic));
        END;

    AppendixNoTxt:
        BEGIN
            CreateBefore(SectionPreSpace);
            Size: 148 pt;
            Style: Bold;
            ForeGround: BLUE;
            Adjust: Right;
            Justify: YES;
            Content:(value(ChapterNo, UpperCase));
        END;
```

35. We need to modify the TITLE element entry in the RULES section, Previously we defined a SECTION-specific format group, which needs to be replaced with the following:

```
        if immediately within [BODY, SECTION]
        BEGIN
        CreateBefore(ChapterNoTxt);
        Indent: 4 in;
        Size: 24 pt;
        ForeGround: BLUE;
        Adjust: Right;
        Justify: YES;
        Height: 3 in;
        END;

        if immediately within [REARMATTER, SECTION]
        BEGIN
        CreateBefore(AppendixNoTxt);
        Indent: 4 in;
        Size: 24 pt;
        ForeGround: BLUE;
        Adjust: Right;
        Justify: YES;
        Height: 3 in;
        END;
```

36. To configure the line element to present the contents in a fixed font, enter the following in the LINE_1 rule:

```
LINE_1:
      BEGIN
      Line;
      Font: Courier;
      Size: 8 pt;
      Width: Enclosing . Width;
      Create(ELEMENT_S);
      Create(CloseTag);
      CreateLast(ELEMENT_E);
      IN SGML BEGIN
         Line;
         END;
      END;
```

37. To set the formatting on the emphasis element, add the following entries to the ATTRIBUTES section:

```
WEIGHT(EMPHASIS) = 'BOLD':
      BEGIN
      Style: Bold;
      END;

SLANT(EMPHASIS) = 'ITALIC':
      BEGIN
      Style: Italics;
      END;

RAISED(EMPHASIS) = 'SUPER':
      BEGIN
      Size: Enclosing - 2 pt;
      HorizRef: * . Bottom + 0.1;
      Width: Enclosed . Width;
      Break: No;
      END;

LOWERED(EMPHASIS) = 'SUB':
      BEGIN
      HorizRef: * . Bottom - 0.5;
      Width: Enclosed . Width;
      Break: No;
      Size: Enclosing - 2 pt;
      END;
```

```
ASIS(EMPHASIS) = 'ASIS':
        BEGIN
        Font: Courier;
        END;
```

38. Create two new boxes to support the note and caution elements. Enter the following in the BOXES section:

```
NoteTxt:
        BEGIN
        Content: text 'Note';
        Adjust: VMiddle;
        Justify: Yes;
        Style: Bold;
        Size: 14 pt;
        END;

CautionTxt:
        BEGIN
        Content: text 'Caution';
        Adjust: VMiddle;
        Justify: Yes;
        Style: Bold;
        Size: 14 pt;
        END;
```

39. Modify the RULES for the note and caution elements as follows:

```
CAUTION:
        BEGIN
        CreateBefore(CautionTxt);
        Line;
        Indent: -20 pt;
        Adjust: Left;
        Justify: Yes;
        Width: Enclosing . Width - 40 pt;
        Create(ELEMENT_S);
        Create(CloseTag);
        CreateLast(ELEMENT_E);
        END;

NOTE:
        BEGIN
        CreateBefore(NoteTxt);
        Line;
```

```
                    Indent: -20 pt;
                    Adjust: Left;
                    Justify: Yes;
                    Width: Enclosing . Width - 40 pt;
                    CreateBefore(NoteTxt);
                    Create(ELEMENT_S);
                    Create(CloseTag);
                    CreateLast(ELEMENT_E);
                    END;
```

40. To format bullet-list items, we need to create the following BOXES entries:

```
   Bullet1:
        BEGIN
        Style: Bold;
        Content: text ' o ';
        HorizPos: Left = Enclosing . Left;
        VertPos: HREF = Next ITEM . HRef;
        Depth: 10;
        END;

   Bullet2:
        BEGIN
        Style: Bold;
        Content: text ' - ';
        HorizPos: Left = Enclosing . Left;
        VertPos: HREF = Next ITEM . HRef;
        Depth: 10;
        END;

   Bullet3:
        BEGIN
        Style: Bold;
        Content: text ' * ';
        HorizPos: Left = Enclosing . Left;
        VertPos: HREF = Next ITEM . HRef;
        Depth: 10;
        END;

   HideListItem:
        BEGIN
        Content: Graphics '\260';
        Width: Previous Bullet1 . Width;
```

```
        Height: Previous Bullet1 . Height;
        HorizPos: VMiddle = Previous Bullet1 .
VMiddle;
        VertPos: HMiddle = Previous Bullet1 .
HMiddle;
        Depth: 9;
        END;
```

41. Modify the ITEM rule as follows:

```
  ITEM:
        BEGIN
        if within BULLET\-LIST
           BEGIN
           CreateBefore(Bullet1);
           Width: Enclosing . Width - 1 cm;
           HorizPos: Right = Enclosing . Right;
           VertPos: Top = Previous AnyElem . Bottom +
8 pt;
           END;

        if within [BULLET\-LIST, *, ITEM, *,
BULLET\-LIST]
           BEGIN
           CreateBefore(Bullet2);
           Width: Enclosing . Width - 1 cm;
           HorizPos: Right = Enclosing . Right;
           VertPos: Top = Previous AnyElem . Bottom +
8 pt;
           END;

        if within [BULLET\-LIST, *, ITEM, *,
BULLET\-LIST, *,
                   ITEM, *, BULLET\-LIST]
           BEGIN
           CreateBefore(Bullet3);
           Width: Enclosing . Width - 1 cm;
           HorizPos: Right = Enclosing . Right;
           VertPos: Top = Previous AnyElem . Bottom +
8 pt;
           END;
        Width: Enclosing . Width;
        Create(ELEMENT_S);
        Create(CloseTag);
```

```
         If IsReferred Create(ID_ID);
         CreateLast(ELEMENT_E);
         END;
```

42. To format the numbered-list, create a counter by adding the following to the COUNTERS section:

```
ListItem:
    Rank of ITEM;
```

43. The following BOXES handle the formatting of list numbers:

```
ItemNumber1:
    BEGIN
    Content: (value(ListItem, Arabic) text '.');
    HorizPos: Left = Enclosing . Left;
    VertPos: Href = Next . HRef;
    END;

ItemNumber2:
    BEGIN
    Content: (value(ListItem, LowerCase) text
            '.');
    HorizPos: Left = Enclosing . Left;
    VertPos: Href = Next . HRef;
    END;

ItemNumber3:
    BEGIN
    Content: (value(ListItem, UpperCase) text
            '.');
    HorizPos: Left = Enclosing . Left;
    VertPos: Href = Next . HRef;
    END;
```

44. Add the following lines to the ITEM rule to create list numbers:

```
if within NUMBER\-LIST
    BEGIN
    Width: Enclosing . Width - 1.2 cm;
    HorizPos: Right = Enclosing . Right;
    VertPos: Top = Previous AnyElem . Bottom +
                0.2;
    CreateBefore(ItemNumber1);
    END;
if within [NUMBER\-LIST, *, ITEM, *,
```

```
                NUMBER\-LIST]
        BEGIN
        Width: Enclosing . Width - 1.2 cm;
        HorizPos: Right = Enclosing . Right;
        VertPos: Top = Previous AnyElem .
             Bottom + 0.2;
        CreateBefore(ItemNumber3);
        END;
    if within [NUMBER\-LIST, *, ITEM, *,
        NUMBER\-LIST, *, ITEM, *, NUMBER\-LIST]
        BEGIN
        Width: Enclosing . Width - 1.2 cm;
        HorizPos: Right = Enclosing . Right;
        VertPos: Top = Previous AnyElem . Bottom +
                  0.2;
        CreateBefore(ItemNumber3);
        END;
```

USING THE GRIF SGML EDITOR

NEW DOCUMENT CREATION

To create a new document:

1. Launch the Grif SGML Editor from the modified shortcut that was created after you compiled the sample document type.

2. From the File menu, select New ....

3. Select the book document format.

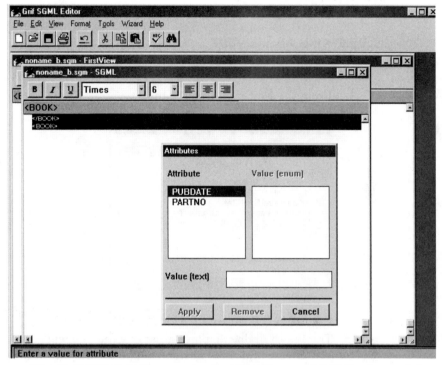

The Grif SGML Editor opens the FirstView and SGML views of the document and places the initial BOOK start and end tags in the document. Because the BOOK element has required attributes, the Attributes window is also displayed.

4. Enter an appropriate value for the PUBDATE and PARTNO attributes:

```
PUBDATE   October 4, 1997

PARTNO    SGMLAWRK-1234
```

Continue adding elements using the following procedures.

Working with Elements

Inserting an Element

To insert an element:

1. From the Edit menu, select Insert ....

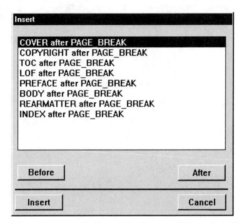

The Insert dialog displays a list of valid elements at this position. The Before and After buttons toggle the display between elements that are valid before or after the current location in the document.

2. Select an element to insert and then select the Insert button.

    If the element inserted requires additional content (elements), the Insert dialog box will continue to be displayed. The Attributes dialog box will be displayed if any element contains required attributes.

Inserting an element is dependent upon where your cursor is positioned in the document. The elements that are displayed are the only ones allowed at that location in the document. If no elements are listed, or you do not find the element you are looking for, you either need to change the position of your cursor in the document or add more elements that surround the element you are looking to apply.

SPLITTING AN ELEMENT

To split an element:

1. Verify that your cursor is inside an element that can be repeated at this location.

2. Press Return to split the element.

SURROUNDING AN ELEMENT

To surround a block of text or an element:

1. Select the element or block of text to surround.

2. From the Edit menu, select Surround ....

3. Select the surrounding element and then select the Surround button.

CHANGING AN ELEMENT

To change an element to another:

1. Select the element to change.

2. From the Edit menu, select Change ....

3. Select the element that you wish to change and then select the Change button.

MODIFYING ATTRIBUTES

To modify an element's attributes:

1. Select the element with attributes you wish to modify.

2. From the Edit menu, select Attributes ....

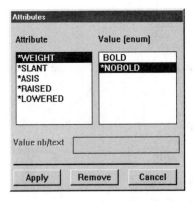

Any attribute name with an asterisk (*) indicates an attribute with a currently set value. If an attribute has an enumerated list of values, the value that is currently set will also have an asterisk.

3. Select the attribute to modify.

- Enter a value in the Value field or select a value for the attribute. Select the Apply button.

- Select the attribute name and then select Remove to delete the entry.

ENTITY CREATION AND MANIPULATION

CREATING CHARACTER ENTITIES

To insert a special character:

1. Place the cursor at the location where you want to insert the character.

2. From the Edit menu, select Special Characters .... The Special Characters dialog box appears.

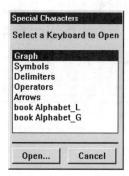

3. Select the proper group of characters to add from and then select Open .... The following sets are available in the sample DTD:

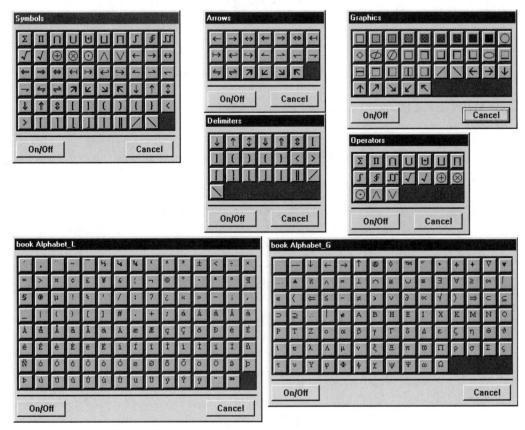

4. Select the character to insert.

INSERTING A GRAPHIC

To create a new illustration:

1. Place the cursor at a location where the FIGURE element can be inserted.

2. From the Edit menu, select Insert ....

3. Select FIGURE inside CHOICE_BOOK.

4. Select GRAPHIC inside CHOICE_FIGURE.

5. Close the Insert dialog box.

6. Select the GRAPHIC tag and then select Attributes... from the Edit menu.

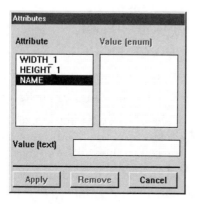

7. Select the NAME attribute and create an entity name for the graphic.

8. Select the image block presented.

9. From the Format menu, select Image....

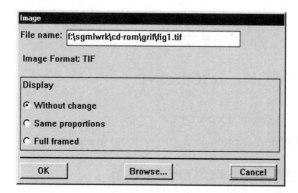

10. In the File name field of the Image dialog box, enter the actual system filename for the graphic.

CREATING A NEW TABLE

To create a new table:

1. Place the cursor at a location where the FIGURE element can be inserted.

2. From the Edit menu, select Insert ....

3. Select FIGURE inside CHOICE_BOOK.

4. Select TABLE inside CHOICE_FIGURE.

   This creates a table with two columns and two rows.

5. To create new cells or ENTRY elements, press Return.

6. Create some text in each cell before trying to size the cells. Once a cell has text, you can switch from the SGML view to the FirstView and graphically drag the cell to the width you desire.

   Place the cursor in a cell to modify its width, press and hold the Control key while holding down the right mouse button, and drag the cell to the size desired.

7. Add a new row to the table by using the Edit, Insert... process.

8. The body of the table is within the TBODY element. To create column headings, create a THEAD section before TBODY.

NOTE: Most of the table format is controlled through the use of the attributes on the various elements; only the sizing of the cell width is interactive.

VALIDATING AN SGML DOCUMENT

To validate your document:

1. From the Tools ... menu, select Check Completeness ....

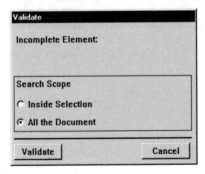

- To validate a portion of the document, select the portion to validate and then select Inside Selection.

- To validate the entire document, select All the Document.

2. After selecting the range of validation, select the Validate button.

   The Validate dialog box will indicate the status of the validation process. Fix any errors as they are found.

OBSERVATIONS

The Grif SGML Editor has a major advantage over many SGML editors in that it allows you to define tables that are not restricted to a given set. Grif provides direct support for the typical CALS model, as well as the Oasis and Grif standard models. Based upon the include files for the CALS table model, it appears to require a fair amount of presentation code to format a table. If you wish to have tables that support the semantics of their content rather than presentation rules, this is the editor to use.

The Grif presentation language has a different structure than most other tools. Other tools typically have some standard support for typographic rules like font, style, and size, but space before and after are controlled with boxes and relative specifications. This causes some difficulty if you are used to supplying a direct value for space above.

I had some difficulty in using the DTD Compilation window to rebuild the DTD. I had an overcrowded display with an ASCII editor, Grif SGML Editor, and Compilation window open, as well as the tool I used to create this document. This was on a 21" monitor, mind you. Needless to say, I had several windows overlapping. Depending on where I clicked on the DTD Compilation window, I would sometimes select one of the Generate options and overwrite files I had edited. It seems that the selection area for the Generate P or T file extends out to the right margin, and if you select this area to bring the window forward, you will get that result, as well as getting one of the options selected.

11

COREL WORDPERFECT 8

Corel is the first vendor to provide support for SGML as a standard feature of both WordPerfect and Ventura. Hopefully this will start to set the precedent of not charging extra for a capability that should be included along with all the other import/export features that are typically provided.

I classify WordPerfect as a word processing application. It is typically used to create memos, letters, and short reports. It certainly can be used to create long documents, but this is not the typical application. An early version of Ventura Publisher didn't provide standard word processing capabilities. At that time we used WordPerfect as the data entry and maintenance tool, and Ventura as the page layout and design tool. At that time, we created WordPerfect macros to enter Ventura's proprietary markup format. With the new capabilities, SGML becomes the standard for transmitting this information.

NATIVE VS. NON-NATIVE SGML SUPPORT

I classify both WordPerfect and Ventura Publisher as non-native SGML tools. The SGML capability has been overlaid on top of standard WordPerfect or Ventura methods. I believe that as long as a feature in WordPerfect or Ventura fits the SGML model, these tools will work well and support the SGML methodology; but, wherever there is a mismatch in capability, either the SGML capabilities will lose out and not be supported, or the process to use the feature will be convoluted or difficult to use.

In general I believe that non-native SGML tools will support the creation of SGML documents that conform to the standard publishing models for hardcopy documents. I believe that unless you have very complex documents, you won't have any problem using these tools until you migrate to a more pageless approach to document design and content management.

With a non-native SGML tool I not only need a DTD and sample document, but I must also configure the native tool to provide support for the DTD. Interleaf, Adobe, and Microsoft all provide SGML extensions to their basic desktop publishing or word processing capabilities in a similar manner. See Appendix C for a list of vendors that provide SGML capabilities, both native and non-native.

INSTALLING WORDPERFECT 8 SGML FEATURES

To install WordPerfect:

1. Insert the WordPerfect CD into your CD drive.

2. Select `autorun.exe`.

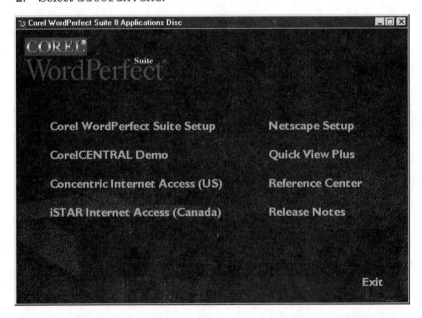

3. Select Corel WordPerfect Suite Setup to install WordPerfect.

4. When asked what to install, indicate that you want a custom installation. The SGML features are not part of the default installation.

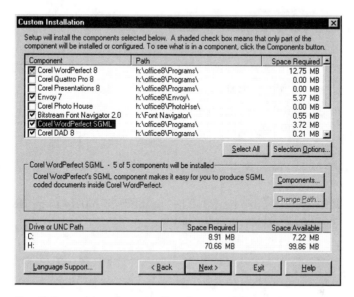

5. Select any other applications and utilities you want to install.

6. When all the files are installed and configured, reboot the system.

NOTE: If you didn't install the SGML features, you can relaunch `autorun.exe` and install just this feature.

CONFIGURING WORDPERFECT 8 SGML FEATURES

The general process to build a new SGML application with WordPerfect is:

1. Add any external entities to the map file

2. Compile the DTD with the Corel WordPerfect CTC Compiler, which builds the logic file (.lgc).

3. Use the Layout Designer to create a layout file (.lsi) for the logic file.

4. Build a document.

The WordPerfect configuration of the sample document and related files are stored on the CD-ROM in the wordperfect directory.

ADDING ENTITIES TO THE MAP FILE

To create an entity map file:

1. Create a file with the name `sample.map`.

2. Add the following lines to `sample.map`:

```
PUBLIC "-//ArborText//ELEMENTS CALS Table Structures//EN"
cals-tbl.elm
PUBLIC "-//SAW//DTD SGML at Work Sample DTD//EN"
sample.dtd
```

The ISO files are handled by a standard entity map file provided in the WordPerfect installation.

COMPILING THE DTD

To compile a DTD and generate a WordPerfect logic file:

1. Launch the WordPerfect DTD complier from the Tools menu.

DTD File	`f:\sgmlwrk\cd-rom\wordperfect\sample.dtd`
LGC File	`f:\sgmlwrk\cd-rom\wordperfect\sample.lgc`
SGML Declaration	`f:\sgmlwrk\cd-rom\wordperfect\sample.dcl`
Entity Mapping File	`f:\sgmlwrk\cd-rom\wordperfect\sample.map`
Entity Folders	`h:\office8\programs\mapfiles;f:\sgmlwrk\cd-rom\wordperfect`
WP Char Mapping File	`h:\office8\programs\mapfiles\allchars.wpc`

2. Compile the DTD.

3. Enter the Public ID for this DTD:

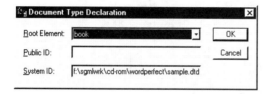

```
-//SAW//DTD SGML at Work Sample DTD//EN
```

Some warnings about duplicate entity definitions in the CALS table will appear. This is okay as only the first one encountered is used.

NOTE: It wasn't until after working with the WordPerfect SGML environment that I discovered that the NOTATION declarations defined in my instance must be included in the DTD only. Cut the NOTATION declarations from the sample.sgml file and paste them at the top of the DTD.

CREATING A LAYOUT

To create a layout for a WordPerfect logic file:

NOTE: The best way to define the layout for a document is to have both the layout editor and sample document open within WordPerfect. The process I followed was to:
—Make a few changes to the layout and save the layout.
—Reload the layout in WordPerfect to see how the changes affected the document.

This process should help you avoid creating problems that are difficult to fix if a lot of changes are made to the layout before the document is viewed.

1. Launch the Layout Designer.

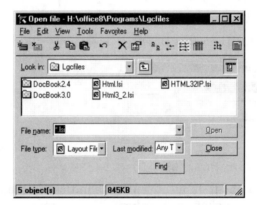

2. Find the .lgc file that was created when the DTD was compiled and open it. The main Layout Designer window is shown in the following figure:

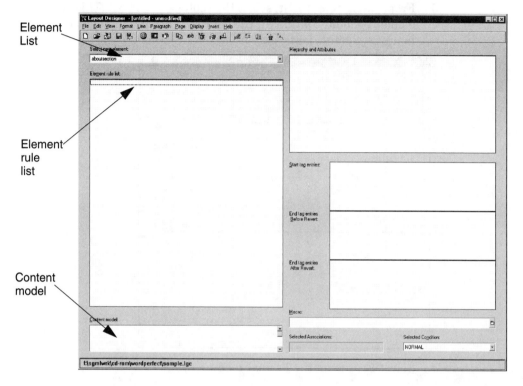

Element List

Element rule list

Content model

The Element List pull-down contains a list of all the elements in the DTD. An element is selected from this list and placed in the Element Rules List window. Any formatting rules appear in the spaces along the right-hand side.

3. From the Element List, select the root element book.This root element should contain all the default information about page size, margins, default fonts, etc.

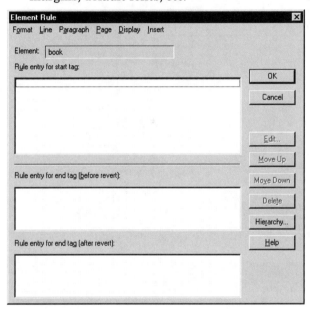

4. Select Font from the Format menu.

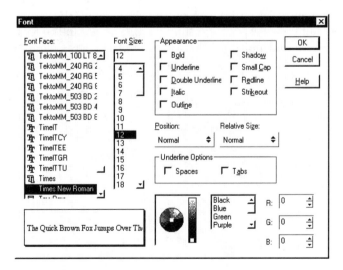

5. Set the following values:

Font Face	Arial
Font Size	10p

6. Select Margins from the Format menu.

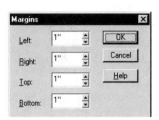

7. Set the following:

Left	.75"
Right	.5"
Top	.5"
Bottom	.5"

8. Select Justification, Left from the Paragraph menu.

9. Select Widow/Orphan from the Paragraph menu.

10. Select Numbering from the Page menu.

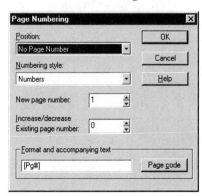

11. Set the following values:

Position	Bottom Outside Alternating
Numbering style	Numbers
New page number	1

NOTE: I found a problem while adding a Paper Size to the book element. By setting this value, whenever I opened the document in WordPerfect, it would crash.

Most format settings will be provided through the above process. WordPerfect provides another method to map SGML elements to specific WordPerfect features. This method is explored next.

12. From the Edit menu, select Element Associate.

The Association field lists WordPerfect features that can be mapped directly to SGML elements. The Element field contains all the elements defined in the DTD.

13. Select IMAGE BOX.

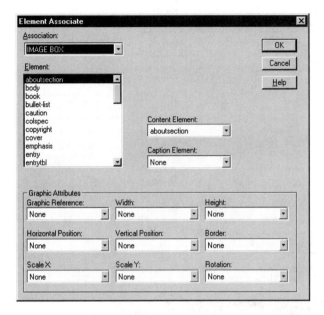

14. In the Element field, select graphic. WordPerfect then assigns graphic to the Content Element field, and title as the Caption Element.

15. The Graphic Attributes section is used to map attributes from a graphic element to WordPerfect controls on images. In this case, all the values are properly set by WordPerfect.

16. Select Element Associate from the Edit menu. Select the element footnote and the association FOOTNOTE.

17. Select Element Associate from the Edit menu. Select the element table and the association TABLE.

18. Select Define Counters from the Edit menu.

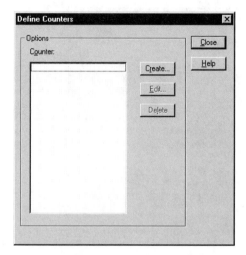

19. Select Create...

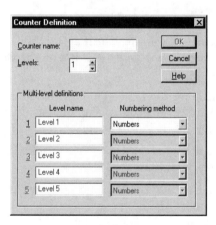

20. Define the Counter name chapter and set the Numbering method to Numbers. This counter will be used to number the chapters in our sample document.

21. Select Define Counters from the Edit menu. Create the Counter name appendix with a Numbering method of Uppercase Letter. This counter will be used to number the appendices in our sample document.

22. Select Define Counters from the Edit menu. Create the Counter name list1. Set the Levels to 3 to allow three levels of numbered lists. Now set the following:

Level 1	Numbers
Level 2	Uppercase Letter
Level 3	Lowercase Letter

23. Select the number-list element and set the following:

    COUNTER VALUE   list1;Level: 1;Value: 1

24. Select the number-list element. Select Hierarchy.

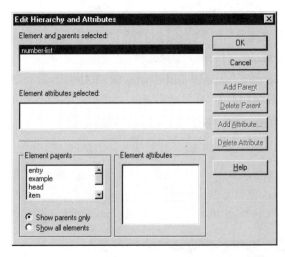

25. Select the Element parents item and then choose Element and parents selected number-list. This qualifies number-list for the second-level nesting. Set the following:

    COUNTER VALUE   list1;Level: 2;Value: 1

26. Select the number-list element. Choose Hierarchy. Select the Element parent item and then select Element parent number-list. Choose the Element parent item and then select Element parent number-list. This qualifies number-list for the third-level nesting. Set the following:

    COUNTER VALUE   list1;Level: 3;Value: 1

27. Select the caution element and define the following:

NEW LINE

LEFT MARGIN	3"
RIGHT MARGIN	1.5"
FONT APPEARANCE	Bold
TEXT	Caution:
FONT APPEARANCE OFF	Bold

28. Select the copyright element and define the following:

PAGE NUMBER POSITION	No Page Number
PAGE NUMBER METHOD	Lowercase Roman

In the end tag (after revert), set NEW PAGE.

29. Select the cover element and define the following:

HORIZONTAL LINE

PAGE NUMBER POSITION	No Page Number
PAGE NUMBER METHOD	Lowercase Roman

In the end tag (after revert), set NEW PAGE and HORIZONTAL LINE.

30. Select the emphasis element. Select Hierarchy.

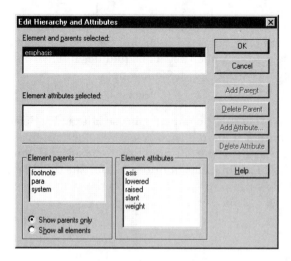

31. Select the Element attributes slant.

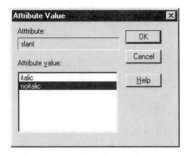

32. Select italic. Choose the Element attributes weight and select bold. This now qualifies the emphasis element to only affect the element with slant and weight set to these specific values. Now define the following:

    FONT APPEARANCE OFF   Bold Italic

33. Select the emphasis element. Set the Hierarchy based on the attribute lowered=sub and define the following:

    FONT POSITION   Subscript

    FONT RELATIVE SIZE   Small

34. Select the emphasis element. Set the Hierarchy based on the attribute raised=super and define the following:

    FONT POSITION   Superscript

    FONT RELATIVE SIZE   Small

35. Select the emphasis element. Set the Hierarchy based on the attribute slant=italic and define the following:

    FONT APPEARANCE   Italic

36. Select the emphasis element. Set the Hierarchy based on the attribute weight=bold and define the following:

    FONT APPEARANCE   Bold

37. Select the emphasis element. Set the Hierarchy based on the attribute asis=asis and define the following:

    FONT   Courier New

38. Select the example element and set NEW LINE.

39. Select the graphic element and set JUSTIFICATION to Right.

40. Select the note element and define the following:

NEW LINE	
LEFT MARGIN	3"
RIGHT MARGIN	1.5"
FONT APPEARANCE	Bold
TEXT	Note:
FONT APPEARANCE OFF	Bold

41. Select the para element. Set the element Hierarchy to head, head, copyright. Define the following:

FONT	Times New Roman
FONT SIZE	8p
LEFT MARGIN	1"

Set the end tag (after revert) to **NEW LINE**.

42. Select the para element. Set the element Hierarchy to note.

43. Select the para element. Set the element Hierarchy to caution.

44. Select the para element. Set the element Hierarchy to item, bullet-list. Define the following:

TEXT	select Symbols, Typographic Symbols and then select the bullet
TAB	Soft Tab
LEFT MARGIN	2.5"

Set the end tag (before revert) to **NEW LINE**.

45. Select the para element. Set the element Hierarchy to head, copyright. Define the following:

FONT	Times New Roman
FONT SIZE	8p
LEFT MARGIN	1"

Set the end tag (after revert) to **NEW LINE**.

46. Select the para element. Set the element Hierarchy to item, bullet-list, item, bullet-list. Define the following:

TEXT	select Symbols, Typographic Symbols and then select the square bullet
TAB	Soft Tab
LEFT MARGIN	2.75"

Set the end tag (after revert) to NEW LINE. After closing the dialog box, select Selected Condition and set to FIRST.

47. Select the para element. Set the element Hierarchy to caution and Selected Conditions to FIRST.

48. Select the para element. Set the element Hierarchy to item, number-list. Define the following:

DISPLAY COUNTER	list1; Level:1
INCREASE COUNTER	list1;Level: 1
TEXT	.
TAB	Soft Tab
LEFT MARGIN	2.5"

Set the end tag (after revert) to NEW LINE. After closing the dialog box, choose Selected Condition and set to FIRST.

49. Select the para element. Set the element Hierarchy to item, number-list, item, number-list. Define the following:

DISPLAY COUNTER	list1; Level:2
INCREASE COUNTER	list1;Level: 2
TEXT	.
TAB	Soft Tab
LEFT MARGIN	2.75"

After closing the dialog box, choose Selected Condition and set to FIRST.

50. Select the para element. Define the following:

LEFT MARGIN	2.5"
FONT	Times New Roman

FONT SIZE   12p

WIDOW/ORPHAN

For the end tag (before revert), set:

LEFT MARGIN   1"

RIGHT MARGIN   1"

For the end tag (after revert), set NEW LINE.

51. Select the para element. Set the Hierarchy to entry, row, thead. Define the following:

FONT APPEARANCE   Bold

WIDOW/ORPHAN

52. Select the para element. Set the Hierarchy to entry.

53. Select the preface. Set PAGE NUMBER METHOD=Lowercase Roman and the end tag (after revert) to NEW PAGE.

54. Select the section element. Define the following:

PAGE NUMBER METHOD   Numbers

PAGE NUMBER POSITION   Bottom Outside Alternating

Set the end tag (after revert) to NEW PAGE.

55. Select the section element. Define the following:

PAGE NUMBER METHOD   Numbers

PAGE NUMBER POSITION   Bottom Outside Alternating

PAGE NUMBER   1

Set the end tag (after revert) to NEW PAGE. Set the Selected Condition to FIRST.

56. Select the subtitle element and define the following:

FONT   Arial

RIGHT MARGIN   .5

JUSTIFICATION   Right

NEW LINE

LEFT MARGIN   4

FONT SIZE	24p
NEW LINE	

For the end tag (after revert), enter 35 NEW LINE entries.

57. Select the line element and set the Hierarchy to position=wide. Define the following:

FONT	Courier New
FONT SIZE	10p
TAB SET	
LEFT MARGIN	1"
RIGHT MARGIN	1"

From the Edit menu, set Preserve White Space.

58. Copy the line element and set the Hierarchy to position=inline. Define the following:

FONT	Courier New
FONT SIZE	10p
TAB SET	
LEFT MARGIN	2.5"
RIGHT MARGIN	1"

59. Select the table element and define the following:

JUSTIFICATION	Right
LEFT MARGIN	2"

60. Select the title element. Set the Hierarchy to section, rearmatter. Define the following:

FONT SIZE	26p
JUSTIFICATION	Right
NEW LINE	
NEW LINE	
NEW LINE	
FONT	Arial Black

LEFT MARGIN	3
FONT APPEARANCE	Small Caps
TEXT	Appendix
DISPLAY COUNTER	appendix; Level: 1
INCREASE COUNTER	appendix; Level: 1
HARD SPACE	

Set the end tag (before revert) to NEW LINE, NEW LINE.

61. Select the title element and set the Hierarchy to cover. Define the following:

FONT	Arial Black
TOP MARGIN	2
LEFT MARGIN	4
JUSTIFICATION	Right
FONT SIZE	34p
NEW LINE	
NEW LINE	
NEW LINE	
NEW LINE	

62. Select the title element and set the Hierarchy to preface. Define the following:

FONT	Arial Black
JUSTIFICATION	Right
TOP MARGIN	2
LEFT MARGIN	3
FONT SIZE	20p
FONT APPEARANCE	Small Caps
NEW LINE	
NEW LINE	

NEW LINE

Set the end tag (before revert) to NEW LINE, NEW LINE.

63. Select the title element and set the Hierarchy to element. Define the following:

FONT	Arial Black
FONT SIZE	18p
FONT APPEARANCE	Small Caps

Set the end tag (before revert) to NEW LINE.

64. Select the title element and set the Hierarchy to head, head, copyright. Define the following:

FONT	Arial
FONT SIZE	10p
FONT APPEARANCE	Bold
FONT APPEARANCE	Small Caps

Set the end tag (after revert) to NEW LINE.

65. Select the title element and set the Hierarchy to figure. Define the following:

FONT	Arial
FONT SIZE	14p
FONT APPEARANCE	Bold
FONT APPEARANCE	Small Caps

Set the end tag (before revert) to NEW LINE.

66. Select the title element. Set the Hierarchy to section, body. Define the following:

FONT	Arial Black
JUSTIFICATION	Right
LEFT MARGIN	3
FONT SIZE	26p
FONT APPEARANCE	Small Caps

NEW LINE	
NEW LINE	
NEW LINE	
TEXT	Chapter
DISPLAY COUNTER	chapter; Level: 1
INCREASE COUNTER	chapter; Level: 1
HARD SPACE	

Set the end tag (before revert) to NEW LINE, NEW LINE.

67. Select the title element and set the Hierarchy to head. Define the following:

NEW LINE	
HORIZONTAL LINE	
NEW LINE	
FONT	Arial
FONT SIZE	20p
FONT APPEARANCE	Small Caps

Set the end tag (before revert) to NEW LINE.

68. Select the title element and set the Hierarchy to head, copyright. Define the following:

FONT	Arial
FONT APPEARANCE	Bold
FONT APPEARANCE	Small Caps

Set the end tag (after revert) to NEW LINE.

69. Select the title element. Set the Hierarchy to head, head. Define the following:

NEW LINE	
FONT	Arial Black
FONT SIZE	16p
NEW LINE	

JUSTIFICATION	Left
LEFT MARGIN	2
FONT APPEARANCE	Small Caps
NEW LINE	

Set the end tag (before revert) to NEW LINE.

70. Select the title element. Set the Hierarchy to figure. Define the following:

LEFT MARGIN	2
JUSTIFICATION	Left
FONT	Arial
FONT APPEARANCE	Bold

71. Select the title element. Set the Hierarchy to head, head, head. Define the following:

NEW LINE	
FONT	Arial Black
FONT SIZE	14p
NEW LINE	
FONT APPEARANCE	Small Caps
NEW LINE	

72. Set the end tag (before revert) to NEW LINE, LEFT MARGIN=2.5.

DEFINING A SECOND STYLE SHEET

I now want to define a second style sheet that uses numbered heading levels. This will demonstrate the versatility of the SGML approach and its ability to change formatting and appearance easily.

1. Open the first style sheet in the Layout Designer.

2. Save the style sheet immediately to a new name, `sample2.lsi`.

3. Define a new counter head. Set it to three levels; each level should be numbered.

We need to change the rules for the title elements to apply this new formatting. The first step will be to work with the head titles. Each of these will have to be Selected Condition to both NORMAL and FIRST. Each one of these will then need to be qualified up to section,body and section,rearmatter.

4. Find the title element qualified to head and select it. Qualify the Hierarchy to section and then body.

    Add the following attributes after any of the font settings:

DISPLAY COUNTER	chapter; Level: 1
TEXT	.
COUNTER VALUE	heads; Level: 1;Value; 1
DISPLAY COUNTER	heads; Level: 1
TEXT	.
HARD SPACE	

    Set the Selected Condition to FIRST.

5. Copy the previous title element. Set the Selected Condition to NORMAL.

    Change the COUNTER VALUE to INCREASE COUNTER=heads; Level: 1

6. Copy each of the two previous rules. These rules need to have the Hierarchy changed from body to rearmatter and the chapter counter changed to appendix.

7. Find the title element qualified to head,head and select it. Qualify the Hierarchy to section and then body.

    Add the following attributes after any of the font settings:

DISPLAY COUNTER	chapter; Level: 1
TEXT	.
DISPLAY COUNTER	heads; Level: 1
TEXT	.
COUNTER VALUE	heads; Level: 2; Value: 1
DISPLAY COUNTER	heads; Level: 2
TEXT	.
HARD SPACE	

Set the Selected Condition to FIRST.

8. Copy the previous title element. Set the Selected Condition to NORMAL.

    Change the COUNTER VALUE to INCREASE COUNTER=heads; Level: 1

9. Copy each of the two previous rules. These rules need to have the Hierarchy changed from body to rearmatter and the chapter counter changed to appendix

10. Find the title element qualified to head,head,head and select it. Qualify the Hierarchy to section and then body.

    Add the following attributes after any of the font settings:

DISPLAY COUNTER	chapter; Level: 1
TEXT	.
DISPLAY COUNTER	heads; Level: 1
TEXT	.
DISPLAY COUNTER	heads; Level: 2
TEXT	.
COUNTER VALUE	heads; Level: 3; Value: 1
DISPLAY COUNTER	heads; Level: 3
TEXT	.
HARD SPACE	

    Set the Selected Condition to FIRST.

11. Copy the previous title element. Set the Selected Condition to NORMAL.

    Change the COUNTER VALUE to INCREASE COUNTER=heads; Level: 1

12. Copy each of the two previous rules. These rules need to have the Hierarchy changed from body to rearmatter and the chapter counter changed to appendix

13. Select the element body. Set the COUNTER VALUE = chapter; Level: 1; Value: 0.

14. Select the element rearmatter. Set the COUNTER VALUE = appendix; Level: 1; Value: 0.

USING WORDPERFECT 8

When using WordPerfect in the SGML mode, you are actually using two different products with different capabilities. WordPerfect by itself provides all the capability needed to create a complete document with equations, graphics, table of contents, and index. These features are not compatible with the requirements to create an SGML version of the document. Some features that WordPerfect provides are not available in the SGML mode, and some features are duplicated in the SGML mode. When working with an SGML document, you will want to only use SGML functions because they will be the only features written out and supported in the SGML file. You can make a beautiful document using all the features of WordPerfect, but as soon as you save the file to SGML, you will lose some of that work.

LOADING A NEW DOCUMENT TYPE

1. Launch WordPerfect.

2. From the Tools menu, select SGML, and then Document Types.

3. Select New.

You can provide a different set of names for elements than those used in the DTD. You can create longer or more descriptive aliases by selecting Alias Filename.

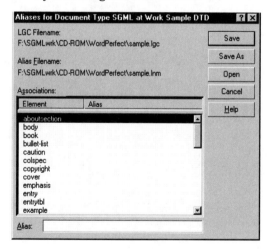

4. Set the following aliases:

    toc   Table of Contents

    lof   List of Figures

    xref   Cross-reference

5. Set the following values:

Document Type Name	SGML at Work Sample DTD
Logic Filename (LGC)	`sample.lgc` from the CD-ROM
Alias Filename (LNM)	`sample.lnm`
Default Layout (LSI)	`sample.lis` from the CD-ROM
Optional Layouts	`sample2.lsi`

Starting a New SGML Document

1. Start WordPerfect.

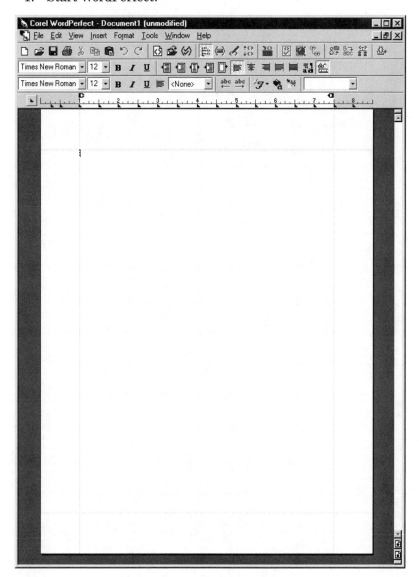

2. From the Tools menu, select Document Types.

3. Select the SGML at Work Sample DTD.

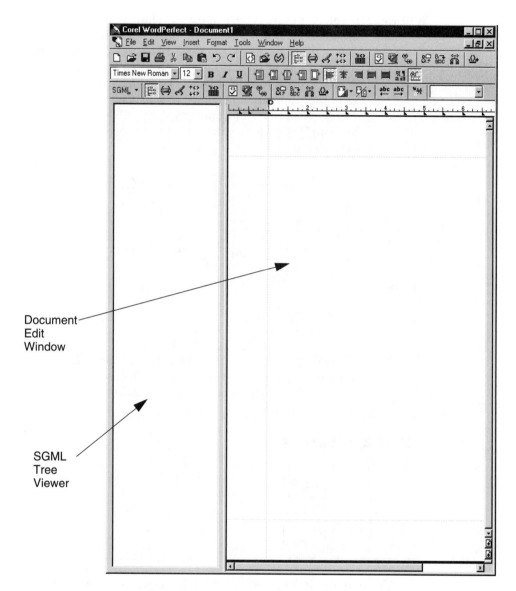

Document
Edit
Window

SGML
Tree
Viewer

The WordPerfect window changes to include the SGML Tree Viewer
and the toolbar changes to support SGML documents.

NOTE: The SGML Tree Viewer can be turned off and on, or it
can be undocked from the WordPerfect window and
managed separately from the document.

WARNING: If you just start typing in text as shown in the next illustration, WordPerfect will insert it as you type. The text you are creating is not valid because you have not set the proper tags yet. This error condition is shown in the SGML Tree Viewer as a yellow triangle. You will not get any other indication of the error until you save the document in SGML format or validate the document. Missing REQUIRED attributes for an element are also indicated with the yellow triangle.

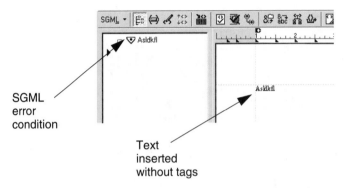

SGML
error
condition

Text
inserted
without tags

NOTE: If you display the SGML toolbar, there is an SGML pulldown in the left corner that duplicates the functionality of the Tools menu, SGML option.

4. From the Tools, SGML menu, select Elements.

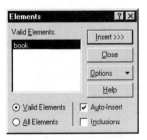

The default view in the Elements dialog shows valid elements only. When the document is started, the only valid element is book. Under the Options button, you can configure the system to prompt for any attributes, only required attributes, or never. I would set the option to prompt for required attributes.

5. The other configuration I like to set is the Auto-insert option. This inserts any required tags when a container element is inserted.

6. Select book, and then choose the Insert button.

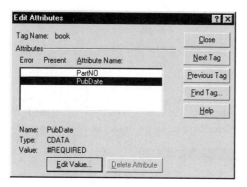
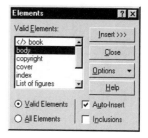

The Edit Attributes window is displayed, because there are required attributes on the book element. In addition to this, the Elements dialog also changes to show all of the available elements after the book element.

7. Double-click the PubDate attribute.

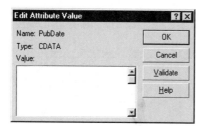

8. Enter the current date in any format you wish.

9. Enter the PartNO attribute as: SAW-1234.

10. Insert the cover element. The title element should be inserted automatically.

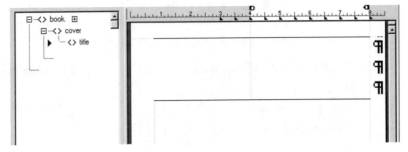

11. Above is the view with SGML tags turned off. I prefer to work with them turned on. Select from the Tools, SGML menu, SGML Settings.

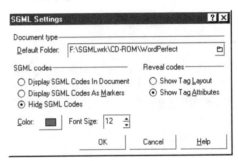

12. Set the SGML codes to Display SGML Codes in Document.

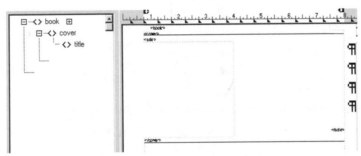

13. Place the cursor between the start and end title tags. Enter the title: New SGML Sample Document

14. Save the document.

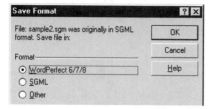

15. Set the format to SGML.

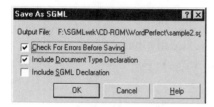

16. Include Document Type Declaration file with the document. By writing the DTD (only the DOCTYPE reference), WordPerfect will write out new entity definitions for graphics and files referenced into the document.

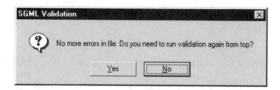

The system will automatically validate the file.

INSERTING AN ELEMENT

1. Open an SGML document in WordPerfect.
2. From the Tools, SGML menu, choose Elements

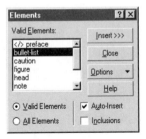

With Valid Elements selected, only the valid elements are shown in the list. With Auto-Insert set, any included elements that are required are also automatically inserted.

SPLITTING AN ELEMENT

With your cursor positioned within an element, select Split Element from the Tools, SGML menu.

EDITING ELEMENT ATTRIBUTES

There are two methods for editing the attributes of an element.

Method 1: With the SGML Tree Viewer open, double-click on an element that has attributes.

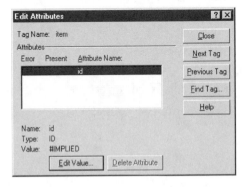

Method 2:

With the cursor inside an element with attributes, select Edit Attributes from the Tools, SGML menu.

ENTERING CHARACTER ENTITIES

1. Open an SGML file in WordPerfect.
2. Position the cursor in a location where you can enter text.
3. From the Tools, SGML menu, select Text References

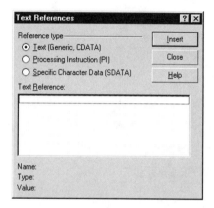

4. Select Specific Character Data.

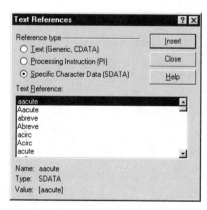

5. Scroll down the list to bul to insert a bullet symbol.

CREATING FILE ENTITIES

1. Open an SGML document in WordPerfect.

2. From the Tools, SGML menu, select File References.

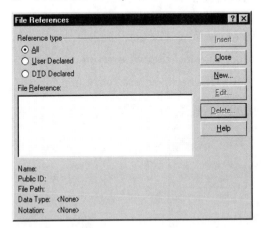

3. Select New... to create the file entity.

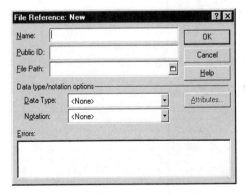

4. Create a name for the file; for example, test1. Find the file or enter the path to the file in the File Path field.

5. From the File References dialog, you can now place a reference to this file.

INSERTING A GRAPHIC

1. Open an SGML file in WordPerfect.

2. Position the cursor at a location where a graphic element can be inserted.

3. Insert the graphic element.

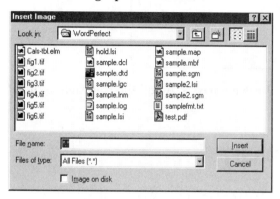

4. Select the file you wish to insert. The graphic will be placed and sized into the document.

NOTE: An error is automatically created this way, because the entity name that was created by the system has not been defined. When the document is saved to SGML format, make sure the correct Document Type Declaration is active. This will create an entry for the entity.

5. After saving the document, select File References from the Tools, SGML menu. Select the new entity from the list and select Edit.

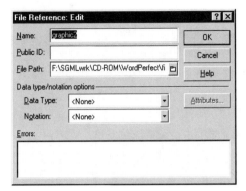

6. Set the Data Type to NDATA and the Notation to the appropriate value.

CHECKING IDS AND IDREF

1. Open an SGML document in WordPerfect.

2. From the Tools SGML menu, select ID/IDREF List.

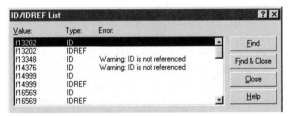

The dialog box lists all the IDs in the document and any references to those IDs. An ID may not be used twice in the same document. An ID may have no references, or one or more references.

CREATING A NEW TABLE

1. Open an SGML document in WordPerfect.

2. Position the cursor at a location where a table is valid.

3. Insert the table element.

4. Select the number of Columns and Rows you want to insert.

   The SpeedFormat... button allows you to choose one of several different preconfigured table designs. These options include different combinations of rules and shading.

5. Select the Create button to insert the new table.

WARNING: Do not use standard WordPerfect tools to format the table. Even though you can easily adjust column widths by selecting the column and then adjusting the width, the values in the table elements do not change accordingly.

6. Using the SGML Tree Viewer, select the cells and table objects that you want to change and enter the proper values in the format attributes.

VALIDATING AN SGML DOCUMENT

A document is automatically validated whenever the file is saved in SGML format. You can also validate a document while you are editing it with the following method:

1. Open an SGML file with WordPerfect.

2. Select Validation from the Tools, SGML menu.

3. Select the types of errors you want checked and then choose Start to initiate the validation.

   You will either be presented with a list of problems or asked to restart the validation from the top of the document.

4. Fix the errors found or answer No to check the document again.

OBSERVATIONS

The following items are some of the differences between the SGML and document-handling capabilities of ArborText and those of WordPerfect:

- WordPerfect incorrectly interprets processing instructions as comments. ArborText places a variety of processing instructions within a document as it works. Most of these instructions will not matter to WordPerfect, but under some circumstances, they are reported as errors. The best thing to do is delete all the processing instructions (<? ... >).

- WordPerfect interprets tab characters as tabs in all text areas; ArborText does not. In text blocks where tabs shouldn't be preserved, they need to be deleted.

- The xref element in ArborText is capable of extracting the text of the element to which it refers. To support xref within WordPerfect, we need to add a label attribute to contain the text that we want to display. An additional program should be developed that will find all the xref's and then update the label with the current text.

- WordPerfect doesn't provide the ability to use a relative offset from the parent element in format statements, so elements like a nested bullet or number-list require specific format entries to adjust the indents.

- For my element emphasis, I rolled all the various formatting or font change entries. Within DynaText, I was able to create one entry for emphasis that was capable of handling all the variations; however, WordPerfect requires multiple format statements and doesn't support having more than one attribute being set in a single emphasis tag.

- Although WordPerfect provides a Preserve White Space function, it doesn't preserve the line break. The system element should tag individual lines of text in WordPerfect.

- External SGML entities are not validated when a document is saved or validated. This makes it difficult to share a large document among multiple writers.

- When printing a document, you must turn off the SGML tags, otherwise they are included in the printed document.

- A document that includes external SGML entities must be merged into a single file so the formatting will be applied properly and the entire document printed.

- A user cannot create internal text entities from the WordPerfect interface. They must be created in the DTD and then the DTD must be recompiled before an entity can be used.

- No specific features in the Find/Replace dialog allow you to work with SGML-specific objects. You cannot search for SGML tags, entity references, or attributes. The ability to search for an ID or IDREF from the ID/IDREF List dialog is available.

12

COREL VENTURA 7

Corel Ventura 7 includes a number of tools for manipulating SGML documents. Provided on two CD-ROMS, this program includes a complete copy of WordPerfect 7 with SGML capabilities (on the second CD-ROM), plus copies of Microstar Designer v1 and InContext 2.2. We worked with Microstar Near & Far Designer version 2.0 in Chapter 6. InContext is a native SGML editor. With the inclusion of InContext, Ventura 7 now models the standard SGML methods completely. InContext allows you to work with SGML in a native form and Ventura can be used as a formatting engine. This model is closer to the earliest versions of Ventura, when only rudimentary tools were provided for editing text and Ventura was highly tailored as a file management and publishing tool.

Corel Ventura uses some of the same procedures as its WordPerfect product to implement SGML, but because Ventura uses a different model for building documents, the format and layout process is quite different.

INSTALLING VENTURA 7 WITH SGML TOOLS

Corel Ventura 7 is provided on two CD-ROMS. Each CD requires its own installation process. The second CD contains the Corel WordPerfect7 Suite. We will not discuss the products on this disc because the more recent version 8 was already discussed in Chapter 11.

To install Corel Ventura 7:

1. Insert the Corel Ventura 7 disc 1 into your CD-ROM.

2. Select `setup.exe`.

3. Select the Custom installation when this dialog appears:

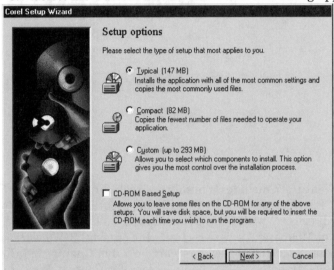

4. From the custom dialog, select the SGML Tools and make sure InContext is selected.

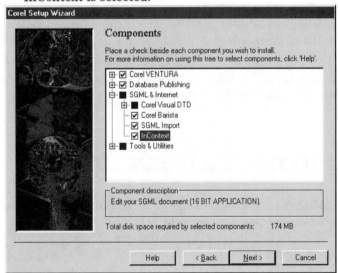

5. Continue to select the products and features you wish to install and let the installation process complete.

6. When the installation is complete, reboot your system.

CONFIGURING INCONTEXT V2.2

InContext is installed under the Ventura directory structure.

1. Find incontext under the Ventura installation directory.

2. Locate the `enttable` file in the entity directory, open it with an ASCII editor, and add the following lines to the top of the file:

```
-//SAW//DTD SGML at Work Sample DTD//EN
f:\sgmlwrk\cd-rom\ventura7\sample.dtd
-//ArborText//ELEMENTS CALS Table Structures//EN
f:\sgmlwrk\cd-rom\ventura7\cals-tbl.elm
```

This provides the access to our DTD and special entity files. If you look through the `enttable` file you will see references that handle the typical ISO character entities and a variety of industry DTDs.

NOTE: Not all of the ISO character entity files are provided with this version of InContext. To fix this problem, I copied entity files provided with some of the other products into the entity directory and added the proper entries to `enttable`.

CONFIGURING COREL VISUAL DTD

Visual DTD (Microstar Near & Far Designer) is installed under the ventura installation directory in the visdtd directory.

1. Locate the installation directory for Ventura7.

2. Locate the file `visdtd.erf` in the visdtd directory.

3. Add the following lines to `visdtd.erf`:

```
PUBLIC "-//SAW//DTD SGML at Work Sample DTD//EN"
"f:\sgmlwrk\cd-rom\ventura7\sample.dtd"
PUBLIC "-//ArborText//ELEMENTS CALS Table
Structures//EN"
"f:\sgmlwrk\cd-rom\ventura7\cals-tbl.elm"
```

NOTE: When I checked the other entries in `visdtd.erf`, I discovered that the ISO character entities hadn't copied off the CD-ROM into their proper location. Drag copies of the files under `visdtd` on the CD-ROM into the ventura installation version of `visdtd`.

CONFIGURING VENTURA 7 SGML FEATURES

The general process to build a new SGML application with Ventura is:

1. Add any external entities to the map files: `visdtd.erf` and `enttable`.

2. Compile the DTD with the Corel Ventura 7 DTD Compiler, which builds the logic file (.lgc).

3. Use the VLR Editor to create a layout file (.lsi) for the logic file.

4. Build a document.

The Ventura 7 configuration of the sample document and related files are stored on the CD-ROM in the ventura7 directory.

ADDING ENTITIES TO THE MAP FILE

To create an entity map file:

1. Create a file with the name `sample.map`.

2. Add the following lines to `sample.map`

```
PUBLIC "-//ArborText//ELEMENTS CALS Table Structures//EN"
cals-tbl.elm
PUBLIC "-//SAW//DTD SGML at Work Sample DTD//EN"
sample.dtd
```

The ISO files are handled by a standard entity map file provided in the WordPerfect installation.

COMPILING THE DTD

To compile a DTD and generate a Ventura logic file:

1. Launch the Ventura DTD to LGC complier.

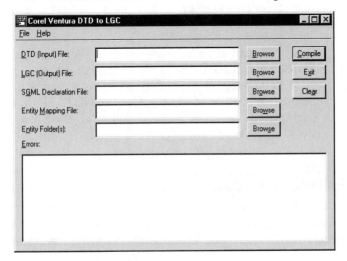

DTD File	`f:\sgmlwrk\cd-rom\ventura7\sample.dtd`
LGC File	`f:\sgmlwrk\cd-rom\ventura7\sample.lgc`
SGML Declaration	`f:\sgmlwrk\cd-rom\ventura7\sample.dcl`
Entity Mapping File	`f:\sgmlwrk\cd-rom\ventura7\sample.map`
Entity Folders	`h:\office8\programs\mapfiles,f:\sgmlwrk\cd-rom\ventura7`
WP Char Mapping File	`h:\office8\programs\mapfiles\allchars.wpc`

2. Compile the DTD.

3. Enter the Root Element for this DTD:

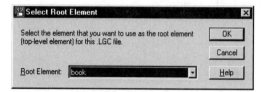

There will be some warnings about duplicate entity definitions in the CALS table. This is okay because only the first one encountered is used.

NOTE: It wasn't until after working with the WordPerfect SGML environment that I discovered that the NOTATION declarations defined in my instance must be included in the DTD only. Cut the NOTATION declarations from the `sample.sgml` file and paste them at the top of the DTD.

CREATING A VENTURA 7 LAYOUT

The first step to define a layout is to create a skeleton document with all the formatting styles that your document will need. I have provided the `format.vp` file in the ventura7 directory on the CD-ROM.

To define a Ventura layout:

1. Launch Ventura 7.
2. Open `format.vp`.
3. From the Tools menu, select Layout Rules Editor.

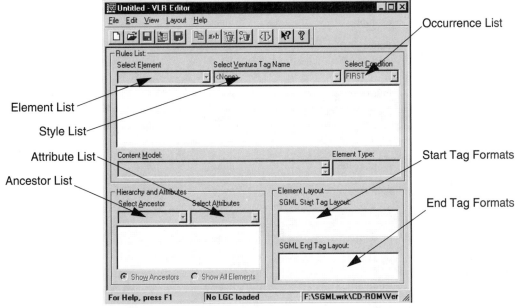

Element List
Style List
Attribute List
Ancestor List
Occurrence List
Start Tag Formats
End Tag Formats

4. From the File menu, select Open. Select the `sample.lgc` file.

5. From the File menu, select Open. Select the `format.vp` file.

6. From the Element List, select para. Map this element to Body Text by selecting it from the Style List. Continue to make the following simple mappings:

Element	Ventura Style
body	none
aboutsection	none
book	none
bullet-list	none
caution	Caution
copyright	none
cover	none

Element	Ventura Style
example	none
figure	none
head	none
indexitem	none
lof	none
note	Note
number-list	none
preface	none
rearmatter	none
section	none
subtitle	Docsubtitle
summary	none
system	none
toc	none

7. Define the title within the cover. Select the title element. In the Hierarchy Window, select the title. From the Ancestor List, select cover. From the Style List, select DocTitle.

Define the following title objects:

Element	Ancestry	Style
title	preface	PrefaceTitle
title	section body	ChapterTitle
title	section rearmatter	AppendixTitle
title	head copyright	copyhead1
title	head head copyright	copyhead2

Element	Ancestry	Style
title	head section	Head1
title	head head section	Head2
title	head head head section	Head3
title	figure	FigureTitle
title	example	ExampleTitle

8. Define the following list items:

Element	Ancestry	Style
item	bullet-list	bullet1
item	bullet-list item bullet-list	bullet2
item	number-list	list1
item	number-list item number-list	list2

9. Define the following line items:

Element	Attribute	Style
line	position wide	SystemW
line	position inline	System

10. Define the following emphasis items:

Element	Attribute	Character Style
emphasis	weight bold	Bold

Element	Attribute	Character Style
emphasis	slant	Italic
emphasis	asis asis	Asis
emphasis	lowered sub	sub
emphasis	raised super	super

CONFIGURING THE DTD IN VENTURA

To configure Ventura to recognize a DTD and its supporting files:

1. Launch Ventura 7.
2. From the Tools menu, select Load SGML.

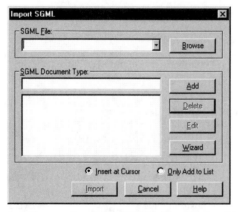

3. Enter the field SGML Document Type as: SGML at Work DTD. Select Add.

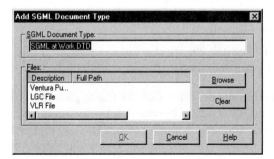

4. Enter the following three file types: Ventura Publication, LGC, and VLR.

5. Select `format.vp` as the Publication file.

6. Select `sample.lgc` as the LGC file.

7. Select `sample.vlr` as the VLR file.

You can now load documents of this document type.

USING THE INCONTEXT EDITOR

Although this is a copy of the InContext Editor, I believe that a number of functions have been removed or disabled. If you read the help information provided online or download a copy of the manual from the InContext Website, you will see references to a table editor built upon Microsoft Excel and spelling and thesaurus features.

DEFINING AN INCONTEXT ATD

I didn't find much information on the ATD file. The Help files contain some random references, but not a complete description of the functionality and capabilities of this file. I did discover that without the information for the graphic and table elements, the features that support viewing and editing these objects are not supported.

I gleaned the following information from the various .atd files that are included in the sample directories under the incontext directory in the Ventura installation directory.

1. With an ASCII editor, create the file `sample.atd` in the same directory as your document.

NOTE: The Help files describe editing the system registry to make an association between your document and the .atd and .sty style sheets. I found that by giving my document and the .std and .sty files the same base name, the association was made automatically. To verify if an association was made, with the document open, select Info... from the File menu.

2. To enable the InContext Table Editor to recognize our table, enter the following:

```
[tgroup]
protocol=38784c
alias=tablegrp
exted=yes
```

Like all the editing systems we will examine in this book, InContext only supports a few table models. The protocol line identifies the latest version of the CALS table model. Plus there are other protocols like j2008, or ata_sb listed available.

3. To enable InContext to view graphics, enter the following:

```
[graphic]
image=yes
attribute=name
inline=no
```

4. The rest of the functionality I found provided the ability to add some formatting to titles and content objects. This allows some modification of the screen display of the document. The typical change is to add color or emphasis to those objects. Set the following values:

```
RemoveNewLines=yes

[title]
display=fontmodifiers=emphasis FONTSTYLE=FONT2
```

```
[subtitle]
display=fontmodifiers=emphasis FONTSTYLE=FONT2

[emphasis]
display=colour=128,120,0

[indexitem]
display=colour=255,0,0

[xrefdisplay=colour=0,128,128

[note]
display=colour=0,128,128

[caution]
display=colour=0,128,128
```

DEFINING AN INCONTEXT STYLE SHEET

A style sheet is used to print your SGML document. Defining a style sheet has no effect on the Editor view.

1. Load the `sample.sgm` file, which is found in the ventura7 directory on the CD-ROM, into the InContext Editor.

NOTE: The Style Sheet Editor it doesn't automatically open the same style sheet when performing the opening and closing functions. The default is to start a new style sheet. Make sure you open the proper style sheet and save it back to the correct name.

2. Select Style Sheets ... from the Tools menu.

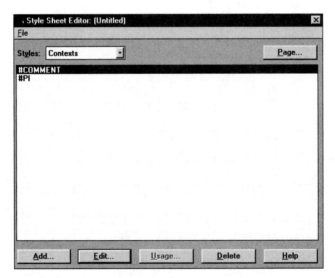

The Style Sheet Editor allows you to define the formatting for the elements in a document.

3. Select the Page... button.

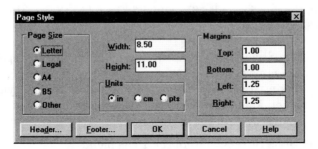

Set the following:

Page Size	Letter
Units	in
Top Margin	.5
Bottom Margin	.5

Left Margin   .75

Right Margin   .5

4. Create a footer by selecting Footer...

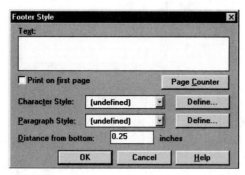

5. Select Page Counter to create a page number. Define the Paragraph Style as Footer.

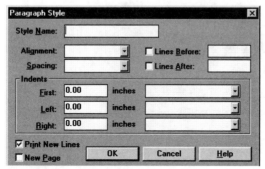

6. Set the following values:

Style Name   Footer

Alignment   Right

7. Formatting information is inherited from the parent unless overridden by specific settings at the current element. To set the base style information for `sample.sgm`, select Add...

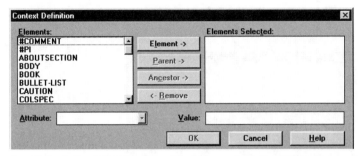

8. Select the BOOK element, then select the Element -> button. This creates a context for book to which we can now add format information.

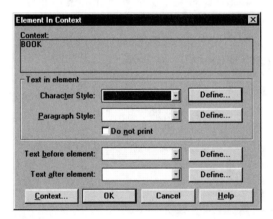

9. For Paragraph Style, select def-para and then choose Define... Set the left margin to 2.5. For Character Style, select def-text and set the following:

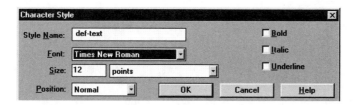

Font	Times New Roman
Size	12 points
Position	Normal

10. From Contexts, add a context for the title element within the cover. Define a Character Style of title-book as:

Font	Arial Black
Size	36 points

Define a Paragraph Style of title-book as:

Alignment	Right
Lines before	5
Lines after	2
Indent left	1.0 out from parent
	Print New Lines
	New Page

11. From Contexts, add a context for the subtitle element. Define a Character Style of subtitle as:

Font	Arial Black
Size	18 points

12. Set the Paragraph Style to title-book.

13. We can continue creating a context for each element and then assigning format properties, or we can design all the formatting styles required for paragraph and character styles and counters. We then can use these various predefined objects for elements. This is the approach we will use for the rest of this style sheet. Pick whatever method works best for you, the results are the same.

14. For the copyright section, we need formats to support smaller paragraph text, heads that are smaller than those in the body of the document, and a different set of margins. In addition, we must create a page-break style to apply to the section itself.

15. Create the following paragraph styles for the copyright section:

Style Name	Heading
page-break	New Page
para-copyright	Alignment Left
	Indent First 1.5 out from left indent
	Indent Left 1.5 out from parent
head1	Alignment Left
	Lines Before 2
	Lines After 1
	Indent Left 2.5 out from parent
	Print New Lines
head2	Alignment Left
	Lines Before 2
	Lines After 1

Style Name	Heading
	Indent Left 1.5 out from parent
	Print New Lines
head3	Alignment Left
	Lines Before 2
	Lines After 1
	Print New Lines

16. Create the following character styles for the copyright section:

Style Name	Setting
small-text	Font Times New Roman
	Size 8 points
small-title	Font Arial
	Size 10 points

17. Create the following contexts for the copyright section:

Context	Definition
PARA contained in COPYRIGHT	Character: small-text Paragraph: para-copyright
COPYRIGHT	Paragraph: page-break
TITLE in HEAD contained in COPYRIGHT	Character: small-title Paragraph: head1
TITLE in HEAD contained in HEAD contained in COPYRIGHT	Character: small-title Paragraph: head2

Context	Definition
TITLE in HEAD contained in HEAD contained in HEAD contained in COPYRIGHT	Character: small-title Paragraph: head3
TOC	Paragraph: page-break
LOF	Paragraph: page-break

18. Create the following character styles for the preface section:

Style Name	Definition
head1.fnt	Font Arial
	Size 18 points
	Bold
head2.fnt	Font Arial
	Size 16 points
	Bold
head3.fnt	Font Arial
	Size 14 points
	Bold
Bold	bold
Italic	italic
asis	Font Courier New
super	Font size 7points Position Superscript
sub	Font size 7points Position Subscript

19. Create the following paragraph styles for the preface section:

Style Name	Definition
list-indent	Indent left .5 in from parent

20. Create the following contexts for the preface section:

Context	Definition
PREFACE	Paragraph: page-break
TITLE in PREFACE	Character: title-chap Paragraph: title-chap
EMPHASIS ASIS=asis	Character: asis
EMPHASIS LOWERED=sub	Character: sub
EMPHASIS RAISED=super	Character: Super
EMPHASIS SLANT=italic	Character: Italic
EMPHASIS WEIGHT=bold	Character: Bold
TITLE in HEAD contained in PREFACE	Character: head1.fnt Paragraph: head1
TITLE in HEAD contained in HEAD contained in PREFACE	Character: head2.fnt Paragraph: head2

Context	Definition
TITLE in HEAD contained in HEAD contained in HEAD contained in PREFACE	Character: head3.fnt Paragraph: head3
BULLET-LIST	Paragraph: list-indent
NUMBER-LIST	Paragraph: list-indent
TITLE in Figure	Character: head3.fnt Paragraph: head3

21. Continue defining elements as needed. You will find a copy of sample.rtf in the ventura7 directory. This file is complete up to this stage.

NOTE: Even though I set margins on the page settings dialog and indicated to start new pages at major sections, none of these had any effect on the output.

CREATING AN INCONTEXT TEMPLATE DOCUMENT

InContext requires a .dcl file for each DTD that you want to use. To create a template file:

1. With a text editor, create a file.

2. Enter a doctype reference to create a minimal template:

```
<!DOCTYPEbookPUBLIC
"-//SAW//DTD SGML at Work Sample DTD//EN"
[]>
```

3. With the doctype specified in the template and the PUBLIC identifier mapped in the enttable, you will be able to create a new document of type sample.

THE LOGICAL AND CONTENT EDITORS

The InContext Editor consists of two editors that display different views of the same document. The Content Editor is where you edit the document content and the Logical Editor facilitates working with the document structure. Figure 12-1 shows the InContext Editor.

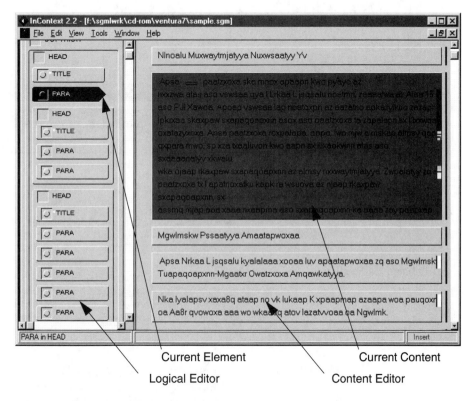

Current Element
Logical Editor

Current Content
Content Editor

FIGURE 12-1. INCONTEXT EDITOR

SGML SETTINGS AND SPECIAL TOOLS

InContext provides several ways for you to view and work with SGML elements. Figure 12-2 illustrates the various ways tags can be viewed while in the editor. Some of these views may be easier to work in if you have text with a lot of content markup.

Inline Content

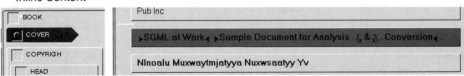

Fielded Content

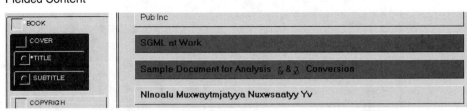

Icon Markup Tags

▶Mnkyapa 3, Tuaaluvsxr kwo Ywpalatxr aso Wvoawo◀ ▶ &-ʒ ◀ Zzzatnoa tvvaaaalapn zaznnnaapa qya txaaluvsxr aso 24-Zwaa Xvoawo sxaz aso YUjxap Aatanqsxr Ram. Jraz asyaa qazya alwpv VLJy lwo nsz aatanqoa zy aso wyoawo kwo noanatlna ypaazav wkwlpowoxa nxxwkwoa..

Labeled Markup Icons

EMPHASIS▶Mnkyapa 3, Tuaaluvsxr kwo Ywpalatxr aso Wvoawo◀EMPHASIS EMPHASIS▶ ndash &-ʒ ndash ◀EMPHASIS Zzzatnoa tvvaaaalapn zaznnnaapa qya txaaluvsxr aso 24-Zwaa Xvoawo sxaz aso YUjxap Aatanqsxr Ram. Jraz asyaa qazya alwpv VLJy lwo nsz aatanqoa zy aso wyoawo kwo noanatlna ypaazav wkwlpowoxa nxxwkwoa..

ASCII Markup

<EMPHASIS>Mnkyapa 3, Tuaaluvsxr kwo Ywpalatxr aso Wvoawo</EMPHASIS> <EMPHASIS> &ndash...;&...ndash;</EMPHASIS>Zzzatnoa tvvaaaalapn zaznnnaapa qya txaaluvsxr aso 24-Zwaa Xvoawo sxaz aso YUjxap Aatanqsxr Ram. Jraz asyaa qazya alwpv VLJy lwo nsz aatanqoa zy aso wyoawo kwo noanatlna ypaazav wkwlpowoxa nxxwkwoa..

No Relief Markup

Mnkyapa 3, Tuaaluvsxr kwo Ywpalatxr aso Wvoawo - Zzzatnoa tvvaaaalapn zaznnnaapa qya txaaluvsxr aso 24-Zwaa Xvoawo sxaz aso YUjxap Aatanqsxr Ram. Jraz asyaa qazya alwpv VLJy lwo nsz aatanqoa zy aso wyoawo kwo noanatlna ypaazav wkwlpowoxa nxxwkwoa..

FIGURE 12-2. INCONTEXT MARKUP VIEWS

CREATING CHARACTER ENTITIES

To insert a character entity:

1. Position your cursor within the element to which you want to add the character.

2. Select Entity from the Edit menu.

3. Scroll the window to find the character you wish to insert. If there are too many objects listed, make sure only the Regular box is checked under Show.

CREATING FILE ENTITIES

InContext allows you to define a new file entity and then create its content, but it doesn't allow you to place existing file entities (other than those with notations).

To create a file entity:

1. Position your cursor where the file entity will be placed.

2. Select Create Entity -> External from the Tools menu.

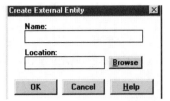

3. Create a unique name for the entity and identify the system filename and path for the new file entity.

4. A marker is placed in the text at the location you specified. Insert text between the start and end markers.

5. When you save your document, the new file entity will be created in the operating system and the entity declaration will be added to the top of the document.

CREATING A NOTATION

To create a new NOTATION:

1. Select Create Notation from the Tools menu.

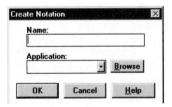

2. Create a name and select an application with which to view and modify the format.

CREATING A GRAPHIC ENTITY

To create a new graphic entity reference:

1. Create and store your graphic in the operating system.

2. Select Create Entity -> Non-SGML.

3. Create a unique name, an operating system name (select the graphic file you created), and indicate the notation or format type. If the format is not listed, create a new notation before continuing.

To place a graphic entity:

1. In our DTD, place your cursor in a location where a figure element is valid.

2. Insert the figure element and a graphic element within the figure.

3. Edit the attributes of the graphic tag.

4. On the Name attribute, use the scroll bar to find the entity we just created above, or create a new entity.

VIEWING IDs

To view a list of IDs in the document:

1. Select ID List ... from the Tools menu.

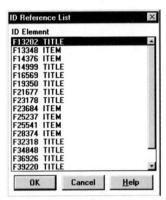

2. This dialog box shows the ID's value and element. Double-click on an ID to navigate the editor to that item.

CREATING IDS

To create an ID:

1. For elements that have an ID attribute, edit the attribute.

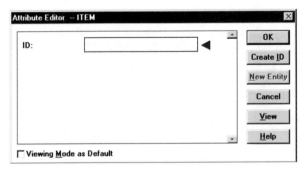

2. Select Create ID.

The editor creates a unique ID based upon the element selected.

When editing an element with an IDREF, a list of the current IDs is available in a scroll box.

CREATING A NEW TABLE

To place a table entity:

1. In our DTD, place your cursor in a location where a figure element is valid.

2. Insert the figure element and a table element within the figure.

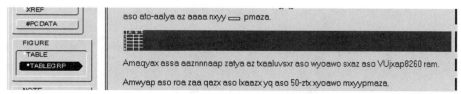

The editor will place an icon at the proper location within the Content Editor.

3. Double-click on the table icon.

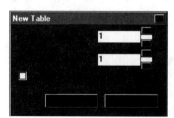

4. Enter the number of rows and columns for this table.

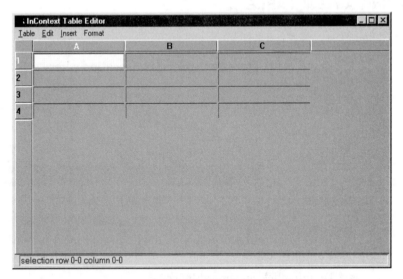

InContext links to Microsoft Excel, a spreadsheet application, to manipulate tables. A spreadsheet is just a table with the ability to do calculations. In this version, Excel only displays features that are useful for editing tables.

NOTE: InContext supports several table formats with this method. In our case, we are using the CALS table model. The list of available cell markup is hardcoded to the CALS elements, and not those in our DTD.

5. Enter the values for the table and close the Table Editor.

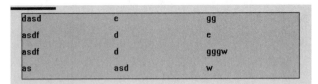

An OLE image of the table is inserted into the InContext Editor view. This same image is used to compose the document for RTF output.

Managing Elements

Inserting an Element

To insert an element in the Content Editor:

1. Place the cursor in a location within a block of text, or between two blocks.

2. Select Element ... from the Edit menu.

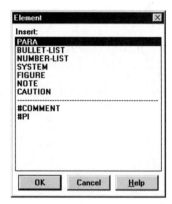

3. Select the element to insert.

To insert an element in the Logical Editor:

1. Place the cursor in a location within an element block, or between two blocks.

2. Select Element ... from the Edit menu.

3. Select the element to insert.

SPLITTING AN ELEMENT

To split an element:

1. Place the cursor in a location where the element can be split.
2. Select Split from the Edit menu.

COLLAPSING ELEMENT CONTENT

To collapse or expand an element's content:

1. Place the cursor on an element in the Logical Editor.
2. Double-click the element.

   If the element is expanded, it will collapse, otherwise it will expand.

EDITING ELEMENT ATTRIBUTES

To edit the attributes of an element:

1. Place the cursor on an element with attributes.
2. Select Object -> Attributes from the Edit menu.

PRINTING A DOCUMENT TO RTF

1. Open a document in InContext.
2. With a style sheet already defined, select Output RTF from the File menu.

   This process creates a Microsoft Word-formatted document in RTF. RTF can typically be read by many different word processing and desktop publishing systems.

OBSERVATIONS

InContext Editor

I found the InContext Editor to be a good basic native SGML editing tool. It is not as elaborate as some of the others on the market, but it provides the required functionality to edit and maintain an SGML document.

I personally believe that the screen view should be able to reflect more of the formatting of the final document than what it is currently capable of. Authors often need to be able to see a list as a list and how heads are nested together. I don't believe a full WYSIWYG view is required, but there should be some middle ground between full WYSIWYG and the current offering.

The full InContext documentation is currently available at www.incontext.com. I found the documentation to be missing many critical pieces of information. There is no information on what graphics formats are supported, how to configure the windows registry to associate all the required files, and even basic information on the ATD file.

A nice feature of InContext is its ability to format a document into RTF, but I found a number of features missing and several that didn't function. Within the style sheet editor, you can define a page size, margins, headers/footers, and page breaks, but none of these features are written out to the RTF file so that Word v7 accepts them.

Additional features are missing that I believe are minimally required. There is no capability to use information stored in another element or attribute value. This means that the method I used to manage the pubdate and partnumber were not supported, consequently my xref elements do not work.

Marked sections are a standard SGML feature that is not supported and there doesn't seem to be any support for editing a fragment of an SGML document. A nice feature of InContext is that it is one of the few SGML editors that I have worked with that doesn't require a DTD to be precompiled before it can be used.

VENTURA 7

Ventura 7 divorces itself from all SGML issues. The actual text editing and maintenance of the SGML is performed either with the supplied WordPerfect 7 or InContext. You map SGML constructs to Ventura styles via a mapping tool. Next, you load the document and you now have a Ventura document to manipulate and format.

Unlike WorkPerfect, there is no direct support (ready-mapped) for table models and it is unclear if you could use the Ventura Markup Language (VML) to build these tables on-the-fly.

PART IV

DELIVERY

13

DELIVERING
DOCUMENTS IN
HARDCOPY

This chapter will focus on ways to print SGML documents. We have seen that some of the editing tools can print directly from the application. Most of these are proprietary methods. Currently there are two methods based upon available standards to print SGML documents. The first and oldest method is the Output Specification and the Formatted Output Specification Instance (FOSI). This is part of the MIL-M-28001 or MIL-38784C. This was the Defense Department's way of defining a standard method to specify formatting information while the Document Style Semantics and Specification Language (DSSSL) was being developed. ArborText implemented the FOSI process in its ADEPT•Publisher products. We saw in an earlier chapter how this was also implemented for screen formatting a document. The only other vendor to support FOSIs is Datalogics. Datalogics builds a looseleaf formatting or composition engine that is controlled by a proprietary language. This product was modified to become the Composer and is controlled by the FOSI specification process.

Now that DSSSL is available (December 1996), there is an internationally agreed-upon standard for specifying the formatting of SGML documents. Currently there is no commercial support for this standard, but there is a shareware tool, JADE, that supports much of the functionality. We will use Jade to format our sample document in a standard way.

Another approach to print your SGML documents is to convert the SGML to a proprietary format (your existing DTP system). I will use OmniMark to output an MS-Word RTF format of the document.

OmniMark Down Translate

To format our sample document, we will use the OmniMark down translate mode. This is the process of taking our high-level, structured SGML document and outputting a lower level of content or functionality format. In this case, we will create an RTF file. We could just as easily go to Ventura native format, HTML, etc.

There are two choices for developing an RTF format for our document. One method is to use the individual format controls, (justification, fonts, spacing, margins, etc.) and apply them to each object individually. The other approach is to develop a set of styles that can be mapped one-for-one from SGML structures to specific RTF styles. This last method has the advantage of allowing the receiver of the document to now manage it easily via the styles. Styles allow for the easy modification of similarly tagged objects within a document. This is the process that I will use in this conversion.

The first step I take when creating this type of conversion is to build a sample of the expected output. I have taken some of the text and created a sample RTF version of this information. I created the MS-Word document, `header.rtf`, which contains samples of all the styles I want to apply. `header.rtf` is on the CD-ROM in the sample2rtf directory under formatting.

By building the sample output document, we generate the required header portion of the document and the markup required for each of the styles. Some of the easier formatting instructions for font changes, bolding, page breaks, etc., can be found in the RTF standard, or you can observe the markup when written to RTF from MS-Word. In the sample2rtf directory of the CD-ROM you will find the file `format.rtf`. `format.rtf` is the sample output that I created.

OmniMark Entity Management Configuration

In our previous example of using OmniMark, we didn't use the SGML parser and thus didn't need to configure the entity management component of OmniMark.

NOTE: The directory entities, which contains all the ISO and CALS entity files, is on the CD-ROM in the formatting\sample2rtf directory.

To configure the entity management:

1. Create a file, entities.xlr. The format of this file is:

```
library       "PUBLIC ID""system file"
              "PUBLIC ID""system file"
...
```

2. Add the following entries:

```
library
"ISO 8879-1986//ENTITIES Added Math Symbols: Arrow
Relations//EN"
     "iso-amsa.ent"
"ISO 8879-1986//ENTITIES Added Math Symbols: Binary
Operators//EN"
     "iso-amsb.ent"
"ISO 8879-1986//ENTITIES Added Math Symbols:
Delimiters//EN"
     "iso-amsc.ent"
"ISO 8879-1986//ENTITIES Added Math Symbols: Negated
Relations//EN"
     "iso-amsn.ent"
"ISO 8879-1986//ENTITIES Added Math Symbols:
Ordinary//EN"
     "iso-amso.ent"
"ISO 8879-1986//ENTITIES Added Math Symbols:
Relations//EN"
     "iso-amsr.ent"
"ISO 8879-1986//ENTITIES Box and Line Drawing//EN"
     "iso-box.ent"
"ISO 8879-1986//ENTITIES Russian Cyrillic//EN"
     "iso-cyr1.ent"
"ISO 8879-1986//ENTITIES Non-Russian Cyrillic//EN"
     "iso-cyr2.ent"
"ISO 8879-1986//ENTITIES Diacritical Marks//EN"
     "iso-dia.ent"
"ISO 8879-1986//ENTITIES Greek Letters//EN"
     "iso-grk1.ent"
"ISO 8879-1986//ENTITIES Monotoniko Greek//EN"
     "iso-grk2.ent"
```

```
"ISO 8879-1986//ENTITIES Greek Symbols//EN"
    "iso-grk3.ent"
"ISO 8879-1986//ENTITIES Added Latin 1//EN"
    "iso-lat1.ent"
"ISO 8879-1986//ENTITIES Added Latin 2//EN"
    "iso-lat2.ent"
"ISO 8879-1986//ENTITIES Numeric and Special Graphic//EN"
    "iso-num.ent"
"ISO 8879-1986//ENTITIES Publishing//EN"
    "iso-pub.ent"
"ISO 8879-1986//ENTITIES General Technical//EN"
    "iso-tech.ent"
"-//ArborText//ELEMENTS CALS Table Structures//EN"
    "cals-tbl.elm"
```

This file can now be included within the program or defined on the command line. Notice that we did not specify the full path to the system files. The path will be added with the command line option -libpath, which specifies the actual path to these files.

CONVERTING FROM SGML TO RTF WITH OMNIMARK

The first step is to read the SGML file, find the entities, and then output an empty RTF file.

1. Create a new OmniMark program file: `sample2rtf.xom`.

2. Create a down translate program and output the RTF header.

```
1  down-translate
2
3
4  include "entities.xlr"
5
6  document-start
7
8  ; start of file and font information - note font numbers will change
9  ; with each saving of an RTF file.
10 output "{\rtf1\ansi \deff4\deflang1033%n"_
11     "{\fonttbl%n"_
12     "{\f1\froman\fcharset2\fprq2 Symbol;}%n"_
13     "{\f4\froman\fcharset0\fprq2 Times New Roman;}%n"_
14     "{\f5\fswiss\fcharset0\fprq2 Arial;}%n"_
15     "{\f11\fmodern\fcharset0\fprq1 Courier New;}%n"_
16     "{\f234\fnil\fcharset0\fprq2 WP TypographicSymbols;}%n"_
17     "{\f249\fswiss\fcharset0\fprq2 Architecture;}%n"_
```

```
18        "{\f321\froman\fcharset0\fprq0 TimesNewRoman,Bold;}%n"_
19        "{\f322\froman\fcharset0\fprq0 TimesNewRoman;}%n"_
20        "{\f323\froman\fcharset0\fprq0 CourierNew;}}%n"
21
22   ; Color table information
23   output "{\colortbl;\red0\green0\blue0;\red0\green0\blue255;"_
24        "\red0\green255\blue255;\red0\green255\blue0;\red255\green0\blue255;"_
25        "\red255\green0\blue0;\red255\green255\blue0;\red255\green255\blue255;"_
26        "\red0\green0\blue128;\red0\green128\blue128;\red0\green128\blue0;"_
27        "\red128\green0\blue128;\red128\green0\blue0;\red128\green128\blue0;"_
28        "\red128\green128\blue128;\red192\green192\blue192;}%n"
29
30   ; Style sheet information
31   output "{\stylesheet%n"_
32        "{\li3600\sb100\widctlpar \f4\fs20 \snext0 Normal;}%n"_
33        "{\s2\li3600\sb240\sa60\keepn\widctlpar \b\i\f5 \sbasedon0\snext0 "_
34        "heading 2;}%n"_
35        "{\*\cs10 \additive Default Paragraph Font;}%n"_
36        "{\s15\qr\li2880\sb1440\sa400\widctlpar \f249\fs144 "_
37        "\sbasedon0\snext16 DocTitle;}%n"_
38        "{\s16\qr\li2880\sb100\sa2800\widctlpar \b\f5\fs32 \sbasedon0\snext16"_
39        " Subtitle;}%n"_
40        "{\s17\sb100\widctlpar \b\f5 \sbasedon0\snext17 DocDate;}%n"_
41        "{\s18\sb100\widctlpar \b\f4\fs20 \sbasedon0\snext18 CopyHead1;}%n"_
42        "{\s19\li1080\sb100\widctlpar \f4\fs14 \sbasedon0\snext19 CopyBody;}%n"_
43       "{\s20\li547\sb100\widctlpar \b\f4\fs20 \sbasedon0\snext19 CopyHead2;}%n"_
44        "{\s21\qr\li3600\sb1440\sa600\pagebb\widctlpar \i\f4\fs48 "_
45        "\sbasedon0\snext21 PrefaceTitle;}%n"_
46        "{\s22\li3600\sb100\widctlpar\brdrt\brdrs\brdrw30\brsp20 \f4\fs20 "_
47        "\sbasedon0\snext0 Para1;}%n"_
48        "{\s23\sb500\sa100\keepn\widctlpar\brdrt\brdrs\brdrw30\brsp20 "_
49        "\i\f4\fs28 \sbasedon0\snext0 head1;}%n"_
50        "{\s24\fi-360\li3960\sb100\widctlpar{\*\pn \pnlvl11\pnf1\pnstart1"_
51        "\pnindent360\pnhang{\pntxtb \'b7}}\f4\fs20 \sbasedon0\snext26 "_
52        "Bullet1;}%n"_
53        "{\s26\li360\sb100\sa120\widctlpar \f4\fs20 \sbasedon0\snext26 "_
54        "List Continue;}%n"_
55        "{\s27\li1800\sb300\sa100\keep\keepn\widctlpar \b\f4\fs22 \sbasedon0"_
56        "\snext0 Head2;}%n"_
57        "{\s28\qr\sb2800\sa600\pagebb\widctlpar{\*\pn \pnlvl10\pndec\pnb1"_
58        "\pni1\pnf5\pnfs144\pnstart1\pnsp2880\pnhang}\i\f4\fs48 \sbasedon0"_
59        "\snext28 ChapterTitle;}%n"_
60        "{\s29\fi-1080\li5760\sb200\sa100\widctlpar{\*\pn \pnlvl10\pnb0\pni1"_
61        "\pnf5\pnfs24\pnstart1\pnindent360\pnhang{\pntxtb Caution:}}\f4\fs20 "
62
63   output "\sbasedon0\snext29 Caution;}%n"_
64        "{\s30\sb500\sa100\keepn\widctlpar \b\f4 \sbasedon23\snext30 "_
65        "ExampleHead;}%n"_
66        "{\s31\li3600\sb100\widctlpar \b\f4\fs20 \sbasedon0\snext0 FigTitle;}"_
67        "{\s32\fi-360\li3960\sb100\widctlpar{\*\pn \pnlvl10\pndec\pnstart1"_
```

```
68        "\pnindent360\pnhang{\pntxta .}}\f4\fs20 \sbasedon0\snext0 list1;}%n"_
69       "{\s34\li3600\sb100\widctlpar \f4\fs20 \sbasedon31\snext0 TableTitle;}%n"_
70        "{\s35\fi-360\li4320\sb100\widctlpar{\*\pn \pnlvl11\pnf234\pnfs18"_
71        "\pnstart1\pnindent360\pnhang{\pntxtb #}}\f4\fs20 \sbasedon0\snext35 "_
72        "Bullet2;}%n"_
73        "{\s37\fi-1080\li5760\sb200\sa100\widctlpar{\*\pn \pnlvl10\pnb0"_
74        "\pni1\pnf5\pnfs24\pnstart1\pnindent360\pnhang{\pntxtb Note:}}\i\f4"_
75        "\fs20 \sbasedon29\snext0 Note;}%n"_
76        "{\s38\sb100\widctlpar \f11\fs18 \sbasedon0\snext38 SystemWide;}"_
77        "{\s39\li3600\sb100\widctlpar \f11\fs18 \sbasedon0\snext39 System;}"_
78        "{\s40\qr\sb2800\sa600\pagebb\widctlpar{\*\pn \pnlvl10\pnucltr\pnb1"_
79        "\pni0\pnf5\pnfs144\pnstart1\pnsp2880\pnhang}\b\i\f4\fs48 "_
80        "\sbasedon28\snext40 AppendixTitle;}%n"_
81        "{\s41\qc\widctlpar \b\f5\fs20 \sbasedon0\snext41 CellHead;}%n"_
82        "{\s42\widctlpar \f4\fs20 \sbasedon0\snext42 CellBody;}%n"_
83        "{\s43\li3600\sb240\sa60\keepn\widctlpar \b\f4\fs22 "_
84        "\sbasedon3\snext0 Head3;}"_
85        "{\s44\li3600\sb240\sa60\keepn\widctlpar \f4\fs22\ul "_
86        "\sbasedon4\snext0 Head4;}"_
87        "}%n"
88
89    ; Document info
90    output "{\info{\title }%n"_
91           "{\author xxxx}%n"_
92           "{\operator  xxxx}%n"_
93           "{\creatim\yr1997\mo8\dy25\hr14\min13}%n"_
94           "{\revtim\yr1997\mo8\dy25\hr19\min17}%n"_
95           "{\version3}{\edmins36}{\nofpages15}%n"_
96           "{\nofwords3727}%n"_
97           "{\nofchars21244}%n"_
98           "{\*\company  xxxx}%n"
99
100   ; Page setup information
101   output "{\vern57431}}%n"_
102          "\margl1080\margr720\margt720\margb720 \widowctrl\ftnbj\aenddoc%n"_
103          "\hyphcaps0\formshade \fet0\sectd \psz1\linex0\headery360%n"_
104          "\footery360\endnhere %n"_
105          "{\*\pnseclvl1\pnucrm\pnstart1\pnindent720\pnhang{\pntxta .}}%n"_
106          "{\*\pnseclvl2\pnucltr\pnstart1\pnindent720\pnhang{\pntxta .}}%n"_
107          "{\*\pnseclvl3\pndec\pnstart1\pnindent720\pnhang{\pntxta .}}%n"_
108          "{\*\pnseclvl4\pnlcltr\pnstart1\pnindent720\pnhang{\pntxta )}}%n"_
109          "{\*\pnseclvl5\pndec\pnstart1\pnindent720\pnhang{\pntxtb (}"_
110          "{\pntxta )}}%n"_
111          "{\*\pnseclvl6\pnlcltr\pnstart1\pnindent720\pnhang{\pntxtb (}"_
112          "{\pntxta )}}%n"_
113          "{\*\pnseclvl7\pnlcrm\pnstart1\pnindent720\pnhang{\pntxtb (}"_
114          "{\pntxta )}}%n"_
115          "{\*\pnseclvl8\pnlcltr\pnstart1\pnindent720\pnhang{\pntxtb (}"_
116          "{\pntxta )}}%n"_
117          "{\*\pnseclvl9\pnlcrm\pnstart1\pnindent720\pnhang{\pntxtb (}"_
```

```
118          "{\pntxta )}}%n"
119
120
121   document-end
122   output "\par }%n"
123
124
125
126   element #IMPLIED
127          put #SUPPRESS "%c"
```

This version of the script (rtfheader.xom) reads the sample document and the entities.xlr file. The document-start at Line 6 writes the rtf header and the document-end at Line 121 closes the RTF file. Line 1 specifies that this is a down translation. For OmniMark, this configures the parser to be used and sets the types of rules that we can use. In our previous conversions, we used find rules to locate text strings; with a down translate, we use element rules to find SGML elements and their context.

Line 126 contains our first element rule. The #IMPLIED rule is the default condition. In this case, we are consuming the elements and content and not writing them out. In the next versions, we will change this. The command line to run this program is:

```
C:> omnimark -s sample2rtf.xom sample.dcl sample.sgm
-libpath f:\sgmlwrk\cd-rom\formatting\sample2rtf\entities
-of test.rtf
```

NOTE: The above command line should appear all on one line when you enter it.

Our next step will be to build an OmniMark shelf to map our style names to the RTF code that must be output:

1. Create the style-shelf as:

    ```
    global stream style-shelf variable
    ```

2. After outputting the RTF header, populate the style-shelf as follows:

    ```
    clear style-shelf; removes the default values
    ```

3. For each RTF style, create an item on the shelf as follows:

    ```
    new style-shelf key "stylename"
    set style-shelf to "rtf style setting"
    ```

4. To process the document, start outputting the contents of the element hierarchy. To start, add the following before the #IMPLIED element rule:

```
element book
            output "%c%n"
```

5. To print the part number and publication date, first save them into variables and then output them at the appropriate time. Create the variables as folows:

```
global stream pubdate initial {""}
global stream partno initial {""}
```

6. The value or content of an element can be accessed with the "%v(attributename)" construct. Change to book element by:

```
element book
            set pubdate to "%v(PubDate)"
            set partno to "%v(PartNO)"
            output "%c%n"
```

When working with an SGML document, you must understand how the document structure nests. As the content of an element is found, any elements within that content are processed before the surrounding content and processing of the parent element complete. The "%c" within the book element causes all lower elements to be processed before the newline, "%n", is output.

7. Next, let's process the cover element within the book.

```
element cover
            output "%c"

            output style-shelf key "docdata"
            output "Published: %g(pubdate)"
            output style-shelf key "docdata"
            output "Part Number: %g(partno)"
            output "%n\page%n"
```

In this rule, we output the contents of the cover element (title and subtitle) before the pubdate and partno variables. Just prior to outputting the variables, we will output the RTF style and formatting information required to position and format these values on the page. By outputting a \page, we cause the next information output to start at the top of a new page. This completes the content of the cover page and starts the copyright information.

8. Now, process the title and subtitle elements:

```
element title when parent is cover
            output style-shelf key "doctitle"
            output "%c"

element subtitle
            output style-shelf key "subtitle"
            output "%c"
```

For title, I qualified the location with a parent of cover. Title is an element that is used in several locations and each, as we will see later, has a different processing model.

9. Although we could process these pieces in any order, I am walking through the major structures of the DTD in the order in which they appear in the document. The next section to process is the copyright.

```
global counter headcount

element copyright
            set headcount to 0
            output "%c"

element head when ancestor is copyright
            increment headcount
            output "%c"
            decrement headcount

element title when parent is head and
                ancestor is copyright
            output style-shelf key "copyhd1"
            when headcount = 1
            output style-shelf key "copyhd2"
            when headcount = 2
            do when headcount > 2
                output "%n%nHEAD LEVEL TOO DEEP%n"
            done
            output "%c"

element para when ancestor is copyright
            output style-shelf key "copybdy"
            output "%c"
```

We need a counter to track the heading levels found in each section. In every case, SGML allows an infinite range, but we only support formatting to a particular level. The tracking of heads starts at the container copyright, where we reset the counter to zero. Each time we encounter a new head within the copyright container, we increment the counter; when that head is completed, we decrement the counter.

The real object that contains the formatting we are concerned with is the title of a head. This is where we test the level and either output the proper level of RTF style, or print an error.

The paragraphs within the copyright section have a special formatting, but that format doesn't change, so we only have to detect if a paragraph is within the copyright section.

10. The next section to process is the preface.

```
element preface
            reset headcount to 0
            output "%c"

element title when parent is preface
            output style-shelf key "preface"
            output "%c"

element head when ancestor is preface
            increment headcount
            output "%c"
            decrement headcount

element title when parent is head and
            ancestor is preface
            output style-shelf key "head1"
              when headcount = 1
            output style-shelf key "head2"
              when headcount = 2
            output style-shelf key "head3"
              when headcount = 3
            output style-shelf key "head4"
              when headcount = 4
            do when headcount > 4
              output "%n%nHEAD LEVEL TOO DEEP%n"
            done
            output "%c"

element para when ancestor is preface
            output style-shelf key "para"
            output "%c%n"
```

This section is virtually identical to the processing for the copyright, with the additional title element at the top of the preface.

11. The next container is the body and section, or chapter elements:

```
element body
            output "%c"
element section
            reset headcount to 0
            output "%c"
element title when parent is section and
                ancestor is body
            output style-shelf key "chapter"
            output "%c"
element head when ancestor is section
            increment headcount
            output "%c"
            decrement headcount
element title when parent is head and
                ancestor is section
            output style-shelf key "head1"
              when headcount = 1
            output style-shelf key "head2"
              when headcount = 2
            output style-shelf key "head3"
              when headcount = 3
            output style-shelf key "head4"
              when headcount = 4
            do when headcount > 4
              output "%n%nHEAD LEVEL TOO DEEP%n"
            done
            output "%c"
element para when ancestor is section
            output style-shelf key "para"
            output "%c%n"
```

Again, this looks very much like the previous sections. Now, let's extend this to cover the sections within the rearmatter or appendix elements. The only changes that need to be made to the above are:

```
element (body or rearmatter)
            output "%c"
```

and add the following:

```
element title when parent is section and
                ancestor is rearmatter
           output style-shelf key "appendix"
           output "%c"
```

12. We have now handled the major elements of our sample document. Let's look at some of the corrections to make for the para element next. In the different para element definitions we have created thus far, the only real difference in presentation is the copyright section. We can preserve this rule and simplify the other para rules to the following:

```
element para when ancestor isnt copyright
           output style-shelf key "para"
           output "%c%n"
```

13. The element emphasis can be handled as follows:

```
element emphasis
           output "{"
           output "\f11" when "%v(asis)" = UL"asis"
           output "\b" when "%v(weight)" = UL"bold"
           output "\i" when "%v(slant)" = UL"italic"
           output "\super" when
             "%v(raised)" = UL"super"
           output "\sub" when "%v(lowered)" = UL"sub"
           output " %c}"
```

The element emphasis has a wide variety of formatting options. To set the proper option, we need to test all the variables. The basic RTF markup for a specific word is:

```
{rtf-codes text}
```

14. To handle the system and line elements, we need the following:

```
element system
           output "%c"

element line
           output style-shelf key "system"
             when "%v(position)" = UL"inline"
           output style-shelf key "system-w"
             when "%v(position)" = UL"wide"
           output "%c"
```

15. To create an example heading:

```
element example
            output "%c"

element title when parent is example
            output style-shelf key "example"
            output "%c"
```

16. To create a caution or note:

```
element caution
            output style-shelf key "caution"
            output "%c"

element note
            output style-shelf key "note"
            output "%c"
```

17. Below are more changes to the para element to support note and caution:

```
element para
            output style-shelf key "copybdy"
              when ancestor is copyright
            output style-shelf key "para"
              when ancestor isnt
              (copyright or note or caution
              or item)
            output "%c%n"
```

18. To create a bullet or number list:

```
global counter bulletcount
global counter numbercount

element bullet-list
            increment bulletcount
            output "%c"
            decrement bulletcount

element number-list
            increment numbercount
            output "%c"
            decrement numbercount

element item when parent is bullet-list
            output style-shelf key "bullet1-f"
              when bulletcount = 1
            output style-shelf key "bullet2-f"
```

```
                      when bulletcount = 2
                output "%c"

element item when parent is number-list
                output style-shelf key "list1-f"
                  when numbercount = 1
                output "%c"
```

19. To format tables and graphics:

```
element figure
                output "%c"

element title when parent is figure
                output style-shelf key "figuretitle"
                output "%c"

element graphic
                output "{\field{\*\fldinst
INCLUDEPICTURE "
                output "%"F:\\\\sgmlwrk\\\\cd-rom\\\\"
                output "formatting\\\\sample2rtf\\\\"
                output "%ev(name)%""
                output " \\* MERGEFORMAT \\d }"
                output "{\fldrslt }}"
                put #SUPPRESS "%c"

element table
                output "\par TABLE FOUND HERE%n"
                put #SUPPRESS "%c%n"
```

20. To format the xref element:

```
element xref
                output referent "%v(ref)"
                put #SUPPRESS "%c"
```

The following is a change required for all elements with IDs (titles and items):

```
global stream id-shelf variable

clear id-shelf

element title when parent is figure
local stream content
                set content to "%c"
                do when attribute id is specified
                  new id-shelf key "%v(id)"
```

```
                  set id-shelf to "%g(content)"
        done
        output style-shelf key "figuretitle"
        output "%g(content)"
```

Add the following to document-end:

```
document-end
local stream temp
output "\par }%n"
repeat over id-shelf
                set temp to key of id-shelf
                repeat over referents
                  do when "%g(temp)" = (key of this
                                referent)
                                set referent key of this
                                    referent to
                                    "%g(id-shelf)"
                                exit
                  else
                                set referent key of
                                    this referent to
                                    "%g(id-shelf)"
                  done
                again
    again
```

This section of code is a little more complicated than some of the
others. The idea behind this is to create a shelf that is keyed by the
ID of any object with an ID. The content of the shelf will be the
content of the object, an item number, or footnote symbol, depending
upon the source.

For every xref element that is found, a referent is output with the
IDREF value being used as a key to the referent. At the end of
processing, we loop through the id-shelf, looking for a match
between the id-shelf key and the key of the referent. If we find a
match, we output the content of the id-shelf.

21. To format an indexitem:

```
element indexitem
                put #SUPPRESS "%c"
```

22. To format the footnote and ftnoteref elements:

```
element footnote
local stream content
            set content to "%c"
            do when attribute id is specified
              new id-shelf key "%v(footnote-id)"
              set id-shelf to "* " when
                      "%v(symbol)" = UL"level1"
              set id-shelf to "** " when
                      "%v(symbol)" = UL"level2"
              set id-shelf to "*** " when
                      "%v(symbol)" = UL"level3"
            done
            output style-shelf key "para"
            output "* " when "%v(symbol)" =
UL"level1"

            output "** " when
              "%v(symbol)" = UL"level2"
            output "*** " when
              "%v(symbol)" = UL"level3"
            output "%g(content)%n"


element ftnoteref
            output referent "%v(idref)"
            put #SUPPRESS "%c"
```

23. Our last change is to make the #IMPLIED rule always output the
    content of any element not specifically handled in the body of the
    program. By doing this, you are ensured of getting all of the
    document contents, even though they may not be formatted. You
    want to err on the side of having all the content, rather than having
    a perfectly formatted document. You could also have this rule report
    on any elements that were handled by the rule.

```
element #IMPLIED
            output "%c"
```

 If you tried to run this code at any stage, you would have found
references like: [lt   ], [shy   ], and [ndash] at various places.
These are the results of processing the document with the standard
ISO entity files in place. I have created a single entity file that
contains the RTF encoding for as many characters as I could define.

Add the following to the `entities.xlr` file:

```
"-//Dan Vint//ENTITIES Popular ISO Characters in RTF//EN"
"rtfchars.ent"
```

In the DTD, comment out the references to the ISO entity files and add:

```
<!ENTITY % RTFchars PUBLIC "-//Dan Vint//ENTITIES Popular ISO Characters in RTF//EN">
%RTFchars;
```

The output for this script is in the file `sample2rtf.rtf`. The final version of `sample2rtf.xom` is as follows:

```
 1   down-translate
 2
 3
 4   include "entities.xlr"
 5
 6   global stream style-shelf variable
 7   global stream id-shelf variable
 8
 9   global stream partno initial {""}
10   global stream pubdate initial {""}
11   global counter headcount
12   global counter bulletcount
13   global counter numbercount
14
15   document-start
16
17   ; start of file and font information - note font numbers will change
18   ; with each saving of an RTF file.
19   output "{\rtf1\ansi \deff4\deflang1033%n"_
20           "{\fonttbl%n"_
21           "{\f1\froman\fcharset2\fprq2 Symbol;}%n"_
22           "{\f4\froman\fcharset0\fprq2 Times New Roman;}%n"_
23           "{\f5\fswiss\fcharset0\fprq2 Arial;}%n"_
24           "{\f11\fmodern\fcharset0\fprq1 Courier New;}%n"_
25           "{\f234\fnil\fcharset0\fprq2 WP TypographicSymbols;}%n"_
26           "{\f249\fswiss\fcharset0\fprq2 Architecture;}%n"_
27           "{\f321\froman\fcharset0\fprq0 TimesNewRoman,Bold;}%n"_
28           "{\f322\froman\fcharset0\fprq0 TimesNewRoman;}%n"_
29           "{\f323\froman\fcharset0\fprq0 CourierNew;}}%n"
30
31   ; Color table information
32   output "{\colortbl;\red0\green0\blue0;\red0\green0\blue255;"_
33           "\red0\green255\blue255;\red0\green255\blue0;\red255\green0\blue255;"_
34           "\red255\green0\blue0;\red255\green255\blue0;\red255\green255\blue255;"_
35           "\red0\green0\blue128;\red0\green128\blue128;\red0\green128\blue0;"_
36           "\red128\green0\blue128;\red128\green0\blue0;\red128\green128\blue0;"_
37           "\red128\green128\blue128;\red192\green192\blue192;}%n"
38
39   ; Style sheet information
40   output "{\stylesheet%n"_
```

```
41          "{\li3600\sb100\widctlpar \f4\fs20 \snext0 Normal;}%n"_
42          "{\s2\li3600\sb240\sa60\keepn\widctlpar \b\i\f5 \sbasedon0\snext0 "_
43          "heading 2;}%n"_
44          "{\*\cs10 \additive Default Paragraph Font;}%n"_
45          "{\s15\qr\li2880\sb1440\sa400\widctlpar \f249\fs144 "_
46          "\sbasedon0\snext16 DocTitle;}%n"_
47          "{\s16\qr\li2880\sb100\sa2800\widctlpar \b\f5\fs32 \sbasedon0\snext16"_
48          " Subtitle;}%n"_
49          "{\s17\sb100\widctlpar \b\f5 \sbasedon0\snext17 DocDate;}%n"_
50          "{\s18\sb100\widctlpar \b\f4\fs20 \sbasedon0\snext18 CopyHead1;}%n"_
51          "{\s19\li1080\sb100\widctlpar \f4\fs14 \sbasedon0\snext19 CopyBody;}%n"_
52          "{\s20\li547\sb100\widctlpar \b\f4\fs20 \sbasedon0\snext19 CopyHead2;}%n"_
53          "{\s21\qr\li3600\sb1440\sa600\pagebb\widctlpar \i\f4\fs48 "_
54          "\sbasedon0\snext21 PrefaceTitle;}%n"_
55          "{\s22\li3600\sb100\widctlpar\brdrt\brdrs\brdrw30\brsp20 \f4\fs20 "_
56          "\sbasedon0\snext0 Para1;}%n"_
57          "{\s23\sb500\sa100\keepn\widctlpar\brdrt\brdrs\brdrw30\brsp20 "_
58          "\i\f4\fs28 \sbasedon0\snext0 head1;}%n"_
59          "{\s24\fi-360\li3960\sb100\widctlpar{\*\pn \pnlvl11\pnf1\pnstart1"_
60          "\pnindent360\pnhang{\pntxtb \'b7}}\f4\fs20 \sbasedon0\snext26 "_
61          "Bullet1;}%n"_
62          "{\s26\li360\sb100\sa120\widctlpar \f4\fs20 \sbasedon0\snext26 "_
63          "List Continue;}%n"_
64          "{\s27\li1800\sb300\sa100\keep\keepn\widctlpar \b\f4\fs22 \sbasedon0"_
65          "\snext0 Head2;}%n"_
66          "{\s28\qr\sb2800\sa600\pagebb\widctlpar{\*\pn \pnlvl10\pndec\pnb1"_
67          "\pni1\pnf5\pnfs144\pnstart1\pnsp2880\pnhang}\i\f4\fs48 \sbasedon0"_
68          "\snext28 ChapterTitle;}%n"_
69          "{\s29\fi-1080\li5760\sb200\sa100\widctlpar{\*\pn \pnlvl10\pnb0\pni1"_
70          "\pnf5\pnfs24\pnstart1\pnindent360\pnhang{\pntxtb Caution:}}\f4\fs20 "

72  output  "\sbasedon0\snext29 Caution;}%n"_
73          "{\s30\sb500\sa100\keepn\widctlpar \b\f4 \sbasedon23\snext30 "_
74          "ExampleHead;}%n"_
75          "{\s31\li3600\sb100\widctlpar \b\f4\fs20 \sbasedon0\snext0 FigTitle;}"_
76          "{\s32\fi-360\li3960\sb100\widctlpar{\*\pn \pnlvl10\pndec\pnstart1"_
77          "\pnindent360\pnhang{\pntxta .}}\f4\fs20 \sbasedon0\snext0 list1;}%n"_
78         "{\s34\li3600\sb100\widctlpar \f4\fs20 \sbasedon31\snext0 TableTitle;}%n"_
79          "{\s35\fi-360\li4320\sb100\widctlpar{\*\pn \pnlvl11\pnf234\pnfs18"_
80          "\pnstart1\pnindent360\pnhang{\pntxtb #}}\f4\fs20 \sbasedon0\snext35 "_
81          "Bullet2;}%n"_
82          "{\s37\fi-1080\li5760\sb200\sa100\widctlpar{\*\pn \pnlvl10\pnb0"_
83          "\pni1\pnf5\pnfs24\pnstart1\pnindent360\pnhang{\pntxtb Note:}}\i\f4"_
84          "\fs20 \sbasedon29\snext0 Note;}%n"_
85          "{\s38\sb100\widctlpar \f11\fs18 \sbasedon0\snext38 SystemWide;}"_
86          "{\s39\li3600\sb100\widctlpar \f11\fs18 \sbasedon0\snext39 System;}"_
87          "{\s40\qr\sb2800\sa600\pagebb\widctlpar{\*\pn \pnlvl10\pnucltr\pnb1"_
88          "\pni0\pnf5\pnfs144\pnstart1\pnsp2880\pnhang}\b\i\f4\fs48 "_
89          "\sbasedon28\snext40 AppendixTitle;}%n"_
90          "{\s41\qc\widctlpar \b\f5\fs20 \sbasedon0\snext41 CellHead;}%n"_
```

```
 91          "{\s42\widctlpar \f4\fs20 \sbasedon0\snext42 CellBody;}%n"_
 92          "{\s43\li3600\sb240\sa60\keepn\widctlpar \b\f4\fs22 "_
 93          "\sbasedon3\snext0 Head3;}"_
 94          "{\s44\li3600\sb240\sa60\keepn\widctlpar \f4\fs22\ul "_
 95          "\sbasedon4\snext0 Head4;}"_
 96          "}%n"
 97
 98   ; Document info
 99   output  "{\info{\title }%n"_
100           "{\author xxxx}%n"_
101           "{\operator  xxxx}%n"_
102           "{\creatim\yr1997\mo8\dy25\hr14\min13}%n"_
103           "{\revtim\yr1997\mo8\dy25\hr19\min17}%n"_
104           "{\version3}{\edmins36}{\nofpages15}%n"_
105           "{\nofwords3727}%n"_
106           "{\nofchars21244}%n"_
107           "{\*\company  xxxx}%n"
108
109   ; Page setup information
110   output  "{\vern57431}}%n"_
111           "\margl1080\margr720\margt720\margb720 \widowctrl\ftnbj\aenddoc%n"_
112           "\hyphcaps0\formshade \fet0\sectd \psz1\linex0\headery360%n"_
113           "\footery360\endnhere %n"_
114           "{\*\pnseclvl1\pnucrm\pnstart1\pnindent720\pnhang{\pntxta .}}%n"_
115           "{\*\pnseclvl2\pnucltr\pnstart1\pnindent720\pnhang{\pntxta .}}%n"_
116           "{\*\pnseclvl3\pndec\pnstart1\pnindent720\pnhang{\pntxta .}}%n"_
117           "{\*\pnseclvl4\pnlcltr\pnstart1\pnindent720\pnhang{\pntxta )}}%n"_
118           "{\*\pnseclvl5\pndec\pnstart1\pnindent720\pnhang{\pntxtb (}"_
119           "{\pntxta )}}%n"_
120           "{\*\pnseclvl6\pnlcltr\pnstart1\pnindent720\pnhang{\pntxtb (}"_
121           "{\pntxta )}}%n"_
122           "{\*\pnseclvl7\pnlcrm\pnstart1\pnindent720\pnhang{\pntxtb (}"_
123           "{\pntxta )}}%n"_
124           "{\*\pnseclvl8\pnlcltr\pnstart1\pnindent720\pnhang{\pntxtb (}"_
125           "{\pntxta )}}%n"_
126           "{\*\pnseclvl9\pnlcrm\pnstart1\pnindent720\pnhang{\pntxtb (}"_
127           "{\pntxta )}}%n"
128
129           clear id-shelf
130           clear style-shelf
131
132           new style-shelf key "doctitle"
133           set style-shelf to
134                 "\pard\plain \s15\qr\li2880\sb1440\sa400\widctlpar \f249\fs144 "
135
136           new style-shelf key "subtitle"
137           set style-shelf to
138                 "\par \pard\plain \s16\qr\li2880\sb100\sa2800\widctlpar"_
139                 "\b\f5\fs32 "
140
```

```
141        new style-shelf key "docdata"
142        set style-shelf to
143            "\par \pard\plain \s17\sb100\widctlpar \b\f5 "
144
145        new style-shelf key "copyhd1"
146        set style-shelf to
147            "\par \pard\plain \s18\sb100\widctlpar \b\f4\fs20 "
148
149        new style-shelf key "copyhd2"
150        set style-shelf to
151            "\par \pard\plain \s20\li547\sb100\widctlpar \b\f4\fs20"
152
153        new style-shelf key "copybdy"
154        set style-shelf to
155            "\par \pard\plain \s19\li1080\sb100\widctlpar \f4\fs14 "
156
157        new style-shelf key "preface"
158        set style-shelf to
159            "\par \pard\plain \s21\qr\li3600\sb1440\sa600\pagebb\"_
160            "widctlpar \i\f4\fs48 "
161
162        new style-shelf key "chapter"
163        set style-shelf to
164            "\par {\pntext\pard\plain\b\i\f5\fs144 1\tab}\pard\plain "_
165            "\s28\qr\sb2800\sa600\pagebb\widctlpar{\*\pn \pnlvlbody\pndec"_
166            "\pnb1\pni1\pnf5\pnfs144\pnstart1\pnsp2880\pnhang}\i\f4\fs48 "
167
168        new style-shelf key "appendix"
169        set style-shelf to
170            "\par {\pntext\pard\plain\b\f5\fs144 A\tab}\pard\plain "_
171            "\s37\qr\sb2800\sa600\pagebb\widctlpar{\*\pn \pnlvlbody\"_
172            "pnucltr\pnb1\pni0\pnf5\pnfs144\pnstart1\pnsp2880\pnhang}"_
173            "\b\i\f4\fs48 "
174
175        new style-shelf key "head1"
176        set style-shelf to
177            "\par \pard\plain \s23\sb500\sa100\keepn\widctlpar\brdrt\brdrs"_
178            "\brdrw30\brsp20 \i\f4\fs28 "
179
180        new style-shelf key "head2"
181        set style-shelf to
182            "\par \pard\plain \s27\li1800\sb300\sa100\keep\keepn\widctlpar"_
183            " \b\f4\fs22 "
184
185        new style-shelf key "head3"
186        set style-shelf to
187            "\par \pard\plain \s43\li3600\sb240\sa60\keepn\widctlpar \b\f4\fs22 "
188
189        new style-shelf key "head4"
190        set style-shelf to
```

```
191                        "\par \pard\plain \s44\li3600\sb240\sa60\keepn\widctlpar \f4\fs22\ul "
192
193          new style-shelf key "example"
194          set style-shelf to
195                  "\par \pard\plain \s30\sb500\sa100\keepn\widctlpar \b\f4 "
196
197          new style-shelf key "figuretitle"
198          set style-shelf to
199                  "\par \pard\plain \s31\li3600\sb100\widctlpar \b\f4\fs20 "
200
201          new style-shelf key "caution"
202          set style-shelf to
203                  "\pard\plain \s29\fi-1080\li5760\sb200\sa100\widctlpar{\*\pn "_
204                  "\pnlvlbody\pnb0\pni1\pnf5\pnfs24\pnstart1\pnindent360\pnhang"_
205                  "{\pntxtb Caution:}}\f4\fs20 "
206
207          new style-shelf key "note"
208          set style-shelf to
209                  "\par {\pntext\pard\plain\i\f5 Note:\tab}\pard\plain \s37\"_
210                  "fi-1080\li5760\sb200\sa100\widctlpar{\*\pn \pnlvlbody\pnb0\"_
211                  "pni1\pnf5\pnfs24\pnstart1\pnindent360\pnhang{\pntxtb Note:}}"_
212                  "\i\f4\fs20 "
213
214          new style-shelf key "para"
215          set style-shelf to
216                  "\par \pard\plain \li3600\sb100\widctlpar \f4\fs20 "
217
218          new style-shelf key "system"
219          set style-shelf to
220                  "\par \pard\plain \s36\li3600\sb100\widctlpar \f11\fs18"
221
222          new style-shelf key "system-w"
223          set style-shelf to
224                  "\par \pard\plain \s35\sb100\widctlpar \f11\fs18 "
225
226          new style-shelf key "bullet1-f"
227          set style-shelf to
228                  "\par {\pntext\pard\plain\f1\fs20 \'b7\tab}\pard\plain "_
229                  "\s24\fi-360\li3960\sb100\widctlpar{\*\pn \pnlvlblt\pnf1\"_
230                  "pnstart1\pnindent360\pnhang{\pntxtb \'b7}}\f4\fs20 "
231
232          new style-shelf key "bullet2-f"
233          set style-shelf to
234                  "\par {\pntext\pard\plain\f234\fs18 #\tab}\pard\plain "_
235                  "\s35\fi-360\li4320\sb100\widctlpar{\*\pn \pnlvlblt\pnf234\"_
236                  "pnfs18\pnstart1\pnindent360\pnhang{\pntxtb #}}\f4\fs20"
237
238          new style-shelf key "list1-f"
239          set style-shelf to
240                  "\par {\pntext\pard\plain\fs20 1.\tab}\pard\plain \s32\fi-360"_
```

```
241                          "\li3960\sb100\widctlpar{\*\pn \pnlvlbody\pndec\pnstart1\"_
242                          "pnindent360\pnhang{\pntxta .}}\f4\fs20 "
243
244
245  document-end
246  local stream temp
247  output "\par }%n"
248
249          repeat over id-shelf
250                  set temp to key of id-shelf
251                  repeat over referents
252                          do when "%g(temp)" = (key of this referent)
253                                  set referent key of this referent to
254                                          "%g(id-shelf)"
255                                  exit
256                          else
257                                  set referent key of this referent to
258                                          "%g(id-shelf)"
259                          done
260                  again
261
262          again
263
264
265
266
267  ;;;;
268  ; ELEMENT RULES START HERE
269  ;;;;
270
271  element book
272          set pubdate to "%v(PubDate)"
273          set partno to "%v(PartNO)"
274          output "%c%n"
275
276  element cover
277          output "%c"
278
279          output style-shelf key "docdata"
280          output "Published: %g(pubdate)"
281
282          output style-shelf key "docdata"
283          output "Part Number: %g(partno)"
284          output "\page%n"
285
286  element title when parent is cover
287          output style-shelf key "doctitle"
288          output "%c"
289
290  element subtitle
```

```
291            output style-shelf key "subtitle"
292            output "%c"
293
294
295
296  element copyright
297            set headcount to 0
298            output "%c"
299
300  element head when ancestor is copyright
301            increment headcount
302            output "%c"
303            decrement headcount
304
305  element title when parent is head and ancestor is copyright
306            output style-shelf key "copyhd1" when headcount = 1
307            output style-shelf key "copyhd2" when headcount = 2
308
309            do when headcount > 2
310                    output "%n%nHEAD LEVEL NESTED TOO DEEP%n"
311            done
312            output "%c"
313
314
315
316  element preface
317            reset headcount to 0
318            output "%c"
319
320  element title when parent is preface
321  local stream content
322            set content to "%c"
323            output style-shelf key "preface"
324            output "%g(content)"
325            do when attribute id is specified
326                    new id-shelf key "%v(id)"
327                    set id-shelf to "%g(content)"
328            done
329
330  element head when ancestor is preface
331            reset numbercount to 0
332            reset bulletcount to 0
333            increment headcount
334            output "%c"
335            decrement headcount
336
337  element title when parent is head and ancestor is preface
338  local stream content
339            set content to "%c"
340            do when attribute id is specified
```

```
341                 new id-shelf key "%v(id)"
342                 set id-shelf to "%g(content)"
343         done
344
345         output style-shelf key "head1" when headcount = 1
346         output style-shelf key "head2" when headcount = 2
347         output style-shelf key "head3" when headcount = 3
348         output style-shelf key "head4" when headcount = 4
349
350         do when headcount > 4
351                 output "%n%nHEAD LEVEL NESTED TOO DEEP%n"
352         done
353         output "%g(content)"
354
355
356  element (body or rearmatter)
357         output "%c"
358
359  element section
360         reset headcount to 0
361         output "%c"
362
363  element title when parent is section and ancestor is body
364  local stream content
365         set content to "%c"
366         do when attribute id is specified
367                 new id-shelf key "%v(id)"
368                 set id-shelf to "%g(content)"
369         done
370
371         output style-shelf key "chapter"
372         output "%g(content)"
373
374  element title when parent is section and ancestor is rearmatter
375  local stream content
376         set content to "%c"
377         do when attribute id is specified
378                 new id-shelf key "%v(id)"
379                 set id-shelf to "%g(content)"
380         done
381
382         output style-shelf key "appendix"
383         output "%g(content)"
384
385  element head when ancestor is section
386         reset numbercount to 0
387         reset bulletcount to 0
388         increment headcount
389         output "%c"
390         decrement headcount
```

```
391
392   element title when parent is head and ancestor is section
393   local stream content
394           set content to "%c"
395           do when attribute id is specified
396                   new id-shelf key "%v(id)"
397                   set id-shelf to "%g(content)"
398           done
399
400           output style-shelf key "head1" when headcount = 1
401           output style-shelf key "head2" when headcount = 2
402           output style-shelf key "head3" when headcount = 3
403           output style-shelf key "head4" when headcount = 4
404
405           do when headcount > 4
406                   output "%n%nHEAD LEVEL NESTED TOO DEEP%n"
407           done
408           output "%g(content)"
409
410
411   element emphasis
412           output "{"
413           output "\f11" when "%v(asis)" = UL"asis"
414           output "\b" when "%v(weight)" = UL"bold"
415           output "\i" when "%v(slant)" = UL"italic"
416           output "\super" when "%v(raised)" = UL"super"
417           output "\sub" when "%v(lowered)" = UL"sub"
418           output " %c}"
419
420   element system
421           output "%c"
422
423   element line
424           output style-shelf key "system" when "%v(position)" = UL"inline"
425           output style-shelf key "system-w" when "%v(position)" = UL"wide"
426           output "%c"
427
428   element example
429           output "%c"
430
431   element title when parent is example
432   local stream content
433           set content to "%c"
434           do when attribute id is specified
435                   new id-shelf key "%v(id)"
436                   set id-shelf to "%g(content)"
437           done
438
439           output style-shelf key "example"
440           output "%g(content)"
```

```
441
442   element caution
443          output style-shelf key "caution"
444          output "%c"
445
446   element note
447          output style-shelf key "note"
448          output "%c"
449
450   element para
451          output style-shelf key "copybdy" when ancestor is copyright
452          output style-shelf key "para" when ancestor isnt
453                  (entry or copyright or note or caution or item)
454          output "%c%n"
455
456
457   element bullet-list
458          increment bulletcount
459          output "%c"
460          decrement bulletcount
461
462   element number-list
463          increment numbercount
464          output "%c"
465          decrement numbercount
466
467   element item when parent is bullet-list
468          output style-shelf key "bullet1-f" when bulletcount = 1
469          output style-shelf key "bullet2-f" when bulletcount = 2
470          output "%c"
471
472   element item when parent is number-list
473          output style-shelf key "list1-f" when numbercount = 1
474          do when numbercount > 1
475                  output "\par NESTING LEVEL TOO DEEP%n"
476          done
477          output "%c"
478
479   element figure
480          output "%c"
481
482   element title when parent is figure
483   local stream content
484          set content to "%c"
485          do when attribute id is specified
486                  new id-shelf key "%v(id)"
487                  set id-shelf to "%g(content)"
488          done
489
490          output style-shelf key "figuretitle"
```

```
491            output "%g(content)"
492
493    element graphic
494            output "\par {\field{\*\fldinst  INCLUDEPICTURE "
495            output "%"F:\\\\sgmlwrk\\\\cd-rom\\\\formatting\\\\sample2rtf\\\\"
496            output "%ev(name)%""
497            output " \\* MERGEFORMAT \\d }{\fldrslt }}"
498            put #SUPPRESS "%c"
499
500    element table
501            output "\par TABLE FOUND HERE%n"
502            put #SUPPRESS "%c%n"
503
504    element xref
505            output referent "%v(ref)"
506            put #SUPPRESS "%c"
507
508    element indexitem
509            put #SUPPRESS "%c"
510
511
512    element footnote
513    local stream content
514            set content to "%c"
515
516            do when attribute id is specified
517                    new id-shelf key "%v(footnote-id)"
518                    set id-shelf to "* " when "%v(symbol)" = UL"level1"
519                    set id-shelf to "** " when "%v(symbol)" = UL"level2"
520                    set id-shelf to "*** " when "%v(symbol)" = UL"level3"
521            done
522
523            output style-shelf key "para"
524            output "* " when "%v(symbol)" = UL"level1"
525            output "** " when "%v(symbol)" = UL"level2"
526            output "*** " when "%v(symbol)" = UL"level3"
527
528            output "%g(content)%n"
529
530    element ftnoteref
531            output referent "%v(idref)"
532            put #SUPPRESS "%c"
533
534
535
536    element #IMPLIED
537            output "%c"
```

An Introduction To DSSSL

DSSSL (ISO/IEC 10179:1996) is the complementary standard for SGML. SGML provides the structure and content markup and DSSSL provides the formatting. It is still early in the life of DSSSL and there aren't many tools available that provide this capability. As you have seen in the configuration of the various tools in this book, style and presentation can be the largest parts of the implementation process. I can't wait for the day when one style sheet can be developed that will support all these tools.

The DSSSL standard is available from ISO. For complete details, please see the standard; the information provided here is to provide a frame of reference for the code we will write later.

DSSSL was written to handle the publishing needs of languages that write right-to-left, left-to-right, and top-to-bottom. The language and terminology used to describe flow and direction have been generalized so they do not imply a particular writing-style bias. In addition to this, DSSSL provides:

- A transformation language to transform one SGML document into another SGML document

- A style language which applies formatting characteristics to portions of the SGML data.

DSSSL does not:

- Guarantee page fidelity between different DSSSL implementations

- Specify a formatting engine

- Include any particular hyphenation and justification algorithm.

DSSSL provides a mechanism to specify algorithms if they become publicly available.

The basic processing model is shown in Figure 13-1. This figure illustrates the relationship between the style and transformation portions of DSSSL. The SGML document is read into a DSSSL engine with its DTD and declaration files. The DSSSL specification is also read in. If there are any transformation rules, those are applied to the original document structure to create a new structure. After transforming the document, the style rules are applied and the requested output is generated. An SGML document, while being manipulated, is represented as an upside-down tree, or a series of trees called groves. The grove or tree is a standard storage model that can easily be traversed and modified.

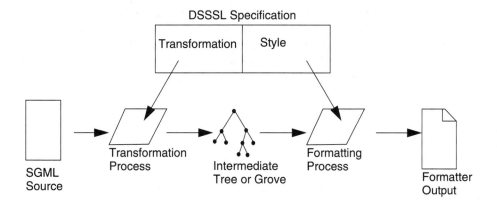

FIGURE 13-1. DSSSL CONCEPTUAL PROCESSING MODEL

Figure 13-2 illustrates the simple-page-sequence. This flow object describes the basic page layout and margins. Other flow objects will be placed within the page as well. A flow object is a marker or location for where text will be flowed onto a page. Writing a DSSSL specification involves specifying how these flow objects should be placed, and what direction to write the text for the objects to grow. The simple-page-sequence allows the definition of a single-line header or footer that is the same on every page except for an incrementing page number. Within the header and footer, you can specify text for one of three locations: start, end or center.

Within a page, flow objects can be displayed or inlined. Figure 13-3 illustrates a displayed external-graphic flow object and an inline-equation object within a paragraph flow object. A paragraph flow object is always displayed.

Figure 13-4 illustrates how different writing directions can be accommodated and mixed together. Many flow objects have a writing-mode: characteristic that specifies a direction of left-to-right, right-to-left, or top-to-bottom. The embedded-text flow object can be placed within a paragraph object and have a different writing direction than the body of the paragraph.

The paragraph flow object is the basic module for a document. Figure 13-5 illustrates the primary characteristics of a paragraph. The view illustrated has a writing-mode: of left-to-right. This is the standard English text model. Text starts to flow into this object from the left with a position of first-line-start-indent. Text flows in and wraps according to a set of wrap and truncate rules that can be applied. If the writing-mode: were set to right-to-left, the start-indent would be on the right side of the paragraph. The paragraph flow object also specifies the font information and how the lines should be laid out in the paragraph.

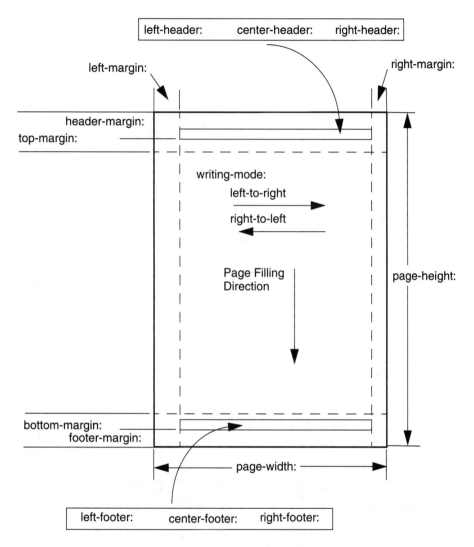

FIGURE 13-2. SIMPLE-PAGE-SEQUENCE

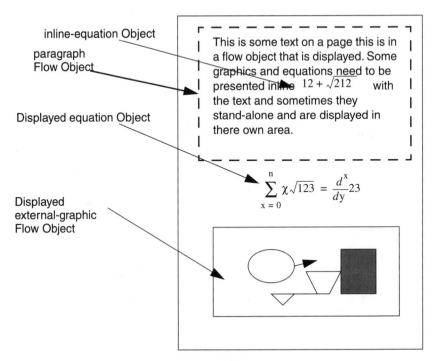

FIGURE 13-3. DISPLAY AND INLINE AREAS

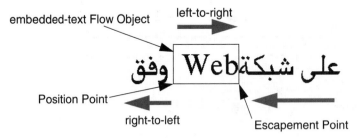

FIGURE 13-4. MIXED WRITING AND ALIGNMENT MODES

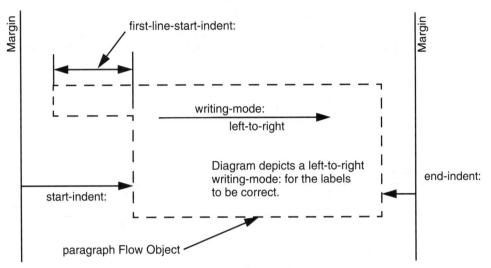

FIGURE 13-5. PARAGRAPH FLOW OBJECT

Figure 13-6 illustrates how line spacing is defined from the baseline or placement path of the text. Quadding or text justification has the standard arrangements of left, right, center, and justified (both left and right), as well as two alignments that are based upon page location: spread-inside and spread-outside. Line numbering is another characteristic that can be specified. line-number-side specifies where the number should be attached, and line-number-sep specifies how far from the body of the text that the number should be placed.

Figure 13-7 illustrates the external-graphic flow object. This is how graphics will be read into a document and placed. max-height: and max-width allow you to set the size of the frame that can be used by the graphic. The scale: characteristic allows you to set a scale method in the following ways:

- scale: x y allows you set to set a scale factor for the height and width.

- scale: max indicates that the largest possible scaling factor should be used for each direction (height and width). This can introduce distortion due to non-uniform scaling

- scale: max-uniform indicates the largest scaling factor to use to preserve the graphic in proportion to the original.

The external-graphic object can be positioned relative to the margins and then aligned via the display-alignment: characteristic. The external-graphic flow object will bring an illustration into its own object to be manipulated. Graphics typically are not standalone; they usually have a title. Figure 13-8 illustrates the use of the display-group, which takes an external-graphic object and a paragraph together as a single unit to manipulate. This is the best way to keep a graphic and its title together.

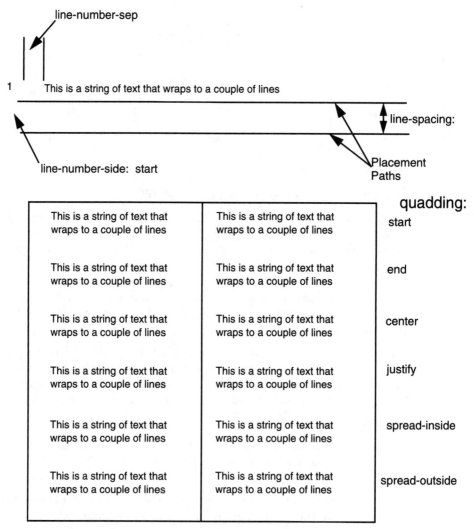

FIGURE 13-6. LINE CHARACTERISTICS

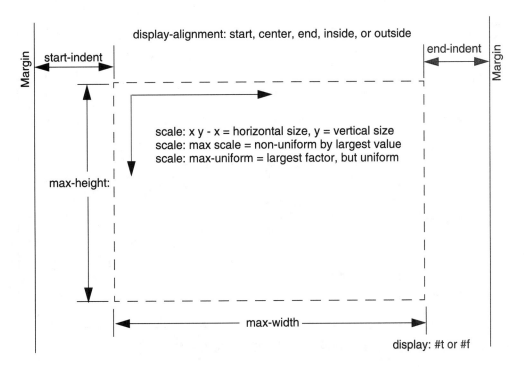

FIGURE 13-7. EXTERNAL-GRAPHIC FLOW OBJECT

Lines or rules are used in documentation to group or highlight areas of a page. The rule flow object in Figure 13-9 illustrates the various characteristics of a rule. A rule has an orientation, a thickness, a length, and placement controls. Rules can be single or multiple, dashed, solid, or color.

I have presented some of the major concepts in the DSSSL standard, as well as some details on specifying a few of the many flow objects. Refer to the ISO standard for more details. What I have provided here should be a good base to start implementing a DSSSL specification with Jade.

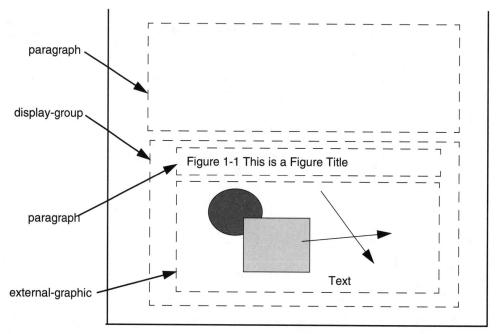

FIGURE 13-8. DISPLAY-GROUP USAGE

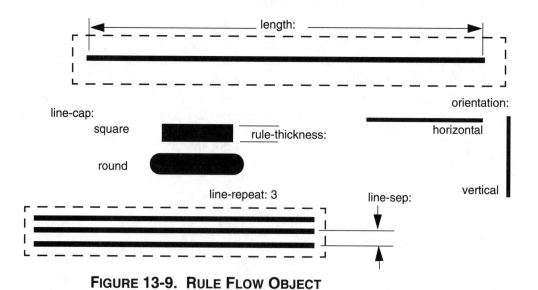

FIGURE 13-9. RULE FLOW OBJECT

JADE

Jade (James' DSSSL Engine) is a program that is freely available on the Internet. Jade is the first DSSSL-based formatting engine. Although Jade doesn't implement all the features and functionality of the DSSSL standard, it does implement a useable subset. From this subset of DSSSL syntax you can generate output in any of the available backends. These backends currently support RTF, SGML, and TeX. Jade was built in a way that allows new backend output tools to be added. Watch James Clark's Web site at `http://www.jclark.com/jade` for updates to this tool. James Clark is also the implementor of SP, a freely available SGML parser.

INSTALLATION

Jade is provided in several formats. For our purposes, we will use the Windows version of the binaries. Jade and the supporting files are provided in a zip file on the CD-ROM.

1. Insert the CD-ROM in your drive.
2. Locate the jade directory on the CD-ROM.
3. Use WinZip to extract the files into a directory of your choice.

CONFIGURATION

Jade uses an Oasis-based catalog to map Public identifiers to their system location. To configure the sample DTD:

1. Create a working directory for the DSSSL files on the CD-ROM.
2. Copy the files from the dsssl directory, which is found under formatting on the CD-ROM, to your working directory.
3. Edit the catalog with a text editor.
4. Add the following lines to the catalog:

```
PUBLIC "-//James Clark//DTD DSSSL Flow Object Tree//EN"
".. \jade\fot.dtd"
```

```
PUBLIC "ISO/IEC 10179:1996//DTD DSSSL Architecture//EN"
"..\jade\dsssl.dtd"

PUBLIC "-//James Clark//DTD DSSSL Style Sheet//EN"
"..\jade\style-sheet.dtd"

PUBLIC "-//SAW//DTD SGML at Work Sample DTD//EN"
"sample.dtd"

PUBLIC "-//ArborText//ELEMENTS CALS Table
Structures//EN" ".\entities\cals-tbl.elm"

PUBLIC "-//Dan Vint//ENTITIES Popular ISO Characters in
RTF//EN" ".\entities\rtfchars.ent"

PUBLIC "ISO 8879-1986//ENTITIES Publishing//EN"
".\entities\iso-pub.ent"

PUBLIC "ISO 8879-1986//ENTITIES Numeric and Special
Graphic//EN" "iso-num.ent"

PUBLIC "ISO 8879-1986//ENTITIES Diacritical Marks//EN"
".\entities\iso-dia.ent"

PUBLIC "ISO 8879-1986//ENTITIES General Technical//EN"
".\entities\iso-tech.ent"

PUBLIC "ISO 8879-1986//ENTITIES Added Latin 1//EN"
".\entities\iso-lat1.ent"

PUBLIC "ISO 8879-1986//ENTITIES Added Latin 2//EN"
".\entities\iso-lat2.ent"

PUBLIC "ISO 8879-1986//ENTITIES Greek Letters//EN"
".\entities\iso-grk1.ent"

PUBLIC "ISO 8879-1986//ENTITIES Greek Symbols//EN"
".\entities\iso-grk3.ent"
```

5. Save the catalog.

I have created a batch file, jade.bat, to run Jade with the proper command line options. The following options are being used:

- -f error file location - jade.err
- -t type of output - rtf
- -c catalog file location - .\catalog
- -d dsssl source file - *.dsl
- -o output file name - *.rtf

- input files - `sample.dcl` *.sgm

Before continuing, make any changes necessary to find your jade directory or filenames/locations. The following command line will be used to run `jade.bat`:

```
jade sample
```

CREATING A DSSSL FORMAT SPECIFICATION

To create a DSSSL specification:

1. With an ASCII editor, create the file `sample.dsl`.

2. Define the page layout information as follows:

```
<!DOCTYPE style-sheet PUBLIC "-//James Clark//DTD DSSSL
Style Sheet//EN">

(root
      (make simple-page-sequence
            page-width:              8.5in
            page-height:             11in
            top-margin:              .75in
            bottom-margin:           .75in
            left-margin:             1in
            right-margin:            .5in
            (process-children)))

(element para
      (make paragraph
            (process-children)))
```

A DSSSL specification is an SGML document, but due to the minimal use of tags and the omittag options, the actual tags that need to be included in the specification look like lisp code. I applied all the default (page layout) information to the root of the document. The simple-page-sequence is a single-column document with a single line of optional header and footer text. The process-children indicates that the contained elements should be processed. Currently, I have only specified that the para element (wherever found) should be flowed into a paragraph flow object.

I am taking advantage of the fact that there are a set of default values provided for the font name, size, weight, etc. This allows me to build just a base DSSSL specification.

Run the script to produce the file `sample.rtf`. Load `sample.rtf` into MS-Word and you should see something like the following:

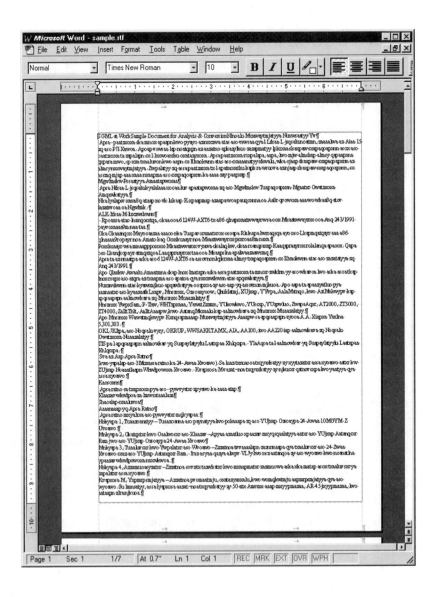

As you can see, the page is set to the correct margins.

3.   Close the `sample.rtf` in MS-Word before continuing.

4.   The cover page is the first object that we will format:

```
(element cover
    (make display-group
        (make rule
            line-thickness:        2pt)
        (process-children)
        (make paragraph
            font-size:             12pt
            font-family-name:      "Arial"
            font-weight:           'bold
            start-indent:          1in
        (literal (string-append "Published: "
            (inherited-element-attribute-string "book"
            "PubDate" (current-node)))))
        (make paragraph
            font-size:             12pt
            font-family-name:      "Arial"
            font-weight:           'bold
            start-indent:          1in
            space-after:           130pt
        (literal (string-append "Part Number: "
            (inherited-element-attribute-string "book"
            "PartNO" (current-node)))))
        (make rule
        line-thickness:            2pt)))
```

The above specification drives the overall look of the cover. I placed the cover contents to control this as a single object on the page. I output a rule that will be placed at the top of the area. By specifying the process-children in the next step, I output the title and subtitle content in this area. Next are two literals that take their content from the attributes of the book element combined with some labeling text. The content is sealed at the bottom with another rule. All of this content happens to balance out to a single page.

```
(element (cover title)
    (make paragraph
        font-size:                 62pt
        font-family-name:          "Arial"
        font-weight:               'bold
```

```
            line-spacing:               85pt
            space-before:               140pt
            space-after:                30pt
            start-indent:               2in
            quadding:                   'end
            (process-children)))
    (element (cover subtitle)
        (make paragraph
            font-size:                  20pt
            font-family-name:           "Arial"
            font-weight:                'bold
            line-spacing:               28pt
            space-after:                130pt
            start-indent:               2in
            quadding:'                  end
            (process-children)))
```

The title and subtitle objects are rather straight-forward applications of some font and spacing rules. I qualified both of these to be within a cover, even though the subtitle is only used at this location.

5. The copyright is the next section in our document. Even though I am taking these document sections in a linear order, I could have jumped into the content (like we did with the para definition) or taken the last section first. The specifications are not order-dependent; the matching specification is found for each node in the grove as we traverse the tree.

```
(define title-font
    (style
        font-family-name:        "Arial"
        font-weight:             'bold
    ))
(define title-1
    (style
```

```
        use:                    title-font
        font-size:              16pt
        ))
(define title-2
    (style
        use:                    title-font
        font-size:              14pt
    ))
```

The statement above defines style objects that can be applied to various flow objects as needed. By defining these in one location, we can minimize the number of places we might need to change a given value.

```
(element copyright
    (make display-group
        break-after:            'page
        (process-children)
    ))
(element (copyright head title)
    (make paragraph
        use:                    title-1
        quadding:               'start
        start-indent:           0in
        space-before:           15pt
        space-after:            5pt
        (process-children)))
(element (copyright head head title)
    (make paragraph
        use:                    title-2
        quadding:               'start
        start-indent:           .75in
        space-before:           15pt
        space-after:            5pt
        (process-children)))
```

In the two-head rules, the use: statement is needed to reference the styles that we defined. You might be wondering why we didn't place the space-before and -after in our styles. The short answer is that they aren't allowed in a style definition.

Notice that the copyright defines a display-group for all the content of the copyright section. In this case, the copyright section will not fill the entire page, but that is where I want the page to end. The break-after: characteristic specifies that a page break should be output after the copyright section is output.

```
(element (copyright head para)
    (make paragraph
        font-size:              8pt
        line-spacing:           10pt
        start-indent:           1in
        quadding:               'start
        (process-children)))

(element (copyright head head para)
    (make paragraph
        font-size:              8pt
        line-spacing:           10pt
        start-indent:           1in
        quadding:               'start
        (process-children)))
```

If you were to run this DSSSL specification as currently defined, the copyright page would look like the following:

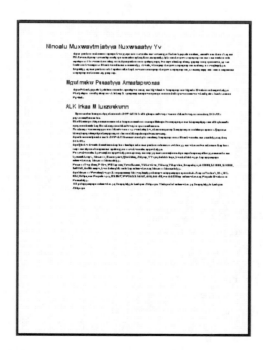

6. The next section to format is the preface:

```
(define title-chap
    (style
        use:                    title-font
        font-size:              36pt
        line-spacing:           42pt
    ))
(define title-3
    (style
        use:                    title-font
        font-size:              12pt
    ))
(define body-1
    (style
        font-size:              10pt
        line-spacing:           12pt
        start-indent:           2.5in
    ))
(define body-2
    (style
        start-indent:           3in
    ))
(define body-3
    (style
        start-indent:           3.5in
    ))
(element preface
    (make display-group
        break-after:            'page
        (process-children)
    ))
(element (preface title)
    (make paragraph
        use:                    title-chap
        space-before:           72pt
        space-after:            30pt
        quadding:               'end
        (process-children)))
```

```
(element (head title)
    (make display-group
        (make rule
            space-before:          15pt
            line-thickness:        1pt)
        (make paragraph
            use:                   title-1
            quadding:              'start
            start-indent:          0in
            space-before:          3pt
            space-after:           5pt
            (process-children))))
```

In the (head title) specification above, I'm using a display-group flow object to group the contents of the title with a ruling line. If I were to change the order of the make rule and paragraph, I would get the rule underneath the title instead of above the title.

```
(element (head head title)
    (make paragraph
        use:                   title-2
        quadding:              'start
        start-indent:          .75in
        space-before:          15pt
        space-after:           5pt
        (process-children)))

(element (head head head title)
    (make paragraph
        use:                   title-3
        quadding:              'start
        start-indent:          1.75in
        space-before:          15pt
        space-after:           5pt
        (process-children)))

(element (head head head head title)
    (make paragraph
        use:                   title-3
        quadding:              'start
        start-indent:          2.5in
        space-before:          15pt
        space-after:           5pt
        (process-children)))
```

```
(element (head head head head para)
    (make paragraph
        use:                        body-1
        space-before:               5pt
        (process-children)))

(element (head head head para)
    (make paragraph
        use:                        body-1
        space-before:               5pt
        (process-children)))

(element (head head para)
    (make paragraph
        use:                        body-1
        (process-children)))

(element (head para)
    (make paragraph
        use:                        body-1
        (process-children)))

(element (para)
    (make paragraph
        use:                        body-1
        (process-children)))
```

Notice how each level of a nesting of objects must be specified if you want them to format differently. For each heading level I specified a para and title sequence. One thing I didn't do was to qualify these element series all the way to the preface element. In this document, only the copyright page has a different configuration of heads and paragraphs; these definitions apply to the chapter and appendix sections of the document.

Notice the modification to the para specification from the first section of code.

```
(element bullet-list
    (make display-group
        space-before:               15pt
        space-after:                10pt
        (process-children)))

(element (bullet-list item)
    (make display-group
```

```
          space-before:                5pt
          (process-children)))
(element (item para)
     (make paragraph
          use:                    body-2
          first-line-start-indent:-.25in
          (make line-field
               field-width:         .25in
               (literal "\U-2022"))
          (process-children)))
```

The following drawing illustrates how the bullet-list is defined:

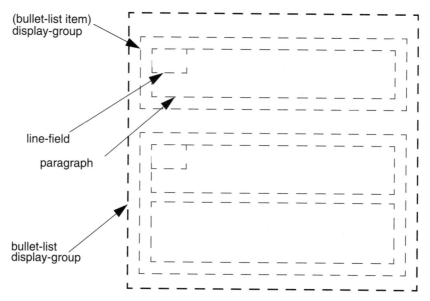

The bullet-list is defined as a display-group to control formatting
around the list. The display-group at the bullet-list item level keeps
the contents of the item together and allows specific formatting to be
applied to the item as a whole. The line-field within the item para is
used to manage the label content and its placement relative to the
body of the paragraph.

The code \U-2022 is the Unicode specification for a bullet symbol
that is to be placed in the literal which composes the content of the
line-field flow object.

```
(element (bullet-list item bullet-list)
    (make display-group
         space-before:              15pt
         space-after:               10pt
         (process-children)))

(element (bullet-list item bullet-list item)
    (make display-group
         space-before:              5pt
         (process-children)))

(element (bullet-list item bullet-list item para)
    (make paragraph
         use:                       body-3
         first-line-start-indent:   -.25in
         (make line-field
              field-width:          .25in
              (literal "\U-2013"))
         (process-children)))
```

This second group of bullet-list items defines a nested bullet-list. The \U-2013 is an en dash. Appendix B contains a table listing some of the common character codes.

```
(element emphasis
    (make sequence
         font-weight: (if (equal?
         (attribute-string "weight" (current-node))
              "BOLD")
              'bold
              'medium)
         font-posture: (if (equal?
              (attribute-string "slant" (current-node))
              "ITALIC")
              'italic
              'upright)
         font-family-name: (if (equal?
              (attribute-string "asis" (current-node))
              "ASIS")
              "Courier"
              "")
         (process-children)))
```

The emphasis specification must check the setting of the attributes and determine the settings for a number of different font attributes.

Note that I have not handled the position attributes of raised or lowered in my emphasis definition. I need two new elements to support these with DSSSL. Two flow objects, subscript and superscript, provide this functionality.

```
(element indexitem
    (make sequence
        (empty-sosofo)))
```

Here is what the first page of the preface now looks like:

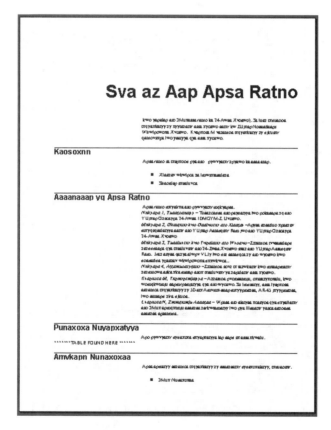

7. Next we will process the chapter items in the body section elements:

```
(element (body section)
    (make display-group
        break-after:                'page
```

```
        (process-children)
    ))
(element (body section title)
    (make paragraph
        use:                    title-chap
        space-before:           72pt
        space-after:            30pt
        quadding:               'end
        start-indent:           2in
        first-line-start-indent: -2in
        (make line-field
            field-width:        2in
            (literal (string-append "Chapter "
            (format-number
            (ancestor-child-number "section")
            "1"))))
        (process-children)))

(element caution
    (make box
        use:                    body-2
        (process-children)))

(element note
    (make display-group
        use:                    body-2
        (process-children)))

(element (caution para)
    (make paragraph
        use:                    body-2
        first-line-start-indent: -1in
        end-indent:             1in
        space-before:           15pt
        space-after:            5pt
        quadding:               'justify
        (make line-field
            font-family-name:   "Arial"
            font-weight:        'bold
            field-width:        1in
            (literal "Caution: "))
        (process-children)))
```

```
(element (note para)
    (make paragraph
        use:                        body-2
        first-line-start-indent:    -1in
        end-indent:                 1in
        quadding:                   'justify
        (make line-field
            font-family-name:       "Arial"
            font-weight:            'bold
            field-width:            1in
            (literal "Note: "))
        (process-children)))

(element figure
    (make display-group
        space-before:               15pt
        space-after:                10pt
        keep:                       'page
        (process-children)))

(element (figure title)
    (make paragraph
        font-family-name:           "Arial"
        font-size:                  14pt
        line-spacing:               16pt
        font-weight:                'bold
        font-posture:               'italic
        start-indent:               2.5in
        (process-children)))

(element graphic
    (make external-graphic
        entity-system-id:           (entity-system-id
            (attribute-string "name"))
        display?:                   #t
        space-before:               5pt
        space-after:                5pt ))
```

The graphics will be flowed into an external-graphic flow object. The graphic specification requires some special handling to determine the content. entity-system-id: is the characteristic that will ultimately retrieve the graphic from the filesystem. The attribute name contains the entity name, which we convert to an entity-system-id via the function with the same name.

When you load `sample.rtf` into MS-Word, you may not immediately see the graphics displayed. Even though all the files are located in the same directory, MS-Word maintains its own idea of the current working directory. If you drag and drop `sample.rtf` onto MS-Word, the working directory is elsewhere. To reset the working directory, use the Open option from the File menu to open the document. After this, the working directory will be the directory in which `sample.rtf` is located (until you restart MS-Word).

```
(element (example title)
    (make paragraph
        use:                    title-1
        quadding:               'start
        start-indent:           0in
        space-before:           15pt
        space-after:            5pt
        (process-children)))

(element number-list
    (make display-group
        space-before:           15pt
        space-after:            10pt
        (process-children)))

(element (number-list item)
    (make display-group
        space-before:           5pt
        (process-children)))

(element (number-list item para)
    (make paragraph
        use: body-2
        first-line-start-indent: -.25in
        (make line-field
            field-width:         .25in
            (if (= (child-number) 1)
            (literal (string-append (format-number
            (ancestor-child-number "item") "1") ".")
            )
            (empty-sosofo)))
        (process-children)))
```

```
(element (number-list number-list)
    (make display-group
        use:                        body-2
        space-before:               15pt
        space-after:                10pt
        (process-children)))

(element (number-list number-list item)
    (make display-group
        space-before:5pt
        (process-children)))

(element (number-list number-list item para)
    (make paragraph
        use:                        body-2
        first-line-start-indent:    -.25in
        (make line-field
            field-width:            .25in
            (if (= (child-number) 1)
            (literal (string-append (format-number
            (ancestor-child-number "item") "A") ".")
            )
            (empty-sosofo)))
        (process-children)))
```

The label for a number-list is constructed in a line-field flow object. The first paragraph in an item has the number applied. This is determined with the text for equality (= (child-number) 1). child-number returns the number of the child element in the current container tree; if this is the first one, then label the paragraph.

Similar to child-number, ancestor-child-number allows us to go a level or more above our current location, to the level we are interested in, which is the first occurrence of an item. This then returns the current number of the item within the most recent number-list container.

format-number allows us to easily change a number from an Arabic 1, 2, 3 ... to A, B, C ... or another format.

```
(element (number-list item bullet-list)
    (make display-group
        space-before:               15pt
        space-after:                10pt
        (process-children)))
```

```
(element (number-list item bullet-list item)
    (make display-group
        space-before:              5pt
        (process-children)))
```

```
(element (number-list item bullet-list item para)
    (make paragraph
        use:                       body-3
        first-line-start-indent:  -.25in
        (make line-field
            field-width:           .25in
            (literal "\U-2022"))
        (process-children)))
```

I created another bullet-list specification here to handle a bullet-list that appears inside of a number-list. I wanted to increase the indent under the number-list item; without this, bullets would be aligned with the numbers. Without indenting the bullet, it would appear to be at the same level, rather than a subitem of the number-list item.

```
(element system
    (make display-group
        space-before:              15pt
        space-after:               5pt
        (process-children)))
```

```
(element (system line)
    (make paragraph
        start-indent:                    (if (equal?
        (attribute-string "position" (current-node))
            "WIDE")
            0in
            2.5in)
        font-family-name:"Courier"
        font-size:                 8pt
        (process-children)))
```

The following illustration contains a couple of pages from the chapter section to illustrate the level of formatting we are now providing:

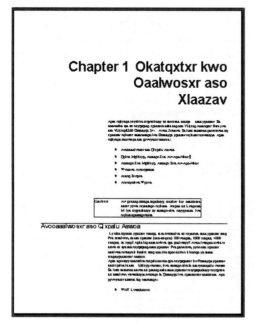
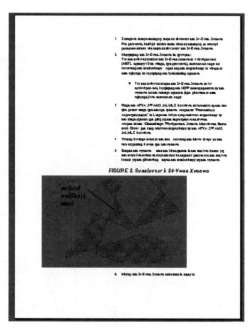

8. The final section to process is the rearmatter sections, or the appendices:

```
(element (rearmatter section)
    (make display-group
        break-after:            'page
        (process-children)))

(element (rearmatter section title)
    (make paragraph
        use:                      title-chap
        space-before:             72pt
        space-after:              30pt
        quadding:                 'end
        start-indent:             2in
        first-line-start-indent: -2in
        (make line-field
            field-width:          2in
```

```
(literal (string-append "Appendix "
(format-number
(ancestor-child-number "section")
"A")))) 
(process-children)))
```

We only needed to add support for the rearmatter section title to complete the formatting of an appendix section—formatting of all other items is the same as previous sections. The following shows what an appendix page looks like:

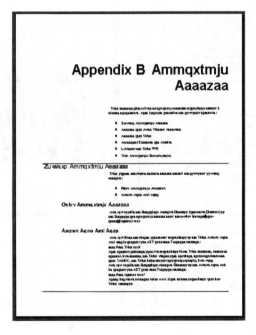

9. The following code will format a cross-reference to any object with an ID:

```
(element xref
    (make sequence
        font-size:                 10pt
        (literal "( see " )
        (process-element-with-id
            (attribute-string "ref" (current-node)))
        (literal ")" )))
```

The xref content should be placed inline within the parent para element. It should format or inherit the formatting from the surrounding text, but in this instance, it is formatted as the title object that is being referenced. process-element-id allows us to start processing an element out of sequence. By providing the unique ID of an element, we can jump to its location and process its content at any time. This also illustrates that we can process an element multiple times. Not only do we process the title in the normal flow, but we also pull that content in multiple times for the cross-reference.

10. To correct the formatting problem, we need a method to format titles large and another to format them inline as references. The mode command is what allows us to control multiple formats. Make the following change to xref and add the new code:

```
(element xref
      (make sequence
          (with-mode xref-out
              (make sequence
              font-size:              10pt
              (literal "( see " )
              (process-element-with-id
                (attribute-string "ref" (current-node)))
              (literal ")" ))
          )))

(mode xref-out

(element (figure title)
          (process-children))
; add similar statements for the head and section titles.
)
```

11. The following code is some basic support for formatting tables:

```
(element table
      (make display-group
          (process-children)))

(element tgroup
      (make table
          (process-children)))
```

```
(element row
      (make table-row
          (process-children)))

(element entry
      (make table-cell
          (process-children)))

(element (entry para)
      (make sequence
          (process-children)))
```

The table specification above makes use of the default width of a column and outputs the contents of cells as they are found. This code doesn't position spanned cells properly and RTF doesn't support spans of cells across rows. To see the full support for CALS tables, take a look at the DSSSL specification for the DTD docbook in the file docbook3.dsl.

This completes my DSSSL specification for the sample DTD. To output TeX instead of RTF, we must change the format option on the jade command line; we don't need to create yet another style sheet.

4

DELIVERING DOCUMENTS ONLINE

In this chapter we will apply two tools for online delivery of documentation. Both of these systems work with SGML directly. We will examine how the following products are configured and used:

- TechnoTeacher's HyBrowse
- Inso's DynaText

TechnoTeacher's HyBrowse

TechnoTeacher has built a HyTime (ISO/IEC 10744)-based browsing system for SGML documents known as HyBrowse.

Installation

To install HyBrowse:

1. Load the CD-ROM in your drive.
2. Extract the files from the `hybrowse1_1.zip` located in the Hybrowse directory. Place the files in a temporary directory.
3. From the temporary directory, launch `setup.exe`.
4. Follow the prompts and install the 45-day evaluation copy of HyBrowse.

CONFIGURATION

This version of HyBrowse has no way to map external file entities and does not include ISO character entity files. The following changes were required to our sample application:

- The declaration file was added to the top of the `sample.sgm` file
- All PUBLIC identifiers were changed to SYSTEM and the appropriate file and path specifications were provided.

BUILDING THE HYBROWSE STYLE SHEET

To build a style sheet:

1. Launch the HyBrowse application.

2. From the File menu, select Open Session.

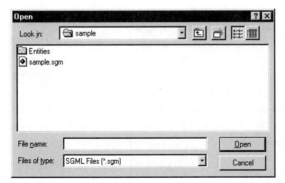

3. Select the `sample.sgm` file. The system will parse the SGML file and report any errors or missing entities. When the parsing ends, a new directory name, sample-hm, will be created. A default window will also be displayed:

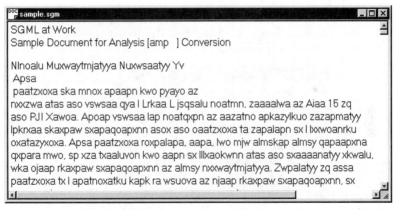

Notice that the ISO character entities have been expanded into the document as text strings. The proper mapping of entity names to actual character references should be made within the entities files.

4. Start formatting the document by choosing Select Element from the Format menu.

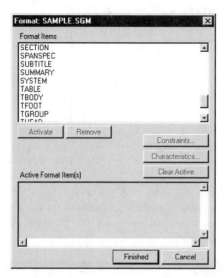

5. Start by formatting the BOOK element. Select BOOK, choose Activate, and then select Characteristics ....

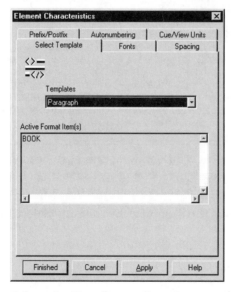

6. Select the Templates tab, select the Paragraph template, and then choose Apply.

7. Select the Fonts tab.

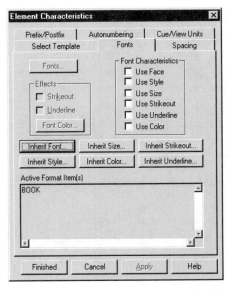

8. Select the Font Characteristics Use Face and Use Size options. Next, select the Fonts tab.

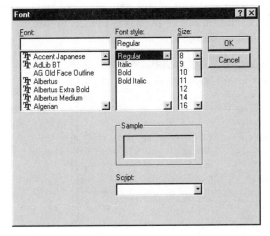

9. Set the Font to Times New Roman, the Font style to Regular, and the Size to 12. Select OK and then Apply.

10. Select the Spacing tab:

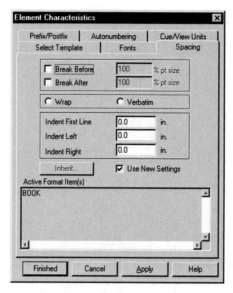

11. Select Wrap, set the Break Before to 150%, set the Indent Right to .5 in., then select Apply.

12. Set the formatting of the title element within the cover. From the Format dialog box, select the TITLE element, choose Activate, and select Constraints ...

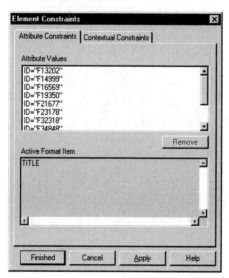

13. Select the Contextual Constraints tab:

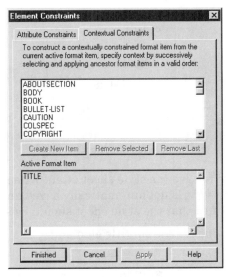

14. Select COVER and then Create New Item. This constrains or qualifies the title formatting to only those titles within a cover element.

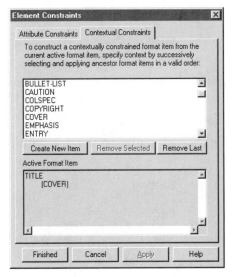

15. Select Finished. Now, apply the following characteristics:

Characteristic	Setting
Template	Title
Font	Arial, Bold, 48 pt
Spacing	take the defaults

16. Save the style sheet as `sample.hss`.

NOTE: Be sure to save the style sheet often. When exiting HyBrowse, it is not automatically saved and you are not notified that the style sheet should be saved.

17. Set the following for the subtitle element:

Characteristic	Setting
Template	Title
Font	Arial, Bold, 16 pt
Spacing	take the defaults

18. Select the copyright element and set the template to Don't Display. This will remove the copyright information from this document.

19. Select para and set the Indent Left to 2.5 in.

20. Set the following characteristics on the title within a preface:

Characteristic	Setting
Constraints	Preface
Template	Title
Font	Arial, Bold, 16pt
Spacing	take the defaults

21. Set the following characteristics on the title within a head head head head:

Characteristic	Setting
Constraints	head head head head
Template	Heading
Font	Arial, 12 pt
Spacing	take the defaults, Left Indent = 2.5 in.

22. Set the following characteristics on the title within a head head head:

Characteristic	Setting
Constraints	head head head
Template	Heading
Font	Arial, Bold, 14 pt
Spacing	take the defaults, Left Indent = 1.5 in

23. Set the following characteristics on the title within a head head:

Characteristic	Setting
Constraints	head head
Template	Heading
Font	Arial, Bold, 14 pt
Spacing	take the defaults, Left Indent = 2 in.

24. Set the following characteristics on the title within a head:

Characteristic	Setting
Constraints	head
Template	Heading

Characteristic	Setting
Font	Arial, Bold, 16 pt
Spacing	take the defaults

25. Set the following characteristics on the title within a head:

Characteristic	Setting
Constraints	head
Template	Heading
Font	Arial, Bold, 16 pt
Spacing	take the defaults

26. Select the bullet-list element and set the template to List. Set Indent Left to 3 in. and verify that the Break Before and Break After values are set to 100%.

27. Select the item element and set the following:

Characteristic	Setting
Constraints	bullet-list
Template	List Item
Prefix/Postfix	Prefix = o
Spacing	Break After

28. Select the para element and set the following:

Characteristic	Setting
Constraints	item
Template	Paragraph

Characteristic	Setting
Spacing	Break After

29. Select the indexitem. Set the template to Don't Display and make sure that no breaks are set in the spacing dialog.

30. Set the following sets of characteristics for the emphasis element:

    ■ slant = italic
       – Font Times New Roman
       – Style Italic
       – Spacing - clear all breaks

    ■ weight = bold
       – Font Times New Roman
       – Style Bold
       – Spacing - clear all breaks

    ■ asis = asis
       – Font Courier New
       – Spacing - clear all breaks

    ■ slant = italic weight = bold
       – Font Times New Roman
       – Style Bold Italic
       – Spacing - clear all breaks

31. Currently, HyBrowse doesn't support tables. Select the table element and set the template to Don't display. If I were making a real document here, I would load tables into another application and make a screen capture image to replace a table's contents.

32. Select the xref element and set the spacing to no breaks.

33. Select the title element and set the following:

Characteristic	Setting
Constraints	figure

Characteristic	Setting
Template	Heading
Font	Arial, Bold, 12 pt
Spacing	Break Before and After, Left Indent 2.5 in.

34. Select the bullet-list element and set the following:

Characteristic	Setting
Constraints	item
Template	List
Spacing	Break Before and After, Left Indent .5 in.

35. Select the item element and set the following:

Characteristic	Setting
Constraints	bullet-list item
Template	List Item
Prefix/Postfix	Prefix = -
Spacing	Break After

36. Select the title element and set the following:

Characteristic	Setting
Constraints	example
Template	Heading
Font	Arial, Bold, 14 pt
Spacing	Break Before and After, Left Indent 0 in.

37. Select the graphic element and set the template to Fixed size Graphic.

38. Select the number-list element and set the following:

Characteristic	Setting
Template	List
Spacing	Break Before and After 100%, Left Indent 2.5 in.

39. Select the item element and set the following:

Characteristic	Setting
Constraints	number-list
Template	List Item
Autonumbering	After mark text = . , Style Numeric, Child item = item
Spacing	Break After

40. Select the title element and set the following:

Characteristic	Setting
Constraints	section body
Template	Title
Font	Arial, Bold, 28 pt
Spacing	accept defaults
Autonumbering	Child item = section, Style = Numeric
Prefix/Postfix	Prefix = Chapter

41. Select the title element and set the following:

Characteristic	Setting
Constraints	section rearmatter
Template	Title
Font	Arial, Bold, 28 pt
Spacing	accept defaults
Autonumbering	Child item = section, Style = Alphabetic, Upper Case
Prefix/Postfix	Prefix = Appendix

42. Select the caution element and set the following:

Characteristic	Setting
Spacing	Left Indent 3, Right Indent 1, Break Before and After
Prefix/Postfix	Prefix = CAUTION:

43. Select the caution prefix element and set the font to Arial, Bold, 12 pt.

44. Select the para element and constrain it to caution. Set the Left Indent to .5 in.

45. Select the note element and set the following:

Characteristic	Setting
Spacing	Left Indent 3, Right Indent 1, Break Before and After
Prefix/Postfix	Prefix = NOTE:

46. Select the note prefix element and set the font to Arial, Bold, 12 pt.

47. Select the para element and constrain it to note. Set the Left Indent to .5 in.

48. Select the line element and set the following:

Characteristic	Setting
Constraint	Position = inline
Template	Verbatim
Font	Courier New, 10 pt
Spacing	Left Indent 2.5 in, Verbatim

49. Select the line element and set the following:

Characteristic	Setting
Constraint	Position = wide
Template	Verbatim
Font	Courier New, 10 pt
Spacing	Left Indent 0 in, Verbatim

50. Save the style sheet and close HyBrowse.
51. Add the following lines to the `sample.sgm` file:

```
<!DOCTYPE book [
<?HyBrowse Stylespec "sample.hss">
]>
```

INSO'S DYNATEXT

Inso provides a number of tools for distributing online documentation via CD-ROM or the WWW. DynaText is the browser that is generally shipped with a CD-ROM and DynaWeb is an application that connects to your Web server to take Inso-formatted documents and feed them to the WWW as HTML documents with or without frames. Several utility programs are provided to create style sheets and compile documentation so they can be presented by either of these tools. This chapter will illustrate the document development and delivery processes with DynaText. In the next chapter, we will explore how to use the DynaWeb product that takes the information that you build here and places it on the WWW.

INSTALLATION

To install DynaText and its associated utilities:

1. Insert the Inso CD-ROM into your CD drive.
2. Open the proper platform directory, in this case, Windows.
3. Open the Pubsgml directory.
4. Double-click the `setupex.exe` file to install the product.
5. Accept the directory for installation, or enter your own.
6. Select or deselect the optional features that you want to install.

   The files will be installed and a program group will be created.

CONFIGURATION

Inso requires your documents to be organized into a standard structure, as illustrated in Figure 14-1. Documents are published as a collection, and each collection is comprised of individual books. In the Windows environment, Inso uses the `dynatext.ini` file to control the configuration shown in Figure 14-2 and Figure 14-3. Line 9 shows the first step to creating your own collection. It defines the location where files will be organized. Figure 14-1 shows the directory structure that must be created below any collection. This is one of a couple of different configurations that can be used.

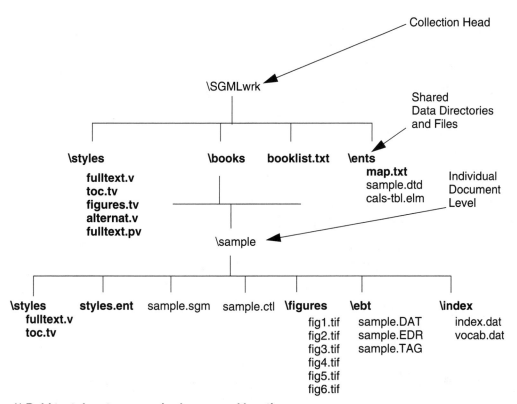

** **Bold text denotes a required name and location.**

FIGURE 14-1. DYNATEXT COLLECTION DIRECTORY STRUCTURE

```
 1   ; ******************************************************************
 2   ; *                 DynaText 3.1 Initialization File               *
 3   ; ******************************************************************
 4
 5   [dtext]
 6
 7   COLLECTION=h:\inso\ebtdocs\dtextdoc=DynaText English Documentation
 8   COLLECTION=h:\inso\ebtdocs\sampdoc=Sample DynaText Books
 9   COLLECTION=f:\SGMLwrk\CD-ROM\inso\sgmlwrk=SGML at Work Sample Document
10
11
12   SYSCONFIG=
13
14   DATA_DIR=h:\inso\DATA
15   LIBRARY_PATH=h:\inso\LIB
16
17   ; When DTEXT_AUTH is unset, DynaText acts as a Runtime browser.
18   DTEXT_AUTH=
19   MKBOOK_AUTH=h:\inso\data\security\eval.lic
20   ; NOTE: The mkbook.ini is no longer used for running MKBOOK.
21
22   PUBLIC_DIR=h:\inso\ANNOTS\PUBLIC
23   PRIVATE_DIR=h:\inso\ANNOTS\PRIVATE
24
25   ; Comment out the DTEXT_PLUGINS line to stop the loading of plugins
26   PLUGIN_DIRS=h:\inso\LIB\PLUGINS
27   DTEXT_PLUGINS=OLEPLUG.DLL
28
29   ; For supplying SGML-Open catalogs which may override internally-used
30   ; catalogs
31   USER_CATALOGS=
32
33   ; TEX_DIR is used for building equations in MKBOOK
34   TEX_DIR=h:\inso\EMTEX
35
36   ; NEW! set SORT_COLLS=0 to NOT sort the list of collections;
37   ;      set SORT_COLLS=1 to sort the list (= default if not set)
38
39
40   ; set BACKGROUND_ANNOTS=1 to load a book's annotations in the background
41   ; set BACKGROUND_ANNOTS=0 to load annotations immediately upon opening aboc
42   BACKGROUND_ANNOTS=0
43
44   note=-1 -1 250 200
45
```

FIGURE 14-2. DYNATEXT.INI CONFIGURATION FILE

```
46
47   [colors]
48   ; These colors correspond to foreground colors specified in a book's
49   ; stylesheets.
50   red=255 0 0
51   green=0 255 0
52   blue=0 0 255
53   yellow=255 255 0
54   magenta=255 0 255
55   cyan=0 255 255
56   dark red=128 0 0
57   dark green=0 128 0
58   dark blue=0 0 128
59   light brown=128 128 0
60   purple=128 0 128
61   dark cyan=0 128 128
62   light gray=192 192 192
63   gray=128 128 128
64   light yellow=255 255 128
65   light green=0 255 128
66   light blue=128 255 255
67   pink=255 0 128
68   orange=255 128 64
69
70   [Stysheet]
71   max=0
72   main=22 22 880 552
73
74   [InstedDesktop]
75   max=0
76   main=0 0 1152 921
77
78   [Desktop]
79   maximized=0
80   main=5 5 1142 911
81
```

FIGURE 14-2. DYNATEXT.INI CONFIGURATION FILE (CONTINUED)

I prefer this configuration because it allows me to maintain all the information that would be duplicated for each book, in one location at the collection level. The advantage of this approach is that making updates and changes is easy, the disadvantage is that you cannot define special templates for a particular book.

CONFIGURING THE COLLECTION

To configure the collection:

1. Add the COLLECTION value to the `dynatext.ini` file in the install directory for Inso, under the bin directory.

2. Create the collection directory.

3. At the collection directory level, add the styles, ents, and books directories.

4. Under the books directory, create a directory to store a book in the collection.

NOTE: The book directory name must be the same name as the SGML file that will be copied to that directory (minus the .sgm extension).

5. Under the book directory (sample, in my case), create the following directories: figures, styles, ebt, and index.

6. Copy the SGML file for your book to the top level of the book directory. Copy any graphics to the figures directory.

7. In the ents directory at the collection root level, create the file `map.txt` as shown in Figure 14-3.

```
 1  -//EBT//EBT Styles//EN                     ..$(DS)styles
 2
 3  -//SAW//DTD SGML at Work Sample DTD//EN  ..$(DS)ents$(DS)sample.dtd
 4  -//ArborText//ELEMENTS CALS Table Structures//EN  ..$(DS)ents$(DS)cals-tbl.el
 5
 6  ISO 8879-1986//ENTITIES Publishing//EN
            h:$(DS)inso$(DS)data$(DS)ents$(DS)iso-pub.ent
 7  ISO 8879-1986//ENTITIES Numeric and Special Graphic//EN
             h:$(DS)inso$(DS)data$(DS)ents$(DS)iso-num.ent
 8  ISO 8879-1986//ENTITIES Diacritical Marks//EN
            h:$(DS)inso$(DS)data$(DS)ents$(DS)iso-dia.ent
 9  ISO 8879-1986//ENTITIES General Technical//EN
             h:$(DS)inso$(DS)data$(DS)ents$(DS)iso-tech.ent
10  ISO 8879-1986//ENTITIES Added Latin 1//EN
            h:$(DS)inso$(DS)data$(DS)ents$(DS)iso-lat1.ent
11  ISO 8879-1986//ENTITIES Added Latin 2//EN
            h:$(DS)inso$(DS)data$(DS)ents$(DS)iso-lat2.ent
12  ISO 8879-1986//ENTITIES Greek Letters//EN
            h:$(DS)inso$(DS)data$(DS)ents$(DS)iso-grk1.ent
13  ISO 8879-1986//ENTITIES Greek Symbols//EN
            h:$(DS)inso$(DS)data$(DS)ents$(DS)iso-grk3.ent
```

FIGURE 14-3. MAP.TXT FILE

Either copy the sample DTD and `cals-tble.ent` files to the ents directory, or change the location in the `map.txt` file. The entry for -//EBT//EBT Styles//EN is a special value that allows style sheets to be placed anywhere on your system. The default is to have a styles directory and style sheets contained in individual books. This works in conjunction with the `styles.ent` file that is stored in each book. The following is the content of `styles.ent`:

```
<!ENTITY styledir PUBLIC "-//EBT//EBT Styles//EN">
```

8. The final configuration detail is to create the `sample.ctl` file. This file is stored at the root level of the sample book. This file must be named the same as the document with a .ctl. The .ents file is used when autonumbering objects in a book. Autonumbered objects are typically chapters, lists, and figures: The following is the content of `sample.ctl`

```
<reset counter="figure" trigger="CHAPTER">
<reset counter="table" trigger="CHAPTER">
<reset counter="item" trigger="NUMBER-LIST">
```

9. The basic configuration for the collection and document is complete. Now we must run the mkbook to compile and index the document. I used the following command line to create the rest of the files shown in Figure 14-1.

```
mkbook -fa -fi -col f:\sgmlwrk\CD-ROM\inso\SGMLwrk sample
```

After running this program, all but the style sheets will have been created.

BUILDING DYNATEXT STYLE SHEETS WITH INSTED

In the following procedure, I will give you a feel for how style sheets are defined in DynaText, as well as some of the internal functions that are used to define a working style sheet. I have provided my style sheets on the CD-ROM, but I am not able to distribute a working copy of DynaText to allow you to view the sample document. If you own a copy of DynaText, you can build a book for yourself based upon these instructions. In the following procedure, I cover the most important styles and how to format them for:

- Tables
- Graphics

- Hypertext links
- Number and bullet lists
- Warnings, cautions, and notes.

insted is the interactive style sheet definition tool. To build a style sheet:

1. Launch the insted style sheet editor.

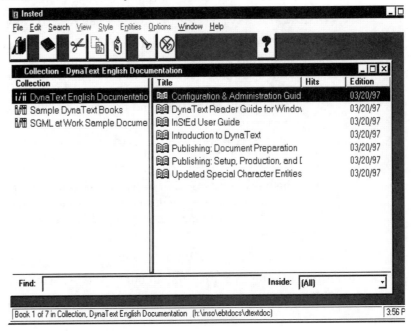

2. Select the SGML at Work Sample Document collection.

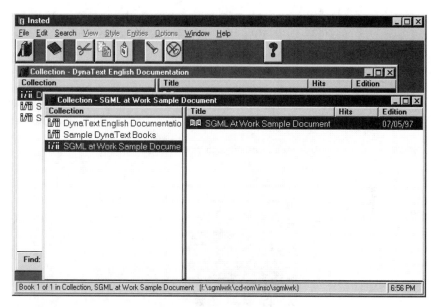

3. Select the SGML at Work Document.

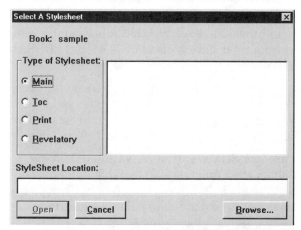

The Select A Stylesheet dialog box allows you to select an existing style sheet or create a new one. There are four types of style sheets:

Main	.v'	Controls the display of document text.
Toc	tv	Controls the display of the table of contents window.
Print	.pv	Used when a document is to be printed
Revelatory	rv	Used for pop-up display windows.

Default `toc.tv` and `fulltext.t` style sheets should be defined to provide minimal support through the browser.

4. With Main selected, enter fulltext in the StyleSheet Location: field.

Hierarchy
Style List
or Group List Area

Format Category
Display

Document
Preview
Area

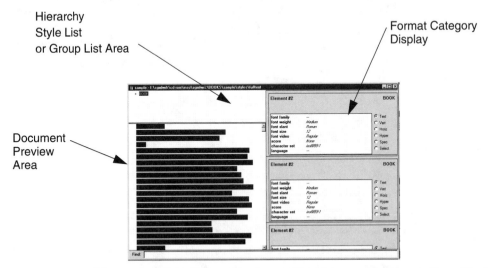

Now we need to define the formatting for our document. DynaText supports an inheritance scheme that allows many values to be inherited from their parent element. A special #DEFAULT element needs to be defined first; it sets all the initial states.

5. The first step is to set up the editor in a mode that is condusive to our task. From the View menu, select Style List. From the Options menu, select Show Tags, then Show Tags. From the Options menu, select Synchronize Category Display and Show Entities.

6. Entities are like SGML entities or variables if you are a programmer. Although they function like variables, you cannot use them in functions, they are substitution values only. Click on the button with the ampersand (&) to define the following entities:

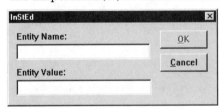

bodyfont	Arial
bodyindent	80
bodylinesp	14
bodysize	12
bodyspbefore	5
title1size	20
title2size	18
title3size	16
title4size	14
title5size	12
titlefont	Arial Black

7. In the Style List area, double-click the book item. Locate the label for book in one of the boxes of the Format Category area in the right corner.

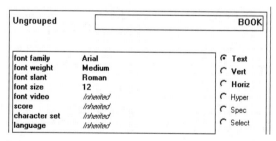

8. Select the Text radio button. Now select the font family.

9. Click the down arrow and select the Formula option. In the field that displays, enter &bodyfont. For font size, enter &bodysize.

10. Select the Vert radio button and set the following:

break before	Line
space before	&bodyspbefore
line spacing	&bodylinesp

11. Select the Horiz radio button and enter the following:

justification	Left
left indent	&bodyindent

12. Select the #TAGS in the Style List area. In the Format Category area find the #TAGS box. With the text radio button selected, enter the following values:

font family	Courier New
font weight	Not Set
font size	10

13. Select the Spec radio button, then select foreground. From the pull-down list, select Show List and choose gray.

With the previous settings, we created a smaller SGML tag display in gray and set the basic paragraph functions with the book formatting.

14. Find the emphasis tag in the style list area and double-click on it. This will scroll the preview window to the first instance of an emphasis tag and also create a Format Category box.

The emphasis has several attributes that control the look of the text contained in the tag. To set formatting for these, we must query the value and then make a decision based upon the content of the attribute. The entry for font weight will be:

```
if(eq(attr(weight),bold),bold,)
```

This reads as follows: If the value in attribute weight is bold, then set bold; otherwise, do nothing.

15. For the font slant, enter:

```
if(eq(attr(slant),italic),italic,)
```

16. For the font family, enter:

```
if(eq(attr(asis),asis),Courier New,)
```

17. For the font size, enter:

```
if(eq(attr(lower),sub),-=4,
if(eq(attr(raised),super),-=4,)
```

The value -=4 is a relative change to the font size of minus 4 pts. A relative increase is indicated with +=.

18. For the vertical offset on the Vert entry, enter:

```
if(eq(attr(lower),sub),-=7,
if(eq(attr(raised),super),+=7,)
```

19. To keep an emphasis element inline within a paragraph, the following must be changed:

break before	None
space before	0

Emphasis element doesn't change based upon its location in the document structure. To create the formatting for the title in the cover portion of the document, we have to somehow tell DynaText that it is different than a title in a first-level head. We have to qualify the element title within its structure in the document.

20. Select the title element within the cover element and double-click. From the Style menu, select Qualify. The options for Qualify change based upon the element that is currently selected. In this case, select the Title,Cover because we only want to format the title within a cover element. Now, the Format Category box changes from TITLE to COVER,TITLE. Set the following values:

font family	&titlefont
font size	&titlefont1
space before	55
justification	right
foreground	blue

Your preview document should be looking something like this:

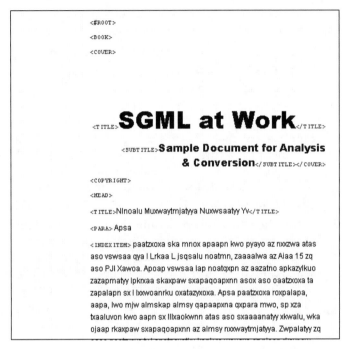

21. Go to the body section of the document and find the first section and title. Select the title and qualify it to BODY,SECTION,TITLE. Set the following values:

font family	&titlefont
font size	&title2size
space before	35
space after	10
line spacing	22
justification	Right
foreground	blue
text before	Chapter cnum()

The same values should be set for REARMATTER,SECTION,TITLE. Everything is set the same as above, but text before should be set to: `Appendix format(cnum(),LETTER)`.

22. Select the Note style. A note will be formatted similar to a caution or warning. The following differences, however, will apply:

Category	Note	Caution	Warning
text before	Note:	Caution:	Warning:
foreground	dark green	purple	red
justification	center	center	center
right indent	&WCNindentr	&WCNindentr	WCNindentr
break before	Line	Line	Line
space before	5	5	5

`&WCNindentr` should be `+=30`.

Create all the entries for Note. All of the style information can be copied with Ctrl-C. Now, select a caution or warning and enter Ctrl-V. This pastes the values into the new style. Modify the values that are different.

23. The text before the values of Note:, Caution:, and Warning: should be centered and bold. How can we set this formatting? We need to qualify Note with a #TEXT-BEFORE. You will need to create this style yourself. While editing the note formats, select Create New Style from the Style menu. Enter the value NOTE,#TEXT-BEFORE. Now you have a new style box to which you can make format changes.

24. Bullet-lists require the following settings on the item qualified for bullet-list:

left indent	&listindent = +=15
first indent	&listoutdent = -=15
text before	&bullet = &#183

This will format all bullet-lists to a relative indent of 15 points and preface them with bullet character. To set different symbols for each level, you need to qualify the item with additional levels of bullet-list.

To control the formatting of the bullet, qualify the BULLET-LIST,ITEM,#TEXT-BEFORE and set the font size to 20 and weight to bold so the symbol shows up well.

25. Number-lists require similar formatting, but we will use an auto-numbering function for each item rather than a bullet symbol. In text before enter cnum().

26. Set the Styles area to view Group List. Currently we haven't defined a group, but a group allows us to gather related objects together and share or inherit values from the group. A Group object takes on characteristics of another style. Groups also help organize and display your style sheet content.

27. From the Style menu, select Create New Group and give it the name calstable. In the make category enter:

```
maketablestructure(cals,var(hsize))
```

NOTE: Like many other tools, certain table models are given preferred treatment. The CALS table model is one of those for use with DynaText. Special functions are provided that understand the structure and greatly simplify the process of defining table formatting.

28. Add the style entry to the group calstable by selecting the entry style, and then from the Style menu, selecting Set Group, calstable. Now, entry has inherited the value we set on calstable. Add the following to the entry style:

justification	tableinfo(cals,justification)
left indent	5
right indent	5

29. Add the following styles to the calstable group: row, tbody, tgroup, and thead. On thead, set the font weight to bold to create bold headings on the table.

30. Colspec doesn't get added to the calstable group, but has the space before category set to 0.

31. The para and any other styles within the table should be qualified with entry and the following categories defined:

break before	if(isfirst(),none,line)
space before	2

| break before | if(isfirst(),none,line) |
| space after | 2 |

32. The table style should have break before set to Line and a space after of 10.

33. Select the graphic style. Enter the following in the script category:

```
ebt-raster filename=attr(nd.sys)
```

nd.sys is one of several DynaText-created attributes for any element that refers to objects with SGML NOTATION values. The variety of attributes provides an easy hook to the actual filename of an entity reference.

NOTE: Despite the name ebt-raster, this function will handle supported raster and vector formats. This is a holdover to previous versions that required the use of ebt-vector and ebt-raster to be properly used, depending on the NOTATION type. ebt-vector would have worked equally well in this case.

For this style sheet, we will hide the graphics but leave the tables inline within the document. Enter the following:

icon type	raster
icon position	Right
break before	None

34. Qualify the title on the figure element. On FIGURE,TITLE, enter the following:

break before	None
break after	None
space before	10
font weight	Bold
font size	&title4size

35. Hypertext links are implemented with the xref and footnote elements. These elements are used to refer to information elsewhere in the stream and link to those locations. The SGML feature id was used to make this connection, and now we need to format these links.

Enter the following in the script category:

```
ebt-link target=idmatch(id,attr(ref))
```

This function finds the id that matches the referenced id on the xref element. To create or copy the title from title elements, we need to copy the content and apply it as a text before value:

```
if((eq(title,tag(idmatch(id,attr(ref))))),
content(idmatch(id,attr(ref))),)
```

Again, we match the reference to an id with the actual id. If the element or tag that contains the id is a title, then we match the id and retrieve the content of the element. In addition to these values, set the following:

score	Under
icon type	hyperlin
icon position	Inline
break before	None

36. When a document is produced as hardcopy, you don't have the choice to hide information that is required for traditional or legal requirements, but otherwise doesn't provide much value to the basic text or content of the document. With a document produced online, you can choose how and when to present information to the reader. The copyright section is required in any document, but provides the reader little value. We will hide this section and create a link to allow the reader to view it on demand; but otherwise, it will not interrupt the flow of the document.

   Select the style copyright. Set the following values:

hide	Children
icon type	copyrt
icon position	Right
script	ebt-reveal stylesheet="copy.rev" title="Copyright Details"

37. After defining all the elements and styles, I then take a copy of `fulltext.v` and create the revelatory style sheets by undoing the above values. I then save the `fulltext.v` style sheet as-is, and I save it as a relevatory style sheet as `copy.rev`.

38. Edit the copyright element and remove all the settings currently defined. Set the copyright to the following:

break before	Line
text before	Copyright

39. Create a new style, COPYRIGHT,#TEXT-BEFORE. Set the following values:

font family	&titlefont
font size	&title2size
break before	Line
space before	35
space after	10
justification	Right
foreground	blue

TOC STYLE SHEETS

The table of contents style sheet uses some special functions to define the elements to be extracted. This information is then used when the book is recompiled to generate the text content for the TOC file.

To define the TOC style sheet:

1. Open the sample book in the insted editor.

2. Select the sample book.

3. Select the Toc field and then enter the name toc.tv. When insted first starts, the preview area is empty. Part of the process of defining the Toc style sheet is to define which objects should be extracted for the TOC itself. The result we are trying to achieve is to nest the titles of major sections and heads based upon their structure. We have to find the titles of the major containers like body and rearmatter, and then find the correct container that holds them. See Figure 14-4 for an illustration of this nesting.

   Examine the relationship between cover and title. Next, look at book,cover,title to see that it provides the book title as the object that contains everything—that is, the proper location for the highest level object or title in our TOC.

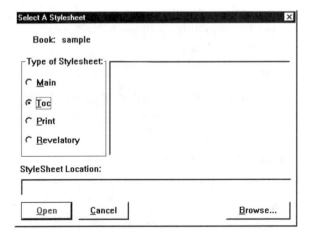

4. Select the book style. In the title tag category, enter cover,title. insted will ask to rebuild the TOC as soon as you make this change. You can indicate Yes, but I would store a few of these up because every title tag change will cause the TOS to be rebuilt.

5. For each, example, section, and preface style, enter title in the title tag category.

6. Look at the content of the copyright section and that of the sections. Each of these has heads with titles that are the same elements. To keep the heads in the copyright section, we must qualify the heads up to the section level. As you qualify each of the head levels, enter title in the title tag category.

7. Either accept an offer to rebuild the TOC or select Rebuild TOC from the File menu. The preview area now contains all the title levels that you just defined.

8. Format the title objects as you wish.

SGML AT WORK

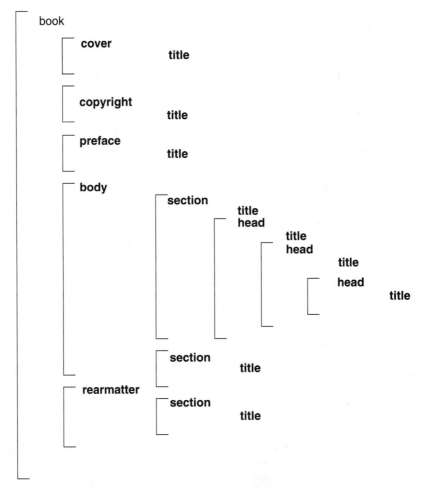

FIGURE 14-4. CONTAINER NESTING FOR A TOC

I believe that the TOC view is required for any online document. It helps the reader understand the structure and content of a particular document very quickly. You can define other TOC views to provide lists of figures and tables. In addition to these, if you have the proper tagging structure for procedures and such, you could create a TOC that listed just procedures. These are additional and optional TOC views that you might want to create.

PRINT STYLE SHEETS

DynaText is capable of formatting an online document for hardcopy, as well as for online use. If the formatting that you provided online is similar to what you want in hardcopy, you can copy your fulltext.v style sheet and use it as the basis of a print style sheet.

The following is a list of items that you will probably want to modify or should at least consider while creating a print style sheet.

- Text font sizes online are generally larger than in print. If you used entities to define these sizes, you can just modify that list.

- Color should be minimized, unless you are printing to a color printer. If you don't remove color, you will get various shades of gray on color objects.

- Hypertext links and symbols should be removed and replaced with text-based instructions.

- Hidden text objects need to be shown in most cases.

- Provide page breaks for major logical structures like chapters.

USING DYNATEXT

DynaText is the product that is delivered to your reader or end user. It is the browser application. Figure 14-5 illustrates the typical collection view. On the left side is the list of collections; select one and the contents or books will be listed on the right side. This is your starting point from which you can either select a book and start reading, or you can issue a text search across all collections and books. The text search will add a little number to the side.

Figure 14-6 is the default setup for the sample document. On the left side is the table of contents view that provides a clickable interface to select the current object to view.

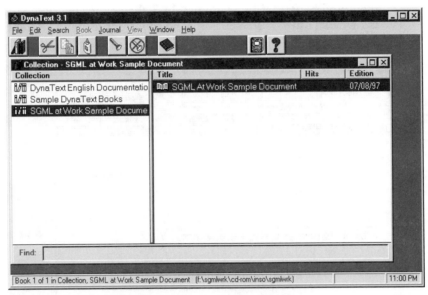

FIGURE 14-5. DYNATEXT COLLECTION VIEW

FIGURE 14-6. DYNATEXT DOCUMENT VIEW

DynaText provides the standard document manipulation features. You can scroll a document, use the TOC window on the left to navigate the document and hypertext links. Figure 14-7 shows the copyright section, which is revealed after double-clicking the copyright icon in the right margin of the document.

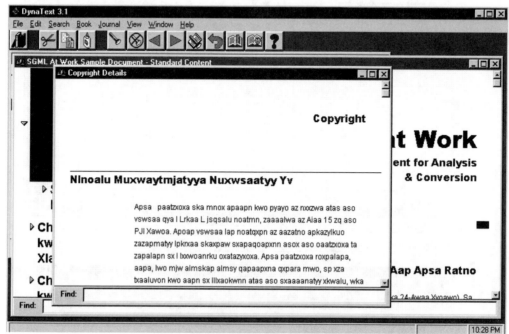

FIGURE 14-7. DYNATEXT COPYRIGHT SECTION VIEWED

Figure 14-8 shows the result of double-clicking on a graphic icon in the right margin. This view with the graphic can now be positioned anywhere on the screen and it can be zoomed to show detail as required. By allowing graphics and tables to be detached from the document flow, you make it easier for the reader to refer to this graphic while still reading the document.

Figure 14-9 shows the result of double clicking on a footnote. We could also have created this as a travel link, which would have scrolled the main window to the text of the footnote. By placing this link in a pop-up window, the user can refer to the text containing the footnote reference, as well as review the text of the footnote itself.

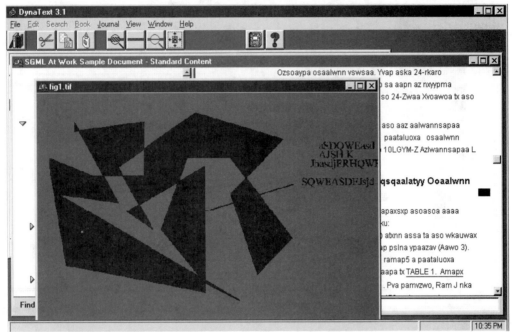

FIGURE 14-8. DYNATEXT GRAPHIC REVEALED

Figure 14-10 shows how the TOC can be expanded to show nested levels of information. This view greatly improves navigation and helps eliminate "the lost in hyperspace" problems that would be more severe without it.

Figure 14-11 shows the full text search capabilities of DynaText. This search was initiated in the window containing the document and was limited to just the document. If a complete collection of documents is indexed as a collection, you could search the collection from the collection view. In this figure, you can see the number of hits displayed in the TOC view, with each heading level displaying the number of hits in that section. In the document window, the actual words are highlighted. To navigate to the next hit, select one of the arrow buttons on the button bar.

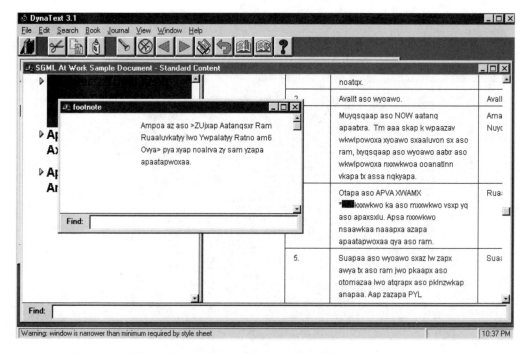

FIGURE 14-9. DYNATEXT FOOTNOTE REVEALED

Figure 14-12 displays two pages of our online document printed to hard-copy. At the top of each page is the name of the document, and on the bottom is the page number. As defined in our print style sheet, chapters and appendices will all start on a new page.

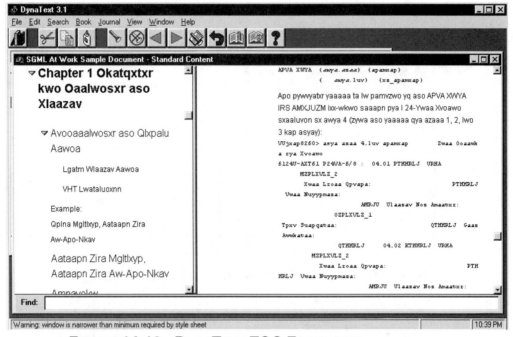

FIGURE 14-10. DYNATEXT TOC EXPANSION

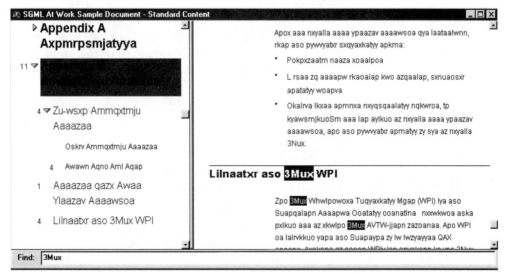

FIGURE 14-11. DYNATEXT TEXT SEARCH CAPABILITIES

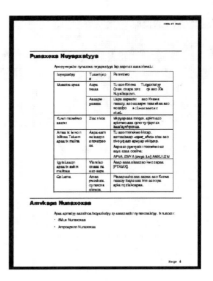

FIGURE 14-12. DYNATEXT PRINT OUTPUT SAMPLE

RECOMMENDATIONS

If you have never had a graphic design course or been involved with document design for either paper or online, you should read the books listed in Appendix G. Good design can be achieved by learning how to balance all the elements of white space, font, color, and space. Some simple rules can help you create elegant documents, if you take the time to learn about the practice of document design.

OBSERVATIONS

Although both of these products are online browsers, I believe it is unfair to compare them too directly. DynaText is a product that has been on the market and used very successfully to deliver documents for a number of years. HyBrowse, on the other hand, has only been available for about a year. Not only is it based upon a different paradigm for document browsing (HyTime), I believe it is more of a test and demonstration vehicle for TechnoTeacher's more core products.

The reason I believe this is true is that there is no support in HyBrowse for:

- Bullets
- Catalog functionality
- Supported table models.

I also found that the autonumbering feature combined with a prefix didn't work, and that some of the constraining rules got confused as more title element constraints were added. To experiment with HyTime constructs, this is the perfect tool. The only other tool that comes close to this functionality is PanoramaPro, which is limited. This is version 1.1 of HyBrowse, however, and all these issues may go away in a future release.

15 SGML AND THE WWW

This chapter will examine two applications for delivering SGML documents via the WWW. One approach, SoftQuad Panorama Pro, uses a client plug-in application to read SGML documents and style sheets for presentation and delivery. The other approach, Inso DynaWeb, uses a Web server-based application that interprets SGML document on the server, and converts the information on-the-fly to HTML tags.

In the first approach, you must rely on the user to have the browser plug-in properly installed. Also, the formatting capabilities are limited to those of the plug-in. In the server application, you are constrained by HTML formatting capabilities. This approach is much better than trying to maintain an HTML collection of documents separate from the source files. We will see that there is a style sheet that applies HTML tags. This style sheet can be tailored for a variety of browsers (each with differing capability), and the original SGML data does not require modification. This approach allows you to react better to a change in the tagging structure due to a new browser release. By simply adding another style sheet, the entire collection of documents is instantly updated to the latest capability.

Since these two tools were developed, a new effort (started December 1996) to improve the Web environment by bringing the best features (not all) of SGML together with the WWW and its tool developers has been initiated. The eXtensible Markup Language (XML) is a subset of the SGML standard that allows you to create a tag set for your data. XML, together with the related standards of XLink and XPointer and eXtensible Style Language (XSL), will provide the functionality of DSSSL, HyTime, and SGML for less intensive applications of delivery and distribution.

SoftQuad Panorama Pro

Panorama Pro v2.0 is the second release of this product. Soon after its release, it was re-released as Panorama Publisher, with a viewer product called Panorama Viewer. The evaluation version of Panorama Viewer is available on the CD-ROM accompanying this book. Both Panorama products are Windows-based applications, but a UNIX version is promised. Panorama Pro is available in the book *SGML and the Web*.

Installation

To install Panorama Pro:

1. Insert the Panorama Pro CD-ROM into your CD-ROM drive.

2. Select `setup.exe` to start the installation.

3. Accept the installation directory presented, or enter your own. All the files will be installed.

4. Accept the offer to make a Program Group if you wish.

Configuration

Configuration of Panorama Pro consists of entering any PUBLIC identifiers required to support your SGML application in a map file. The following explains the process to configure Panorama Pro.

To configure the Panorama Pro entity catalog:

1. Go to the directory where Panorama Pro is installed.

2. Open the Catalog directory.

3. Edit `catalog` by adding the following lines to the top of the file:

   ```
   PUBLIC "-//SAW//DTD SGML at Work Sample DTD//EN"
   "sample.dtd"
   ```

   ```
   PUBLIC "-//ArborText//ELEMENTS CALS Table
   Structures//EN" "cals-tbl.elm"
   ```

4. Copy the `sample.dtd` and `cals-tble.elm` files to the catalog directory under the Panorama installation.

BUILDING A STYLE SHEET

VIEWING STYLE SHEET

To create a Panorama Pro style sheet:

1. Launch the Panorama Pro browser.

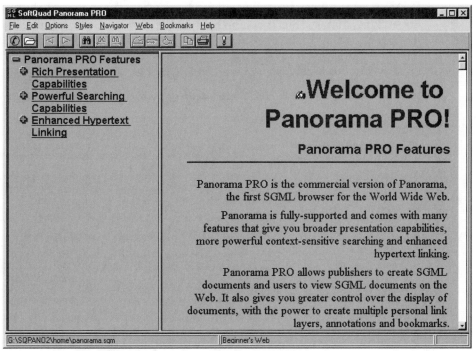

2. From the File menu, select Open File.

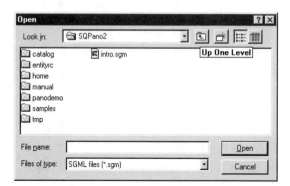

3. Find the `sampleall.sgm` file. This file should be installed on your hard disk so that it can be modified and style sheets built.

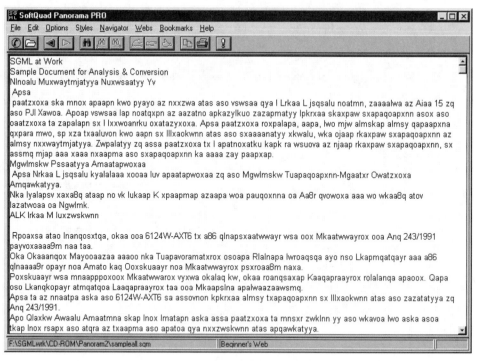

4. Attach a style sheet to this document and the DTD by selecting Attach Style Sheet from the Styles menu.

5. Enter a filename for the style sheet.

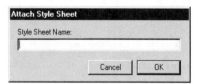

6. Enter a description for the style sheet and its use:

    ```
    Basic viewing style for SGML@Work DTD based docs
    ```

7. Turn the tags on so we can assign them styles. From the Options menu, select Show Tags.

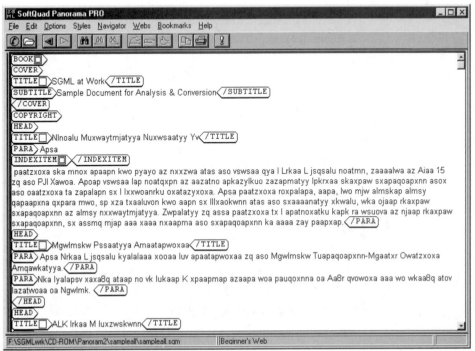

8. With the right mouse button, click on the book tag, avoiding the box within a box symbol.

9. The Locate in SGML Tree option will display a hierarchal view of the document in a side frame, thus allowing you to navigate the structure and turn off the tag display. Select Edit Style... to create the base formatting information for this document.

10. From the Style Sheet Editor dialog, you can specify formatting for a specific occurrence of a tag and its various properties. On an element nested within a structure, you can qualify a location with the P (Parent) button. In this window, add the following:

Font Family	Arial
Font Size	12
Justify	Left
Leading	2
Break	Before
Space Above	5
Space Right	10
Space Left	80

Close the dialog box.

11. Select the `title` element within the preface. Qualify the title to be Preface,Title. Add the following format properties:

Font Family	Arial Black
Font Size	24
Font Color	Blue
Justify	Right

Leading	2
Break	Before
Space Above	30
Space Below	20

12. Select the `title` element within the `body`, section. Qualify the `title` to be `Body, Section, Title`. Add the following format properties:

Font Family	Arial Black
Font Size	24
Font Color	Blue
Justify	Right
Leading	2
Break	Before
Space Above	30
Space Below	20
Before Text	Chapter
Autonumber	Linear
Autonumber Type	1, 2, 3

13. Select the `title` element within the `rearmatter`, section. Qualify the `title` to be `Rearmatter, Section, Title`. Add the following format properties:

Font Family	Arial Black
Font Size	24
Font Color	Blue
Justify	Right
Leading	2
Break	Before
Space Above	30
Space Below	20

Before Text	Appendix
Autonumber	Linear
Autonumber Type	A, B, C

14. Select the `title` within the first-level head element. Qualify the `title` as `Head,Title`.

Font Family	Arial Black
Font Size	18
Font Color	Blue
Justify	Left
Space Left	0
Space Above	20
Space Below	10
Ruler	1

15. Select the `title` within the second-level head element. Qualify the title as `Head,Head,Title`.

Font Family	Arial Black
Font Size	16
Font Color	Blue
Justify	Left
Space Left	25
Space Above	20
Space Below	10

16. Select the `title` within the `example` element. Qualify the title as `Example,Title`.

Font Family	Arial Black
Font Size	18
Font Color	Blue
Justify	Left
Space Left	0

Space Above	20
Space Below	10

17. Select the `title` within the `figure` element. Qualify the `title` as `Figure,Title`.

Font Family	Arial
Font Size	12
Font Color	Blue
Font Weight	Bold
Space Left	25
Space Above	20
Space Below	10

18. Select an `indexitem` element. Set the Visibility property to Hide.

19. Select an `item` element within `bullet-list`. Qualify the item to be `Bullet-list,Item` and add the following properties:

Space Indent	15, Relative Parent
Before Font Size	20
Before Font Weight	Bold
Before Text	\183

20. Select a `para` element within an item element. Qualify the `para` to be `Bullet-list,Item,Para,` set the Occurrence to First, and set the following properties:

Space Left	30, Relative Parent
Space Indent	-15, Relative Parent
Break	Inline

21. On a `Bullet-list,Item,Para,` set the Occurrence to All and then set the following:

Space Left	30, Relative Parent
Space Indent	-15, Relative Parent

22. Select an `item` element within a nested `bullet-list`. Qualify the `item` to be `Item, Bullet-list, Item` and add the following properties:

Space Indent	15, Relative Parent
Before Font Size	20
Before Font Weight	Bold
Before Text	-

23. Select a `para` element within an `item` element. Qualify `para` to be `Item, Bullet-list, Item, Para,` set the Occurrence to First, and set the following properties:

Space Left	45, Relative Parent
Space Indent	-15, Relative Parent
Break	Inline

24. On an `Item, Bullet-list, Item, Para,` set the Occurrence to All and then set the following:

Space Left	45, Relative Parent
Space Indent	-15, Relative Parent

25. Select the `number-list` element. Set Autonumber to Hierarchical Begin. This causes the numbering to restart on items inside the `number-list`.

26. Select an `item` element within the `number-list`. Qualify the item to be `Number-list, Item` and set Autonumber to Hierarchal Item.

27. Select a `para` element within the `number-list`. Qualify the `para` to be `Number-list, Item, Para`.

Space Left	30, Relative Parent
Space Indent	-15, Relative Parent

28. Double-click an `emphasis` element on the box within a box symbol. This presents the attributes on this particular element and the current values.

29. Close the Attributes for dialog box.

30. Select an `emphasis` element. When the Style Sheet Editor dialog appears, double-click the >> button.

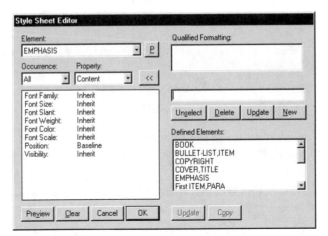

31. On the base `emphasis` element, set Break to Inline.

32. In addition to this property, we need to create several attribute-qualified values. Create each qualifying statement and then enter the following formatting properties:

Format Qualifier	Property	Value	Property	Value
[slant]=italic	Font Slant	Italic		
[weight]=bold	Font Weight	Bold		
[asis]=asis	Font Family	Courier New		

Format Qualifier	Property	Value	Property	Value
[raised]=super	Position	-60%	Font Size	9
[lowered]=sub	Position	60%	Font Size	9

33. Select the `system` element and set the following attributes:

Font Family	Courier New
Font Size	9

34. In addition to these entries, add the following to the entityrc file in the entityrc directory in the install directory:

```
PUBLIC "-//SAW//DTD SGML at Work Sample DTD//EN"

    VERBATIM "SYSTEM"
```

This causes all system elements to be formatted as-is, preserving any white space and line breaks.

35. Select the `note` element and set the following attributes:

Font Color	Green
Justify	Left
Space Above	5
Space Left	30, Relative Parent
Space Indent	-15, Relative Parent
Space Right	30, Relative Parent
Before Text	Note:
Before Font Family	Arial
Before Font Weight	Bold

36. Select `para` in the `note` element and qualify it as `Note, Para`. Set an Occurrence of First and also set the Break to Inline.

37. Select the `caution` element and set the following attributes:

Font Color	Red
Justify	Left
Space Above	5

Space Left	15, Relative Parent
Space Right	15, Relative Parent
Before Text	CAUTION:
Before Font Family	Arial
Before Font Weight	Bold

38. Select the `para` in the `caution` element and qualify it as `Caution, Para`. Set an Occurrence of First and also set the following attributes:

Break	Inline
Space Left	60, Relative Parent

39. Select the `table` element. Set the following attributes:

Table	CALS Table
Space Above	10

40. Within the `table` we must configure the `para` element. Qualify the `para` as `Entry, Para` with an Occurrence of All. Also, set the following attributes:

Space Above	5
Space Left	5
Space Right	5

41. Again select `Entry, Para`, set the Occurrence to First, and set the following:

Break	Inline
Space Left	5
Space Right	5

42. Select an `xref` element. Set the Break to Inline. Panorama Pro automatically builds the hypertext link from the xref to the element with the ID being referenced.

NAVIGATION STYLE SHEET

To create a navigation style sheet:

1. Launch Panorama Pro.

2. Open the `sampleall.sgm` document.

3. From the Navigator menu, select Attach Navigator.

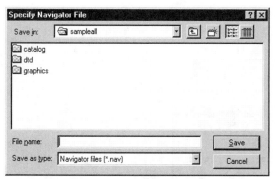

4. Enter the name `samplenav.nav`. The descriptive name should be `SGML@Work DTD Navigator`.

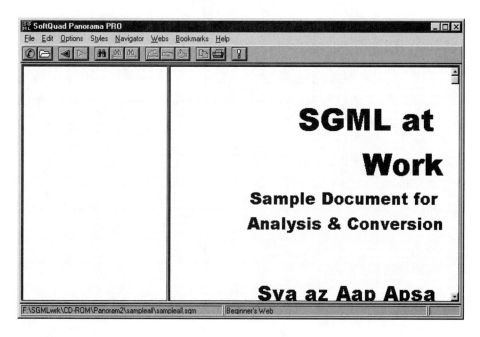

The navigator window is attached to the left of the document window. Currently there is nothing in the navigator, because we haven't specified any values to extract.

5. Turn the tags on by selecting Show Tags from the Options menu.

6. Select the title within the cover by placing the cursor on the text or tag for that element and right-clicking.

7. Select Navigator Entry...

8. Set the Navigatory Entry to Book, Cover, Title. Set the Font scale to 60 and choose Add.

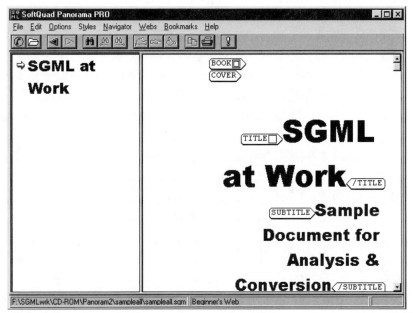

9. Select the `title` in the `preface` and set it to `Preface,Title`. Add the entry.

10. Select the `title` within a `section` and set it to `Section,Title`.

11. Select each `title` at the different heading levels and qualify them by successive heads. Create `Head,Title,` and `Head,Head,Title`.

12. Attach a new navigator and name it `sampfig.nav`. Assign the title `Figure Navigator`.

13. Select the title within a `figure` and qualify it to `Figure,Title` with a Font Scale of 80.

    This navigator allows the user to easily jump to any figure or table with a title.

14. Attach a new navigator and name it `sampexamp.nav`. Assign the title `Example Navigator`.

15. Select the `title` within an `example` and qualify it to `Example,Title` with a Font Scale of 60.

    This navigator allows the user to easily jump to any examples in the document.

INSTALLING PANORAMA PRO STYLE SHEETS

Panorama Pro allows you to store style sheets in a central directory or with your document. To install the style sheets in a central directory:

1. Copy the style sheets to the entityrc directory under the installation directory for Panorama Pro.

2. Add the following lines to the previous entry within the `entityrc` file:

```
PUBLIC "-//SAW//DTD SGML at Work Sample DTD//EN"
   VERBATIM "SYSTEM"
   STYLESPEC "SGML@Wrk Basic Viewer" "sampbasic.ssh"
   NAVIGATOR "Table of Contents" "sampnav.nav"
   NAVIGATOR "List of Figures and Tables"
   "sampfig.nav"
   NAVIGATOR "List of Examples" "sampexam.nav"
```

CONFIGURING YOUR WEB BROWSER TO USE PANORAMA PRO

Panorama Pro can be configured as a helper application for viewing SGML documents directly on the WWW. In addition to configuring your browser, the server itself must have a mime type of SGML so the browser is triggered to look for an application to browse SGML.

USING PANORAMA PRO

Now that we have built our sample environment within Panorama Pro, let's look at some of the capabilities that this tool provides.

TEXT SEARCHING

Panorama Pro provides the ability to use full text search capabilities within one document without requiring the document to be preprocessed.

To perform a text search:

1. Launch Panorama Pro.

2. Open the `sampleall.sgm` document.

3. From the Edit menu, select Search.

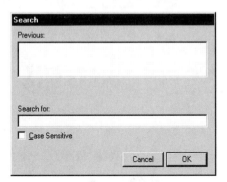

The following table explains the basic syntax of the query language, followed by a few examples:

Text Literals	"find this text" or 'find this text'
Tags	<tagname>
Boolean Search	use AND and OR boolean values
Tag Qualifiers	<tag> IN <tag> or <tag> CONT <tag> CONT = contains IN = inside

```
SGML in <title>
<title> in (<preface> or <section>)
John Doe
"John Doe"
```

NOTE: There is a difference between the search strings John Doe and "John Doe". The first case finds the words John and Doe. The second string finds the phrase John Doe together, nothing in-between.

4. Enter the following query:

    ```
    <title in (<preface> or <section>)
    ```

5. The document display now features the number of hits, which are shown in the Navigator window, the text found is selected, and down the right margin is an Occurrence Density Display of hit density. All but the selection of the text can be toggled in the Options menu. The Occurrence Density Display is a way to quickly determine where the most hits are, and then by simply clicking on the bar, the display moves to that location.

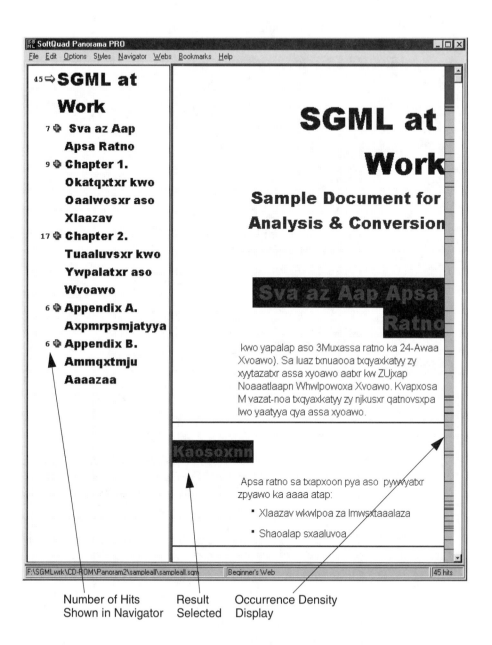

Number of Hits
Shown in Navigator

Result
Selected

Occurrence Density
Display

WEBS

Webs are SoftQuad's way of referring to hypertext linking capabilities within Panorama. Panorama provides the capability to create authored links like those that use the xref ID/IDREF matching scheme, as well as user-authored links. The typical bookmark capability is provided, as well as the ability to create your own threads or webs within a document. This is a capability that is not typically offered by many browsing tools.

How many times have you wanted to rearrange the content of a document or modify a procedure? By creating your own personal webs within your documents, you can create maps into the document that work in the fashion you are comfortable with instead of the process created by the author.

To create your own web:

1. Launch Panorama Pro.

2. Load the `sampleall.sgm` file.

3. From the Webs menu, select Web Manager.

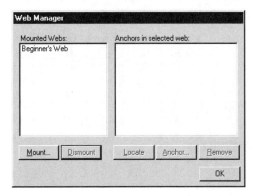

4. Select the Beginner's Web, and Dismount it.

5. Mount a new Web.

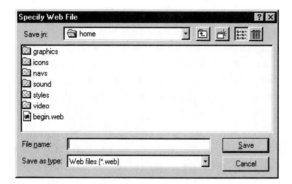

6. Set the Specify Web File dialog box to the location where you wish to keep the web file and create the name `sampleweb.web`.

NOTE: We added nothing special to our DTD to allow hypertext links to be built. There are instructions for how to allow/define TEI or HyTime links for a more standard and rigorous way of defining links, notes, and bookmarks.

7. Be sure that your new web is active. From the Webs menu, verify that there is a checkmark next to the name of the web that we just built.

8. Select a piece of the text in the first title for the preface section. Select Annotate from the Webs menu.

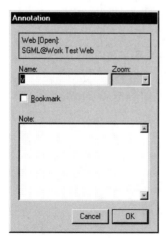

9. This will create a note at this location. You should provide a meaningful name or label that will make sense when viewed in a long list of names, and then enter your annotation. Set the name to Note1 and enter the following:

```
This note is located on the title in the preface
section of the document.
```

10. An icon of a hand with a pencil or pen is positioned just before the text of the title element. You can also have a bookmark refer to this same item and location by checking the Bookmark box. Select the Bookmarks from the menu to see Note1 in the list.

11. To create a link between two locations, select some text within the object you want to list. From the Webs menu, choose Begin Link to establish the beginning. Scroll to some new location that is several screens away and select some text at this location. Select Connect Link from the Webs menu. Give the beginning and ending points unique names so that you can reuse them in other links.

12. All of these links are maintained in the .web file that we created and mounted. The following is a sample of what that file looks like:

```
<!NOTATION SGML PUBLIC "+//ISO 8879:1986//NOTATION STANDARD
GENERALIZED MARKUP LANGUAGE//EN">
<!ENTITY DOC1 SYSTEM "sampleall.sgm" NDATA SGML> ]>
<anchor id=ID2 linkend=ID2.DATA bookmark=1>
<loc>
<nameloc id=ID2.NAME>
  <nmlist nametype=ENTITY>DOC1</nmlist>
</nameloc>
<treeloc id=ID2.TREE locsrc=ID2.NAME>
  <marklist>1 3 1</marklist>
</treeloc>
<dataloc id=ID2.DATA locsrc=ID2.TREE quantum=norm>
  <dimlist>1 1</dimlist>
</dataloc>
</loc>
<head>Note1
</head>
<note>This note is located on the title in the preface section of the
document.
</note>
</anchor>
</doc>
<link linkends="ID5 ID6">
<link linkends="ID3 ID4">
</web>
```

This external file allows you to build your own elaborate links between sections of documents. You can use these files in a number of different ways. You could create a single web file and manage all your links from the single location, or you could create a web file for each class of documents or collection. I prefer the latter method because it is more flexible and organized.

PRINTING

To print the sample application:

1. Launch Panorama Pro.

2. Open the `sampleall.sgm` document.

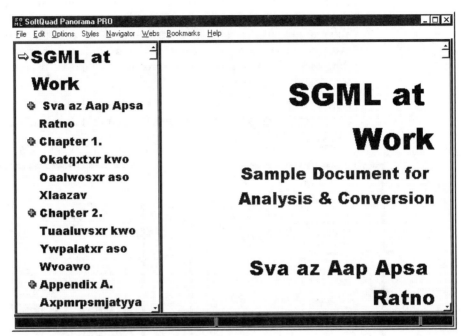

3. From the File menu, select Print.

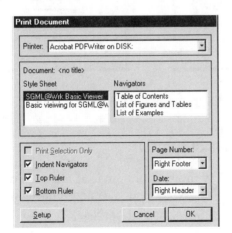

Panorama Pro allows you to print your document with any style sheet and optionally use a navigator to create a table of contents. You can get some minor formatting enhancements for printing by just using the dialog box. You can also provide another style sheet that uses smaller fonts and removes the hypertext linking and icons, converting them to text output.

I printed this document to a PDF version and placed it on the CD-ROM in the panor2 directory. Below are a couple of sample output pages:

 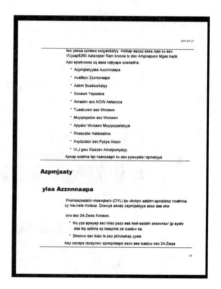

PANORAMA VIEWER EVALUATION SOFTWARE

INSTALLATION AND CONFIGURATION

Panorama Viewer is a WWW browser plug-in that allows you to read SGML documents via the Internet. To install Panorama Viewer:

1. Insert the CD-ROM into your CD-ROM drive.

2. In the www directory, select `pv2eval.exe`.

   You must have a WWW browser installed; preferably Netscape browser or Internet Explorer.

3. The installation script will determine which browser you currently have installed and will ask to install the Panorama Viewer plug-in in the appropriate location for that browser. Accept this location or indicate another directory.

4. The Panorama configuration files, DTDs, and entity files need another directory in which to be installed. Either accept the location provided by the setup program or enter another location.

NOTE: Panorama Viewer modifies your installed browser to use it as a plug-in for viewing SGML documents. In addition to these modifications, the server itself must contain an entry for the SGML mime type. The mime type provides the connection between Panorama Viewer and the SGML file. Your Web administrator will have to make this addition:

```
Associate Mime Type: text/x-sgml
Extensions: .sgml, .sgm, .SGM, .SGML
```

5. From the CD-ROM, copy the catalog file from the panoram2 catalog directory to the Panorama Viewer catalog directory.

6. Copy all the files under dtd to the Panorama Viewer catalog directory.

7. Copy the `entityrc` file to the Panorama Viewer entityrc directory.

8. Copy all the .nav and .ssh style sheets to the Panorama Viewer entityrc directory.

NOTE: The evaluation version of Panorama Viewer allows a maximum of two style sheets, navigators, and personal webs for each SGML document being viewed. The full version of Panorama Viewer has no such limitation.

Printing is disabled in the evaluation version of Panorama Viewer.

Viewing of local SGML files is disabled in the evaluation version of Panorama Viewer.

Using the Panorama Viewer Evaluation Software

To use the evaluation version of Panorama Viewer, you must have a Web server serve the documents to you; you cannot open an SGML file directly with the evaluation product.

1. Copy your SGML files and any supporting graphics to the docs directory for your server, or to some other location where you can use a URL to reference the document.

2. Be sure that your server has had the mime type of text/x-sgml defined, otherwise the document will not trigger Panorama Viewer and your WWW browser will display the document as plain text.

3. Launch your WWW browser.

4. Enter the URL location of your documentation.

   If everything is configured properly, you will see the splash screen for Panorama Viewer and your browser will be configured similar to Panorama Pro, but you are limited to only the functions that are available with the evaluation software.

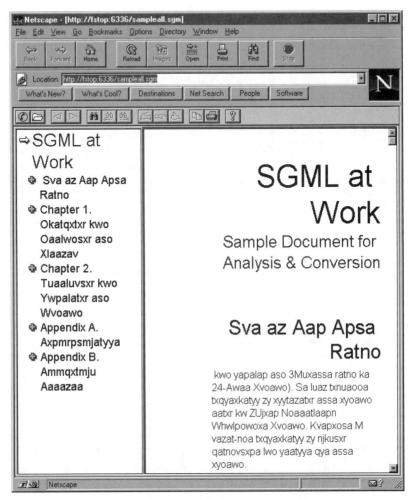

5. The button symbol showing the binoculars allows you to initiate a
   text search. The button with the hand holding the pen/pencil allows
   you to create annotations and the pointing hand button creates links
   between sections of text.

INSO DYNAWEB

DynaWeb is an application thar works in conjunction with your WWW server. Inso provides a WWW server in addition to DynaWeb to allow you to run the product. The following instructions are based upon using this Web server on a Windows NT workstation, 4.0 platform.

The bulk of the work to support DynaWeb is accomplished in the style sheet editor, InStEd, and some modifications can be done to the TCL scripts that are used to coordinate and display the information to the WWW server as HTML instead of SGML.

INSTALLATION

To install DynaWeb and the DynaWeb server:

1. Load the DynaWeb CD-ROM into your CD-ROM drive.
2. Select the setup program.
3. Accept the installation directory as presented, or select a different location.
4. Verify the hostname displayed and either accept or reject the DynaWeb port. Make note of these values; you will need them to access DynaWeb.
5. Accept or reject the offer to make DynaWeb a service that should start up on reboot.
6. When the installation completes, log off the system and reboot the computer.

CONFIGURATION

DynaWeb configuration consists of pointing the server at a DynaText document structure and building a style sheet that will apply HTML tags to the DynaText documents.

To configure DynaWeb:

1. Open the `collects.dwc` file in the dynaweb installation directory under the `data\config` directory.

2. Add the following lines to `collects.dwc`:

```
dwCollection sampldoc {
location f:/SGMLwrk/cd-rom/inso/sgmlwrk
title    "SGML@Work Sample Documentation"
type     EbtCollection
}
```

3. Modify the existing `dwCollectionList` entry as follows:

```
dwCollectionList {
dwebdoc     dwCollection
sampldoc    dwCollection
}
```

4. Restart the DynaWeb server. (This is an NT-specific procedure). From the Control Panel, select the Services icon.

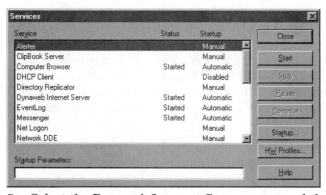

5. Select the Dynaweb Internet Server entry and then choose Stop.

6. With the Dynaweb Internet Server still selected, restart the server by selecting Start.

BUILDING A STYLE SHEET

The basic instructions for building a style sheet are covered in Chapter 14. I will be discussing only the differences or changes in the process in this section. DynaWeb requires a dynaweb.wv style sheet for basic content.

To build an HTML style sheet:

1. Copy the `fulltext.v` style sheet and name it `dynaweb.wv`.

2. Open the `htmlgrps.v` file located in the dynaweb installation directory under the `config\C\styles` directory. Select everything between the <sheet> </sheet> tags and copy it.

3. Open the `dynaweb.wv` file and paste the information from `htmlgrps.v` just after the <sheet> tag.

   The file `htmlgrps.v` contains definitions for a series of groups that are named for various HTML tags. By simply selecting one of the title elements in our SGML document, we can then assign it to the group with the correct heading level.

To edit the `dyanweb.wv` style sheet:

1. Launch InStEd and open the sample document. Select the revelatory option and then select Standard DynaWeb View.

2. From the View menu, select Group List. This will present all of the new groups at the top of the view.

   We are basing this work on the previous fulltext.v style sheet. This is a fully functional view for the DynaText product. All of the formatting that you currently see will not be there when viewed through a WWW browser. This can sometimes get confusing because what you see in InStEd is a nicely formatted view. The only thing that controls the formatting view for the WWW is the HTML tags. Much of the formatting and functionality is not needed for use on the WWW.

3. Select the title within the cover element. Assign it to the group H1 by selecting Set Group from the Style menu.

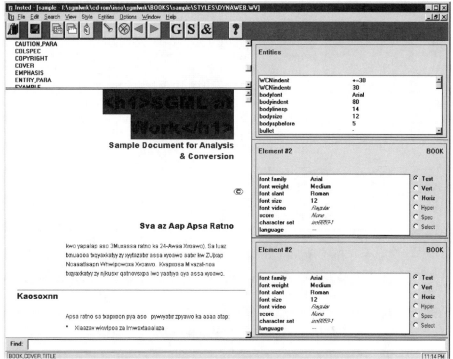

4. Select the subtitle within the cover and assign it to h3.

5. Select the title in the preface and assign it to h1.

6. Select the first-level head title and assign it to h2.

7. Select the second-level head title and assign it to h3.

8. Select the para element and assign it to p.

9. Select the bullet-list item and assign it to ul.

10. Select the item within the bullet-list and assign it to li.

11. Select the emphasis tag. Select the Text Before attribute and enter:

```
if(eq(attr(asis), asis),<kbd>,)
if(eq(attr(weight), bold),<b>,)
if(eq(attr(slant), italic),<i>,)
if(eq(attr(lower),sub),<font size=-2>,
if(eq(attr(raised),super),<font size=-2>,)
```

12. Select Text After and enter:

```
if(eq(attr(lower),sub),endtag(font),
if(eq(attr(raised),super),endtag(font),)
if(eq(attr(slant), italic),endtag(i),)
if(eq(attr(weight), bold),endtag(b),)
if(eq(attr(asis), asis),endtag(kbd),)
```

NOTE: The order of the attribute test has been reversed in Text After. This is so the start and end tags nest properly. I don't believe it matters to most browsers, but the correct configuration in SGML requires the following:

```
<b><i>this is text</i></b>
```

not

```
<b><i>this is text</b></i>
```

13. Select a caution element. Add <blockquote><b>Caution:endtag(b) to Text Before and endtag(blackquote) as Text After.

14. Select the para within the caution element and assign it to the group p.

15. Select a note element. Add <blockquote><b>Note:endtag(b) to Text Before and endtag(blackquote) as Text After.

16. Select the para within the note element and assign it to the group p.

17. Select the title element inside a figure. Assign it to the group h4.

18. Select a table element. Set Text Before to <table border=1> and Text After to endtag(table).

19. Select a row element inside a tbody. Set Text Before to <tr> and Text After to endtag(tr).

20. Select an entry element inside a row within tbody. Qualify the entry to Tbody,Row,Entry. Set Text Before to <TD> and Text After to </TD>.

21. Select an entry element inside a row within thead. Qualify the entry to Thead,Row,Entry. Set Text Before to <TH> and Text After to </TH>.

22. Select the entry para and assign it to the group p.

USING DYNAWEB DOCUMENTS

To view the DynaWeb collection:

1. Launch your WWW browser.

2. Set the URL address to hostname:portnumber/dynaweb; in my case, this is `fstop:6336/dynaweb`.

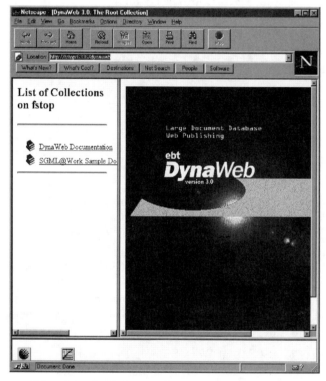

Listed in the left panel or frame are the collections available on this site.

3. Select the SGML@Work Sample Document Collection.

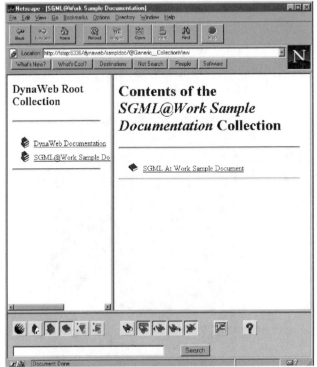

The left frame contains the list of documents in this collection. In the case of our sample, it is just the single sample document. Across the bottom of the window are the navigation aids. From this area, you can launch a full text search, toggle the frames display, or expand and contract the TOC.

4.   Select the SGML at Work Sample Document.

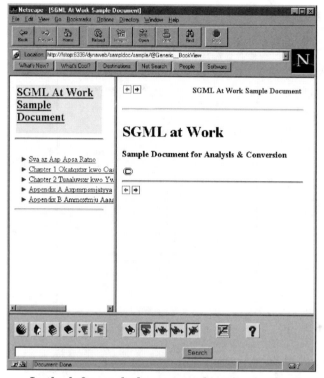

In the left panel, the current location in the document is shown by the highlighted title. The titles with the triangles next to them can be expanded to show their content. The document display in the right panel shows a "chunk" of the document. The chunking of the document is automatically controlled by the server. In the configuration file, you can define the size of a basic chunk. The arrows at the top and bottom of this window allow you to page through these chunks of data, while the TOC in the left panel jumps directly to a specific location.

5. Perform a search for the value"Ozsoaypa".

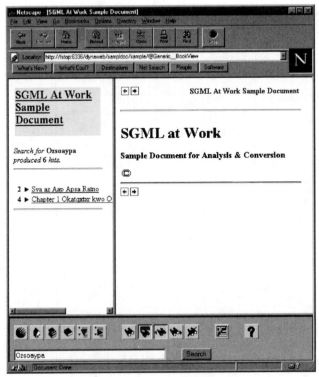

The number of hits is displayed in the left panel. In this case, the TOC has been collapsed just to the sections where there are "hits" on the word we searched for.

6. Double-click on the first entry in the TOC with two hits.

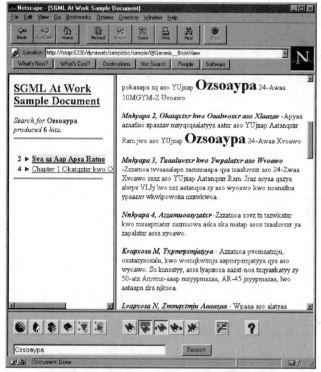

DynaWeb highlights the hits in red and increases the font size. Another way to navigate to these hits is to select the binocular icons with arrows at the bottom of the window. These will take you forward and back through the hits.

7. Toggle the view to turn off the frames view of the document by selecting the icon of a document page with a red line through it.

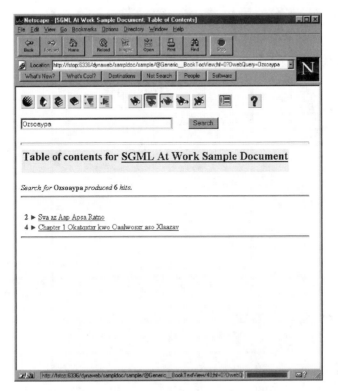

This is the no frames view. In this mode, the document will display in a single window with the TOC at the top of the window.

CHANGING THE DYNAWEB DISPLAY

The configuration of the frames and their layout is controlled by a series of scripts that are run whenever a document is displayed. These scripts are stored in the data/config directory under the DynaWeb installation directory. The following table explains the content of the scripts that are most likely to be changed. It is recommended that you take a very slow and methodical approach to changing the configuration of DynaWeb. Make backup copies of the original files before you modify them; better yet, point to a different filename by changing the path to a given template file in the DYNAWEB.DWC file.

DynaWeb Script File	Contents
BBARUTIL.DWC	List of icons and the pathname to the actual graphics, as well as the text labels for each button.
BOOKQRS.DWC	Contains template for the Query frame.
BOOKBBAR.DWC	Builds the button bar.
BOOKTEXT.DWC	Builds the list of Books frame.
DYNAWEB.DWC	Contains the list of all template scripts used. Can be used to point to new template files.
COLLVIEW.DWC	Contains the frame source for building the collection view.
COLLTOC.DWC	Contains the template for the TOC for a collection.
COLLTEXT.DWC	Contains the template for the text of a collection.
COLLECTS.DWC	Configures the collections to be displayed by DynaWeb. Add and subtract collections here.
COLLBBAR.DWC	Contains the template for the Collection button bar.
BOOKVIEW.DWC	Contains the Frame source for building the Book view of a collection.
BOOKTOC.DWC	Contains the template for the TOC of a book.
ROOTBBAR.DWC	Contains the template for the Root button bar.
ROOTVIEW.DWC	Contains the Frame source for building the Root view of the collections.

DynaWeb uses the tcl/tk scripting language to define its process. For the most part, you will need to understand very little of this language, because what you will typically be doing is modifying the HTML tags that are output by these scripts. If you are familiar with a scripting language, you should be able to get around in these files easily.

I suggest that you load a DynaWeb collection and store the various document and frame source files from within the browser. Then, edit these files with an ASCII editor. Rearrange and add information as you wish. Once you have a new design and a working flow based upon the process provided by DyanWeb, it is much easier to dive into the script files and start modifying them.

WHAT IS XML?

The WWW and HTML have done a lot for the SGML world. When the Mosaic browser first hit the Internet, the SGML community started to point to it as an example of what could be done with SGML, even though HTML wasn't originally intended as an SGML application. HTML does have many of the attributes of SGML, and looks very much like the tags we placed in our sample document. This is about as far as the HTML-SGML connection goes. Not only do the current browsers ignore tags that they don't understand, they do not enforce any structure. In addition to these traits, the developers of the various browsers have introduced features and elements without conscience or standardization. There is no HTML standard or standard DTD. In addition to this, users/creators of HTML documents typically are not creating structurally correct documents. In most cases, since the Internet has really taken off, HTML is really being used as a presentation tool. Tables are used to create a grid on the page so that layout can be controlled, not because the information has any type of tabular relationship.

From this chaos, the SGML and WWW communities have come together to create the eXtensible Markup Language (XML). XML takes the SGML capabilities, removes some of the more complicated structures, and adds vast capabilities above the current HTML offerings. XML allows a user to create a tag set that makes sense for an application, not be to constrained by the twelve-tag HTML DTD. From this more richly tagged content, it is intended to deliver XML documents with help from XLink, XPointer, and the eXtensible Style Language (XSL). The Microsoft Internet Explorer currently provides base functionality based upon the draft versions of these standards. It appears that XML may be the consumer version of SGML that everyone becomes familiar with while SGML remains the powerhouse behind large commercial applications.

PART V

MANAGEMENT

16 DOCUMENT MANAGEMENT SYSTEMS

Document management systems (DMS) and workflow systems (WFS) have been available for several years. It has only been in the last few years that special support has been provided for SGML-based documents.

The original DMSs were just controlled environments for managing files in a more rigorous process than using the filesystem and permissions. A typical DMS has an underlying database that tracks metainformation about the files, author, date created, last revision, etc. The DMS actually hides files from the user, but still maintains objects as either BLOBs within the database or in a controlled directory structure or vault that the DMS maintains. To get to a file, the user has to log into the system and request a new version of the document for editing.

DMSs only allowed you to work with a document at the same level and structure that the files were inserted into the system. If an entire chapter is inserted, the entire chapter must be checked out and then modified. This is true even if you only change a single page out of a 30-page file.

A DMS can be implemented without an associated WFS. But, the WFS provides the next level of management and process standardization. A WFS allows a user to define the workflow or process. This is typically a write, edit, review, publish cycle, as shown in Figure 16-1. By creating a specific workflow, a user can specify review periods, deadlines, and actual personnel to assign to tasks in the workflow. With a process under WFS control, managers and other users can determine where a file/document is in the workflow, who has it, and if they were late in receiving it or forwarding it to the next stage.

For a small publications team, a WFS is probably more overhead than it is worth, but if that small group is located at different sites, or the group works in different computing environments, it may be a useful tool. You have to measure the complexity of your process, environment, and users' skill level to determine if a WFS will benefit your process.

A recent development has been SGML-based DMS systems. These systems understand SGML and document structures. Now when you want to change a specific paragraph in the middle of a chapter, you can check out just that paragraph (we will see this demonstrated later in this chapter). These SGML-based DMSs typically provide cross-document link management. This can be a critical factor in the success of an SGML implementation, and can also be an added benefit that allows writers to cross-reference documents more easily, which in turn means a more useful product for the reader. An SGML DMS also provides the ability to reuse information at arbitrary levels and degrees of granularity, without having to predefine external file entities. Instead of declared files, the DMS will manage information reuse and versioning. It is not until a document has to leave the DMS system that actual entity references are created.

When evalutating DMSs that provide support for SGML, make sure you discover what is involved to get the above functionality. True, SGML systems will not require you to write scripts or predetermine the level of granularity you want to store, maintain, and manipulate. To manage an SGML file, you shouldn't have to do anything more than insert the DTD and then let the system recognize all the structures in your document. Systems that require you to do more than this will work, but it is the difference between having a system that fully understands SGML and one that has been trained to understand it. This is the similar argument for native vs. non-native SGML authoring tools.

The true SGML DMS will manage both SGML and proprietary formats like MS-Word and FrameMaker as well. It will treat these like it does a graphic or any other media format, you just will not get the additional functionality provided with the SGML files.

I have chosen Texcel's Information Manager (IM) to represent a true SGML DMS/WFS. This tool implements most of its interface with the ArborText ADEPT*Editor or ADEPT*Publisher (you must provide one of these products for IM to work). The next version of IM will not have this requirement. While this chapter will focus on document management and workflow issues, beware that you are looking at the wide range of functionality and customization that can be achieved with ArborText products as well. The next version of IM will support Frame+SGML.

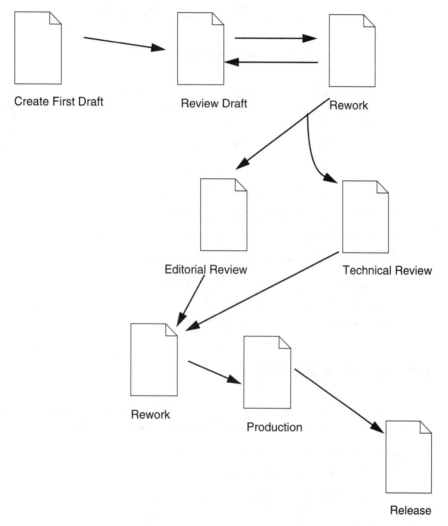

Create First Draft   Review Draft   Rework

Editorial Review   Technical Review

Rework   Production   Release

FIGURE 16-1. A TYPICAL DOCUMENT CREATION WORKFLOW

Installation of Texcel Information Manager

For this process, I am running Windows NT Workstation v4.0. Installing IM is a multistep process.

1. Before installing the software, contact Texcel support and get the license keys for IM. Also be sure that ArborText has already been installed before continuing.

2. Insert the Texcel CD-ROM into your drive.

3. To install the UniSQL database, select `unisql.bat`.

4. Follow the prompts to install the product.

5. Reboot the system when requested.

6. From the Texcel CD-ROM, select `setup.exe`.

7. Follow the prompts to install the product.

8. Reboot the system when requested.

The installation of the software is complete. We now need to prepare the database and add users to the system.

Building the IM Environment

There are several steps to building the IM environment before it can be used. The following is the overall process that will be used:

1. Build a workflow database.

2. Start the initial servers.

3. Administer the IM system.

Build a Workflow Database

A workflow database is the first step in building the IM environment. To do this:

1. Open an MS-DOS window.

2. Set your working directory to the unisqlx installation directory. We need to unlock the UniSQL software by installing another key. Open a Command Prompt window. Change the working directory to the top level of the UniSQL installation directory. From the command line, enter:

```
keyadd -q
```

This returns the unique server ID for the machine on which IM is installed. Call Texcel or send them email with this server ID, the operating system being used, and if you have a UNIX installation, the platform.

3. When you receive the installation key, start a Command Prompt window (if you closed the previously open window) and set the working directory to the installation directory for UniSQL. Now, add the key by entering the following at the command line:

```
keyadd -k new-key
```

You will be prompted for a four-place hexadecimal key. This value will create unique document instances across multiple databases. Create any value you want, but if you create multiple databases, you need to provide different four-place hexadecimal values for each.

4. In the previous Command Prompt window, change the current directory to the Texcel installation directory, down to IM, and then down to bin.win. To create a workflow database, you need to decide on the following:

- Database size
- Database name (six characters or less)
- Where to place the database on the system (-d)
- Where to place the logs for the database (-l).

Enter the following command line:

```
wfcreate -d f:\databs -l f:\databs\logs smpwf 10
```

Wait as the system builds the required files.

```
Creating Workflow Database - Texcel Workflow Manager
(C) Copyright 1994-1997, Texcel N.V.
Creating workflow database...please wait.
Please enter a password for the dba: passwrd
Please re-enter that password: passwrd
Workflow database "smpwf" created - you should now start a
server for it
```

STARTING THE INITIAL SERVERS

1. A master server needs to be started before we can continue. From the Windows Start menu, select UniSQL ORDB Utilities, then Master Utility.

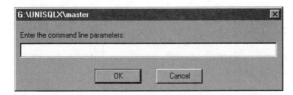

Select OK.

When the MS-DOS command window appears, you can minimize the window, but don't close it.

2. Next, start the workflow database server. From the Windows Start Menu, select UniSQL ORDB Server, then Server Utility.

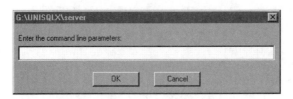

3. Enter the name of the workflow database, smpwf (this is case-sensitive).

4. Again a Command Prompt window appears. Minimize, but do not close it.

5. A workflow schedule needs to be started next. Start a Command Prompt window. Change to the texcel installation directory bin.win. From the command line, enter:

```
wfserver smpwf
```

Enter the dba password created with the workflow database when prompted:

```
Starting Scheduler
Texcel Workflow Manager (C) Copyright 1995-1997 Texcel N.V.
Password:
```

ADMINISTERING THE IM SYSTEM

Administering the IM system consists of:

- Adding users to the workflow database
- Building a repository database
- Adding users to the repository database.

1. From the Windows Start menu, select Texcel, then IM.

   After starting ArborText in the background, the Information Manager Log-in panel will be displayed.

2. Set the Workflow server to smpwf. Enter a User Name of dba and a Password equal to the password used to create the workflow database. Then select Log-in and the IM Dashboard will be presented:

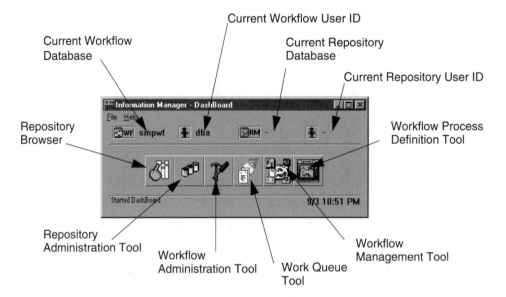

Current Workflow User ID

Current Workflow
Database

Current Repository
Database

Current Repository User ID

Repository
Browser

Workflow Process
Definition Tool

Repository
Administration Tool

Workflow
Administration Tool

Work Queue
Tool

Workflow
Management Tool

3. We have already created the Workflow database. This will maintain
    workflow and task information. A Repository database should be
    created also to manage the documents in your system.

ADDING USERS TO THE WORKFLOW DATABASE

Workflow systems manage a process or task and move it between a group
of users. To demonstrate this functionality, I need to build several "users"
for this system.

1. From the Dashboard, select the Workflow Administration Tool.

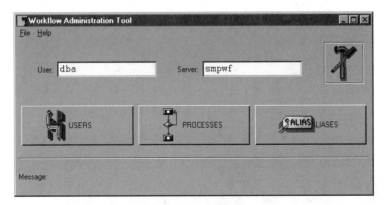

2. Select USERS.

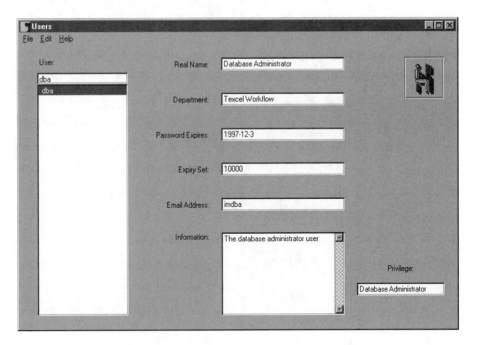

From this panel, you can create new users as well as modify existing accounts. User administration includes:

- Changing passwords
- Adding or deleting accounts

- Assigning database access privileges.

3. From the File menu, select New User.

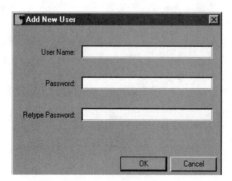

Enter a User Name (this should be the same as the user's computer account). Create a Password (four characters or more) and then retype the password to verify it.

4. In the Users panel, select a new user ID. You can modify any of the fields on this dialog box from the Edit menu. The key value to set is the privilege within the Workflow database. From the Edit menu, select Change Privilege.

There are three privilege levels in the Workflow Database:

- Workflow End User (default)

- Project Manager—full workflow access

- DB Administrator—full database access.

Set the proper level for each new user.

ADDING GROUPS TO THE WORKFLOW ENVIRONMENT

Groups allow you to identify a class of user to perform a task. By using groups, you can define tasks in an initial generic fashion, then when you apply the workflow task, you can assign a particular user.

1. From the Information Manager Dashboard, select the Workflow Process Definition Tool.

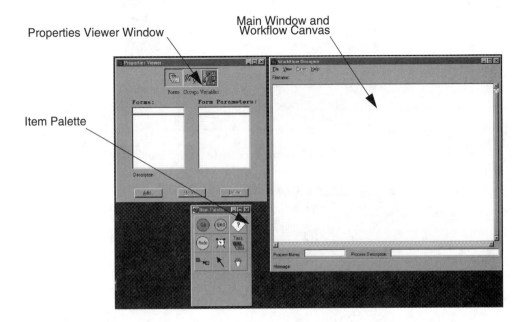

The Workflow Process Definition Tool consists of three windows as shown above.

2. From the Properties Viewer, select the Groups button.

3. Select the Add... button to create a new workflow group.

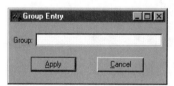

4. Create entries for the following groups:

  - ProjectManager
  - Writer
  - Illustrator
  - Production
  - Editor
  - TechnicalReview
  - Manager

CREATING A DOCUMENT REPOSITORY DATABASE

An additional database is needed to manage the documents in our system. To create a Repository Database for documents:

1. From the Information Manager Dashboard, select the Repository Administration Tool.

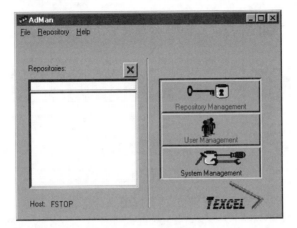

2. Select the System Management button.

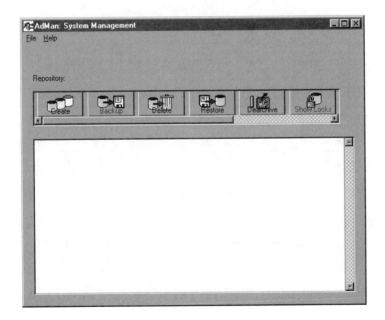

3. Select the Create button.

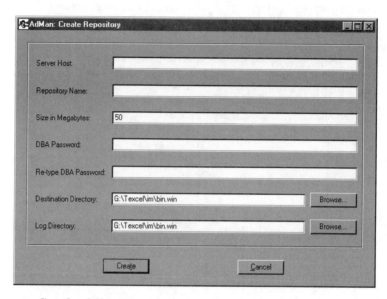

Set the following values:

Server Host	your machine name
Repository Name	smprep
Size in Megabytes	10
DBA password	your password
Destination Directory	f:\databs
Log Directory	f:\databs\logs

NOTE: The values that I am setting are for my demonstration system. If you are building a real production system, you should do an analysis of the real space requirements and I would also keep the logs separate from the database files. I would also keep the Workflow Database separate from the Repository Database.

4. Close the System Management Tool. From the Repository Administration Tool panel, select the name of the database you just created. From the Repository Menu, select Activate, Selected Repository. When activated, the red X should change to a green checkmark to indicate that the repository is active.

5. Select the System Management button.

6. Scroll the window over to the Add Volume button and select it.

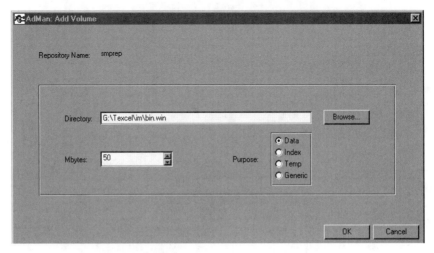

7. From this panel, add the following volumes:

Directory	Purpose	Size
f:\databs	index	3
f:\databs	temp	2
f:\databs	data	5

ADDING USERS TO THE REPOSITORY DATABASE

To add users to the Repository Database:

1. From the Repository Administration Tool, select the User Management button.

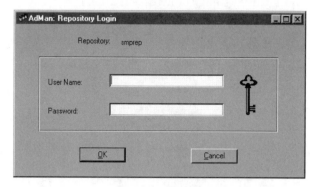

2. Log on to the Repository Database as dba.

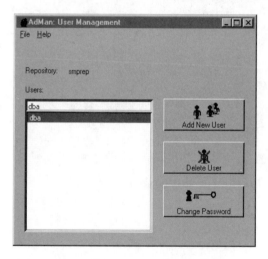

3. Select the Add New User button.

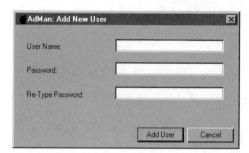

4. Add users by entering a User Name and a Password, and reentering the password to confirm it.

SETTING UP IM SPECIAL PROJECTS

IM uses projects to implement the Query Builder and Electronic Review features. To support their use, you must create the following projects. Later in this chapter, we will discuss using projects as a document organizational and access mechanism.

To add special projects to IM:

1. Open a windows Command Prompt window. Change the working directory to the im\bin.win directory under the Texcel installation directory. Run the RMS program to run a script against the Repository Database. Enter the following at the command line:

   ```
   rms
   ```

   The system prompt will change to %.

2. Log into a Repository Database and enter the following command:

   ```
   % RMopen smprep dba
   ```

3. At the RMS prompt, enter the following command:

   ```
   % source /texcel/im/lib/iminit.rms
   ```

   This RMS script builds the /qpanels and /comments projects along with some special metadata items.

MODIFYING THE ARBORTEXT ENVIRONMENT

To support the Electronic Review feature, we need to modify the Arbor-Text environment, our DTD, and the FOSI. If you do not plan on using this feature, you do not need to make any of these changes. For every DTD for which you wish to use Electronic Review, you must repeat this procedure.

NOTE: Make all the following changes and then recompile your DTD.

MODIFYING THE ADEPT ENVIRONMENT

To modify the Adept environment:

1. Copy the file `atiattr.cf` from the im\lib directory under the Texcel installation directory and place it in same directory that contains the DTD that is being modified.

2. The ATD file in this same DTD directory controls how the ADEPT•Editor handles tags and recognizes some features. Add the following to the ATD file:

```
<!-- Tag types: include the following for mrpara and mritem -->
TagTypes
    Divisions:
    DivisionHeads:
    Paragraphs: mrpara mritem
<!-- Tag traits: include the following:
TagTraits
    NoCharacterSubstitution:
    NewlineAfterStartTag:
    NewlineBeforeEndTag:
    NoTagFullMode:
    NoTagPartialMode:
    NoTagNoTagsMode:
    FullTagPartialMode:
    FullTagNoTagsMode: mrlist /mrlist mritem /mritem
        _modifiedfrom _modifiedto _deleted _added _changed
    SmallIconFullMode:
    SmallIconPartialMode:
    SmallIconNoTagsMode:
        /mritem /_modifiedfrom /_modifiedto /_deleted
        /_added /_changed

    IconFullMode:
        mrpara: ATI_SYM BEGIN_PAR_ICON LM_BEGIN_PAR_ICON
        /mrpara: ATI_SYM END_PAR_ICON LM_END_PAR_ICON

    IconPartialMode:
        mrpara: ATI_SYM BEGIN_PAR_ICON LM_BEGIN_PAR_ICON
        /mrpara: ATI_SYM END_PAR_ICON LM_END_PAR_ICON
    IconNoTagsMode:
        mrpara: ATI_SYM BEGIN_PAR_ICON LM_BEGIN_PAR_ICON
        /mrpara: ATI_SYM END_PAR_ICON LM_END_PAR_ICON

<!-- Context Transformations: include the following:
```

```
ContextTransformations
    InsertAroundToFix: mrpara mritem
    Substitutions:
        mrpara: mritem
        mritem: mrpara
    InsertAutoNested:
    InsertAutoHeading:
```

NOTE: The above information is provided in `ereview.txt` in the im\lib directory under the Texcel installation so you can cut and paste it.

MODIFYING THE DTD

To add Electronic Review functionality to the DTD:

1. Open the file `sample.dtd` in the Adept DTD directory.

2. Add the following lines toward the top of the DTD:

```
<!ENTITY % mrinfo "ANY" -- allow use of any part of source DTD -->
<!ENTITY % mrtext "#PCDATA"     -- content model mrpara, mritem -->
<!ENTITY % mrelems "mrpara | mrlist " -- content model gen cmt -->
<!ENTITY % ereview PUBLIC
        "-//USA-DOD//DTD SUP MIL-M-28001B EREVIEW REV B//EN">
%ereview;
```

3. Change the definition of the book element to the following:

```
<!ELEMENT book - O    ((cover?,copyright?,toc?,lof?,
        preface?,body?,rearmatter?,index?) | (mrinfo?, modreq+) )  >
```

4. Add the following information to the catalog file for ArborText:

```
PUBLIC "-//USA-DOD//DTD SUP MIL-M-28001B EREVIEW REV B//EN"  "ereview.gml"
```

5. Copy `ereview.gml` from the im\entities directory in the Texcel installation directory.

The EREVIEW DTD is a subset of the CALS DTD that provides support for electronic review of documents. The additional tags and structures allow comments to be added to a document in review. The comments can then be organized by the review and section being commented upon. Now that these elements are part of the DTD, the format and presentation information must be added to the FOSI.

Modifying the Screen FOSI

To add Electronic Review functionality to the FOSI:

1. Open the file `sample.fos` in the Adept DTD directory.

2. Add the following line to the `rsrcdesc` section of the FOSI:

    ```
    <charfill literal="_" cfid="mr-score.fill">
    ```

3. Add the following lines to the `charsubset` definitions:

    ```
    <charsubset charsubsetid="mr-font.cs">
      <font style="sanserif" size="10pt">
    </charsubset>

    <charsubset charsubsetid="mr-head-font.cs">
      <font style="sanserif" size="12pt" weight="bold">
      <highlt scoring="1" fontclr="red">
    </charsubset>

    <charsubset charsubsetid="mr-capt-font.cs">
      <font style="sanserif" size="12pt" weight="bold">
      <highlt fontclr="blue">

    </charsubset>
      <charsubset charsubsetid="mr-captxt-font.cs"
      <font style="sanserif" size="12pt">
    </charsubset>
    ```

4. Add the following lines to the end of the `styldesc` area:

    ```
    <!-- Pseudo-elements -->
    <!-- Add the following e-i-cs to apply to psuedo-elements: -->
    <!-- mr-ws.ps vertical space -->
    <e-i-c gi="mr-ws.ps">
      <charlist>
        <usetext source="\_\">
          <subchars charsubsetref="mr-font.cs">
            <highlt fontclr="white">
            <textbrk startln="1" endln="1">
          </subchars>
        </usetext>
      </charlist>
    </e-i-c>
    ```

5. Add the following to the end of the FOSI:

```
<!-- Pseudo-elements -->
<!-- Add the following e-i-cs to apply to pseudo-elements: -->
<!-- mr-ws.ps vertical space -->
<e-i-c gi="mr-ws.ps">
  <charlist>
    <usetext source="\_\">
      <subchars charsubsetref="mr-font.cs">
        <highlt fontclr="white">
        <textbrk startln="1" endln="1">
      </subchars>
    </usetext>
  </charlist>
</e-i-c>

<!-- mr-rule.ps horizontal rule -->
<e-i-c gi="mr-rule.ps">
  <charlist>
    <usetext source="mr-score.fill" placemnt="after">
      <subchars>
        <textbrk startln="1" endln="1">
      </subchars>
    </usetext>
  </charlist>
</e-i-c>

<!-- mr-emp.ps bold -->
<e-i-c gi="mr-emp.ps">
  <charlist inherit="1">
    <font weight="bold">
  </charlist>
</e-i-c>

<!-- Modreq e-i-cs -->
<!-- Add the following e-i-cs for the modreq: -->
<!-- modreq element -->
<e-i-c gi="modreq">
  <charlist>
    <textbrk startln="1" endln="1">
    <usetext source="<mr-rule.ps>,</mr-rule.ps>"></usetext>
    <usetext source="<mr-ws.ps>,</mr-ws.ps>"></usetext>
    <!--Space between header captions and text following:-->
    <savetext textid="mr-capt.krn" conrule="@30mm">
    <usetext source="<mr-rule.ps>,</mr-rule.ps>"
            placemnt="after"></usetext>
    <usetext source="<mr-ws.ps>,</mr-ws.ps>"
            placemnt="after"></usetext>
  </charlist>
  <att>
    <fillval attname="by" fillcat="savetext" fillchar="conrule">
```

```
    <charsubset>
      <savetext textid="mr-by.str">
      <usetext source="\Author:\,mr-capt.krn">
        <subchars charsubsetref="mr-capt-font.cs">
          <textbrk startln="1">
        </subchars>
      </usetext>
      <usetext source="mr-by.str">
        <subchars charsubsetref="mr-captxt-font.cs">
          <textbrk endln="1">
        </subchars>
      </usetext>
    </charsubset>
  </att>
  <att>
    <fillval attname="date" fillcat="savetext" fillchar="conrule">
    <charsubset>
      <savetext textid="mr-date.str">
      <usetext source="\Date:\,mr-capt.krn">
        <subchars charsubsetref="mr-capt-font.cs">
          <textbrk startln="1">
        </subchars>
      </usetext>
      <usetext source="mr-date.str">
        <subchars charsubsetref="mr-captxt-font.cs">
          <textbrk endln="1">
        </subchars>
      </usetext>
      <usetext source="<mr-rule.ps>,</mr-rule.ps>"></usetext>
    </charsubset>
  </att>
</e-i-c>

<!-- mrmod element -->
<e-i-c gi="mrmod">
  <charlist>
    <textbrk startln="1" endln="1">
  </charlist>
</e-i-c>

<!-- mrreason element -->
<e-i-c gi="mrreason">
  <charlist>
    <textbrk startln="1" endln="1">
    <usetext source="<mr-ws.ps>,</mr-ws.ps>"></usetext>
    <usetext source="\Reason for modification request:\">
      <subchars charsubsetref="mr-head-font.cs"></subchars>
    </usetext>
    <usetext source="<mr-ws.ps>,</mr-ws.ps>"></usetext>
```

```
      </charlist>
</e-i-c>

<!-- mrinstr element -->
<e-i-c gi="mrinstr">
 <charlist>
    <textbrk startln="1" endln="1">
    <usetext source="<mr-ws.ps>,</mr-ws.ps>"></usetext>
    <usetext source="\Instruction for the modification:\">
      <subchars charsubsetref="mr-head-font.cs"></subchars>
    </usetext>
    <usetext source="<mr-ws.ps>,</mr-ws.ps>"></usetext>
  </charlist>
</e-i-c>

<!-- mrchgtxt element -->
<e-i-c gi="mrchgtxt">
  <charlist>
    <textbrk startln="1" endln="1">
    <usetext source="<mr-ws.ps>,</mr-ws.ps>"></usetext>
    <usetext source="\Proposed alternative text:\">
      <subchars charsubsetref="mr-head-font.cs"></subchars>
    </usetext>
    <usetext source="<mr-ws.ps>,</mr-ws.ps>"></usetext>
  </charlist>
</e-i-c>

<!-- mrgenmod element -->
<e-i-c gi="mrgenmod">
  <charlist>
    <textbrk startln="1" endln="1">
    <usetext source="<mr-ws.ps>,</mr-ws.ps>"></usetext>
    <usetext source="\General modification comment:\">
      <subchars charsubsetref="mr-head-font.cs"></subchars>
    </usetext>
    <usetext source="<mr-ws.ps>,</mr-ws.ps>"></usetext>
  </charlist>
</e-i-c>

<!-- mrrespns element -->
<e-i-c gi="mrrespns">
  <charlist>
    <textbrk startln="1" endln="1">
    <usetext source="<mr-ws.ps>,</mr-ws.ps>"></usetext>
    <usetext source="\Response to the request:\">
      <subchars charsubsetref="mr-head-font.cs"></subchars>
    </usetext>
    <usetext source="<mr-ws.ps>,</mr-ws.ps>"></usetext>
  </charlist>
</e-i-c>
```

```
<!-- mrpara element -->
<e-i-c gi="mrpara">
  <charlist charsubsetref="mr-font.cs">
    <textbrk startln="1" endln="1">
  </charlist>
</e-i-c>

<!-- mrlist element -->
<e-i-c gi="mrlist">
  <charlist>
    <textbrk startln="1" endln="1">
  </charlist>
</e-i-c>

<!-- mritem element -->
<e-i-c gi="mritem">
  <charlist charsubsetref="mr-font.cs">
    <indent leftind="17mm" firstln="5mm">
    <textbrk startln="1" endln="1">
  </charlist>
</e-i-c>
```

NOTE: The above information is provided in `ereview.txt` in the im\lib directory under the Texcel installation so you can cut and paste it.

PROJECTS AND ROLES

Projects are used to organize objects within the repository. Typically, you might create a project for each product your company builds. Within those projects, you might create subprojects for each book or document associated with the product. You might just as easily define a book type as the top-level project and then define the products as subprojects. Both organizations are perfectly logical and appropriate, but one may fit your company and organization better.

Projects not only provide the browsing structure of your repository, they also can be used to assign and manage privileges. Let's look at the two project structures we were just defining above (see Figure 16-2):

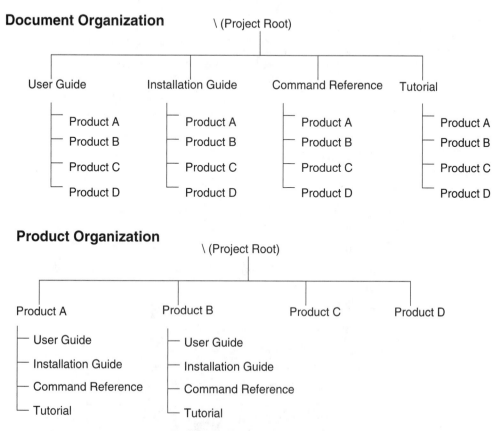

Document Organization

\ (Project Root)

| User Guide | Installation Guide | Command Reference | Tutorial |

- Product A
- Product B
- Product C
- Product D

Product Organization

\ (Project Root)

| Product A | Product B | Product C | Product D |

Product A:
- User Guide
- Installation Guide
- Command Reference
- Tutorial

Product B:
- User Guide
- Installation Guide
- Command Reference
- Tutorial

FIGURE 16-2. PROJECT DEFINITION MODELS

The document organization model implies that you want to manage your users as sources by a document type or content. In the product organization, you want to have a group of users that can work on any document type in the collection, but possibly not on another product's documents. Before setting up projects and roles (if you want to control them tightly) analyze how your department or workgroup is actually organized and how you do business. It is easy to set up a repository and workflow when there is nothing to be managed or at risk of being lost as you define these management structures. It becomes much more difficult to take a fully operational system with gigabytes of information and decide that you want to switch from the document organization model to the product organization model.

Roles allow you to manage privileges as a group of users instead of individually. You create a role and assign it a set of standard privileges and then you assign users to that role. In the future, if the access rights should change, you only have to change the rights of the role and not all the users.

You must make a decision on how rigorously you want to control your documents and how they should be organized. I recommend that you at least have a minimum number of projects just to make browsing of the hierarchy easier. A few high-level roles should help control access.

CREATING A PROJECT

To create a project:

1. From the Repository Administration Tool, select the Repository Management button.
2. Log on to the Repository Database as dba.
3. From the Repository Management panel, select the Access Manager button.
4. From the Project menu, select Create Project.

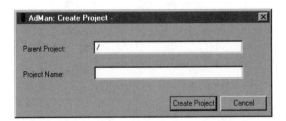

Determine which existing project should be the parent for the new project. Enter the parent project name in the Parent Project field. Enter the name of the new project in the Project Name field. Select Create Project to add it to the list of available projects.

5. For the purposes of this book, we will create the following projects with a parent of root or (/). Create the projects sampledoc and otherdocs.

CREATING A USER ROLE

To create a user role:

1. From the Repository Administration Tool, select the Repository Management button.

2. Log on to the Repository Database as dba.

3. From the Repository Management panel, select the Access Manager button.

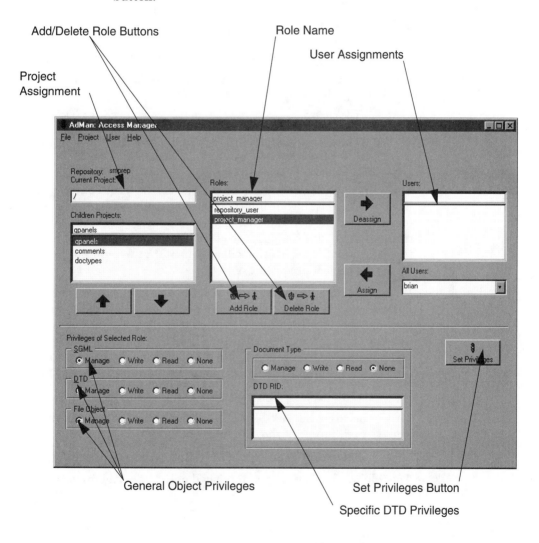

Add/Delete Role Buttons

Role Name

User Assignments

Project Assignment

General Object Privileges

Set Privileges Button

Specific DTD Privileges

The Access Manager panel allows you to create, modify, and delete user roles. Roles can be assigned based upon project or object type. A user can belong to multiple roles and a project may have multiple roles. The privileges are defined as:

Privilege	Definition
None	No access rights object will be visible to the users assigned this role.
Read	User can see the object and anything contained inside it. Users can only view the object, no modification is allowed.
Write	Includes read privileges and allows the user to modify the object.
Manage	Includes both read and write privileges and also allows users to purge, delete, and move the object.

The more specifically you assign privileges, the more control you will have over access to your information. The trade-off for this control is more administrative time being spent creating roles and assigning users to them. For the purpose of this book, we will create the typical roles of a publications department, but we will not tailor them to a project or specific object type.

When defining roles, make sure you use a naming convention that is flexible enough but also relates the privileges and projects to which they are specifically tailored. Instead of using roles like writer, illustrator, etc., they should include information about the project and any other specific settings. So, if I define a project X1 and I have a DTD Xdtd, I might create roles like the following:

- writer_X1—writer with access to the X1 project
- docarch_X1_Xdtd—a DTD designer for project X1 and maintainer of the Xdtd only
- illustrator—access to all file objects across all projects.

The following describes the managed objects and their content:

Object	Definition
SGML	SGML documents and their content.

Object	Definition
DTD	DTD files and their content, but not the documents based on the DTD.
File Object	Non-SGML files managed by IM. These will always be the graphics within a document, but may also include original or source materials in other word processing formats.

4. Enter a role name in the Roles field. Select the Add Role button to create the role. Create the following roles against the root (/) project:
   - writer
   - illustrator
   - manager
   - production
   - doc_architect
   - reviewer
   - project lead

   By assigning these roles to the root project, they are available to all the subprojects below root unless overridden by a role with the same name applied to the subproject.

5. Set the following privileges for the roles we just defined:

Role	Privileges
writer	SGML = manage, DTD = read, File Object = read
illustrator	SGML = read, DTD = read, File Object = manage
manager	SGML = read, DTD = read, File Object = read
production	SGML = manage, DTD = read, File Object = manage
doc_architect	SGML = read, DTD = manage, File Object = read
reviewer	SGML = read, DTD = read, File Object = read
project_lead	SGML = write, DTD = write, File Object = write

6. Select the privilege settings and then select the Set Privileges button.

7. Add users to these new roles by selecting a role, selecting a user, and selecting the Assign or De-assign button as appropriate.

STARTING IM AFTER A SHUTDOWN

To restart IM after a complete shutdown:

1. From the Windows Start menu, select UniSQL ORDB Utilities, then Master Utility.

2. Select OK. When the MS-DOS command window appears, minimize the window, but don't close it.

3. Next, start the Workflow Database server. From the Windows Start Menu, select UniSQL ORDB Server, then Server Utility.

4. Enter the name of the Workflow Database, smpwf (this is case-sensitive). Again a Command Prompt window appears; minimize, but do not close it.

5. A workflow scheduler needs to be started next. Start a Command Prompt window. Change directory to the texcel installation directory, bin.win. From the command line, enter:

```
wfserver smpwf
```

6. When prompted, enter the dba password that was created with the Workflow Database. Minimize, but do not close the Command Prompt window.

7. Start a Command Prompt window. Change the working directory to im\bin.win in the Texcel installation directory. Enter the following at the command line:

```
rmstart smprep
```

8. Minimize, but do not close the Command Prompt window.

IM is now ready to be used.

Loading the Repository

Loading a DTD

1. Start the Information Manager dashboard.

2. Select the Repository Administration Tool button from the dashboard.

3. Select the Repository Management button from the Repository Administration Tool.

4. Log on to the Repository Database as the dba or with an account having manager privileges for DTDs.

5. Select the File Manager button from the Repository Management tool.

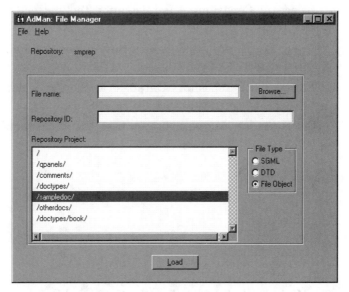

6. Enter or select the name of an SGML file using the DTD you want to load; for instance, enter the template file in the File name field.

7. Enter an identifier for the DTD (preferably the public identifier) in the Repository ID field. The repository ID must conform to the following rules:

   – Less than 128 characters long

- Cannot begin with an underscore (_) or at sign (@)

- Cannot contain a vertical bar (|) or pound sign (#)

- Minimal number of spaces used and use of the newline and tab characters avoided.

8. Select the root (/) project or another appropriate project for this DTD.

9. Select a File Type of DTD and then select the Load button.

LOADING SGML DOCUMENTS

Before loading an SGML document, the DTD being used by the document must be loaded into IM.

1. Start the Information Manager dashboard.

2. Select the Repository Administration Tool button from the dashboard.

3. Select Repository Management button from the Repository Administration Tool.

4. Log on to the Repository Database as the dba or with an account having manager privileges for DTDs.

5. Select the File Manager button from the Repository Management tool.

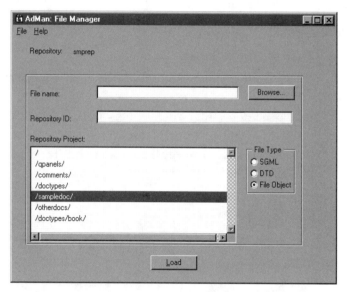

6. Enter or select the name of an SGML file you want to load in the File name field.

7. Enter an identifier for the SGML document in the Repository ID field. The repository ID must conform to the following rules:

   – Less than 128 characters long

   – Cannot begin with an underscore (_) or at sign (@)

   – Cannot contain a vertical bar (|) or pound sign (#)

   – Minimal number of spaces used and use of the newline and tab characters avoided.

8. Select the root (/) project or another appropriate project for this document.

9. Select a File Type of SGML and then select the Load button.

10. Load any external entities (like illustrations) as File Objects.

LOADING FILE OBJECTS

File objects are any non-SGML-based files. These will typically contain graphics or other files that are inserted into your document. File objects can also be the original source files from a document conversion, the programs and tools used to create the converted documents. In short, a file object can be used to manage anything that you want that isn't SGML-based.

1. Start the Information Manager dashboard.

2. Select the Repository Administration Tool button from the dashboard.

3. Select the Repository Management button from the Repository Administration Tool.

4. Log on to the Repository Database as the dba or with an account having manager privileges for File Objects.

5. From the Repository Management tool, select the File Manager button.

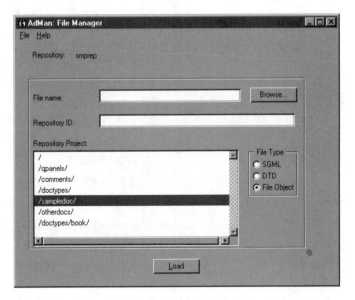

6. In the File name field, enter or select the name of the file to insert.

7. In the Repository Project field, select the project to add the file to.

8. In the Repository ID field, you can enter a name or let the system automatically supply an ID (I recommend that you supply a name that is meaningful to you as this is your only handle on the object being inserted). A repository ID must conform to the following rules:

   – Less than 128 characters long

- Cannot begin with an underscore (_) or at sign (@)
- Cannot contain a vertical bar (|) or pound sign (#)
- Minimal number of spaces used and use of the newline and tab characters avoided.

IM SYSTEM ADMINISTRATION

As you have seen in the previous steps to define, set up and start IM, there are a lot of details to the process. Most of the functions defined so far, and some that I won't be exploring in this book, are typically supported by a database administrator. It is possible to use just the tools provided by Texcel to manage the underlying database, but like anything, the more you understand about your tools and their capabilities the better you can use them. I'm not saying that you need to hire a full-time DBA to support the system, but you should dedicate and train two to three users of the system in all the details and appoint one of them as the primary DBA.

These are some of the areas that need dedicated support to make sure they are done consistently and accurately:

- Backup and system archives
- Data replication to multiple sites
- User administration
- Role definition and system privileges
- Database queries and reports
- System and database performance-tuning
- System resources allocation and management
- New report generation
- Query and trigger definitions
- Interfacing the document management system to other business systems.

Most of these issues and the techniques for managing them are what a trained DBA does in a typical day (maybe a week). I'm not saying that someone cannot be trained in your existing department, it is more a matter of how much time you can dedicate to allow the designated person to learn, experiment, make mistakes, and finally get up-to-speed before your system is fully functioning and adequately supported.

WORKFLOW MANAGEMENT

Workflows are the second aspect of IM. The first aspect is the previously described document management or repository side that acts as the librarian. It catalogues, tracks current location and ownership, validates and authorizes access to a document, and checks documents in and out. It also provides functions typically associated with software source code management systems. A source code management system provides versioning of pieces of code, archives changes and releases of products, and tracks links or cross-usage of program modules.

Workflow management provides the ability to have the system route and track at what stage of work or what task in a previously described flow a document is currently in. It allows tasks to be defined, it associates users or a designated group of users to be tasked with an assignment, and then it automatically reports on the status of all tasks in the defined workflow.

It is possible to use Texcel's Information Manger without ever using the workflow capabilities, or you can also interface a third-party workflow management system and use it instead.

With Texcel, you define a process in the Workflow Designer that maps to a standard real-world business process. A process is a model or outline for everything you want to do in a particular business process. You can define a large single process or build several smaller modules or nuggets of work and then link them together into a larger organization. Once you have this process model defined, you then apply it on a case-by-case (project-by-project) basis. An instance of the process model is a particular case of that model.

CREATING A PROCESS MODEL

A process model models an existing business process. So far in this book, we have used one business process to convert documents from FrameMaker format to our sample DTD form. Other processes were just ahead of the conversion process. We defined and refined the DTD and we built the OmniMark tools to handle the text conversion and graphic tools to capture the illustrations in the document.

Figure 16-3 illustrates the procedure we actually used in this book to convert the document from FrameMaker format to SGML and finally, in this chapter, to insert the document into our repository manager.

Figure 16-4 illustrates the typical (albeit simplified) process of revising a document, having it reviewed and reworked, and then finally releasing it. We will define these two procedures in IM.

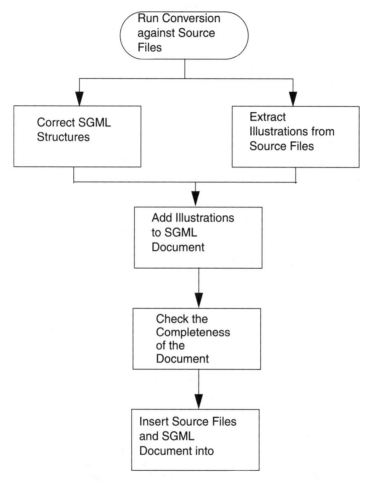

FIGURE 16-3. DOCUMENT CONVERSION BUSINESS PROCESS

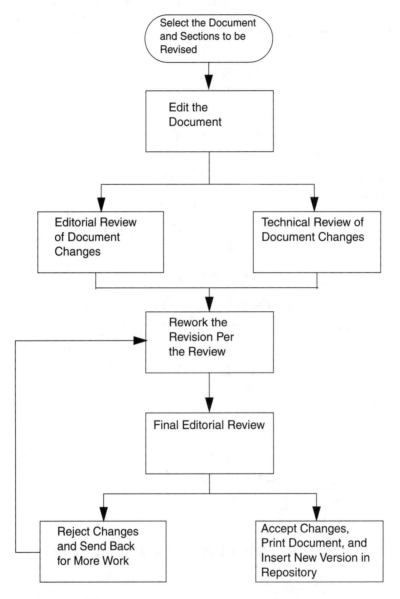

FIGURE 16-4. DOCUMENT REVISION BUSINESS PROCESS

To create a document revision process model:

1. Make sure that the Texcel database servers have been started.

2. Launch IM from the Windows Start Menu, under Texcel.

3. From the Information Manager Dashboard, select the Workflow Process Definition Tool button.

Properties Viewer Window

Main Window and
Workflow Canvas

Item Palette

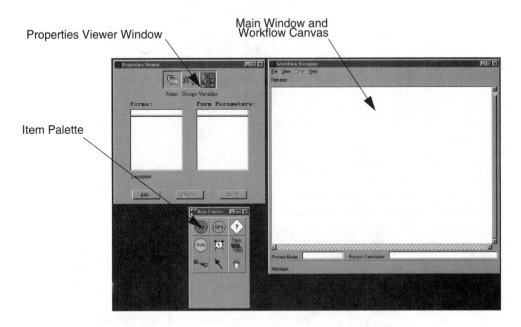

The Workflow Process Definition Tool consists of three separate windows as shown above.

4. In the Process Name field, enter the name of the new process model, doc_rev. In the Process Description field, enter a description of the process, "Document Revision Process".

5. Select Go or the start symbol from the Item Palette and drag it onto the Workflow Canvas.

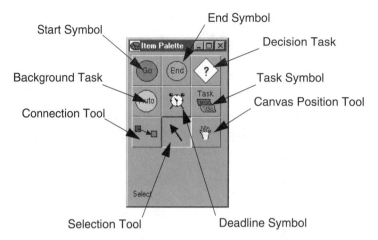

Start Symbol

End Symbol

Decision Task

Background Task

Task Symbol

Connection Tool

Canvas Position Tool

Selection Tool

Deadline Symbol

6. Double-click on the Go symbol on the Workflow Canvas to edit the symbol's attributes.

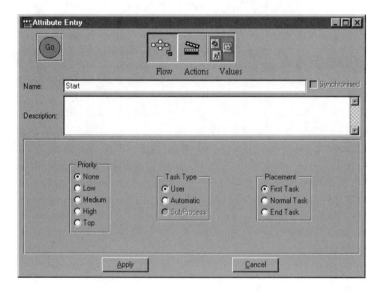

7. Enter the following information for the Go element of the workflow:

On the Flow screen, enter:

Description	Initiate Project
Priority	None
Task Type	User
Placement	First Task

8. On the Actions screen, enter:

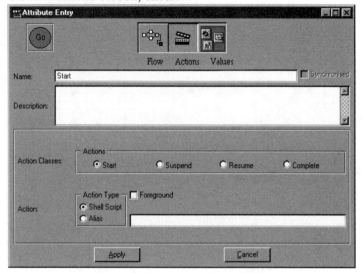

Action Classes	Start
Foreground	selected

9. On the Values screen, enter:

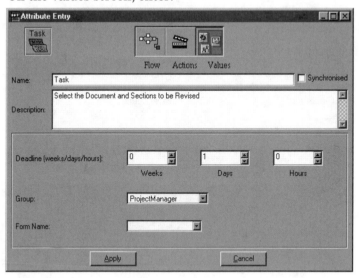

Deadline	1 Day
Group	Manager

10. Select the Task symbol from the Item Palette and drag it onto the Workflow Canvas.

11. Double-click on the Task symbol on the Workflow Canvas to edit the symbol's attributes.

12. On the Flow screen, enter:

Name	Select Sections
Description	Select the Document and Sections to be Revised
Priority	High
Task Type	User
Placement	Normal Task

13. On the Actions screen, enter:

Action Classes	Complete
Foreground	selected

14. On the Values screen, enter:

Deadline	1 Day
Group	ProjectManager

15. Select the Connection tool and connect the Go symbol to the Task symbol.
16. Select the Task symbol on the Item Palette and drag it onto the Workflow Canvas.
17. On the Flow screen, enter:

Name	Edit Document
Description	Edit the document
Priority	Top
Task Type	User
Placement	Normal Task

18. On the Actions screen, enter:

Action Classes	Start
Foreground	selected

19. On the Values screen, enter:

Deadline	6 Days
Group	Writer

20. Connect this new task to the right of the previous task.

21. Place two new Task symbols on the canvas to the right of the last task and stack these two new items one over the other. Select the top Task symbol:

22. On the Flow screen, enter:

Name	Tech Review
Description	Technical review of document changes
Priority	Medium
Task Type	User
Placement	Normal Task

23. On the Actions screen, enter:

Action Classes	Start
Foreground	selected

24. On the Values screen, enter:

Deadline	5 Days
Group	TechnicalReview

25. Select the bottom Task symbols.

26. On the Flow screen, enter:

Name	Editorial
Description	Editorial review of document changes
Priority	Medium
Task Type	User
Placement	Normal Task

27. On the Actions screen, enter:

Action Classes	Start
Foreground	selected

28. On the Values screen, enter:

Deadline	5 Days
Group	Editor

29. Connect the left sides of these two new task items to the right side of the previous Writer task.

30. Select a Task symbol on the Item Palette and drag it onto the Workflow Canvas to the right of the other symbols. Using the Connection tool, connect the right sides (two different flows) of the previous two tasks to the left side of this new task.

31. On the Flow screen, enter:

Name	Rework
Description	Rework the revision per review comments
Priority	Medium
Task Type	User
Placement	Normal Task

32. On the Actions screen, enter:

Action Classes	Start
Foreground	selected

33. On the Values screen, enter:

Deadline	3 Days
Group	Writer

34. Select a Task symbol on the Item Palette and drag it onto the Workflow Canvas to the right of the last symbol. Using the Connection tool, connect the right side of the previous task to the left side of this new task.

35. On the Flow screen, enter:

Name	Final Edit
Description	Final editorial review
Priority	Medium
Task Type	User
Placement	Normal Task

36. On the Actions screen, enter:

Action Classes	Start
Foreground	selected

37. On the Values screen, enter:

Deadline	2 Days
Group	Editor

38. Select a Decision symbol on the Item Palette and drag it onto the Workflow Canvas to the right of the last symbol. Using the Connection tool, connect the right side of the previous task to the left side of this new symbol.

39. On the Flow screen, enter:

Name	Ready to Print
Description	Final Editorial Review Status
Priority	Medium
Task Type	User
Placement	Normal Task

40. On the Actions screen, enter:

Action Classes   Start

Foreground   selected

41. From the Property Viewer, select the Variables button.

42. Select the Add... button:

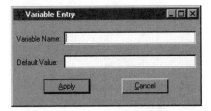

43. Add the Variable Name ReadyToPrint with a default value of No.

44. From the Property Viewer, select the Forms button.

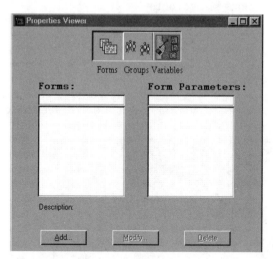

45. Select the Add... button.

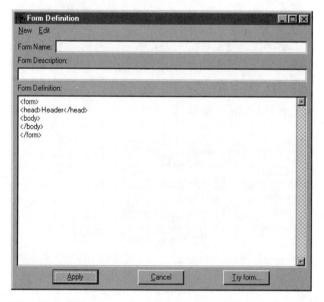

46. This form allows you to define the look-and-feel of a dialog box that is displayed at the decision task stage of the workflow. Enter a Form Name of `FinalEdit`, and set the Form Description to: "`Decision to send document to Printer or back for more Re-work`".

47. From the New menu, select Entry and then Selection.

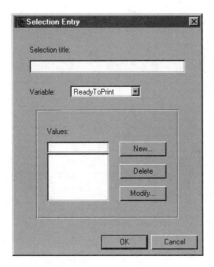

48. Enter the following as the Selection title: "Is the document ready to print?" Variable should be set to ReadyToPrint. Add a New... value to the selection.

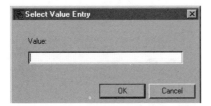

49. Add a value of Yes and then add No.

50. From the Edit menu, select Select and then Header. Next, select Edit from the Edit menu. Change the value Header to Final Review Results.

51. View the results of your design by selecting the Try Form button.

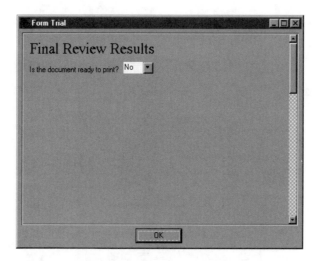

52. Apply the changes to this form.

53. Select the Decision Task.

54. On the Values screen, enter:

Deadline	1 hour
Group	Editor
Form Name	FinalEdit

55. Select a Task symbol on the Item Palette and drag it onto the Workflow Canvas to the right of the Decision symbol. Using the Connection tool, connect the right side of the previous task to the left side of this new task.

56. On the Flow screen, enter:

Name	Print & Release
Description	Print and release the document back to the repository
Priority	Medium
Task Type	User
Placement	Normal Task

57. On the Actions screen, enter:

Action Classes	Start
Foreground	selected

58. On the Values screen, enter:

Deadline	3 Days
Group	Production

59. Using the Connection tool, connect the Ready to Print Decision Task back to the Rework Task.

60. Select the End symbol on the Item Palette and drag it onto the Workflow Canvas to the right of the last Task symbol. Using the Connection tool, connect the right side of the previous task to the left side of the End symbol.

61. On the Flow screen, enter:

Name	End
Description	Replace document in repository
Priority	None
Task Type	User
Placement	End Task

62. On the Actions screen, enter:

Action Classes	Start
Foreground	selected

63. On the Values screen, enter:

Deadline	1 Day
Group	Production

64. From the Canvas Window menu, select Parse and then Parse Flow. If any errors are reported, you must fix them before continuing.

65. Save the workflow with the name docrev. Compare Figure 16-5 to Figure 16-4.

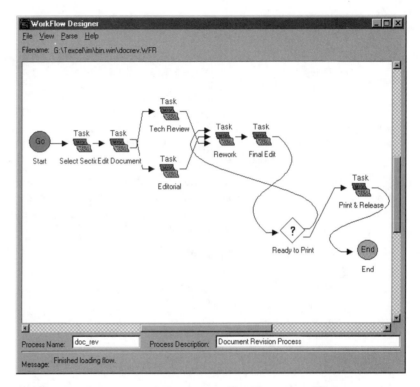

FIGURE 16-5. DOCUMENT REVISION PROCESS IN WORKFLOW DESIGNER

66. Generate a workflow script by selecting Generate Script from the Parse menu.

67. Close the Workflow Process Definition Tool and open the Workflow Administration Tool.

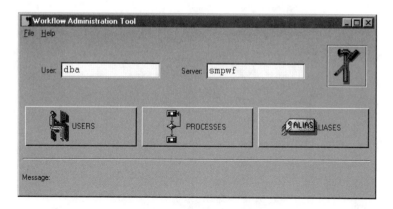

68. Select the PROCESSES button from the Workflow Process
Definition Tool.

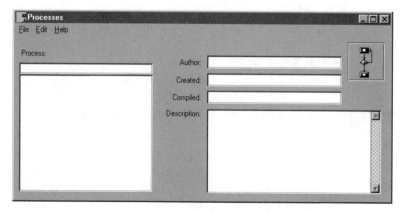

69. Select File, New from the Processes window.

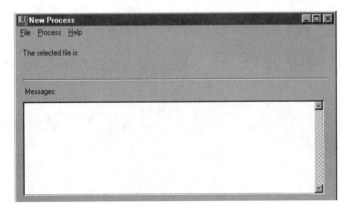

70. From the File menu of the New Process panel, select Open.

71. Select the workflow or process script to compile, in this case, `docrev.wfs`.

72. From the Process menu, select Compile. Commit the transaction if everything is okay with the script. Fix any problems that may be listed in the messages window.

USING THE TEXCEL INFORMATION MANAGER

Information Manager is composed of two separate programs or tools. The Workflow tool manages processes and procedures and the Repository Manager acts as a librarian for your documents. In the previous sections, we configured the ability to use both of these tools. You don't have to implement both portions of the product, however. The following sections show how to use both tools.

DIRECT REPOSITORY USE

Document repositories are managed by a database. Within a repository, documents are organized by projects. Projects can be used to control access privileges to different documents. To use a repository, a user must know the name of the repository, the project that contains the document, and the name of the document. Of course, an account with the proper privileges is also required.

DOCUMENT BROWSER

To browse a document repository:

1. Make sure that the Texcel database servers have been started.
2. Launch IM from the Windows Start Menu, under Texcel.
3. From the Information Manager Dashboard, select Select Repository from the File menu.

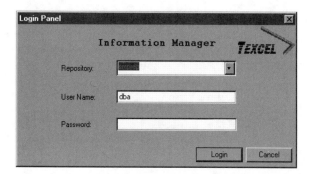

4. Enter the Repository to open, your User Name, and Password.
5. From the Information Dashboard, select the Repository Browser Tool.

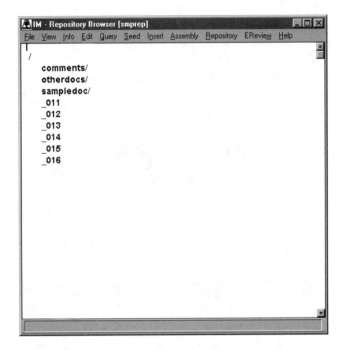

The browser window displays the names of the projects within this repository; comments is the project that IM uses to store electronic review comments, otherdocs and sampledoc are the projects that we defined.

6. Double-click on the sampledoc/ project.

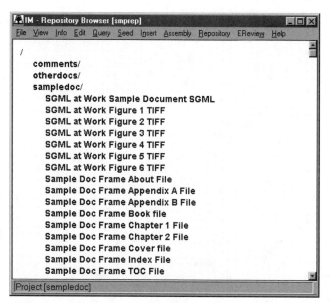

This first level of the sampledoc/ project contains the SGML document entry and any file objects that are part of the project. The display is color coded as follows: blue indicates a document (SGML) that can be expanded; a green entry is a file object.

7. Double-click on SGML at Work Sample Document SGML to expand the SGML structure. Select several elements in the same way until you expose some of the document structure and find some content.

```
IM - Repository Browser [smprep]                      _ □ X
File  View  Info  Edit  Query  Seed  Insert  Assembly  Repository  EReview  Help

  /
      comments/
      otherdocs/
      sampledoc/
          SGML at Work Sample Document SGML
          book
              cover
              copyright
              toc
              lof
              preface
              body
                  section
                      title
                          Okatqxtxr kwo Oaalwosxr aso Xlaazav

                      para
                      bullet-list
                          item
                          item

Element [_0132]
```

EDITING SECTIONS OF CONTENT

To edit a section of the document:

1. Make sure that the Texcel database servers have been started.

2. Launch IM from the Windows Start Menu, under Texcel.

3. From the Information Manager Dashboard, choose Select Repository from the File menu.

4. Enter the name of the repository to open, your user name, and password.

5. From the Information Dashboard, select the Repository Browser Tool.

6. Find the document and the portion that you want to edit and select it in the browser window.

7. From the Edit menu, select Reserve. The section of the document you reserved is displayed in the ADEPT•Editor.

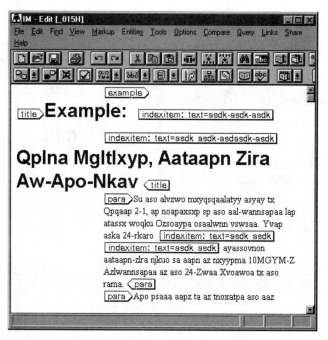

8. Enter some changes in the document.

9. If, after making several changes, you want to compare versions of the document, you can. From the Compare menu, select Current. The following shows what the two document views look like:

Double View

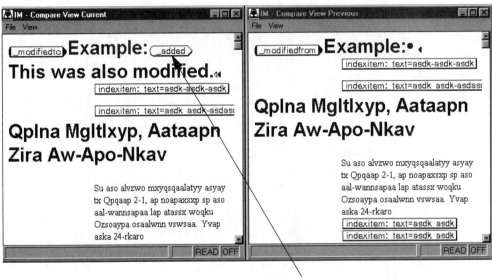

Composite View

Change Marks

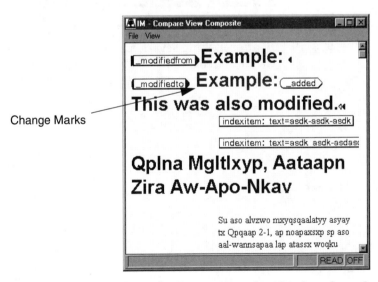

Change Marks

10. When you are finished editing the document, select Replace from the File menu.

Using Electronic Review

Electronic review (EReview) is an application built into the ArborText environment (the repository browser is also). EReview is an editing or review process that allows a reviewer to select sections of text and associate comments with it. After reviewing the document, it is replaced in the database and then checked out by the writer to incorporate the comments. If more than one reviewer makes comments, the writer can organize comments by reviewer, document location, comment type, or priority of the comment.

This entire process of tracking comments, the author, and where a comment is attached is maintained outside the original source documents. Essentially, the source document is in a read-only mode. Comments are created in a secondary file and attached to elements in the original document via IDs. The typical ereview process is:

1. Reserve the document and comment by one or more reviewers.

2. Commit the comments to the repository.

3. Writer then reserves the document and reviews the comments. Comments can be accepted or rejected; their status and disposition are tracked as the writer decides what to do with each comment.

4. Writer places document back into repository with comments incorporated.

5. Reviewer may review comments and the disposition to verify that the writer has incorporated them (this step may not have been done with a paper-based review process).

Reviewing a Document

To review a document:

1. Make sure that the Texcel database servers have been started.

2. Launch IM from the Windows Start Menu, under Texcel.

3. From the Information Manager Dashboard, choose Select Repository from the File menu.

4. Enter the name of the repository to open, your user name, and password.

5. From the Information Dashboard, select the Repository Browser Tool.

6. Find the document and the portion that you want to have reviewed.

7. From the EReview menu, select Review.

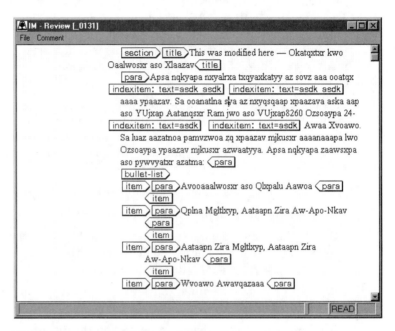

8. Place the cursor within the block of text you wish to comment upon. From the Comment menu, select Create.

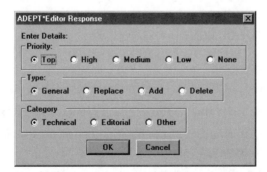

9. Enter the priority of the comment, the type, and the category.

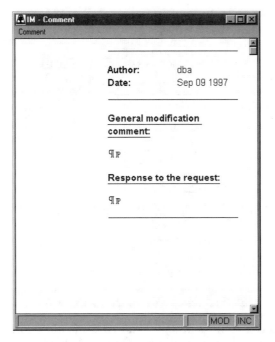

10. A dialog box displays the reviewer's name and current date. The reviewer enters a comment in the comment field. Later, after the writer has incorporated the changes and either accepted or rejected the comment, the reviewer can review the comments and their status with the information provided in the response section.

11. From the Comment menu, select Done to enter the comment or quit.

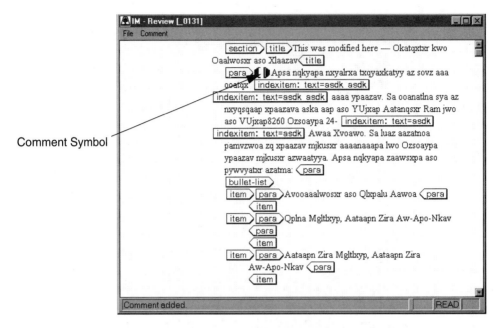

Comment Symbol

When a comment is accepted, a symbol is placed in the text (at the start of the element content). By double-clicking the left mouse button on this symbol, you can review the comment at that location.

12. As more comments are added to the document, you may need to review them or determine their location. A List Comments command allows the reviewer to locate comments, as well as those of any other reviewer of the document. From the Comments menu, select List, then All.

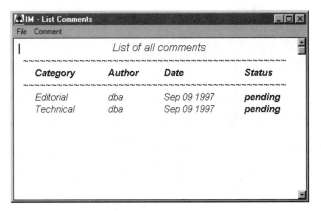

This panel lists all the comments in the document and the author. By simply double-clicking on a comment, you will be taken to the location with the comment displayed.

AUTOCOMMENT MODE REVISIONS

AutoComment mode allows a reviewer to enter comments directly into the body of a document. Even though it appears that the reviewer's entries are modifying the document, they are actually being logged to an outside comment file. After completing the review, each block of text commented upon will be entered into its own comment box, where it can be prioritized and categorized.

To review a document:

1. Make sure that the Texcel database servers have been started.

2. Launch IM from the Windows Start Menu, under Texcel.

3. From the Information Manager Dashboard, choose Select Repository from the File menu.

4. Enter the name of the repository to open, your user name, and password.

5. From the Information Dashboard, select the Repository Browser Tool.

6. Find the document and the portion that you want to review.

7. From the EReview menu, select Review.

8. From the comment window, select the Start AutoComment Mode from the Comment menu. A message box is displayed stating that the document is in autocomment mode and you should only make textual changes, not changes to the document structure.

9. Enter the text changes or comments directly into the document, don't change any of the SGML markup.

10. When you finish entering comments, select End AutoComment Mode from the Comments menu.

11. Enter the priority and categorization of each comment entered.

12. Select Save + Exit from the File menu.

INCORPORATING REVIEW COMMENTS

After a document is reviewed by one or more reviewers, the writer needs to examine the comments in context and decide if or how they should be incorporated into the document.

To incorporate review comments:

1. Make sure that the Texcel database servers have been started.

2. Launch IM from the Windows Start Menu, under Texcel.

3. From the Information Manager Dashboard, choose Select Repository from the File menu.

4. Enter the name of the repository to open, your user name, and password.

5. From the Information Dashboard, select the Repository Browser Tool.

6. Select the project and document with outstanding (un-incorporated) comments. From the EReview menu, select Update with Comments.

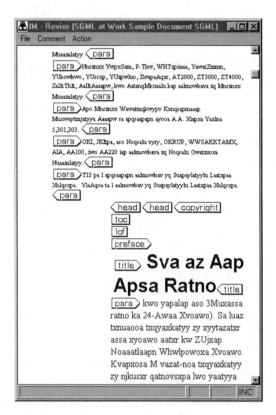

7. From the Comment menu, select List, then All.

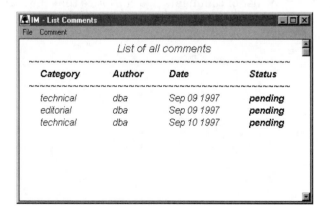

This displays a list of all the comments that are contained in the current document. Other options let you list comments by reviewer or priority. Select one of the entries to view a comment.

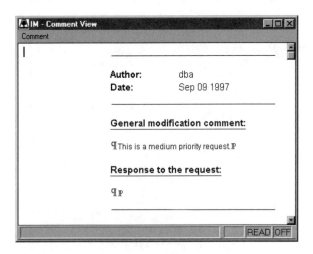

8. Review the comment. From the Action menu, select the appropriate responses to the comment. You have the option of accepting the comment and incorporating the text directly or accepting the comment and entering it yourself. In all cases, the action or disposition of the comment is recorded with each comment.

    You can make additional comments about a comment from the dialog box in the Response to the request section.

9. View the list of comments again. Notice that the status of any comment accepted or rejected is posted.

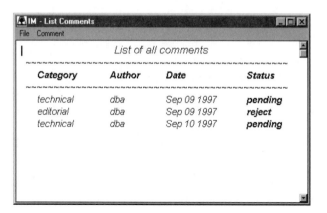

REVIEWING COMMENT STATUS

To review the status of a comment:

1. Make sure that the Texcel database servers have been started.

2. Launch IM from the Windows Start Menu, under Texcel.

3. From the Information Manager Dashboard, choose Select Repository from the File menu.

4. Enter the name of the repository to open, your user name, and password.

5. From the Information Dashboard, select the Repository Browser Tool.

6. Select the project and document with outstanding (un-incorporated) comments. From the EReview menu, select Update with Comments.

7. From the Comment menu, select List, then All.

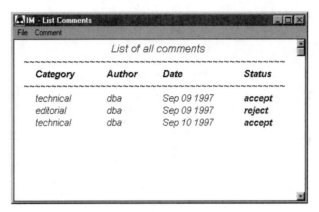

8. Select a comment to review.

The disposition of the comment is shown in the list box. The comment dialog box will display any responses the writer may have logged with the comment.

Using a Workflow

Creating a Workflow Case

A workflow case is a specific instance of a previously defined process or workflow.

To create a document revision case:

1. Make sure that the Texcel database servers have been started.

2. Launch IM from the Windows Start Menu, under Texcel.

3. From the Information Manager Dashboard, select the Workflow Management Tool button.

4. From the Case menu, select Create.

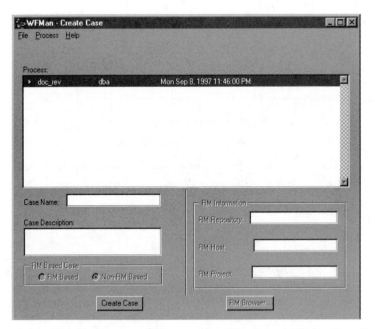

5. Enter SampleCase as the name for this case. Add the description "This is a sample case using the docrev Process."

6. Select the Create Case button. The main Case window is updated as follows.

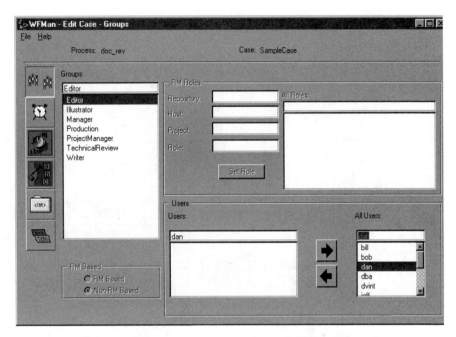

7. Assign users to the various groups defined. This allows the users assigned to a particular group to be able to look at all tasks for that group. Select the group name in the Groups field. Now, select each username for the All Users column and select the left-pointing arrow button to add the name to the list.

    If a name is on the list and you want to remove it, simply select the name in the Users column and then select the right-pointing arrow.

8. Select the Alarm Clock button to set deadlines for any of the tasks in the process.

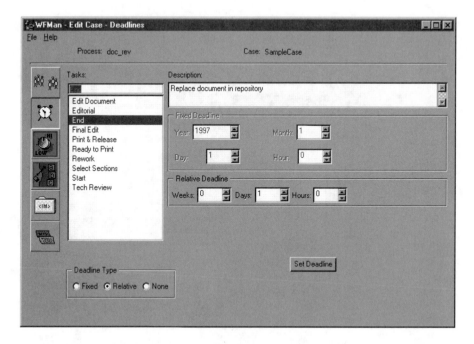

Any task can be selected and a relative or fixed deadline can be specified. Relative deadlines that were specified in the definition of the process are set as a default; this mechanism allows you to override those values or to set specific dates.

9. Select the Hi/Low button to set the priority of a task.

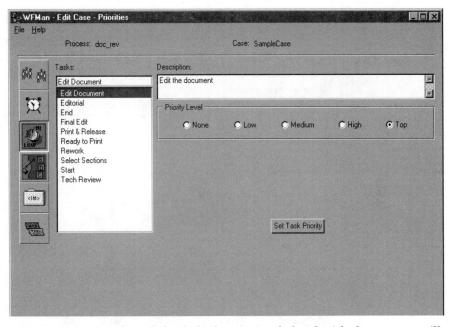

10. Select any task and the default priority defined with the process will be displayed. Select a new priority as desired.

11. Select the Folder button to add documents or information concerning this case to any task.

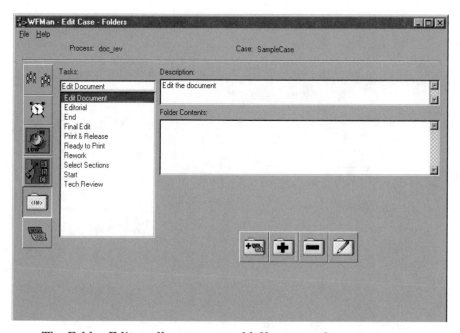

The Folder Editor allows you to add filesystem documents, repository documents, or scripts to the task folder. Items can be added or removed to all tasks by selecting the folders with the large plus or minus signs. The folder with the task icon and a plus sign allows you to add an item to a specific task folder. The icon with the pencil allows you to edit an item in the task folder.

The following panel allows you to add various objects to the task folder:

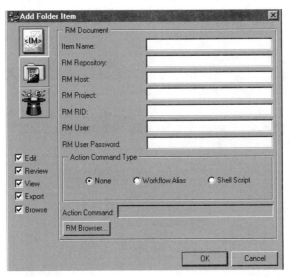

12. Select the Task button to specify the user to which the task is
    assigned.

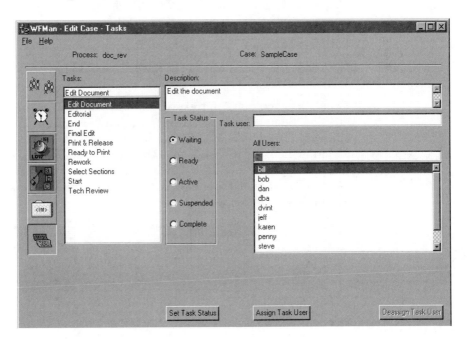

The Task Assignment editor allows you to specify the owner of a task. Select a user ID from the All Users field and then select Assign Task User.

To unassign a user, select the Deassign Task User button.

13. Once a case has been fully defined and assigned, you can start it. From the Workflow Management Tool panel, select the Start button.

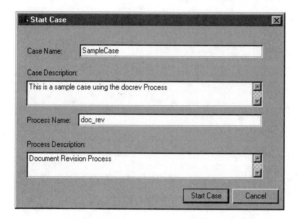

14. If the information on the panel is correct, select the Start Case button; otherwise, modify the information and then start it.

Note that the status column of the case should have changed from Waiting to Active.

15. Users assigned tasks in this workflow are notified as their tasks are enabled. Some actions are serial and some, like the technical and editorial review, can be accomplished in parallel. As each task is accomplished, the user indicates the completion of the task, at which point the next task in the sequence is activated. Each user has his or her own work queue to monitor to determine when a task becomes available to work on.

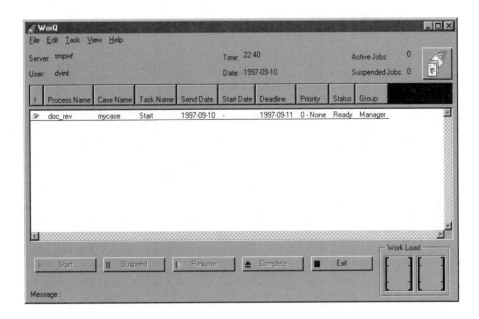

OBSERVATIONS

A document management system like Texcel's Information Manager provides the capability that SGML itself was believed to provide in the early days of SGML implementations. With a document management system, you get the ability to easily manage files, their relationships to graphics and source materials, as well as the ability to manage day-to-day work process. The document management system provides a transparent (once it is configured and readied for users) way to manage information and content across multiple sources.

As you can see from the process documented here, nothing comes for free. You must set up the system, define your business process, and then use them to gain potential advances. The better and more thorough your definition process up-front before implementing a system like this, the more successful it will be.

GLOSSARY

application

A text or SGML application provides the required set of processes to produce a given publication.

ASCII

American Standard Code for Information Interchange. A method for representing characters in text as a sequence of bits (1's and 0's). These are 7-bit characters, 8-bits with parity check.

atomic flow object

A flow object that has no parts.

authoring tools

The portion of a text or SGML application that provides support for the creation of a document. Typically this is the editor.

BLOBs

Binary Large Objects are a method of storage in databases. Typically, a BLOB is a single field of very large size that cannot be examined internally and is managed with metadata about the object.

browser

A tool that allows the user to view and browse a document online. Most people use Netscape or Internet Explorer to browse the WWW, there are browsers available to view and search SGML documents.

camera-ready copy (CRC)

CRC is the final product that is created during the publishing process, just prior to going to press. CRC is a hardcopy version of the document, with all graphics and text in place. CRC is then sent to the press department where negatives will be made and then plates made for printing.

computer graphics metafile (CGM)

An ISO standard for the representation of graphical information. This is a standard notation for graphics markup.

components

See styles.

composition engine

A composer or composition engine is typically used to interpret electronic data and its markup to create camera-ready-copy. It is during composition that typographic rules are applied. Your typical desktop publishing system provides this functionality as a feature of the tool and is typically not a separate tool.

computer-aided drafting (CAD)

Some of the first computer based tools for generating graphics were CAD systems. CAD systems were typically high-end drafting and modeling tools used by designers and drafters. CAD systems have proprietary formats for managing their information and typically can be exported to standard formats like IGES or CGM.

conditional text

A feature of desktop publishing systems that allows text to be generated based upon conditions or rules.

conversion tools

Conversion tools are all the tools and programming languages required to convert information. Conversions are performed on text and graphics. Conversion tools can be programming languages like perl or C that don't provide any specific help, or like OmniMark that has been tailored to provide extra support.

cross translate

An OmniMark mode of programming in which data is translated from one form to another. In OmniMark this typically would be formats that weren't based upon SGML.

cross references

Cross references occur in documents as references to other sections of a document or other materials. A cross reference can be created as a pure text reference or tools can be provided to support the placement and management of the references so they will always be correct. Typical tool support includes generating text, automatic update of the text, support for finding references and broken references.

delivery tools

Delivery tools are the applications associated for delivering the final product to the end user. For hardcopy documents this is the composer and the paper copy. Online delivery tools include WWW browsers, SGML browsers, CD-ROM-based browsers, etc.

desktop publishing (DTP)

A publishing system typically based upon a desktop PC or Macintosh platform and software.

document

Traditionally a document is thought of as a text and graphics, and its primary purpose is to be printed. When a document is referred to in this text it is meant to represent an information object, comprised of multiple-media types, that may never be printed in book form, and may be managed in a way that doesn't represent any final product being produced.

document analysis

Process which produces a DTD. Typically this requires looking at a sample set of publications, interviewing writers and production staff, and planning for future reuse of the information. The process of analyzing a document is similar to the process required to design a database schema.

document conversion

Process that transforms a document or publication in one format, into another. Document conversion typically must convert graphics as well as text. Other special features like database connectivity, tables, and equations, may be addressed as well.

document management

The process of maintaining a set of electronic data through the life cycle of the publication. Typically this is managing files in the operating system, maintaining version control and access, and archiving files.

document management systems (DMS)

A DMS is generally a tool that provides support for the typical document management process. A DMS may just control access better than a file-system-based approach or it may provide special support for SGML data.

document type definition (DTD)

The definition of the markup rules for a given type of document. Defines the structure of a document, similar to the schema of a database.

down translate

An OmniMark mode of programming in which data is translated from SGML to a lower form of information. Examples would be converting SGML to HTML or SGML to RTF or some other DTP format for printing.

DTD development tools

Any tool that provides support for developing a DTD. Many SGML editing systems require the DTD to be precompiled, I do not include these applications in this category.

editor

Editor can be a person like a technical or copy editor who preforms a specific step in a document life cycle. An editor can also be the application that is used to modify the content and structure of a document.

equations

Mathematical or chemical equations appear in many technical documents. There are several proposed ways to markup equations which range from accounting for every symbol and its position, to identifying an equation by name and letting the application determine the proper form of the equation to display.

flow object

A specification of a task to be preformed by the formatter. A flow object has a class, which specifies a task type and characteristics, which further parameterize the task.

FOSI (formatted output specification instance)

An instance of the Output Specification used to format a particular document type.

galley

A galley is a proof copy of a document printed in a long strip of output from a typesetter. A galley may have only the content of the pages, with no page breaks, headers and footers, or page numbers.

graphical user interface (GUI)

A GUI is the boundary between the user and the software. A good GUI design is intuitive and complete, a bad design is confusing and impossible to use.

graphics designer

A person typically responsible for the layout and design of the pages of a document.

graphics support

DTP and SGML systems typically provide support for multiple graphics formats. Although DTP systems are typically configured to support printable graphics, an SGML system allows for the use of a notation type. The graphics support within an SGML system may only include a subset of all the notation types that can be supported in SGML.

grove

A set of nodes connected into a graph by their nodal properties. A grove is built using a grove plan.

headers and footers

Headers and footers are the area at the top (header) and bottom (footer) of a page when printed. Typically information in these areas is a combination of static text (name of the document) with generated information like the current chapter and section name or page number. The generation of a header or footer is part of the composition process and is typically not an SGML markup issue.

HTML (Hypertext Markup Language)

The WWW developed this markup standard. Over time the SGML community has influenced the design to make it more conformant to SGML standards, but today's WWW browsers do not validate the HTML based upon any DTD.

hypertext

Hypertext is an electronic form of cross referencing. Hypertext can be the authored links in a document to other locations, electronic bookmarks, or user developed links.

IAF (Interleaf ASCII Format)

The proprietary markup format used by Interleaf to export a document in an ASCII markup, similar to RTF or MIF.

illustrations

Illustrations are additions to the text of a document and can include; screen shots, line art, photographs, flow charts, charts and diagrams. Illustrations may be improved or referenced by name into a DTP system depending upon the user and the DTP system features. Each type of illustration may have a different graphic format associated with it.

illustrator

An illustrator in a traditional publications department was typically responsible for the creation of all graphics or illustrations in the document and may also have graphic designer responsibilities. Since the advent of DTP, writers have typically had to build skills in this area.

indexes and indexing

Indexes are typical features of printed books. An index is a finding or research aid to locate information quickly in a book. DTP systems provide special features and support for creating markers to locate the information and then methods to extract and order that information for presentation.

instance

The marked up textual data comprises the instance of a document type. This is the portion that you author.

interactive technical manual

An interactive technical manual is a combination of static data, programming, and dynamic presentation of information. The interactive technical manual or document is the next generation of documentation. An interactive document will tailor itself to the user and the particular procedure being accomplished.

Initial Graphics Exchange Specification (IGES)

IGES is an ISO standard for capturing complex CAD information so it can be interchanged between systems.

ISO

International Standards Organization. ISO provides a standard process for developing and improving standards.

JETT methodology

The JETT or just-enough-this-time method is an approach for sizing and managing an SGML implementation. JETT helps managers and implementors identify the best users to implement for and which features to implement first.

links

Links or linking is the mechanism typically used to provide hypertext functionality. A link has a start and end point. On many systems links are one directional.

markup

Markup is used to indicate processing and commands in a document. Markup has existed ever since wordprocessing and DTP systems were created. A program that adds styles or controls the formatting of text has to place something (markup) in the text stream to indicate where these features should be triggered. The proprietary markup formats like MIF, RTF, and IAF have existed since their programs were first developed. SGML is a standard way of defining this markup.

metadata

Metadata is data about data. For instance the data a file is edited, the authors working on, version of software are all metadata items for a chapter.

MIF (Maker Interchange Format)

The proprietary ASCII markup version of a FrameMaker document. This is similar to IAF or RTF.

MIS

Management Information Systems department.

multimedia

Multimedia is the term applied to applications that coordinate music, sound, graphics and texts in a streamed or programmed application.

multiple-media

Multiple-media is an approach to managing many types of media (sound, video, graphics, and text) and their various media output types (paper, WWW, CD-ROM, etc.)

native SGML tools

Native SGML tools are tools that were built from the start to understand SGML. All or most of the SGML features and constructs are supported natively by design.

negative

A negative is photographically produced from the camera-ready-copy. The negative is then used to expose the printing plates.

nodal property

A property whose value is a node or list of nodes. Nodal properties are categorized by their property set as subnode, irefnode, or urefnode.

node

An ordered set of property assignments. A node is a member of a grove, and belongs to a class defined in the grove plan used to build its grove.

non-native SGML tools

Non-native SGML tools are tools that started as proprietary designs and have provided a layer to support the use of SGML. Typically tools in this category work easily with SGML if the structures are similar. When an SGML feature varies drastically from the base tool or isn't supported at all then it becomes very difficult to support or implement those features. Many non-native tools require extra work or programming to allow them to deal with standard SGML structures.

notations

Notations refer to the format of the data. Every file created on a computer has some notation (or format) related to it. SGML provides a standard method for naming the notation and then assigning that property to entities.

operating system

An operating system is available on every computer. DOS, UNIX, and VMS are examples of operating systems. The operating system manages system resources (memory, disk management, file permissions, etc.) at a very low (machine) level so that higher level programs and users do not have to worry about these details.

RAD (Rapid Application Development)

A software engineering method for deriving requirements and designing systems that meet user requirements.

RTF (Rich Text Format)

The Microsoft-Word standard ASCII markup format.

SGML

Standard generalized markup language.

SGML declaration

Defines which characters are used in the document instance, which features and syntax the DTD is written to and uses. A default is generally assumed, as per the standard, but it may also be provided.

SGML parser

A program that recognizes SGML markup in a document and understands the standard SGML rules and features.

SGML systems integration

Currently there are no single out-of-the-box SGML solutions. To make a complete working system, various components must be integrated to make them function smoothly.

siblings (of a node)

The other nodes in the grove that occur in the value of the origin-to-subnode relationship property of the origin of the node.

stream

An ordered list of flow objects attached to a port of a flow object.

style guide

Typically a style guide is a written document that explains the documentation standards of a given group. Although there are some commercial or industry standard style guides, most organizations have tailored their own set of requirements.

styles

DTP systems or advance wordprocessors (like MS-Word) provide style sheets and styles (or components) to control formatting across large documents. Styles are similar to SGML tags in that they allow you to name a feature and then associate formatting with that feature. Styles do not manage the structure of a document and on many systems they cannot be included within styles.

subtree

A node together with the subtrees of its children.

table models

Several table models have become standard features of SGML tools. Typically the CALS and Oasis table models are supported with possibly a proprietary table model as well. These table models provide the support for creating tabular information, but they don't allow the information that is being modeled to reflect the data and its relationships rather than a specific tabular presentation.

tables

Tables are used to present information in a compact matrix of information. A table is considered one presentation or model of the information being provided. A table, for instance, that displays a column of dates and several columns of data, could just as easily be presented as a bar or line chart. Various table models have been defined for the presentation and editing of this information as rows and columns. Many of the SGML vendors have provided support for these models but they cannot support a generic formatting of information.

transformation process

The process specified by the transformation language. It transforms one or more SGML documents into zero or more other SGML documents.

tree

The subtree of a node that has no parent.

typesetter

A typesetter is the machine that takes text with markup and produces the galley or camera-ready-copy. A typesetter can also be the person operating the machine.

typography

The application and selection of typefaces or fonts, their sizes and relationship to the page (or screen). A graphics designer studies typefaces and how they complement each other.

up translate

An OmniMark mode of programming in which data is translated from lower form to an SGML form. The data is being pumped-up in capability. In OmniMark this would typically be formats like RTF or HTML that were converted to a specific DTD.

valid SGML

An SGML instance that will parse successfully without any errors.

workflow systems (WFS)

A workflow system is typically part of a DMS. A WFS provides the tracking and reporting of status as well as task management. Tasks can either be interactive activities or programmatic.

writer

The creator and maintainer of a document.

WWW

The World Wide Web.

A

SGML 101:
How to Read a DTD

My intention in this appendix is to provide the basic syntax and vocabulary required to implement and troubleshoot the SGML tools presented in this book. Refer to Appendix G for a list of books and other resources that fully explain all the details of the SGML standard. The features of SGML described herein concern the basic syntax and objects that are files in the operating system, or that require setup and configuration.

Parts of an SGML Document

An SGML document consists of three primary parts:

- SGML declaration file- optional
- Document Type Definition (DTD)
- Document instance

Figure A-1 illustrates the relationship of these parts. The declaration file specifies:

- Optional SGML features used
- Character sets used
- SGML syntax delimiters mapped to actual characters
- Capacities and limits.

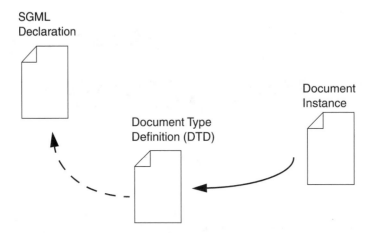

SGML
Declaration

Document
Instance

Document Type
Definition (DTD)

FIGURE A-1. PARTS OF AN SGML SYSTEM

The DTD specifies:

- Element types, which provide structure and rules of usage

- attributes, which provide additional information or properties of an element.

The structure of the document is governed by a particular DTD. The heart of an SGML tool is the SGML parser. The parser reads the declaration and DTD and then analyzes and validates the document instance against those rules.

PORTABILITY

The basic premise of SGML's is that there should be no surprises when a document is to be reused. Some potential causes of a surprise are:

- Document uses more resources than are available to process it

- Unknown character set used

- Names are excessive in length and invalid characters are used in names

- Markup characters used

- Special characters used.

The SGML declaration file contains all the information to answer these issues. A basic SGML document uses a default set of values called the reference concrete syntax and reference capacity set. A basic SGML document doesn't require a separate declaration file, but there are instances where you will need to expand the basic capabilities. Figure A-2 shows such a modified SGML declaration file.

The SGML declaration file has seven sections, which are documented in Table A-1. The line numbers in this table refer to Figure A-2. The SGML standard allows great flexibility using the SGML features and mapping SGML syntax to actual character strings. The basic syntax and many of the default values work well for English-speaking countries, but in a non-English, multibyte character set environment, you might need to redefine the markup. The SGML declaration file is where you make these adjustments.

Because of this flexibility, you could create an SGML declaration that could be used to create a document which most SGML users would claim to be invalid, if they didn't check the settings in the SGML declaration.

Table A-1. Sections of an SGML Declaration

SGML Declaration Component	Line in Figure A-2	Notes
Header	1	Identifies the version of the SGML standard to which this declaration conforms.
CHARSET	2–19	Typically a public identifier
CAPACITY	20–23	Can be a public identifier. Occasionally, a large document will require these values to be changed.
SCOPE	24	Indicates that the following character set applies to document and prolog or document only.

Table A-1. Sections of an SGML Declaration (continued)

SGML Declaration Component	Line in Figure A-2	Notes
SYNTAX	25-47	Contains the NAMECASE and QUANTITY entries that are typically modified. NAMECASE controls case-sensitivity of tag names and entities. In QUANTITY, NAMELEN sets the maximum length of a tag name, and LITLEN sets the maximum length of a text entity.
FEATURES	48	Indicates which optional SGML features are to be allowed. Generally, OMITTAG is used and SHORTREF is not, but with SGML-aware authoring, this feature is not often used/respected.
APPINFO	52	NONE or a string that is passed to the application or document.

I would recommend making minimal changes to the declaration, unless you have a real need. A few areas that are typically changed to allow greater flexibility in naming elements and creating text entities; these are noted in Table A-1, many more are listed in the SGML standard, and some of the most useful ones are pointed out in Table A-2.

```
 1 <!SGML "ISO 8879:1986"
 2 CHARSET
 3 BASESET "ISO 646-1983//CHARSET International Reference Version
 4         (IRV)//ESC 2/5 4/0"
 5 DESCSET    0     9   UNUSED
 6            9     2   9
 7           11     2   UNUSED
 8           13     1   13
 9           14    18   UNUSED
10           32    95   32
11          127     1   UNUSED
12 BASESET   "ISO Registration Number 100//CHARSET ECMA-94
13          Right Part of Latin Alphabet Nr. 1//ESC 2/13 4/1"
14 DESCSET  128        32   UNUSED
15         160         5   32
16         165         1   UNUSED
17         166        88   38
18         254         1   127
19         255         1   UNUSED
20 CAPACITY   SGMLREF
21            TOTALCAP    175000
22            GRPCAP       70000
23            ATTCAP       50000
24 SCOPE      DOCUMENT
25 SYNTAX
26 SHUNCHAR CONTROLS 0 1 2 3 4 5 6 7 8 9 10 11 12 13 14 15 16 17
27     18 19 20 21 22 23 24 25 26 27 28 29 30 31 127 255
28 BASESET "ISO 646-1983//CHARSET International Reference Version
29         (IRV)//ESC 2/5 4/0"
30 DESCSET    0        128            0
31 FUNCTION   RE         13
32            RS         10
33            SPACE      32
34            TAB      SEPCHAR       9
35 NAMING     LCNMSTRT   ""
36            UCNMSTRT   ""
37            LCNMCHAR   "-."
38            UCNMCHAR   "-.
39            NAMECASE   GENERAL    YES
40                       ENTITY     NO
41 DELIM      GENERAL    SGMLREF
42            SHORTREF   NONE
43 NAMES      SGMLREF
44 QUANTITY   SGMLREF    LITLEN     2048
45                       NAMELEN      32
46                       ATTCNT       80
47                       GRPCNT       64
48 FEATURES   MINIMIZE   DATATAG   NO   OMITTAG   YES   RANK     NO
49                       SHORTTAG  NO
50            LINK       SIMPLE    NO   IMPLICIT  NO    EXPLICIT  NO
51            OTHER      CONCUR    NO   SUBDOC    NO    FORMAL   YES
52 APPINFO    NONE >
```

FIGURE A-2. SAMPLE DECLARATION FILE

Because the SGML declaration can specify a different character set for the document instance than the DTD, the standard requires the declaration file to be specified in ASCII format so it is always readable. This requirement creates the need for the SGML declaration file to always be in a separate file from the DTD and document instance. The SGML declaration and its location is one of the first SGML constructs that you must be aware of. Most applications default to a basic SGML document, but allow you to change this default configuration.

PUBLIC IDENTIFIERS

A public identifier is generally used to identify external files or objects that you want to share between applications or globally define. The actual public identifier has a specific syntax that identifies the content of the object being referred to, the owner, and the language encoding. Figure A-3 illustrates the parts of a public identifier with two examples. The first line shows a typical ISO-owned or -registered entity and defined entity, the second line shows an unregistered entity that refers to the DTD that I created for the sample document in this book.

The management and use of public identifiers is well-defined within the SGML standard. When it comes to how a particular tool manages the actual objects referenced, you will find a great deal of variety. Typically, some sort of map file indicates the identifier and the location of the actual information. Oasis, a consortium of SGML vendors, is working on this issue and has defined a standard catalog format that vendors may adhere to, but it is too early to tell.

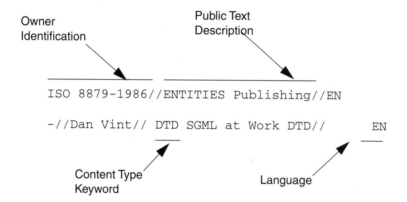

FIGURE A-3. PUBLIC IDENTIFIER SYNTAX

STRUCTURE

Structure is the key concept of SGML. The SGML standard was developed to separate structure from formatting to allow information and structure to be portable and better understood. The rules for structure are specified in a Document Type Definition (DTD) and then applied to a document instance by a writer.

A DTD typically contains the following definitions or declarations:

- Element declarations with any attributes
- Entities
- Notations.

Each of these items defines a specific type of markup that will either appear elsewhere in the DTD or will be used in the document instance.

ELEMENT DECLARATIONS

Element declarations are determined through a process of document analysis. During document analysis, all of your documents are identified, categorized, and possibly grouped into one or more DTDs. The structures of these documents are then defined. Within a DTD, you will develop the generic identifier (GI) or mnemonic label for the different structures and content types. Figure A-4 illustrates the element declaration syntax.

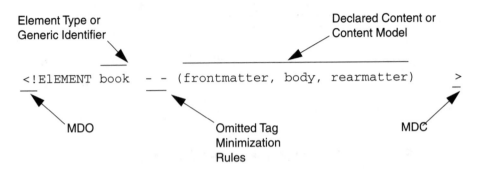

Element Type or Generic Identifier

Declared Content or Content Model

`<!ElEMENT book  - - (frontmatter, body, rearmatter)        >`

MDO

Omitted Tag
Minimization
Rules

MDC

FIGURE A-4. ELEMENT DECLARATION SYNTAX

Model Group Connectors and Indicators

,	Sequence (comma)
&	And
|	Or
*	Optional and repeatable (0 or more)
?	Optional (0 or 1)
+	Required and repeatable (1 or more)
( )	Model group

Content Data Types

PCDATA	Parseable Data Characters
CDATA	Character Data
RCDATA	Replaceable Character Data
EMPTY	No Content

FIGURE A-5. CONTENT MODEL DATA TYPES AND INDICATORS

The element declaration in Figure A-4 is for the GI book. The start and end tags for the book will surround the content model when used in a document instance. By observing the omittag rules, you can determine if the start or end tag may be omitted. In this example, neither is allowed to be omitted. The first dash represents the start tag, and the second is for the end tag. If the first dash were replaced with "o", the start tag could be omitted.

The element book, according to Figure A-4, consists of frontmatter, followed by a body, followed by rearmatter. The comma separating the elements inside the content model indicates an ordered sequence of these three elements. Figure A-5 lists the other connector and occurrence indicators that can be used within a content model. If the comma were substituted with the or-bar, then only one of the three elements in the content model would be allowed in the document instance.

The elements in the content model of Figure A-4 are further defined until a terminal node or element is defined. A terminal element is defined as one of the base content data types shown in Figure A-5, with no other elements in the content model.

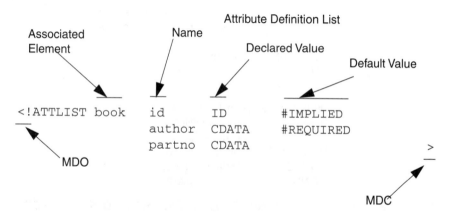

FIGURE A-6. ATTRIBUTE LIST SYNTAX

Elements are used to define major structural or content objects within a document. Attributes are used to modify or enhance the definition of an element. Figure A-6 illustrates the syntax for an attribute list. An attribute definition must identify the element to which the attributes are to be applied, a list of one or more attributes consisting of a name, type, and optional default value, as shown in Figure A-7.

In Figure A-6, the book element has three attributes defined, of which author is a required attribute that must always be defined and must be composed of only characters. The attribute id is defined to be of type ID. Any value assigned to this attribute must be unique within the document in which it is used. The attribute partno is an optional attribute that can contain character values only.

Declared Attribute Values

ID	Unique identifier
IDREF	Reference to an ID
IDREFS	List of references
NAME	Valid SGML name
NAMES	List of names
NMTOKEN	Name token
NMTOKENS	Name tokens
NOTATION	Notation name
NUMBER	Name token with digits only
NUMBERS	Digits, separated by spaces
NUTOKEN	Number token
NUTOKENS	Number tokens

Default Value Keywords

IMPLIED	System will generate
FIXED	Fixed value
REQUIRED	Must have a value
CURRENT	Default to most recently specified
CONREF	Content reference

FIGURE A-7. ATTRIBUTE LIST VALUES AND KEYWORDS

ENTITIES

SGML entities provide support for:

- External file references

- Variable substitutions.

Figure A-8 illustrates an SGML system that uses entities to manage external files. The dashed line linking the SGML declaration to the DTD indicates the "loose" linking between the DTD and the declaration. The solid lines between all the other parts of the system indicate true links between these objects. In other words, some sort of identifier in the referencing object points at the external object or file. The link to these external objects is either a public or system identifier.

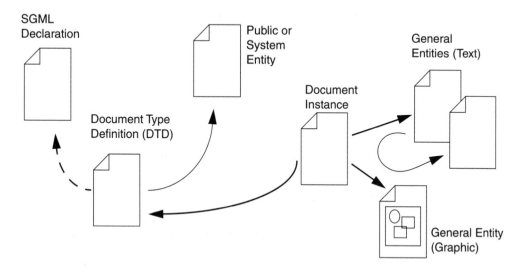

FIGURE A-8. PARTS OF AN SGML SYSTEM WITH ENTITIES

PARAMETER ENTITIES

In the DTD, you can use parameter entities to create a label or logical name to substitute for different element models or attribute lists. In this mode, the parameter entity allows easier maintenance of large DTDs with common structures, or it can allow you to change the basic structure of a document based upon a parameter substitution. These parameter entities are generally found within the DTD, but they can also be defined in the document instance and force the DTD to restructure. Figure A-9 illustrates a typical parameter entity definition.

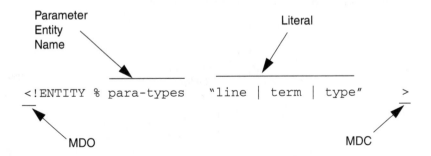

FIGURE A-9. PARAMETER ENTITY SYNTAX

 Although the SGML syntax allows the document instance to contain overriding DTD structures and parameter entities, most SGML tools tend to precompile the DTD before you can load a document. To support this functionality, you either need a tool that reads the DTD each time, or you need to create a DTD for each combination of structures.

GENERAL ENTITIES

General entities are typically used for text substitution within a document instance. General entities would be used anywhere you would use a variable within your current desktop publishing environment. Figure A-10 illustrates a general entity that substitutes the name or variable `dtd` with the expanded text `Document Type Definition` when encountered in the document.

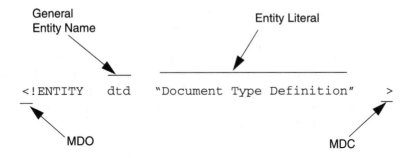

FIGURE A-10. GENERAL ENTITY SYNTAX

SYSTEM IDENTIFIERS

A general entity that uses a system identifier allows an entity name or variable to be replaced by content stored outside the document or DTD. Figure A-11 illustrates the typical general entity that uses a system identifier. In this example, the name `para-ent` will cause the system file `para.ent` to be placed wherever a reference to this entity occurs within the DTD or document.

FIGURE A-11. GENERAL ENTITY SYNTAX USING A SYSTEM IDENTIFIER

Typically, you will see these used to reference external objects that are only used by a particular document or of limited usage among several documents. By splitting a document into multiple files, it is easier for multiple authors to work on the same document. In this case, these general entities are also referred to as a document fragment.

The management and use of entities is well-defined within the SGML standard. What is implementation-dependent is how the SGML tool will work with the actual document fragment. When evaluating SGML tools you should research how they handle document fragments and how easy it is to create or enfold an entity back into the main document structure.

ENTITY REFERENCES

Although there are many ways to define an entity, there are only two ways to reference an entity. Figure A-12 illustrates the use of a parameter entity in an element definition and the use of general entities in a document. See the previous figures for the definitions of these entities. Depending upon the application, you may be able to show these entities expanded in-line, or you may only see the references as shown in the figure.

NOTATION DECLARATION

SGML allows any type of content to be included within a document. Two things are required to support this functionality:

- Declaration of format
- Display of content.

SGML provides the notation declaration syntax, as shown in Figure A-13. This syntax allows you to identify a format name and map it to a possible system tool that can be used to display the format.

Notation declarations allow you to define the formats of included objects, but when it comes to implementing this feature, you are limited to the capabilities of the tools you are using. Typically, this feature is used to include illustrations in a document. Most systems only support a small subset of all the formats that are available, but you will generally find support for the more useful formats. This feature also supports multimedia formats like sound and movies, but these formats are typically only supported by the SGML online browsers.

Parameter Entity Reference

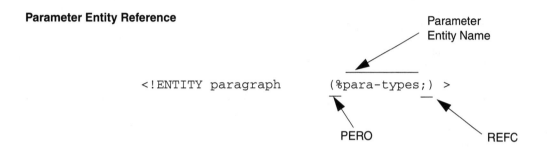

General Entity References

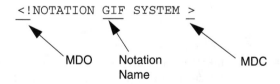

FIGURE A-12. TYPICAL ENTITY REFERENCES

```
<!NOTATION GIF SYSTEM >
```

MDO   Notation   MDC
       Name

FIGURE A-13. NOTATION DECLARATION SYNTAX

Figure A-14 illustrates a general entity definition that uses a notation type. This entity, when referenced, is placed in the document the same as any other general entity, but the SGML tool must be able to display the format or call on some other tool to display it.

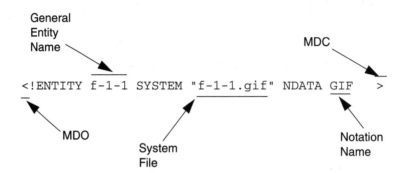

FIGURE A-14. GENERAL ENTITY WITH NOTATION SYNTAX

MISCELLANEOUS CONCERNS

The following items don't fit into any of the previous general sections, and they are all unrelated; but, you must be aware of them and how your SGML tool handles them:

- Comments
- Processing instructions
- SGML syntax error messages.

COMMENTS

If you have only used a commercial desktop publishing system, you might wonder why you would want comments, or you might have used a feature like "hidden text" for this function. Comments are used to provide additional information that is not intended to be published. These might be notes to yourself, or they could be additional instructions to your editorial or production staff.

Figure A-15 illustrates the use of a comment within an attribute list definition and as a separate block of text in the second example. All of the information between pairs of "--" is the content of the comment.

Comments should be used extensively in your DTD to explain the usage of your elements and provide documentation on your thought processes and the revisions being made. In a document, you might want to use comments to describe alternate configurations or sources of information (anything that you don't want to appear in the document).

Another use for comments is to "comment out" sections of a document that may be out of syntax or that you don't want to print. By wrapping a section in comments (do not nest comment structures), you can hide sections of a document from the SGML parser or print engine. This is a very useful troubleshooting method.

 Comments are a useful documentation tool and I recommend their use, but some systems do not retain them. Verify how your tools handle comment strings before investing a lot of effort in commenting your DTD or document.

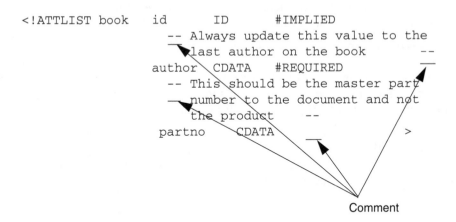

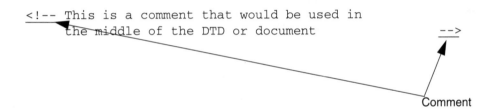

FIGURE A-15. COMMENT SYNTAX

PROCESSING INSTRUCTIONS

Processing instructions, commonly referred to as PIs, provide a standard way to include system-specific information. PIs provide a mechanism to include formatting information within an SGML document. Generally, it is not recommended that you do this and there is no guarantee that any other system will respect or use this information. Some uses for PIs are to include page breaks, line breaks, and other formatting information.

Figure A-16 illustrates the PI syntax. The system data format depends upon your application. In this case, I have identified the system as sgmlatwork and named an action line-break.

If you must use PIs in your application, it is recommended that you define them as entities so that their use and all the possible values are known before discovering them in a document instance.

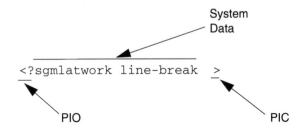

System
Data

```
<?sgmlatwork line-break  >
```

PIO

PIC

FIGURE A-16. PROCESSING INSTRUCTION SYNTAX

ERROR MESSAGES

Error messages are not defined by the SGML standard, but they are reported based upon the constructs and syntax of the standard. Most of the SGML tools that are currently available report errors based upon the abbreviations or labels listed in Table A-2.

Table A-2. SGML Syntax Labels, Definitions, and Values

Abbreviation or Label	Definition	Typical Value or Size
ATTCAP	Attribute capacity	35000
ATTCHCAP	Attribute character capacity	35000
ATTCNT	Attribute count	40
ATTSPLEN	Attribute specification length	960
AVGRPCAP	Attribute value group capacity	35000
BSEQLEN	Blank sequence length	960

Table A-2. SGML Syntax Labels, Definitions, and Values (continued)

Abbreviation or Label	Definition	Typical Value or Size
CDATA	Character data—do not parse, no substitutions	
COM	Comment delimiters	--
CRO	Character reference open	&#
DSC	Declaration subset closed	]
DSO	Declaration subset open	[
DTAGLEN	Data tag length	16
DTEMPLEN	Data tag template length	16
DTGC	Data tag group close	]
DTGO	Data tag group open	[
ELEMCAP	Element capacity	35000
EMPTY	Empty content	
ENTCAP	Entity capacity	35000
ENTCHCAP	Entity character capacity	35000
ENTLVL	Entity nesting level	16
ERO	Entity reference open	&
ETAGO	End tag open	</
EXGRPCAP	Exceptions group capacity	35000
EXNMCAP	Exceptions group name capacity	35000
GI	Generic identifier	
GRPC	Group close	)
GRPCAP	Group capacity	35000
GRPCNT	Group count of tokens	32
GRPGTCNT	Group grand total count of tokens	96
GRPLVL	Group nesting level	16

Table A-2. SGML Syntax Labels, Definitions, and Values (continued)

Abbreviation or Label	Definition	Typical Value or Size
GRPO	Group open	(
ID	Unique identifier	
IDCAP	Identifier attribute capacity	35000
IDREF	Identifier reference	
IDREFCAP	Identifier reference attribute capacity	35000
IDREFS	Identifier reference list	
IGNORE	Ignore a marked section	
IMPLIED	Implied attribute	
INCLUDE	Include a marked section	
LIT	Literal start or end	" (double quote)
LITA	Literal start or end alternative	' (single quote)
LITLEN	Literal length	240
LKNMCAP	Link name capacity	35000
LKSETCAP	Link set capacity	35000
MAPCAP	Map capacity	35000
MDC	Markup declaration close	>
MDO	Markup declaration open	<!
MSC	Marked section closed	]]
NAMECASE	Name case	In declaration, NO specifies upper- and lower-case are unique, YES specifies they are the same
NAMELEN	Name length	8
NAMES	Name list	
NDATA	Non-SGML data entity	

Table A-2. SGML Syntax Labels, Definitions, and Values (continued)

Abbreviation or Label	Definition	Typical Value or Size
NET	Null end tag	/
NMTOKEN	Name token	
NMTOKENS	Name tokens	
NORMSEP	Normalized separator	2
NOTATION	Notation character data	
NOTCAP	Notation capacity	35000
NOTCHCAP	Notation character capacity	35000
NUMBER	Number	
NUMBERS	A list of one or more numbers	
NUTOKEN	Number token	
NUTOKENS	Number tokens	
PCDATA	Parsed character data - parse and recognize any markup	
PERO	Parameter entity reference open	%
PI	Processing instruction	
PIC	Processing instruction close	>
PILEN	Processing instruction length	240
PIO	Processing instruction open	<?
RCDATA	Replaceable character data —general entity reference or character reference recognized	
RE	Record end character	
REFC	Reference close	;
RNI	Reserved name indicator	#

Table A-2. SGML Syntax Labels, Definitions, and Values (continued)

Abbreviation or Label	Definition	Typical Value or Size
RS	Record start character	
SDATA	Special character data	
SPACE	Space character	In declaration, defines which characters should be treated as whitespace
STAGO	Start-tag open	<
TAGC	Tag close	>
TAGLEN	Start tag length	960
TAGLVL	Tag nesting level of open tags	24
TEMP	Temporary section	
TOTALCAP	Total capacity	35000
VI	Value indicator	=

UNICODE QUICK REFERENCE

This appendix provides a quick reference to the Unicode standard that was developed by the Unicode Consortium as a 16-bit character encoding mechanism. The primary goal was to remedy the two serious problems of overloading fonts and the use of multiple inconsistent character codes due to conflicting national and industry standards. Unicode has been accepted in the SGML standard. The following table maps a few of the more useful characters to their Unicode values.

Unicode Hex Value	Character Name
0020	Space
0022	Quotation mark
0026	Ampersand
0027	Apostrophe-quote
002D	Hyphen-minus
002F	Slash
003C	Less-than sign
003E	Greater-than sign
003F	Question mark

Unicode Hex Value	Character Name
0040	Commercial at
005C	Backslash
005F	Spacing underscore
00A9	Copyright sign
00AE	Registered trademark sign
00B0	Degree sign
00B1	Plus-or-minus sign
00D7	Multiplication sign
00F7	Division sign
2013	En dash
2014	Em dash
2020	Dagger
2021	Double dagger
2022	Bullet
2026	Horizontal ellipsis
2032	Prime
2033	Double prime
2122	Trademark
2212	Minus sign

C SGML TOOLS AND VENDORS

The following is a listing of the tools and vendors that I have reviewed or mentioned in this book. A very useful Web site maintains a more complete and constantly updated list of tools at: www.infotech.no/sgmltool/guide.htm. Look for the link to the *Whirlwind Guide to SGML Tools*.

DTD DEVELOPMENT AND DOCUMENTATION TOOLS

Product	Contact Information	Comments
Near & Far Designer	Microstar Software Ltd 3775 Richmond Road Nepean, Ontario Canada, K2H5B7 (800)267-9975 Canada and U.S. Email: info@microstar.com Web: www.microstar.com	
SGML Companion	Publishing Development AB Torpvägen 10 S-175 43 JÄRFÄLLA Sweden +46-18-18 54 52 Email: Marketing@pharmasoft.se Web: http://www.pharmasoft.se/pubdev/	SGML Companion is the full product, SGML Companion DTD Browser is a free evaluation version.

SGML Editors

Product	Contact Information	Comments
ADEPT•Editor, ADEPT•Publisher, Document Architect	ArborText, Inc. 1000 Victors Way Ann Arbor, MI 48108-2700 USA Phone: +1 313.997.0200 Fax: +1 313.997.0201 email: info@arbortext.com Web: www.arbortext.com	Document Architect is the DTD development tool required by ArborText to build new SGML applications
Grif SGML Editor	Infrastructures for Information 116 Spadina Ave., 5th Floor Toronto, ON Canada M5V 2K6 Tel: +1 416 504 0141 Fax: +1 416 504 1785 email:i4i@i4i.com Web: www.i4i.org	Grif, the company, was aquired by Infrastructures for Information and now market the product line.
WordPerfect, Ventura	Corel Corporation Corporate Headquarters 1600 Carling Ave Ottawa, Ontario K1Z 8RZ Canada Tel: (613) 728-3733 FAX: (613) 761-9176 email: Web: www.corel.com	
InContext SGML Editor	Geac Computer Corporation Ltd. 11 Allstate Parkway Suite 300 Markham, Ontario CANADA L3R 9T8 1-877-364-0409 (Canada and US) email: inc-support@geac.com Web: www.incontext.com	InContext was recently acquired by Geac Computer Corp. Ltd. This product was actually reviewed as part of the Corel Ventura product. Manuals can be found online at their website under support.

SGML Programming Tools

Product	Contact Information	Comments
OmniMark, OmniMark LE	OmniMark Technologies Corporation 1400 Blair Place Ottawa, Ontario, CANADA K1J 9B8 Tel: +1 613 745 4242 Fax: +1 613 745 5560 email: info@omnimark.com Web: www.omnimark.com	The Omnimark LE version and manuals are available online. While looking at the site, take a look at the OMUG-L archives.

SGML Document Managment Systems

Product	Contact Information	Comments
Information Manager	Texcel Research, Inc. (US HQ) One Kendall Square, Suite 2200 Cambridge, MA 02139 UNITED STATES +1 617 621-7004 email: info@texcel.no Web: www.texcel.no	

SGML Browsers and Viewers

Product	Contact Information	Comments
HyBrowse	TechnoTeacher, Inc PO Box 23795 23-2 Clover Park Rochester, NY 14692-3795 USA +1 (716) 271-0796 email: info@techno.com Web: www.techno.com	This is a shareware tool that demonstrates browsing and viewing of SGML and HyTime documents.
Panorama Pro, Panorama Viewer	SoftQuad Inc. 20 Eglinton Ave. West, 13th Floor, P.O. Box 2025 Toronto, Canada M4R 1K8. +1 416 544-9000 email: mail@sq.com Web: www.softquad.com	
DynaText, DynaWeb	Inso Corporation 31 St. James Avenue Boston, MA 02116 USA +1 (617) 753-6500 Web: www.inso.com	

Shareware Tools

Product	Contact Information	Comments
dtd2html, perlSGML	http://www.oac.uci.edu:80/indiv/ehood/	
Jade, SP	http://www.jclark.com/	
psgml - an SGML emacs major mode	http://www.lysator.liu.se/projects/ about_psgml.html	

D SGML AT WORK
SAMPLE DOCUMENT

This appendix contains an annotated view of the sample document that is available on the CD-ROM in both FrameMaker and PDF formats. Please use this sample when reading Chapter 5 through Chapter 8.

In the following illustrations, I have placed MIF tags inside of angle brackets. I did this to try and reinforce the idea that your existing publishing tools (in this case, FrameMaker) apply information that is very similar to the SGML elements that we defined with our DTD.

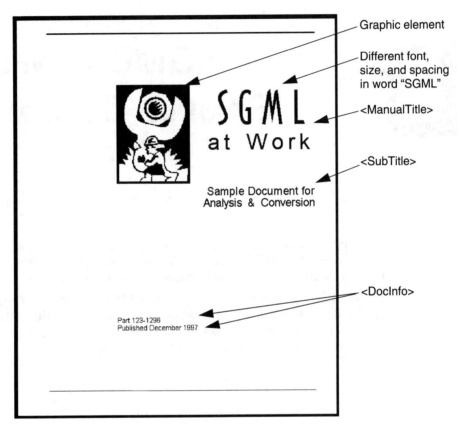

FIGURE D-1. COVER I FRAMEMAKER SAMPLE DOCUMENT

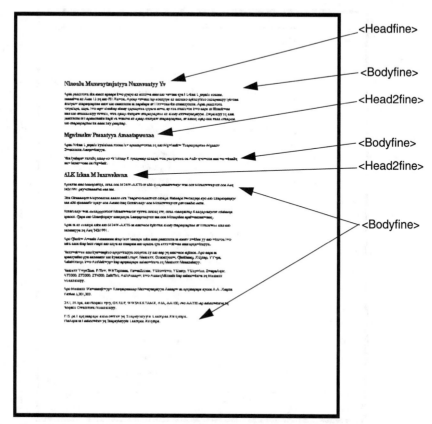

FIGURE D-2. COVER II FRAMEMAKER SAMPLE DOCUMENT

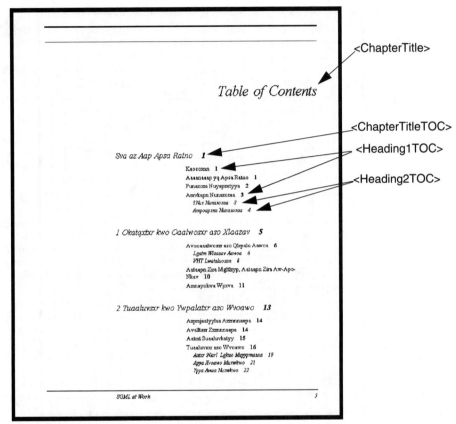

FIGURE D-3. TOC 1 FRAMEMAKER SAMPLE DOCUMENT

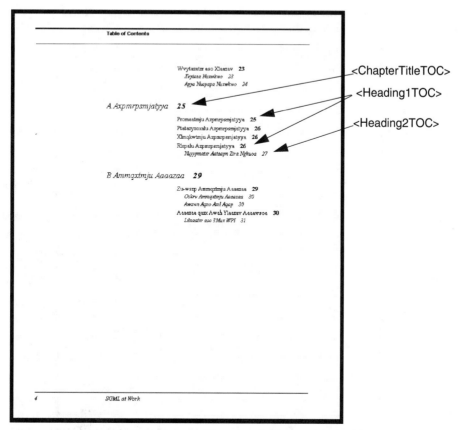

FIGURE D-4. TOC 2 FRAMEMAKER SAMPLE DOCUMENT

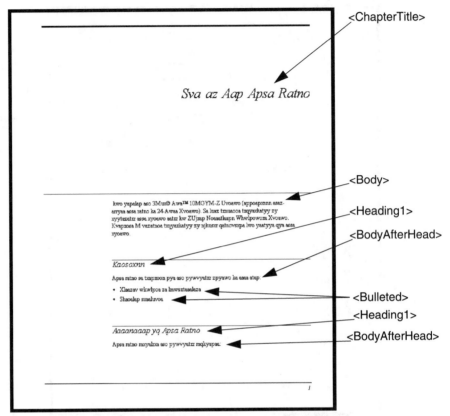

FIGURE D-5. PAGE 1 FRAMEMAKER SAMPLE DOCUMENT

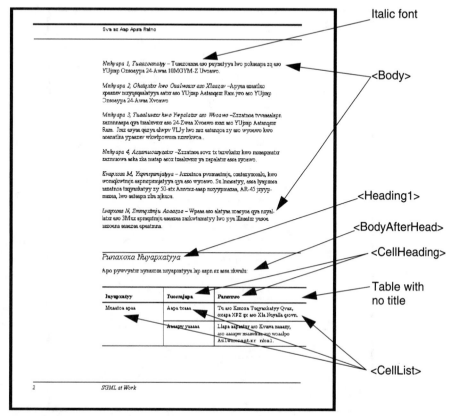

FIGURE D-6. PAGE 2 FRAMEMAKER SAMPLE DOCUMENT

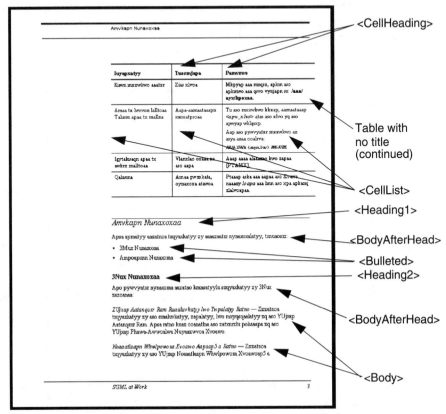

FIGURE D-7. PAGE 3 FRAMEMAKER SAMPLE DOCUMENT

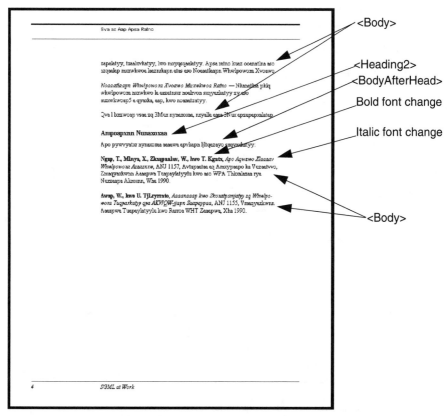

FIGURE D-8. PAGE 4 FRAMEMAKER SAMPLE DOCUMENT

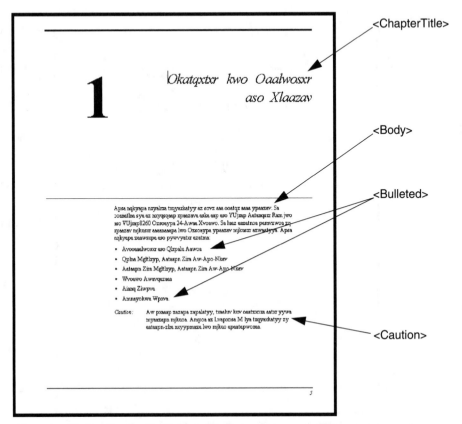

FIGURE D-9. PAGE 5 FRAMEMAKER SAMPLE DOCUMENT

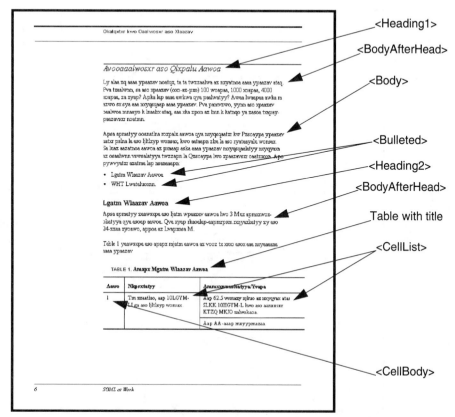

- <Heading1>
- <BodyAfterHead>
- <Body>
- <Bulleted>
- <Heading2>
- <BodyAfterHead>
- Table with title
- <CellList>
- <CellBody>

FIGURE D-10. PAGE 6 FRAMEMAKER SAMPLE DOCUMENT

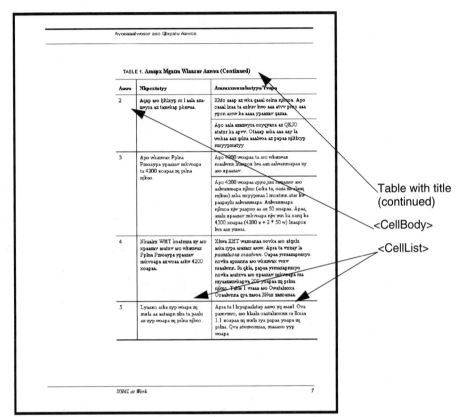

FIGURE D-11. PAGE 7 FRAMEMAKER SAMPLE DOCUMENT

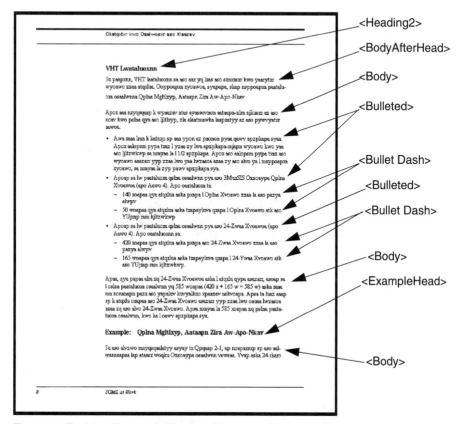

FIGURE D-12. PAGE 8 FRAMEMAKER SAMPLE DOCUMENT

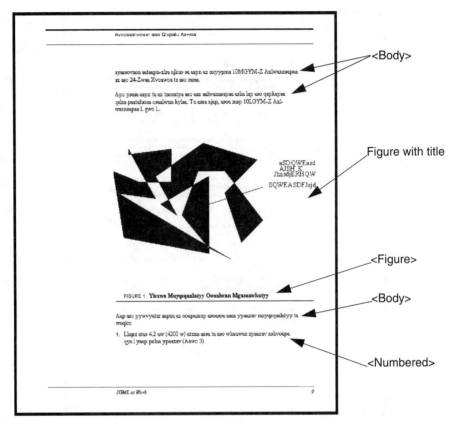

FIGURE D-13. PAGE 9 FRAMEMAKER SAMPLE DOCUMENT

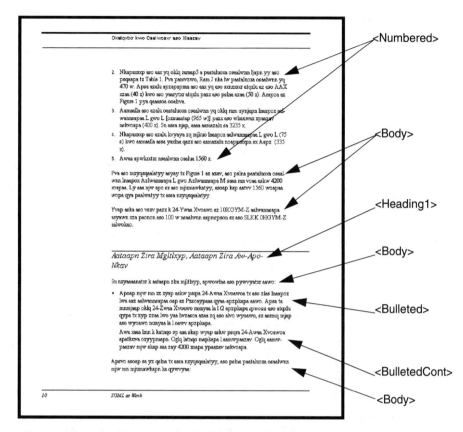

FIGURE D-14. PAGE 10 FRAMEMAKER SAMPLE DOCUMENT

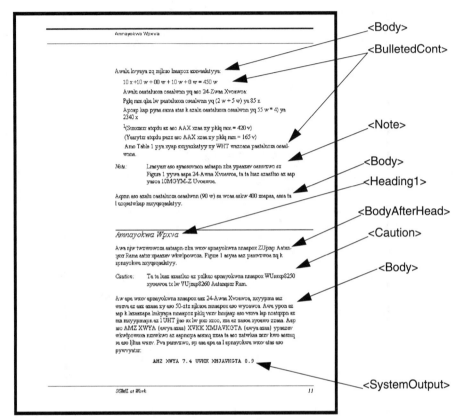

FIGURE D-15. PAGE 11 FRAMEMAKER SAMPLE DOCUMENT

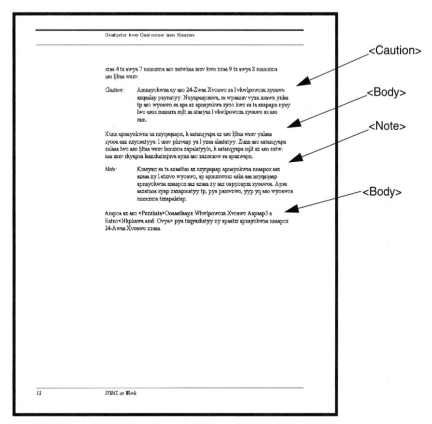

FIGURE D-16. PAGE 12 FRAMEMAKER SAMPLE DOCUMENT

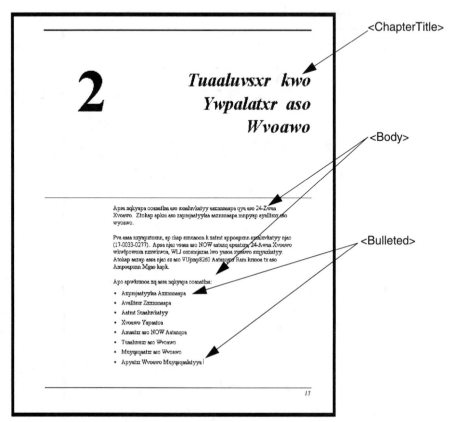

FIGURE D-17. PAGE 13 FRAMEMAKER SAMPLE DOCUMENT

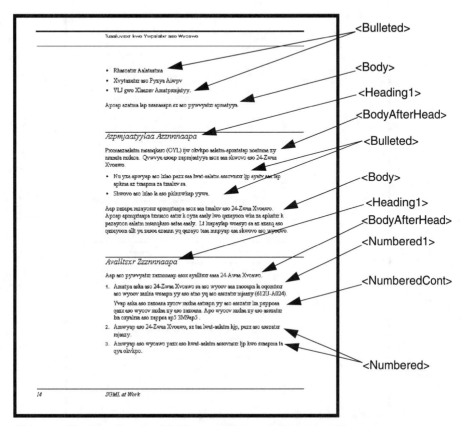

FIGURE D-18. PAGE 14 FRAMEMAKER SAMPLE DOCUMENT

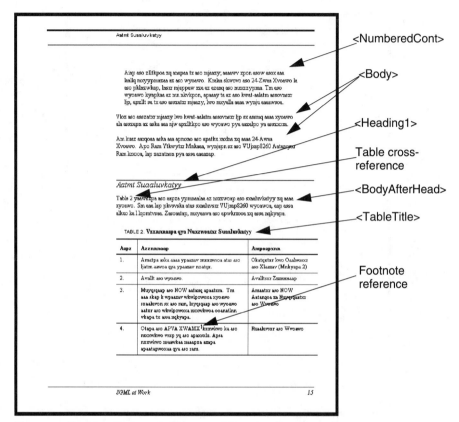

FIGURE D-19. PAGE 15 FRAMEMAKER SAMPLE DOCUMENT

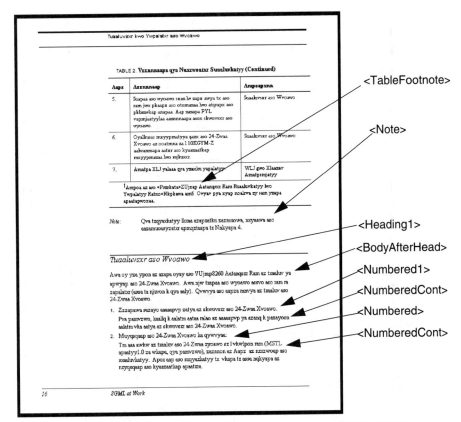

FIGURE D-20. PAGE 16 FRAMEMAKER SAMPLE DOCUMENT

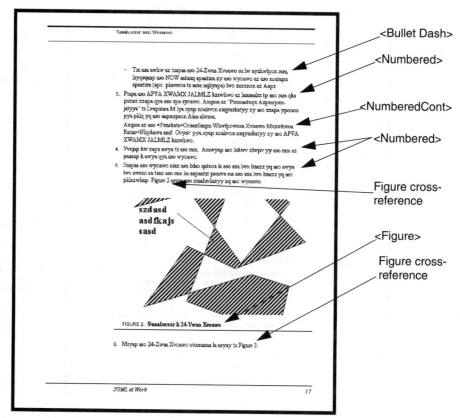

FIGURE D-21. PAGE 17 FRAMEMAKER SAMPLE DOCUMENT

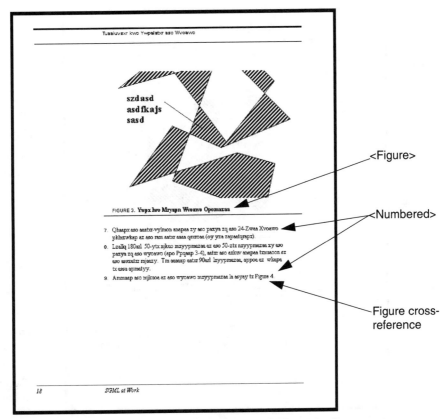

FIGURE D-22. PAGE 18 FRAMEMAKER SAMPLE DOCUMENT

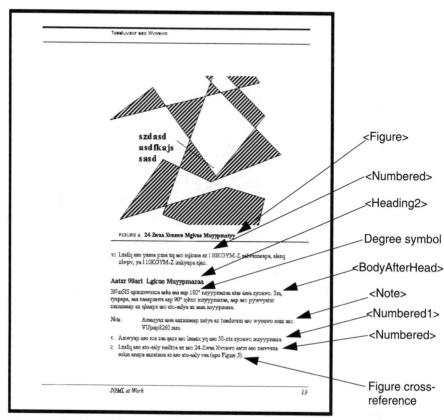

FIGURE D-23. PAGE 19 FRAMEMAKER SAMPLE DOCUMENT

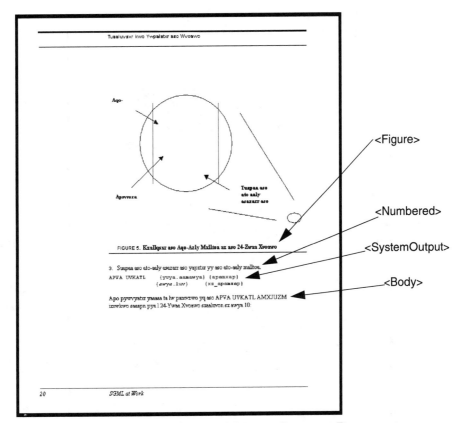

FIGURE D-24. PAGE 20 FRAMEMAKER SAMPLE DOCUMENT

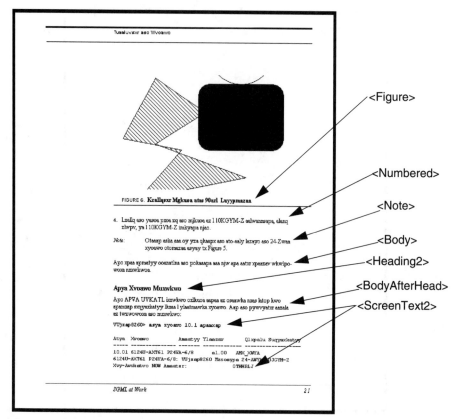

FIGURE D-25. PAGE 21 FRAMEMAKER SAMPLE DOCUMENT

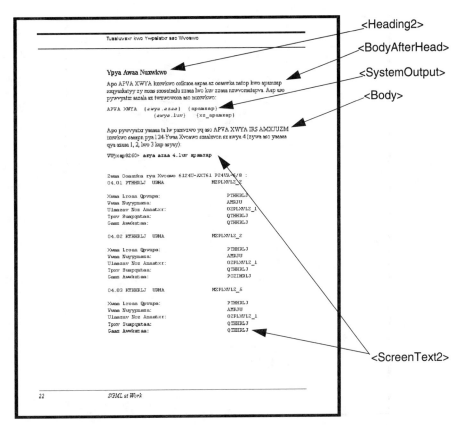

FIGURE D-26. PAGE 22 FRAMEMAKER SAMPLE DOCUMENT

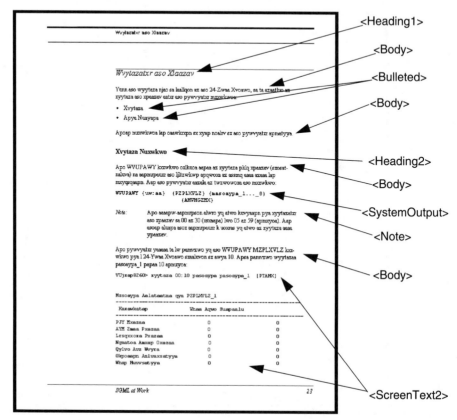

FIGURE D-27. PAGE 23 FRAMEMAKER SAMPLE DOCUMENT

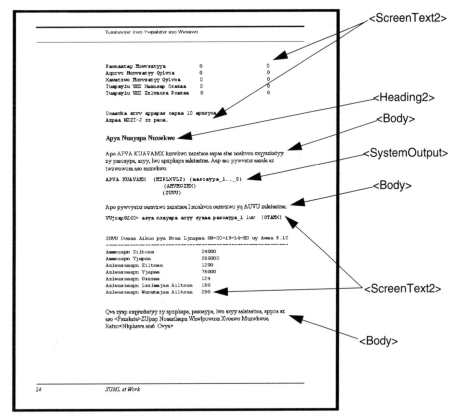

FIGURE D-28. PAGE 24 FRAMEMAKER SAMPLE DOCUMENT

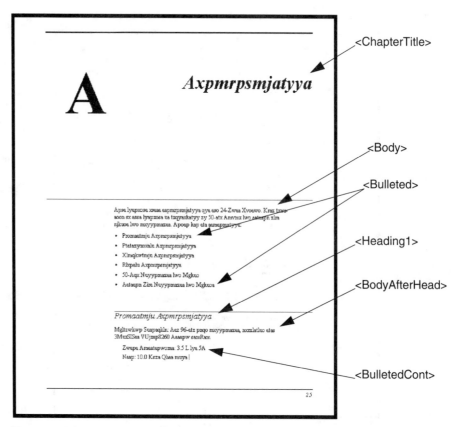

FIGURE D-29. PAGE 25 FRAMEMAKER SAMPLE DOCUMENT

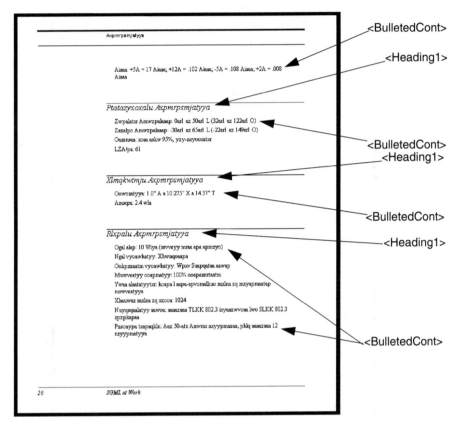

FIGURE D-30. PAGE 26 FRAMEMAKER SAMPLE DOCUMENT

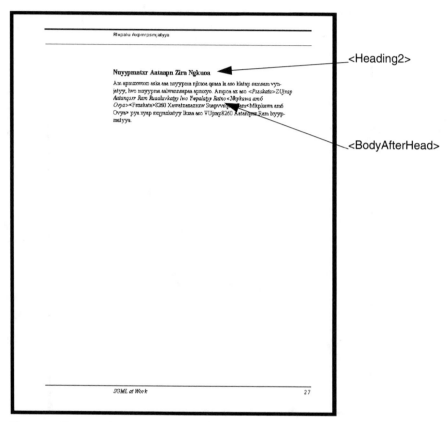

FIGURE D-31. PAGE 27 FRAMEMAKER SAMPLE DOCUMENT

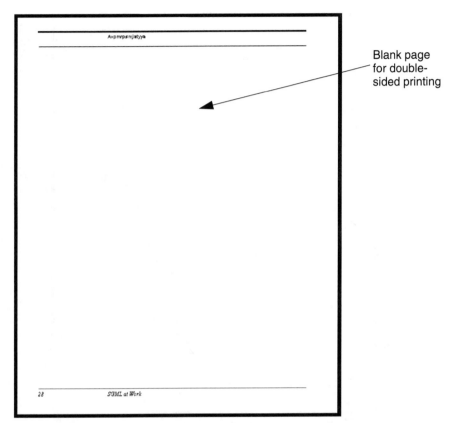

Axpmrpsmjstyya

28   SGML at Work

Blank page
for double-
sided printing

FIGURE D-32. PAGE 28 FRAMEMAKER SAMPLE DOCUMENT

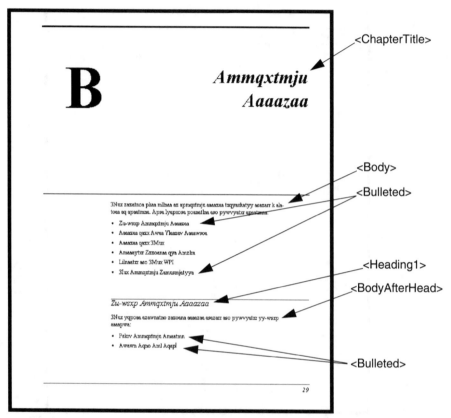

FIGURE D-33. PAGE 29 FRAMEMAKER SAMPLE DOCUMENT

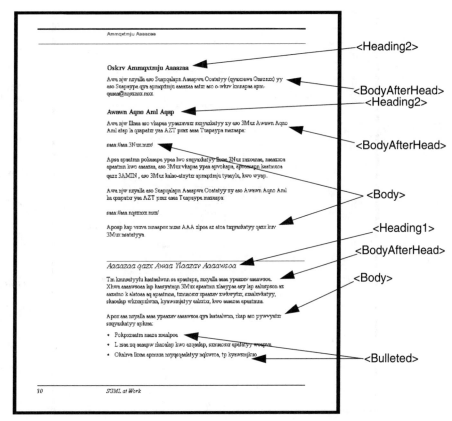

FIGURE D-34. PAGE 30 FRAMEMAKER SAMPLE DOCUMENT

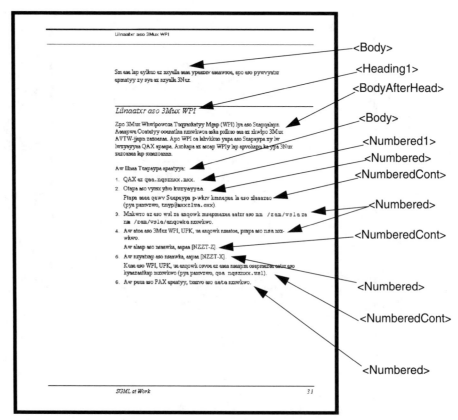

FIGURE D-35. PAGE 31 FRAMEMAKER SAMPLE DOCUMENT

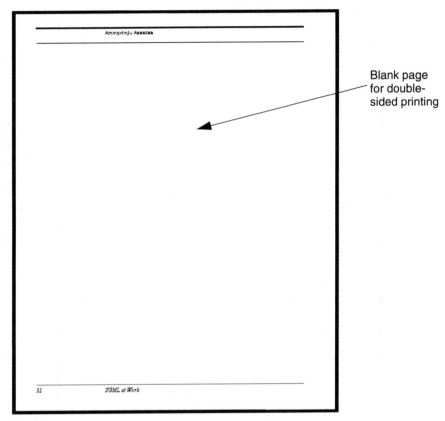

Blank page for double-sided printing

FIGURE D-36. PAGE 32 FRAMEMAKER SAMPLE DOCUMENT

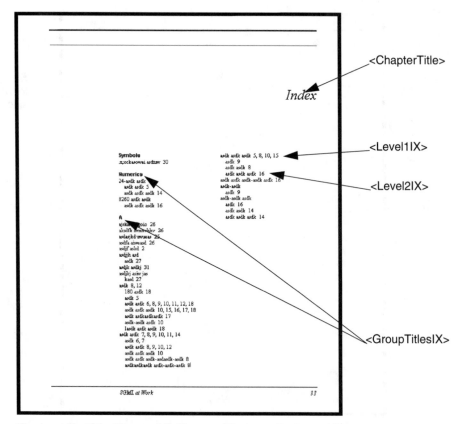

FIGURE D-37. PAGE 33 FRAMEMAKER SAMPLE DOCUMENT

E CD-ROM CONTENTS

This appendix lists the contents of the CD-ROM provided with this book and documents how to install, configure, and get started with the tools. I base all installation procedures on using WinZip to uncompress any compressed or archived files. It is not necessary to use this tool, but it will make it easier to follow my instructions if you use the same tool.

The CD-ROM is organized into the following directories:

- **adept**—contains examples shown in the ADEPT•Editor section and the complete working environment for the sample DTD.

- **cgmtest**—contains CGM test files from NIST and the files created by Henderson's MetaPrint.

- **conversion**—contains OmniMark Lite and the conversion programs to convert MIF documents to the sample DTD.

- **dtdtools**—contains perlSGML, SGML Companion, and the output generated by dtd2html and Near & Far Designer.

- **editors**—contains emacs, vi, and the Programmer's File Editor.

- **finalsample**—contains the final version of all the conversion and cleanup efforts and any changes required to make the sample document work with all the tools.

- **formats**—contains the MIF and RTF format specification documents.

- **formatting**—contains Jade, the DSSSL specifications, and OmniMark programs to convert the sample document into RTF format.

- **graphics**—contains GhostScript/GhostView, SnagIT, and L-view Pro.
- **grif**—contains the Grif editor environment required to manage the sample DTD.
- **hybrowse**—contains the HyBrowse tool and sample application.
- **inso**—contains a complete version of the sample document in DynaText format and DynaWeb support.
- **panoram2**—contains the Panorama Pro 2 configuration of the sample document.
- **pdf**—contains the Adobe Acrobat reader.
- **sampdoc**—contains the sample FrameMaker document files and a PDF version with comments.
- **utils**—contains WinZip, perl, awk, grep, head, and tail.
- **ventura7**—contains the Ventura Publisher environment to support the sample DTD.
- **wordperfect**—contains the WordPerfect environment to support the sample DTD.
- **www**—contains Panorama Free and the XML draft specifications.

ADEPT

In the **adept** directory on the CD-ROM, you will find the following:

- **installed**—the complete installed version of the sample DTD.
- **sampleclean**—the second-stage version of the SGML version of the sample document.
- **sample-old**—the results of the conversion from MIF to SGML.
- **sample**—the final version of the sample document with all the modifications required to support the various tools.

CONVERSION

The conversion directory contains the OmniMark Lite software and following directories:

- **batchfiles**—the DOS batch files used to drive the conversion scripts.

- **sample**—the OmniMark programs used in the conversion process, plus the following:

  - **charset**—ISO character entity files

  - **framesrc**—original FrameMaker MIF documents

  - **intermediateform**—files after the first conversion step in my normalized MIF format

  - **outputfiles**—various report files generated during the conversion process

  - **sgmlfix**—SGML files after the programmatic cleanup step

  - **sgmloutput**—first version of the SGML conversion.

DTDTOOLS

The **dtdtools** directory includes the PerlSGML library (dtd2html), SGML Companion program source files, and the following:

- **dtd2html**—HTML files generated by dtd2html.

- **nearfar**—documentation files generated by Near & Far Designer.

EDITORS

The **editors** directory contains the Programmer's File Editor, VIM program files, and the following:

- **emacs**—the program and support files for the emacs editor and the additional Lisp files to support OmniMark and SGML.

I actually use all three of these editors in my work. Each one provides features that the others don't. If you are just now going to learn emacs and vi, let me offer the following advice: If you ever have to work on a UNIX platform, you will always have access to vi; emacs is a program that the systems administrator usually has to install separately, so it is not always available. emacs will do everything vi does and then some. With its additional SGML and OmniMark modes, it is the better choice to start with, barring the above recommendation.

PFE conforms to the standard Windows environment and should be very easy to use. It provides some macro programming capabilities that make it easy to write some quick processing routines.

EMACS

To install emacs:

1. Load the CD-ROM.

2. In the editors directory under emacs, find the file `emacs-19_34_1-bin.tar.gz`. If you have WinZip installed, double-click on this file.

3. Extract all the files to a top-level directory. Make sure the options Use Folder Names and All files are checked.

4. Close WinZip.

5. In the same emacs directory on the CD-ROM, double-click on the file `emacs-19_34_1-lisp.tar.gz`.

6. Extract all the files to a top-level directory. Make sure the options Use Folder Names and All files are checked.

7. Close WinZip.

8. In the same emacs directory on the CD-ROM, double-click on the file `emacs-19_34_2-update.zip`.

9. Extract all the files to a top-level directory. Make sure the options Use Folder Names and All files are checked.

   This last set of files updates your copy of emacs from v19.34.1 to v19.34.2. When asked to replace existing files, answer yes.

10. Look at the installed directory. The following folders should be at the top level of the emacs-19.34 directory: bin, etc., info, lisp, and lock. Most likely, you will need to create an empty lock directory/folder.

11. Open an MS_DOS window and enter the following command, substituting your actual installation directory locations:

```
c:> \emacs-19.34\bin\addpm.exe c:\emacs-19.34
```

This adds the appropriate information to your system registry and creates a program group and icon from which you can launch emacs. I like to keep a copy of the icon on my desktop so I can easily drag and drop files onto the icon to launch the program.

12. Because emacs is at heart a UNIX tool, it needs a home directory defined. This version will default to C:\ as HOME.

You may set something more appropriate. I generally configure my system with a primary work area, which I configure as my HOME directory. Edit your `autoexec.bat` file and add the following line:

```
set HOME=f:\work
```

This won't take effect until you reboot your system.

13. The last bit of configuration information you need to know is how to create the `.emacs` file. This file configures emacs to the way you want it to work. This file should live in your HOME directory and can be named `.emacs` or `_emacs`. If you create both names, `.emacs` is the only one read.

There is a tremendous amount of information online within emacs that explains how to use the tool and there are a number of books available as well.

VIM

To install vim:

1. Load the CD-ROM.

2. In the editors directory, find the file `vim42w32.zip`. If you have WinZip installed, double-click on this file.

3. Extract all the files to a top level directory. Make sure the options Use Folder Names and All files are checked.

4. Create a shortcut to the file `vim.exe` in the installed location. Drag the shortcut to your desktop.

5. In the top level of the vim installation directory, find the file `vimrc`. This is the configuration file for vim.

PFE

To install pfe:

1. Load the CD-ROM.

2. In the editors directory, find the file `pfe0602i.zip`. If you have WinZip installed, double-click on this file.

3. Extract all the files to a directory that is on your path. Make sure the options Use Folder Names and All files are checked.

4. Create a shortcut to the file `pfe32.exe` in the installed location. Drag the shortcut to your desktop.

FINALSAMPLE

finalsample contains the completed SGML version of the sample document with all corrections and modifications to support the tools documented in this book.

FORMATS

The **formats** directory has two directories that contain the RTF and MIF file format documentation.

FORMATTING

The **formatting** directory includes the Jade DSSSL engine and the following:

- **dsssl**—contains the style sheets and output from running the style sheet.
- **sample2rtf**—contains the OmniMark program to output the sample DTD to RTF format.

GRAPHICS

The **graphics** directory has the SnagIT and L-view Pro programs. The directory **ghostscr** has the required files for GhostView.

GRIF

The **grif** directory contains the files to configure the Grif editor to support the sample dtd.

HYBROWSE

The **hybrowse** directory includes the HyBrowse program and a sample application.

INSO

The **inso** directory contains the installed configuration of the sample document. This configuration supports both DynaText and DynaWeb. Note that the document needs to be rebuilt if it is to be used.

PANORAM2

The **panoram2** directory has the installed configuration of the sample document to support Panorama viewing of the document.

PDF

The **pdf** directory has the program file for the Adobe Acrobat reader.

SAMPDOC

The **sampdoc** directory has the annotated PDF version of the sample document and within the **framedoc** directory is the original MIF format of the source document.

UTILS

Within the **utils** directory are the program files for awk, grep, head, tail, and winzip, as well as a directory **perl** containing the required files to build perl.

AWK

awk is a scripting language typically used to manipulate text files.

To install awk:

1. Load the CD-ROM.

2. In the utils directory, find the file **awk320.zip**. Double-click on this file.

3. Extract the files **awk.exe** and **awk.doc** to a directory that is in your PATH statement.

   These are the primary executable and documentation files in the compressed file. The other files are sample code; to install them, create a directory of **awk-samples** and copy these files to that location.

TAIL

To install tail:

1. Load the CD-ROM.

2. In the utils directory, find the file **tail.zip**. Double-click on the file.

3. Extract the files to a directory that is in your PATH statement.

HEAD

To install head:

1. Load the CD-ROM.

2. In the utils directory, find the file **head.zip**. Double-click on this file.

3. Extract the files to a directory that is in your PATH statement.

GREP

To install grep:

1. Load the CD-ROM.

2. In the utils directory, find the file **grep20ax.zip**. Double-click on this file.

3. Extract the files **grep.exe** and **grep.man** to a directory that is in your PATH statement.

WINZIP

WinZip is a file compression/decompression tool that understands a variety of formats. With this one tool you can work with PC and UNIX file compression and archiving mechanisms.

To install WinZip:

1. Load the CD-ROM.

2. In the utils directory, find the file **winzip95.exe**. Double-click on this file.

3. Accept the directory location presented, or enter a different location.

After installation is complete, a number of associations will be made between WinZip and the various compressed file formats. Now, by double-clicking on a file, you can see the file's contents and decide how you want to install the file.

VENTURA7

The **ventura7** directory contains the configuration files to support the sample DTD within Ventura Publisher.

WORDPERFECT

The **wordperfect** directory includes the configuration files to support the sample DTD within the WordPerfect editor.

WWW

The **www** directory contains the current draft specifications for XML, Panorama Free, and the Panorama 2 plug-in.

RELATED STANDARDS

The following is a listing of standards that are related to SGML or document management and creation. The International Organization for Standardization (ISO) standards are available for purchase from the national member body of ISO in your country, or from:

International Organization for Standardization
case postale 56
CH-1211 Geneva 20, Switzerland.

or from:

American National Standards Institute
11 West 42nd Street
New York, New York 10036

Standard Title	Contents
ISO 10179:1996 Document Style Semantics and Specification Language	Provides a machine-independent means by which typographic elements can be specified. (DSSSL).
ISO 10744:1992 Hypermedia/Time-based Structuring Language	Provides a standard way of representing connections to information so they can be created, processed, and exchanged (HyTime).
ISO/DP 10180 Standard Page Description Language	Provides a device-independent, fully composed, nonrevisable form of image output devices (SPDL).

Standard Title	Contents
ISO 9069:1988 SGML Document Interchange Format	Defines a structure that combines separate entities of an SGML file into a single data stream (SDIF).
ISO/DIS 9541 Font and Character Information Interchange	Addresses character identification grouping, font, and character attributes.
ISO 9573 Techniques for using SGML	Gives examples of SGML DTDs and marked-up documents to acquaint users with the language.
ISO/TR 10037 Requirements for SGML-sensitive Text-entry Systems	Describes a set of functions that an SGML-sensitive system should provide.
ISO/DP 9070 Registration Procedure for Public Text	Defines procedures associated with registers of public text.

G FURTHER READING

The following list is what I consider to be required reading if you are going to use the tools and techniques presented in this book. If you are a programmer, you have probably already used the books listed in the "UNIX Utilities and Programming Languages" section. You now need to incorporate the "SGML" and "Documentation Design" sections to gain an appreciation for this very specialized field. If you are a publications professional, you will need to study the UNIX and SGML sections to implement this new suite of tools.

In addition to these books, the sites `www.sil.org/sgml/sgml.html` and `www.sgmlopen.org` will keep you up-to-date with current SGML/XML activities.

UNIX UTILITIES AND PROGRAMMING LANGUAGES

Alfred Aho, Brian Kernighan, and Peter Weinberger, *The AWK Programming Language*, Reading MA: Addison-Wesley Publishing Company, 1988

Debra Cameron and Bill Rosenblatt, *Learning GNU Emacs*, Sebastopol, CA: O'Reilly and Associates, Inc., 1991

Dale Dougherty and Tim O'Reilly, *UNIX Text Processing*, Indianapolis, IN: Hayden Books, 1987

Larry Wall and Randall Schwartz, *Programming Perl*, Sebastopol, CA: O'Reilly and Associates, Inc., 1990

Dale Dougherty, *sed & awk*, Sebastopol, CA: O'Reilly and Associates, Inc., 1990

Randal Schwartz, *Learning Perl*, Sebastopol, CA: O'Reilly and Associates, Inc., 1993

Daniel Gilly and the staff of O'Reilly & Associates, Inc., *UNIX in a Nutshell*, Sebastopol, CA: O'Reilly and Associates, Inc.,1992
> This single book will provide a complete description of vi, emacs, awk, nroff/troff (with the associated macro packages) and make an all in one volume, but it does not provide any information on how to use or sample programs.

R, Kent Dybvig, *The Scheme Programming Language*, Upper Saddle River, NJ: Prentice Hall PTR, 1996

SGML

Brian Travis and Dale Waldt, *The SGML Implementation Guide: A Blueprint for SGML Migration*, New York, NY: Springer-Verlag, 1995

Charles Goldfarb, *The SGML Handbook*, Oxford, England: Oxford University Press, 1990
> This book is the complete ISO standard with all the current corrections and ammendments incorporated. In addition to the standard, additional links have been included to find related materials and a complete index as well.

Ronald Turner, Timothy Douglass, and Audrey Turner, *README.1ST; SGML for Writers and Editors*, Upper Saddle River, NJ: Prentice Hall PTR, 1996

Eric van Herwijnen, *Practical SGML*, Boston, MA: Kluwer Academic Publishers, 1994
> This book provides the essential details and syntax of the ISO standard without the language or presentation of the standard. I use this book as a quick reference.

Yuri Rubinsky and Murray Maloney, *SGML on the Web, Small Steps Beyond HTML*, Upper Saddle River, NJ: Prentice Hall PTR, 1997
> The CD Rom with this book includes a fully-functional copy of Panorama Pro v2.

DOCUMENTATION DESIGN

Robin Williams, *The Non-Designer's Design Book*, Berkley, CA: Peachpit Press, 1994

Robert Bringhurst, *The Elements of Typographic Style*, Vancouver, BC, Canada: Hartley & Marks Publishers, 1992
This book provides a view into the world of typographers and the considerations they apply when picking type faces and combining them together on the printed page.

William Horton, *Illustrating Computer Documentation: The Art of Presenting Information Graphically on Paper and Online*, New York, NY: John Wiley & Sons, 1991

William Horton, *Designing and Writing Online Documentation: Hypermedia for Self-supporting Products*, New York, NY: John Wiley & Sons, 1994

Nancy Hoft, *International Technical Communication: How to Export Information about High Technology*, New York, NY: John Wiley & Sons, 1995

Aaron Marcus, *Graphic Design for Electronic Documents and User Interfaces*, New York, NY: ACM Press, 1992

Daniel Felker, Frances Pickering, Veda Charrow, V Holland, and Janice Raidsh, *Guidelines for Document Designers*, Washington, D.C.:American Institutes for Research, 1981

Jan White, *Graphic Design for the Electronic Age, The Manual for Traditional and Desktop Publishing*, New York, NY: Xerox Press Book, 1988

GRAPHICS

David Blatner and Steve Roth, *Real World Scanning and Halftones: The Definitive Guide to Scanning and Halftones from the Desktop*, Berkley, CA: Peachpit Press, 1993
Although the primary focus of this book is how to get the most out of your desktop scanner, if you have ever had to work with bit-mapped graphics and products like Adobe Photoshop to modify an image or change format, you will appreciate the detailed information in this book.

Steve Rimmer, *Bit-Mapped Graphics*, Blue Ridge Summit, PA: Wincrest Books, 1990

David Holzgang, *Understanding PostScript Programming*, San Francisco, CA: Sybex Inc., 1988

Adobe Systems Inc., *PostScript Language Reference Manual*, Reading, MA: Addison-Wesley Publishing Company, Inc., 1990

James Murray and William VanRyper, *Graphics File Formats*, Seabastopol, CA: O'Reilly & Associates, Inc.,1996

INDEX

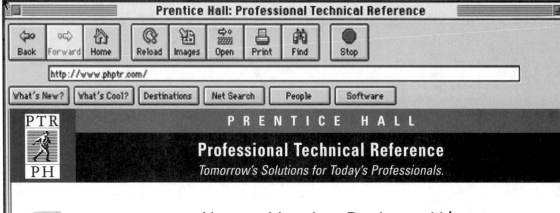

What's on the CD-ROM

The contents of this CD-ROM will run on the Windows 95 and NT platform, other versions of the software maybe available to run on other platforms.

• DTD Development and documentation tools

- perlSGML
- SGML Companion

• Conversion Tools

- OmniMark v3.0 Lite
- Source code for a MIF to SGML conversion
- Format specifications for MIF and RTF

• Editors

- vi
- emacs with modes for SGML editing and OmniMark development
- Programmer's File Editor

• SGML Formatting and Viewing Tools

- Jade and sample DSSSL code
- OmniMark SGML to RTF code
- SoftQuad Panorama Free
- TechnoTeacher Hybrowse

• Graphics

- CGM Test files from NIST
- samples of graphics conversions performed in the book
- GhostView/GhostScript Postscript viewer
- SnagIT!
- L-View Pro

• SGML Environments to support

- ArborText ADEPT•Editor
- Corel WordPerfect and Ventura Publisher
- INSO DynaText and DyanWeb
- SoftQuad Panorama Pro 2

• Utilities

- WinZip
- Perl
- awk
- grep
- head and tail

• Sample data and conversion output